THE GROWTH OF
RESPONSIBLE GOVERNMENT
IN STUART ENGLAND

TO MY WIFE, ANNE

THE GROWTH OF
RESPONSIBLE GOVERNMENT
IN STUART ENGLAND

BY

CLAYTON ROBERTS

*Associate Professor of History at
Ohio State University*

CAMBRIDGE
AT THE UNIVERSITY PRESS
1966

PUBLISHED BY

THE SYNDICS OF THE CAMBRIDGE UNIVERSITY PRESS

Bentley House, 200 Euston Road, London, N.W. 1
American Branch: 32 East 57th Street, New York, N.Y. 10022
West African Office: P.M.B. 5181, Ibadan, Nigeria

Printed in Great Britain at the University Printing House, Cambridge
(*Brooke Crutchley, University Printer*)

LIBRARY OF CONGRESS CATALOGUE
CARD NUMBER: 66–11033

CONTENTS

Preface   *page* vii

Abbreviations and Location of MSS   xi

1   The Revival of Impeachment (1603–1625)   I

2   The Rise and Fall of Irresponsible Government
      (1625–1640)   42

3   The Failure of Impeachment (1640–1642)   77

4   The Separation of Powers and the Principle of
      Accountability (1642–1660)   120

5   The Breakdown of the Balance of Government
      (1660–1674)   155

6   The Crisis of Confidence (1674–1688)   197

7   The Logic of Parliamentary Supremacy (1688–1697)   245

8   The Tory Conversion to Responsible Government
      (1697–1702)   286

9   Political Parties and Responsible Government
      (1702–1714)   329

10   The End of Impeachment (1715–1717)   379

Conclusions   428

Index   447

v

237185

PREFACE

The responsibilities assumed by Sir Robert Walpole as the leading minister of George I differed markedly from those borne by Lord Burghley as the most trusted servant of Queen Elizabeth. Walpole assumed responsibility for any advice upon which the King acted; Lord Burghley claimed no such responsibility for the counsels upon which the Queen acted. If necessary Lord Burghley could plead the Queen's commands to justify his actions; Walpole knew that he could not plead the King's commands in his defence. If worst came to worst, Lord Burghley could rely on the Queen's pardon to excuse any unlawful act that he had committed; Walpole could not. Walpole had to answer for his conduct to Parliament, where he was liable to criticism, censure, and impeachment. Lord Burghley answered to the Queen alone for his management of her affairs, and feared no impeachment. To gain office and to remain in office, Burghley needed only the confidence of the Queen; Walpole needed both the King's and Parliament's. Walpole gained high office by making himself indispensable to the King in the House of Commons, while Lord Burghley gained high office by making himself indispensable to the Queen in the Secretary's office. Walpole, when out of office, systematically obstructed the King's business in Parliament in order to force his way back into office. Lord Burghley would have regarded such conduct as at best factious, at worst treasonous.

My purpose in this study is to show how and to explain why these changes in the responsibilities of ministers of state occurred. I do not intend to argue that ministerial responsibility to Parliament was fully achieved by 1714. It was not in fact fully achieved until 1841, when Sir Robert Peel, with no protest from the nation, formed a government that did not possess the confidence of the Queen. Macaulay may have believed that the great English Revolution of the seventeenth century transferred supreme control over executive power from the Crown to Parliament, but the facts of political life in the eighteenth century contradict his opinion. Yet the lateness of the achievement of responsible government does not preclude the antiquity of its beginnings. As early as the year 1341 Parliament demanded that ministers of the King answer to it for their conduct in office. Five centuries later it secured its demand. My purpose is to write the history of this struggle during one of these centuries, during the century when the House of Stuart reigned in England.

Two historians, Miss Mary Taylor Blauvelt and Professor A. H. Dodd, have previously written concerning this epoch in the history of responsible government. Miss Blauvelt's *The Development of Cabinet Government in England*, published in 1902, deserves praise as a thoughtful pioneering work. Professor Dodd's *The Growth of Responsible Government from James the First to Victoria*, published in 1956, is a book of much greater value, sketching the history of responsible government from 1603 to 1837 with an admirable clarity and an enviable soundness of judgment. I have written this study in the belief that Miss Blauvelt and Professor Dodd have not between them exhausted what could be usefully discovered and profitably said about the growth of responsible government in Stuart England.

Throughout this study I shall use the phrase 'responsible government' to mean all those laws, customs, conventions, and practices that serve to make ministers of the King rather than the King himself responsible for the acts of the government, and that serve to make those ministers accountable to Parliament rather than to the King. This double aspect of ministerial responsibility ought not to go unnoticed. There is a responsibility *for*, and there is an accountability *to*. In the thirteenth century the King assumed responsibility *for* the actions of the government, and ministers of the King answered *to* him for their conduct. In the reign of Queen Victoria ministers of state assumed responsibility *for* what the government did, and answered *to* Parliament for the wisdom of it. The history of responsible government is the history of both these transformations. It is the story of the denial of all responsibility to the King; and it is the story of Parliament's insistence that his ministers answer to it for their conduct in office.

This book would have been far more imperfect than it is had I not had the help of others in writing it. To three scholars I am particularly indebted: to Professor Frederick George Marcham of Cornell University, to Robert Latham, Reader in History at Royal Holloway College, University of London, and to my brother, David Roberts, Professor of History at Dartmouth College. Each of these persons read the entire book in typescript. Their timely counsels and wise comments saved me from innumerable solecisms, inaccuracies, inconsistencies, and blunders. The debt of gratitude that I owe them is immeasurable. To Brian Hill, Lecturer in History at the University of East Anglia, I owe a debt of gratitude hardly less great. He read the last six chapters of the book in typescript, commented on them, and corrected the errors he found there. Other experts similarly helped me. Professor Thomas Moir, author of *The Addled Parliament*, read chapter 1 in typescript; my former colleague, John Sperling, now of San Jose State College, read chapter 9, and my present colleague, John Rule, read chapter 10. Each of these scholars, out of their special knowledge of the period in question, made invaluable suggestions and corrections. Another colleague, Professor William McDonald, graciously helped by translating important passages in Latin for me. In particular he wrote, from two corrupt versions, an uncorrupted version of James I's final remark to the four Privy Councillors at Theobalds in 1610. To all these persons I owe a great debt, for they gave generously of their time and knowledge that my book should be less faulty.

I should also like to thank the Marquis of Bath for permission to examine the Coventry and Thynne Papers at Longleat and Miss Dorothy Coates, the archivist at Longleat, for the help and kindness she extended to me when I visited there. Earl Spencer extended a similar kindness to me when I travelled to Althorp to examine the Halifax Papers which he possesses. I should like to thank him for the kindness he then showed me and for the permission he gave me to read the Halifax Papers. For permission to read and quote from microfilms of the Cecil Papers in the Folger Library, I should like to thank the Marquis of Salisbury, and for permission to read and quote from the Portland Papers on loan to the University of Nottingham and to the British Museum, I should like to thank the Duke of Portland; I should also like to thank the University of Nottingham and the British Museum for making those papers available to me. I am indebted to William Ellis of the Historical Manuscript Commission for allowing me to read the Sackville [Knole] Papers in the Commission's possession and to the Right Honourable the Lord Sackville for permission to quote from them. A substantial part of chapter 5 appeared previously as an article in the *Cambridge Historical Journal* (XIII, no. 1, pp. 1–18), entitled 'The Impeachment of the Earl of Clarendon'. I should like to thank the editors of the *Journal* for permission to reprint it in my book. In 1959 the American Philosophical Society granted me sufficient money to pay my travel expenses to London and back, for which I am most grateful. I am similarly indebted to Ohio State University for granting me research leave in 1959, thus making it possible for me to come to England to pursue my researches.

Though I cannot repay, I can acknowledge, the kindness which these persons have shown me and the help which these institutions have given me. Without that kindness and without that help, this book could not have been written.

C.R.

ABBREVIATIONS USED IN
THE FOOTNOTES

Add. MSS	Additional Manuscripts
B.M.	British Museum
C.J.	*Commons Journals*
C.S.P. Dom.	*Calendar of State Papers Domestic*
C.S.P. Ven.	*Calendar of State Papers Venetian*
Cal. Tr. Books	*Calendar of Treasury Books*
Cl. St. Pap.	*Clarendon State Papers*
C.U.L.	Cambridge University Library
E.H.R.	*English Historical Review*
Fr. Trans.	French Transcripts
H.M.C.	*Historical Manuscript Commission*
H. of L. MSS	*House of Lords Manuscripts*
L.J.	*Lords Journals*
P.R.O.	Public Record Office
S.P.D.	State Papers Domestic
S.T.	Stowe Transcripts

LOCATION OF MSS CITED IN
THE FOOTNOTES

Ballard MSS	Bodleian Library
Brydges Papers	Huntington Library, San Marino, California
Carte MSS	Bodleian Library
Cecil Papers	Hatfield House, Hertfordshire. Microfilms in the British Museum and Folger Library
Clarendon MSS	Bodleian Library
Cottonian MSS	British Museum
Coventry Papers	Longleat, Wiltshire
Sackville [Knole] Papers	Historical Manuscript Commission Office, Quality Court, Chancery Lane, London

Egerton MSS	British Museum
French Transcripts	Public Record Office
Harleian MSS	British Museum
Lansdowne MSS	British Museum
Portland Papers	University of Nottingham
Rawlinson MSS	Bodleian Library
State Papers Spanish	Public Record Office
Stowe MSS	British Museum
Tanner MSS	Bodleian Library
Thynne Papers	Longleat, Wiltshire
Wentworth Woodhouse MSS	Sheffield City Library
Wynn of Gwydir Papers	National Library of Wales, Aberystwith

Unless otherwise stated, London is the place of publication of all works cited in the footnotes.

When quoting from contemporary sources I have modernized the spelling, capitalization, and punctuation.

CHAPTER I

THE REVIVAL OF IMPEACHMENT
(1603–1625)

On a summer morning in 1610 four great councillors of state rode into the King's park at Theobalds. Sent not by the Council, but by the two Houses of Parliament, they sought out James I among his beagles and horses and companions of the chase, and there amidst the hills of Hertfordshire presented His Majesty with a petition from the two Houses. Among the many favours that the two Houses begged in this petition, one in particular angered the prophet of a Free Monarchy: a request that he allow his servants to be arrested and sued as freely as were other men. Parliament begged this favour because it had just prosecuted Mr Henry Spiller and Sir Stephen Proctor, two unpopular servants of the Crown, and because it wished to prosecute the whole tribe of purveyors and cart-takers. Mr Spiller was a clerk in the Exchequer, who, it was said, neglected to prosecute recusants. Sir Stephen Proctor was a Commissioner of Concealed Debts, who had allegedly abused his commission in order to line his pockets with gold. The House of Commons had questioned Spiller before a committee of the House, and had imprisoned Proctor, but James demanded the release of Proctor and told the two Houses that he was to judge the delinquency of his own servants. The result of this impasse was the humble request made at Theobalds on the morning of 17 July 1610.

James's reply to Parliament's request was voluble, learned, prompt, and unfavourable. He had read the records of the past. He knew that when the people demanded this favour of their King, either the Kings were unjust and the people trampled underfoot, or the Kings were in eclipse and the people wanton and insolent. Since neither was true of these times, when his servants used such moderation as no man could justly complain of them, he must refuse their petition. *Non placet exemplum, nec placet petitio.*[1]

This confrontation at Theobalds ushered in a new epoch in the

---

[1] B.M. Lansdowne MSS 486, ff. 148–148v, 151, 152; B.M. Add. MSS 48053, ff. 86–89v, 96–97.

history of responsible government. No Tudor Parliament had ever asked a monarch for permission to arrest and sue his servants. Nor had any Parliament since 1388 imprisoned one of the King's officers. The last time that Parliament had complained of a servant of the Crown was in 1449. To those Elizabethan statesmen still alive in the seventh year of James's reign, Parliament's request must have seemed strange and unprecedented, even revolutionary. Elizabeth, and Elizabeth's father before her, had never allowed Parliament to attack their servants.

And in truth Parliament's request was, when compared to the practices and theory of Tudor government, revolutionary. The responsibility of officers and ministers of the Crown under the Tudors was to the King, not to Parliament, nor to the people. If a councillor gave foolish advice, the King, not Parliament, had the right to remove him. If a great minister of the Crown abused his authority and rode roughshod over the law, the obligation to punish him lay on the King, not Parliament. If there was corruption in the Exchequer, it was the King's duty, not Parliament's, to stop it. As Henry VIII told the leaders of the Pilgrimage of Grace in 1536, 'We would you knew, that it appertains nothing to any of our subjects, to appoint us our Council...' And in 1542 Henry again showed the world that he would not brook malicious attacks on his servants. In that year he sent two members of the House of Commons to the Fleet for exhibiting to the Council 'sundry heinous articles against the President of the Council of the Marches of Wales'. Those great ministers under Henry who did pay with their lives for their mistakes—the Empsons and Dudleys, the Wolseys and Cromwells—did so because they had lost the King's favour, their only shield against harm.[1]

Queen Elizabeth, in asserting her mastery over her servants, was less sanguinary but no less tenacious than her father. She allowed neither royal favourites nor court factions nor members of Parliament to dictate to her whom she should choose as her servants. When the Earl of Leicester, the first courtier in the realm, threatened to have the Gentleman of the Black Rod dismissed for not admitting

---

[1] *State Papers Published under the Authority of His Majesty's Commission. King Henry the Eighth* (1830–6), I, 508; N. H. Nicolas (ed.), *Proceedings and Ordinances of the Privy Council of England* (1834–7), VII, 306. I am indebted to Professor S. T. Bindoff for the reference to Henry's imprisoning two members of the House of Commons for attacking his servant.

one of his followers to the Privy Chamber, the Queen retorted, 'God's-death, my Lord, I have wished you well, but my favour is not so locked up for you, that others shall not participate thereof; for I have many servants unto whom I have and will, at my pleasure, bequeath my favour...and if you think to rule here, I will take a course to see you forthcoming: I will have here but one mistress, and no master...'[1] The northern rebels in 1569 and the faction that took up arms with the Earl of Essex in 1591, both of whom sought to remove evil counsellors from about the Queen, fared much worse than did Leicester, paying with their lives for their temerity. Nor did the House of Commons escape the Queen's chastisement. In 1589 they passed two bills concerning abuses in the Exchequer and in Purveyances. The Queen at once sent a message to the Commons informing them that she would not have them touch 'the officers and ministers of her own Household' or 'the officers and ministers of her own Court of her own revenue'. If any officials had demeaned themselves unlawfully or untruly, she was 'both able and willing to see due reformation', and would do so, to the public example of others. And when the House grumbled at this message, she sent another reminding them that she had 'as much skill, will, and power to rule and govern her own Household, as any subject to manage his without the aid of his neighbours'.[2]

Though there is no recorded instance in the whole of Tudor history of a parliamentary attack upon a minister enjoying the King's favour, there were many such attacks in the two hundred years before Henry Tudor won the Crown at Bosworth Field. These were the years that James spoke of, the years when Kings were either tyrannous or in eclipse, the people either cowed or insolent. Compared to the practices of these times the conduct of Parliament in 1610 was not strange, or unprecedented, or revolutionary. Parliament was merely reviving old habits and long-forgotten claims. Indeed, James Whitelocke, a bold champion of the Common Law, reminded the Commons in 1610 that Parliament had condemned Lord Latimer in the fiftieth year of the reign of Edward III for advising the collection of impositions not voted by Parliament. Another member told the House that Richard Lyons, a Farmer of the Customs under

[1] Sir Robert Naunton, 'Fragmenta Regalia', in *Harleian Miscellany* (1808–11), v, 124.
[2] Sir John Neale, *Elizabeth I and Her Parliaments, 1581–1601* (1957), pp. 207–13.

Edward III, had lost his goods and lands for the same reason.[1] The medieval heritage had not vanished during the golden age of monarchical government.

The important question is, exactly what legacy did these medieval proponents of responsible government leave to the parliamentarians of Stuart England? Just what did the councillors at Oxford, the Lords Ordainers, and the Lords Appellant leave behind them when their day was over? What sedimentary deposits remained after the high flood of baronial demands had subsided? The most concrete and practical answer is the Year Books that James Whitelocke read in Gray's Inn, the Parliament Rolls that committees of the House of Commons consulted in the Tower, and the chronicles of Matthew Paris and Thomas Walsingham that gentlemen read in their libraries. These ancient records survived the Tudor monarchy and lay close at hand to jog the memories of Stuart politicians and to furnish them with a rich mine of precedents to justify their conduct.

Viewed in another way, the medieval legacy consisted of a legal doctrine, a parliamentary power, and a political tradition. The legal doctrine was the maxim that the King can do no wrong; the parliamentary power was that of impeachment; and the political tradition was the belief that the King should act on the advice of councillors acceptable to Parliament. Stuart politicians were to seize firmly upon each of these weapons in their hour of need.

The maxim that the King can do no wrong was rarely, if ever, heard in the twelfth and thirteenth centuries. Englishmen then believed that their Kings could do, and often did, wrong. Article 61 of Magna Carta is testimony enough to the existence of this belief. But the coercion of a King charged with wrong-doing by a Council of Barons was not the path leading to constitutional monarchy in England. That path was a more devious one, and the signposts along it bore the maxim: the King can do no wrong. This maxim of law, which first appears in its modern guise in the fifteenth century, really conceals three distinct, though related, principles. The first principle states that the King cannot act himself, but must always act through a servant. The second asserts that a servant of the King should refuse to execute an unlawful command. The third declares that a servant cannot plead the King's command to justify an unlawful act. To-

---

[1] S. R. Gardiner (ed.), *Parliamentary Debates in 1610* (Camden Soc. LXXXI), p. 108; B.M. Add. MSS 48053, f. 159.

gether these three principles free the King from all legal responsibility for the acts of his government and place that responsibility on his ministers.

In the thirteenth century the law had not yet imprisoned the King in the doctrine that his will could only be expressed by a writ or a warrant, by letters patent or a charter, sealed or countersigned by one of his servants. Sir Edward Coke's assertion that the King's will is always a 'matter of record' was far distant. In fact in the thirteenth century the King's will expressed by word of mouth carried more force than his own writs. The King could give verbal orders for the arrest of one man or the disseisin of another or the enfeoffment of a third.[1] Furthermore, if his Chancellor balked at putting the Great Seal to an unlawful grant he could devise a new seal to give force to his wishes, and he could entrust it to any person he wished. But slowly this personal, immediate, and private lordship gave way to a more impersonal, formal, and public kingship. Englishmen began to argue that the King's commands ought to be expressed in formal writs and his favours granted in solemn charters. By 1485, largely to protect the King from fraud, an elaborate procedure had arisen for the expression of the royal will. In the Chancery royal commands bore the Great Seal, in the Exchequer the Privy Seal, in the Secretary's office the Signet; and often all three were required to give expression to the royal will. The King could no longer grant lands to a favourite, make payments out of the Exchequer, pardon a felon, summon an adviser to Council, or arrest a man, without acting through one of his servants.

These developments in the procedures by which the King expressed his will acquired constitutional significance when the judges began to rule that the King could do no wrong. In 1457 Justice Moyle maintained that the King could not himself seize any man's property, for then there would be no remedy. Two years later Choke, a Serjeant-at-law, declared that the King could not grant land or arrest a man 'except by a written matter of record, for all that the King did was of record'. The doctrine that these two men pleaded soon won a wider acceptance. Sir John Markham, Chief Justice of Common Pleas, told Edward IV that the King could not arrest a man on suspicion of felony or treason, for if he did so wrongly, the man would have no remedy at law. Henry VII heard the same story

---

[1] L. Ehrlich, *Proceedings Against the Crown* (Oxford, 1921), pp. 68, 127, 141–2.

from Chief Justice Hussey, who told him in 1485 that there were certain acts which the King could not do, for if he did wrong the subject would have no remedy.[1]

At the same time Englishmen began to argue that the Chancellor should not put the Seal to an illegal charter, and that the judge should disregard an unlawful order. In the courts Letters Patent were voided because they were unlawful and charters were overturned because they contravened the Common Law. Henry IV in 1406 agreed to the Commons' demand that the Chancellor and Privy Seal should not pass grants contrary to the law; and judges were sworn, as Sir John Fortescue observed, to do justice according to the law, even if the King ordered the contrary.[2] It was the combination of these two principles—that the King could not act himself, personally and immediately, and that those who acted for him must act lawfully—that divided the King from any direct responsibility for the lawfulness of his own government.

These two principles implied that a Chancellor or judge or Treasurer could not plead the King's command to justify an unlawful act. This third principle also appeared for the first time in the fifteenth century. Before that century the opposite doctrine prevailed in the courts. An escheator who wrongfully seized lands for the King could successfully plead that he had done it at the King's command. A royal officer who falsely imprisoned a man could plead that he had acted under a royal commission.[3] But during the reign of Edward III there arose a clamour for change. In response to this clamour Edward in 1341 promised that anyone who did anything against the law, even at the King's command, should answer for it, either in Parliament or elsewhere. And in 1354 he granted a request of the House of Commons that purveyors should not be allowed to hide behind the King's commands.[4] In the fifteenth century the judges accepted this new doctrine. In 1483 all the judges gathered

[1] Sir William Holdsworth, *A History of English Law* (Boston, 1924), III, 388, 464–8; S. B. Chrimes, *English Constitutional Ideas in the Fifteenth Century* (Cambridge, 1936), pp. 45, 50, 364; Sir Edward Coke, *The Second Part of the Institutes of the Laws of England* (1797), pp. 186–7.

[2] Ehrlich, *Proceedings Against the Crown*, pp. 15, 70, 128–30, 146; T. P. Taswell-Langmead, *English Constitutional History* (9th ed. Boston, 1929), p. 280; Sir John Fortescue, *De Laudibus Legum Angliae* (Cambridge, 1942), pp. 126–7, 204–5.

[3] Ehrlich, *Proceedings Against the Crown*, pp. 50, 110–11, 141.

[4] Ehrlich, *Proceedings Against the Crown*, pp. 131, 158; G. T. Lapsley, *Crown, Community and Parliament in the Middle Ages* (Oxford, 1951), p. 269.

in Chancery agreed that if a man disseised another for the King, where the King had no right, the King could not be said to be the disseisor, for the King can do no wrong.[1] Yet Sir Edward Coke was unable either in his *Institutes* or his *Reports* to cite an instance when the plea of the King's command was made before, and disallowed by, a court of law. The reason for this is clear. Medieval and Tudor Kings had the power to stop any litigation in the courts that affected their servants, and so to prevent the creation of such precedents. But though explicit precedents were lacking, the principle that no one could plead the King's command to justify an illegal act was part of the Common Law of late medieval England; and Stuart parliamentarians seized upon it, and applied it to the greatest ministers in the realm.

Though medieval Kings could prevent the prosecution of their servants in the ordinary courts of the land, three of them, Edward III, Richard II, and Henry VI, could not prevent the impeachment of their ministers in Parliament. In a strictly legal sense, the power of impeachment first appeared in the Good Parliament of 1376. It emerged then, as T. F. T. Plucknett has ingeniously shown, by the transformation of the ancient procedure of conviction by notoriety into the modern practice of impeachment by common fame. In the twelfth century a local court could, simply on the notoriety of the fact, pronounce a thief guilty. In the fourteenth and seventeenth centuries the House of Commons could, simply on the notoriety of his faults, accuse a great minister of state.[2] But in a more general sense, in a political sense, the power of impeachment had its origins in the stormy Parliament of 1341, when King and Parliament alike accepted the principle that the King's ministers were to answer in Parliament for their misdeeds. As Gaillard Lapsley observes, 'The right of impeachment seems to be explicitly granted except that no corporate accusation is contemplated.'[3] And even this corporate accusation was foreshadowed in 1341 when Archbishop Stratford asked to be tried before Parliament because he was 'notoriously defamed throughout the realm'.[4] From this year the desire of the Commons and the Lords to punish royal officials who broke the

---

[1] *Year Book, Edward V* (1579), p. viii; Chrimes, *Fifteenth Century*, p. 375.
[2] T. F. T. Plucknett, 'The Origin of Impeachment' and 'The Impeachments of 1376', in *Transactions of the Royal Historical Society*, 4th ser. xxiv, 47–71, and 5th ser. i, 153–64.
[3] Lapsley, *Crown, Community and Parliament*, p. 269.
[4] Plucknett, *Trans. R. Hist. Soc.* 4th ser. xxiv, 68.

law grew in strength and vehemence. Between 1376 and 1397 the House of Commons impeached no fewer than eighteen royal officers and judges for their crimes, real or alleged. The Lords found each and every one of them guilty.[1] And though impeachments gave way to Acts of Attainder in the fifteenth and sixteenth centuries, the right of the House of Commons to impeach great ministers of state and of the House of Lords to judge them was indelibly inscribed on the Parliament Rolls in the Tower. The record was there for William Noy and William Hakewill to read on 27 February 1621.

By impeachment Parliament could punish those who violated the law, but impeachments were a poor instrument for controlling the King's policies. And the control of royal policy was as much the concern of the baronial opposition in medieval England as the punishment of offenders against the law. The problem that confronted the barons was the problem of counsel, of who should advise the King. No monarchy, unless a constitutional monarchy, can avoid this problem, and the English monarchy from the reign of Aethelred the Counsel-less to the reign of Queen Victoria was no exception. One solution to the problem, a solution attendant with much violence, was to compel the King to act upon the advice of a Council forced upon him. The magnates of England proposed this solution in 1244 and carried it into effect in 1258, but with no lasting success. The Lords Ordainers during the reign of Edward II and the Lords Appellant during the reign of Richard II likewise used force to make the King heed their counsels, but with no more success. Nor did any of these attempts to force councillors on the King establish a tradition to which Stuart parliamentarians might look back with reverence. Quite the contrary: a Sandys, a Coke, or a Hakewill was most unlikely to mention these experiments, knowing that they were attempted in times of rebellion. Until 1642 Stuart politicians ignored all precedents for coercing the King. The tradition to which they did hearken was that which appeared as early as 1341, but found its fullest expression under the first Lancastrian

---

[1] The Commons impeached and the Lords condemned Lord Latimer, Lord Neville, and Richard Lyons in 1376, the Earl of Suffolk in 1386, Sir Robert Bealknap, Sir John Holt, Sir William Burgh, Sir Robert Fulthrop, Sir John Cary, Sir Simon Burley, Sir John Beauchamp, Sir James Berners, Sir John Salisbury, John Blake, Thomas Usk, John Lokton, and Bishop Rushook of Chichester in 1388, and Thomas Arundel, Archbishop of Canterbury, in 1397. In 1449 the Commons impeached the Duke of Suffolk, but Henry VI banished him from the realm before the Lords could try him.

King: the tradition that the King should act on the advice of councillors acceptable to Parliament. Henry IV promised his subjects that he would always act on the advice of his Council, and he dismissed four of his servants from Court because they were displeasing to Parliament. This heritage, and not the memory of rebellious barons confronting their King at Runnymede or Lewes, proved valuable to Englishmen in the seventeenth century. Parliament should not name the King's councillors, but neither should the King listen to irresponsible courtiers who were hateful to the people.

Under the Tudors little was heard of the maxim that the King can do no wrong, nothing of impeachments, and hardly a word about the King's listening to councillors in whom Parliament could confide. It is true that Henry VIII, by further regulating the use of the three seals in 1536, made the King's will more than ever a matter of record. It is true that the judges in 1584 refused to obey an unlawful command sent to them by Queen Elizabeth. It is also true that Parliament, by voting Acts of Attainder, shared indirectly in the condemnation of ministers of state (in 1621 'Empson and Dudley' was on every man's lips). And there were grumblings in 1536 and 1569 about upstart councillors around the throne.[1] But for the most part these particular constitutional issues slept. Yet the constitution did not; for the sixteenth century witnessed two developments that profoundly influenced the nature of English government. G. R. Elton has thoroughly described the first of these, the final transformation of a personal household administration into an impersonal public administration.[2] This development greatly weakened the logical force of Elizabeth's plea (echoed later by James I and Charles I) that she had as much right to choose her own servants as any subject to choose his. The comparison was inept in an age when the King's servants were public ministers, not keepers of the King's robes and custodians of his plate. What the Stuart parliamentarians sought to superintend was unmistakably a public, not a personal, administration.

The second development was the emergence of the House of

---

[1] Sir William Anson, *The Law and the Custom of the Constitution*. Part II. *The Crown* (Oxford, 1896), p. 50; W. E. Hearn, *The Government of England* (Melbourne, 1886), pp. 103–4. Sir Edward Coke and his friends were mistaken to cite Empson and Dudley as a precedent for attacking Mompesson, for it does not appear that Parliament carried out its threat to vote an Act of Attainder against them (D. M. Brodie, 'Edmund Dudley: Minister of Henry VII', *Transactions of the Royal Historical Society*, 4th ser. xv, 150–1).

[2] G. R. Elton, *The Tudor Revolution in Government* (Cambridge, 1953).

Commons as an assembly proud of its independence, jealous of its privileges, possessed of a corporate will, and driven by new-found ambitions. Sir John Neale has written the history of this development and has noted its great importance.[1] To the historian of responsible government the emergence of the Commons has this significance: it meant that ministerial responsibility, when finally won, would be to the House of Commons and not to the House of Lords. The barons in the fourteenth and fifteenth centuries had missed their chance. They had failed to make ministers answerable to a Parliament which they dominated. Their failure arose both from a habit of returning after each crisis to their own estates and their own concerns, and from an inability to see that capturing the Council did not suffice if the machinery of daily administration remained in the hands of servants of the King.[2] As a result of their default, and of the growing power of the House of Commons under the Tudors, the initiative for making ministers responsible to Parliament passed in the seventeenth century to the Commons of England. And they did not fail, for they did not lack persistence or fail to superintend those who were entrusted with the day-to-day administration of the realm.

Medieval legacies and Tudor developments explain why Parliament in the reign of James I could justify its renewed demands for responsible government, but they do not explain why it chose to renew them. They do not explain why from 1610 to 1625 the House of Commons impeached seven servants of the Crown, arrested eight others, expelled four of them from the House, censured one, named the Treasurers for the Subsidies in 1624, and required the Council of War to answer to Parliament for wisely spending the Subsidies. These impeachments, arrests, and expulsions took place not because there existed Year Books and Parliament Rolls to justify them, but because there existed members of Parliament who desired them. Who were these members and why did they in 1610, again in 1614, and then in 1621 and 1624, challenge the King's undoubted right to choose, to protect, to consult, and to remove from office his own councillors and ministers?

In the Parliament of 1610 members of the House of Commons for the first time directly attacked the King's lesser servants, obliquely

---

[1] Neale, *Elizabeth I and Her Parliaments.*

[2] E. C. Lodge and G. A. Thornton, *English Constitutional Documents 1307–1485* (Cambridge, 1935), pp. 46–9.

threatened his Privy Councillors, and complained of his irresponsible advisers.

Sir Stephen Proctor and Mr Henry Spiller were the lesser servants attacked in the House. The author of the complaint against Proctor was Sir John Mallory, a Yorkshire knight who sat for the borough of Ripon. The author of the complaint against Spiller was Thomas Felton, who, not being a member of Parliament, persuaded Sir Francis Hastings, a knight of the shire from Somerset, to introduce his petition for him.[1] The motives of these men were largely personal. Mallory was engaged in a feud with Proctor, which reached its climax in 1609 when Mallory, with forty men behind him, at the open fair at Thirsk, proclaimed himself Lord Salisbury's High Steward, and put out Proctor's deputy. Felton, who had a grant of the sixth part of recusancy fines increased by his efforts, felt wronged by Spiller's negligence. Hastings was a meddling politician whom the Council in 1605 placed under house arrest for drawing up a petition for some Puritans in Northamptonshire.[2] Mallory and Spiller acted out of personal pique; Hastings out of a spirit of faction.

Why the Commons entertained these complaints is a question of more importance than why Mallory and Hastings introduced them. Did the members of the House listen to them because abuses by royal officials were greater now than they had been under Elizabeth, or because James, enjoying less popularity, was less able to protect his servants? Were the Commons concerned with good government or an increase in their own power? The charges that Mallory made against Sir Stephen Proctor suggest that abuses had got out of hand. He accused Proctor of wrongfully despoiling Englishmen of their money and goods, of illegally searching their houses, of taking bribes from some and compounding with others, and of defrauding the King by pocketing a third part of the money he collected. The only trouble with these allegations is that Mallory failed to prove them before a committee of the House of Lords on 18 July; and the witnesses called to substantiate them were a singular lot. They included a keeper of pigeon holes and his wife, a keeper of a bawdy house, one perjurer, one cut-purse, and two felons.[3]

---

[1] Lansdowne MSS 486, f. 148; *L.J.* II, 650–1.
[2] S.P.D. 14/12:74; 14/43:115; 14/74:104; 14/216:72, 94; *C.S.P. Dom. 1603–1610*, p. 393; *1610–1618*, p. 41.
[3] S.P.D. 14/54:32; Lansdowne MSS 513, f. 97v.

Yet the House of Commons not only accepted the charges when Mallory brought them into the House, but continued to press them, even after the committee of the House of Lords dismissed them as worthless. Why did they do so? There are three possible reasons. One lies in another of Mallory's charges: that Proctor had collected 'debts concealed upon good cause'.[1] This might well have struck a responsive chord in gentlemen who believed that such ghosts should not be raised, that ancient debts owed the Crown should not be searched out. Another reason, perhaps, is that James had also granted to Proctor, at his suggestion, the office of Collector and Receiver of Fines on Penal Statutes. The effect of this office was to wrest power and profit from justices of the peace, many of whom sat in the House of Commons.[2] These members could hardly look with favour on a man sent out from Whitehall to pry into their business. A third possible reason was the ambition of members of Parliament to win for themselves the right to proceed against royal officials on common fame. This determination was best expressed by those peers in the Upper House who supported the desire of the Commons to act against Proctor. They argued that 'many times things are not at the hearing of causes opened so fully as were fit, and many times proofs may be...kept from the knowledge and understanding of such as are to judge the cause'. Therefore the House of Lords should not dismiss the accusations brought by the House of Commons against Sir Stephen Proctor.[3] The argument of these lords echoed the determination of fourteenth-century Parliaments to proceed on 'notoriety' and foreshadowed the willingness of Parliament in 1626 to impeach the Duke of Buckingham on 'common fame'.

Henry Spiller's case likewise showed that the House of Commons did not intend to allow a want of proof to stand in their way. Mr Spiller's fault was 'his partial proceedings against recusants, the trust of proceeding against them being his'. Mr Felton, however, failed to prove before a committee of the House of Commons that Spiller had neglected his duty in prosecuting recusants. The House accordingly ordered that the proceedings against Spiller be dropped.[4]

[1] S.P.D. 14/54:32.
[2] S.P.D. 38/9:411; 14/47:57. J. Spedding, *The Letters and the Life of Francis Bacon* (1861–74), IV, 96–105.
[3] Lansdowne MSS 513, f. 98.   [4] Lansdowne MSS 486, ff. 148–148v.

Then unexpectedly, three weeks later, on 6 July, the House returned to Felton's charges against Spiller. The best guess, and it can only be a guess, why the House took up the matter again is that many of its members wanted the penal laws against Catholics more vigorously enforced. In April the House had voted that not executing the laws against recusants was a grievance, and in June Lawrence Hyde proposed that a clause demanding the execution of laws against Jesuits and Seminarists be added to the Subsidy Bill.[1] Quite obviously, James's remissness in prosecuting recusants had taught the House to be concerned with the execution, as well as the formulation, of laws.

In the debate on 6 July the Commons betrayed an uneasiness at their own intrepidity. They had imprisoned Proctor and examined Spiller, yet how could they justify themselves to the world at large? In May the King had ordered them to release Proctor and had told them that they might proceed against him either 'by way of Bill, or as a Grievance, leaving to His Majesty to do therein as he saw fit'. The House dutifully obliged, surrendered Proctor to James, and proceeded against the errant Commissioner by a Bill of Particulars. Both James's demand and the Commons' obedience to it conformed to the theory of the constitution at the time. The Commons had the right to proceed by bill for the redress of acts done against the law, and by petition for the redress of grievances that were merely onerous, not unlawful; but they could not proceed on their own authority to examine, imprison, or punish the King's servants.[2] Unfortunately for James, the House of Commons was losing patience with this arrangement. Not only Proctor and Spiller caused this unease, but the purveyors also, and the officers of the Green-Cloth who superintended them. In 1604 the Commons had petitioned James for relief from the oppressions of these officials, and in 1606 they had passed a bill to correct the worst abuses perpetrated by them. But James had not heeded the petition and the House of Lords had not passed the bill. To one member of the House of Commons, to Sir Edwin Sandys, the loss of the bill meant little. If thirty-seven laws against abuses in purveyance produced no effect, he observed, then thirty-eight will produce no more.[3] The logic of

[1] *C.J.* I, 420, 438.
[2] Lansdowne MSS 486, ff. 145v–146. The expressions 'Bill of Particulars' and 'Bill for the Punishment of Sir Stephen Proctor' (*L.J.* III, 650–1) were used to describe the bill that the Commons sent to the Lords against Proctor. No one ever called it a Bill of Attainder, although that is what it must have been.   [3] *C.J.* I, 281.

13

this observation was ominous: merely passing another law would serve no purpose, the Commons must see to it that the King's servants observed those laws already on the statute book.

The immediate result of the debate on 6 July was a decision to resume the investigation into Spiller's delinquencies. But that decision was not the sole result. These events in early July coincided with the Earl of Salisbury's negotiations for the Great Contract. Someone, there is no indication who, put two and two together, and moved that one of the terms of the contract be that the King's servants might be sued and imprisoned as freely as other men. On 16 July the House of Commons agreed to this motion, and sent it (with six other proposals for easing the subject) to the House of Lords. The Lords agreed that the seven Heads of Ease should be part of the Great Contract, and sent the Earls of Salisbury, Northampton, Suffolk, and Worcester to present them to James at Theobalds on the 17th.[1] Thus came about the confrontation at Theobalds and James's voluble and angry speech.

When the Earl of Salisbury informed the House of Commons of James's refusal to allow his servants to be arrested and sued as other men, the Commons agreed 'to rest satisfied with the answer'. They also dropped any further prosecution against Mr Spiller. The Lords, for their part, refused to examine the Bill of Particulars against Proctor. The only gain for the Commons in this whole affair was the agreement of the King and the Lords to except Proctor from the General Pardon passed that session.[2] The gain was trivial. The victory in this opening round clearly went to the apostle of a Free Monarchy. His victory was as complete, in its way, as Elizabeth's in the year 1589, when she told the Commons that she would punish her servants if they did wrong. The tragedy was that James, unlike Elizabeth, did not recognize the need to put his own house in order. As a result the Commons, eleven years later, in 1621, sought to do it for him.

July must have been a vexatious month for James. Not only did the House of Commons ask permission to arrest his servants, but members of the House attacked those who had advised him to collect

---

[1] Lansdowne MSS 486, ff. 148v–152; B.M. Add. MSS 48053, ff. 86–88; *C.J.* I, 450.
[2] Lansdowne MSS 486, ff. 154v–155; B.M. Add. MSS 48053, f. 97; *L.J.* II, 657–8. Lord Huntingdon believed that James's unwillingness to allow his prerogative to be subject to the law contributed to the failure of the Great Contract (Hastings MSS, Box 1, f. 4).

impositions. The authors of these attacks were not country gentlemen from Yorkshire and Somersetshire. They were lawyers from Gray's Inn and Lincoln's Inn. Two of them in particular, James Whitelocke and William Hakewill, distinguished themselves as tribunes of the people in the great debate of 2 July on impositions. Both of them attacked impositions as unlawful, and both of them reminded the House that Parliament in 1376 had condemned Lord Latimer and Richard Lyons for 'procuring impositions to be set without assent of Parliament'. Another member hazarded a comparison between the present Lord Treasurer and Empson and Dudley.[1] To quiet these audacious men, James met both Houses in the Banqueting Hall a week later, and asked his Lord Treasurer to explain to them the necessity for impositions. But the Earl of Salisbury devoted more time to clearing himself than to justifying impositions. He began his apology for his past conduct with a reminder, rendered ironical by the presence of both Houses, that he was accountable only to the King. He then went on to plead that the Earl of Dorset had originated the scheme for collecting impositions, that the Council had concurred in it, that the principal merchants had assented to it, that the Court of Exchequer had declared it lawful, and that the King had commanded him to put it into execution. He concluded that, these things being true, it showed a want of charity in any man to liken him to Empson and Dudley.[2] But Salisbury's mending of political fences did not end with his formal defence before both Houses. That same night he drove to Hyde Park to meet privately with a select number of House of Commons men, and to justify further his conduct in the matter of impositions. Sir Edwin Sandys, that redoubtable champion of the privileges of the Commons, was present, as was Sir Henry Neville, who perhaps saw in that night's meeting the model for his undertaking in 1614. Six others were also present. But it is questionable whether this meeting did Salisbury, or the eight leaders of the House, any good. When news of the

[1] Gardiner, *Parliamentary Debates in 1610*, p. 108; B.M. Add. MSS 48053, ff. 159–159v.

[2] *H.M.C. Downshire*, II, 330–8; *L.J.* II, 639. Though Salisbury did not emphasize the plea that he had acted at the King's command, there is reason to believe that he held such a plea to be perfectly valid. In 1608, along with other counsellors, he signed a letter to the King, which bears this title: 'A Letter written by the Lords of the Councell to the King...touching means to advance the King's revenues by unusual means so as the King will take the Act upon himself and be their protection.' In the letter the Lords of the Council recommended raising revenue by examining defective titles, recovering assart lands, compounding for wards, examining entails, and exacting provisions (Harleian MSS 2207, f. 2).

meeting spread through the environs of Westminster, all those present at the meeting were suspected of plotting some new design. All, perhaps, except Salisbury, whose reputation, according to Sir Dudley Carleton, did not really suffer because of the reflections made on him in the House of Commons.[1] Sir Dudley's judgment is credible, for most Englishmen recognized the fundamental rectitude of the Lord Treasurer. The persons whom they really distrusted were the courtiers and clergymen who urged James to be a true King.

The parliamentary enemies of these courtiers and clergymen withheld their fire until November, when the failure of the Great Contract precipitated an attack upon them. Henry Martin began the attack by firing a broadside at the clergy. He observed on the 14th of November, '...now the Contract is like to break...the King's wants may drive him to extremities', men may counsel him to extend 'the prerogative beyond the bounds...This cannot be done but by two sorts of men. The one Privy Counsellors, but there is no fear of them, they are noble and honourable. [They] themselves have fair possessions and posterity, and it cannot be imagined they will advise that which shall make their posterity servile.' But it is different with the clergy. They have advised the King to do things that 'none of his predecessors in England ever did'. They preach daily 'against the fundamental laws of the Kingdom'. They urge that 'Kings are not bound by their laws'. They say that His Majesty 'may of right take things without Parliament that are granted in Parliament'. They know that 'the highway to a double benefice is to tread on the Common Law'. Martin then proposed that the House pass a bill to deprive such clergymen of their dignities and to prosecute them for praemunire.[2] In these fulminations against the high prerogative notions of the clergy, and in the violent action proposed against them, one can glimpse the seeds of that mingled rage and fear which would destroy Laud a generation later.

The turn of the Scots came nine days later, when they fell under the lash of a lawyer named John Hoskyns, who once told his wife that he 'had rather die with wit than live without it', and who very nearly died for want of it in 1614.[3] He rose in the House on 23 November

---

[1] R. F. Williams (ed.), *The Court and Times of James the First* (1848), I, 123.

[2] B.M. Add. MSS 48119, ff. 203–204v.

[3] L. B. Osborne, *The Life, Letters and Writings of John Hoskyns* (New Haven, 1937), p. 71. For Hoskyns's folly in 1614 see below, p. 22.

1610 in order to complain of those who had begged so much from the King that Parliament must now deliberate on the means to relieve him. This was not a question, he said, of this or that person, but of a whole nation. This nation was not the Irish, 'for they would sooner turn costermongers', nor the Dutch, for they were 'too industrious', nor the English, for he could clear them of this offence. 'But a fault there was', and he therefore moved the House to examine what had caused the King's want, 'for without a doubt the royal cisterne had a leak, and until stopped it was of little use to consult how to bring money into it'. His fellow members fully agreed, and accordingly voted that a Committee of the Whole House should, the very next morning, enter into consideration of the causes of the King's wants. There was talk of a petition to the King to remove the Scots from Court, and of refusing to vote supplies unless he did so. But the Committee of the Whole House never met, for James, to prevent either inquiry or petition, prorogued and then dissolved Parliament. In this rupture the intrigues of Sir Robert Carr, James's Scottish favourite, cast a sinister shadow. Not only had Carr urged the prorogation, but in the preceding months he had stirred up members of the House of Commons against Salisbury. It was a sad day for the House of Stuart when one trusted servant began to intrigue in Parliament against another.[1]

The Earl of Salisbury's failure to control the House of Commons in 1610 was, as Professor Willson remarks, 'more than a failure of a single minister. It was the failure of a system...The Elizabethan system, without Elizabeth, had broken down and was not to be restored.'[2] If it was not to be restored, then it had to be replaced, for some system of some kind was needed to reconcile an impecunious King with a distrustful Parliament. Some means must be found to keep all in tune. Two men, one a politician and the other a philosopher, confidently offered James the magic wand for securing such harmony. The politician was Sir Henry Neville, a Berkshire

---

[1] B.M. Add. MSS 48119, ff. 212–212v; Cecil Papers 134/143; D. H. Willson, *The Privy Councillors in the House of Commons* (Minneapolis, 1940), p. 127. Sir Thomas Lake reported that James 'discoursed long to show in what degree of treason they were that would seek to remove servants from a Prince...'. To which Lake answered, 'perhaps the party that had the conceit, being some rash man, took it for no treason to move to the House to go by Petition'. But this did not satisfy James, who demanded that Lake and Salisbury name those in the Commons that dared attack his Scottish servants (Cecil Papers, 128/168).

[2] Willson, *Privy Councillors*, pp. 128–9.

gentleman who had sat in six Parliaments since 1584. The philosopher was Sir Francis Bacon.

Sir Henry Neville, despite the fact that he had been one of 'the parliamentary mutineers' in 1610, was the first to come forward with a plan. In the summer of 1612 he followed James to Windsor, on the hunt, into the field, in order to urge him to rely on the affections of his House of Commons rather than on the fullness of his prerogative. He urged him to win their affections by redressing the grievances of which they complained and by giving office to those in whom they could confide. Neville did not himself ask to be appointed Secretary of State; his friends at Court did so for him. His only purpose was to persuade the King that he knew 'the inwardest thoughts' of the principal gentlemen in the Commons, and that he could undertake to secure their support for the King, if the King would grant them the graces they sought. His scheme came to nothing, for, as James himself said, he would 'not have a Secretary imposed on him by Parliament', nor would he hear of Neville's bringing in with him 'his man Sir Ralph Winwood and his champion the Earl of Southampton, and whosoever he thinks good'. Neville's 'great pains to reconcile and set all in tune' came to naught. As Professor Moir observes, 'he had to reconcile the irreconcilable'.[1]

At some time between June 1613 and January 1614 Sir Francis Bacon wrote down the counsels that he believed the King should pursue. He first offered the King some advice that was characteristically Elizabethan: avoid any quarrel over privileges, be silent about impositions, have projects ready for Parliament to fall upon. He then advanced proposals of a less traditional nature. James should win over or bridle the lawyers in the House, 'that they may further the King's causes or at least fear to oppose them'. He should take measures to secure the loyalty of the burgesses in the House; even more, he ought to consider how to win the support of 'that great body of the House which consists of Justices of the Peace and gentlemen of the country'. Measures should also be taken to retain the support of the 'courtiers and the King's servants', who in the last session deserted, either from fear or from a desire to be popular.

---

[1] S.P.D. 14/74:44; *H.M.C. Buccleuch*, I, 111, 113–14; N. E. McClure (ed.), *The Letters of John Chamberlain* (Philadelphia, 1939), I, 358–60, 384–5, 387; T. L. Moir, *The Addled Parliament of 1614* (Oxford, 1958), p. 16. James later described the undertaking as 'a combination of divers for their own preferment...' (W. Notestein, F. H. Relf and H. Simpson, eds., *Commons Debates 1621*, New Haven, 1935, IV, 10).

The King should also seek to intimidate, or win over with hopes of preferment, those who 'made the popular party' in the last Parliament. Bacon then turned from the arts of parliamentary management to those of parliamentary electioneering. Fit persons should be brought in and 'violent and turbulent' ones kept out. To this purpose use should be made of 'the boroughs of the Cinque Ports and of the Duchy, and other boroughs at the devotion of divers [of] the King's counsellors'. The King should not leave things 'to chance', yet so handle affairs that there is 'no show nor scandal nor nature of the packing...of a Parliament'. And in order that Parliament may be 'truly free', measures should be taken 'to make men perceive that it is not safe to combine or make parties in Parliament'. To these grave admonitions, Bacon then added some encouraging words. The opposition in the last Parliament is 'now much weaker than it was, and that party almost dissolved; Yelverton is won, Sandys is fallen off, Crew and Hyde stand to be serjeants: Brooke is dead: Neville has hopes: Berkeley I think will be respective: Martin has money in his purse: Dudley Digges and Holles are yours.' But lest James's hopes leap too high, Bacon warned him to regard this coming Parliament as a *coup d'essai*, for 'until Your Majesty tune your instrument, you will have no harmony'.[1]

True to his careless nature, James heeded the advice of neither man until it was too late, and then in a panic simultaneously adopted the counsels of both. Hearing that the elections were going badly for him, he looked to his Cinque Ports and to the Duchy of Lancaster and sent out letters to all his great counsellors urging them to secure the election of loyal men. Then, when these loyal men proved to be too few in number, he offered the Commons on 8 April some of the concessions that Neville had urged him to grant.[2] The result of these hurried letters and desperate concessions was a violent explosion against those who dared 'undertake' to manage Parliament in return for preferment at Court, and against those who presumed to secure the election of courtiers to Parliament. Bacon himself had heaped scorn on those who 'for particular promotions will undertake to carry this Parliament for His Majesty's profit and ends', and who presumed 'to command the tongues, hearts, and consciences of

---

[1] Spedding, *Letters and Life of Bacon*, IV, 363–73.
[2] McClure, *Letters of John Chamberlain*, I, 158; Moir, *Addled Parliament*, p. 88; Cottonian MSS Titus F. IV, f. 342.

those that are strangers to them'.[1] Yet the House of Commons showed far more charity towards these 'undertakers' than they did towards those who used their authority to pack Parliament. For imprisoning men who would not vote as he commanded and for ordering a bailiff to make a false return, the Commons fell furiously on the aged Sir Thomas Parry, Chancellor of the Duchy of Lancaster and Privy Councillor. And though Bacon pleaded that Parry, as a councillor of state, represented the King, the Commons expelled him from the House. Yet they listened, with respect, to Sir Henry Neville, when he took upon his shoulders the guilt for undertaking to manage Parliament for the King. In doing so, 'he acquitted himself so happily', reported Thomas Lorkin, 'and with so much satisfaction to the House and honour to himself, as they presently superseded from all farther search, declaring in favour and justification of him, that he had done nothing which became not a good subject and an honest man'.[2]

Sir Henry Neville's 'pragmatical invention' (as the Earl of Northampton called it) and Bacon's alternative to it have a particular significance for the growth of responsible government, for while the one opened the way to its ultimate attainment, the other impeded its progress. Neville was the first of the great parliamentary undertakers, the first who sought to reconcile King and Parliament by bringing the leaders of the opposition into the government. Bacon was the first of the great parliamentary managers, the first who sought to reconcile King and Parliament by holding out to loyal Parliament men the hope of preferment. Neville sought to use his influence in the House of Commons as a lever to force his way into office. Bacon sought to use the power of patronage as a lever to force the Commons to serve the King. Neville would have the government more dependent on the Commons, Bacon the Commons more dependent on the King. Neville was the precursor of Sir Richard Temple, Sir William Jones, Lord Wharton, and Charles James Fox; Bacon of Sir Thomas Clifford, the Earl of Danby, the Earl of Sunderland, and the Duke of Newcastle. Intertwined, tangled, and often indistinguishable, these two threads weaved their way through the fabric of English politics until 1841, when the

---

[1] Cottonian MSS Titus F. IV, ff. 351–352v; Spedding, *Letters and Life of Bacon*, v, 42–8.
[2] *C.J.* I, 477–9; Williams, *Court and Times of James I*, I, 315. John Chamberlain reported (*Letters*, I, 532) the same triumph: '...he not only calmed their troubled spirits but won himself much credit and commendation.'

favourite who controlled the King's patronage finally gave way to the politician who controlled the Houses of Parliament.

The Addled Parliament witnessed four other significant events: James's ungrateful reflections upon the late Earl of Salisbury, an attack upon monopolists, an attack upon the judges who had ruled in favour of impositions, and John Hoskyns's inflammatory speech against the Scots.

James's reflections, gratuitously made in his opening speech, were not only ungrateful but unwise. Their purpose was to shift the blame for the failure of the last Parliament on to the late Lord Treasurer, thus clearing himself.[1] But a Free Monarch is less free if he cannot assume responsibility for the acts of his ministers. To yield this responsibility is to yield the pass to the enemy. The most that can be said for James is that he shared with his son and grandsons this weakness for turning on a too-faithful and too-rigid minister. Strafford, Clarendon, and Rochester were to learn in their turn not to put their trust in princes.

Sir Francis Bacon believed that Sandys 'had fallen off' and that Crew had been silenced by the hope of becoming a serjeant; he was mistaken on both counts. On 8 April Sir Edwin Sandys moved that the House appoint a committee for receiving petitions, for 'this Parliament was not called for making of laws; rather for the execution'. And on 20 April, Sir Thomas Crew, acting on the Sandys doctrine, urged that Parliament punish those who had procured a patent for a monopoly of trade with France. The ever-prepared Whitelocke supported him by citing precedents from the Good Parliament to justify Parliament's fining and imprisoning monopolists. The House heeded the words of Crew and Whitelocke by ordering the patentees to appear before them. But for the sudden dissolution in June, the Commons might have embarked on the road they took in 1621.[2]

---

[1] According to a parliamentary diary in the Bodleian Library (MSS English History C. 386, ff. 146v–147) James said to the two Houses that he hoped that this Parliament would end more amicably than the last, 'wherein some whom he prayed God to forgive had dealt doubly, breeding jealousy betwixt him and them, which [interpolated the diarist] seemed to touch the late Lord Treasurer'. The young Thomas Wentworth, who was to be betrayed by James's son twenty-seven years later, wrote to his father (Wentworth Woodhouse MSS, Strafford XXIA, Letter 7) that the King 'made mention of some that did ill offices the last Parliament, whom he prayed God to forgive, intimating a great little man, as I conceive'.

[2] *C.J.* I, 457, 469. In February Lord Chancellor Ellesmere had delayed putting the Seal to a patent for manufacturing glass because it 'might give more occasion of speeches and questions in this hopeful Parliament than is yet foreseen or thought of' (S.P.D. 14/76:12).

On 12 May the House of Commons voted that the King had been misinformed about the subject's right in the matter of impositions. They also declared that the Barons of the Exchequer ought to have asked Parliament's advice before ruling on impositions, and that precedents existed for Parliament's censuring judges who did not seek its advice in matters touching the subject's liberties. Language of this nature had not been heard in the Commons since the Merciless Parliament of 1388, when Richard II's judges paid with their lives for ruling in favour of the prerogative.[1]

Hoskyns's celebrated solecism—his threatening the Scots with a Sicilian Vespers when he knew not what the Sicilian Vespers was—has concealed a fact of considerable importance: the House took no exception to anything in his inflammatory speech. In fact when Sir Henry Wotton, courtier, scholar, and ambassador, called the speech into question, the House justified it, as containing nothing that 'exceeded the bounds of modesty'. Not only did a lunatic fringe consisting of the witless Hoskyns, the pedantic Christopher Neville, and the Bible-quoting son of Peter Wentworth object to the presence of Scotsmen and Papists at Court: a majority of the House agreed. They agreed because they believed that naming Papists to the Council had caused an increase in recusancy, and that the importunity of Scotsmen had impoverished the King. Faced with this spirit in the Commons, a spirit not limited to fools bribed by the Earl of Northampton (as Hoskyns might have been), James had no alternative but to dissolve Parliament. In no other way could he keep an unfettered grasp on the sceptre.[2]

James did not meet Parliament again for seven years, not until the need to rescue his son-in-law in the Palatinate and the failure to collect a benevolence for that purpose forced him to ask Parliament for money. His financial adversity proved Parliament's opportunity. The rumblings heard in 1610 and 1614 now erupted in violent attacks upon the King's servants. The House of Commons arrested seven of them, questioned fourteen more, expelled three and suspended one from sitting in the House. They also revived the long

---

[1] *C.J.* I, 481–2.

[2] Williams, *Court and Times of James I*, I, 345–6; Notestein *et al. Commons Debates 1621*, VII, 652. The Piedmontese envoy, Gabaleone, wrote (B.M. Add. MSS 32023B, f. 256): 'It is said that the dissolution of Parliament is not displeasing to many of the more important councillors, since it appears there was to be an investigation of some of them, which would have caused them much trouble and embarrassment.'

dormant power of impeachment. Three times that spring members of the Commons marched through the Painted Chamber; three times they crowded before the bar of the House of Lords; three times their Speaker demanded judgment against one whom they had impeached.[1] What was the explanation for these extraordinary events? Sir Henry Wotton attributed them to the youthfulness of the House, for those of the 'weakest wing' are often 'the highest flyers'. James suggested that the House acted from private spleen and a wish to abridge his prerogative. Bacon and Buckingham regarded the impeachments as a calculated attack upon greatness, which would begin with the King's ministers and end with the King's person. But the Commons denied that private spleen and factious opposition caused them to inquire into the King's administration or to impeach his servants. They said that their true motives were to pass laws correcting abuses in the realm and to punish wrong-doers as an example to others.[2]

Where does the truth lie? With the King and courtiers who suspected private passions and a desire to limit the prerogative? Or with the Commons who pleaded a wish to reform? In large measure an answer to this question can be found in an inquiry into the motives that led the Commons to accuse Sir Giles Mompesson on 8 March and Sir Francis Bacon on the 17th, for the impeachment of these two men opened the dikes to a flood of further accusations.

Of a personal vendetta against Sir Giles Mompesson and Sir Francis Bacon there is little evidence, other than Coke's well-known

[1] The House of Commons arrested Sir Francis Michell, Sir Giles Mompesson, Mathias Fowle, Richard Dike, George Geldard, John Churchill, and Sir John Bennet; they questioned Alexander Harris, John Ferrar, James Thurborne, John Sparrow, Sir Francis Blundell, Sir John Townshend, Sir Allen Apsley, Henry Goldsmith, Sir Henry Britain, Sir Eubule Thelwall, Robert Dixon, Dr George Eglisham, John Lepton, and Sir Samuel Tyron; they expelled Sir Robert Floyd, Sir Giles Mompesson, and Sir John Bennet, and suspended Mr Giles Bridges; they impeached Sir John Bennet, Dr Theophilus Field, Sir Giles Mompesson, Sir Francis Bacon, and Sir Francis Michell; and they demanded judgment against Mompesson, Bacon, and Michell. Patentees and commissioners are included in this list, because they acted by the King's authority—their crimes were done in his name. Contemporaries regarded them as the King's servants. The author of the Belasyse diary (*Commons Debates 1621*, v, 35) wrote, 'Note that Blundell and Mompesson were called in person, though they were the King's servants.' Sir Walter Raleigh (*Works*, Oxford, 1829, viii, 46) held that commissioners, because they had power to command, were magistrates. James himself in 1610 regarded Sir Stephen Proctor, a patentee and commissioner, as his servant.

[2] Sir Henry Wotton, *Reliquiae Wottoniae* (1672), p. 67. W. Cobbett, *Parliamentary History of England* (1806–20), i, 1367. Fr. Trans. 21/31 March and 22 Apr./2 May 1621. McClure, *Letters of John Chamberlain*, ii, 367–8, 380–1. Spedding, *Letters and Life of Bacon*, vii, 213. Notestein et al. *Commons Debates 1621*, ii, 114, 158, 194–5, 309, 406–7; iv, 111, 406–7. *C.J.* i, 589.

rivalry with Bacon. Of a party opposed to Court and prerogative there is rather more. Lawyers like Coke were anxious to subordinate the prerogative to the law as interpreted by Parliament. Men of rank and pride like Sir Edward Sackville, brother of the Earl of Dorset, resented the dominance of Buckingham and his friends at Court, and wished to end it. Protestant gentlemen like John Pym looked for any pretext to abridge the prerogative of a King who sought counsel from a Spanish ambassador. But these ambitious lawyers, resentful courtiers, and stout Protestants were too few in number to dictate to the House. The total number of these 'patriots' was less than thirty.[1] They offered leadership and they gave guidance, but that does not explain why nine-tenths of the House, men of loyalty and little ambition, supported the impeachments of Mompesson and Bacon.

The truth is these men had lost confidence in the King. They no longer believed in his ability to remedy the abuses that disgraced his courts and his administration. The history of James's dealings with Mompesson gave them good reason for losing confidence. On the pretence of suppressing disorderly inns, James granted Mompesson a patent for licensing inns and hostelries. He then looked the other way as Mompesson sold licences to disorderly alehouses, intimidated justices of the peace who protested, and brought 3,120 *quo warrantos* against innkeepers who would not compound with him. In order to prevent the melting down of English bullion, James made Mompesson a Commissioner for the Manufacture of Gold and Silver Thread. He then permitted Mompesson to melt down £20,000 worth of English bullion a year, to extort 3s. 8d. per pound of thread from poor workmen, to gaol or threaten to gaol gold finers, silver men, silk men, haberdashers, and button makers, and to imprison a maid for not testifying that her mistress spun gold thread. Ostensibly to reduce the number of officials in the Exchequer, James granted Mompesson a patent for concealed lands. He then allowed him to harry hospitals in Yorkshire, almshouses in Reading, and householders in Holborn for an odd 5s. here, 1s. there.[2] These

---

[1] W. M. Mitchell, *The Rise of the Revolutionary Party in the English House of Commons* (New York, 1957), p. xv; Fr. Trans. 14/24 June 1621.

[2] *C.J.* I, 540–2. Notestein *et al. Commons Debates 1621*, II, 109–10, 113, 165–6, 181–92, 221; IV, 121, 127–8; V, 475–80; VI, 25–6, 300–1. *L.J.* III, 62–3. F. H. Relf (ed.), *Lords Debates in 1621, 1625, and 1628* (Camden Soc. 3rd ser. vol. XLII), p. 13. Hastings MSS, Box 1 and 2, Parliamentary Papers.

patents profited James and England nothing, and went far towards substituting the sale of law for the enforcement of law, and government by patentees for government by justices of the peace. An enraged, not a factious, House voted the impeachment of Sir Giles Mompesson.[1]

The House of Commons were able to revive the power of impeachment because precedents justified it, the House of Lords welcomed it, and the King was powerless to prevent it. Precedents not only justified impeachment, they militated against more radical action. On 23 February the Commons pronounced judgment against Sir Francis Michell, the lean-faced Clerkenwell magistrate who was Mompesson's colleague in the Commission for Gold and Silver Thread. Four days later, prompted by Coke, they were about to take similar action against Mompesson, when Sir Robert Phelips and Sir Edward Sackville intervened. Phelips warned the House to search for precedents for what they were about to do. Sackville suggested that they had better ask the Lords to join with them in pronouncing judgment on Mompesson. The House prudently heeded these warnings, drew back, and sent Hakewill and Noy to the Tower to search its records. The next day the two lawyers reported that there were no precedents for the House of Commons alone passing judgment on delinquents. Upon this self-denying report, the Commons resolved 'according to former precedents to address ourselves to the Lords'. It is a singular fact that precedents guided the Commons away from, not into, a rash act. The revival of impeachment on 28 February 1621 was a triumph for moderation, not innovation. And this explains in part the welcome that the Lords gave the Commons' initiative. Flattered by the respect paid to their power of judicature and convinced (by their own search in the Tower) that precedents justified their exercising it, the Lords examined, judged, and condemned Sir Giles Mompesson.[2]

James was powerless to withstand the revival of the power of impeachment because Mompesson was an unparalleled extortionist

---

[1] The House of Commons had good reason not to place their confidence in James. Tilliers reported that James suffered these attacks on patents only because he could restore them after Parliament had risen (Fr. Trans. 28 Feb./9 March 1621).

[2] Notestein *et al. Commons Debates 1621*, II, 127–31, 145–6, 148; V, 14; VI, 14–15, 286, 301–2, 453. *L.J.* III, 65, 67, 68–70. Relf, *Lords Debates*, pp. 33, 39–48. The Commons impeached Mompesson at 2 p.m. on the afternoon of 8 March at a conference between the two Houses in the Painted Chamber. At that hour and in that place Parliament revived the power of impeachment.

and bully, who promptly sought safety in flight. Faced with a thoroughly bad situation, James sensibly followed the strategy offered him by Dr John Williams, Dean of Westminster. Williams urged James to allow, even to encourage, Parliament to prosecute and condemn monopolists. In this way he and Buckingham could win friends in both Houses, friends who would prevent any attack upon officers of state or favourites at Court. Retreat from the crumbling outworks, he said in effect, and defend a line drawn around the Council Chamber and the Bedchamber.[1]

This strategy was shrewdly conceived, but its adoption did not mean the end of the battle, for the Commons soon discovered that great officers of state had approved of these hated patents. The real struggle in the 1621 Parliament revolved around the referees who had certified patents to be legal and convenient. And the greatest of these referees were the Lord Chancellor and the Lord Treasurer, that is, Sir Francis Bacon, lately created Viscount St Alban, and Henry Montagu, lately created Viscount Mandeville. The storm broke against these two great lords on 9 March, when the Commons ordered a committee to lay open before the Lords the faults of those who had certified Mompesson's patents. On hearing this, James flew into a rage, hastened the next morning to the House of Lords, and addressed the peers. In his speech he loaded Mompesson with reproaches and invited the Lords to punish Bacon and Mandeville for any delinquencies they may have committed. But he also insisted that his judges should rule on the legality of patents, not Parliament, and that his councillors should not suffer for declaring patents convenient before their inconvenience had become evident. He then urged the Lords to punish those who were most at fault in executing patents, but only to 'advise like wise men' concerning the referees who had declared them lawful and convenient.[2] James's interposition of his authority between the referees and the anger of the Commons had its intended effect. The Commons made no attempt to impeach them. The Commons in fact were more intent on preventing like extortions in the future than on attacking the King's ministers. Place it on record that the Lord Chancellor and

---

[1] John Hacket, *Scrinia Reserata* (1693), part I, 49–51.

[2] *C.J.* I, 546–7; Relf, *Lords Debates*, pp. 12–15; Lady de Villiers (ed.), *The Hastings Journal of the Parliament of 1621* (Camden Soc. 3rd ser. vol. CXXXIII), pp. 26–9. Throughout this chapter I shall call Sir Francis Bacon by his surname rather than his title, since he is far better known as Bacon than as St Alban.

Lord Treasurer had erred, and pass a law to prevent similar errors in the future: that was their plan of attack. And in pursuance of that plan they set to work on a bill to remove from the Council, and place in the courts, responsibility for certifying grants of monopolies and penal laws. In order to insure the safe passage of the bill through Parliament, the Commons were willing, when they sent up written charges against Mompesson, to say nothing about the referees. Events seemed to have vindicated triumphantly the Dean of Westminster's strategy.[1]

Then the Committee for Grievances in Courts of Justice discovered that Sir Francis Bacon had accepted gifts from suitors in the Court of Chancery. This discovery breached the fortifications that James had sought to hold against parliamentary inquiry into the actions of great officers of state. In themselves these discoveries proved nothing unusual. Other judges besides Bacon had accepted gifts and gratuities. No gift seems to have warped his judgment. And the thousands of decrees that he handed down as Lord Chancellor were good law and good equity.[2] One can hardly escape the conclusion that the Commons were not impeaching the corrupt judge so much as the sycophantic minister. Of the nineteen patents condemned in the 1621 Parliament, Bacon had certified thirteen. His servant Vaudry was a registrar of licences for inns; another servant, Bassano, was a patentee for the lobster monopoly; he himself was a Commissioner for Gold and Silver Thread. Where his predecessor Ellesmere had stoutly resisted, he had readily complied with, James's prodigal grants of monopolies, concealments, and penal laws. No man in England had possessed more power to stop vexatious patents; no man had done less to stop them; no man so justly deserved to be punished for them. Furthermore, he had too often exalted the prerogative at the expense of the law. He had publicly called the prerogative the perfection of the Common Law, and had urged James to protect the prerogative by using the writ *de non procedendo Rege inconsulto* to draw cases involving his rights from the Common Law courts to Chancery. He sought a similar immunity for himself from the criticism of the Commons when he

[1] *C.J.* I, 539. Notestein *et al. Commons Debates 1621*, II, 167–8, 210, 218–19; v, 289–90.
[2] As Lord Saye, no friend of Bacon, remarked in the Lords (Relf, *Lords Debates*, p. 39), 'If giving shall make a decree void, many just decrees, nay most of them will be voided, for money was given commonly for all.'

told them in early March that he 'wondered how the Lower House would or dared go about to question his honour'. The gage that he threw down in this peremptory fashion the Commons picked up on 17 March, by voting to send to the Lords the evidence they had uncovered concerning his venality.[1]

James hurriedly intervened. On 19 March he proposed that Commissioners named by Parliament should examine Bacon's conduct and report to him, that he might pronounce judgment. The Commons hesitated, then rejected the proposal. It was an important turning point in English history. Confronted with the choice, the Commons of England resolved that servants of the Crown should answer for their crimes to the High Court of Parliament and not to the King's Commissioners. There were to be no *tribunaux administratifs* in England as in France, no *conseil d'état* enforcing a *droit administratif*. What led them to make this choice? In part they must surely have possessed the natural ambition of any court to preserve and extend its own jurisdiction. When Coke rose to oppose accepting the King's proposal, he warned the Commons against any 'interruption of our parliamentary course'.[2] But even more they must have lacked confidence in James himself. No Englishman dared voice this want of confidence on the floor of the House of Commons, but justification for it was everywhere. The French and Venetian ambassadors both reported to their governments the unfitness of the King to reform his own courts and his own administration.[3] Oppressions, extortions, and corruptions advertised the fact throughout the realm. The ease with which the Commons revived the power of impeachment was commensurate with the extent of corruption in the government and the depth of despair that James would ever remedy it.

The fate of Bacon's cause in the House of Lords further shows how easily Parliament revived the power of impeachment. Not a single lord, not the Prince himself, not Buckingham, dared question the right of the House to judge Bacon. The severity of the sentence caused a dispute between those who followed Southampton and those who followed Buckingham. But these twistings and turnings

[1] Notestein *et al. Commons Debates 1621*, II, 146–7; VII, 386, 403–4, 562–4. McClure, *Letters of John Chamberlain*, II, 321. *C.S.P. Dom. 1619–23*, p. 229. Spedding, *Letters and Life of Bacon*, V, 236.

[2] *C.J.* I, 563; Notestein *et al. Commons Debates 1621*, IV, 170.

[3] *C.S.P. Ven.* XVI, 535, 603. Tilliers wrote to Puisieux, 'the King wishes to do all and does nothing' (Fr. Trans. 30 Dec. 1621/6 Jan. 1622).

of faction only explain why Bacon was not degraded from his viscountcy. They do not explain the Lords' assertion of a power to sit in judgment on the King's Lord Chancellor. Pride in their ancient judicature, the memory of passing judgment on Richard II's Lord Chancellor, disgust at the sordid patents that Bacon had certified, astonishment at Bacon's carelessness in accepting gifts, and doubt that James would or could cleanse the Augean stables, these were the motives that persuaded the peers of England to examine, to judge, and to sentence Sir Francis Bacon.[1]

Lord Mandeville escaped impeachment, though as deeply engaged in the iniquities of the Alehouse Patent as Bacon was in the oppressions of the Gold and Silver Thread Commission. He escaped because James interposed his authority between the Commons and his minister, warning the House on 24 April that they should not accuse those who had advised him to the best of their ability. They should condemn only corruption, not error, for *humanum est errare*.[2] The House yielded to James's definition of the limits appropriate to the use of impeachment because they did not wish to drive him to a dissolution that would end their great work of reformation. Throughout the spring of 1621 the House followed the rule that only where His Majesty did not interpose his power to protect a servant would they proceed to impeach him. Taking bribes was a personal fault, which in no way involved the King. Where it could be proved, the King was powerless to interpose his authority and Parliament free to accuse his minister. This doctrine of interposition, clearly perceived by no one but instinctively pursued by all, divided the extortions of Mompesson and the briberies of Bacon from the questionable certificates of Mandeville and the whispered counsels of Buckingham; and distinguished the areas where the King assumed no responsibility from those where he assumed final responsibility.[3]

The whispered counsels of Buckingham could not long be ignored. Most men suspected (and a few men knew) that the great Marquis was the Minotaur at the centre of this labyrinth of patents and

---

[1] Relf, *Lords Debates*, pp. 27–9; *L.J.* III, 53; *C.J.* I, 564; S. R. Gardiner (ed.), *Lords Debates in 1624 and 1626* (Camden Soc. n.s. XXIV), pp. 13–17, 20–2, 62–3; McClure, *Letters of John Chamberlain*, II, 371.

[2] Notestein *et al. Commons Debates 1621*, III, 42, 67–71; IV, 252–3; V, 87. *C.J.* I, 586. E. Nicholas, *Proceedings and Debates in the House of Commons* (Oxford, 1760), I, 308–9.

[3] James told the Commons, concerning Bacon's accepting bribes, 'No Prince could answer for the faults of all his servants, yet he took contentment in this, that his own honour remained clear' (Notestein *et al. Commons Debates 1621*, IV, 170).

projects. The wretched Mompesson was known to be his creature; Sir Edward Villiers, a commissioner of Gold and Silver Thread, and Mr Christopher Villiers, a sharer in the Alehouse Patent, were his brothers. Buckingham regarded the patents as family perquisites, and opposed Bacon's suggestion in the autumn of 1620 that James revoke the worst of them before meeting Parliament.[1] Yet he, the chief sinner of all, escaped impeachment. One obvious reason for this was his entire capitulation (on John Williams's advice) to Parliament. He told the Lords and Commons in March that he had been misled by the referees, that he would not protect his brothers, that he would now be a good scholar of Parliament, and that they should strike while the iron was hot. Both Houses took him at his word, struck while the iron was hot, embarked on a search through the labyrinth of patentees, referees, suitors, and projectors. They checked their search neither at the Council nor the Court. The Marquis took fright at this unanticipated zeal, and, throwing himself at James's feet, implored him to dissolve Parliament in order to save his servants. In March hope had converted him to parliamentary government. In April fear converted him back to prerogative rule.[2]

When Parliament reassembled after the Easter recess, the coldness of the Court towards its efforts at reformation became immediately evident. As a result men began to murmur against the great favourite; a faction formed in Parliament, which sought to discredit him with the King by exposing his crimes and follies to the world. Those Lords in the Upper House who grouped themselves around the Earl of Southampton formed the core of this faction. According to rumour men from the House of Commons also attended their meetings at Southampton House in Holborn.[3] The problem facing the Holborn 'patriots' was to find someone who would expose Buckingham's misconduct; their misfortune was to believe that Sir Henry Yelverton was that man. Yelverton, who had served

---

[1] Nicholas, *Proceedings and Debates*, I, 76; Notestein *et al. Commons Debates 1621*, VI, 303; Spedding, *Letters and Life of Bacon*, VII, 145–52; Arthur Wilson, *The History of Great Britain* (1653), p. 157. According to Salvetti, the Tuscan envoy, the people believed that Buckingham aided Mompesson in his flight; and would vent their rancour against him if they could (B.M. Add. MSS 27962A, f. 418v).

[2] *C.J.* I, 537, 552; Notestein *et al. Commons Debates 1621*, II, 212; IV, 149; V, 270; VI, 303; Fr. Trans. 21/31 March and 3/13 Apr. 1621.

[3] Notestein *et al. Commons Debates 1621*, VII, 615–17; McClure, *Letters of John Chamberlain*, II, 384–5; Egerton MSS 2651, f. 33; *Cabala, Sive Scrinia Sacra* (1691), p. 2.

James as Attorney General from 1617 to 1621, was a man of fits and starts, neither a coward nor a hero, but both by turns. By resisting the Villiers gang, he had incurred the favourite's wrath and earned imprisonment in the Tower. By eventually complying with its schemes, he had angered Parliament and drawn accusations upon himself. While defending himself in the Lords against those accusations he excited the greatest expectations among Buckingham's opponents. He pleaded that he had imprisoned silk men because Buckingham was prepared 'to hew him down' if he did not; that he had prosecuted innkeepers because the Marquis threatened him with imprisonment if he refused. The story he told of being bullied by Mompesson and the Villiers brothers was odious and shocking, vivid and credible. Unfortunately for himself, he made two blunders. He reflected on James by saying that he suffered for serving him too well; and he made allegations which he lacked the courage and witnesses to prove when he appeared again before the Lords. These blunders saved Buckingham and cost Yelverton dear.[1] The Lords sentenced him to pay the King and the Marquis heavy fines and to be imprisoned in the Tower during His Majesty's pleasure. They did not, however, condemn him for advising illegal indentures, penning unlawful proclamations, or issuing warrants dormant, though these were the charges brought against him by the Commons. Nor did the House of Commons complain that their accusations were ignored. Parliament to the very end refused to reflect on any man for giving the King bad advice or executing his unlawful commands.[2]

Yet it showed no reluctance to punish extortionists and receivers of bribes. The House of Commons impeached Sir John Bennet, for nineteen years Judge of the Prerogative Court of Canterbury, for briberies that make Bacon appear an honest man. They impeached Sir Francis Michell, the Clerkenwell Justice of the Peace, for exacting bonds from London merchants and extorting money

---

[1] *L.J.* III, 77–8, 115, 121; Gardiner, *Lords Debates*, pp. 42–53, 79–84, 87–9. Tillières reported (Fr. Trans. 19/29 May 1621) that James threatened Yelverton with perpetual imprisonment in the Tower unless he disavowed his earlier charges. Yelverton himself referred to this threat in his final appearance before the Lords (Gardiner, *Lords Debates*, p. 89). Salvetti (B.M. Add. MSS 27962B, f. 16) offers another reason why Buckingham escaped impeachment. He observes that James's warm defence of the Marquis in late April destroyed any illusion that Parliament could attack the royal favourite without inviting a dissolution.

[2] Gardiner, *Lords Debates*, pp. 5–6, 85–90; *L.J.* III, 77–8, 124.

from alehouse keepers. They impeached Dr Theophilus Field, Bishop of Llandaff, for serving as a broker in one of Bacon's bribes. They drew up an impeachment against Alexander Harris, Warden of the Fleet, for extorting higher fees from his prisoners than they were required by law to pay. And they were preparing impeachments against Dr John Lambe (Chancellor to the Bishop of Peterborough) and Dr John Craddock (Chancellor to the Bishop of Durham) for selling letters of administration, taking bribes, and fining Puritans, when James adjourned Parliament.[1] In all these prosecutions the end was the reformation of abuses and not the venting of private spleen or party hatreds. Bennet was immensely popular in the House; Michell and Harris were too unimportant to have personal or party enemies; and the Bishop of Llandaff was more pitied than hated. In the prosecution of Lambe and Craddock, however, the spirit of party did come to the aid of the spirit of reformation, for the Puritans in the House drove on the prosecution with an eagerness not to be explained solely by a hatred of bribery.

The sudden adjournment of Parliament in June saved Bennet from judgment and Harris, Lambe, and Craddock from impeachment. But their escape was of little moment compared with the wreckage that lay all about. Parliament's wrath against the 'Justice Greedys' and 'Sir Giles Overreaches' of England had shattered the King's power to protect his own servants. In particular it had restored to Parliament rights that it had not exercised for a century and a half. The restoration of these rights, in turn, raised issues about the responsibilities of ministers which were not to be resolved for a century to come, and placed the King's servants in a dilemma from which they were not to escape for two centuries.

The word 'impeachment' was used only once in the 1621 Parliament,[2] but the Commons asserted and won the right to inquire into the actions of the King's servants and to present those whom they found faulty to the Lords; and the Lords promptly secured the right to judge those whom the Commons had accused. James did not yield these rights to Parliament gracefully. In late April he forbad the Commons to inquire into abuses committed by his servants in

---

[1] Notestein *et al. Commons Debates 1621*, II, 185–8, 310–15, 346–7, 365–6, 373; III, 260–2, 266, 275–6.

[2] It was used by William Hakewill on 23 Apr. (Notestein *et al. Commons Debates 1621*, II, 314). I have used impeachment in this chapter to describe any vote by the Commons to send to the Lords a charge or accusation or information against a servant of the King.

Ireland; to which the House replied that they hoped that 'public information' concerning abuses would be as acceptable to the King 'as private'. Without yielding their right of inquiry, they gave up their inquiry in this instance.[1] The right of presentment James countered by interposing his authority between the accused servant and the Commons' accusation, but the Commons immediately circumvented this manœuvre by presenting men for crimes that could not possibly involve the King's authority. The Lords' right of judgment James challenged both in speech and deed. He told the peers in March that, though they were undeniably a court of record, it was questionable how far their jurisdiction extended. In May he sought to limit that jurisdiction by claiming for himself the right to judge Yelverton, but the Lords clung tenaciously to their right to judge a man who had come under their jurisdiction. Once again James gave way.[2] Parliament thus emerged from the 1621 Parliament with three undoubted rights inscribed on its Journals: the right of inquiry, the right of presentment, and the right of judgment.

Two men who were later to confront each other as protagonists across the vastness of Westminster Hall saw, each in his own way, the significance of the winning of these rights. Thomas Wentworth, concerned now as ever with efficient government, told the citizens of Rotherham that, 'The censure of Mompesson is of more good to the Commonwealth than six of the best laws made in the six last Parliaments.' John Pym, jealous now as ever of the privileges of Parliament, boasted in the House of Commons that, 'The power of judgment in Parliament, which this great while has slept, has been awakened to the terror of such offenders.' The question was no longer whether impeachment was to be or not to be, but whether it should be used as a legal procedure to secure good government, or as a political weapon to terrorize political opponents.[3]

The revival of impeachment in 1621 raised four new constitutional issues. Was a counsellor responsible for advice that later proved unsuccessful? Must he answer for advice which Parliament later declared unlawful? Could he plead in his defence the concurrence

---

[1] *C.J.* I, 597–8; Notestein *et al. Commons Debates 1621*, IV, 281, 285. Professor Elizabeth Foster has described very fully the procedures used by the Commons in making these inquiries (W. A. Aiken, ed., *Conflict in Stuart England*, New York, 1960, pp. 57–78).
[2] Relf, *Lords Debates*, p. 15; Gardiner, *Lords Debates*, pp. 55–9; *L.J.* III, 104, 112, 115.
[3] Wentworth Woodhouse MSS, Strafford XXI A, Letter 17; Notestein *et al. Commons Debates 1621*, v, 18.

of other counsellors? And could he plead the King's commands to justify the wrong he had done? Bacon and Mandeville, the two men who had certified the greatest number of patents, pleaded that they were not to blame if patents that they had certified later proved grievous in execution. They might have committed errors, but not crimes.[1] Sir Francis Goodwin fixed the principle in a Latin phrase, *Nullum concilium ab eventu est estimandum*. Fair play certainly dictated that advice which was good in intent but unfortunate in execution should not condemn the adviser. Fair play also suggested that a man who had the opinion of the King's Learned Counsel for the lawfulness of his patent ought not to suffer; yet this plea, voiced by Sir Robert Floyd, a Patentee for the Sole Engrossing of Wills, did not prevent the Commons from expelling him from the House. And what if the King's Learned Counsel pleaded 'misconusance of the law', as Noy described a mistaken legal opinion? Were they to be punished for not understanding the law as a future Parliament might understand it?[2] And who ultimately was to declare what was good law? James said his judges, and urged the Lords to consult with them before condemning patents. Coke and his friends said Parliament, and showed that they meant it by introducing a bill ('for the better securing the subject from imprisonment against Magna Carta'), with a clause requiring the judges to stand to the censure of Parliament if they transgressed the law.[3]

Yelverton was the first to plead the concurrence of others in his counsels and deeds, but his plea earned him only the contumely of those whom he implicated. But Sir Edward Coke pleaded it with entire success. Accused of drawing up, when Attorney General, a Patent for the Sole Making of Bills and Letters in the Presidency of York, he told the Commons that he had at first refused to draw it, but, the King's councillors overruling his objections, he could not refuse to draw it. The Commons exhibited their great devotion to impartial justice by accepting the plea from one former Attorney General and rejecting it from the other.[4]

[1] Notestein *et al. Commons Debates 1621*, III, 43; V, 389; VI, 52–4, 383. *C.J.* I, 550, 618. Nicholas, *Proceedings and Debates*, I, 144–5. Relf, *Lords Debates*, pp. 13–15.
[2] Notestein *et al. Commons Debates 1621*, V, 59–61, 347; *C.J.* I, 566–7, 589.
[3] Relf, *Lords Debates*, pp. 13–15; Notestein *et al. Commons Debates 1621*, III, 324; *C.J.* I, 628.
[4] Relf, *Lords Debates*, pp. 43–53. Notestein *et al. Commons Debates 1621*, IV, 336–7; V, 142. *C.J.* I, 620. A committee of the House of Commons heard Yelverton's defence on 4 March (Notestein *et al. Commons Debates 1621*, II, 164–6; V, 271–2) and the House accused him before the Lords on the 10th (*ibid.* VI, 52; V, 286–7. *C.J.* I, 549).

The gravest issue raised in this Parliament was the validity of the King's command. Michell and Yelverton both pleaded it, and the King hinted at it when he told the Lords, 'because I am the giver of all patents, it [their condemnation] cannot but reflect on me'. But Coke would not hear of this doctrine. 'Every grant against the liberty of the subject', he insisted, 'is void...for the King is Lieutenant of God, and as God can not do wrong, neither in law can the King.'[1] The doctrine was not wholly new. The first session of James's first Parliament had heard it enunciated; and judges in the fifteenth century had proclaimed it.[2] In fact the chief significance of the 1621 Parliament is that submerged Lancastrianism then came to the surface, never to sink from sight again.

If the King's commands could not justify a minister in an illegal act, what should he do when ordered to act illegally? This was the dilemma that faced all ministers of the King after 1621. The first to be trapped in it was Dr John Williams, whom James had named Lord Keeper on Buckingham's recommendation. In many ways Williams was the heir of Sir Henry Neville. Both men kept a finger on the pulse of Parliament and both men sought to persuade the King to heed its quickening beat. In March Williams had advised Buckingham to rely on the support of friends in Parliament and in September he told Sir Lionel Cranfield, the new Lord Treasurer, 'You were stated in this place by the voice of the people, before you understood the pleasure of the King.'[3] But Williams was an ambitious man, and soon found it impossible to serve both Parliament and the favourite. Asked by Buckingham to draw a pardon for Bacon that he knew would anger Parliament, he pleaded with the Duke not to ask it of him, but ended his letter with an avowal that he would draw the pardon if his Lordship commanded him to do so. Buckingham commanded him to draw it and he did so.[4] Despite the revival of impeachment, Parliament's power was but a fraction of the favourite's.

The significance of James's next Parliament, which the pursuit of a costly war policy and the failure of another benevolence forced

---

[1] Relf, *Lords Debates*, pp. 13–14, 43–53. Gardiner, *Lords Debates*, pp. 26, 45. Notestein *et al. Commons Debates 1621*, V, 59; VI, 286.

[2] *C.J.* I, 940. In his speech enunciating this principle, Coke cited the judges in 13 Edward IV (Notestein *et al. Commons Debates 1621*, II, 253).

[3] Hackett, *Scrinia Reserata*, part I, 50, 103–4.

[4] Harleian MSS 7000, f. 80.

him to meet in 1624, was that the favourite then placed his great authority behind a parliamentary impeachment, and one designed to terrorize a political opponent, not to promote good government. Vexatious administrative abuses caused the impeachments of 1621. Profound differences over the advisability of war with Spain led in 1624 to the impeachment of Sir Lionel Cranfield, Lord Treasurer since 1621 and Earl of Middlesex since 1622.

Unlike the charges against Mompesson and Bacon, those against Middlesex did not arise from an inquiry into abuses within the realm. On 5 April Sir Miles Fleetwood unexpectedly rose in the Commons and charged Middlesex with doubling a fee, with creating a new stamp in the Court of Wards, and with taking two bribes of £500 each. Fleetwood reported from no committee and these charges arose from no petitions before the House. In all likelihood Middlesex's enemies at Court, led by the Duke of Buckingham, persuaded minor officials in the Court of Wards to search them out. Fleetwood himself was a Receiver of the Court of Wards; and the trivial character of the charges suggest that they sprang from artifice, not the anger of an indignant nation.[1]

Sir Edwin Sandys and Sir Robert Phelips had, to be sure, complained on 2 April of those who had advised the placing of impositions on groceries and wines, grievances that a committee looking into the causes for the decay of trade had unearthed. And on 9 April Sandys and Phelips named Middlesex as the author of these impositions. Yet even here the shadow of the favourite loomed ominously, for Sandys and Phelips were suspected of being 'undertakers'. The nature of their undertaking has never come to light, but contemporaries suspected that they had offered to support Buckingham in his quarrel with Middlesex, if he would engage the King to break once and for all with Spain.[2]

James later taxed Buckingham with fashioning a rod with which his enemies would one day scourge him, but Buckingham had little choice in the matter. His enemies at Court, led by Middlesex, were

[1] Tanner MSS 392, ff. 80–82; Harleian MSS 6383, ff. 118–119v. Fleetwood had earlier angered Middlesex by issuing £8,000 from the Court of Wards to Prince Charles, solely on the Prince's personal command (Rawlinson MSS B 151, ff. 65–65v).

[2] Harleian MSS 6383, ff. 116–117; B.M. Add. MSS 18597, ff. 126–129; G. Goodman, *The Court of King James the First* (1839), I, 255; *C.S.P. Ven.* XVIII, 211; McClure, *Letters of John Chamberlain*, II, 549–50; Hacket, *Scrinia Reserata*, part I, 189–90; Harleian MSS 7000, ff. 151–152v.

seeking to supplant him in the King's favour and to discredit him in Parliament. The Earl of Pembroke argued in January that Parliament ought to inquire into and punish Buckingham's past errors, and Middlesex openly sought the Duke's downfall. Yet Pembroke remained Lord Chamberlain, and Middlesex Lord Treasurer.[1] The truth is no man made a parliamentary impeachment more likely in 1624 than James himself. He publicly advocated war with Spain, yet retained as Lord Treasurer the declared enemy of that war. He secretly cherished a Spanish alliance, yet kept as his favourite the open enemy of such an alliance. He would not remove Middlesex at Buckingham's insistence, or Buckingham at Middlesex's. He would not choose between the Spanish and anti-Spanish factions at Court, but vacillated, trimmed, procrastinated, and avoided London. Both factions feared the other; both sought any and every ally; both saw in Parliament an ally that they dared not ignore. James unwittingly forced his servants to extend into Parliament their intrigues against each other. He deplored these intrigues, but, old and sick and senile, he lacked the will to put an end to them.[2]

James was unable in the next two months to prevent the condemnation of his Lord Treasurer, for Middlesex had (or appeared to have) taken the two bribes, had offended both Houses with his arrogant behaviour and financial exactions, and had won the furious enmity of the Prince of Wales by rudely lecturing him at the Council table. Yet James still clung to the right, where his authority was concerned, to interpose his royal person between Parliament and an accused minister: Parliament might condemn Middlesex for corruption, but should not condemn him for advising or obeying the King. On 5 May James told the Lords that the imposition on wines was for his service, and that they might as well arraign him for it as his Lord Treasurer. Prince Charles then interrupted his father, saying that Middlesex was not questioned for advising the imposition on wines. James told him he lied, and bade the House

---

[1] R. H. Tawney, *Business and Politics under James I* (Cambridge, 1958), pp. 234–8; *C.S.P. Ven.* xvIII, 210–11, 216, 267–8; Fr. Trans. Dec. 1624.

[2] The Duke of Richmond wrote to Middlesex on 18 Jan. that the King is 'very careful and earnest to suppress anything that makes evil blood among his counsellors and servants...' (Sackville [Knole] Papers, O/N 126), but, as the French ambassador observed three months later, James lacked the vigour to suppress such intrigues (Fr. Trans. 5/15 Apr. 1624).

proceed with greater care.[1] James was right. The Prince had lied. The Commons had charged the Lord Treasurer with advising impositions on wines, as also on sugar and groceries. Furthermore, their spokesman, Sir Edwin Sandys, going beyond his brief, had accused Middlesex of advising the dissolution of the last Parliament and the collection of a benevolence. These last two charges never appeared in the formal indictment but they, more than the two bribes, explain the resentment felt towards the Lord Treasurer in the House of Commons.[2] The Lords, however, pursued a more correct policy. They did not condemn Middlesex for advising impositions, either on wines or sugar or groceries. Neither did they condemn him for advising the new Instructions in the Court of Wards, nor for securing a favourable lease of the sugar farm. James sent messages to the peers assuming responsibility for all these actions. In the end the Lords condemned him only for doubling a fee and making a new stamp in the Court of Wards, for failing to keep accounts in the Wardrobe, for mismanagement and extortion in the Ordnance, and for taking bribes. For these crimes they sentenced him to pay a heavy fine, to remain in the Tower during the King's pleasure, and to be forever incapable of holding office. Once again Parliament wrested a faithful minister from the King without actually challenging the King's right to protect those who gave him counsel and those who yielded him obedience.[3]

Middlesex's impeachment was significant, as James himself told the Lords, because it established a precedent for condemning men for faults dug up by their enemies. But the significance of the 1624 Parliament did not end there, as James too painfully realized.[4] For the Commons had also exercised in a conscious and deliberate manner their right to inquire into and accuse faulty servants of the Crown; and the Lords, also with an eye to posterity, asserted their right to judge them. The Commons were the more aggressive of the two Houses. As 'the inquisitors general of the grievances of the Kingdom', they inquired into crimes allegedly committed by the Lord Keeper, by numerous patentees, by the Heralds in the Earl Marshall's office, by Sir Simon Harvey of the Green Cloth, by the

---

[1] Tawney, *Business and Politics*, pp. 234–6, 244, 247, 258–62, 265–7; *C.S.P. Dom. 1623–25*, p. 240.

[2] Harleian MSS 4289, ff. 191–195.

[3] *L.J.* III, 375, 380; Gardiner, *Lords Debates*, pp. 73–90.

[4] Harleian MSS 4289, f. 150v; S.P.D. 14/165:61.

Bishop of Norwich, and by Lambe, Craddock, and Harris. In the debates arising from these inquiries the same issues emerged as in 1621. The King's servants pleaded that they had committed mistakes, not crimes; that the Council had concurred in their actions; that the King's Learned Counsel had ruled in their favour; that the King had sanctioned what they had done. The Lord Keeper, for example, pleaded that he had ruled against Lady Darcy out of ignorance of the law, not corruption; and the House indulgently accepted the plea, probably because Williams had made his peace with Buckingham in January.[1] The Commons, however, ruled completely out of court the plea of the concurrence of the Council. They did so by sending a formal protestation to the House of Lords, declaring that in charging Middlesex with advising impositions they meant to cast no reflections on those in the Council who had concurred in the advice.[2] The House likewise rejected Mr Nichols's plea that the King's Learned Counsel, and not he, should defend the Patent for Praetermitted Customs, since he had only executed what they had declared to be lawful.[3] No one in 1624 actually pleaded the King's command to defend his actions, but the Solicitor General did urge the House to judge the Lord Keeper kindly, 'lest through his sides we stick into his master's honour for putting him into that place'. To which Sir Robert Coke retorted, that if they accepted that doctrine they would receive no complaints at all. The Solicitor's doctrine was not heard of again, and the House went on to impeach the Bishop of Norwich for putting down preaching and setting up images, and to censure Sir Simon Harvey, Clerk of the Green Cloth, for unlawfully collecting malt and commandeering carts. The House petitioned James to remove Harvey from office, but James did not remove him. Instead he prorogued Parliament as soon as it had passed the Subsidy Bill, thereby protecting his servants from further attacks.[4]

The Subsidy Bill was yet another blow to the King's prerogative, for it provided that the Commons should name the Treasurers to spend the money collected, and it made those Treasurers, and the Council of War, accountable to the Commons for the proper

---

[1] Rawlinson MSS B 151, ff. 66v–67; *C.J.* I, 784; Harleian MSS 7000, ff. 139, 140–141v.   [2] B.M. Add. MSS 18597, ff. 141–143v; *L.J.* III, 349, 378.
[3] Harleian MSS 159, f. 110; *C.J.* I, 768; S.P.D. 14/167:10.
[4] Harleian MSS 6383, f. 140v; *C.J.* I, 702, 784; *L.J.* III, 388–90; Wynn of Gwydir Papers, no. 1226.

expenditure of the money. When this unusual Bill came before the House of Lords, the peers objected to it because it enlarged the privileges of the House of Commons. But their objections were silenced when the judges, called in for advice, declared that the Bill was not unlawful, for the Commons did not claim these new privileges by right, but only by an Act of Parliament, to which the King and Lords could or could not assent. Furthermore, said the judges, the King had first proposed that the House of Commons name the Treasurers.[1] And in fact James had first suggested this inroad on his prerogative. He had done so upon the advice of, or more accurately upon the insistence of, the Duke of Buckingham. Why Buckingham wished to add to the powers of the Commons is uncertain. Possibly it was part of his agreement with the leaders of the opposition, for the opposition in 1621 had talked of a similar plan. More likely he saw that the Commons would never vote money to be wasted by a prodigal King. Buckingham desperately wanted a war against Spain; but the Commons would pay for such a war only if the money they voted were spent by officials in whom they had confidence, and they did not have confidence in the King or his appointees. Once again a want of confidence in James drove men, for immediate and practical ends, to demand responsible government.[2]

The last words James ever spoke to a Parliament were words spoken against its presumption in attacking his servants. On 28 May 1624 he ordered the two Houses to forbear such attacks in the future. He forbad them to examine and judge his servants, any of them, 'from the greatest ministers of state to the scullion in the kitchen'.[3] James's remark echoes across the centuries Richard II's brave words at Eltham, that he would not dismiss even one of his scullions at Parliament's request. And like Richard in 1386, James in 1624 sought to conceal with high pretensions a real loss of power. His favourite knew better. Whether he was negotiating with the French

---

[1] J. R. Tanner (ed.), *Constitutional Documents of the Reign of James I* (Cambridge, 1952), pp. 374–9; Cobbett, *Parl. Hist.* I, 1485–6.

[2] *C.S.P. Dom. 1623–25*, p. 178; Philip Yorke, 2nd Earl of Hardwicke, *Miscellaneous State Papers* (1778), I, 466–7; Egerton MSS 2651, f. 33v. If Salvetti can be believed, the Commons' want of confidence in James was justified. He wrote that James never gave up hope to regain the Palatinate for his son-in-law by negotiations with Spain, and only awaited Parliament's prorogation to return to that policy (B.M. Add. MSS 27962 C, ff. 156v–158v).

[3] S.P.D. 14/165–61 and 14/167:10; *C.S.P. Dom. 1623–25*, p. 445; Salvetti to the Duke of Tuscany, B.M. Add. MSS 27962 C, ff. 160–160v.

or directing supplies to Count Mansfeld, Buckingham heard Parliament's clamorous presence hurrying near. And though he did not sufficiently heed the danger, he did perceive the truth that the King's servants would have to face a Parliament in the end, and that their position was less secure in 1624 than it had been in 1603.[1]

The House of Commons could now impeach a minister, and (if he were not a peer) arrest or question or censure him. The Lords for their part now possessed the right to judge and sentence those whom the Commons impeached. Standing accused at the bar of the House of Lords, a minister could not be certain that a plea that he had committed errors, and not crimes, would be accepted. If he pleaded the concurrence of other councillors, he might only multiply his enemies. If he pleaded that he had followed the advice of Learned Counsel, he might find the plea politely ignored. The most unacceptable plea of all was that he had obeyed the King's command, for that would reflect on His Majesty, who could do no wrong. At most a minister could hope, if he had taken no bribes and committed no extortion, for the King's intervention to save him. Parliament had not yet formally condemned any man for giving the King wicked advice or yielding obedience to an illegal command.

Parliament revived the power of impeachment between 1610 and 1625 not for a single reason but for a number of reasons. The House of Commons was filled with confident, aggressive, and ambitious men, and the House of Lords with peers jealous of their privileges. James's prodigality drove the tight-fisted gentry to oppose importunate courtiers. Government by patentees angered every justice of the peace in the land. The grant of monopolies persuaded the merchants to join in the hunt for monopolists. The collection of impositions aroused the lawyers and merchants. The failure to enforce the laws against recusants exasperated the Puritans. The prevalence of extortion in the administration angered all who had to pay its price. Indecision at Court impelled courtiers to seek support in Parliament against their enemies. In sum, the revival of impeachment became inevitable the day that an impoverished King, indifferent to good government and the opinions of his subjects, met an ambitious Parliament, determined to use its power to secure good government and the pursuit of national policies.

[1] S. R. Gardiner, *History of England* (1883), v, 262, 269; Fr. Trans. 16/26 Jan. 1626.

CHAPTER 2

THE RISE AND FALL OF IRRESPONSIBLE
GOVERNMENT (1625–1640)

During the medieval ages Englishmen believed that their monarchs should act on the advice of a Council composed of the great magnates of the realm. In Tudor times they believed that they should act on the advice of a Privy Council chosen from the wisest in the realm. Today they believe that they should act on the advice of a Cabinet Council responsible to Parliament. But at no time, not even under the Tudors, did they believe that their monarchs should by-pass all Councils, and act on the advice of Court minions, personal favourites, gentlemen of the Bedchamber, and foreign ambassadors. Yet James I and Charles I followed that course from 1612 to 1628, and gave to England a government more irresponsible than any it had known since the days of Gaveston and Spencer, and of Bushy and Bagot.

The rise of irresponsible government, in the sense of government by courtiers rather than by councillors, dates from the end of the Cecilian epoch in 1612. Freed by the death of Salisbury from an irksome tutelage, James ceased to submit important affairs of state to the Privy Council. He fell into the easier habit of resolving all things alone with his Scottish favourite, Robert Carr, Viscount Rochester, later Earl of Somerset. So great became Somerset's power that he could advance or depress whomever he wished at Court.[1] But his ascendancy was shortlived; from 1616 onwards George Villiers, later Marquis and then Duke of Buckingham, swayed all. Guided by the whispered counsels of his new favourite, James ignored his Privy Council more than ever. In 1619 he refused to ask its advice concerning the Elector of the Palatinate's election as King of Bohemia, for fear that it would support the Elector's claims. In 1622 he forced a silent and sullen Council to acquiesce in his decision to dissolve Parliament, though all the Council disapproved. In 1623 he kept secret from the Council the

---

[1] State Papers Spanish 94/20:82; J. O. Halliwell (ed.), *The Autobiography and Correspondence of Sir Simonds D'Ewes* (1846), I, 70.

Prince's intended voyage to Spain, until it was too late to act. In March of the same year he agreed to the surrender of Frankenthal to the Infanta Isabella for eighteen months, though his councillors advised unanimously against it. The Privy Council, swollen in numbers and disregarded, became a mere shadow of what it had been under Elizabeth.[1]

Meanwhile the Duke of Buckingham, who could brook no rival, filled all the great offices of state with those who were, or feigned to be, his creatures. Only one other man in the whole realm enjoyed an influence comparable to his. He was the Spanish ambassador, Sarmiento de Acuna, Count of Gondomar. From 1613 to 1623 Gondomar acted as one of James's chief counsellors, being night and day at the Palace of Whitehall, where he heard the most secret counsels and gave the most imperious advice. James placed an entire confidence in him, even dismissing a Secretary of State upon his advice. But Buckingham in 1624, having driven the Earl of Middlesex from the government, drove Gondomar's successor, Inojosa, from the Palace and the realm.[2] The favourite was now the sole counsellor of the King, the sole means of access to Court, the sole means of preferment in Church and State. The death of James and the accession of Charles confirmed rather than destroyed Buckingham's ascendancy. James's infatuation with the comely youth merely gave way to Charles's diffidence before the experienced man of the world. And Charles was no more able than his father to appreciate the truth of Sir Walter Raleigh's remark that, 'To govern without council is not only dangerous in aristocracies and popular states, but unto independent princes an occasion of utter ruin.'[3]

Though Charles preferred 'to govern without council', his subjects found such a government highly objectionable. At Oxford, in August 1625, their representatives in Parliament said so in unmistakable words. 'An advised Council for the government of present affairs is necessary', said one member. Another appealed to the saying of Solomon, that in the multitude of counsellors there is health. A third observed that Queen Elizabeth 'governed by a grave and wise Council'. Before the debate had run its course no

---

[1] Gardiner, *History*, III, 313; IV, 265; V, 74. *C.S.P. Dom. 1619–23*, p. 496.
[2] *C.S.P. Ven.* XVII, 438–42.
[3] Sir Walter Raleigh, *Works* (Oxford, 1829), VIII, 145.

one could doubt that the target of the House's anger was the exorbitant and irresponsible power exercised by the Duke of Buckingham.[1]

Buckingham did not regard these sentiments as those of the nation. He believed that Bishop Williams, the Lord Keeper, supported by Pembroke, the Lord Chamberlain, had fomented these attacks upon his monopoly of all counsels. He accused Williams of stirring up the leaders of the House against him, of urging them to bring in charges against him, and of promising to supply them with evidence to support such charges. All this Williams did, said Buckingham, in order to divert the Commons from an inquiry into his own misconduct as Lord Keeper. Williams denied the entire accusation, and retorted that Buckingham sought to destroy him in Parliament. He charged that the Duke's henchmen had promised members of the House of Commons the support of the Duke if they would fly against him. Those, he added, who showed the greatest malice against him, as Sir William Stroud and Sir Nathaniel Rich, 'were never out of my Lord Duke's chamber and bosom'.[2]

To discover the truth amidst such a barrage of charges and counter-charges is difficult. Buckingham and Williams assuredly quarrelled in July, when the Bishop opposed the Duke's proposal to adjourn Parliament to Oxford; the enraged Buckingham probably then threatened to ruin Williams for daring to oppose him; and the fearful Williams most likely sought safety by studying the Duke's ruin in Parliament. Certainly Williams did not appease Buckingham's anger by announcing in Council, a fortnight later, that His Majesty should promise Parliament that in actions of great importance he 'would take the advice of a settled and a constant Council'. To a man of Buckingham's tender sensibilities, to a man who could believe that even the Queen of Bohemia in the Hague was plotting against him, the mere voicing of such sentiments proved that the Lord Keeper sought his ruin in Parliament. And Williams, for his part, ever mindful of Middlesex's fate, attributed to Buckingham a power to sway Parliament that he no longer possessed. That either man actually instigated an intrigue against

---

[1] S. R. Gardiner (ed.), *Debates in the House of Commons in 1625* (Camden Soc. n.s. VI), pp. 78, 156; J. Rushworth, *Historical Collections* (1721), I, 180.

[2] Rushworth, *Historical Collections*, I, 198; Hacket, *Scrinia Reserata*, II, 17–18, 20–1; W. Sanderson, *A Compleat History of the Life and Raigne of King Charles* (1658), p. 17; P. Heylyn, *Observations on the History of the Reign of King Charles Published by H.L.* (1656), p. 36; W. Knowler (ed.), *The Earl of Strafford's Letters and Dispatches* (1739), I, 28.

the other in the Oxford Parliament is unlikely, but Williams hovered as close to the flame of intrigue as he could without being consumed by it, and Buckingham declined the game only because he saw no hope of success.[1]

The importance of the quarrel between Buckingham and Williams is not that the Bishop's intrigues caused the Commons to attack the Duke, for they would have launched that attack had Williams remained Buckingham's staunchest supporter. Rather the quarrel is significant because it demonstrates that courtiers would, if they believed they could succeed, use Parliament to destroy a rival. As Williams himself remarked five years later, when justifying his conduct in 1625, no man who had both the Duke and the King against him dared offend Parliament also. But the young King Charles did not perceive that the extension of Court intrigues into Parliament could and would do him irreparable harm. When the Lord Keeper in November 1625 begged Charles to make peace between the Duke and himself, the King replied, 'It became not him, a King, to take up the quarrels between his subjects.' Charles failed to see that a King who could not rule his Court could not long rule his realm.[2]

The real authors of the attack on Buckingham in August 1625 were not Williams and Pembroke, but the leaders of the House of Commons, Sir Robert Phelips, Sir Francis Seymour, and Sir Edward Coke, men set apart from their colleagues by a more than ordinary eloquence and a more than usual boldness. The memorialist Sir Philip Warwick accuses these men of acting from envy at Buckingham's greatness, and the historian Sir Edward Walker accuses them of acting in a spirit of revenge, not being 'so countenanced and advanced by the Duke as they expected'. These charges fell easily from the pens of royalists like Warwick and Walker; they may contain a grain of truth. But they do not answer the far more important question, why the House followed the lead of Phelips, Seymour, and Coke, and not that offered by Sir Humphrey May,

[1] Sir John Eliot, *Negotium Posterorum* (1881), II, 78–9; Hacket, *Scrinia Reserata*, II, 20; Harleian MSS 6988, f. 29. Sir John Wynn wrote to his father on the Lord Keeper's dismissal in October, 'The cause of his remove was only the malice of the Duke towards him, who (when he could not by the means of Parliament displace him) used all his power with the King and [to the] grief of most of the lords, he at length prevailed' (Wynn of Gwydir Papers 1376).

[2] S.P.D. 16/361:206; Hacket, *Scrinia Reserata*, II, 24.

Sir Robert Heath, and Sir Richard Weston, all of whom spoke eloquently and boldly for the Duke.[1]

The moralists of the age, Edward Hyde and Sir Henry Wotton, attributed the willingness of the Commons to listen to Buckingham's opponents to the inconstancy of popular assemblies, observing that they now pulled down the very man whom they had made a hero the year before. Peter Heylyn, William Laud's chaplain and biographer, offered yet another reason for the willingness of the Commons to follow Phelips, Coke, and Seymour in their attack on Buckingham. They did not, he said, wish to lose through disuse that power to remove ministers from the King that they had won by impeaching Bacon and Middlesex. With both of these insinuations, Sir Thomas Wentworth, a member of the House, would have quarrelled. He joined in the opposition to the Court and the Duke in August, and wrote to his friend Wandsworth in December, '...my rule, which I will not transgress, is never to...contest with a King, but when I am constrained thereto, or else make shipwreck of my inward integrity and conscience...'. What forced men like Wentworth to contest with the King in August of 1625 was the folly of the Duke of Buckingham's conduct. The opinions of Clarendon and Wotton notwithstanding, it was Buckingham, not the House of Commons, who displayed an astonishing inconstancy in the years 1624 and 1625.[2]

In 1624 Buckingham had broken the marriage negotiations between Charles and a Catholic princess, had urged the enforcement of penal laws against recusants and priests, had demanded the summoning of Parliament, had favoured a war at sea against Spain, and had favoured parliamentary control of the money voted for that war. In 1625 he reversed his field. He promoted the King's marriage with a Catholic princess, Henrietta Maria of France. He helped negotiate a Treaty with France guaranteeing protection to English recusants and Catholic priests. He did not send out the English fleet to plunder Spanish treasure, but allowed it to lie at anchor at Plymouth, wasting its victuals and stores. As Lord Admiral, he loaned one warship and seven merchant men to France,

---

[1] Sir Philip Warwick, *Memoirs of the Reign of King Charles I* (1701), p. 12; Sir Edward Walker, *Historical Discourses* (1705), p. 332; Eliot, *Negotium Posterorum*, II, 48.

[2] Edward Hyde, Earl of Clarendon, *The History of the Great Rebellion* (Oxford, 1888), I, 31–2; L. P. Smith, *The Life and Letters of Sir Henry Wotton* (Oxford, 1907), II, 295; P. Heylyn, *Cyprianus Anglicus* (1671), p. 188; Knowler, *Letters and Dispatches*, I, 33.

with no security that the King of France would not use them against the Protestants of La Rochelle. Without consulting the Council of War, he advised Charles to embark on an extravagant policy of subsidizing a continental war. England paid in one year £360,000 to the King of Denmark, £240,000 to support Mansfeld's expedition, and £100,000 for the support of troops in the Low Countries. Mansfeld's army of 12,000 men, unwanted by the French and Dutch alike, ill-equipped, and badly provisioned, perished in Holland of disease and starvation, having accomplished nothing.[1] Unsteady, reckless, incompetent, Buckingham was more than the House of Commons could endure. His arrogance towards others (many of whom boasted a more ancient lineage than he), his taking all upon himself, his disordered purposes, his refusal to listen to advice, his jealousy of rivals, all these faults discredited him beyond hope of redemption.

The House of Commons in August 1625 did not demand the removal of the Duke of Buckingham from the Council, though Sir Edward Coke believed that ancient precedent justified Parliament's demanding the removal of incompetent ministers. Nor did the House of Commons wish to name the King's Council for him, though the antiquarian, Sir Robert Cotton, believed that precedent also justified this. Neither did the Commons wish to make the King's councillors answer to them in Parliament for the advice they gave the King, though again Sir Robert Cotton produced precedents justifying it. All that the Commons desired was that His Majesty choose 'a wise, religious, and worthy Council', and advise with it concerning every important act of state. They wanted an end to single counsels. Their desire was modest, but the difficulty of persuading Charles to grant it was immense.[2]

The ever-confident, ever-meddling Lord Keeper was the first man who sought to persuade Charles to grant the desire of the House. In July he told the King that Buckingham's enemies in the Commons had complaints ready to prefer against him. If, however,

---

[1] Gardiner, *History*, v, 269–71, 287–90, 336; vi, 9–12. Parliament learned of the secret Treaty with France from the Earl of Carlisle, who told the two Houses that the King and his ministers agreed to the article about English Catholics only to please the Pope, and had no intention to observe it (*Histoire de ce qui s'est passé en Angleterre depuis le voyage de Madame jusqu'au bannissement des français*, 1626, Fr. Trans.).

[2] Gardiner, *Commons Debates in 1625*, pp. xx–xxiii, 130–2; Cobbett, *Parl. Hist.* ii, 14–17; *C.J.* i, 814.

His Majesty would make the way easy for other men to enter his Council, he would undertake that the Duke's enemies remained silent. Charles refused to accept Williams's undertaking, with the result that the Duke's enemies did voice their complaints in the House.[1] On 5 August Phelips, Seymour, and Coke charged that English ships were loaned to France to be used against the Protestants of Rochelle, that the Treaty with France was no better than the abortive Spanish treaty, and that men of no experience served in the Admiral's office. To assuage the fierceness of the House, Sir Nathaniel Rich, a close friend of Buckingham's, proposed an accommodation. He offered five measures of reconciliation, the third of which provided that His Majesty should employ grave and wise counsellors in the government of the realm. Buckingham at first listened sympathetically to the proposed accommodation, but he ultimately rejected it, choosing instead to defend his conduct of the King's affairs before the two Houses assembled in the Hall of Christ Church. In a speech that was at once sincere and arrogant, he insisted that the King had done nothing without the advice either of the Privy Council or the Council of War. The King had laid before the Privy Council the details of the summer's campaign, and had resolved nothing concerning the fleet without first consulting the Council of War. The speech was at heart a denial that Charles governed by courtiers rather than councillors.[2]

The opponents of Buckingham in the House of Commons now faced a twofold task. They must persuade the House that neither the King nor the Duke had consulted the Privy Council and the Council of War, and they must find a way to drive the Duke from the King's side. Sir Robert Phelips, the wealthy knight from Montacute, the son of a former Speaker of the House, the imprisoned tribune of the people in 1622, proposed, on 10 August, the means to accomplish both tasks. He first suggested that the House ask Sir Thomas Mansell, a member both of the House of Commons and

---

[1] Hacket, *Scrinia Reserata*, II, 14–15.

[2] Eliot, *Negotium Posterorum*, II, 50, 53–5; Gardiner, *Commons Debates in 1625*, pp.91, 95–102. In order to save himself, Buckingham not only defended himself before both Houses, he also persuaded the King to issue a proclamation against the Catholics of England, a proclamation which the French ambassador found to be 'the most rigorous and inhumane that has ever been made against them in England'. He did this, believed the ambassador, in order to win over the Puritans in Parliament and to find his accommodation in the ruin of the Catholics (*Histoire de ce qui s'est passé en Angleterre depuis le voyage de Madame jusqu'au bannissement des français*, 1626, Fr. Trans.).

the Council of War, whether Buckingham had sought the advice of the Council of War in drawing up his military designs. Mansell, an old Elizabethan sea-salt and a friend of the great Earl of Pembroke, heeded Phelips's suggestion, and informed the House that he had never heard any plan of operation discussed in the Council of War. Sir Robert Heath, the Solicitor General, protested that this was not true, but the House found Mansell's testimony more convincing than the Solicitor's protestation, and proceeded to condemn government by single counsels.[1]

Phelips's suggestion for driving the Duke from the King's side was to refuse to vote money until the King took other counsels. He reminded the House that in the reign of Henry VI the Duke of Suffolk had engrossed the favour of the King, had treated alone of the King's marriage, and had assumed the government of the realm to himself; and that Parliament had then refused to vote supplies until he was censured. Furthermore, both the Cortes in Spain and the Estates General in France had in earlier centuries refused to vote money until their Kings had removed faulty ministers. England was now the only monarchy left in Christendom that retained its original rights and constitutions. The safety of the kingdom lay in adhering to these original rights, these ancient precedents. In answer to this confident prescription, the Chancellor of the Duchy protested that ancient precedents were not infallible. But the House followed Phelips's lead, declined to vote supplies, and resolved to draw up a remonstrance expressing the reasons why they could not give the King money.[2] The stubborn acts of Charles and Buckingham, their refusal to listen either to the Lord Keeper's undertaking, or Sir Nathaniel Rich's accommodation, or the complaints of the nation, impelled the House to use the power of the purse to attack irresponsible government. The revival of impeachment in 1621 challenged the King's power to rule unlawfully; the revival of the power of the purse in 1625 challenged his right to govern irresponsibly.

In the short run, to withhold supplies proved a frail reed. Charles broke it by dissolving Parliament on 12 August; thereby saving his

[1] Gardiner, *Commons Debates in 1625*, pp. 108–16; Eliot, *Negotium Posterorum*, II, 83, 93; *C.J.* I, 814.
[2] Gardiner, *Commons Debates in 1625*, pp. 108–16; Eliot, *Negotium Posterorum*, II, 82–94; Rushworth, *Historical Collections*, I, 190.

favourite from the threatened remonstrance against him. Two days later he declared to his Council, meeting at Woodstock, that he would employ 'one or many or nobody', as he saw fit. Charles acted in this peremptory fashion not only because he loved Buckingham, but also because he felt touched in his own sovereignty. As his faithful servant Lord Conway wrote, the Commons in attacking the Duke treated the King 'as a man incapable of governing himself', as a man wholly 'in the power and direction of another', as a man whom they must redeem from that power by putting 'into the tutelage of a Council'.[1] But Charles felt no need for redemption and disdained to be placed under the tutelage of a Council. He would no more admit the truth of Sir Francis Seymour's maxim that 'Princes must see and hear with other eyes and ears', than his father would admit Coke's maxim that in his courts the King's reason was the artificial reason of his judges. In October Charles proclaimed to the kingdom his independence of Council and Parliament (and by inference his dependence on the Duke) by dismissing the one man left in the government who was not the Duke's creature, Bishop Williams, the Lord Keeper. With his dismissal a King who would employ 'one or many or nobody' in his government confronted a Parliament that would have him employ 'a grave and religious and worthy Council'.[2]

The Commons in August 1625 attacked irresponsible government in another of its guises, that of government by foreign ambassadors. They objected to the continual and illegal intervention of foreign ambassadors in the government of England. There is no doubt that this intervention occurred. The Marquis of Villa Clara, the French ambassador, persuaded Charles to grant a pardon to a seminary priest and ten other Papists in Exeter. The Duke of Chevreux, who came over with the young Henrietta Maria, importuned Charles into restoring certain relics to a woman in Dorsetshire. The hapless Lord Conway drew up the warrant for the pardon and wrote the letter to the Dorset justices. The House of Commons spent many days inquiring into both incidents, and pressed Lord Conway hard to defend his actions. But he escaped censure. He escaped it because, as Sir Edward Coke told the House of Lords, the chief end of the House of Commons was to stop the importunity of foreign

[1] S.P.D. 16/21:86.
[2] *C.S.P. Ven.* xix, 146–7; Gardiner, *Commons Debates in 1625*, pp. 78, 177.

ambassadors hereafter. Even Sir Henry Martin, the Prerogative Judge who strove so manfully to gain Charles a vote of supply in the Oxford Parliament, confessed that 'the exorbitant and irregular power of foreign ambassadors is fit to be looked into and to be restrained'. Charles's sudden dissolution of Parliament on the 12th, however, foreclosed both inquiry and restraint.[1]

The short-lived Oxford Parliament is significant in the history of responsible government for three reasons: the Commons for the first time attacked a minister, the Duke of Buckingham, whom they did not charge with breaking the law; the Commons for the first time withheld supplies because the King would not listen to worthy councillors; and the Commons for the first time challenged the King's right to order them to desist from proceeding against one of his servants. This third encroachment on the King's prerogative occurred in the case of Richard Montagu, author of *A New Gagg for an Old Goose* and *Appello Caesarem*. In 1624 the Commons had condemned him for propagating Arminian tenets in *A New Gagg for an Old Goose*. Montagu replied to this censure by writing *Appello Caesarem*, in which he expressed even more extreme opinions, maintaining that the Pope was not the Antichrist, and that Puritans were worse than Papists. The Commons replied to this contempt of their authority by arresting him in June 1625. At this point Charles intervened, sending a message to the House declaring that Montagu was his servant, his Chaplain in Ordinary, and that he had taken the case into his own hands and would give the House satisfaction in it. He asked that they free Montagu from the custody of their serjeant. For the moment the Commons evaded the issue, replying that Montagu was already free on bail; but when Parliament met once again at Oxford in August the Commons seized the nettle firmly. Mr Alford, described by a contemporary as 'one of the faction', took the initiative. He reminded the House of the dangers of exempting the King's servants from questioning in Parliament. In 1621 the Commons had foreborne inquiring into abuses in Ireland, upon a message from the King, and in 1624 they had left it to James to punish Sir Simon Harvey for his delinquencies; and what fruit had either action borne? 'All Justices of Peace', he continued, 'all Deputy Lieutenants are the King's servants, and indeed no man

---

[1] *Ibid.* pp. 118–19, 136–7, 144–5; Cobbett, *Parl. Hist.* II, 19–20; *H.M.C. Buccleuch,* II, 250.

can commit a public offence but by colour and opportunity of public employment and service to the King: so that, if we admit this message, we shall take the way to destroy Parliaments.' The House assented to these views by commanding the serjeant, at his peril, to bring Montagu to the House to answer for his contempt. By pleading sickness, Montagu escaped for the moment the inquisitors general of the realm, but the Commons had proclaimed their determination not to allow messages from the King to dissuade them from inquiring into the misdeeds of his servants.[1]

Between 12 August 1625, when Charles dissolved Parliament, and 6 February 1626, when he met a new Parliament, the single counsels of the Duke of Buckingham were tried, and found wanting. As a result the Parliament of 1626 was the Parliament of 1625 writ large. As Buckingham's power grew more transcendent, the determination of the Commons to put an end to it grew more resolute. Buckingham had fair warning that his desire to engross all counsels would be his undoing. Lord Cromwell admonished him in September, '...let Parliament sit when it will, begin they will where they ended. They say the best Lords of the Council knew nothing of Count Mansfeld's journey or this Fleet, which discontents even the best sort, if not all. They say it is a very great burden your Grace takes upon you, since none knows anything but you. It is conceived that not letting others bear part of the burden you now bear, it may ruin you.'[2] The Duke ignored these warnings. In the next four months he neglected, packed, and abused the Privy Council. He reached decisions without seeking its counsels; he appointed obsequious colleagues to it; and he caused the council to approve plans and policies he had already resolved on, thereby forcing it to share the opprobrium for his counsels. But he deceived no one, and, when Parliament met on 6 February, the Commons were ready to charge him with responsibility for all that had gone wrong in the realm for the past six years.

The past six years had been years of depression at home and dishonour abroad. The outbreak of the Thirty Years War, by closing German markets to English cloth, helped cause a decay in trade, a fall in prices, and a decline in rents. The rise of the House

---

[1] B.M. Add. MSS 48091, ff. 14v–20v; Gardiner, *Commons Debates in 1625*, pp. 33–4, 47–53, 69–71, 179; *C.J.* I, 809–10; J. Forster, *Sir John Eliot* (1864), II, 472.
[2] *Cabala, Sive Scrinia Sacra*, p. 378.

of Austria in Europe brought dishonour to England, when the armies of Spinola drove James's daughter and son-in-law from their newly won kingdom of Bohemia and their ancient patrimony of the Palatinate. The piratical raids of Dunkirkers, Turks, and Spaniards in the Channel added disgrace to dishonour, and imperilled English shipping. Meanwhile, in the eyes of most Englishmen, a more profound danger arose to threaten their spiritual welfare. Indulgences granted to Papists and favours shown to Arminians threatened the purity and privileges of the English Church, and endangered the salvation of Englishmen. These were years of mounting anxiety and frustration for squires and merchants, for Puritans and patriots; and, as men have done in all ages when faced with forces they do not understand, they sought and found a scapegoat. They blamed the Duke of Buckingham for their ills. Though a distant war caused the decay of trade, though Parliament in 1621 voted only a tithe of the money needed for the recovery of the Palatinate, though the Admiralty had only £22,000 to spend on guarding the Narrow Seas, though Charles's marriage policy and religious predilections led him to indulge Papists and favour Arminians, the House of Commons in the spring of 1626 branded the Duke as the cause of all these evils. The Commons erred in their belief, an irrational belief, but their irrationality did not diminish their conviction that the Duke was to blame for all.

Yet Buckingham's innocence of these faults does not lessen the magnitude of the follies that he did commit. Those follies proclaimed to the world that the Duke (whose dancing all admired) was fitter to be *premier danseur* in a ballet company than *premier ministre* to a mighty monarch. Governed by pride and passion, swept by unreasonable hopes and unreal dreams, devoid of wisdom and prudence, he rushed from one disaster to another. He had promised a toleration for English Catholics in the Marriage Treaty with France, but a few months later turned against those same Catholics for the political advantage to be gained by persecuting them. He had loaned the French eight English ships, with no guarantee that they would not be used against the Protestants at Rochell; yet four months later he seized twenty-two French ships for allegedly carrying Spanish goods. By sending out an ill-equipped, badly provisioned, poorly manned, and incompetently commanded expedition against Cadiz, he yielded to the clamour for a war at sea; but he then embarked simultaneously on an extravagant policy of subsidizing a continental war. He pledged £30,000 a month to Denmark for help in recovering the Palatinate, though he had not yet heard that the money for this purpose had been captured at Cadiz. He was unable to finance a war against Spain, yet he allowed England to drift into a war with France.[1] His follies were not trivial, occasional, or of a kind that can be explained away. They were continual, gross, and palpable. Two facts about the Duke of Buckingham must be kept steadily in view: he did not cause the Great Depression of the 1620's or the rise of the House of Austria in Europe, but neither was he fit to rule a kingdom which faced these perils.

Most Englishmen opposed the Duke because they knew him to be incompetent and believed him to be the author of their miseries. But others had more particular reasons for their opposition. There was a phalanx of disappointed courtiers, whom the Duke had excluded from office because they would not cringe before him; an ancient nobility, who saw a *parvenu* monopolize all favour and dispense all honours; and the merchants of the Levant Company, who resented Buckingham's recalling a competent ambassador from the Porte in order to name a favourite to the post. In addition a group of Welsh members followed the Earl of Pembroke in his private quarrels with the Duke; returning colonels and sea-captains opposed him for blaming the failure of the Cadiz expedition on old Captain Geer, a veteran of Elizabethan campaigns; and Puritans denounced him as the great protector at Court of the Montagutians. Contemporaries who saw these men arrayed against the Duke did not err greatly when they said that Charles placed Buckingham in the balance against the whole nation.[2]

And place him in the balance Charles assuredly did. Charles never wavered for a moment in his support of Buckingham during the spring of 1626. He sought to prevent any inquiry into his actions, he accepted responsibility for everything that he had done, he sent messages threatening to dissolve Parliament if the Commons continued to prosecute him, and in the end he dissolved Parliament to save him. The importance of the 1626 Parliament lies in the fact

---

[1] Gardiner, *History*, v, 307–8, 378–94, 398; vi, 22–3, 36–7, 41.

[2] Willson, *Privy Councillors*, pp. 176–88; Clarendon, *History*, i, 12; *C.S.P. Ven.* xix, 367, 391; A. H. Dodd, 'Wales in the Parliaments of Charles I', *Transactions of the Honourable Society of Cymmrodorion, 1945 Session* (1946), pp. 47, 49; Harleian MSS 390, f. 61.

that never before had there been such a direct confrontation between a King determined to defend his minister and his prerogative and a House of Commons determined to wrest that minister from him, even if it injured his prerogative. This confrontation in turn brought into bold relief three problems that the Commons would have to solve before they could destroy irresponsible government in England: how to discover those who were, in fact, responsible for the maladministration of the realm; how to clear the King from any blame; and how to force the King to dismiss those who were at fault.

The first task was to discover the authors of the disasters of the last few years. The House of Commons saw this clearly, and had no sooner assembled than they launched their inquiries. They summoned before them members of the Council of War appointed in 1624, and the Speaker asked each of them whether his counsels and advice had been followed in the management of the war. The Committee for Religion, led by John Pym, searched the Signet-Office for letters written by Secretaries of State ordering reprieves for convicted Jesuits, priests, and recusants. Sir John Eliot led a committee to investigate the seizure of the *St Peter de Havre Grace*. Before his committee had completed its labours it had examined the Lieutenant of the Tower, the Constable of Dover Castle, and a Marshal of the Admiralty. This vigorous exercise of the right of inquiry met prompt opposition from the King. Charles ordered the members of the Council of War not to answer any questions about the advice they had given in Council, because they had taken oaths as councillors not to do so. Then Charles told the House he would not suffer their committees to send general warrants to his Signet-Office, commanding his officials to produce books, records, and private notes. Finally, he reminded his own servants not to testify before the House, without first securing his leave. The Commons, led by the lawyer and scholar John Selden, protested that the Subsidy Act of 1624 gave them authority to examine the Council of War and that 'the laws of the realm and the constant usage of Parliaments' permitted them to search into public records. But Selden and the House were wrong. The Subsidy Act held the Council of War accountable only for the warrants it issued, not for the advice it gave, and earlier Parliaments had not searched the Signet-Office for proof of the delinquencies of Secretaries of State. The ineluctable fact was that the ancient oath of secrecy taken by councillors did prevent the Commons from discovering who advised the King.[1]

Neither the learned John Selden, nor the eloquent Sir John Eliot, nor the determined John Pym ever found a path around the councillor's oath of secrecy. A physician named Dr Samuel Turner, a man better known for diverting noble lords at Court than for advocating popular causes, found that path. On 11 March members of the Council of War refused to say whether their advice had been taken in the management of the war. The very next day Dr Turner rose in the House, and in the name of common fame blamed the Duke of Buckingham for the failure of the Cadiz expedition, for the neglect to guard the Narrow Seas, for the sale of honours and offices, for the impairment of the King's revenues, and for disregarding the Council of War. Charles, furious at these unsupported charges, immediately sent a message to the Commons chastising them for allowing Dr Turner to accuse the Duke without producing any proofs; he demanded that they punish him. The House of Commons did not punish him, nor did they abandon the principle which the inconsiderable Court-dependent had so unexpectedly pronounced. In the ensuing debates on the validity of common fame, the lawyers of the House (led by William Noy, who was later to advise Charles to collect Ship Money) argued that the Canon law, the Civil law, early English law, and the law of Parliament permitted one to accuse a man, though not to condemn him, on common fame. But more forceful than arguments from law were those drawn from necessity. As William Noy observed: 'If we should not proceed on Fame, I know not how we shall proceed.' The House of Commons concurred by voting that common fame was a sufficient ground for transmitting complaints against delinquents, either to the King or to the House of Lords.[2]

The Commons were not, however, prepared to act on every

---

[1] *C.J.* I, 824, 826–8, 829, 832–3, 835. The Parliamentary Journal of Bulstrode White-locke, C.U.L. Dd 12–20, ff. 31–32, 35v–36v, 40v, 45v, 48v, 55v, 68v; Dd 12–21, ff. 120, 136v. S.P.D. 16/22:17, 19, 57, 60. Harleian MSS 390, ff. 23v–24, 25. Hamond Le-strange, *The Reign of King Charles* (1656), p. 23. Cobbett, *Parl. Hist.* II, 58, 68–70.

[2] Warwick, *Memoirs*, pp. 16–18; Cobbett, *Parl. Hist.* II, 50–1; Whitelocke's Diary, C.U.L. Dd 12–21, ff. 119, 136v, 147v–155. Dr Turner began his speech, 'To enquire the cause of the evils of this kingdom; especially *causa generalissima*; by Common Fame the Lord Admiral.' Five days later he admitted to the Speaker, 'Saturday last I did deliver in certain accusations of Common Fame into the House of Parliament against the Lord Admiral' (Huntington Library, HM 213, pp. 11–12).

rumour overheard on Paul's Walk. As Noy remarked, 'We must not have all Fame, neither must we refuse some Fame, but take the middle way.' The grand architect of this middle way was Sir John Eliot, who carefully guided the proceedings of the House of Commons in the spring of 1626. As chairman of the Committee on Grievances he examined such witnesses and searched such records as were available to him. Yet for want of evidence, he and the House were willing to believe Walsingham Crisly when he said that he heard the Earl of Bristol say that the Duke of Buckingham had hindered the recovery of the Palatinate. More significantly, Eliot and the House willingly blamed Buckingham for anything done wrongly in the Admiralty, since he commanded there; and for anything done wrongly by the King, since, as Eliot said, 'We know well who had the King's ear then.'[1] The Duke of Buckingham protested against both assumptions in a speech before the two Houses on 30 March. He said he hoped that he would not be blamed for the Cadiz expedition, he being not there in person, and he confidently asserted that the King had done nothing by single counsels. 'For myself,' he said, 'I have ever been an obedient servant and minister to the Council's resolutions.' But the Commons would not allow the Duke to hide behind the individual responsibility of subordinates or the collective responsibility of the Council. John Selden observed that the Duke of Buckingham appointed the officers deputed to guard the Narrow Seas, 'so that whatsoever is wanting in the safeguarding of the Seas is his fault'. And Mr Matthew declared, in the debate on the loan of the eight ships to France, 'Seeing the Duke had power enough to have prevailed with the King in this, and did not, I think him guilty.' The Commons declared their belief in the particular responsibility of the departmental head and the chief responsibility of the royal favourite by voting that the Duke was the principal cause of all the evils under which the kingdom suffered.[2]

The principle that the royal favourite must answer for everything could hardly be defended in equity. What if the King acted on the advice of others, perhaps in opposition to the advice of his favourite? Must the favourite then answer for the King's conduct? Sir John Eliot

---

[1] Whitelocke's Diary, C.U.L. Dd 12–21, ff. 119, 140–140v; H. Hulme, *The Life of Sir John Eliot* (1957), p. 112; Rawlinson MSS B 151, f. 76.

[2] B.M. Add. MSS 18016, ff. 34–43v. Whitelocke's Diary, C.U.L. Dd 12–20, ff. 13v–19v, 85–87; Dd 12–21, f. 148v. *L.J.* III, 595, 598. *C.J.* I, 841, 849. S.P.D. 16/23:68.

said yes, unless he publicly disavowed the counsels that the King pursued. In his celebrated summation of the charges against Buckingham, he argued that even had the King followed the advice of others in loaning the eight ships to France, the Duke should have entreated the King not to lend them, should have carried the matter to the Council, should have entered a protestation there against the policy. Eliot did not say that the Duke should have resigned if his advice were refused, but that was logically the next step in his argument.[1]

Buckingham not only sought to hide behind the collective responsibility of the Council, he also sought to hide behind the King's commands. In fact his readiness to save himself by involving the King in everything he had done was only equalled by Charles's eagerness to save his authority by assuming responsibility for all that Buckingham had done. The one would bring down the Crown to save himself, the other would endanger the Crown to secure his prerogative. 'The King', wrote the Bishop of Mende to Richelieu, 'is so persuaded that Parliament intends to put him in tutelage, that he holds that he cannot abandon the Duke without ruining his reputation and credit.' With both men determined to pursue the same strategy, it is not strange that Charles frequently intervened on the Duke's behalf and that the Duke repeatedly pleaded the King's commands. Charles first intervened by forbidding Parliament to question the Duke at all. On 15 March he boldly announced to the Speaker of the House of Commons, 'I would not have the House to question my servants.' On the 29th the Lord Keeper told the House that His Majesty, believing that these proceedings against the Duke wounded his and his father's honour and judgment, commands you to 'cease and desist from these enquiries'. But the House, finding that precedents both ancient and modern justified such inquisitions, sent Charles a remonstrance on 5 April, in which they declared that it was the undoubted right of Parliament to question and complain of all persons, of whatsoever degree, who were grievous to the Commonwealth. They matched the deed to the word by continuing their inquisition into the Duke's misconduct.[2]

---

[1] Forster, *Life of Eliot*, I, 544.

[2] *C.S.P. Ven.* XIX, 344, 351–2, 365, 400; *H.M.C. Rutland*, I, 477; Fr. Trans. 17/27 May and 27 May/6 June 1626; B.M. Add. MSS 22474, ff. 10, 18–21, 33v; Whitelocke's Diary, C.U.L. Dd 12–21, ff. 117–119v.

Charles also intervened by assuming responsibility for Buckingham's actions. On 6 March the Attorney General told the House of Commons that Buckingham had seized the *St Peter de Havre Grace* a second time 'by the King's express commandment'. On 15 March the King told the Speaker, 'And for some particulars wherewith the Duke has been pressed...certain it is that I did command him to do what he has done therein.' On 10 May the Commons, not deterred by Charles's intervention, impeached the Duke. On the following day, Charles told the peers, '...as touching the accusations against him, I myself can be a witness to clear him in everyone of them'. But Sir Dudley Digges in his prologue to the Commons' impeachment anticipated Charles. 'And if there have been any commands...pretended,' he said, 'the Duke's misinformations have procured them; for the laws of England teach us that Kings cannot command ill, or unlawful things. Whenever they speak, though by Letters Patent, if the thing be evil, those Letters Patent are void, and whatsoever ill event succeeds the executioner of such commands must ever answer for them.' From this maxim that the King can do no wrong the Commons steadfastly refused to retreat.[1]

The third problem facing the Commons proved the most intractable: how to force Charles to dismiss the Duke. The least disloyal manner of proceeding was to petition the King to dismiss him, in much the same way that the House petitioned the King to redress grievances. From the opening of Parliament until 24 April the House of Commons, guided by Eliot, pursued this method. In February a Committee of the Whole House for Evils, Remedies, and Causes carefully inquired into the grievances of the kingdom, with the alleged intent of petitioning the King for redress. The disguise was thin. As February gave way to March, and March to April, the truth slowly emerged that the Committee was searching out the faults of the Duke, not seeking the causes for the decay of trade and the diminution of the nation's honour. The Commons half-dropped the disguise on 20 March, when Eliot suggested the naming of a subcommittee to find the 'cause of causes', and Sir William Waller openly declared that the 'cause of causes' was the fact that 'all counsel rode on one horse'. On 24 April the House set aside all pretence of a dispassionate search for remedies by voting 228 to 168

---

[1] Whitelocke's Diary, Dd 12–20, f. 43v; *H.M.C. Eleventh Report, Part 1*, p. 49; B.M. Add. MSS 22474, f. 10; *L.J.* III, 592, 596; Huntington Library, HM 905, ff. 207–207v.

to empower a Select Committee to consider, not only such grievances as had been already brought before the House, but any new matter that might concern the Duke.[1] This Select Committee prepared charges against Buckingham and laid them before the House on 2 May. The Duke's friends worked hard that day to have them presented to the King, not the Lords; but the opponents of the Duke, citing the precedents of Bacon and Middlesex, prevailed. By 36 votes the House resolved to present the charges to the Lords. Eight members of the Select Committee did so at a conference with the Lords on 8 and 10 May. The delay in openly resorting to impeachment is wholly explicable: Charles had repeatedly told the House that they might search out remedies for grievances, but they should not search out the faults of his favourite. That the House finally went by impeachment rather than by petition is equally understandable: Charles had clearly shown that he would never give a favourable reply to a petition requesting the Duke's removal.[2]

To vote an impeachment was one thing, to prove its accusations another. This was especially true in 1626, for Buckingham, though guilty of many follies, was guilty of no crimes. He had sent out an ill-prepared expedition to Cadiz, but he had not desired its failure. He had loaned ships to France, but only in order to help an ally besiege Genoa. He was at fault for staying the *St Peter de Havre Grace*, but he had no thought of enriching himself with its goods. He did neglect to guard the Narrow Seas against pirates, but only for want of money to send out more ships. He had extorted £10,000 from the East India Company, but by means that were nominally legal. He was guilty of presumption in prescribing a physic for the late King, but he had no intention of causing his death. He was a pluralist, he did buy and sell offices and honours, he did accept exorbitant gifts from the King: but these were the common practices of the day. As the Duke said in his own defence, '...though I confess there be some errors...They are no errors of wilfullness, nor of corruption, nor oppressing of the people, nor injustices...'[3] To

---

[1] *C.S.P. Ven.* xix, 358, 380. S.P.D. 16/23:37. Whitelocke's Diary, C.U.L. Dd 12–20, f. 63; Dd 12–21, ff. 147v, 155v–156. *C.J.* i, 847, 849.

[2] Whitelocke's Diary, C.U.L. Dd 12–21, ff. 172–174v; Harleian MSS 390, ff. 29, 51v; S.P.D. 16/23:9; *H.M.C. 11th Report, Part 1*, pp. 51, 52; Fr. Trans. 17/27 Apr. 1626.

[3] Cobbett, *Parl. Hist.* ii, 66; S. R. Gardiner, *Documents Illustrative of the Impeachment of the Duke of Buckingham* (Camden Soc. n.s. xlv); G. E. Aylmer, *The King's Servants* (1961), pp. 228–9.

demonstrate his criminality, the eight members of the Commons who charged the Duke before the Lords had no other course but to plead ancient and unused statutes, the dicta of Bracton, the law of nations, the custom of the Exchequer, and doubtful law declared in earlier impeachments. Of the eight prosecutors, John Pym displayed the greatest audacity (and foreshadowed the case against Strafford) by appealing to the fundamental laws of England, laws 'that are co-essential and co-natural with government, which being broken all things run into confusion'. But appeals to Bracton and the fundamental laws of England carried little weight with the Lords. Especially was this true when Buckingham, deserting his habitual arrogance, made a modest and persuasive defence of his innocence before the Lords. At the same time Charles created three new peers and spoke with the Bishops, in order to ensure a party for the Duke in the Upper House. In the face of possible defeat in the Lords, the Commons fell back on a weapon that they had carefully held in reserve: the power of the purse.[1]

The Commons had always been ready to use this weapon, but they were reticent to say so. It was an innovation as difficult to justify as it was mandatory to introduce. The House first hinted at their willingness to use it on 27 March, when they resolved to give the King money, but only after they had presented their grievances and he had returned them an answer. Charles two days later told the House that he found this manner of voting supplies entirely unacceptable. He commanded them to vote supplies, without conditions, by the following Saturday. The House did not do so; instead they fell to justifying their actions. Having read (in Sir Walter Raleigh's *A Dialogue Between a Counsellor and a Justice of the Peace*) about the Commons' refusal to vote Richard II supplies until he removed the Earl of Suffolk, Sir John Eliot was able to cite it as a precedent. Two further arguments were heard more often than the appeal to precedent: the argument that the House had a right to know that the money they gave was not misspent, and the argument that they might demand the redress of grievances before voting supplies. Sir Benjamin Rudyerd's remark, 'No man will be willing to give his money into a bottomless gulf...', seemed not

---

[1] *L.J.* III, 597–608, 610–16; Rushworth, *Historical Collections*, I, 302–56; Huntington Library, HM 905, ff. 163–176; Cobbett, *Parl. Hist.* II, 166–83; Harleian MSS 390, ff. 64, 73; H. Wharton (ed.), *The History of the Troubles and Tryals of William Laud* (1695), I, 32.

disloyal, but the merest prudence. Those whom the House represented paid the subsidies and the fifteenths; surely they had a right, through their representatives in Parliament, to see that it was wisely spent. The argument that the House might demand redress of grievances before voting supplies was as old as the reign of Henry IV and had echoed through St Stephen's Chapel in James's reign. What was new was the willingness of the House to refer to a minister of the King as a grievance. By this legerdemain the House could use an old weapon for securing a favourable reply to a petition as a new instrument for encroaching on the King's control of the executive. Both arguments—the appeal to the right of superintendence and the appeal to the right of redress—were to be heard again and again in Stuart England. They were rationalizations, but they convinced the burgesses from the towns and the knights from the shires that they might justly refuse to vote supplies until the King dismissed a prodigal minister, grievous to the realm.[1]

The power of the purse was effective only because the King was impoverished and the kingdom secure from foreign invasion. These two circumstances, more than any others, explain why responsible government came in England rather than on the continent. As the Bishop of Mende observed in May, what encouraged the opposition was the fact that, if the King dissolved Parliament, he would have to meet a new one in two months. 'His necessity', he added, 'gives them their audacity.' Denied by law the right to levy taxes on his own authority, £500,000 in debt, and spending £20,000 a year more than his revenues brought in, Charles could not withstand the power of the purse. The only argument that his servants in the House made for the immediate granting of supplies was the threat of danger from abroad. As the Vice-Chamberlain said on 5 May, 'Those that are so sick of grievances here at home, do not think of the grief and danger that hangs over them abroad...shall we be talking of grievances until the enemy comes upon us?' It is true that the opponents of Buckingham were not thinking of the danger from abroad; but neither was there a pressing need for them to do so, for Kent was not contiguous to Flanders, Spanish armies could not march into England. The facts of geography allowed the Commons to indulge

---

[1] *C.J.* 1, 842. Whitelocke's Diary, C.U.L. Dd 12–20, ff. 5v–10v, 30v, 91–93, 143–144v; Dd 12–21, ff. 119v–120. Cobbett, *Parl. Hist.* II, 59. Fr. Trans. 29 March/8 Apr. and 19/29 Apr. 1626. S.P.D. 16/23:37 and 16/27:18.

in the luxury of driving Buckingham from office while England fought with Spain. They enjoyed an island luxury, denied to states with no 'moat defensive to the realm'.[1]

The Commons in their remonstrance to the King on 5 April declared that by ancient custom Parliament had voted supplies at the end of the session. They then proceeded to the impeachment of Buckingham. Charles at once rushed to the defence of his favourite, imprisoning Sir John Eliot and Sir Dudley Digges for speaking too vehemently against Buckingham at the conference with the Lords on 8 and 10 May. This led the Commons to prepare another remonstrance, justifying their privileges. While the House was preparing this new remonstrance, Charles named Buckingham President of the Council of War and secured his election as Chancellor of the University of Cambridge. His contempt of popular and parliamentary opinion persuaded the Commons, already fearful that the Lords might find the Duke innocent, to convert their second remonstrance into a demand for Buckingham's dismissal. Charles replied by threatening on 9 June to dissolve Parliament unless the Commons passed the Subsidy Bill within a week. Once again the House of Commons stood up to Charles's intimidations. On 12 June, after a debate lasting from eight in the morning until nine in the evening, with over 200 members speaking, they voted by a large majority to go first to their remonstrance, and then to the Subsidy. Two days later they voted their remonstrance, and with that act dropped all pretence that they were not bargaining with the King. The pace of events had overtaken Eliot's scruples against, and had justified Pym's insistence on, stating conditions to the King. In their remonstrance the Commons made the removal of the Duke a condition for the voting of supplies. The remonstrance also announced the new principle that there were faults that were not criminal and yet justified the removal from office of those who were guilty of them. In order to prevent the House from presenting this revolutionary document, Charles dissolved Parliament on 15 June.[2]

[1] Fr. Trans. 14/24 May and 14/24 June 1626; *H.M.C. Lonsdale*, p. 16; Whitelocke's Diary, C.U.L. Dd 12–21, f. 180. The sums given for Charles's debt and deficit are only rough approximations, based on figures given by Gardiner for 1623 and 1635 (Gardiner, *History*, VIII, 81; x, 222–3).

[2] Fr. Trans. 27 May/6 June and 14/24 June 1626; *H.M.C. Lonsdale*, pp. 31–3; S.P.D. 16/29:12; B.M. Add. MSS 22474, ff. 183–183v; Harleian MSS 390, ff. 77, 79; Whitelocke's Diary, C.U.L. Dd 12–21, f. 121; Cobbett, *Parl. Hist.* II, 201–7. Buckingham begged Charles to dissolve Parliament. The Bishop of Mende wrote on 14 June, 'I found the

Charles did so for a very good reason: the remonstrance of 14 June threatened to take from him control of the executive power. Yet the more puzzling question remains: why had Charles earlier sought to prevent Buckingham's trial before the Lords? Acquittal might have been the result of such a trial, and a Duke of Buckingham declared innocent by the Lords would have been more powerful than ever. Two motives persuaded Charles to seek to prevent such a trial: he feared that the Earl of Bristol would make disclosures in the trial that would embarrass both him and the Duke, and he could not entirely depend on the Lords to acquit the Duke. Through the spring of 1626 Bristol had prosecuted his own personal charges against Buckingham, and the Earl possessed letters of state that might reveal more than Charles wished known about the Spanish journey. When Charles attempted to dissuade Bristol from revealing what he knew, the Earl replied (according to the Bishop of Mende) that if it were a matter of his life or property, he would rather lose both than to continue to justify his conduct, but where his honour was concerned he would justify the Devil against Jesus Christ. Charles had no desire to allow such a fearless man to produce state secrets before the House of Lords. His disclosures might persuade the Lords, who had just contravened the royal will by demanding the Earl of Arundel's release from the Tower, to resist the royal will again by passing judgment against Buckingham.[1] In fact the whole nation was united in a desire to see the Duke, who wholly engrossed the King's favour, removed from office. The tragedy for Charles was that he had manœuvred himself into a position which forced him to place the Duke in the balance against both Houses of Parliament in order to defend his prerogative. Charles acted wisely in dissolving Parliament to save the Duke, for in no other way could he maintain his hold on the sceptre. But he had erred grievously in employing the Duke in the first place.

The attack of the House of Commons upon the Duke of Buckingham kept them from considering much else. Yet they did find time

Duke yesterday at the feet of His Majesty, shedding more tears than words, and with a visage more fitting a condemned man than a favourite. He was most vexed at my surprising him, and tried to persuade me that he was rendering rather than demanding grace of the King. But if I pretended to believe him, it was only in order to please him' (Fr. Trans. 14/24 June 1626).

[1] *C.S.P. Ven.* xix, 429–32; *H.M.C. 11th Report, Part 1*, pp. 59–60, 68–9, 73; Harleian MSS 390, ff. 47, 53, 56; Fr. Trans. 17/27 Apr., 29 Apr./9 May, 15/25 May, 23 May/2 June, 27 May/6 June, 14/24 and 16/26 June 1626.

to propose, though not to perfect, censures against the Court of High Commission, against the Bishop of Bangor, and against Richard Montagu. The quarrel of the Commons with the Court of High Commission arose out of that Court's excommunication of a member of Parliament, Sir Robert Howard, in 1621. The House interrogated three lay members of the Court, and considered censuring them for violating the privileges of one of their members. In the end, however, they merely resolved to request the Court to vacate all proceedings against Howard. Against the Bishop of Bangor the House heard charges of simony, incontinence, bribery, and extortion. Having heard the charges, the House gave their Committee for Religion power to examine witnesses and to send for papers concerning the Bishop's alleged crimes. But the dissolution of Parliament prevented any further prosecution of the Bishop. The dissolution of Parliament also prevented further prosecution of Richard Montagu, whose two books, *A New Gagg for an Old Goose* and *Appello Caesarem*, had earned him the censure of Parliament in 1625. The House reopened his prosecution in 1626, when John Pym spoke for two hours on Montagu's crimes, and so amazed Montagu's friends by the brilliance of his performance, that not one of them spoke for Montagu; they left the House when the question to impeach him was put. In his speech Pym charged that Montagu had, by publishing his books, disturbed the peace of the Church, set the King against his subjects, and promoted popery. The House agreed, and voted his impeachment. By 15 June the House had proceeded to the engrossment of articles against him, but Charles that same day dissolved Parliament. These attacks on the High Commission, on the Bishop of Bangor, and on Richard Montagu failed, but not before they had enlisted the zeal of the Puritan faction behind Parliament's demand for responsible government. William Laud saw in the attack on Montagu 'a cloud arising and threatening the Church of England'. Did he also see a cloud arising that would threaten with destruction any man who advised the King to pursue a religious policy hostile to that of Parliament?[1]

Between June 1626 and February 1628 irresponsible government in England reached its zenith. The power of the Duke of Buckingham

---

[1] Whitelocke's Diary, C.U.L. Dd 12–20, ff. 69–71; Dd 12–21, ff. 132v, 133v–136. *C.J.* 1, 839, 845, 850–2. Harleian MSS 390, f. 45. *Calendar of Wynn (of Gwydir) Papers 1515–1690* (1926), pp. 227–8. Wharton, *Troubles and Tryals of William Laud*, 1, 27.

had never been greater and the reputation of the Privy Council had never been lower. Few men could respect a Council from which the Duke had driven in the first year of Charles's reign the Earl of Bristol, Lord Keeper Williams, and the Earl of Arundel. In place of these Charles named to the Council in July 1626 the Earls of Dorset, Salisbury, and Bridgewater, all of them dependents of the Duke, and men who had spoken for him in the late Parliament. A year later Charles drove the Archbishop of Canterbury from Court for showing signs of independence. Yet even this obsequious Council Buckingham ignored. The Council might busy itself with expedients for raising more revenue, but Buckingham rarely brought important matters of state before it.[1] Government by a single Court favourite was a visible reality in the year 1627; nor did the arrogant Duke seek to conceal the fact. Instead he sought to justify it by a signal triumph abroad, by bringing succour to the hard-pressed Huguenots of La Rochelle. Hoping to demonstrate both his Protestant sympathies and his military talents, he led an expedition to the Isle of Rhé, outside the harbour of La Rochelle. There, while walking the rounds at night and superintending the mining of the counterscarp of St Martin's by day, he received from King Charles a letter congratulating him on the success of the campaign, a success which 'forces all men to approve my judgment of you'. But Charles spoke too hastily, for Buckingham had undertaken the siege of St Martin's without any assurance of adequate supplies from home, or rather, in the full knowledge that the government did not have the money to purchase such supplies. Reinforcements therefore did not arrive, a disastrous retreat ensued, and England lost two thousand men. 'Since England was England', Denzil Holles remarked, 'it received not so dishonourable a blow.'[2]

That Charles, in the face of so dishonourable a blow, decided to meet Parliament in February 1628 is puzzling. He had, however, two good reasons for doing so: forced loans had not provided the money he needed to defend the realm against Spain and France,[3]

---

[1] *C.S.P. Ven.* XIX, 462, 495; Fr. Trans. 16/26 July 1626; Harleian MSS 390, f. 167v.

[2] Fr. Trans. 15/25 March 1627; Harleian MSS 6988, f. 40; Knowler, *Letters and Dispatches*, I, 42.

[3] In December 1627 anticipations on the revenue amounted to £319,000; in addition Charles needed £200,000 a year to pay the soldiers and sailors levied for the Cadiz expedition. A loan of £120,000 from the City was quite inadequate to meet these needs (Pearl Valerie, *London and the Outbreak of the Puritan Revolution*, Oxford, 1961, pp. 73–4).

and the leaders of Parliament promised him that they would not attack Buckingham if Parliament met. The leaders of Parliament made this promise because they saw clearly that Charles would rather introduce arbitrary government than surrender the Duke. Because Buckingham's removal was not negotiable, prudence dictated that Parliament should not negotiate about it. Parliament should act where there was hope of success. Wentworth, with his usual political realism, saw that the Commons might better wrest from the King a clear declaration of the law. 'Put such a mark on the law', he said, 'as no licentious spirit will dare to break into it.'[1] Out of this strategy emerged the Petition of Right. By declaring the law (as Parliament interpreted it) to be supreme, and by implying that ministers had a duty to act within the framework of law, the Petition of Right furthered the growth of responsible government in England.

Though the leaders of Parliament promised not to attack Buckingham, they made no promise to spare other delinquents. Their thorough and earnest investigation into the misdeeds of these delinquents suggests that inquiries into maladministration had become not only a right, but a habit. They interrogated Mr Mowden, High Constable of Kingston, for billeting soldiers on those who did not pay a levy imposed on the hundred. A committee of the House recommended the impeachment of Sir William Welby, a Deputy Lieutenant of Lincoln, for imprisoning two men who refused to pay a similar levy. The House voted to impeach Mr Burgess for collecting a similar levy in his county, and Lord John Mohun, for arbitrary and extortionate conduct as Vice-Warden of the Stannaries. A committee of the House found Sir Edward Moseley, Attorney of the Duchy, guilty of extortion and bribery, and the whole House voted that Mr Thornall should answer for grievances in the execution of the saltpetre commission.[2]

The Commons pressed even more diligently charges against two of their own members, Mr Baber, Recorder of Wells, and Sir Edmund Sawyer, a Revenue Auditor. Accused of levying money for the billeting of soldiers, Baber replied that he knew that it was illegal, but having been called once before the Council table for

---

[1] Harleian MSS 4771, ff. 20v–21.

[2] *Ibid.* ff. 20v–21; *C.J.* I, 881, 895, 905–7, 908, 917–19; *H.M.C. Cowper*, I, 354; Stowe MSS 367, ff. 193–194.

5-2

resisting the saltpetre men, he dared not oppose the levy. This prompted the eminent and learned lawyer, Edward Littleton, to cry out, 'He should have rather suffered than done an injustice. Chief Justice Markham in the reign of Edward IV resigned rather than do an injustice.' The Commons suspended Baber from the House. Sir Edmund Sawyer voiced the same plea when accused of being the projector of a new book of rates, by which the King could collect 2*s.* where he had collected 1*s.* before. He told the House, 'I did nothing but by the King's command', a statement that Charles confirmed the next day. This plea caused Sir Thomas Wentworth to exclaim, 'It makes my blood boil within me to hear this man lay all upon the King.' It made the blood of most members of the House boil also, for they expelled Sawyer from the House and imprisoned him in the Tower. The one doctrine that the Commons would not stomach was that men owed obedience to the King's every command. They also showed their detestation of the doctrine in this same Parliament by impeaching Dr Roger Manwaring for preaching and publishing two sermons advocating it. Perhaps no principle lies closer to the heart of responsible government than the duty of a servant of the King to suffer disgrace and dismissal before committing an illegal (or unpopular) act.[1]

Through the months of April and May the leaders of the House kept their promise not to attack the Duke of Buckingham, but in June the flood gates flew open and their rage poured out on the royal favourite. A belief that Buckingham had advised Charles to give an unsatisfactory answer to the Petition of Right on 2 June released their anger. Suspicion that the Duke would continue to advise Charles to invade their liberties and to attack their property caused them to resume their attack, even after Charles had given a satisfactory answer to their Petition on 7 June. There was an atmosphere of fear and alarm in the land, which was not present in 1626. No longer did the Commons confront a minister guilty only of folly. They now faced a minister who had advised Charles to impose extra-parliamentary taxes on his subjects, who had coun-

---

[1] *C.J.* I, 881, 916; Stowe MSS 366, ff. 61–63, 275–275v; Harleian MSS 390, f. 387. Sir William Crofts, suspended from his place as Gentleman of the Privy Chamber for speaking against the Duke in 1626, also argued in 1628 that a minister should resign before obeying an unlawful command. He told the House of Commons, on their discovering the Great Seal attached to the Commission for the Raising of Money by Imposition or Otherwise, 'Should I have had the Great Seal in my keeping, I should rather have given it up than set it to such a commission' (Stowe MSS 366, f. 245).

selled him to bring over 1,000 Dutch Horse to help collect such taxes, and who was General of a standing army garrisoned in their towns.

As in 1626, so now, the Commons had to prove Buckingham's fault, free the King from all responsibility, and find a means to drive the Duke from the King's person and councils.

The Commons set out to demonstrate Buckingham's guilt by the usual inquisitorial methods; once again they failed. Neither by examining the Commission for Raising of Money by Imposition or Otherwise, nor by interrogating Burlamachi concerning the plan to bring over the Dutch Horse, could they prove that Buckingham had advised such schemes. The House therefore fell back once more on common fame. In part this meant relying on mere rumour. Eliot had heard that all was done at the Isle of Rhé without the advice of the Council of War. Mr Long had heard that Montagu found protection at York House. Pym reminded the House that the Duke's mother was a Papist.[1] But rumour and guilt by association were no basis for a serious parliamentary charge. So the Commons, prompted by Sir Edward Coke, resorted once more to the particular responsibility of the departmental head and the general responsibility of the royal favourite. Coke asked rhetorically, 'If there be a fault in the Treasury, who is answerable but the Treasurer?' And then argued, 'The Duke has engrossed sea and land. Necessity enforces us to name him.' The Solicitor objected, 'You say he is in great favour, but you are to prove the particular misdemeanours of his power.' The House decided, however, that they need not prove particular misdemeanours, and voted that 'the excessive power of the Duke of Buckingham and the abuse of that power are the chief cause of these evils and dangers to the King and Kingdom'.[2]

On 6 June Charles informed the House of Commons that they were not to tax him under the name of his ministers. Sir Robert Phelips instantly replied, '...if anything falls out unhappily, it is not King Charles that advised himself, but King Charles misadvised by others and misled by disordered counsels'. This interpretation of the maxim that the King can do no wrong went beyond the usual

---

[1] *C.J.* I, 912; Stowe MSS 366, ff. 224–225 v, 238; Cobbett, *Parl. Hist.* II, 383; L. M. Sumner, 'A Critical Edition of Nicholas' Notes on the Parliament of 1627–8' (A thesis submitted to the Faculty of the Graduate School of the University of Minnesota, 1913), p. 191.
[2] Stowe MSS 366, f. 239v; *C.J.* I, 911.

argument that those who executed his illegal commands were at fault. The truth is the House wished to punish councillors who gave the King evil advice, not underlings who executed his orders. And in order to focus responsibility on such councillors they were forced to deny the King any judgment at all. As Coke said, repeating the maxim that Seymour first voiced in 1625, 'I do free my sovereign. He sees with other men's eyes and hears with other men's ears.' The logic of this maxim, pushed to its uttermost, reduced the King to a cipher in the government of his own realm.[1]

The third problem confronting the Commons proved the most intractable of all: how to force Charles to dismiss Buckingham. To solve it they resorted neither to impeachment nor to the withholding of supplies. Instead they drew up a remonstrance explaining why they feared innovations in religion, alterations in the government, and future ill success in war, if the Duke remained in office. Where coercion had failed, they now tried persuasion. They sought to convince Charles that the Duke was indubitably 'the grievance of grievances', as Coke passionately characterized him on that memorable 5 June, when members of the House openly wept for grief at the state of the realm. But persuasion also failed. Charles received the remonstrance, which not only asked for Buckingham's removal but also censured Bishop Neile and William Laud, on 17 June. On receiving it, he told the Commons, with a singular want of tact, that he now saw that they understood less of matters of state than he had thought. He refused even to consider dismissing from his councils the three men against whom the Commons remonstrated.[2]

Charles never published an answer to the remonstrance against Buckingham, Neile, and Laud, but he did commission Laud to write an answer. This state paper, now in the Public Record Office,[3] is the most cogent presentation of the royalist view of the responsibilities of ministers written in the seventeenth century. Laud began his answer by insisting that misfortunes should not be made crimes and that the government should not be traduced because of disasters abroad, 'for neither is good success a sure proof of wise counsel, nor ill success of weak'. And if the forts of the realm are decayed and the regality of the Narrow Seas lost, everyone knows that it is

[1] Cobbett, *Parl. Hist.* ii, 406–7; Stowe MSS 366, f. 239v.
[2] Cobbett, *Parl. Hist.* ii, 404, 420–7; Harleian MSS 390, ff. 410–411; Stowe MSS 366, ff. 255–256.
[3] S.P.D. 16/108:67.

because the House of Commons would not trust the government with the means to make the forts strong and the seas safe. Nor can the King in justice be expected to remove any man from office or Council merely on general accusations, without particular proof. Then Laud came to the heart of his case. Speaking in His Majesty's name he wrote: And what does this remonstrance 'make us to our people', when

it proclaims that we can be led up and down by Buckingham, or any man living, to do what he, or they, please? Does it mean to persuade our people we have lost our judgment, or have none to lose? Or that we give excessive power to any of our ministers, and then are so weak that we see not how ourself and our power is abused? In the beginning it calls us a good, a just, a wise, a judicious Prince...But if we be wise and judicious, how comes it to pass we are thus ignorant of imminent dangers, as the same Remonstrance would make us? And if we be good and just, how is it that what our wisdom sees amiss in the State, or the ministers of it, is not punished or amended?...We would not have our people only but the world know that neither Buckingham nor any man living does or can lead us to or from any action or business of state, but as we see cause and reason to move us.

This was the royalist reply to Seymour's maxim that the King must see with other men's eyes and hear with other men's ears. The King was not a prisoner of his ministers: he had a mind of his own.

On 26 June Charles prorogued Parliament because the House of Commons dared to question his right to collect tonnage and poundage. Still confident that wisdom, loyalty, and ability resided preeminently in the person of the Duke of Buckingham, still preferring to govern his realm through courtiers rather than councillors, he sent the Duke to Portsmouth to superintend the preparation of yet another expedition to win renown for the King and applause for the Duke. At Portsmouth a Suffolk gentleman, John Felton, brooding over the state of the realm and the Duke's unwillingness to grant him a captaincy, drove a dagger through Buckingham's heart. The impeached minister who refused to resign from office, the unpopular courtier who declined to leave the King's side, the royal favourite who defied all remonstrances against him, was finally driven from the King, not by Parliament, but by the dagger of an assassin.

The assassination of Buckingham was not an ephemeral event in English politics. The consequences were lasting. It ended government by a Court favourite in England. Charles never again entrusted the destinies of England wholly to the hands of a royal favourite. The pattern of government employed after Buckingham's death may have been unpopular, may have stretched the prerogative to its uttermost, but it was government by a Council over which no single minister tyrannized. Neither Weston nor Laud nor Wentworth, not even the Queen herself, attained the transcendent power that Buckingham had once enjoyed. Yet the definition of responsibility changed with the passage of time. Where Parliament once objected to government by courtiers rather than councillors, it now objected to government by councillors who followed policies of doubtful legality and less popularity. Charles's troubles were not over, as the Parliament of 1629 proved.

In 1629 the House of Commons resumed their attacks on the King's ministers. That the Commons should do so even after Buckingham's death gave clear proof, said Charles, that their secret design had always been to abate the power of the Crown. Mr Corriton dissented, proclaiming, to the applause of the greater part of the Commons, that they came with a full purpose to give His Majesty satisfaction, but that once assembled they discovered so many treasons in his servants, that they had first to punish them. Both Charles and Mr Corriton were in error: there existed no conscious design to abate the power of the Crown, and the King's servants had committed no treason. The clash between King and Commons occurred because Charles was determined to promote Arminians, to reprieve Papists, and to collect tonnage and poundage before Parliament voted it, while the Commons were equally determined to punish Arminians, to hang Papists, and to refuse to pay tonnage and poundage until they had voted it.[1]

No sooner did Parliament meet on 20 January 1629 than they began their usual inquiries into the authors of past misdeeds. They empowered committees to send for persons and papers. They refused to vote tonnage and poundage until they had completed their inquiries. They asked the Attorney-General who had sent him orders to draw up pardons for Manwaring, Montagu, Cosin, and Sibthorpe, four notorious Arminians. They asked Chief Justice Hyde why he

---

[1] *His Majesties Declaration to All His Loving Subjects of the Causes which Moved Him to Dissolve the Last Parliament* (London, 1628/9), p. 40; W. Notestein and F. Relf (eds.), *Commons Debates in 1629* (Minneapolis, 1921), p. 261.

reprieved Mr Moore, a condemned Catholic priest. They asked the officers of the Customs why they seized the goods of Mr Rolle, a member of Parliament who refused to pay tonnage and poundage. The Attorney-General answered that he had a warrant from the King to draw up the pardons. Chief Justice Hyde replied that he had reprieved Mr Moore because the King commanded him to do so. The officers of the Customs pleaded that they had a Commission from the King authorizing them to seize the goods of those who would not pay tonnage and poundage. Confronted by this plea wherever they turned, the House decided not to contest but to circumvent it. Thus they read the Commission to the officers of the Customs and discovered that it gave them authority to levy the duty but not to seize the goods of a member of Parliament who would not pay it. A sigh of relief could be heard from friends and opponents of the Crown alike, for they could now punish the Customs officers without dishonouring the King.[1]

Members of the House of Commons had not counted on the tenacity and clarity of purpose of Charles. He refused to allow an oversight in a commission to rob him of his authority to exact obedience from his servants. On 23 February he informed the Commons that he had ordered the officers of the Customs to seize the goods of those who would not pay tonnage and poundage. He added that he would not allow the House to sever him from the actions of his servants. Charles's message, like a bolt of lightning, illuminated briefly and vividly a constitutional scene that Eliot and his friends preferred to keep in darkness. The persistent obfuscation of the House, said Charles in effect, should not be allowed to obscure the fact that the King, and not his servants, bore responsibility for the government of the realm. Caught off-guard by this message, the House adjourned for two days in order to take counsel privately. Charles suspected that this private counsel boded no good for him; he further adjourned Parliament until 2 March.[2] The Commons then reassembled, and before the tumultuous events of that day were played out, Eliot had, without offering any proof, named

---

[1] *C.J.* I, 921, 926, 928, 930; Notestein and Relf, *Commons Debates in 1629*, pp. 38–9, 47, 89–93, 125–6, 130, 150, 155–6, 165, 211, 225.

[2] *Ibid.* pp. 94–5, 167–8, 237–8. Salvetti, the Tuscan envoy, reported that the leaders of the House of Commons decided, presumably as a result of their private counsels, to resume the prosecution of delinquents when they met again on 25 Feb., despite the King's message of the 23rd (B.M. Add. MSS 27962 E, f. 244 v).

The Rise and Fall of Irresponsible Government

Lord Treasurer Weston as the councillor 'in whose person is contracted all the evil that we do suffer'; Corriton had asked,' Shall every man that has broken the law have the liberty to pretend the King's command?'; and the House had voted that whoever introduced innovations in religion or advised the taking of tonnage and poundage 'shall be reputed a capital enemy to this kingdom and commonwealth'. In these words and resolves the House resorted once again to accusation by common fame, to the maxim that the King can do no wrong, and to the voting of remonstrances against evil counsellors. They could find no other solution to the three perennial problems of responsible government: how to focus responsibility on those most at fault, how to clear the King of all responsibility, and how to secure the dismissal of those found to be at fault. Charles, however, rendered ineffectual each of these solutions by immediately adjourning, and then dissolving, Parliament. He did not meet another Parliament for eleven years.[1]

Charles also issued a declaration justifying his dissolution of Parliament. In it he challenged the right of the Commons to interrogate his servants and defended his right to exact obedience from them. He objected heatedly to their forcing officers of the Customs to wait on them day after day, to their examining the Attorney-General, 'an officer of trust and secrecy', to their demanding to see Letters Patent under the Great Seal and Warrants by the Privy Council, to their examining Chief Justices touching judicial proceedings, to their asking Privy Councillors what this or that man said at Council Table, and to their imprisoning the Sheriff of London for not answering them as they wished. He then repeated his message of 23 February, that they should not sever him from the actions of his servants. And he concluded with an answer to the terrible votes of 2 March, 'For our ministers, we will not that they be terrified by those harsh proceedings that have been strained against some of them. For, as we will not command anything unjust or dishonourable, but shall use our authority and prerogative for the good of our people; so we will expect that our ministers obey us, and they shall assure themselves we will protect them.'[2]

[1] Sir Thomas Crew, *The Proceedings and Debates of the House of Commons, in the Session of Parliament, begun the twentieth of January, 1628[9]* (1707), pp. 146–57; Notestein and Relf, *Commons Debates in 1629*, pp. 101–5, 170–2, 253–66.

[2] *His Majesties Declaration...of the Causes which Moved Him to Dissolve the Last Parliament*, pp. 5–43. The Venetian ambassador wrote in October that Charles refused to meet

74

From 1629 to 1640 Charles returned to the Tudor ideal of government by a Privy Council. For eleven years England knew neither the egregious irresponsibility of Buckingham's days nor the responsibility of ministers to Parliament that Pym and Eliot obscurely demanded. No great man engrossed all power or reversed the decisions of the Council Table or monopolized the favour of the King. Men of genuine administrative talent, such as Laud and Wentworth, served the King in high office and sat at the Council Table. In 1640 Parliament did not take exception to the form of government, but to the policies pursued by the government.

Yet the years of irresponsible government left a legacy that the passage of eleven years did not erase. The House of Commons now regarded inquiry into misdeeds as a duty as well as a right. They quietly assumed to themselves the right to interrogate the King's servants and to search through his state papers. They asserted a right, where such inquiries proved barren, to accuse ministers on common fame; which often meant common rumour, but occasionally meant the particular responsibility of the departmental head or the overall responsibility of a royal favourite. They even suggested that ministers enter a formal protest or resign when the King acted on illegal advice. The most insistent principle they voiced was the maxim that the King can do no wrong. Their frequent iteration of this maxim tended to divorce the King from responsibility for the legality, and even for the wisdom, of acts of government. His ministers must answer for all. And if they persisted in illegal, dishonourable, and unsuccessful policies, then the Commons might impeach them for their crimes, or declare them to be 'the grievance of grievances', and withhold supplies until they were removed. The sum total of these new principles added up to a revolution in English government.

Loyal knights of the shire, modest burgesses from the towns, and eminent peers of the realm accepted this revolution for two reasons. No one among them (unless it were John Pym) saw what the sum total of these principles logically meant. And most of them had been too enraged by Buckingham's incompetence to reflect on what they

Parliament again because it would injure his authority by inquiring into the acts of his servants, and because he had discovered that making himself responsible for decisions had met with no success. The ambassador added that everyone was very cautious about doing anything to the prejudice of the people, even though the King offered to make himself responsible and pledged his word to protect them (*C.S.P. Ven.* XXII, 204).

were doing by attacking him. The Duke's government of England had been an abject failure, a failure that flouted the dignity of the King's rightful councillors, offended the patriotism of the whole nation, and excited the mirth of foreign ambassadors. Had James not become infatuated with this handsome youth, and had Charles not been awed by his grandeur, the first two Stuarts might have successfully resisted the growing inclination of Parliament to encroach on the prerogative. No doubt a wish to participate more fully in government would in time have led the two Houses to attack the King's ministers, but Buckingham's folly and pride offer a sufficient explanation why they did so in the 1620's.

CHAPTER 3

THE FAILURE OF IMPEACHMENT
(1640–1642)

I know no reason [wrote Sir Thomas Wentworth, the King's Deputy in Ireland, to Archbishop William Laud in England] but you may as well rule the Common Lawyers in England as I, poor beagle, do here; and yet that I do (and will do in all that concerns my master's service) upon the peril of my head. I am confident that the King...is able by his wisdom and ministers to carry any just and honourable action through all imaginary opposition, for real there can be none; that to start aside for such panic fears, phantastic apparitions, as a Prynne or an Eliot shall set up, were the meanest folly in the whole world; that the debts of the Crown taken off, you may govern as you please.[1]

Wentworth wrote these brave words in 1633. Seven years later the Crown debts remained unpaid, the Common Lawyers set out to rule rather than be ruled, the 'phantastic apparitions' of a Prynne or an Eliot took on flesh, and Wentworth's life stood in imminent peril. The ensuing impeachment and attainder of Wentworth (created Earl of Strafford in January 1640) sprang directly from his contempt for the Prynnes and Eliots and Common Lawyers of England, a contempt he so openly expressed in his letter to Laud.

The House of Commons impeached Strafford in November 1640 because they believed that servants of the Crown should answer to Parliament for any illegal or unjust actions that they had done. Responsible government as their predecessors had defined it in the 1620's, the Commons now wished to secure finally and irrevocably. For this reason they impeached not only the great statesman, Strafford, but also the great churchman, Laud, the great judge, Sir John Finch, and the Principal Secretary, Sir Francis Windebank. Against each of them the House of Commons in the autumn of 1640 voted or resolved to vote an impeachment. Nor was this the work of a faction, a party, or a handful of plotters; the whole nation represented in Parliament voted the impeachments. Except for Arminians

---

[1] Knowler, *Letters and Dispatches*, I, 173. Archbishop Laud replied to Wentworth, 'But let me tell you, the Common Lawyers are another manner of body here for strength and friends, than they are with you' (Wentworth Woodhouse MSS, Strafford Papers, VI, f. 26).

and Divine Right Monarchists, men of every religious and political persuasion joined to indict these men. There were popular lawyers like John Selden and John Pym, constitutional royalists like Lord Falkland and Edward Hyde, middle-of-the-road Anglicans like Sir Benjamin Rudyard and Thomas Lane, and moderate Presbyterians like Sir Harbottle Grimstone and Sir John Maynard. There were also men later to become Straffordians, as Lord Digby and Sir Orlando Bridgman, and future Commonwealth men, such as Arthur Hasel-rigge and Oliver St John. All these men, despite the diversity of their views, joined in 1640 to impeach Strafford, Laud, Finch, and Windebank.[1]

Behind this solid phalanx of members of Parliament lay, to be sure, enemies whose opposition was private, foreign, or factious. In Ireland, the Earl of Cork, Viscount Ranelagh, and Lord Mount-norris sought to use Parliament as a means to destroy Strafford, their hated foe. The Scottish nation passionately demanded the condemnation of Strafford and Laud for attempting to force an English liturgy on them. And John Pym led a faction that supped with him nightly in his lodgings behind Westminster Hall and that sought Strafford's death. But the Irish enemies were few and had only a negligible influence on the Commons; the assistance of the Scots was sought by, not foisted on, the English; and Pym and his friends could not dictate to the House of Commons. True, they did persuade the Commons to purge themselves of monopolists, and of royalists whose elections were disputed. This purge, however, excluded only twelve monopolists and ten royalists from the House. The absence of twenty-two royalists in a House of 493 could have affected the results of few divisions.[2] Neither private passion nor

---

[1] No one dissented from the votes to impeach Strafford and Laud, only seven or eight dissented from the vote to impeach Finch, and no one opposed the decision to proceed to an impeachment of Windebank (W. Notestein, ed., *The Journal of Sir Simonds D'Ewes*, New Haven, 1922, pp. 176, 395; Clarendon, *History*, i, 225; *C.J.* ii, 26, 41–2; *The Diurnall Occurrences, or Dayly Proceedings of Both Houses, in this Great and Happy Parliament from the Third of November 1640 to the Third of November 1641*, 1641, p. 15).

[2] H. F. Kearney, *Strafford in Ireland* (Manchester, 1959), pp. 185, 194, 199–206; M. F. Keeler, *The Long Parliament* (Philadelphia, 1954), p. 10; B.M. Add. MSS 15567, ff. 30–30v. Clarendon (*History*, i, 229, 240, 245–7) argues that a few governed the House and a multitude followed them, that Pym, Hampden, and St John were 'the engine which moved all the rest', and won over the multitude either by promise of preferment or intimidation. It is undoubtedly true that (as in all political assemblies) the few led and the many followed, but Clarendon failed to see that Pym, Hampden, and St John could not lead the multitude where the multitude did not want to go. Yet he relates a story that demonstrates exactly this. It is the story of Pym's inability to prevent the

foreign dictation nor the machinations of politically ambitious men can explain why the Commons impeached these four great ministers of the Crown. The simple fact is the great majority of politically conscious Englishmen, in and out of Parliament, clamoured for their impeachment, and clamoured for it because they believed that these men had endeavoured to destroy what Lord Falkland called 'the excellent constitution of this kingdom'. So persuaded were the Commons of the danger, that they accused these men, not of misdemeanours, as their predecessors had accused Bacon, Middlesex, and Buckingham, but of high treason.[1]

But had Strafford, Laud, Finch, and Windebank sought to destroy the English constitution? Had they counselled Charles to subvert the fundamental laws of the realm? For such beliefs compelling reasons existed in 1640. Strafford had disrupted the Short Parliament by insisting upon a vote of supply before the redress of grievances, had urged that sheriffs be prosecuted for not collecting Ship Money, and had favoured debasing the coinage and seizing silver stored in the Tower. He had threatened to fine and ransom aldermen who would not loan the King money, had levied money on the inhabitants of Yorkshire without their consent, had executed martial law in Ireland in time of peace, and had refused to parley with the Scots or listen to their demands. Above all else, he had raised an army in Ireland which could be used to destroy English liberty. These arbitrary acts were his; so common fame proclaimed far and wide in November 1640.[2]

impeachment of Lord Keeper Finch, who had sought safety by deserting to the camp of the patriots. Not only Clarendon, but also Sir Edward Nicholas (B.M. Add. MSS 4180, f. 170v) describes Pym's failure. Nicholas wrote that as a result of Pym's efforts to save the Lord Keeper he 'is reported in the town to be grown cold in the business of the Commonwealth'. This fact does irremediable damage to the plot theory that colours Clarendon's history of these early months of the Long Parliament.

[1] Cobbett, *Parl. Hist.* II, 696. Observers as various in their points of view as the Venetian ambassador (*C.S.P. Ven.* xxv, 94, 96, 128), the French ambassador (Fr. Trans. 12/22 Nov. 1640 and 4/14 March 1641), the Tuscan envoy (B.M. Add. MSS 27962 I, ff. 137, 149, 155v, 168), the Earl of Northumberland (A. Collins, ed., *Letters and Memorials of State*, 1746, II, 663), and Edmund Percival (*H.M.C. Egmont*, I, 128) reported the universal hatred of these men.

[2] Fr. Trans. 7/17 May, 10/20 Aug., 12/22 Nov. 1640; *C.S.P. Dom. 1640*, pp. 56–7, 639–41; Sir Walter Trevelyan and Sir Charles Trevelyan (eds.), *Trevelyan Papers, Part III* (Camden Soc. cv), pp. 197–8; A. Grosart (ed.), *The Lismore Papers, Second Series* (1887), IV, 124–6; *C.S.P. Ven.* xxv, 58–9, 96; Gardiner, *History*, IX, 171–2, 220–1. The Earl of Manchester observed that the people were particularly violent against Laud and Strafford, 'for common fame had rendered these in the highest ranks of evil counsellors' (B.M. Add. MSS 15567, f. 31).

The Failure of Impeachment

The alleged crimes of Laud, Finch, and Windebank were equally notorious. Laud had favoured prerogative government, suppressed lecturers, licensed Arminian books, extended the jursdiction of ecclesiastical courts, imposed severe sentences on Puritans in Star Chamber, and forced an Anglican liturgy on Scotland. As Hugo Grotius wrote, the Archbishop is impeached for having 'promoted the growth of royal power, frightening the English with the example of France, where royal power has attained the fullest development possible'. Finch's faults were four: he had refused to put Eliot's motion to the House in 1629 when Speaker; he had driven on the enforcement of ancient Forest Laws; he had solicited the extrajudicial opinions of the judges in favour of Ship Money; and he had written the King's Declaration justifying the dissolution of the Short Parliament. Windebank, for his part, discredited himself for all time by signing seventy-eight Letters of Grace to recusants and issuing twenty-nine warrants for the discharge of priests from prison. In the eyes of men as varied in temperament and belief as the accomplished and radical Denzil Holles, the moderate and self-righteous Sir Simonds D'Ewes, and the conscientious and loyal Falkland, these crimes amounted to a subversion of religion and a destruction of English liberty.[1]

Yet the accusers were wrong to believe that Strafford, Laud, Finch, and Windebank had sought to destroy 'the excellent constitution of this kingdom'. They had not. They had wished merely to exercise the same conciliar and prerogative powers used so effectively by their Tudor forebears. Not one of their acts lacked a Tudor or medieval precedent. Yet there was a decisive difference: the Tudors had exercised those powers to enforce a Protestant and national policy which had the support of most Englishmen, while Charles's ministers exercised them to enforce policies that most Englishmen hated. The original quarrel between Parliament and Charles was not constitutional. Parliament opposed him on political and religious grounds. It charged that in religion he favoured ceremony rather than simplicity, rites rather than preaching, free will rather than predestination, and in politics, peace with Spain rather than war with Spain, the granting of monopolies rather than their suppression, and the toleration of Catholics rather than their perse-

---

[1] H. Grotii, *Epistoliae* (Amsterdam, 1687), p. 672; H. Trevor-Roper, *Archbishop Laud* (1940), pp. 118, 136, 165, 222, 231; *Trevelyan Papers, Part III*, pp. 199–202; *C.J.* II, 41; D'Ewes, *Autobiography*, II, 113–14; B.M. Add. MSS 11045, f. 137; M. A. E. Green (ed.), *Diary of John Rous* (Camden Soc. LXVI), pp. 105–8; Notestein, *D'Ewes Journal*, p. 353.

cution. Had Charles been a Puritan, breathing hatred for Spain, and inclined to leave economic life alone, his ministers would have had no need to resort to Ship Money and Star Chamber proceedings to carry on the King's government. Parliament would have granted supplies and asked for redress of few grievances. Strafford and Laud violated the law only when the niggardliness of Parliament and the obstructiveness of the law courts forced them to do so. Two truths about Strafford in particular explain his conduct: he never intended to violate the law one iota further than was necessary to carry on the King's government; yet, if necessary, he would subvert it totally to protect the King's right. His closest friend, Sir George Radcliffe, understood his political philosophy best. Radcliffe wrote of Strafford, 'He always thought that regal power and popular privileges... were best preserved when they went hand in hand and maintained one another...Yet it being most hard and difficult to keep the interest of the King and people from encroaching one upon another, the longer he lived, his experience taught him that it was far safer that the King should increase in power than that the people should gain advantages on the King.'[1] In other words, if irreconcilable differences between King and people threatened to wreck the harmonies of the Tudor constitution, then the King, not Parliament, should prevail. Because Strafford held this opinion, Parliament dared not leave him by the King's side.

Members of the House of Commons not only agreed on the necessity of impeaching the four ministers, they also concurred in their right to do so. Opinions expressed in the opening debates of the Long Parliament on 7 and 9 November demonstrate this. On those days members of the House revived and repeated the constitutional ideas that their predecessors had enunciated in the 1620's, ideas which had become received opinion in Westminster Hall and St Stephen's Chapel by 1640. Parliament had a duty to remedy the grievances of the realm, the causes of which lay not in the want of good laws, but in the violation, the mis-interpretation, and the lack of enforcement of existing laws. The King himself was not at fault, for he could do no wrong; his servants had violated, mis-interpreted, and neglected to enforce the laws. Parliament therefore had the duty to inquire into these sins of omission and commission and to expose the authors of them. The faults should hunt out the

---

[1] Knowler, *Letters and Dispatches*, II, 434.

man, so that the King might see that the House did not vindictively pursue any man; the Commons should then impeach the guilty, that their punishment might be an example to others. How false a maxim to say, 'If a King suffers men to be torn from him, he shall never have any good service done him.' Far better to impeach those who served him ill, in order to encourage others to serve him well.[1]

Within four days of the opening debate, the Commons violated their own precept. On 11 November, before any inquiry into any fault could hunt out any man, they impeached the Earl of Strafford for High Treason. John Pym asked the House to vote an impeachment before conducting an inquiry. He did so not to vindicate the principle of common fame, for he had earlier proposed an inquiry into the misgovernment of Ireland, but in order to remove at once a dangerous councillor from the side of the King. He feared that if he did not persuade the Commons to impeach Strafford today, Strafford would persuade the King to impeach him and others tomorrow. He and his friends would then suffer all the disabilities that hindered Bristol in his prosecution of Buckingham in 1626, while Strafford would enjoy all the advantages that Buckingham had then enjoyed. The Earl of Manchester, who wrote a memoir of these times, was uncertain whether Strafford really intended to persuade Charles to arrest the leaders of the Commons, but he had no doubts that Pym believed that Strafford did.[2] Pym acted now on the principle of conduct that Marat urged on the Parisians during the French Revolution: it is better to kill the devil than to let the devil kill you. Constitutional scruples gave way to revolutionary action. One would do better to go to Jean-Paul Sartre's *Les Mains Sales* to defend the rightness of Pym's decision, than to Coke's *Institutes*.

Pym used three arguments to persuade the House of Commons to vote an impeachment before conducting an inquiry: first, he accused Strafford of being the principal author of all those counsels that had exposed the kingdom to ruin, and gave as many instances as possible of Strafford's treasonous conduct; secondly, he argued

---

[1] These constitutional ideas are drawn from speeches given by Pym, Rudyard, Digby, Grimstone, Bagshaw, and Seymour (Cobbett, *Parl. Hist.* II, 640–51; *Speeches and Passages of this Great and Happy Parliament*, 1641, pp. 207–9; Notestein, *D'Ewes Journal*, pp. 3–12; B.M. Add. MSS 15567, ff. 23v, 29).

[2] B.M. Add. MSS 15567, ff. 31v–32. William Sanderson (*Compleat History of King Charles*, p. 337), Peter Heylyn (*Observations on 'the History of King Charles'*, p. 212), and John Rushworth (*The Tryal of Thomas Earl of Strafford*, 1680, pp. 1–2) concur in Manchester's explanation of Pym's extreme haste.

that the House, being only accusers, and not judges, need not prove the charges alleged against the Earl; and thirdly, he insisted that they must impeach him at once, and for High Treason, in order to persuade the Lords to remove him from the King's presence, otherwise 'he would be able to render all their endeavours for the Commonwealth fruitless'. These arguments from fact, from law, and from necessity—reinforced by fears engendered by Charles's reviewing the troops in the Tower that very day—helped to persuade the House to impeach Strafford before the Lords that very afternoon. The Commons thereby deserted the principle (favoured by Rudyard and Digby) of letting the faults hunt out the man, and embraced instead the principle of first accusing a man, and then searching out the faults with which to charge him, a principle that Sir Philip Warwick thought no better than 'trailing for an hare'.[1]

The impeachment voted against Strafford with such desperate haste was destined to fail, but no one can say that it failed because the House of Commons lacked the power to inquire into Strafford's iniquities. In the winter of 1641 the Commons vindicated their right of inquiry with a vengeance. They empowered the Committee preparing the impeachment to send for records, papers, parties, and witnesses. They summoned witnesses from Ireland, Yorkshire, and the City of London. They impeached Sir George Radcliffe to insure both that he be brought from Dublin to testify against Strafford and that he be made incapable of testifying for him.[2] Yet in seizing records and examining witnesses and impeaching Radcliffe, they did nothing that the Commons had not done in the 1620's. Their decision, however, to examine witnesses on oath and to question Privy Councillors concerning proceedings at the Council table did depart radically from past practices. Since the House of Commons lacked power to administer an oath, and since the House of Lords possessed that power, the Commons asked the Lords to appoint some of their members to a Committee of Both Houses for examining witnesses. The Lords willingly agreed to this arrangement, but they

---

[1] Clarendon, *History*, I, 219–26; Notestein, *D'Ewes Journal*, pp. 28–9, 532–3; B.M. Add. MSS 15567, ff. 24, 28v; Warwick, *Memoirs*, p. 153. Pym could have cited an earlier argument from necessity that was uniquely apposite. According to Sir John Bramston (*Autobiography*, Camden Soc. XXXII, p. 45), Strafford, then Sir Thomas Wentworth, had urged Parliament in 1626 to imprison the Duke of Buckingham, saying, 'Take him from the King's ear, and you [will] have witnesses enough; but whilst he is so near the King, few will dare to speak their knowledge.'

[2] *C.J.* II, 28, 42; B.M. Add. MSS 11045, f. 133.

balked momentarily at the request that Privy Councillors testify before this Committee. Not only were such councillors usually peers, but all were sworn to secrecy. In the end the Lords gave way before the argument that the Privy Councillor's oath was not meant to conceal from Parliament treasons whispered at the Council table. They also yielded before the undeniable fact that the King might excuse councillors from the oath of secrecy. Since it was well known that the King might do this, all eyes turned to see what Charles would do. Advised by his Council that a refusal to excuse his councillors would suggest that treason had been whispered at the Council table, he granted them permission to testify on oath before the Committee of Both Houses. Guistinian, the Venetian ambassador, observed that the Commons had, by demanding that councillors violate the oath of secrecy, 'laid the sickle to the most noble part of the royal sovereignty'.[1]

Insufficient powers of inquiry, then, did not cause the failure of the impeachment. Neither did Strafford's efforts to escape responsibility for the crimes charged against him cause its failure, though he strove manfully to evade all responsibility. In the course of his trial before the Lords, he voiced no less than six different pleas, pleas which he deftly wove, like *leit motifs*, into a long and artful defence. Morning after morning in Westminster Hall, through late March, into early April, he insisted that the crimes with which the Commons charged him had been done either (1) with the concurrence of the whole Council, or (2) on the advice of Learned Counsel, or (3) by others, or (4) in the course of giving counsel, or (5) at the King's command, or (6) with the consent of the governed. These six pleas and the prosecution's answers to them illuminate, as do few other events in these years, the various and confused ideas about ministerial responsibility that men held on the eve of the Great Rebellion.

Strafford saw no reason why he should suffer while men who acted with him went free, and during his trial he never missed an opportunity to remind the Lords of this inequity. Only with the full concurrence of either the Privy Council or the Castle Chamber

---

[1] *C.J.* II, 30, 39, 42; *L.J.* IV, 95, 104; B.M. Add. MSS 10045, f. 145; Clarendon, *History*, I, 255–7; *C.S.P. Ven.* xxv, 105–6. The Commons reminded the Lords that three years earlier, Strafford, then Sir Thomas Wentworth, had demanded that the Earl of Holland violate the oath of secrecy in order to testify against Sir Pierce Crosby (Fr. Trans. 26 Nov./6 Dec. 1640).

had he taken the Great Seal from Lord Loftus, removed Sir Pierce Crosby from the Council, issued a decree against Lady Hibbots, dispossessed Lord Mountnorris of a manor, committed the Earl of Kildare to prison, censured Henry Parry, fined Henry Steward, and executed Thomas Denwit. In the management of the public revenues he 'always submitted to the major part of the Council'. The entire Council published the Proclamations that prohibited the private sale of tobacco, regulated the manufacture of flax, billeted soldiers on disobedient subjects, and forbad anyone to leave Ireland without the Deputy's permission. Why, asked Strafford, should these Proclamations be particularly laid on him? He 'is not particularly answerable for things done by the advice of the Council'. And on another occasion he complained, 'I conceive it a hard case, that having the honour to be King's Deputy sitting in Council, where there be twenty who voted as well as myself, that I should be voted to answer for them all, though I did constantly submit myself to the major part.'[1]

Strafford's plea of the collective responsibility of the whole Council carried even greater weight when applied to the English scene, for during his trial Strafford steadfastly proclaimed what most of his judges knew to be true, that in January 1640 the Privy Council had voted unanimously that the demands of the Scots were unreasonable, and in May had voted to dissolve Parliament, not one man dissenting. Concerning the refusal of the Scots' demands, Strafford pleaded the concurrence of a Cabinet Council as well as a Privy Council. 'All at the Council for Foreign Affairs voted the demands of the Covenanters such as might not with honour and safety be accepted by His Majesty.' Strafford, the first minister in the history of England to invoke the collective responsibility of a Cabinet Council, was not to be the last.[2]

Strafford's plea discomfited, but did not rout, the Commons. It discomfited them because equity clearly demanded either that other councillors be punished also, or Strafford be pardoned. It failed to rout them because the ascendancy of Strafford in the government of Ireland and in Charles's counsels after he left Ireland were matters

---

[1] J. Bruce (ed.), *Verney Papers* (Camden Soc. xxxi), pp. 17, 20, 32; J. Nalson, *An Impartial Collection of the Great Affairs of State* (1682), ii, 43, 118; Rushworth, *Tryal of Strafford*, pp. 11, 24, 26, 201, 231, 409, 421, 474, 505; Notestein, *D'Ewes Journal*, p. 404; D'Ewes Journal (unpublished portion), Harleian MSS 162, f. 396.

[2] Rushworth, *Tryal of Strafford*, pp. 28, 29, 548; Bruce, *Verney Papers*, p. 22.

of common fame. Sir John Maynard conceded that others joined with Strafford in removing Sir Pierce Crosby from the Council, 'but I am sure', said Maynard, 'he moved it'. Bulstrode Whitelocke admitted that it was not Strafford alone but the Castle Chamber that sentenced Henry Steward, but 'if others join with him in a hard sentence against law, his fault is not the less, but rather the greater, to draw others into the same fault. His opinion had more harshness and severity than the rest, and, being his opinion, it was sufficient to carry all the rest with him.' Whitelocke even held Strafford responsible for the Irish Parliament's declaration against the Scots, since he was 'the chief governor there'. Sir John Maynard was more explicit, 'My Lord might say he is not the only man that deserves punishment, but he cannot say but that he is the principal man, and indeed, in effect the sole man... They are to blame that follow his misguidance, but he is not innocent that draws others into such actions with him.' The Commons could not deny the collective responsibility of the Council, but they did join to it the special responsibility of 'the chief governor', 'the principal man', 'the sole man'.[1]

Not only had he always acted with the advice of the greater part of the Council, pleaded Strafford, but he had always taken the advice of Learned Counsel. 'For the legality of the proceedings [of the Council at York],' he said, 'divers eminent lawyers were joined with the President, who, for the legal parts, was by them to be directed.' Not only to defend his conduct as President of the Council at York, but also to justify his conduct at the Council Board in Ireland, he pleaded the advice of Learned Counsel. 'In matters of law the Chief Justices sit at the Board, to whom all matters of law are referred, and they are answerable for it.' He defended in the same manner the collection of Ship Money in 1640. 'There being a judgment given in point of law by the judges, it was not for him to dispute what they had done...He would never be more prudent than his teachers, nor give judgment against the judges.'[2]

The managers of the impeachment against Strafford could not tolerate, nor could they easily answer, this plea. Mr Geoffrey Palmer scored the shrewdest blow when he reminded the Lords that

---

[1] Rushworth, *Tryal of Strafford*, pp. 423, 510; Nalson, *Impartial Collection*, II, 48, 88.
[2] Rushworth, *Tryal of Strafford*, pp. 474, 586; *A Brief and Perfect Relation of the Answers and Replies to Thomas Earle of Strafford* (1647), p. 47; Harleian MSS 162, f. 396.

Strafford had, by issuing a Proclamation requiring all men to carry complaints of injustices to him before taking them to England, explicitly assumed responsibility for the administration of justice in Ireland. This reminder struck home, but Strafford, when serving Charles in England, had never assumed such vice-regal powers. How were the managers to answer his plea that the judges had declared Ship Money legal? Sir John Maynard answered very blandly, 'whereas my Lord thinks to excuse himself, because there was a judgment in the Exchequer Chamber, God be thanked, it appears to be a judgment against law'. He then added that the Short Parliament had already condemned the Exchequer's judgment before Strafford set out to collect Ship Money.[1] The conclusion to be drawn from Palmer's and Maynard's remarks was twofold: ministers of the Crown must make up their own minds about, and assume responsibility for, the legality of any intended action; and, if in doubt about its legality, they should consult Parliament rather than Learned Counsel.

Strafford also refused to assume responsibility for faults committed by those who served with or under him in the King's government. He had not prepared the objectionable Commission enlarging the powers of the President of the Council at York; the Secretary of State who prepared it must answer for it. Not he, but others had broken the privileges of the Irish Parliament. The King's revenue officers had raised the Book of Rates before he took his lease of the customs, and they should answer for it. For the tobacco rates, 'the contractors are to justify themselves'. 'For the misdemeanours of the officers in regulating the manufacture of flax, he could not answer.' The Council of War, not he, imposed the sentence on Lord Mountnorris. In Yorkshire, Sir William Pennyman had no warrant of his to levy money for the support of the trained bands. Sir Edward Osborne should answer for those warrants, since he issued them. To these attempts to shift the blame on others, the Commons replied that these subordinate officers merely executed his commands or royal commands arising from his counsels. They only acted 'ministerially', that is, they only administered policies that he devised. He had solicited the enlarged Commission, advised the increase in the Book of Rates, directed the tobacco monopoly, managed the

---

[1] Rushworth, *Tryal of Strafford*, pp. 483, 588; D'Ewes Journal, Harleian MSS 163, ff. 12, 396.

flax scheme, procured Mountnorris's condemnation, and commanded Sir Edward Osborne to issue the warrants for the Yorkshire levy. Sir John Maynard told the Lords, 'He says the execution is nothing to himself, but to his agents. Surely, he that will command unjust and evil things is not a whit less guilty, because he has ministers that will apply themselves to his pleasure, to execute unlawful commands. He commands, they execute.' Where possible the managers sought to prove that Strafford had commanded his subordinates to act as they did, but even where the evidence was wanting, the Commons asserted Strafford's responsibility. John Pym remarked, 'And if my Lord of Strafford were not guilty in his own person of breach of privileges, yet if under his government privileges of Parliament be broken', he is at fault.[1]

Today, in the twentieth century, 'to act ministerially' means to assume responsibility. In the seventeenth century men used the phrase in exactly the opposite sense. 'To act ministerially' meant to act in obedience to the commands of a superior, who was responsible for those commands. Those who 'acted ministerially' in the seventeenth century were the civil servants of Stuart England. Those who directed them to act were the responsible departmental heads, or so Pym and Maynard would have it.[2]

One person in the state could not act as a responsible head of a department, the King himself. His commands could confer no immunity on those who obeyed him. Five Parliaments and Strafford himself had declared as much. Yet Strafford, whose blood once boiled at hearing the King's command pleaded, now pleaded it on every possible occasion. Only in obedience to the King's command did he take the Great Seal from Lord Loftus, become a Farmer of the Customs, restrain the transportation of native commodities, deny Sir Frederick Hamilton a licence to depart from Ireland, impose an oath on the Scots of Ulster, and raise an army of 8,000 Irish. For borrowing £24,000 from the Irish Exchequer, for executing martial law, for deciding cases concerning the possession of land, for

---

[1] Fr. Trans. 25 March/4 Apr. 1641; Rushworth, *Tryal of Strafford*, pp. 145, 147, 195, 246, 409, 413, 422, 625, 629; Nalson, *Impartial Collection*, II, 46, 107–8, 114; Harleian MSS 162, ff. 368–369, 383, 386, 388; R. Baillie, *The Letters and Journals of Robert Baillie* (Edinburgh, 1841), I, 334.

[2] Even a Secretary of State might 'act ministerially'. Lord Mountnorris asked Sir John Coke to lend him letters that he, Coke, had written concerning Irish affairs, and added, to make public these letters 'can be no prejudice to you, you having been employed as a minister only in all Irish affairs...' (*H.M.C. Cowper*, I, 264).

issuing Proclamations, and for billeting soldiers he had the King's warrant.[1]

The reply of the Commons was predictable. In Glynn's words, 'My Lords, the Earl of Strafford does very well know (he may refer to the Petition of Right) that the King's servants are to serve him according to law and no otherwise; he knows very well if an unlawful act be committed, especially to the degree of treason and murder, the King's warrant and authority is no justification at all.' But a careful reading of the records of Strafford's trial shows that the Commons did not blame him for obeying the King. They blamed him instead for misinforming the King. As Maynard said of the King's letters authorizing the tobacco monopoly, '...the King, being misinformed by the Earl of Strafford, directed the same letters, which, being procured by him, do rather aggravate his crime'. Whitelocke commented similarly on the King's letters commanding the enforcement of an oath of loyalty on the Ulster Scots, '...for His Majesty's letters, if Lord Strafford upon misinformation got them, that adds to his crime'. Glynn best expressed the opinion of the Commons, 'For the King's letter justifying the proceedings against Mountnorris, it is written on his information, and if the King's ministers misinformed him, he is just before God and men, and they must answer for it.'[2] The managers of Strafford's impeachment, who had a lively sense of the realities of political life, knew that those who counselled the King were more to blame than those who obeyed him. The maxim that the King can do no wrong was really of less importance to them than the maxim that the King is always advised, badly advised, perhaps, or well advised, but always advised.[3]

Since the Commons sought to punish Strafford as the counsellor and not the administrator of hateful policies, his trial raised the whole problem of counsel in the English monarchy. What responsibilities, what duties, what privileges, what immunities did a counsellor

---

[1] Rushworth, *Tryal of Strafford*, pp. 24–8, 211–12, 407–9; Nalson, *Impartial Collection*, II, 42–3; Harleian MSS 162, f. 368.

[2] Nalson, *Impartial Collection*, II, 142; *Master Glynn's Reply* (1641), p. 50; Harleian MSS 162, f. 386; Rushworth, *Tryal of Strafford*, p. 201. H. F. Kearney writes (*Strafford in Ireland*, p. 182) of the tobacco monopoly, 'Wentworth made out that he entered into the agreement unwillingly, but his disclaimer need not be taken too seriously.'

[3] Even Strafford saw the injustice of blaming those who 'acted ministerially'. He urged Laud in 1637 to divert Charles from a war with Austria, 'for I see nothing in it but distractions to His Majesty's affairs, and mighty dangers to us that must be the ministers, albeit not the authors, of the counsels' (Knowler, *Letters and Dispatches*, II, 66).

possess? Strafford was very clear about it. A counsellor's duty was to speak his mind freely to his monarch, according to the dictates of his conscience, without fear or favour, and his words were to be privileged, and were not to be held against him. 'If to give your opinions in political agitation shall be accounted treason,' argued Strafford, 'who will be willing to serve the King; or what dilemma are you in: if, being sworn counsellors, you speak not your minds freely, you are convicted of perjury, and if you do, perhaps of treason.' To this John Pym replied, 'He pleads that he is a counsellor, and might not be questioned for anything which he advised according to his conscience. The ground is true, there is a liberty belongs to counsellors, and nothing corrupts counsels more than fear...But such treasons as these, the subversion of laws, violation of liberties, they can never be good or justifiable by any circumstance or occasion, and therefore his being a counsellor makes his fault much more heinous.' Pym, forever the realist, could not deny the importance of freedom of speech at the Council table, but he would not allow it to extend to the subversion of the fundamental laws of the realm.[1]

The sixth plea that Strafford propounded was peripheral to the main burden of his defence, and contrary to his growing sympathies for absolute monarchy. It was the plea that he had enjoyed the consent of the governed for what he had done. The Irish Parliament, he maintained, petitioned that the sale of tobacco be taken into the King's care. The Irish gentry approved the oath to be given to the Ulster Scots. The Irish Parliament freely voted money to raise an army for the King. The Great Council of Peers and the gentry of Yorkshire consented to the levy for paying the trained bands. There was only one way that the Commons could counter this plea: to deny that such consent had been freely given. The Petition did not ask that Strafford be given a monopoly of the sale of tobacco. The approval of the Irish gentry was not voluntary. Strafford procured the vote of supply for raising an army. Two hundred gentlemen of Yorkshire cannot lay a charge on the county. The Great Council did not consent to the levy (an assertion whose truth the House of

---

[1] Rushworth, *Tryal of Strafford*, pp. 549, 570–1; *A Brief and Perfect Relation*, p. 43; Nalson, *Impartial Collection*, II, 150. Maynard replied to Strafford (Harleian MSS 164, f. 155), 'Whereas he objects that, if the King's Privy Councillors should be questioned for what they speak there, no man would hereafter dare to speak freely. 'Tis no matter of counsel to destroy all by an army.'

Lords confirmed by a formal vote).[1] Whether Strafford or the Commons were closer to the truth in their assertions is of far less significance than the fact that a minister of the House of Stuart sought safety by pleading the consent of the governed. In the course of time it would be the only sound plea that a minister could enter in his defence.

One caveat must be made concerning these various and contradictory ideas about the responsibilities of the King's ministers. They did not really reflect what men in 1641 thought about the constitution. They reflected rather forces at work shaping that constitution. Strafford was fighting for his very life and therefore in making his defence he pulled out all the stops, grasped at any argument his powerful mind could discern. It is unlikely that anyone in England, least of all Strafford, believed that the Council was collectively responsible to Parliament, but Strafford could not afford to omit this plea, for it appealed to a sense of equity in every man. To omit it might cost him his life. Necessity likewise drove on the House of Commons. They were determined that their quarry should not elude them. They had probably never given thought to the special responsibility of a 'principal minister' or 'chief governor', but if this responsibility must be assumed in order to secure Strafford's condemnation, then they would assume it. Strafford's trial revealed practical forces at work that would in two centuries make the special responsibility of the Prime Minister and the collective responsibility of the Cabinet a reality.

There is no evidence that Strafford's many arguments regarding the nature of his responsibility as a servant of the King impressed his judges in the least. What did impress the peers was his plea that he had not committed those treasons charged against him, and that among those crimes which he had committed none went higher than a misdemeanour. He was innocent either in fact or at law of the treasons charged against him. On these two rocks the Commons' impeachment broke asunder. The House, to begin with, could not prove that Strafford had urged Charles to disregard the wishes of Parliament, or that he had advised him to subvert the laws, seize the silver in the Tower, debase the coinage, and hang the Lord Mayor. Neither could they prove that he told the King in Council,

---

[1] Rushworth, *Tryal of Strafford*, pp. 25, 29, 31, 412, 499–501, 509, 573, 626; Nalson, *Impartial Collection*, II, 117, 123.

'You have an army in Ireland you may employ here to reduce this kingdom', even though on its proof rested the entire impeachment. The Commons could produce only one witness, Secretary Vane, whose testimony Northumberland, Hamilton, Cottington, and the Lord Treasurer promptly contradicted. The embarrassment of having too few witnesses, however, was nothing compared to the embarrassment of having too few treasons. An impeachment by its very nature was an awkward weapon for attacking an unpopular minister, for it concerned the minister's crimes, not his errors. An impeachment for treason was doubly awkward. For such an impeachment ordinary misdemeanours and felonies would not suffice; the accused must be shown to have committed treason. Strafford saw this immediately and made his innocence of treason the heart of his defence. Again and again he told the Lords that the crimes charged against him were not treason, and reminded them that as a hundred misdemeanours made not a felony, so twenty-eight felonies made not a treason. Strafford pressed on even further, and challenged his prosecutors to show that his mistakes and errors were crimes at all. Repeatedly he pleaded that what he had done in Ireland was justified by statute, by precedent, by the custom of the land, and by the practice of previous deputies. But if ever he had mistaken the law, he added, 'he hopes it is no treason...otherwise there would be more actions of treason than trespass in Westminster Hall'. On another occasion he cried out, 'it is a heavy thing to punish me for not being wiser than God Almighty has made me'.[1]

The vigour, the eloquence, and the logic of Strafford's defence forced the Commons to abandon their impeachment. Unable to prove with two witnesses that Strafford had advised Charles to use an Irish army to destroy English liberty, and uncertain whether they could persuade the Lords that an endeavour to subvert the laws fell within the treasons defined by 25 Edward III, they turned to an Act of Attainder, which did not require judicial proof of a known crime. This decision (which John Pym opposed) was not a confession that they believed Strafford innocent, for they believed him guilty. It was only an admission that they could not prove him guilty before the Lords on an impeachment (which Pym believed they could do).[2]

---

[1] Baillie, *Letters and Journals*, I, 320; Harleian MSS 163, f. 36; Rushworth, *Tryal of Strafford*, pp. 146, 181, 626; Nalson, *Impartial Collection*, II, 54, 58, 64.

[2] Montereul, the French ambassador, wrote (Fr. Trans. 15/25 Apr. 1641), 'Wednesday the Commons, not being assured of the Lords' judgment, thought it appropriate to

The Commons read the Act of Attainder for the first time on 10 April; eleven days later they sent it to the Lords, having passed it, on its third reading, by a vote of 204 to 59. Admiration for the courage of the 59 Straffordians should not blind one to the fact that a clear majority of the House was willing to transcend the law in order to destroy Strafford. Why were they?

If those two middle-of-the-road politicians, Sir Simonds D'Ewes and Sir Benjamin Rudyard, may be regarded as typical of the House, the Commons passed the attainder because they sincerely believed that Strafford had intended to subvert the laws of the realm and that such an intent was treason.[1] D'Ewes and Rudyard, and many men like them, had sat morning after morning on make-shift benches in Westminster Hall, had followed intently the massive, detailed indictment presented by the prosecution, had observed the steady accumulation of evidence against the Earl, had listened to the damaging testimony given against him, and had come to believe that he had endeavoured to subvert the laws of England. Had he not extended the jurisdiction of Council Courts at the expense of Common Law courts? Had he not sought to make Proclamations equal in authority to Acts of Parliament? Had he not preferred to enforce obedience with troops rather than win consent through Parliament? Had he not attempted to elevate the King's commands above the objections of Common Lawyers?

No man who sat through the trial could confidently say that Strafford had not sought to do these things; the evidence presented against him was too plain. The Commission for the Presidency of the Council at York gave the Council power to determine all civil cases, to exercise Chancery and Star Chamber jurisdiction, to stay proceedings in Common Law courts, to be free from Prohibitions, and to deny the writ of Habeas Corpus.[2] In Ireland Strafford had decided cases concerning the possession of land and the inheritance of property, had published a Proclamation making the possession of

anticipate it, and so have read the Act of Attainder a second time.' Salvetti (B.M. Add. MSS 27962 i, f. 171) observed that the peers were reluctant to condemn Strafford on insufficient proof because it would establish a precedent that could endanger all of them.

[1] The oft-repeated sentiments of these men, and others, can be found in Harleian MSS 163, ff. 26–28, 42–44, 47–49, 52–55, 75–77; Harleian MSS 164, ff. 162v–163v, 164v–167v, 171, 172–172v, 176v, 178–180, 182–183.

[2] After describing to the House of Commons these vast powers of the Presidency of York, Edward Hyde concluded, 'That by this means no man's estates or liberty was safe' (Harleian MSS 163, ff. 97–98).

powder a felony after Parliament had refused to pass such a law, had used troops to enforce decrees of the Council, and had refused to add 'just' to 'commands' in the oath requiring the Ulster Scots to obey the King. The sum of these arbitrary acts may not have amounted to a total subversion of the laws, but it did imply an habitual contempt for them.[1]

And Strafford's desperate counsels in 1640 persuaded men that he was as willing to subvert, as to brush aside, the law. In that year he openly preached a doctrine that endangered the very existence of Parliament, the doctrine that the King, 'deserted by Parliament', and 'pressed by necessity', was 'loose and absolved' from the rules of government. In words differing only in the degree of their violence, he urged this doctrine on the Lord Primate of Ireland, on Lord Conway, on the Earl of Holland, on the Earl of Bristol, and, according to Vane, on the King himself at a meeting of the Committee of Eight for Scottish Affairs on 5 May.[2] The Commons had good reason to believe that in Strafford's lexicon 'deserted by Parliament' meant denied supplies until grievances were redressed, that 'pressed by necessity' meant faced with a bankrupt Exchequer and disobedient subjects, and that 'loose and absolved' meant extra-parliamentary taxation and Star Chamber proceedings. Strafford had not yet subverted the laws of the realm, the Irish army had not yet set foot on English soil, but the majority of the knights, citizens, and burgesses in Parliament believed that he would subvert the laws, and use the Irish army to this purpose, if given the opportunity. His enlarged Commission for the Presidency of the Council at York, his arbitrary government of Ireland, and his frightening language in 1640 persuaded most of the House that he was guilty of endeavouring to subvert the laws of England.

[1] Rushworth, *Tryal of Strafford*, pp. 184, 211–13, 426–30, 454–5, 492. In answer to the queries sent to them by Charles on 6 Feb. 1641 concerning Strafford's conduct as Lord Deputy of Ireland, the Privy Councillors there returned a long answer (Egerton MSS 2533, ff. 101–115v) which concluded, '...as to his assuming other powers than former Deputies were wont to do, we find that his Lordship assumed some powers, which we remember not to have observed former Deputies to have done'. H. F. Kearney (*Strafford in Ireland*, p. 219) reaches the conclusion that Strafford 'had a vision of absolute monarchy, operating as the only completely free agent in a world of vested interests'.

[2] Rushworth, *Tryal of Strafford*, pp. 523, 525, 533, 536–7, 541–5; Baillie, *Letters and Journals*, I, 281–3. Montereul wrote at the time of the dissolution of the Short Parliament, 'It appears that the Lord Lieutenant of Ireland had desired from the first that affairs should come to a dissolution, for he had insisted from the beginning that the King obtain money before redressing grievances, which is an opinion opposed to that followed in all other Parliaments' (Fr. Trans. 7/17 May 1640).

But was an endeavour to subvert the laws of England treason? Most Englishmen in 1641 found it easier to convict Strafford of the crime than to heighten the crime to a treason. They saw the force in the argument urged by Strafford's counsel that neither Statute Law nor Common Law nor the declaratory power of Parliament could make an endeavour to subvert the law a treason. None of the statutory treasons listed in 25 Edward III comprehended it; Common Law treasons were abolished by that same statute; and 1 Henry IV repealed the clause in 25 Edward III that allowed Parliament to declare new and unforeseen crimes to be treason.[1]

Yet there is more to be said for the position of the House of Commons than Strafford's counsel allowed. In the first place, men as diverse in their politics as Edward Hyde and Nathaniel Fiennes believed in constructive treason, that is, that an endeavour to subvert the laws could be construed as levying war against the King, and so fall within the statute of 25 Edward III. If to kill a judge be treason, argued Hyde, to destroy justice itself must be a greater treason; and Fiennes concluded that 'if it be treason to kill the governor, then sure 'tis treason to kill the government'.[2]

Then there were the persuasive arguments of the proud and sullen, but incomparably able, Oliver St John. St John demonstrated, first to the Commons, and then to the Lords, that Tudor courts had judged it treason to throw down enclosures and free apprentices from prison, because these acts were an overthrowing of the law, and to overthrow the King's law was to levy war against the King. Though St John and his audience could have had no knowledge of it, the historian can reflect that at the close of the eighteenth century the Crown prosecuted members of reform societies for treason because they advocated parliamentary reform. Constructive treason, in fact, was only extinguished in England when Sir Thomas Erskine secured the acquittal of Hardy, Thelwall, and Horne Tooke in 1794. It is likewise open to doubt whether any statute had abolished Common Law treasons and Parliament's right to declare them. St John cast serious doubts on the claim of Strafford's counsel that

[1] Nalson, *Impartial Collection*, ii, 153–6. Conrad Russell ('The Theory of Treason in the Trial of Strafford', *E.H.R.* lxxx, 30–50) has written the clearest exposition of the problem of treason in Strafford's trial. He shows that the trial served as a bridge from the old view that an endeavour to subvert the law was a constructive compassing the King's death to the new view that an endeavour to alter the government was treason in itself.

[2] Gardiner, *History*, ix, 247; *Verney's Notes of the Long Parliament* (Camden Soc. 1st ser. xxi), p. 54.

1 Henry IV had repealed the declaratory power which 25 Edward III gave to Parliament. He maintained that 1 Henry IV merely repealed those treasons that Parliament had actually declared to be treasons since the twenty-fifth year of Edward III. It did not repeal the declaratory power itself.[1] Their consciences assuaged by these arguments, and their belief in Strafford's guilt unaltered, a majority in both Houses voted to attaint Strafford of High Treason for levying war against the King and for endeavouring to subvert the fundamental laws of the realm.

The Commons voted Strafford's attainder because they believed him to be both a guilty and a dangerous man. The Lords passed the attainder less because they believed Strafford to be guilty of treason than because they believed him to be a danger to the realm. They were not prepared to find him guilty upon an impeachment, but they did agree with the Earl of Essex that 'stone dead hath no fellow'. When Essex made this celebrated remark to Edward Hyde in the Bowling Gardens at Piccadilly, he went on to explain that he feared that Charles, once Parliament had disbanded, would grant a banished or imprisoned Strafford a pardon, and bring him back into his service.[2] This prospect, which the Lords feared, Charles ought to have dispelled. But far from dispelling it, he seemed only to confirm it.

He sent money to the north to win over the army there. He permitted Suckling to raise soldiers in London. He made a clumsy attempt to change the officers in the Tower. He listened to a juntilla of plotters led by Percy, Jermyn, Ashburnham, and Wilmot. Above all, he made two disastrous speeches, one on 28 April, and the other on 1 May. On the 28th he told both Houses that he would not dismiss the English Catholics at Court nor would he disband the Irish army until they had voted him money. On the 1st he attempted to intimidate the Lords by telling them in advance that he could never 'in good conscience' accept the Act of Attainder against Strafford. The King's speeches, and not the riots of 3 May (which

[1] Nalson, *Impartial Collection*, II, 162–82. D'Ewes reported (Harleian MSS 164, ff. 179v–180) that St John 'spake not positively' when he argued in the Commons on 19 Apr. that 1 Henry IV had not repealed the declaratory power in 25 Edward III. However St John spoke more positively before the Lords on the 29th. Concerning this speech D'Ewes observed (f. 193v), 'This learned argument gave high satisfaction to all men generally.' He then added, but 'the Earl of Strafford himself said at his going out of the Hall, "What! is this all he can say?".'
[2] Clarendon, *History*, I, 318–20.

they occasioned), frightened the Lords into passing the attainder. The riots had subsided by the 7th, when the Lords gave the Bill its third reading, but rumours of an army plot had grown. The Lords had no confidence in Charles, and therefore dared not allow a man as able and determined as Strafford to stay alive to serve the King another day.[1]

'No man shall suffer for obeying my commands', Charles told the Lord Mayor of London, when the Lord Mayor justified not collecting Ship Money by pleading that his predecessor had been prosecuted for doing so. Charles meant to make good these words for all his servants, but circumstances overwhelmed him in May 1641, and he had to allow his greatest servant to suffer the greatest penalty for obeying him. The situation was truly desperate. The Scots refused to withdraw their army, and the City of London refused to pay the English army, unless Strafford were executed. The people threatened to tear Strafford apart if Charles attempted to save him. And Parliament steadfastly refused to vote supplies until Charles accepted the Act of Attainder. In refusing to vote supplies, Parliament revived the principle first announced by Sir Robert Phelips in 1625, that Parliament had the right to withhold supplies until ill coun- sellors were removed from the King. As the Earl of Essex said in a conference with the Commons in April, 'If any that had been the cause of our grievances were now the cause that we could not be supplied with money, it were good that it were made known, so that they might be the more speedily removed.'[2]

Parliament did not regard the power of impeachment and the power of the purse as temporary expedients. They regarded them as permanent checks upon evil ministers. Lord Digby made this un- equivocally clear in his speech urging the passage of the Triennial Act:

It is true...wicked ministers have been the proximate causes of our miseries; but the want of Parliaments [has been] the primary, the efficient

---

[1] C. H. Firth, *The House of Lords During the Civil War* (1910), pp. 89–91; Gardiner, *History*, IX, 348–51; *C.S.P. Ven.* xxv, 141, 148; Warwick, *Memoirs*, p. 179; Fr. Trans. 8/18 Apr., 29 Apr./5 May 1640, 6/16 and 13/23 May 1641; G. W. Johnson (ed.), *The Fairfax Correspondence* (1848), II, 65. On 19 May D'Ewes wrote to his wife (*Autobiography*, II, 266) of the discovery of the army plot, and commented, 'I hope there will much good come of it, for unless that had fallen out, we had not so easily obtained the Earl of Straf- ford's execution.'

[2] *C.S.P. Dom. 1640*, p. 307; Fr. Trans. 11/21 March, 1/11, 8/18 Apr., 8/18 May 1641; Baillie, *Letters*, I, 283, 302; Dalrymple, *Memorials of Charles I*, pp. 116–19; B.M. Add. MSS 27962 I, f. 200v; Harleian MSS 163, ff. 105–106; Harleian MSS 162, f. 348.

cause...It had been a maxim amongst the wisest legislators that who-soever means to settle good laws must proceed in them with a sinister opinion of all mankind, and I suppose that whosoever is not wicked, it is for want of opportunity. It is that opportunity of being ill, Mr Speaker, that we must take away if ever we mean to be happy, which can never be done but by frequency of Parliaments. No state can wisely be confident of any public ministers continuing good, longer than the rod is over them.

Parliament subscribed to this opinion not only by passing the Triennial Bill, but by passing a bill to perpetuate their own sitting, a bill which contained a clause that Parliament shall not be dissolved 'before justice shall be executed upon delinquents'. When Montereul, the French ambassador, heard that Charles had agreed to the Triennial Act, he remarked, 'As a result of today's decision, the King can no longer withstand anything.'[1]

Charles did not sign the Act of Attainder without first seeking the advice of his councillors, his judges, and his divines. His councillors unanimously urged him to sign the Act; his judges assured him that Strafford had committed treason; and his divines, led by Bishop Williams, the old advocate of popular monarchy, told him that, though in his private capacity as a man he could not condemn Strafford, yet in his political capacity as a King, advised by his Council and Parliament, he could. If Strafford were innocent, the blame for his death would lie on them, just as it would lie on his judges in the King's Bench if they condemned an innocent man.[2] It is not known whether this distinction between his private and his political capacities gave Charles's conscience any ease, but assuredly Parliament could use the doctrine to deny him all responsibility for the government of his realm. James had seen this clearly in 1607 when Coke urged on him the similar doctrine that the King's reason was the artificial reason of his judges. Charles did sign the Act of Attainder on the advice of his councillors, judges, and divines, and against his own conscience. It was an act of high tragedy, as many historians have since observed, but it was also a modest triumph for the corrosive distinction between the King's political and private capacities, a distinction that would in the long run do more to

---

[1] *The Speeches of Lord Digby* (1641), p. 16; Sloane MSS 1467, ff. 63–64; S. R. Gardiner (ed.), *The Constitutional Documents of the Puritan Revolution* (Oxford, 1889), p. 87; Fr. Trans. 18/28 Feb. 1641.

[2] Hackett, *Scrinia Reserata*, ii, 161; Clarendon, *History*, i, 338; Wynn of Gwydir Papers 1685.

establish responsible government in England than Strafford's judicial murder.

Strafford, on 4 May, wrote to Charles urging him to sign the Act of Attainder in order to prevent the evils that would ensue from its veto, but of all men in the kingdom he must have known best that his death would diminish Charles's authority. Since 1629 he had believed that the King's authority to govern and his servants' immunity from attack were one and inseparable. He set forth this doctrine of the inseparability of King and servant most fully in a letter to Laud in August 1638:

And sure howbeit for the present it may seem spoken in my own interest, yet has it appeared in all ages most true, that even the greatest Kings gain or lose much in the person and usage of their ministers. For if some of the School hold that the same worship directed to our Saviour first passes, and that *propria modo*, to and by his image, then sure in a sense less constrained, easier to be understood, it is to be believed that the rights and duties [which] belong to the Kings are in some measure to touch upon their servants, for if the people in their forward way towards sovereignty give no regard, no estimation, to the delegated administrator of it, reverence and subjection will scarce in perfection ever reach so far as to Majesty itself. And infallibly, as the shadow follows the body, great Kings have in all times had great servants; and the obedience and insolence of the subject have first wrought upon, discredited, the servants, before they dared look towards, could attain to, or prejudice Monarchy. And therefore it is a learning worthy a wise Prince, the not discerning whereof may prove very costly, that they are nearly and mightily concerned in such as they appoint to government, that no scorn or contempt can by the inferior be cast upon these but with diminution to themselves, and that it is necessary to sustain, to hold, their ministers up to the height (in their subordination), as the very steps whereby they thereby ascend to their own supreme powers and dominion over all.[1]

Strafford's letter to Laud contains more wisdom, or rather more honesty, than can be found in all the legal distinctions of Coke, the rhetoric of Eliot, and the political maxims of Pym. To attack the King's ministers while pretending to revere his person may be good politics, but it is dishonest political philosophy. Strafford saw more clearly than did his enemies that the consequence of his death would be the end of the English monarchy as fashioned by the Tudors. Persistently to separate the actions of ministers of the Crown from the King's own wisdom, wishes, resolves, and commands was to

[1] Wentworth Woodhouse MSS, Strafford Papers VII, f. 124.

7-2

make necessary a constitutional monarchy. But Charles was unwilling to play the role of a constitutional monarch. On that fact all Parliament's plans came to grief.

There were in 1640 at least five possible schemes for insuring responsible government in England. Some politicians, among them Sir Benjamin Rudyard, would have Parliament continue to rely on the power of impeachment. Others, the chief of whom was the Earl of Bedford, placed their faith in a parliamentary undertaking such as Neville had proposed in 1614; while another group, led by Edward Hyde, believed that the last, best hope for England was to persuade Charles to appoint Privy Councillors in whom the nation could confide. A fourth group followed John Pym, who believed that nothing less than the parliamentary nomination of the King's ministers would suffice. No one advocated the fifth scheme, placing executive power in Parliament itself, but the pressure of events insured that it alone should succeed. Parliamentary impeachments, parliamentary undertakings, conciliar government, parliamentary nomination, and parliamentary committees—these were the five possible alternatives that faced Englishmen after Strafford's death. The paramount question facing the historian is why the first four schemes failed to save England from the fifth.

Strafford's trial and eventual attainder offered the most egregious example of the failure of impeachment, but it was not the only example. The House of Commons in fact failed to secure the condemnation of a single one of those whom they impeached for misleading Charles in the years of Prerogative Government.[1] Secretary Windebank and Lord Keeper Finch, it is true, fled from England to save their lives, but the Commons nevertheless resolved to proceed with their impeachments. The Commons also impeached the judges, six in number, who had ruled in favour of Ship Money, and the bishops, thirteen in number, who had helped Laud pass the new Canons. But in the next two years they failed to secure the condemnation of either Windebank or Finch or Laud or the judges or the bishops. Windebank they probably chose to forget because, as he

---

[1] At the urging of the Lords the Commons finally prosecuted Justice Berkeley and Baron Trevor, and the Lords found both guilty. But the Commons had impeached Berkeley for High Treason and this charge they did not prosecute. The Lords, on 9 Sept. 1643, found him guilty only of high crimes and misdemeanours and merely sentenced him to pay a £20,000 fine. The Lords fined Trevor £6o,ooo, but Parliament believed enough in his innocence to permit him to continue as a Baron of the Exchequer (*L.J.* VI, 211; Clarendon, *History*, III, 210).

pleaded a month before his flight, he had only acted 'ministerially'. Finch they probably forgave because he made a most flattering submission to their authority the day before his flight.[1] Laud they hoped would die from the rigours of imprisonment in the Tower. But why did the House fail to prosecute the bishops who sought to destroy true religion and the judges who sought to subvert the fundamental law? There are two answers. In the first place they did not fear these men, and therefore felt no compulsion to destroy them. In the second place they did not believe that they could persuade the Lords that the religious beliefs and legal opinions of these men were crimes. Least of all did they believe that they could persuade the Lords that Bishop Wren and Justice Berkeley had committed treason. Yet they had impeached these two men for treason. Argue and exhort as they would, fulminate and exaggerate as they would, they knew that they could never persuade the Lords to condemn men for errors of judgment and differences of opinion. The independence of the Lords and the toughness of the law stood like sentries against any abuse of the power of impeachment. The Commons' only alternative was to choose not to prosecute the impeachments which they had voted.[2]

Nothing demonstrates more clearly the bankruptcy of impeachment than the willingness of the Commons to condemn men before they were brought to a legal trial before the Lords. The very day, 20 July, that they impeached Bishop Wren for treason, they voted that he was unfit to hold office, and asked the Lords to join with them in petitioning His Majesty to remove him. Eight days later they asked the Lords to join with them in asking that Laud be removed from office. On 21 July they voted that the impeached judges should not be in the Commission of Oyer and Terminer for the next Assize. In October they voted that the thirteen bishops should be removed from the House of Lords as unfit to exercise a

---

[1] Notestein, *D'Ewes Journal*, p. 26; Cobbett, *Parl. Hist.* II, 689–92. Montereul wrote (Fr. Trans. 24 Dec. 1640/3 Jan. 1641) that Lord Finch 'asked their pardon with the unworthy tears of an inconstant man and with a submission scandalous to a person of his rank'.

[2] The Lords continually pressed the Commons to prosecute their impeachments (*C.J.* II, 251, 493; *State Papers Collected by Edward, Earl of Clarendon*, Oxford, 1767–86, II, 141); and D'Ewes confessed (Harleian MSS 163, f. 368v) that their slowness in proceeding against the judges 'was a delay that we would judge a scandal in any other court'. When the Commons finally did proceed to Berkeley's trial, the lawyers in the House asked to be excused from managing it, because they were 'altogether unsatisfied of any treason in his case' (*H.M.C. Cowper*, II, 315).

vote there. And in November they frankly announced in the Grand Remonstrance that 'the Commons may have just cause to take exception at some men for being councillors, and yet not charge these men with crimes', nor be willing 'to proceed against them in any legal way of charge or impeachment'.[1] Anxious to drive ministers from the King, impatient of the forms of law, the Commons would make an impeachment a presumption of guilt and an accusation of the House a sufficient reason for removal from office.

Charles did not remove these men from office, despite the clamour raised against them. Even had he removed them, the Commons had no assurance that he would replace them with men acceptable to them. The want of this assurance explains the final inadequacy of impeachment. An impeachment could punish a minister who had broken the law, but it could not insure that his successor would be a man in whom Parliament could confide. Strafford's death, purchased at the cost of so much violence to the law and so much dishonour to the King, did not secure the appointment of ministers more acceptable to Parliament.[2] It could have and it might have, but it did not because too few men would countenance the Earl of Bedford's undertaking to serve Charles as Lord Treasurer.

Bedford carried on a tradition begun by Sir Henry Neville in 1614 and continued by Bishop Williams in 1625. He believed, as they believed, that the King should follow the advice of those who could and would undertake to carry on his business in Parliament. As early as December 1640 he expressed a willingness to serve Charles as Lord Treasurer, and the ruling party in Parliament expressed a wish that he should do so. The delicate task of urging this scheme on Charles was entrusted to the Marquis of Hamilton, who then enjoyed a predominant influence at Court. He served as a broker for Bedford, much as Southampton had served as a broker for Neville, and with as little initial success. The first suggestion that Charles bring the leaders of Parliament into his councils met with bitter rejection. But the continued intercession of Hamilton, enforced on occasions by the Queen herself, finally overcame Charles's initial reluctance. In February 1641 he named seven

[1] *C.J.* II, 199, 225, 228, 296; Gardiner, *Const. Doc. of the Puritan Rev.* pp. 153–4.
[2] Henry Parker wrote (*The Contra-Replicant*, 1643, p. 15): '...for aught I can see we have since but changed one Strafford for another, and one Canterbury for another...'

Lords to his Privy Council, Bedford, Essex, Hertford, Bristol, Saye, Mandeville, and Savile—'all Commonwealth men', said Baillie, the Scottish Commissioner. The undertaking had even gone so far that Bedford presumed to confer on Mr Stockdale a messenger's place in the Treasury.[1]

The nature of the undertaking that Bedford proposed was not unlike that which Neville had proposed a generation before. Bedford undertook to secure the King a revenue equal to that enjoyed by his predecessors. In return he asked Charles to grant office to those who desired a reformation in Church and State. These men should come in together, not individually. Before long everyone—Scottish Commissioners, foreign ambassadors, members of Parliament, royalist chaplains—seemed to know who these men were to be. Bedford was to be Lord Treasurer; Lord Saye, Master of the Court of Wards; Pym, Chancellor of the Exchequer; Holles, Secretary of State; St John, Solicitor; Hertford, Governor of the Prince; and Hampden, Tutor of the Prince. Negotiations to make this scheme a reality reached a crisis in late April. Cottington resigned the Mastership of the Wards and the Chancellorship of the Exchequer, and Pym, 'designed by the voice of the people to be his successor as Chancellor of the Exchequer', met with the King twice. But the whole ambitious adventure came to nought, and the stumbling block was the Earl of Strafford. Charles demanded that Bedford undertake to save his minister's life, and Bedford, though personally willing to accept the banishment of Strafford, could not persuade his friends to abate their fury against the Lord Lieutenant. Over this single question the Earl of Bedford's plans came to grief, and a week later he died.[2]

The demand for Strafford's death and Bedford's untimely death do not entirely explain the failure of parliamentary undertaking in 1641. In May Lord Saye persuaded Charles to cancel the appointment of Sir Robert Heath as Master of the Court of Wards and to

---

[1] Collins, *Letters and Memorials of State*, II, 664–6; Clarendon, *History*, I, 258, 279–82; Baillie, *Letters and Journals*, I, 291–3, 300, 305–10; H.M.C. *Cowper*, II, 272. Rossetti, the papal emissary to the Queen, wrote on 19 Feb. (Roman Trans. P.R.O. 31/9, xx, f. 7), 'The King brings six of the chief Puritans, among them the Earl of Bristol and the Earl of Essex, into the Council, and they promise to do great service for His Majesty in Parliament.'

[2] H.M.C. *Cowper*, II, 272; Clarendon, *History*, I, 279–82; *Clarendon State Papers*, II, 157–8; Warwick, *Memoirs*, p. 242; B. Whitelock, *Memorials of the English Affairs...from the Beginning of the Reign of King Charles* (1732), pp. 41, 46; Heylyn, *Cyprianus Anglicus*, pp. 447–8; Fr. Trans. 11/21 Jan. and 27 Feb./7 March 1641; Roman Trans. P.R.O. 31/9, xx, f. 31.

bestow the office on him. At the same time, Charles, presumably on Lord Saye's recommendations, named St John as his Solicitor and Hertford as Governor of the Prince. In June Lord Saye's scheme bogged down, but in July the hopes of the leaders of Parliament for office rose once again. Charles named the popular Earl of Essex as Lord Chamberlain of the Household, and there was talk of his appointing Lord Saye Treasurer, John Hampden Chancellor of the Exchequer, and Holles Secretary of State. But in August Charles extinguished all hope of a parliamentary undertaking by turning to the counsels of Bristol, Digby, and Savile, men now hated by Parliament, and by insisting on a Scottish journey that filled his subjects with dread.[1]

The important truth is not that the undertakings of Bedford and Lord Saye failed, but that they could never have succeeded. They could never have succeeded because the King and the undertakers viewed them in diametrically opposed ways. Charles regarded them (in Edward Hyde's words) as 'a stratagem for winning men by places'. The undertakers regarded them as a means to insure that the King would heed their advice in the future. Charles believed in using the power of patronage to increase his influence in Parliament. Bedford and Lord Saye believed in using their influence in Parliament to increase their power at Court. Charles would bring all into harmony by managing Parliament. The opposition would bring all into harmony by persuading Charles to govern according to the counsels of those in whom Parliament confided. A parliamentary undertaking was a strange and untried invention in 1641, yet it alone could have led Englishmen out of the impasse into which they had driven themselves by May of that year. It alone could have prevented civil war. It alone could have left the King's prerogative formally undamaged, while giving Parliament the assurances it wanted. But Charles was too proud a man, a man too inflexible in his ideals and too unimaginative in his thought, to accept such 'a pragmatical invention'.[2]

Yet Charles was not the only enemy of parliamentary undertakings in England. The rank and file in the House of Commons (and a few of their leaders) also regarded them with suspicion. Just as their predecessors had turned on undertakers in 1614, so did

[1] *H.M.C. Cowper*, ii, 282; *The Autobiography of Sir John Bramston* (Camden Soc. xxxii), pp. 81–2; Sanderson, *Complete History of King Charles*, p. 408; *C.S.P. Dom. 1641–3*, pp. 62–3; *C.S.P. Ven.* xxv, 193, 202–3.   [2] Clarendon, *History*, i, 431.

they in 1641. In February they first expressed their disgust at these intriguers. In that month those newly appointed to the Council deserted the opponents of the Court and worked to secure the King two additional subsidies. Their conduct thoroughly discredited them in the Commons.[1] In June the rank and file took measures to prevent the King from corrupting their members by offering them high office. On 3 June they read 'An Act for the better enabling of the members of Parliament to discharge their conscience in the proceedings of Parliament.' The proposed act would debar members of the House of Commons from accepting office under the King or Queen or Prince unless first 'the leave of both Houses of Parliament be obtained'. This act was the first of those self-denying ordinances of the seventeenth century which honest countrymen passed in order to save themselves from dishonest courtiers. But the Commons in 1641 did not persist in the bill. And though a similar proposal appears in the Causes and Remedies compiled by the Grocers' Hall Committee in January 1642, this proposal did not find its way into the Nineteen Propositions of June 1642, for by then parliamentary undertaking had been stone dead for nearly a year.[2]

John Pym, who seems to have played no part in Lord Saye's schemes though he did in Bedford's, suddenly realized in June 1641 that neither Strafford's attainder nor Bedford's undertaking had brought England one whit closer to responsible government. He therefore turned to a third solution. He rushed through both Houses of Parliament the Ten Heads of 24 June, the third clause of which asked Charles to appoint 'such counsellors and officers as the Parliament may have cause to confide in'.[3] This demand, opposed by no one in either House, was not the progenitor of the Grand Remonstrance and the Nineteen Propositions; otherwise it would have met

[1] Salvetti wrote on 26 Feb. (B.M. Add. MSS 27962 I, ff. 194v–195), 'Saturday there was great strife in the House of Commons concerning the grant of additional money for the maintenance of the English and Scottish armies. Greater divisions were revealed in the House than one believed existed, since the Puritan faction was forced to capitulate to the other faction, conceding two additional subsidies: a considerable point, and one which cannot but serve the royal interests, and much more so if these new Privy Councillors, being drawn to the other faction, will co-operate again. The Puritans are very jealous of this, and show much disgust at those newly advanced to honours.'

[2] Harleian MSS 163, f. 256; 'Resolutions of the Grocers' Hall Committee', B.M. Loan 29/46, No. 7; *C.J.* II, 445. Richard Baxter wrote (*Reliquiae Baxterianae*, 1696, p. 25) that Lord Saye and St John agreed to accept office, but others of them would accept no preferment, 'lest they should be thought to seek [for] themselves, or set their fidelity for sale'.

[3] *C.J.* II, 184–5; *L.J.* IV, 286; Harleian MSS 163, ff. 346–347v.

with the same resistance with which those proposals met. Rather it was the progenitor of Edward Hyde's policy that the King should, of his own volition, appoint and listen to Privy Councillors in whom Parliament and the nation could confide. The only difference between Pym and Hyde is that Pym deserted this policy the day that Charles insisted on visiting Scotland, while Hyde clung to it, despite rebuff, betrayal, and insult, all the days of his life.

Edward Hyde was as persuaded as Pym that Charles had been misled by evil counsellors, but he did not believe that this justified Parliament in taking from Charles his undoubted right to choose his own councillors. Considering Charles's unbending ways, this argument seemed to offer a very bleak prospect for the future, but Hyde did not despair. Instead he sought to persuade Charles to choose his servants more wisely. He urged him, in carefully penned memorials and through intermediaries, to choose as councillors men of independence, men of reputation in their county, men possessed of fair estates and endowed with ability and integrity, men without any obligation to the Court and against whom there was no just cause to take exception. In short, they should be men in whom the nation could confide. And once chosen, said Hyde, Charles should listen to them, and not to irresponsible courtiers. As B. H. G. Wormald observes, Hyde favoured 'a cohesive body of councillors capable of pursuing a responsible line of policy'.[1]

From the beginning of November to the end of December 1641 Charles played with the idea of a cohesive body of councillors pursuing a responsible line of policy. He allowed Hyde to defend this idea in the King's Answer to the Grand Remonstrance. He conceded that the Privy Council should approve of the Answer, and that the Answer should be published with the superscription, 'The King's Answer with the Advice of his Council.' Late in December he agreed, on Hyde's advice, to name Lord Falkland Secretary of State and Sir John Colepeper Chancellor of the Exchequer, men who were acceptable to the nation, if not to the ruling party in the House of Commons. For a brief moment it seemed as if reliance on Privy Councillors in whom the nation had cause to confide might save the monarchy. But Charles was incorrigible. Though he promised the triumvirate of Hyde, Falkland, and Colepeper that he

---

[1] Clarendon, *History*, I, 258–62, 437, 442; B. H. G. Wormald, *Clarendon* (Cambridge, 1951), p. 36.

would take no step without first seeking their advice, he appointed the unscrupulous Thomas Lunsford Lieutenant of the Tower, permitted twelve bishops to challenge the validity of the proceedings of the House of Lords, and attempted in person to arrest five members of the House of Commons—all without asking their advice. Charles's predilection for the private counsels of a Digby or a Murray was altogether too ingrained. He was also far too conscious that he was God's anointed to believe that his judgment needed the discipline of a Privy Council. This betrayal understandably discouraged the triumvirate, but they did not resign from office, even though, in Hyde's words, 'they could not avoid being looked upon as the authors of those counsels to which they were so absolutely strangers, and which they so perfectly detested'.[1] They clung instead to office and to the principle that one should continue to serve a King even though he rejected one's advice.

Charles's attempt to arrest five of their members caused the Commons to desert Hyde's Privy Council scheme, though they had approved of it until then. As late as 29 December, Sir John Holland, an articulate spokesman for Hyde's ideas, persuaded the Commons not to ask the King to remove Bristol as an evil counsellor, but to leave it to the King to appoint new councillors in whom they could confide. But this was the last triumph for those who sought to restore the Privy Council to a semblance of its Elizabethan role. On 25 January, in a long, low room in Grocers' Hall in the City, a Committee of the House flatly rejected conciliar government. They rejected it by omitting from the Causes of Present Evils a complaint that the King had not advised with his Privy Council. And amongst the Remedies, they made no demand that Charles act on the advice of a Privy Council of his own choosing. Instead they demanded that he act on the advice of a Privy Council of their choosing. Not until June did they formally present this demand to Charles (when it appeared as the first of the Nineteen Propositions); but in fact the Commons repudiated in January Hyde's ideal of a King acting on the advice of councillors whom he named and who possessed the confidence of the nation.[2]

[1] Clarendon, *History*, I, 437, 457–9, 484–5, 487; Edward Hyde, Earl of Clarendon, *The Life of Edward Earl of Clarendon* (Oxford, 1761), I, 87, 89–90; Wormald, *Clarendon*, pp. 32–6.
[2] W. H. Coates (ed.), *The Journal of Sir Simonds D'Ewes* (New Haven, 1942), pp. 360–2; Harleian MSS 162, f. 330v; B.M. Loan 29/46, No. 7; Gardiner, *Const. Doc. of the Puritan Rev.* pp. 171–2.

The Failure of Impeachment

Hyde's failure was Pym's opportunity. Month after month, from August through December, from January through June, Pym planned and intrigued and schemed and struggled to persuade his fellow men to accept the parliamentary nomination of the King's councillors and ministers. His proposal was not a simple one, for parliamentary nomination could mean one of three things. It could mean Parliament's naming those ministers and councillors whom it wished the King to remove. Or it could mean Parliament's naming those persons whose intended appointment it found objectionable. Or it could mean naming those persons whom it wished the King to appoint. But whether Parliament voted an address requesting the removal of a minister, or vetoed a royal appointment, or recommended a person for an appointment, it always named a particular person who was acceptable or unacceptable to Parliament.

An insistence on naming particular persons divided all of Pym's schemes from all the proposals of Hyde. When presenting the Ten Heads to the Lords on 24 June 1641, Pym served warning that the third Head, which essentially expressed Hyde's proposal, was only probationary. 'Howbeit this request', he said, 'is by the Commons recommended in general for the present, without pointing or designing particulars, in hope the King will find them out himself, [if it falls out] otherwise, it will cause the House of Commons to reduce this petition to names of particulars.' It did fall out 'otherwise', and the Commons soon gave up hope that Charles would 'find them out himself'. In July they petitioned Charles to name Salisbury Lord Treasurer and Pembroke Lord Steward. But Charles ignored their petition, and set forth on his Scottish journey. This journey, in search of an army, frightened the forward party in the Commons, and persuaded them that petitioning was not enough. Parliament must have, by right and not by grace, a negative voice in the naming of the King's ministers. Never did Charles make a more costly error than his decision to visit Scotland, for he found there not an army, but a demand from the Scottish Parliament that it should have a voice in naming great officers of state in Scotland. Powerless before the might of Argyle and the Scots people, he yielded to their demands. His trip to Scotland had frightened Englishmen, but the concessions he made there emboldened them. While Charles in Edinburgh was conceding the nomination of ministers of state to a

Scottish Parliament, Pym and his friends in London met at Lord Mandeville's house in Chelsea to draft a similar demand.[1] This demand was a radical one, for the parliamentary nomination of the King's ministers was unlawful, unusual, and untested. Most members of Parliament viewed it with emotions ranging from distaste to horror. Pym therefore confronted formidable difficulties. He must first persuade the House of Commons, then the House of Lords, and finally the King to accept a proposal that none cherished.[2]

On 28 October Pym and his allies made their first attempt to persuade the House of Commons to demand the parliamentary nomination of the King's servants. Robert Goodwin then moved 'that it was fit the Parliament should have a negative voice in the choice of great officers and councillors', and William Strode seconded him with great violence. But his violence was no match for Edward Hyde's logic. Hyde argued that the choice of great officers was 'an hereditary flower of the Crown', and that the abolition of Star Chamber, High Commission, and Ship Money gave them security enough against unlawful government. The House did appoint a committee to draw up the heads of that day's debate, but nothing more was heard of Goodwin's proposal.[3]

News of the Irish Rebellion allowed Pym to make a second attempt to win over the Commons. On 5 November he proposed that Parliament enter into no engagement to support the King in Ireland unless the King agree to employ only councillors and officers of whom Parliament approved. Opposition to this proposal was so great that Pym had to alter its wording. Only by making the vote of supplies no longer dependent upon Charles's granting the parliamentary nomination of his servants, could Pym persuade the House to accept his proposal. Even then the decision to request Charles to name councillors and officers acceptable to Parliament passed by the narrow margin of 151 to 110. When the Lords refused to join in the request, the Commons let Pym's proposal die.[4]

---

[1] *L.J.* IV, 286; *C.J.* II, 247-8; *C.S.P. Ven.* xxv, 171; W. Bray, *Memoirs of John Evelyn* (1827), v, 35, 37, 42, 43; Fr. Trans. 21/31 Oct. 1641; Salvetti's dispatches, B.M. Add. MSS 27962 I, f. 281 v.

[2] That Pym dominated the proceedings of the House of Commons is implicit in D'Ewes's account of the debates there, but another diarist (B.M. Add. MSS 4180, f. 170 v) explicitly confirms D'Ewes, by noting, 'The Speaker diligently watches the eye of Pym.'

[3] Coates, *D'Ewes Journal*, pp. 44-7, 94-5; Bray, *Evelyn's Memoirs*, v, 68-70.

[4] Bray, *Evelyn's Memoirs*, v, 86; Coates, *D'Ewes Journal*, p. 99; *L.J.* IV, 421-2, 431-2, 433.

This defeat did not cause Pym to surrender: he merely retreated, regrouped his forces, and entered the fray again. He now decided to appeal to the people of England, over the heads of both King and Lords, in a Grand Remonstrance. Having tasted defeat twice, he now resolved to bring the maximum weight of political pressure to bear on the minimum demands possible. The Grand Remonstrance recited at great length the miseries that fifteen years of evil counsels had brought upon England, and then asked only that Charles employ such councillors and officers 'as the Parliament may have cause to confide in'. The words were the same as those in the Ten Heads of 24 June, but the spirit behind them was different. During the long night's debate that began on 22 and ended on 23 November, Hyde, Falkland, and Colepeper protested that the Remonstrance was in fact a demand that His Majesty take the advice of Parliament in the choice of his servants. Pym did not deny this. Instead he pleaded, 'We have suffered so much by councillors of the King's choosing, that we desire him to advise with us about it.' The Grand Remonstrance passed by 159 votes to 148, a heartening victory, but a majority far too small to allow Pym to believe he had won the battle for the parliamentary nomination of the King's councillors and ministers. The victory appeared even more hollow when Charles, on Hyde's advice, told the Commons that he had in the past protected no man from justice and would in the future name no man to office against whom there was just cause to take exception.[1] Pym's radical schemes could make little headway against the traditional caution of Englishmen and the impeccable logic of Hyde.

Then in one morning Charles gave to Pym what Pym had been unable to secure in three months. By attempting to arrest the five members Charles drove the House of Commons to accept the parliamentary nomination of his ministers and councillors. On 18 January the Grocers' Hall Committee voted that no Privy Councillor or great officer of state shall be chosen 'but by the consent of Parliament'. On the 31st the House of Commons resolved (upon Charles's once again assuring them that he would employ only those in whom they could confide) 'that the confidence of this House is necessarily to be expressed by recommending fit persons to His Majesty'. In early February a Committee of Both Houses for Removing Evil

[1] Gardiner, *Const. Doc. of the Puritan Rev.* pp. 153, 157–8; *Verney Papers*, pp. 123–5; Coates, *D'Ewes Journal*, pp. 183–6.

Counsellors adopted the latter policy of 'recommending fit persons', rather than the Grocers' Hall policy of consenting to the King's choice. Finally, on 19 February the House of Commons added to the Remedies proposed by the Grocers' Hall Committee a demand that Charles appoint as councillors and ministers only such 'as shall be recommended to Your Majesty by advice of both Houses'. Pym, aided by Charles's folly, had finally worn down the reluctance of the Commons to accept the parliamentary nomination of the King's councillors and ministers of state.[1]

The reluctance of the Commons was nothing compared to the recalcitrance of the Lords. The peers' hostility to the parliamentary nomination of the King's servants survived the second Army Plot, the appointment of Lunsford, the protestation of the twelve bishops, and the attempted arrest of the five members. In November they defeated Pym's proposal that the two Houses include in their answer to the King's letter asking for money to suppress the Irish rebellion, a request that he employ only those acceptable to Parliament. In December the Lords, 'because they took the placing and displacing of the King's officers to be a branch of his prerogative', refused to join the Commons in petitioning the King to dismiss Lunsford as Lieutenant of the Tower. On 17 January they refused to join with the Commons in asking for Sir John Byron's dismissal and Sir John Conyers's appointment as Lieutenant of the Tower—although on this occasion twenty-three lords protested against the refusal. Thirty-one lords protested the decision of the House on 24 January not to join with the Commons in requesting the King to place the Tower, the forts, and the militia in the hands of such persons as Parliament may confide in.

Faced with the continued obstinacy of some forty lords, and enjoying the support of only about thirty lords, Pym altered his tactics. Instead of carrying up resolution after resolution, each time giving a little homily on the dangers of evil counsels, he sought to work with the peers by means of a joint Committee of Both Houses for Removing Evil Counsellors. It was Charles's refusal to place Carrickfergus in the hands of the Scots that drove the Lords to co-operate in this joint committee. Yet simultaneously with this effort to win over the peers by co-operation, Pym tried to intimidate them by again appealing to popular opinion. He and his friends

---

[1] *A Continuation of the True Diurnall. Numb. 2* (1642), p. 1; *C.J.* II, 433, 442–5, 505.

incited the people of Hereford, of Kent, of Northampton, of Surrey, and of Oxfordshire to petition Parliament for the removal of evil counsellors.[1] These tactics of Pym's, assisted by the intransigency of Charles, succeeded. In February the Lords joined the Commons in a request that Charles place the forts and militia in the hands of those recommended by Parliament. In April the Lords took the final step, and voted to accept the first Remedy proposed in the Declaration of Causes and Remedies sent up by the Commons. By 27 to 18, they voted to accept this Remedy, which provided that the King shall appoint as councillors and officers only such 'as shall be recommended to Your Majesty by advice of both Houses of Parliament'.[2]

Pym's perseverance succeeded only because of Charles's stubborn reliance on his own erratic judgment, and on the even more erratic judgments of the Queen and Lord Digby. Yet Charles's stubbornness was the very force that finally defeated all Pym's well-laid plans. He would not give up his right to listen to councillors of his own choosing and to employ ministers of his own liking. Against this obduracy Parliament had only one weapon, the power of the purse. By steadfastly refusing to vote tonnage and poundage for more than two months at a time, it kept this power in reserve. In May and June 1642 it exercised the power openly. In the Declaration of the Lords and Commons of 19 May it declared that it could not settle a revenue on His Majesty 'till he shall choose such counsellors and officers as may order and dispose it to the public good...'. In June it refused to settle a revenue on the King until he accepted the Nineteen Propositions.[3] But Charles could now afford to ignore these threats, for he contemplated waging a war against Parliament that would make irrelevant any refusal to vote supplies. The appeal was no longer to the law courts, but to the people, with each side publishing its declarations to win popular support.

[1] Coates, *D'Ewes Journal*, p. 125; Cobbett, *Parl. Hist.* II, 982; *L.J.* IV, 487, 504–5, 532–3, 563–4, 575; *H.M.C. Cowper*, II, 304, 305–6; B.M. Add. MSS 14827, ff. 34, 36v. The Prince of Orange's representative, Heenvliet, wrote (G. C. van Prinsterer, *Archives ou Correspondance inédite de la Maison d'Orange-Nassau*, 2nd ser. IV, 14), 'I asked Vane whether it was not dangerous to incite everyone as they did, and in every county, urging them to come and present their petitions. He answered, no, and added that these petitioners would return satisfied.'

[2] *L.J.* IV, 555–7, 700; Clarendon MSS 21, No. 1603, f. 57.

[3] Bray, *Evelyn's Memoirs*, V, 35, 43; *The Declaration or Remonstrance of the Lords and Commons* (1642), p. 12; Gardiner, *Const. Doc. of the Puritan Rev.* pp. 174–5.

To answer the many declarations published by Parliament, Charles employed the grave and learned pen of Edward Hyde. His choice was wise, for Hyde persuaded Charles to take up a position, to occupy a redoubt, that was nearly impregnable. The principal ramparts of this redoubt were the King's claim that he had never protected any man from the justice of Parliament, his promise that he would never employ any man against whom Parliament could take just exception, and his insistence that he would never dismiss a man at Parliament's behest unless Parliament proved a particular charge against him.[1] To defend the right to choose his own servants Charles invoked the power of impeachment. He assured Parliament that he would employ no man found guilty on an impeachment; but neither would he dismiss a man at their request unless he was found guilty on an impeachment. A power, which began as an instrument by which Parliament could check the King, became in the spring of 1642 a means by which the King could withstand Parliament. This was the measure of the distance travelled towards responsible government in the twenty-one years between 1621 and 1642.

The most forceful of Charles's replies to Parliament was his answer to the Nineteen Propositions, an answer written, not by Hyde, but by Falkland and Colepeper. In the Nineteen Propositions, Parliament asked that Charles appoint only such councillors and officers as 'shall be approved of by both Houses of Parliament'. It did not ask, as it was prepared to ask in April, for the right to recommend to him those whom he should choose. It asked only for the right of approbation. Yet even this retreat to the Grocers' Hall formula was easily and effectively answered by Falkland and Colepeper. They simply appealed to the ideal of a mixed, limited monarchy against Parliament's demand for unlimited sovereignty. The House of Commons debated their persuasive Answer to the Nineteen Propositions on 23 June in a Committee of the Whole House. Two hundred and six members attended, debated, listened, sat until nine at night, and finally resolved (to the anguish of Pym, Holles, and Strode) not to insist on the right to approve those whom Charles named to his Privy Council. Four days later the Commons modified the proposition demanding parliamentary approval of those whom the King named as his great officers of state. The Earl of Northumberland,

---

[1] *His Majesties Answer, To a Book, Intituled the Declaration, or Remonstrance of the Lords and Commons* (1642), pp. 14–15.

113

who probably reflected faithfully the opinion of most Parliament
men, wrote the next day, 'I acknowledge that all things desired in
the Nineteen Propositions are not absolutely necessary for securing
unto us our laws, liberties, and privileges, nor was it intended that
these propositions should be insisted upon, they being petitions of
grace, not of right.' Yet Pym stemmed the retreat of the House from
the Nineteen Propositions by a tactic which he had often used before.
On 1 July, when the House resumed debate on the King's Answer
to the Nineteen Propositions, he warned the Commons that they
must look to their present safety. He then read a letter from Gloucester describing the military preparations of the royalists in that
county. This put a stop to the day's debate, just as the Civil War
itself put a stop to further hopes for a peaceful settlement. The appeal
now was to arms, not to remonstrances.[1]

The most revealing decision made by the House of Commons in
these debates in late June was the decision not to yield on the second
of the Nineteen Propositions. This second proposition asked that the
King always heed the advice of his Privy Council. The intent of the
proposition was not to restore the Privy Council to its historic role
in the government of England. Its intent was to ensure the greatest
publicity of advice and to prevent secret and irresponsible counsels.
During the great debate of 23 June, Pym had cried out against those
who believed that the impeachment of evil counsellors was security
enough, 'The King will not reveal evil counsellors.'[2] To most Parliament men this fact proved embarrassing, for, in the depths of their
English hearts, they wanted to leave the sceptre where it was, in
the King's hands. They did not wish to govern, or nominate those
who governed, or consent to the nomination of those who governed.
They much preferred to play the role of critics. They wished to
impeach, to censure, and to condemn. But how could they impeach
or censure or condemn if they did not know who among the King's
counsellors deserved impeachment, censure, condemnation?

Charles did nothing to help them solve this problem. Instead
he clung to the only two means which he still retained for protecting

---

[1] Rushworth, *Historical Collections*, IV, 728–305; Harleian MSS 163, ff. 207v, 252v,
164, f. 269; B.M. Add. MSS 14827, f. 144; *H.M.C. Buccleuch*, I, 305; *C.J.* II, 642;
G. Bankes, *The Story of Corfe Castle* (1853), p. 138. Pym could not, however, prevent
Parliament from offering peace terms in February 1643 that did not include a demand
to name the King's counsellors and officers (Rushworth, *Historical Collections*, v, 165–8).

[2] Bruce, *Verney Papers*, pp. 181–2.

his counsellors: the right to deny that anyone had counselled him at all; and the right (admitting that he had received counsel) to refuse to name those who had given it to him. Charles resorted to the former practice when the Commons impeached his Attorney-General, Sir Edward Herbert, for preferring articles of impeachment against Lord Kimbolton and the five members. Charles wrote to Parliament that Herbert had not advised the preferring of those articles, and had only obeyed his commands in preferring them. The Commons refused, however, to allow Charles to avow this as his own action, and voted—though they had no shred of evidence to prove it—that Herbert had 'advised and contrived' the articles. Arbitrary votes of this nature finally drove Charles to ask 'that our own immediate actions, which we avow on our honour, might not be so roughly censured and wounded under the common style of evil counsellors'. To insure that he might continue to avow as his own the counsels of others, Charles took care to take advice in secret. He personally copied out messages sent to him by Edward Hyde, in order to protect him. When Hyde suggested that Secretary Nicholas copy them out, Charles replied, 'in this particular, which would be so penal in others, if it should be known, it was not necessary...'.[1]

The two Houses of Parliament were as stubborn as Charles on this supremely important issue. They stated in their Declaration of 19 May that, though His Majesty does not wish his own immediate actions censured under the style of evil counsellors, yet they must act 'according to the maxim in law [that says that] the King can do no wrong, but if any ill be committed in matters of state, the Council, if in matters of justice, the judges, must answer for it'.[2] Parliament clearly designed for the King a lofty eminence, far removed from the arena of government.

Parliament found it possible to breach the King's avowal of responsibility only by dogmatically asserting that he was always advised by others. But they found it far more difficult to pierce the

---

[1] Cobbett, *Parl. Hist.* II, 1121, 1127–9, 1141–2; *C.J.* II, 428; Clarendon, *Life*, I, 107–8. The House of Lords refused to find Herbert guilty of 'advising and contriving' the articles, but they did find him guilty of a breach of the privileges of Parliament in preferring them, and sentenced him to the Fleet for a fortnight, though they did not remove him from office (*L.J.* IV, 645–6; V, 11–12). Because Herbert did violate the privileges of Parliament, the Lords found him guilty. Because he only acted ministerially, and because almost everyone in Parliament believed that Digby had advised the breach of privilege, the Lords gave him a ludicrously light sentence.

[2] *The Declaration or Remonstrance of the Lords and Commons...19 May 1642* (1642), p. 5.

8-2

veil of secrecy that the King threw around his councillors. In December 1641 the Commons sought to penetrate it by asking Charles point-blank who had advised him to violate the privileges of Parliament by taking notice of a bill before the House. Charles replied that 'it was a thing much beneath us to name any that should give us information or counsel'. Despite this frosty answer, the Commons later asked him who had reported to him the Earl of Newport's remarks concerning the safety of the Queen and Prince. In January they asked him who had advised the prosecution of the five members. On both occasions Charles refused to name those who had counselled him.[1] In February the Commons finally conceded that the King ought not to be asked to play the role of an informer. They therefore turned to a different stratagem, to general votes of condemnation, naming no names. On seven different occasions they declared that whoever advised the King to this or that action was 'an enemy to the peace of the Kingdom', 'a mischievous projector', 'an enemy of the state', 'one of the malignant party'. They censured the Duke of Richmond as an evil counsellor and impeached Lord Digby, though confessing they had no proof to substantiate either vote. As John Glynn observed on carrying up the vote against Richmond, 'It is not easy to discover evil counsellors, for it must be either the King that was told it, and he cannot be an accuser, or else by witnesses; and such counsels are works of darkness that cannot be discovered, therefore the House of Commons say, it must be circumstances that must satisfy them.' Denzil Holles then added, 'they see the stone that hit them, but could not discover the arm that threw it'.[2]

Charles answered the Commons with monotonous regularity: let them name his evil counsellors, let them bring particular charges against them, he would not screen any man from the justice of Parliament. His answer of 24 May was typical: 'There will be no end of the discourse [about], and upbraiding us with, evil counsellors, if upon our constant denial of knowing any they will not vouch-

---

[1] *L.J.* IV, 591–3; Cobbett, *Parl. Hist.* II, 981; *C.J.* II, 359.
[2] *L.J.* IV, 550–1, 602. The seven votes (*C.J.* II, 383, 399, 407, 459, 482; and B.M. Add. MSS 14827, f. 98v) were against those who had advised Charles: to distrust Parliament (17 Jan.), to deny the Scots Carrickfergus (27 Jan.), to refuse the Commons' Petition for placing the forts and militia in such hands as they should nominate (1 Feb.), to decline granting the militia for an indefinite time (28 Feb.), to absent himself from Parliament (16 March), to deny the validity of Ordinances (17 March), and to give the answer he did concerning Hull (7 May).

safe to inform us of them, and after eight months amazing the kingdom with the expectation of a discovery of a malignant party and of evil counsellors, they will not at last name any.' It is evident that the Commons felt the justice of such rebukes, for they strove constantly to discover who had given the King evil counsels. They appointed committees of inquiry to search out the authors of wicked advice, but invariably they searched in vain. The Commons therefore sought to banish irresponsible counsellors altogether. First in their Grocers' Hall Committee, and then in the full House, they voted that the King should act on the advice of Parliament or his Privy Council, and not on advice given him by private persons.[1] This vote, accepted by the Lords, became the second of the Nineteen Propositions. This second Proposition really comprehended three demands: first, 'that the great affairs of the Kingdom may not be concluded or transacted by the advice of private men, or by unknown or unsworn councillors'; secondly, that matters appropriate to Parliament be resolved upon there and that matters proper for the Privy Council be decided in Council; and, thirdly, 'that no public act, concerning the affairs of the Kingdom, which are proper for your Privy Council, may be esteemed of any validity, as proceeding from the royal authority, unless it be done by advice and consent of the major part of your Council, attested under their hands...'.[2]

Charles assessed with complete truthfulness the cost to himself of conceding the first three of the Nineteen Propositions. 'These being passed, we may be waited on bare-headed, we may have our hand kissed, the style of Majesty continued to us...we may have swords and maces carried before us, and please ourself with the sight of a Crown and Sceptre...but as to true and real power, we should remain but the out-side, but the picture, but the sign of a King.' Yet the Commons, though they receded from the first, and modified the third, would not surrender the second of the Nineteen Propositions. All the arguments of Selden and all the learning of D'Ewes could not persuade the House to give up their demand that the

[1] *His Majesties Answer to a Printed Book, Intituled the Declaration, or Remonstrance of the Lords and Commons* (York and London, 1642), p. 14; B.M. Loan 29/46, no. 7; *C.J.* II, 442–5. The Lords and Commons (*C.J.* II, 399, 460, 482; *L.J.* IV, 546, 619, 650) joined in the Committees of Inquiry to discover who advised Charles: to refuse Carrickfergus to the Scots (27 Jan.), to refuse to surrender the militia indefinitely (28 Feb.), and to declare Ordinances invalid (17 March).

[2] Gardiner, *Const. Doc. of the Puritan Rev.* pp. 171–2.

King's councillors accept their responsibility in writing. Eight months of frustration in their search for wicked advisers had made them as adamant as steel on that point.[1]

What most members of the House of Commons wanted in June 1642 was the right to vote impeachments against ministers whose faults they could declare to be crimes, and the right to vote censures against counsellors whose advice to the King they could read in Council books. But arbitrary impeachments and the giving of advice in writing did not satisfy Pym and his friends and proved too much for Charles, so England drifted into civil war. Three irreconcilable conflicts led to civil war: reform of the Church, control of the militia, and the right to nominate the King's councillors and officers of state.

The drift into war began with the discovery of the first Army Plot in May 1641 and ended with the raising of Charles's standard at Nottingham in August 1642. During this period no one proposed government by committees of Parliament as a permanent arrangement for ensuring responsible government. But neither could any one find a majority to oppose the *ad hoc* creation of such a government. From 7 May 1641, when Parliament sent commissioners to secure Portsmouth, until 4 July 1642, when it established the Committee of Safety, the two Houses—fearing to be weaker in arms than the King—seized control of the forts, of the militia, of the navy, of the customs, of the Lord Lieutenancies, of the Commissions of Peace—ultimately of everything. It was all the result of expediency, not principle, with one unimportant but interesting exception. In December 1640, long before anyone thought of civil war, the House of Commons resolved that commissioners of their choosing, and not the Exchequer, should collect the two subsidies that they had voted the King. Then in May 1641 Denzil Holles and William Strode urged that tonnage and poundage be collected, not by the King's officers, but by commissioners elected by Parliament, 'in order', they said, 'that liberty of the subject might be asserted'. Swayed by their arguments the Commons voted that commissioners elected by Parliament should collect tonnage and poundage. However, the two Houses could not agree who these commissioners should be, thereby delaying the passage of the bill for tonnage and poundage.

---

[1] Rushworth, *Historical Collections*, IV, 728; Harleian MSS 163, ff. 217v–218v; *C.J.* II, 639.

When Mr Treasurer Vane pleaded that they hasten the passage of the bill, the Commons recanted, and voted tonnage and poundage to the King for two months, to be collected by his officers.[1] Fear of Charles's intentions kept the two Houses from voting him a permanent grant of tonnage and poundage, and therefore King and Parliament did not again dispute who should collect it. Nothing more was heard of a constitutional claim that the Commons had temporarily secured in 1624, briefly advocated in 1641, and would again voice in 1675 and 1678.

This special interest in naming treasurers apart, Parliament made no demand that the executive power be placed directly in the two Houses. That the executive power was in fact placed there, until a Lord Protector stole it away, was an accident. Or rather, it was an unforeseen inevitability, since it was inevitable that in the England of 1640 all other solutions should fail. It was inevitable that impeachments and votes of censure should fail, when voted against innocent ministers and unknown counsellors. It was impossible that parliamentary undertakings should succeed, when the King regarded them as a stratagem for winning men by places and the Commons feared them as a means of corrupting their leaders. It was certain that conciliar government should prove a mockery, when the King persisted in preferring the counsels of private persons to those of sworn councillors. It was inevitable that parliamentary nomination should fail, when the King showed himself unalterably opposed to it and the Lords and Commons only hesitantly in favour of it. The result was really a failure of all solutions and a civil war that solved none of the problems that had provoked it.

[1] Salvetti's dispatches, B.M. Add. MSS 27962 I, f. 234; B.M. Add. MSS 11045, f. 134v; *C.J.* II, 53, 164–5; Harleian MSS 163, ff. 243v–244, 252, 305.

CHAPTER 4

THE SEPARATION OF POWERS AND THE PRINCIPLE OF ACCOUNTABILITY (1642–1660)

When Charles II landed at Dover in May 1660 he took up the sceptre of government as well as the Crown, the executive powers as well as the dignities of kingship. He named his own ministers of state and Privy Councillors, and he dismissed them at his pleasure. These ministers and these councillors answered to him for their conduct and for their counsels, though Parliament might impeach them for violating the law or giving unlawful advice. Yet behind the outward façade of a restored monarchy lay a reality much altered from former years. The extraordinary experiences of the last nineteen years had bitten deeply into the consciousness of Englishmen. The formal constitution of 1660 may have closely resembled that of 1641, but the habits, prejudices, opinions, and predilections of Englishmen in the year of the Restoration differed markedly from what they had been in the year of Strafford's attainder.

This period in the history of England, between the outbreak of civil war and the Restoration, is so chaotic—so many varied, extreme, and ephemeral events occurred during it—that it is difficult for the historian to trace any continuous theme through it. The best that he can do is to ask what survived at the end of the period, what residue remained from the confused alchemy of these years. As concerns the growth of responsible government, the residue was fivefold. Englishmen, looking back on the strange revolutions of two decades, came to prefer impeachments to regicide, to look with less suspicion on parliamentary undertaking, to speak more admiringly of the role of the Privy Council in government, to view with less horror parliamentary addresses against ministers of state, and to distrust more deeply than ever government by parliamentary committees. In the emergence of these altered sentiments, and not in the succession of Committees of Safety, Committees of Both Kingdoms, and Councils of State, lies the true history of the growth of responsible government during these years. The important questions that the historian must ask are why men came to look with more favour on parliamentary impeachments, parliamentary undertakings, conciliar government, and parliamentary addresses, and why they came to look with profound disfavour on government by committees of Parliament. Because these years of strife did alter and shape men's opinions, the historian must ascertain how and why they did so.

At the Restoration far more Englishmen than in 1640 believed that the King could do no wrong, that he invariably acted on the advice of other men, and that Parliament could impeach those men for giving him bad advice. Three events during these years helped persuade men to hold these beliefs: the pamphlet warfare of the 1640's, the trial of Archbishop Laud, and the execution of the King.

In 1641 there existed precedents, stretching back to the fourteenth century, for Parliament's discussing the responsibilities of ministers of state; there existed other precedents, extending back to the fifteenth century, for judges pronouncing on the responsibilities of ministers of state; but there existed no precedents whatsoever for public debate in the press on this subject. Never before could any scribbler write, and any bookseller publish, treatises on the responsibilities of the King's ministers. The importance of the 1640's is that ideas which had previously been the preserve of parliamentarians and judges now became the property of vicars in Coleman Street, Doctors of Divinity in Oxford, and schoolmasters in Avebury. The pamphlets written by these men, even the royalists among them, taught a whole generation of Englishmen that since the King could do no wrong his ministers must answer for whatever wrong was done. Defenders of the parliamentary cause naturally took up this refrain first. Chief among these writers were Henry Parker, whose *Observations upon Some of His Majesties Late Answers and Expresses* drew more replies from royalists than any other pamphlet published during these years, and Philip Hunton, whose *Treatise of Monarchy* likewise entered the main stream of controversy. Parker and Hunton sought to justify Parliament's resort to arms by arguing that Parliament waged war against the King's evil councillors and wicked instruments, not against the King himself.[1] To this argument the

---

[1] H. Parker, *Observations upon Some of His Majesties Late Answers and Expresses*, in W. Haller, *Tracts on Liberty in the Puritan Revolution* (New York, 1934), II, 196–204;

royalists, of whom Dr Ferne was the most prolific and Sir Dudley Digges the most eloquent, replied that there was a difference between a minister's refusing to execute the King's unlawful command and Parliament's waging war against the King. The laws of England required disobedience to unlawful commands; nothing in the laws of England justified war against the King.[1] This clear distinction drove the parliamentarians, notably Philip Hunton, to revive the doctrine of the Despensers, the doctrine that whoever represented the King in his political capacity could justly wage war against those who represented him in his personal capacity. Since no judge, they argued, would permit the verbal commands of the King to obstruct the execution of a judgment pronounced in his court, why should Parliament, the highest court in the land, allow the King's personal commands to hinder the execution of its judgments? Thus did the parliamentarians carry to its logical conclusion the doctrine of the King's twofold capacity, personal and public. The King in his political capacity spoke through his courts, and most highly of all through his highest court, Parliament; and Englishmen should therefore obey it, and not the 'subverting instruments' who represented the King in his personal capacity.[2]

Throughout the 1640's the royalists denounced this doctrine as absurd, branded it as treasonous, denied its logic, and quoted Sir Edward Coke and two Parliaments in condemnation of it. But these same writers stamped their *imprimatur* on the maxim that the King can do no wrong. Dr Ferne even admitted the legitimacy of the doctrine of the King's double capacity. 'Nor is the distinction of his double capacity', he wrote, 'altogether vain, but only in this point of arms and resistance by force. As just sentences of judges, against his personal commands, are for him in his political capacity,

P. Hunton, *Treatise of Monarchy* (1643), pp. 52–6. This same argument is voiced in *A Dialogue Betwixt a Courtier and a Scholar* (1642), p. 4; Mr Hearle, *A Fuller Answer to a Treatise Written by Dr Ferne* (1642), p. 12; J. L., *A Just Apology* (1642), p. 2; *A Speech Delivered in Parliament by J. P. Esquire* (1642), p. 3; and *The Vindication of Parliament*, in *Harleian Miscellany* (1744–6), VIII, 65.

[1] H. Ferne, *A Reply to Several Treatises* (1643), p. 10; Sir Dudley Digges, *The Unlawfulness of Subjects Taking up Arms* (1643), pp. 13, 39, 73, 128. Similar arguments appear in *A Review of the Observations* (1643), p. 21; and *The Case of Our Affairs* (1643), p. 3.

[2] P. Hunton, *A Vindication of the Treatise of Monarchy* (1644), pp. 10, 45, 52, 69. See also *Vox Populi*, in *Harleian Miscellany*, VI, 454; *A Remonstrance of the Lords and Commons . . . Nov. 2, 1642* (1642), p. 21; J.M., *A Reply to the Answer* (1643), pp. 20–2; *A Disclaimer* (1643), pp. 19, 21, 25; *Scripture and Reason* (1643), p. 43; and *A Medicine for Malignancy* (1643), p. 24.

so are all denials of active obedience to unjust commands.' The far shrewder Digges saw a weaker link in his opponents' argument. Though valid for judicial decisions, said Digges, the doctrine of the King's double capacity does not apply to matters of state. He saw that the Civil War concerned differences over policies, not obedience yielded to illegal commands.[1]

Royalists readily admitted that ministers should disobey unlawful commands, but they insisted that to attack the King's policies under the guise of opposing his councillors was 'to wound him through the sides of his Council', and to condemn those councillors without proof was to introduce a 'new mystery into the sciences and senses'. Imputing the King's decisions to his councillors deprived him of all reason. Condemning his councillors without legal proof robbed them of their birth-right as Englishmen.[2] These objections the parliamentarians found difficult to answer, for they were embarrassingly true. Yet answer them they must; otherwise all went by default. Among all those who made the attempt, Henry Parker was the most successful. Where Philip Hunton invariably viewed Parliament as a court of law doing justice and ceaselessly attacked the 'subverting instruments' who obeyed the King, Parker constantly viewed Parliament as a council giving advice and persistently attacked those who gave the King evil advice. Hunton's logic was more rigorous than Parker's, and his premises better grounded in English law, but his view of the problem of responsible government was more old-fashioned. Parker saw that it was not a question of who obeyed the King, but of who advised him. The King, he argued, is always advised, either by the counsels of the Court or the counsels of Parliament; and it injured his reason no more to follow public than private advice. Furthermore, Parliament possessed the right to judge when the whispered counsels of courtiers seduced the King into policies dangerous to the Kingdom. 'The Parliament', he wrote, 'maintains its own counsel to be of honour and power above all other, and when it is unjustly rejected, by a King seduced and abused by private flatterers, to the danger of the

---

[1] Ferne, *Conscience Satisfied* (1643), p. 30; Sir Dudley Digges, *An Answer to a Printed Book Intituled Observations* (1642), p. 21.

[2] T. May, *A Discourse Concerning the Success of Former Parliaments*, in *Harleian Miscellany*, VI, 412; *The Case of Our Affairs* (1643), p. 3; Ferne, *Conscience Satisfied* (1643), p. 3; Digges, *Unlawfulness of Subjects Taking up Arms*, p. 72; *An Answer upon Some Late...Observations* (1642), p. 29; *A Review of the Observations* (1643), p. 21.

Commonwealth, it assumes a right to judge of that danger, and to prevent it.'[1]

It was easier to assume that the King always acted on the advice of someone than to discover who that person was. The writers who rushed to the defence of Parliament frankly confessed that they did not know who had given the King evil counsels.[2] The embarrassment of these men, their silence, their inability to name the authors of evil advice, demonstrated poignantly the importance to the House of Commons of publicity of advice. If the Commons could not find some means to focus responsibility on the counsellors most at fault, they could never justify impeaching them for giving the King wicked counsels. Archbishop Laud's trial in 1644 proved this unmistakably.

The trial of William Laud—undertaken to please the Scots, to justify the Puritans' attack on the Church, and to remove a man who blocked Parliament's nomination of ecclesiastical officials—raised the same questions concerning the responsibilities of ministers of state as had Strafford's trial. Could a minister evade responsibility for his conduct and counsels by pleading that the crimes charged against him had been done either with the concurrence of the whole Council, or on the advice of Learned Counsel, or by others, or in the course of giving counsel, or at the King's command, or with the consent of Parliament?

Upon no other plea did Archbishop Laud lean more heavily than the plea that the Privy Council, the Star Chamber, the High Commission, and Convocation had concurred in everything which he had done. He voiced this plea fifty times if he voiced it once. He even apologized for repeating it so often, but added, '...all acts done in the Star Chamber, at Council Table, High Commission, or Convocation are all joint acts of that body, in and by which they were done; and cannot by any law be singly put upon me, it being a known rule of the law, *Refertur ad universos quod publice fit per majorem partem*'. On another occasion he told the Court, 'The Lords

---

[1] Parker, *Observations*, in Haller, *Tracts*, II, 178–9, 191, 199–200. The Parliament assembled at Oxford had used the phrase 'to wound His Majesty through the sides of his Council'. This goaded Mr Strafford (*The Question Disputed*, 1645, p. 6) to reply, 'They argue that to say that His Majesty is seduced by evil counsel is a "wounding His Majesty through the sides of his Council"'; which exception of theirs must render him either infallible in judgment or so singular in wisdom, as to be above, or to stand in no need of, counsel...or must presume in him such a transcendency of goodness in not inclining to any evil motion as is not competent to a creature.'

[2] *Vox Populi*, and *A Vindication of the Parliament*, both in *Harleian Miscellany*, VII, 454, and VIII, 56.

of the Council are in the ancient Constitution of this Kingdom one body; and whatsoever the major part of them concludes is reputed the act of the whole, not any one man's. And this I must inculcate, because I see such public acts like to be heaped upon my particular.'[1]

The Commons countered Laud's plea of the collective responsibility of courts and councils with the claim that he was, as the 'most potent member' of these councils and courts, chiefly responsible for their acts. They variously described him as 'the chief instrument', 'the principal actor', 'the prime agent', and 'the most potent member'; and they charged him with 'overswaying' the Council, 'causing and contriving' Star Chamber sentences, and 'procuring' unlawful orders.[2] Incensed by these baseless surmises, Laud replied that the Commons insulted the honour of his colleagues. 'And whereas it has been urged that my power was such that I swayed the Lords to go my way, this cannot be said without laying an imputation upon the Lords, as if they could be so easily over-wrought by any one man, and that against law; which is a most unworthy aspersion upon men of honour.'[3] The confrontation was direct. A sense of equity and the law of the constitution proclaimed that responsibility was and ought to be collective. A sense of realism and the necessity of securing a conviction declared that it was and ought to be individual. The Commons had a patently weak case, but then they had the stronger battalions.

Indeed, the Commons more often ignored than sought to refute Laud's appeal to the law of the constitution. At no time, for example, did they seek to answer Laud's defence that he always sought the advice of Learned Counsel for the legality of his actions. He had not deprived Mr Rich of his living, sequestered Mr Ashton's lands, overthrown the feofees, torn down houses near St Paul's, or advised the collection of tonnage and poundage until the Lord Keeper or

[1] *H.M.C. House of Lords MSS*, n.s. XI, p. 374. This volume of the House of Lords MSS contains an account of Laud's trial by John Brown, Clerk of the House of Lords in 1644. For Laud's repeated invocation of the concurrence of others in his counsels see also Wharton, *The Troubles and Tryal of William Laud* (1695), I, 245, 415.

[2] *Ibid.* I, 437; *A Continuation of Certain Special and Remarkable Passages, No. 12* (1644), pp. 5–6; *Mercurius Civicus, No. 43* (1644); *Britain's Remembrancer, No. 1* (1644), p. 1; *The True Informer, No. 26* (1644), p. 187, and *No. 27*, p. 192. *The Parliament Scout, No. 39* (1644), argued thus: 'He who was chief cause of all innovations in Church and State has been the cause of all the miseries in England, Scotland, and Ireland. But my Lord of Canterbury, if any subject, was the chief cause. Ergo, the major none will deny. The assumption has and will be proved before the Lords, and that clearly. Then the conclusion must follow.'

[3] Wharton, *The Troubles and Tryal of William Laud*, I, 259.

the Attorney or the judges had declared these actions to be legal. As he told the Court while justifying the patent for applying High Commission fines to the repair of St Paul's, 'I...took the prime direction of the Kingdom for drawing the patent, the Lord Keeper Coventry, Mr Noy, and Sir Henry Martin. And therefore if anything be found against law in it, it cannot be imputed to me, who took all the care I could to have it beyond exception. And I marvel what security any man shall have that adventures upon any great and public work in this Kingdom, if such counsel cannot be trusted for drawing up of his warrant.'[1] The managers of the impeachment gave no answer to this plea. They simply demanded that he answer for his actions, the concurrence of Learned Counsel notwithstanding.

Laud steadfastly refused to accept responsibility for faults committed by others, even though they were his subordinates. The House of Commons were equally determined to make him answer for the crimes of others, particularly when they were his subordinates. The occasions when Laud spurned responsibility for the actions of his subordinates were many, but the question centred chiefly on his chaplains' licensing Arminian books and refusing to license Puritan ones. Laud argued that his chaplains and not he should answer for the licensing of books. 'Dr Heywood is to answer for licensing Sales's book.' 'Let Mr Weeks answer for licensing *The Lives of the Roman Emperors.*' 'Dr Bray is to answer for censuring Fox's *Martyrology* and licensing Dr Pocklington's treastise.' When the managers protested that these acts were the Archbishop's because his chaplains were his servants, Laud answered, 'No master is to answer for anything done by his servants that is criminal.' The managers replied that his chaplains were his deputies, 'for whom he must answer at his peril'. 'Had not Parliament in Edward I's reign', they asked, 'fined the Archbishop of York because his commissary wrongly excommunicated a man?' This threw Laud on the defensive for the first time. He sought to distinguish his case from the Archbishop of York's. 'The bishop and his official (call him Chancellor, Commissary, or what you will) make but one person in law; and therefore the act of the Commissary...is the act of the bishop in legal construction, and the bishop may be answerable for it. But the bishop and his chaplain are not one person in any construction of

[1] Wharton, *The Troubles and Tryal of William Laud*, I, 233, 248, 300, 372, 413–14, 417; *H.M.C. H. of L. MSS*, n.s. XI, 376, 397, 406, 441–2.

law.' Laud spoke too confidently when he used the phrase 'in any construction of law', for the House of Commons for one chose to construe the law to read that bishop and chaplain were one.[1]

Though in the matter of licensing Arminian books Laud refused to accept responsibility for the actions of those who served under him, when charged with promoting Arminian clergymen he pleaded obedience to those who presided over him. Accused of preferring clergymen such as Montagu and Manwaring, he replied that the Commons offered no proof but the docquet-book, 'which is a full proof who gave order for drawing the Bill at the Signet Office, but is no proof at all who procured the preferment'. He then accused the Duke of Buckingham of preferring Montagu, Lord Conway of preferring Manwaring, the Earl of Dorset of preferring Dr Corbett, the Earl of Danby of preferring Peter Heylyn, and the Earl of Portland of preferring Dr Lyndsell.[2] He had only acted ministerially in ordering the Signet Office to draw bills for their preferments. He made the same plea, of acting ministerially, to the gravest charge brought against him by the Commons, that he had altered the coronation oath. 'If anything be amiss therein,' he said, 'my predecessor gave the oath to the King, not I. I was merely ministerial, both in the preparation and at the Coronation itself...' The Commons did not take issue with this plea, for they too believed that it was a greater crime to advise than to execute a wrongful act. As William Prynne said, *Plus peccat auctor quam actor*. This principle became evident when Laud pleaded the King's commands to justify his actions.[3]

During his trial Laud not only pleaded the King's commands, but sought to shelter himself under his authority and to shift blame on to his shoulders. The King commanded him to consecrate Bishop Manwaring, to print the *Book of Sports*, to punish Mr Wickins for refusing an *ex officio* oath, and to answer the Commons' Remonstrance in 1628. The King had granted him a commission under the Great Seal to demolish houses near St Paul's, to spend the revenue from High Commission fines on the repair of St Paul's, and to alter the statutes of cathedral chapters. The King himself refused to

[1] *H.M.C. H. of L. MSS*, n.s. XI, 427, 436; William Prynne, *Canterburies Doom* (1646), p. 517; Wharton, *The Troubles and Tryal of William Laud*, I, 337.
[2] *Ibid*. I, 239, 356, 366, 367; *H.M.C. H. of L. MSS*, n.s. XI, 368, 430–1, 438–9.
[3] *Ibid*. XI, 413, 416; Prynne, *Canterburies Doom*, p. 539; Wharton, *The Troubles and Tryal of William Laud*, I, 319.

pardon John Bastwick, preferred Richard Montagu to a bishopric, and published the Proclamation forbidding public controversy in the Church. To these pleas the managers of the impeachment replied that it was against the law to lay anything on the King, and that Laud ought to have opposed Montagu's preferment and withstood Manwaring's consecration.[1] Yet the managers did not concern themselves with the obligation of a minister to refuse obedience to illegal commands. Not once during the trial did they pronounce the maxim that the King can do no wrong. Instead they accused Laud of procuring and advising those commands and commissions which he pleaded in his defence. He had procured the letter commanding Wickins's condemnation and the warrant ordering the publication of the *Book of Sports*. He had advised the preferment of Montagu and Manwaring. He had contrived the Proclamation against public controversy in the Church. Laud denied these accusations and derided the proofs upon which they were based. 'A report of a report' is no legal proof. 'It is not proved I had any hand in it.' 'All this proof is a single hearsay.' ' "As he verily believes" is no proof.' 'Inferences are no sworn proof.' The managers, visibly embarrassed by the flimsiness of their proofs, promised to produce 'authentic testimony', but never did. They could not pierce the veil of secrecy that surrounded Charles's counsels. Laud's trial once more revealed the imperative need for the fullest publicity of advice if Parliament ever hoped to make counsellors responsible to it.[2]

By turning from the legal maxim that the King can do no wrong to the political principle that he is always advised, the Commons raised again the question of a councillor's duties and immunities. Strafford had eloquently defended the councillor's duty to speak his conscience freely and his right to suffer no harm for doing so. Archbishop Laud echoed these sentiments. It was his duty to advise the King that the Bishop of Gloucester had not taken the oath contained in the Canons of 1640. If he erred in advising the publication of Robert Sibthorpe's sermon favouring the Loan, yet he erred before Parliament had pronounced against the Loan. If he counselled the

[1] Wharton, *The Troubles and Tryal of William Laud*, I, 239, 246, 302, 342, 349, 356, 406; *Mercurius Civicus*, *No. 43*, p. 439; Prynne, *Canterburies Doom*, pp. 508, 531; *H.M.C. H. of L. MSS*, n.s. XI, 368, 374, 382, 394–5, 408, 422, 430.

[2] *Ibid.* XI, 387, 421, 454–5; *A Continuation of Certain Special and Remarkable Passages*, *No. 12*, p. 5; Prynne, *Canterburies Doom*, pp. 509, 511, 530–1; Wharton, *The Troubles and Tryal of William Laud*, I, 238, 246, 265, 342, 349, 352, 356, 366.

King to suppress the feoffments, he did so, not maliciously, as the impeachment charged, but conscientiously, for the good of the Church. In writing the Proclamation calling in the Commons' Remonstrance, he 'did not err willingly against the Petitition of Right'. In 1628 he recorded, at the King's command, and as a sworn councillor, his hopes and fears of a new Parliament, and he recorded them honestly, lest he perjure himself. He set forth the duties of a councillor most explicitly when justifying the words he spoke at the fatal Council of 5 May 1640. 'For the words unto the King, touching his being absolved from the rules of government, they contained only matter of opinion, and opinion delivered at the Council Table, where all had liberty to speak their own sense... which if it were erroneous and contrary to the sense of others [that were no crime]. He hoped that no man should justly be condemned of treason, for showing himself no wiser than God had made him.' He then admonished the Lords 'seriously to consider what a way was chalked out to ruin them, both in their lives and estates, if for every opinion given in Council...they, who are born to wield the great affairs of the Kingdom, should be arraigned or sentenced as traitors'.[1]

The clearer the Commons chalked out the way to ruin, the more distinctly they delineated the path to safety, which was to plead Parliament's authority or approval for what one had done. Laud was not above taking this path. He never actually pleaded the approval of Parliament, since his ecclesiastical policies had been too unpopular to allow that, but twice he pleaded (to the same charge) that an earlier Parliament had acquitted him of a crime now charged against him. In March he told the Court, 'I was acquitted in open Parliament of licensing the printing of Manwaring's sermons.' In July he reminded his judges again that in 1628, on 14 June, the Commons had branded him an evil counsellor in their remonstrance, 'but the very same day he clearly acquitted himself in open Parliament of all the aspersions cast upon him about Dr Manwaring's sermons'.[2] That this plea benefited Laud is doubtful; certainly it concerned a trivial charge. This cannot be said of his plea that he had parliamentary authority for all that he had done

---

[1] *H.M.C. H. of L. MSS*, n.s. XI, 431, 456–7; Wharton, *The Troubles and Tryal of William Laud*, I, 282–3, 356, 372, 404, 415.

[2] *Ibid.* I, 238, 405; *H.M.C. H. of L. MSS*, n.s. XI, 368.

in Convocation and High Commission. Nothing paralysed the prosecution more than the undeniable fact that statutes passed in the reigns of Henry VIII and Elizabeth gave to Convocation and to the Court of High Commission powers to legislate for, and to enforce discipline in, the Church. Mr John Maynard was so powerless to deny this, that he could only accuse Laud of exercising these powers in a more high-handed fashion than his predecessors.[1]

The law was Archbishop Laud's best armour against his adversaries. The public conduct of Laud may have been unpopular, but it had never been illegal, least of all had it been treasonous. He told the court in March that he had done nothing that his predecessors had not done in the reigns of King James and Queen Elizabeth, nor, he continued, had a single witness yet charged him with overthrowing the laws or introducing arbitrary government. The Commons, painfully aware of this, thereupon charged him with a particular, known treason, with seeking to introduce popery into England; but the witnesses that they produced to substantiate the charge were a pathetic lot. 'A pack of such witnesses', said Laud, 'as were never produced against any man of my place and calling, messengers and pursuivants, and such as have shifted their religion to and fro again, pillory-men and bawds, and these the men that must prove my correspondence with priests.' As in Strafford's trial, so in Laud's, the prosecution could neither prove that he had committed the undoubted treasons contained in the charge, nor demonstrate that the acts he had undoubtedly committed were in any way treasonous. The Commons admitted their failure by deserting their impeachment and going by way of an Attainder.[2]

The Attainder accused Laud, as had the impeachment, of endeavouring to subvert the fundamental laws of England, the true Protestant religion, and the privileges of Parliament. The few remaining peers in the House of Lords readily admitted that the Commons had proved the facts—had demonstrated that Laud sought to subvert the laws, religion, and Parliament of England—but they questioned whether such an endeavour was treason in English law. Laud's legal counsel argued before them that 25 Edward III had abolished all Common Law treasons, that the same

[1] *H.M.C. H. of L. MSS*, n.s. xi, 398; Wharton, *The Troubles and Tryal of William Laud*, I, 299; *The True Informer*, No. 27, p. 195.

[2] *Ibid.* p. 191; *H.M.C. H. of L. MSS*, n.s. xi, 392; Wharton, *The Troubles and Tryal of William Laud*, I, 271, 417.

statute had no meaning if Parliament could construe any and every crime to fall under one of the seven treasons listed in it, and that the declaratory power contained in the statute extended only to declaring felonies, not misdemeanours, to be treasons. In the whole of the seventeenth century no counsel made a more destructive attack on the validity of Common Law, constructive, and declaratory treasons than did the lawyers assisting Laud, the most influential of whom was the young Matthew Hale. Yet five of the nine Lords who attended the House in January 1645 found it possible to interpret the law differently from these lawyers, and to pass an Attainder condemning Laud to death. The House of Commons demanded it, the London mob clamoured for it, and the Lords had not the conviction to stand against it.[1] Laud's Attainder was a vindictive, unnecessary, and cruel act, but his judicial murder discredited only Acts of Attainder, not impeachments. His long trial on an impeachment publicized his responsibility for the counsels he gave the King and the obedience he yielded him. His undeserved death merely proclaimed the malice of his enemies.

No single event in the seventeenth century, not Strafford's trial, not Laud's impeachment, did more to promote ministerial responsibility than the execution of Charles I on 30 January 1649. The shock of that day's deed made sacred the maxim that the King can do no wrong. The impiety of laying hands on the King's person transformed into a badge of respectability a maxim that had once been a trumpet of sedition.

Parliament, purged and cowed by the army, resolved to execute Charles because he would not surrender power and live out his life as a constitutional monarch. First at Oxford, then at Uxbridge, again at Newcastle, and finally at the Isle of Wight, he refused to surrender permanent control over the Church, the Militia, and the sceptre. Not only did he refuse to yield these to Parliament permanently, but he insisted on assuming responsibility for all that had been done of late years in his name. He would neither yield up his servants to the anger of Parliament, nor cease heeding the advice

---

[1] Wharton, *The Troubles and Tryal of William Laud*, I, 422–32, 442; *H.M.C. H. of L. MSS*, n.s. XI, 464–6; *L.J.* VII, 102, 125. Sabran, the French ambassador, wrote (Fr. Trans. 9/19 Jan. 1645), 'only nine of the twenty Lords still in the House chose to attend, five of whom consented to his death, largely from compliance in that which they regarded with indifference and from a knowledge that they were powerless to do otherwise'.

of counsellors whom it condemned, nor give up the right to act according to his own reason. Bereft finally of all counsellors, he continued to resist Parliament's demands, though aware that it might cost him his life.¹ His own stubborn assumption of responsibility finally drove his opponents to concede it to him. In 1643 Henry Parker observed, 'The law says the King can do no wrong, and out of its civility it imputes all miscarriages in government to inferior agents; but policy teaches us that in nature he is strangely blameable, and deeply chargeable, when he makes an ill choice of inferior agents.' John Wildman concluded that the maxim that the King can do no wrong is tantamount to a declaration that he may do as he wishes, 'that the laws are not the rules of his actions'. Richard Overton came to a similar conclusion, and proclaimed it to Parliament. 'You maintain "the King can do no wrong", and apply all his oppressions to "evil counsellors", begging and intreating him in such submissive language to return to his Kingly office...No, it is high time we be plain with you...we do expect according to reason that you should ...declare and set forth King Charles his wickedness openly before the world...' This demand was the voice of armed Puritanism, and it led, by way of Windsor Prayer Meetings and Pride's Purge, to the execution of the King. The wrath of Puritans who feared no man because they feared God so greatly swept to his death a King who feared no fate more than to be deprived of responsibility for the good government of his realm.²

From the day in February 1648 when Parliament declared its resolve to send no more addresses to the King, the royalist pamphleteers took up the refrain that had hitherto been the preserve of the parliamentarians. George Bate, Edward Bagshaw, Edward Hyde, and the anonymous author of *The Kingdom's Brief Answer*, royalists all, insisted that Parliament could not call Charles to account because by the law of the land the King can do no wrong. Majesty itself sanctioned the maxim on 22 January 1649. On that day Charles I submitted in his defence that it was a maxim of English

¹ Charles allegedly wrote, shortly after the Battle of Naseby (*Eikon Basilike*, 1880, p. 158), 'It is probable some men will now look upon me as my own counsellor, and having none else to quarrel with under that notion, they will hereafter confine their anger to myself.'

² H. Parker, *The Oath of Pacification* (1643), pp. 11–12; John Wildman, *Putney Projects*, p. 14; R. Overton, *A Remonstrance of Many Thousand Citizens* (in Haller, *Tracts*, III, 355–6). The authors of *King Charles His Case* (1649), p. 13, *The Second Part of Vox Populi* (1642), and *Plain English* (1643) likewise rejected the maxim that the King can do no wrong.

law that the King can do no wrong. At the very moment when Parliament deserted a maxim it had long maintained, a King who had persistently opposed it embraced it.[1]

Before a dozen years had elapsed, however, the whole English nation, King and Parliament alike, espoused the maxim. Their spokesman was Sir Orlando Bridgman, who gave the summation for the prosecution at the trial of the regicides in 1660. He told the Court, 'The law in all cases preserves the person of the King to be untouched: but what is done by his ministers unlawfully there is a remedy against his ministers for it.'[2]

The remedy of which Bridgman spoke was an impeachment, and by 1660 impeachments had become habitual, respectable, and unexceptionable. The Long Parliament, in the course of its wayward career, impeached 98 persons; the army dissolved the third Protectorate Parliament in 1659 because it threatened to impeach its officers; and Sir Edward Hyde was busy promoting the impeachment of John Thurloe in the revived Long Parliament.[3] Acts of Attainder went out of fashion in 1660, but impeachments did not. As Sir Roger L'Estrange observed in 1660: 'We have done, I hope, with that reason of state which was wont to fill all our prisons, without an impeachment, and which professed the punishing of men for their supposed principles, without anything proved...against them.' But neither L'Estrange nor any other royalist in 1660 questioned

[1] George Bate, *The Regal Apology or, The Declaration of the Commons, Canvassed* (1648), p. 9; George Bate, *Elenchus Motuum* (1660), p. 5; Edward Bagshaw, *The Rights of the Crown* (1660), p. 106; Edward Hyde, *A Full Answer to an Infamous and Trayterous Pamphlet Entituled,* 'A Declaration of the Commons of England in Parliament Assembled' (1648), pp. 19–20; *The Kingdom's Brief Answer, to the Late Declaration of the House of Commons* (1648), p. 15; J. Nalson, *A True Copy of the Journal of the High Court of Justice* (1648), pp. 47–8. Though Bate's *Elenchus Motuum* and Bagshaw's *The Rights of the Crown* were published in 1660, both men wrote their works on the eve of the King's execution.

[2] T. B. Howell, *State Trials* (1809–28), v, 1228. King and Parliament, however, condemned the doctrine of the Despensers, declaring it treason to maintain that anyone can wage war against the person of the King in the name of his authority (Clarendon, *Life*, II, 260).

[3] *C.S.P. Ven.* XXXII, 13; *Cl. St. Pap.* III, 410, 428, 436; Clarendon MSS 72, f. 157. The Long Parliament impeached Strafford, Radcliffe, Laud, Finch, and Windebank in 1640; the 6 Ship Money Judges, the 13 Bishops who passed the Canons, the 12 Bishops who questioned the authority of Parliament, 8 persons involved in the Army Plot, Dr Cosin, and Inigo Jones in 1641; 9 lords who refused to attend Parliament, 22 persons who raised forces against Parliament, Herbert, Digby, and Gardiner in 1642; the Queen in 1643; the Marquis of Ormond in 1644; the Lord Mayor and 5 Aldermen in 1647; Maynard and 7 peers in 1648; and Lord Howard of Escrick in 1651. The last Protectorate Parliament entertained articles of impeachment against Sir William Petty (Clerk of the Council in Ireland) and resolved to impeach Major-General Boteler.

The Separation of Powers

the reason of law which permitted the Commons to impeach and the Lords to try criminal ministers of state.[1]

Parliamentary undertakings did not enjoy in 1660 the respectability that impeachments did. Yet neither did men condemn them as totally as they did in 1641. This was true both of courtiers, who regarded parliamentary undertakings as a stratagem for winning men by the offer of place, and of parliamentarians, who sought to use their influence in Parliament to gain office at Court. Even Charles I, before his death, grew less inflexible in his hostility to such undertakings. In 1644 he gave Secretary Nicholas, who was negotiating with representatives of Parliament at Uxbridge, power to reward particular persons for services rendered him, 'not sparing to engage for places'. In 1646, when his fortunes were yet lower, he offered places to Parliament men on condition they demonstrate their inclination to peace.[2] The times, however, were not propitious for such cynical bargains, and when they finally became so again Charles was dead and his son reigned in his place. What did his son think of the stratagem of winning men by the bestowal of office? Many men must have wondered what Charles II thought of it. Three men did not hesitate to tell him what his thoughts ought to be.

The first of these was the ageing Marquis of Newcastle, brooding over past misfortunes in his abbey at Welbeck. In 1658 he wrote a 'Treatise on Government' for Charles II. In this treatise he condemned many errors committed by Charles's father and grandfather, but no error did he denounce more passionately than the stratagem of seeking to win over Parliament men by the offer of place.

Now, Sir, with Your Majesty's favour, I will speak of the greatest error of state that ever was committed in these two last reigns—and that is, they ever rewarded their enemies, and neglected their friends...This was but a weak policy to take off enemies, nay they would say, 'He is a shrewd man, we must please him, reward him, make him a Lord, give him an office,' but for a friend, 'He is an honest man, give him nothing, he'll do us no hurt'...What man almost has been raised these two reigns that

[1] L'Estrange, *An Eccho to the Plea for Limited Monarchy* (1660), p. 6. Other pamphlets approving impeachments were *England's Monarchy Asserted* (1660), p. 7; *A Full Declaration of the True State of the Secluded Members* (1660), p. 2; and *A Serious Admonition* (1660), p. 35. Though they did not deny that the Commons had the right to impeach the King's ministers, George Searle (*The Dignity of Kingship*, 1660, p. 32) and the author of *An Appeal in the Case* (1660), p. 76, argued that impeachments were really only a screen for attacking the King himself.

[2] *The Works of King Charles* (1735), p. 197; J. Bruce (ed.), *Charles I in 1646* (Camden Soc. LXIII), p. 11.

134

did not oppose the King and the state, nay, they had no other way to raise themselves, they thought, and therefore they plied it, which was the ruin of our Kingdom...This was so much practised, as Henry Martin ...said, 'He would be the greatest man in England with the King'. One asked him how. He answered, 'because he would do him all the mischief he could'...This made Parliaments...refractory to His Majesty, everyone opposing, thinking to be raised...this heated and over-heated every Parliament, as much, if not more, than anything else...The remedy is very easy, reward your friends and punish your enemies...[1]

Matters seemed very different to General Monck, faced with the exigencies of the present, not the mistakes of the past. Badgered by the Presbyterian party, hounded by his Presbyterian wife, and besieged by her brother Dr Clarges, he handed Charles II at Canterbury a long list of men whom he recommended as fit councillors, they being 'most grateful to the people'. Later asked how he dared to recommend notorious Presbyterians and men of faction to the King, he answered that he knew they were not His Majesty's friends, yet the King's 'service would be more advanced by admitting them, than by leaving them out'.[2]

Alan Broderick, one of Edward Hyde's many agents in London, advised neither the policy recommended by Newcastle nor that offered by Monck. He proposed a third course, which was to hold out the hope of preferment as long as possible by leaving vacant the great offices of state. As he wrote from London in May 1660, '...it is the humble desire of...His Majesty's best subjects that His Majesty would only give them all encouragement to expect honours and preferment, but not immediately confer either: the hope being of infinitely more use as affairs stand than the grant.' Edward Hyde and the King acted on this advice for as long as possible, but, once Charles had arrived in London, he could delay no longer. He then named men to office, but in selecting them he neither heeded Newcastle's warning nor followed Monck's advice, but steered a middle course. He named the Earl of Manchester, a leading Presbyterian, his Lord Chamberlain, in order to please

[1] S. A. Strong (ed.), *A Catalogue of Letters and Other Historical Documents Exhibited in the Library at Welbeck* (1903), p. 217. Sir Edward Walker, Secretary of War to Charles I and Clerk of the Council to Charles II, concurred with Newcastle's diagnosis of the ills besetting the monarchy. In his *Historical Discourses* (1705), p. 326, he gives five reasons for 'the usurpation of the House of Commons in our time'. The fifth is, 'The taking off by advancement of such factious persons as opposed the King in Parliament.'

[2] Clarendon, *Life*, II, pp. 9–12.

the Suffolk House cabal, but he did not make him Lord Treasurer or Lord Chancellor, positions he coveted. He appointed another Presbyterian, Lord Robartes, to the Privy Seal, because Robartes had many followers and could prove useful in Council and Parliament. Yet he made the Earl of Southampton, an irreproachable royalist and friend of Hyde's, Lord Treasurer. By October this balancing act had discontented the Presbyterian party and enraged the Cavaliers. Yet their discontent and rage only demonstrated how far removed were the Marquis of Newcastle's principles from the exigencies of the times. In 1660 no King could afford to ignore the ambitions of Parliament men for office and preferment.[1]

The reverse side of the coin was an undertaking by the leaders of the two Houses to manage the King's business in Parliament in return for office. The heir to this tradition in 1660 was the Presbyterian party, or, as they were then called, the Suffolk House cabal. As early as 1650 the Presbyterian exiles in Holland offered to support Charles in a future Parliament if he admitted the Duke of Richmond, the Marquis of Hertford, Denzil Holles, and others to his Council. Secretary Nicholas believed this 'a reasonable desire', but when the Presbyterians offered a similar undertaking in 1660, neither Nicholas nor Hyde nor Charles regarded it as the least bit reasonable. This later undertaking, reported on 19 April by Lord Mordaunt, 'was first laid by Northumberland, St John, Mr Pierrepont, and Lord Manchester, but Mr Holles is come in for Secretary, Sir Gilbert Gerard for Treasurer of the Navy; the two Earls [Manchester and Northumberland] for Admiral and Treasurer; Mr Pierrepont for Privy Seal, and Lewis for President of Wales.' Bordeaux, the French ambassador, got wind of the undertaking, and wrote home that the chief persons in the House of Lords and in the present government propose limitations on the King, but only in order to draw from His Majesty particular advantages in their favour. These particular advantages, however, they never gained, for they lost control of Parliament, the only source of their power. As Bordeaux reported on 1 May, 'There are Presbyterians who desire the Isle of Wight conditions, or at least to secure particular advantages for themselves in return for not insisting on them, and the older Lords are suspected of having divided up the principal offices among themselves, but, the General having brought in the younger Lords [those

[1] Clarendon MSS 72, ff. 157, 280; Clarendon, *Life*, II, 47, 194–5.

who inherited their titles since 1642], their measures are broken.' The Commons also dealt a blow to the proposed undertaking by voting not to entrust to the Earl of Manchester the Great Seal that was in their custody. A party that could persuade neither the Lords nor the Commons to support its designs was in no position to bargain with the King for office.[1]

The real architects of the Restoration Settlement were Edward Hyde and his friends, not the Earl of Manchester and his. As a consequence, the Privy Council, and not Parliament, emerged as the principal, formal check on the King's use of his executive power. Through the long night of the Interregnum Edward Hyde, Sir Edward Nicholas, and Lord Hatton had kept alive this ideal of a King acting on the advice of sworn councillors whom he chose but in whom the nation could confide. Hyde constantly lamented the King's willingness to follow the advice of unsworn councillors, foreign ambassadors, court minions, and royal favourites. Experience taught him the necessity of a small council to advise the King in affairs of great secrecy, but nothing could persuade him to accept the role of a Prime Minister, even though the Duke of Ormond pressed it on him. Nor would he admit the necessity of unanimity in the Council or countenance the practice of resigning if one's advice were refused. His two friends, Nicholas and Hatton, doubted his wisdom in dismissing the need for unanimity in the Council, but in every other respect they subscribed to the ideal of government by a Privy Council. Lord Hatton in 1650 celebrated it in these words, 'I shall never wish the King should impart his secrets, or seek advices to ground resolutions upon, unto or from any but a well chosen, competent number of wise and discreet, but above all religious and faithful, sworn councillors.' A year later Nicholas wrote:

As I am sure our late master (now with God) lost all by despising of councils and by undervaluing of councillors, so Queen Elizabeth kept up her honour and esteem by the value she set on councils and on her sworn councillors. And until the King shall have a well-composed council sworn of honest and thoroughly loyal men that will trust one another, and in whom honest men will and may confide, and that shall have more reputation with the King and respect from his courtiers than in the time

---

[1] *C.S.P. Dom. 1650*, pp. 25–6; *Cl. St. Pap.* iii, 730; Fr. Trans. 23 Apr. 13 May and 1/11 May 1660; Clarendon MSS 72, ff. 17, 180v.

of the late King of blessed memory, I cannot hope that His Majesty's affairs will prosper or that he will have that honour or reverence either at home or abroad that is due to His Majesty.[1]

Englishmen in 1660 did not restore government by King and Council because Hyde, Nicholas, and Hatton favoured it. They restored it because it was traditional. No pamphlet in 1660 advocated Divine Right Monarchy, very few favoured the principle of Popular Sovereignty, but a great host of them urged the restoration of the ancient, regal government of the realm, and the Privy Council was an integral part of that government. In fact, the return to conciliar government began before the restoration of the King. The Instrument of Government in 1654 created a Council on whose advice the Lord Protector must act. The Humble Petition and Advice in 1657 transformed this Council into a body more closely resembling the traditional Privy Council. Where the Instrument embodied the extreme position of the Second of the Nineteen Propositions, the Petition expressed the moderate position advocated by Edward Hyde. The Second of the Nineteen Propositions demanded that the King always act on the advice of the Council. Hyde believed that the King should always ask, but need not always act on, the advice of the Council. For a brief moment in 1657 it seemed as if the House would place a coercive clause in the Humble Petition and Advice, a clause that would read, 'And also, that your Highness will be pleased to exercise your government over these nations, by the advice of your Council, and not otherwise.' But on second thought they voted to omit the last three words, 'and not otherwise'. The Protector should seek the advice of the Council, but he might act without or against such advice. This formula quite fairly expressed the sentiments of Englishmen three years later, when they restored the monarchy. The King should seek the advice of his Privy Council, but (in the words of Charles I) he should regard their 'advice, as advice, not commands'.[2]

Edward Hyde's Privy Council scheme always had about it a hollow ring. As E. I. Carlyle writes, 'Clarendon thought his concept of the Privy Council traditional, but it was really ideal. No such Privy Council had ever existed. The councils of Henry VIII and

---

[1] Clarendon, *History*, III, 224–7. Clarendon, *Life*, I, 189; II, 77, 88–9; III, 676. *Cl. St. Pap.* II, 342, 351; III, 184. *Nicholas Papers*, I, 161–2, 291, 305.
[2] Gardiner, *Const. Doc. of the Puritan Rev.* pp. 314, 340; *C.J.* VII, 513.

Elizabeth were rather a consultative than executive body and were dependent on the personal will of the monarch.' Not only had no such Privy Council ever existed, but the reigning monarch in 1660 had no intention that it ever should. In public Charles II subscribed to the pieties that lay close to Edward Hyde's heart. In 1650 he told Nicholas, 'We are also resolved principally to make use of, and rely on, the faithful advice of our sworn Privy Council in the management and determination of our important affairs.' And in 1661 he told Parliament, 'I never did nor ever will resolve anything of public importance' without first hearing the advice of my Privy Council. But in fact he listened to private counsels constantly, permitted courtiers to set aside decisions reached at the Council table, disclosed secrets to those not sworn to keep them, laughed at libels whispered against his councillors, and showed not the least inclination to play the role Hyde expected of him. Hyde himself could hardly have failed to notice these evasions, but he obstinately refused to admit their existence, that is until it was too late, and he had been driven into exile in 1667. He then wrote, 'It cannot be denied that the King was too irresolute, and apt to be shaken in those counsels which with the greatest deliberations he had concluded, by too easily permitting, or at least not restraining, any men who waited upon him, or were present with him in his recesses, to examine and censure what was resolved; an infirmity that brought him many troubles, and exposed his ministers to ruin.'[1]

The English constitution in 1660 lay in a state of unresolved equilibrium between two worlds. Too much had changed in sixty years to make Tudor conciliar government workable; not enough had changed to cause men to accept the parliamentary nomination of the King's ministers. In the year of the Restoration men distrusted the formal election of the King's servants in Parliament as much as they had in 1641, perhaps even more, since they now associated it with regicide Parliaments and republican experiments. At the same time, however, they believed rather more strongly than before that the King should heed Parliament's wishes in appointing and dismissing his ministers. Parliament should not tell the King whom he should employ, but neither should the King employ those hateful to

[1] E. I. Carlyle, 'Clarendon and the Privy Council', *E.H.R.* xxvii, 251. Bray, *Evelyn's Memoirs*, v, 180. S.P.D. 29/24:89. *Nicholas Papers*, i, 173; iii, 31–2. *L.J.* xi, 241. Clarendon, *Life*, ii, 300.

Parliament. Two events in the 1640's popularized the belief that Parliament had an interest in whom the King employed. These were the public debate provoked by the publication of the Nineteen Propositions and the publicity surrounding the peace negotiations in 1648 on the Isle of Wight.

Those who rushed into print in the 1640's to defend Parliament did not rush to the defence of the parliamentary nomination of the King's ministers. Instead they apologized for 'so high a request', admitted that it seemed 'an unreasonable thing', confessed that it appeared to 'deprive the King of the office of reason', and argued that Parliament had demanded it only after the King had raised an army at York.[1] But though they were reluctant to defend Parliament's right to name the King's councillors for him, they were quick to defend Parliament's right to inform the King who were his evil counsellors. Henry Parker in 1643 put the case this way:

We have as much interest in the King's friends and councillors as we have in our laws, liberties, lives, anything; for we know we can enjoy nothing if the King shall own those for his friends whom we know to be our enemies, and account those as good counsellors, whom we know to be traitors against the state. That Prince that will be arbitrary, and rely upon his own mere opinion and discretion in the employment of councillors and ministers of state, having no regard to public approbation therein, is as injurious altogether as he that will admit of no other law, judge, or rule in property and liberty, but his own breast only.

Parker argued from the needs of the present moment. Sir Roger Twysden, the eminent antiquary and Kentish politician, spoke with the voice of ancient precedent. 'Kings are seldom bad,' he wrote, 'if there can be means found they have no ill men about them; and therefore this Commonwealth has many times taken the freedom to desire His Majesty would remove such as they misliked.' He then related the memorable answer that Henry IV gave to the Commons when they asked that he remove four of his servants from Court. The King replied that, though he knew nothing specially charged against them, yet he would order them from Court, 'being confident that the Lords and Commons would not ordain what was not for the good of his kingdom'. The King then added that he would expel

---

[1] *A Discourse Upon the Question in Debate Between King and Parliament* (1642), p. 9; *Plain English* (1643), p. 10; J.M., *A Reply to the Answer to a Printed Book Intituled Observations* (1643), p. 44; *Scripture and Reason* (1643), p. 56.

from Court anyone else who should fall 'into the hate or indignation of his people'.[1]

In the public debates provoked by the publication of the Nineteen Propositions one can discern three positions. Sir Dudley Digges defended the royalist position that Parliament had no right to remove any man from the King unless it could prove particular charges against him. Henry Parker defended the moderate position that the King should dismiss those ministers whom Parliament declared to be odious to the people. John Pym, loyal to the last to the Nineteen Propositions, defended the radical position in a treatise entitled, *The Parliament's Right to Elect Privy Councellors, Great Officers, and Judges*.[2] Digges spoke for a principle whose glory lay in the past, Parker for a doctrine that had the whole future ahead of it, but Pym's proposal had neither a glorious past nor a hopeful future. It had only an evanescent triumph in the autumn of 1648, when a Presbyterian Parliament and an Anglican King agreed to the parliamentary nomination of ministers of state for twenty years. The history of this compromise, however, reveals its essential insincerity and its enforced nature.

From 1641 until 1648 Parliament's willingness to press for the parliamentary nomination of ministers of state rose and fell with its military fortunes. The King's determination to refuse its demands likewise rose and fell with the fortune of his arms. At the Treaty of Oxford in March 1643, four months after royalist victories at Edgehill and Banbury, Parliament dared not even mention the parliamentary nomination of ministers of state. At the Treaty of Uxbridge in 1645, a year after the parliamentary triumph at Marston Moor, Parliament revived the demand that it had neglected at Oxford. But Charles I still had an army in the field, and so refused to listen to any such proposal. When Parliament next demanded the parliamentary nomination of ministers of state, the Scots held Charles a prisoner at Newcastle. He was now in no position to give a peremptory refusal; yet his high hopes of dividing the English from the Scots led him to request a personal treaty to discuss the demand.

---

[1] H. Parker, *The Contra-Replicant* (1643), pp. 26–7; Sir Roger Twysden, *Certain Considerations upon the Government of England* (Camden Soc. XLV), p. 112. Sir Roger Twysden did not publish his treatise during his lifetime, but as an eminent literary figure and outspoken politician his views were probably well known.

[2] Digges, *Unlawfulness of Subjects Taking up Arms*, pp. 165–6. Pym's treatise is cited and its arguments are summarized and answered in *The Royalist Defence* (1648), p. 65. No copy of Pym's treatise seems to have survived; it may never have existed.

This personal treaty with the English Parliament never took place. Instead civil war broke out again, Cromwell destroyed the Scottish army at Preston, and Charles's hopes lay broken. When Parliament in the autumn of 1648 presented Charles, now on the Isle of Wight, with yet another demand for the parliamentary nomination of his ministers, he could no longer refuse. He conceded Parliament's demand for ten years. Parliament refused the concession. He offered it for twenty years. Parliament, now frightened by the army and desperately in need of an accommodation with the King, accepted.[1] After years of civil war, after more years of intrigue and bargaining, both King and Parliament subscribed to the principles of the Nineteen Propositions, principles which henceforth bore the name 'the Isle of Wight conditions'. Yet this posthumous triumph of Pym's principles was a mockery, for the King who agreed to them languished in prison and the Parliament that demanded them no longer represented the nation. What a desperate Parliament and a defeated King wished in 1648 is of no great importance in the history of responsible government; what a free Parliament and a restored King desired in 1660 is of far greater moment.

During the spring of 1660 it became increasingly clear to most men that Parliament would restore Charles II. But would it restore him on conditions, such as those presented to his father at the Isle of Wight, or would it impose no conditions on him, so that he might be a Free Monarch, in the fashion praised by his grandfather? The Presbyterians, whether of the rigid kind like Lord Saye and Lord Robartes, or of the moderate kind like the Earl of Manchester and the Earl of Northumberland, urged that the Isle of Wight conditions be made the basis of Charles's restoration. In April they met regularly at Suffolk House to define their demands and to plan their strategy. Northumberland and Manchester won over to their party Lord Fairfax, Denzil Holles, William Lewis, William Pierrepont, Sir Gilbert Gerard, and Sir Anthony Cooper. At their second meeting they resolved that Charles II should sign all the Articles of the Treaty of the Isle of Wight, except the Preface. Northumberland insisted particularly that Parliament should dispose of all places of trust, since the people could not otherwise be safe. At the same meeting this cabal mapped out its strategy. They would exclude

[1] Gardiner, *Const. Doc. of the Puritan Rev.* pp. 182–6, 201–2, 220–1, 231; Rushworth, *Historical Collections*, v, 884; *C.J.* vi, 67, 78; *L.J.* x, 574; *C.S.P. Ven.* xxviii, 82.

from the House of Lords any who had fought for, or whose fathers had fought for, the King; and they would exclude from the House of Commons any royalists whom the people might be so foolhardy as to elect. General Monck promised that he would use the army to support these plans.[1]

The design of the Suffolk House cabal failed miserably. Edward Hyde's apprehension of the danger, General Monck's failure to keep his promise, and the English people's opposition frustrated their designs. The King's camp had never hesitated to spurn the Isle of Wight conditions. Edward Hyde regarded them as tantamount to republicanism, and his many correspondents in London, Dr Morley, Lord Mordaunt, Hartgill Baron, John Shaw, and Henry Coventry, worked ceaselessly to prevent their adoption. On one occasion the Presbyterians thought to use their power in the Council of State to force these conditions on the King, but the knowledge that Charles II opposed any conditions whatsoever paralysed their will, and they decided to leave the question to Parliament. Parliament met on 25 April 1660 and the Presbyterians at once sought to exclude the royalist peers from the House of Lords and Cavaliers from the House of Commons. They held to this strategy for two days; then General Monck deserted them, permitting the royalist peers and the Cavaliers elected to the Commons to take their seats. The enraged Presbyterians accused Monck of having plotted this act of treachery, but Monck more likely acted as he did because he saw that he could not do otherwise without precipitating civil war. For not only had the boroughs and shires of England sent royalists to Parliament, they had also deliberately refused to send anyone who wished to place conditions on the King. In many places the electors turned against the principal men of the shire because they favoured conditions. In Surrey the royalists cried out, 'No Rumper, No Presbyterian that will put bad conditions on the King.' The electors of Surrey, and of all England, heeded the cry, and returned men determined to re-establish the ancient monarchy, with no new conditions placed on the King. 'To allow Cavaliers to sit in the Commons and all peers

---

[1] *Cl. St. Pap.* III, 391, 729–30; Clarendon MSS 71, f. 295; Clarendon MSS 72, f. 277; M. Guizot, *Monk* (Bruxelles, 1851), pp. 282, 287. Henry Coventry wrote to Edward Hyde (Clarendon MSS 72, f. 180), 'Sir John Holland told me some days since that the cabal resolved to make very hard propositions, vizt. that the King should recall all his father's Declarations against the Houses, those of the Houses to remain in full power; no power to the King to make any of the Council, nor to have to do with the militia for five years.'

in the Lords', remarks Godfrey Davies, 'made certain the restoration of monarchy without any new legal restrictions on the prerogative.'[1]

A few intrepid souls still dared to raise in a hostile Parliament the question of imposing conditions on the King. Sir Matthew Hale may have been one of these; Colonel Edward King and Sir William Morice certainly were. The willingness of these men to speak out guaranteed that the Convention Parliament would debate the parliamentary nomination of ministers of state. According to a fragmentary record of the debate in the Bodleian Library, it occurred on 1 May in the House of Commons. Sir William Morice began by saying, 'Mr Speaker, there are divers persons that would have the King brought in upon terms, others upon no terms at all. To bring in His Majesty without terms will not be secure for us, nor safe for him.' He then moved that the House immediately fall to work drawing up bills to present to the King for his approval. According to Bishop Burnet, Sir Matthew Hale about this time commended the Isle of Wight conditions. Hale's intervention may have provoked a speech that Colonel Birch remembered many years later, in 1674. He then said in the Commons, 'When once the debate was, in the Convention, of recommending councillors to the King, it was answered, "all the awe you have upon the King's Council hereafter is, if they be such as the people have an ill opinion of, you may remove them, and it is better for us than to name them, for [then] we must be responsible for them".'[2] If Colonel Birch remembered rightly, the Convention rejected only the principles of John Pym, not those of Henry Parker and Sir Roger Twysden. It rejected only the parliamentary nomination of the King's ministers, not Parliament's right to ask the King to dismiss those who were hateful to the people. The Commons in 1660 certainly wanted no responsibility for choosing the King's ministers, but they probably desired the luxury of being able to criticize and censure them.

That the Commons in 1660 wanted no responsibility for naming ministers of state is a fact of great significance. Perhaps the most

---

[1] Mordaunt, *Letter Book*, p. 111; Clarendon MSS 72, f. 69; Guizot, *Monk*, pp. 287, 290; *C.S.P. Ven.* xxxii, 136; *H.M.C. Laing*, i, 310–11; G. Davies, *The Restoration of Charles II* (San Marino, 1955), p. 339.

[2] Clarendon MSS 72, f. 4v; G. Burnet, *Hist. of My Own Time* (Oxford, 1897), i, 160; Anchitell Grey, *Debates of the House of Commons* (1763), ii, 269; *Cl. St. Pap.* ii, 525. The first Protectorate Parliament shared these sentiments, preferring that the Lord Protector name his councillors, and they only approve of them (*C.J.* vii, 395).

imperishable—and the most easily overlooked—effect that the Commonwealth had on the growth of responsible government in England was to insure that it should never take the form of placing executive power in Parliament itself. This was a negative effect, but no less real for that. Englishmen resolved at the Restoration never again to be ruled by parliamentary committees, to always keep separate executive and legislative powers. In 1660 no political principle enjoyed more universal applause than this principle of the separation of powers, a principle which was new to the English scene, for no one before 1648 had spoken of separating legislative, executive, and judicial powers. They had talked instead of a mixed monarchy, a monarchy in which monarchical, aristocratic, and democratic elements enjoyed a co-ordinate power. This co-ordinate power was largely judicial, a resolving of *meum et tuum*. Even as late as Elizabeth's reign, Sir Thomas Smith clung to the medieval belief that government consisted of doing justice, whether in local courts, royal courts, or the high court of Parliament. The Tudor revolution in government and the constitutional quarrels of the early seventeenth century destroyed the last vestiges of this medieval view; while the placing of executive power in Parliament from 1642 to 1653 promoted a different concept of government. Men now spoke of a balance of government in which executive, legislative, and judicial powers were to be separate.

Englishmen came to prize the principle of the separation of powers because they learned to their cost the disadvantages of ignoring it, of placing executive power immediately in Parliament. They learned that it bred inefficiency, that it promoted faction and self-seeking, and that it begat a terrible tyranny. They discovered its inefficiency first.

By July 1643 the Earl of Essex, commander of the parliamentary army, saw the folly of permitting a legislative body to manage the war. He wrote to the House of Commons complaining that their constant intervention in the management of the war caused delays, made secrecy impossible, and encouraged irresponsible criticism. The truth of his complaints eventually became apparent to Parliament. In 1644 it delegated extensive executive powers to a Committee of Both Kingdoms. Even this expedient proved too clumsy. In June 1645 Parliament freed General Thomas Fairfax and his Council of War from the surveillance of the Committee of Both Kingdoms. In 1649 the hard-headed officers of the army concluded that no legislative assembly, not even a Rump Parliament of eighty members, could administer the realm efficiently. They therefore provided in the Instrument of Government for a more workable form of government. They removed executive power from Parliament and placed it in a Lord Protector and Council. By 1660 almost no one believed that Parliament was a fit body to administer the day-to-day affairs of the realm.[1]

To place the executive in a committee or a council rather than in Parliament might promote efficiency, but as long as members of Parliament sat on those committees and councils the door was left open to faction and self-seeking. From the day that the Earl of Bedford proposed his undertaking in 1641 until the last Protectorate Parliament members of Parliament sought, and were accused of seeking, office. Sir Dudley Digges never tired of accusing the patriots of seeking preferment not liberty. The author of *A Narrative of the Late Parliament* took up Digges's refrain under the Protectorate. In 1657 he published his *Narrative*, which is the first sustained philippic in English history against placemen. In it the author listed those in Parliament who enjoyed high office, minor offices, places of profit, and commissions in the army and navy. He concluded that the Protectorate Parliament was a corrupt Parliament.[2]

From the earliest days of the Long Parliament members of the House of Commons felt the justness of these rebukes. In June 1641 the House of Commons voted to pass (but did not ultimately pass) a Self-Denying Ordinance, which would prevent members from accepting office at Court. In the spring of 1644 they finally did pass a Self-Denying Ordinance, but its basic purpose was not to end faction, but rather to insure the triumph of Cromwell's faction over Manchester's. They also wished to silence those who whispered that men in office desired the continuance of the war because it was profitable to them. This same prejudice against members of Parliament who held lucrative office led the Commons to vote in 1646 that no member of Parliament should hold the Great Seal. *The Agreement of the People* spoke the same language in 1648. It asked

---

[1] *C.S.P. Ven.* xxvi, 297; W. Notestein, 'Committee of Both Kingdoms', *A.H.R.* xvii, 482–95; F. Maseres (ed.), *Select Tracts Relating to the Civil War in England* (1815), i, 221; Gardiner, *Const. Doc. of the Puritan Rev.* pp. 190–3, 314.

[2] Digges, *An Answer to a Printed Book Intituled Observations*, pp. 49–50; Digges, *The Unlawfulness of Subjects taking up Arms*, p. 72, and another edition of *Unlawfulness* published in 1647, pp. 159–60; *A Narrative of the Late Parliament* (1657), pp. 1–20.

'That to the end all officers of state may be certainly accountable, and no factions made to maintain corrupt interests, no member of a Council of State, nor any officer of any salary in army or garrison, nor any treasurer or receiver of public money shall (while such) be elected to be a Representative.' The last Protectorate Parliament paid tribute to this ideal by voting against a proposal to name nine members of the House of Commons as Commissioners for Managing the Admiralty and Navy.[1]

Yet the private ambitions of men and the practical needs of the hour triumphed over ideology. The Self-Denying Ordinance of 1644 did not prevent the re-employment of those forced to resign from office. The House of Commons in 1646 repealed three weeks later their order prohibiting members of Parliament from holding the Great Seal. The army in 1649 rejected *The Agreement of the People* and permitted members of the House of Commons to be Councillors of State. In 1658 the Commons, immediately after defeating the proposal to name nine members of the House Commissioners for Managing the Admiralty and Navy, resolved that six of the nine Commissioners should be members of the House.[2] Moralists and idealists may frown on personal ambition and deride political expediency, but throughout the seventeenth century these two motives kept open the door to the development of cabinet government.

Most men considered the unchecked tyranny of a sovereign Parliament to be a worse grievance than administrative blunders or personal corruption. No man expressed more eloquently the indignation this tyranny provoked than Oliver Cromwell himself. In April 1657 he denounced perpetual and supreme Parliaments, arguing that had the Long Parliament continued,

We should have had a Council of State, and a Parliament of four hundred men, executing arbitrary government without intermission...Why it was

---

[1] *C.J.* III, 718; IV, 680; VII, 666; Fr. Trans. 12/22 Dec. 1643; Rushworth, *Historical Collections*, VII, 1359–60. On 29 May 1657, Mr Bampfield moved in the House of Commons that no member be a Commissioner for Buildings, and others supported the motion; but the Speaker prevented the vote by reminding the House that 'it is not fit to set my Lord Protector rules to restrain his appointment'. The Speaker then added: he 'hoped that the self-denying ordinance would hinder any member from seeking those places' (J. Towill, ed., *Diary of Thomas Burton*, 1827, II, 161).

[2] Gardiner, *Hist. of the Great Civil War* (1894), II, 188; and *Hist. of the Commonwealth and Protectorate* (1897–1901), II, 285–8. *C.J.* IV, 700; VII, 666. The Commons were of two minds about their members serving on the Council. In 1654 a member urged that no Parliament man be chosen to the Council and in 1657 a member complained that too few of their members served on the Council (Burton, *Diary*, I, civ; III, 394).

no more but this, that Committees of Parliament should take all upon them, and be instead of Courts at Westminster...and if any man had come and said, 'What are the rules you judge by?' 'Why, we have none! ...we are supreme in legislature and in judicature!' This was the state of the case...And it will be so while and whensoever...the legislative and executive powers are always the same.[1]

Cromwell spoke truly, as every man despoiled, imprisoned, or banished by the Long Parliament would willingly have affirmed.

The spokesmen for Parliament had only one defence against such criticism: the assertion of the infallibility of Parliament. Henry Parker implied it, the author of the *Second Part of Vox Populi* asserted it, and the author of *A Vindication of Parliament* elevated it to a principle. 'It is of dangerous consequence', said Parker, 'to suppose that Parliament will do any injustice, it looseth one of the firmest sinews of law to admit it.' The House of Commons, argued the author of the *Second Part of Vox Populi*, cannot accuse a man wrongly,

because the accusers are not parties, as in other cases, but the Commonwealth, and they are witnesses...it were a weakness in Parliament to be tied to the tedious forms and circumstantial proceedings of inferior courts, or prescribed by the precedent and custom of any other Parliament in matter of justice, since...they are, no less than other Parliaments, the fountain of laws and courts of justice. If delinquents can find out sins which former ages could not think of, the Parliament must find out punishments which former Parliaments did not dream of.

The author of *A Vindication of Parliament* added, '...it is a principle in law, that no unworthy or dishonourable thing is to be imagined or presumed of Parliaments'.[2]

The philosophy of government that these writers enunciated forced men to search for some way to check the arbitrary actions of a sovereign Parliament. John Lilburne proposed that the whole people stand guard over annually elected Parliaments, but very few Englishmen yet believed that democracy was the proper antidote to parliamentary tyranny. Oliver Cromwell proposed that the army check the exorbitancies of Parliament, but the English people showed no more enthusiasm for the rule of the sword than they did for the rule of the demos. The lawyers talked of a fundamental law

[1] *Somers Tracts*, VI, 392. Those who defended the establishment of the Protectorate never tired of reciting examples of the tyranny of an unchecked Parliament and of regal powers assumed by its committees (Burton, *Diary*, I, xxviii, lvi, lviii, cvi; III, 122).

[2] Parker, *Some Few Observations* (1642), p. 6; *The Second Part of Vox Populi* (1642), pp. 8–9; *A Vindication of Parliament*, in *Harleian Miscellany*, VIII, 52.

that bound the Parliament as well as the King, but, as J. W. Gough has shown, no one in Stuart England seriously advocated the doctrine of judicial review.[1] What men did advocate, whether royalists, Presbyterians, Cromwellians, or Levellers, was a balance of government, based on a separation of powers.

At the opening of the civil war men had some conception of a balance of government, but none of the separation of powers. The royalist author of *A Vindication of the King* wished, for example, that Parliament would only counsel, not command, the King, 'for the health of our state is admirably balanced if His Majesty have but his due proportion; the Parliament consisting of three bodies, the King, the Lords, and the Commons, so that if two should be destructive, and the third remain sound...there can be no danger to our Kingdom, but if either of the two can pass at their pleasure what they will, the third must then of necessity stand for a cipher...' The next year another royalist celebrated this balance of government, 'Now division being almost inevitable, and [the royal] power of dissenting [being] necessary for balancing the three differing parts of Parliament, to prevent this power of dissenting were to destroy the balance and being of Parliaments, and to make them courts of popularity, where they that please the people should absolutely carry all things.'[2]

If denying the King the power to dissent endangered the balance of government, refusing to seek his consent wrecked it entirely. Matters came to this extremity in February 1648 when the House of Commons voted to send no more addresses to the King. This provoked the author of *The Kingdom's Brief Answer* to a warm defence of the traditional balance in the English constitution. 'For the sword and the power of raising money were ever distinct', he argued, 'the one was the King's greatness, the other the people's liberty. And when these are joined all freedom is lost. *Quis custodit custodem?* Who will keep the keeper?'[3]

The author of *The Kingdom's Brief Answer* described the division of power in the English monarchy in the traditional manner, the King holding the sword, the people the purse. The first man to describe the doctrine of the separation of powers in the language of

[1] J. W. Gough, *Fundamental Law in English History* (Oxford, 1955).
[2] *A Vindication of the King* (1642), p. 7; *A Review of the Observations* (1643), p. 10.
[3] *The Kingdom's Brief Answer* (1648), p. 5.

Montesquieu and Blackstone was Sir John Wildman in *The Lawes Subversion*, which appeared in February 1648. Wildman wrote his pamphlet because Parliament imprisoned Sir John Maynard without showing cause. In *The Lawes Subversion* he argued that Maynard's imprisonment was illegal and indefensible because it was a 'confounding the legislative power with the power judicial and executive of the laws...'. John Lilburne and his friends then put their trumpets to work popularizing this doctrine. In *The Agreement of the People* of December 1648 they urged 'that the Representative intermeddle not with the execution of laws, nor give judgment upon any man's person or estate...'. Though imprisoned and court martialed, they were still proclaiming five years later 'that Parliaments are not executioners of the law'. The framers of the Instrument of Government agreed in very few things with the Levellers, but they did agree in the necessity of separating the executive from the legislative power. The Instrument of Government placed legislative power in a Parliament and executive power in a Lord Protector and Council. The only written constitution in English history (like the American constitution) explicitly provided for the separation of legislative and executive powers.[1]

In the year 1654 the enemies of the Protectorate proposed a bill that would end this separation of powers by again restoring the executive power to Parliament. This proposal goaded the author of *A True State of the Case* to an eloquent defence of the separation of powers. By this bill, he wrote, 'the supreme powers of making laws and putting them into execution were...to have been disposed in the same hands, which placing the legislative and executive powers in the same persons is a marvellous in-let of corruption and tyranny; whereas the keeping of these two apart, flowing in distinct channels, so that they may never meet in one...there lies a grand secret of liberty and good government.'[2]

[1] J. Howldin [Sir John Wildman], *The Lawes Subversion* (1648), pp. 13–14; Rushworth, *Historical Collections*, VII, 1359–60; *The Faithful Scout, No. 120* (1653), p. 1084; Gardiner, *Const. Doc. of the Puritan Rev.* p. 314. In 1648 a royalist (*The Anarchy of a Limited or Mixed Monarchy*, pp. 1, 24) opposed the separation of powers as destructive to monarchy. In a mixed monarchy, he complained, the King 'is brought from the legislative to the gubernative or executive power only'.

[2] *A True State of the Case of the Commonwealth* (1654), p. 9. Members of Parliament likewise began in 1654 (and continued through all the Protectorate Parliaments) to distinguish between the legislative and executive power, the former residing in Parliament, the latter in 'the sole person' (Burton, *Diary*, I, xxxii, cix, 89; III, 149, 179).

By the year of the Restoration nearly everyone (but John Milton) agreed that in the separation of powers lay the 'grand secret of liberty and good government'. The Republican army officers who occupied Whitehall in December 1659 declared it to be a fundamental law 'that the legislative and executive power be distinct and not in the same hands'. The Long Parliament, clinging desperately to power in January 1660, promised 'not to meddle' with the execution of the law. Commonwealth men like Vane and Harrington defended the doctrine. Royalists like Sir Roger L'Estrange applauded it, and transmuted it into 'our old kingly government'. 'Our old kingly government', L'Estrange wrote, 'included all the perfection of a free state, and was the kernel, as it were, of a Commonwealth in the shell of Monarchy; the essential parts of the Commonwealth are there, the Senate proposing, the People resolving, and the Magistrate executing.' The people, he asserted, possess the legislative power, the King the executive.[1]

The principle of the separation of powers carried with it a collateral principle, the principle of checks and balances. The royalists in 1660 found in this collateral principle the answer to the query posed in 1648, *Quis custodit custodem?*. 'If the Commons are sovereign,' asked a royalist in the year of the Restoration, 'who will be tribunes of the people to check them?...What is to prevent then reiterated burdens on the people?...And who would prevent a Parliament from arbitrarily arresting persons, as Parliament now checks the King's arresting them so?' No one and nothing, he answered; and the architects of the Restoration saw the point, rejecting the idea of sovereignty in favour of a system of checks and balances. As Colonel Gorges said in Parliament in 1659, 'The more checks, the better the constitution.'[2]

Not least among the checks in this system of checks and balances was the accountability of ministers to Parliament for their misuse of the executive power. The gulf separating the legislative and executive branches of government never grew so wide as to destroy the

[1] John Milton, *The Ready and Easy Way to Establish a Free Commonwealth* (E. M. Clark, ed., 1915), p. 21; *C.S.P. Ven.* xxxii, 1–3; *A Declaration of the Parliament Assembled at Westminster Jan. 23, 1659/60* (1660), p. 7; Sir Henry Vane, *A Healing Question Propounded and Resolved* in *Somers Tracts*, vi, 311–12; James Harrington, *Oceana and Other Works* (1737), pp. 393, 543; [Sir Roger L'Estrange], *No King But the Old King's Son, Or, A Vindication of Limited Monarchy As It Was Established Before the Late War* (1660), p. 1.

[2] *A Discourse for a King and Parliament* (1660), p. 12; Burton, *Diary*, iii, 156–7.

principle of accountability, a fact which Sir Roger L'Estrange admitted when he wrote that, we can never hope 'under our Commonwealth, whatever promises be made us, so perfectly to distinguish the legislative from the ministerial authority as once we did, when the House of Commons had not the power of a Court leet to give an oath, nor of a Justice of Peace to make a *mittimus*'. The King chooses his own ministers, he added, but alas they are accountable to a triennial Parliament, 'which none but [those of] the soundest integrity could abide'.[1]

The principle of accountability survived the discredit cast on it by parliamentary misgovernment from 1640 to 1660. The principle may even have become more deeply rooted in English political life than before; and that for two reasons. First, those who advocated the principle found a doctrine for its philosophical justification that was more compelling than the doctrine of the twofold capacity of the King. This new doctrine taught that the people were the source of all political authority. John Locke had not yet given this doctrine its classic exposition, but it gained a wide currency in these years. Henry Parker taught that Parliament entrusts the King with power; John Wildman, Richard Overton, John Lilburne, and Sir Arthur Haselrigge proclaimed that all power resides originally in the people; Captain Baynes urged that 'the Council are trustees of the people'; and Sir Henry Vane and Thomas Scot maintained that the executive power is a gift which Parliament bestows on the Chief Magistrate. These radical men taught a radical doctrine, but it was also a useful one and therefore did not expire at the Restoration. If the people entrusted power to the King, their representatives in Parliament could call to account those to whom His Majesty then entrusted it.[2]

The second reason why the principle of accountability grew in strength during these years concerns the habits of politicians, not their ideas. The constant exercise of the right of inquiry, of the right of interrogation, of the right of surveillance, of the right of criticism, and of the right of censure inculcated in members of Parliament habits that not even a Restoration could erase. During these

---

[1] L'Estrange, *A Plea for a Limited Monarchy*, in *Harleian Miscellany* (1808), I, pp. 21–2.
[2] Burton, *Diary*, II, 288; III, 99, 178–9; Parker, *Observations*, in Haller, *Tracts*, II, 170. Wildman, *Putney Projects* (1647), p. 44. Overton, *An Appeal from the Degenerate Body*, in D. Wolfe, *Leveller Manifestoes* (New York, 1944), p. 162. Lilburne, *A Declaration of Some Proceedings*, in W. Haller and G. Davies, *Leveller Tracts* (New York, 1944), p. 108.

years the two Houses of Parliament served an apprenticeship in the arts of superintending the executive. They questioned ministers of state. They clamoured for information. They objected to oaths of secrecy taken by their own committees.[1] They sent committees of inquiry into the counties. They examined accounts and appropriated revenues. They investigated military failures and criticized naval designs. They opposed, condemned, criticized, and censured those whom they found remiss in the performance of their duties. Gradually they asserted a prescriptive right to these functions, and fell into habits that proved stronger than any philosophy of regal government.

The doctrine of the separation of powers and the principle of accountability were the two most enduring legacies of the Commonwealth period. Englishmen never again placed the executive power immediately in Parliament. Yet they never ceased criticizing in Parliament those to whom the King entrusted it. The line that men drew between a parliamentary executive and an executive accountable to Parliament was a fine one, but it was not an illogical one. Parliament knew what it wanted. It wanted to assume no responsibility, yet to continue to play the role of the critic. 'All the awe you have upon the King's Council hereafter', said the nameless member of the Convention Parliament in 1660, 'is, if they be such as the people have an ill opinion of, you may remove them, and it is better for us than to name them, for [then] we must be responsible for them.' This distinction holds true to this day. A party leader who can find a majority in the House of Commons may assume responsibility for the exercise of the executive power, but the House of Commons itself does not. Its members cling to the right to criticize, to question, to inquire, and to condemn.

It is no mere platitude that man cannot turn back the clock of history. Men may revive earlier forms of government and they may return to former allegiances, but they cannot cast off habits acquired over twenty years or dismiss predilections which they have unconsciously assumed. Englishmen before 1640 talked, as Miss Kemp

---

[1] In June 1657 Mr Bampfield moved that, 'as was agreed on in the last Parliament... the Council may not be under oath not to reveal secrets to the Parliaments in some cases. We remember Lord Strafford's case.' Sir Richard Onslow then suggested, and Bampfield formally moved, that the affirmative and negative of every member of the Council be entered in a Book. The House, however, regarded this as improper and passed to other business (Burton, *Diary*, II, 287–90).

observes, of the King *in* Parliament, men after 1660 of the King *and* Parliament.[1] Before 1640 there existed a unity of government, one King, who governed the realm by the advice of his judges, his Council, his nobility, and his faithful Commons. In 1660 there existed a balance of government, between the King with his prerogatives and Parliament with its privileges. At the centre of this balance lay a vague arrangement for the exercise of executive power. It should reside in the King, and not in the legislature. He should exercise it only after seeking the advice of Privy Councillors, whom he chose but in whom the nation confided. Their advices were advices, not commands. Yet these same councillors should answer to Parliament for the legality of their counsels, just as the King's officers should answer for the legality of their actions. If a councillor gave unlawful advice or a minister obeyed an unlawful command, the House of Commons could impeach and the House of Lords could try him. If the King employed councillors and ministers who were, though guilty of no crime, hateful to the people, Parliament could advise him to dismiss them from office. But it could not take up arms to tear such persons from him.

This balance of government was not an absurd arrangement, nor was it inherently unworkable. It was not a utopian scheme, like Harrington's *Oceana,* but a product of hard-won experience. That by 1667 it had broken down is not to be disputed, but the cause for that breakdown does not lie alone, or even primarily, in the imperfections of the arrangement. It lies in the fact that the men who alone could make it work grew impatient with it; while the architect who created it lacked the will and power to preserve it. The men who tired of it were Charles II and the leaders of Parliament. The hapless architect was Edward Hyde, named Lord Chancellor in 1660 and created the Earl of Clarendon in 1661.

[1] B. Kemp, *King and Commons* (1957), p. 8.

CHAPTER 5

THE BREAKDOWN OF THE BALANCE
OF GOVERNMENT (1660–1674)

Few Lord Chancellors have defended the laws of England with greater steadfastness than the Earl of Clarendon. Yet the House of Commons impeached him in 1667 for attempting to subvert those laws. Standing guardian over the English constitution, he was accused of plotting its ruin. Less guilty than Bacon, he suffered a harsher fate. More innocent than Lord Keeper Finch, he endured the same painful banishment from the England he loved. On 11 November 1667 the House of Commons impeached him for High Treason, and, though they were unable to prove their accusations, they forced him, by the violence of their prosecution, to flee to France. It was Clarendon's tragedy to suffer disgrace, calumny, and banishment; it was England's fate to witness the revival of impeachment and the breakdown of the balance of government.

Two forces conspired to cause the Chancellor's downfall and the revival of impeachment. They were the personal hostility of the King towards Clarendon and the political ambitions of a phalanx of aspiring politicians, eager for the fruits of office. The one led to Clarendon's disgrace, the other to his impeachment, while the vehemence of both insured his final banishment. The combined action of King and Commons, the interweaving of royal displeasure with political opposition, distinguished Clarendon's impeachment from all those that preceded it. The world of Charles II was not the world of Charles I. Motives very different from those that drove Eliot and Pym to attack Buckingham and Strafford impelled the enemies of Clarendon to impeach him. Who these enemies were, however, is a question that must be answered before their motives can be ascertained.

Driven by an inveterate hatred for Sir William Coventry and an insensate jealousy of the Earl of Arlington, Clarendon blamed them for his impeachment.[1] In doing this he confused two widely separate events, events arising from different sources, driven on with different

[1] Clarendon, *Life*, III, 811, 836, 838–9.

155

intentions, and pregnant with different consequences. The two events were Clarendon's dismissal from office in August and his impeachment in November. No proper understanding of Clarendon's fate can be gained if these events are confused, for Sir William Coventry and the Earl of Arlington, who secured the Lord Chancellor's dismissal in August, opposed his impeachment for High Treason in November. Of the two statesmen, Sir William Coventry played the more important role. Secretary to the Lord Admiral, a Commissioner of the Treasury, and a Privy Councillor, he was as much respected in the House of Commons as he was favoured at Court. He was no common intriguer, no Court minion constantly scheming to raise up this man and throw down that one. His interest was the good government of the realm, not his own advancement. No one struck harder at the waste, prodigality, and idleness found in the administration during the second Dutch war. Only recently he had reorganized the Treasury, so long neglected by the Earl of Southampton; and after the disgrace at Chatham he openly spoke out for the summoning of Parliament. In August he told Charles that there was no hope of setting aright what was amiss in the realm unless he dismissed the Lord Chancellor. Charles, much attracted by the ability and integrity of his new councillor, accepted his advice and took the seals from Clarendon.[1]

There was much truth in Coventry's indictment of the great minister. Clarendon, clinging to office in an age which he did not understand, simultaneously monopolized and neglected the management of affairs. At one moment he abused an inferior officer of the Treasury for presuming to meddle in affairs too high for him. At the next he snored peacefully through the Council's deliberation on the state of the Navy. Unwilling to let the young men at the lower end of the Council table manage the Dutch war, he nevertheless disclaimed any responsibility for its mismanagement. It is not difficult to see why those important in public affairs, men such as Coventry and Arlington, clamoured for the Lord Chancellor's dismissal. They wanted a stop put to that mismanagement, that lethargy in administration that had led England down the path to

---

[1] Pepys, *Diary*, 28 Oct. 1667. Court buffoons and ladies of pleasure no doubt contributed to Clarendon's dismissal, but their role has been given undue emphasis. Charles never employed Clarendon because he liked him personally, but because he was indispensable. Sir William Coventry, not Lady Castlemaine, offered Charles the means to dispense with the Lord Chancellor.

defeat. Not that the motives of these administrators were wholly noble and selfless. They desired Clarendon's disgrace, in part at least, in order to protect themselves from the nation's anger at the loss of the Dutch war. They hoped that the sacrifice of one great minister would be a perfect atonement for the faults of all, that the punishment of Clarendon would cleanse the guilt of every public servant. Charles, too, acted from interested motives. He accepted Coventry's advice to dismiss Clarendon because he dared not meet Parliament otherwise. 'I could not retain the Chancellor', he wrote to the Duke of Ormond, 'and do those things in Parliament that I desired.'[1]

But those in public office did not want the impeachment of Clarendon for High Treason and did as much as they dared to oppose it. Sir William Coventry would have no part in the impeachment. He told Pepys that the late Lord Chancellor, though unfit for office, was no rogue, no knave, and had never counselled the King to rule by an army. Much to the displeasure of Charles, he withdrew from the House of Commons when the debates on the impeachment reached their climax.[2] Arlington, on the other hand, acted more circumspectly. Caring more for the fruits of office than the merits of policy, he yielded to the popular outcry against the Chancellor; but he yielded more out of fear than conviction. Threatened by an impeachment against himself unless he joined in the pursuit of the Lord Chancellor, he gave it his support.[3]

Where Clarendon wrongly blamed Arlington and Coventry for his impeachment, the Duke of York, his son-in-law, wrongly blamed the Presbyterians.[4] No doubt the Presbyterians had reason to oppose the Lord Chancellor and to welcome his fall from power. He had failed to soften the terms of the Act of Uniformity passed in 1662 and had supported the Conventicle Act in 1664. Yet the Presbyterians

---

[1] *H.M.C. Rep. 14*, part 9, p. 370; A. Bryant (ed.), *The Letters, Speeches and Declarations of King Charles* (1935), p. 205. Baron Lisola, the Imperial Ambassador, believed (Onno Klopp, *Der Fall des Hauses Stuart*, Vienna, 1875, I, 190–1), that the Earl of Arlington persuaded the King to dismiss Clarendon. There is every reason to believe that Arlington privately urged Clarendon's dismissal, but, as Charles Bate wrote to Sir Charles Savile (Halifax Papers, Althrop, Box. 1, 27 Aug. 1667), only Sir William Coventry publicly opposed Clarendon at Court. Henry Savile agreed with Bate that Coventry's counsels were decisive in securing the Lord Chancellor's dismissal (H. C. Foxcroft, *The Life and Letters of Sir George Savile, Bart., First Marquis of Halifax*, 1898, I, 41).

[2] Carte MSS 220, f. 326.

[3] Fr. Trans. 20/30 Oct. and 30 Oct./8 Nov. 1667; V. Barbour, *Henry Bennet, Earl of Arlington* (1914), p. 115.   [4] J. Macpherson, *Original Papers* (1775), I, 38.

did not plot his impeachment, and when it came into the House of Commons some of them openly opposed it, while those who went along with it counselled moderation. In November the Presbyterians promised to stand by Clarendon if he would stand by himself. The truth is the Presbyterians were offended by the unscupulous conduct of those who sought Clarendon's destruction. They recognized that he was, if an opponent to their principles, at least an honourable opponent. As their chief spokesman, Richard Baxter observed: bad as Clarendon was, he was the chief means of hindering the rule of the army in England.[1]

Equally hostile to Clarendon, though for reasons far removed from those of the Presbyterians, were the old Cavaliers. They had fought stoutly for the King in the days of his adversity, but Charles had not, in their opinion, rewarded them according to their deserts. For this neglect they blamed Clarendon. Had he not persuaded the King to reward his enemies on the premiss that his friends would remain so still? Had he not dispensed honours and office to unworthy Presbyterians? Had he not advised the hated Act of Indemnity and promoted the unjust land settlement? But deep as were their grievances against Clarendon, the old Cavaliers lacked the initiative, the political capacity, and the brazen effrontery to impeach Clarendon for High Treason. There is no evidence that the impeachment of Clarendon proceeded from them. And though many of them supported his impeachment, once it was put in motion, they also clung to his principles of government and defended his friends and allies. In the very Parliament that impeached Clarendon, the Cavaliers demanded the continuance of his policy of securing the Church, and staunchly defended his good friend, the Duke of Ormond, against accusations brought against him in the Commons.

The true authors of Clarendon's impeachment were not those in public office, or the Presbyterians, or the old Cavaliers. They were rather a cabal of ambitious politicians drawn from all factions, welded together by their hatred of Clarendon, and determined to secure office. Their contemporaries called them the anti-Clarendonians. Clarendon was their special enemy because he and his adherents stood in the way of their rapid rise to office. Some of the

[1] Richard Baxter, *Reliquiae Baxterianae* (1696), part III, p. 20. George R. Abernathy maintains ('Clarendon and the Declaration of Indulgence', *The Journal of Ecclesiastical History*, XI, 55–73) that Clarendon favoured rather than opposed the Declaration of Indulgence in 1663.

anti-Clarendonians were old Cavaliers, a few were of the old Commonwealth party, but the greater part were drawn from the independent country gentlemen who formed the backbone of the nation and the majority in the House of Commons. All were led by George Villiers, second Duke of Buckingham, whose political ambitions far outran his political capacities. Ever since the Oxford Parliament of 1665 Buckingham had sought popularity by posing as the people's champion. He demanded the examination of accounts by Parliament, denounced the payment of seamen in worthless tickets, and called for the punishment of those who had cheated the Crown. Angered by this outspoken opposition, Charles, upon the advice of Clarendon and Arlington, imprisoned Buckingham in the Tower in July 1667. But his imprisonment only enhanced his popularity. So loudly did the people acclaim him as he went to the Tower, that Charles found it advisable to release him within a month. Buckingham emerged from imprisonment the martyr of the nation and the declared enemy of the Lord Chancellor.[1]

Allied with Buckingham were the most capable men in the House of Commons, men of great estates, great parts, and great ambition. As early as the 1666 session of Parliament Buckingham began a correspondence with these neglected men of talent, chief of whom were Edward Seymour, Sir Robert Howard, Sir Thomas Osborne, and Sir Richard Temple. The most intrepid of them was Edward Seymour, who came of an ancient and illustrious house in Somersetshire. Haughty and proud to a fault, he was at the same time forthright in speech and fearless in action. In the summer of 1667 he was particularly piqued against Clarendon because he had not received the Privy Seal when it fell vacant the year before.[2] Sir Robert Howard likewise came of a wealthy and famous family, but boasted less of this than of his great wit and literary pretensions. He was the brother-in-law of Dryden and the author of several indifferent tragic plays. In the House of Commons he led the Spanish party that wished to fight for the defence of Flanders. His immediate ambition was to become one of the Commissioners for the Enforcement of the Explanatory Act in Ireland.[3] Sir Thomas Osborne, who seven years

---

[1] Baxter, *Reliquiae Baxterianae*, part III, p. 21. Charles also found it advisable to release the Duke because he could not prove the charges brought against him.
[2] T. Carte, *The Life of James, Duke of Ormond* (Oxford, 1851), IV, 307.
[3] Lady (Winifred Gardner) Burghclere, *The Life of James, First Duke of Ormond* (1912), II, 139.

later became the Earl of Danby, came of an old Yorkshire family. Restless and ambitious, he sought advancement by attaching himself to the Duke of Buckingham.[1] Sir Richard Temple of Stowe, Buckinghamshire, was a meddling politician of indifferent talent who had urged the Earl of Bristol in 1663 and the Duke of Buckingham in 1667 to undertake to manage Parliament for Charles. He was the heir of the great parliamentary undertakers of earlier years, of Sir Henry Neville and Lord Saye. All of these men sought by the impeachment of Clarendon to drive the Clarendonians from office. Others joined with them, men like Sir John Trevor, Sir Thomas Littleton, Lord Vaughan, Lord Andover, and Lord St John. Before these men had even introduced their impeachment against Clarendon into the House, they were calculating how many posts would become vacant on his fall.[2] Buckingham strove for the highest prize of all: the first place in the counsels of the King.

Buckingham's determination to destroy Clarendon grew in proportion to his renewed favour at Court. In July he was released from the Tower. On 4 September, at Whitehall, he had a two-hour *éclaircissement* with Charles. Eleven days later Charles restored him to all offices, honours, and pensions, and received him back at Court. Within a week Buckingham, exploiting this renewed favour, demanded the impeachment of Clarendon, and all that Charles could do was to consent, persuaded as he was that Buckingham ruled all and could do all in Parliament. On 5 October it was decided at Court to impeach Clarendon. But the irresolute, uncertain Charles could not yet bring himself to destroy his trusted servant. To prevent this he ordered the Lord Keeper to draw up articles of impeachment that fell short of treason. They should charge Clarendon with misdemeanours only.[3]

Buckingham found such an impeachment entirely unacceptable. It would tarnish Clarendon's prestige, to be sure, and it would

---

[1] A. Browning (ed.), *The Memoirs of Sir John Reresby* (Glasgow, 1936), p. 71; A. Browning, *Thomas Osborne, First Earl of Danby and Duke of Leeds* (Glasgow, 1944–51), I, 32–3.

[2] Ormond wrote to his son, Lord Ossory (Harleian MSS 7001, f. 264), that the opposition to Clarendon arose largely from those 'seeking public employments'. Sir Richard Temple, in a memorandum written in 1668, confessed that he and the other anti-Clarendonians joined in the impeachment in the full expectation that there would be a change of persons at Court (*Huntington Library Quarterly*, xx, no. 2, p. 142). The Duke of Buckingham admitted the same to John Doddington, Temple's brother-in-law (Doddington to Temple, 28 Jan. 1669, Stowe MSS in the Huntington Library, San Marino, California).

[3] *H.M.C. Rep. 14, Part 9*, p. 370; Fr. Trans. 30 Sept./8 Oct. and 20/30 Oct. 1667.

weaken his support in Parliament, but it would not prevent his return to office, nor would it lead to the rout of the Clarendonians so earnestly desired by the Duke's friends. Furthermore, an impeachment for misdemeanours raised great dangers to its authors. Without ensuring the destruction of Clarendon, it would exacerbate his hostility against those who promoted it. And before Buckingham's mind there floated the spectre of the Duke of York's succession to the throne upon his brother's death, a succession certain to be followed by the restoration of Clarendon to power. Could there be any doubt that Clarendon would then seek vengeance on his enemies? Would he not drive them from office, imprison them, confiscate their estates, perhaps ask their lives in recompense for impeaching him? Politics was a desperate and hazardous game in the seventeenth century, played for the highest stakes, and exacting the severest penalties from the loser. Buckingham therefore resolved to have the late Lord Chancellor's head, believing with Lord Essex that 'stone dead hath no fellow'. The impeachment must therefore be for High Treason, for anything less would not take the Earl's life.[1]

The anti-Clarendonians resolved on 13 October to demand an impeachment for High Treason. A week of conflicting counsels and excited debate then followed at Court. Arlington and Coventry spoke against the new course. The Buckingham faction spoke for it. Charles hesitated and procrastinated until 20 October, when he ended a week of vacillation and changing advice by agreeing to the impeachment of his former Lord Chancellor for High Treason.[2] As a result of the King's decision the impeachment of Clarendon for misdemeanours, appointed for 22 October, was postponed. The articles against him were not yet severe enough. Four more days of feverish activity served to strengthen them. On 26 October the anti-Clarendonians launched their assault. Edward Seymour rose on that fateful Saturday in the House of Commons and accused Clarendon of advising the King to govern by a standing army, and demanded his impeachment for High Treason. Ten days later the anti-Clarendonians introduced into the House formal articles of impeachment against the Earl.[3]

---

[1] Fr. Trans. 19/29 Oct. 1667.
[2] Fr. Trans. 13/23, 18/28, 19/29 and 20/30 Oct. 1667.
[3] Lord Conway wrote to Ormond (22 Oct. 1667, Carte MSS 35, f. 778), 'This day was once designed for bringing in the impeachment of the late Lord Chancellor, but they thought it was not yet strong enough, so 'tis delayed.'

The Breakdown of the Balance of Government

In the seventeenth century it was an easy task to introduce an impeachment for High Treason into the House of Commons; far more difficult was it to persuade the House to vote it. Particularly was this true when few men really believed the accused guilty of the charges brought against him and when many saw that they arose not from a distrustful nation, determined to vindicate the law, but from a scheming faction, eager for office. Of the 500 members of the House of Commons in 1667 few believed Clarendon a traitor, though many believed him guilty of mistakes, negligence, and peculation.

The House of Commons into which the anti-Clarendonians introduced their impeachment was split into many factions. There were the Clarendonians, composed of the churchmen, the lawyers, and the adherents of the Duke of York. There were the old Cavaliers, dwindling in strength and importance as death reduced their numbers and the passage of time assuaged their quarrel with the Puritans. There was the new Court party, about eighty in number, composed of those servants of the King, both menial and honourable, who had secured election to Parliament by royal favour. There were forty Presbyterians, few in numbers, but able, experienced, and sedulous in their attendance in the House. But the largest group in the House belonged to no faction. They were the country gentlemen, who placed the interest of the nation above their own advancement, who sought to save the kingdom's money, and who resented any affront to the honour of English arms. They never led in the House, but, when gained, always carried it.[1]

Since the Clarendonians were obstinately loyal to their master, even to his very flight, Buckingham's problem was to win the support of the old Cavaliers and the new Court party, the Presbyterians and the country gentlemen. The Duke quickly saw that the first two factions, the Cavaliers and Courtiers, could only be won over by the King. Knowing this, he had no intention of embarking on so dangerous a course as the impeachment of Clarendon without Charles's support. And it was not merely Charles's acquiescence that he wanted. He wanted his active participation. The King must use his prestige, his unrivalled influence, and his secret knowledge

---

[1] Sir Richard Temple's description of the House (*Huntington Library Quarterly*, xx, no. 2, pp. 137–44) is the basis for this analysis. It adds much important detail to Wilbur C. Abbott's picture of the House of Commons in the 1660's ('The Long Parliament of Charles II, Part I', *E.H.R.* Jan. 1906), but it does not alter the main features of that portrait.

of affairs to help pursue the Lord Chancellor. He must be the chief witness against him and the chief party whip to bring Parliament into line behind the impeachment. Buckingham wanted no half-way measures.[1]

Why Charles agreed to play the role of chief prosecutor is the most puzzling question of Clarendon's impeachment. The answer is not easily discovered, for various and changing motives governed Charles's conduct from month to month and week to week. Charles agreed to the impeachment in part because he saw no alternative. Facing a Parliament angry at the profligacy of the Court, the waste of public money, the affront given the fleet at Chatham, and the loss of the Dutch war, Charles decided to run before the storm. For this reason he told Parliament on 10 October, at its first meeting, that he would protect no man found at fault and would leave to Parliament the investigation of the late miscarriages at sea.

Charles yielded not only to an angry Parliament but to a determined faction, to Buckingham and his lieutenants, who demanded that Clarendon be impeached for High Treason. Charles agreed to their demand because he believed they governed in Parliament and that they only could win him a vote of supply there. Charles and Buckingham in fact struck a bargain: the Duke undertook to secure a generous vote of supply for the King, to see that his business in Parliament met with no interruption, and to ensure that there was money enough to set out the fleet that spring; in return Charles agreed to make use of the Duke and his friends in the management of the Commons, to entrust them with office, to put the fleet into different hands, and to support the impeachment of Clarendon.[2]

If Charles came reluctantly into the impeachment, he soon showed a warmth far transcending the bounds of enforced consent. No desire to run before the storm, no pact of convenience with Buckingham, could explain his warmth. The truth is Charles was angry with his former Lord Chancellor, and in pursuing him indulged a personal spite. The sources of Charles's hatred were

---

[1] Fr. Trans. 19/29 Oct. 1667.

[2] Lord Conway wrote to Ormond (Carte MSS 35, f. 778), ' 'Tis certain that poor Lord Chancellor of England destined for death and the King is to be the chief witness against him...Buckingham governs all and 'tis like to be well done without morality or judgment...his undertaking that the Parliament shall give money makes him continue very acceptable to the Court.' Buckingham fully described the terms of his undertaking to John Doddington in January 1669 (Doddington to Temple, Stowe MSS in the Huntington Library).

many. He resented Clarendon's belief that the Privy Council should play a central role in government, overshadowing King and Parliament alike. More than once Clarendon had rebuked him for speaking foolishly at the Council table or for ignoring its advice. Charles wished to vindicate himself against so imperious a counsellor and to free himself from such rigid forms. He wished to govern by private advices, not those of the Privy Council. He wished the Privy Purse freed from the dictates of the Exchequer and the Irish Seals set above the Great Seal.[1] He also resented Clarendon's opposition to any scheme for toleration that included Catholics; and there were those who told him that Clarendon had deliberately secured him an inadequate revenue in 1660, in order to make certain that he could not tamper with the Church.[2] But the sharpest hatred, that which put the edge to all else, probably arose from particular and private resentments. The Earl's austere morality, censorious counsels, and ungovernable temper had become quite insupportable to Charles. Clarendon had openly reproached him for his vices, had opposed Lady Castlemaine's appointment as a Lady of the Queen's Bedchamber, and had (thought Charles) removed Miss Stuart from the Court by promoting her marriage to the Duke of Richmond.[3] By 1667 Charles had had enough, and once he had plucked up courage to rid himself of an unwanted servant, he loosed his spite with abandon.

There is no denying the warmth of Charles's opposition to Clarendon. Once the impeachment was before the Commons, he did everything he could to forward it. 'The King', wrote the French ambassador, 'is warmer than anyone for the ruin of the Chancellor.'[4] Charles warned his brother, the Duke of York, to make no effort to defend the Chancellor. Observing Sir Heneage Finch to be silent in the matter, he gave him positive orders to promote the impeachment.[5] The Courtiers he enlisted in the attack by scolding and

[1] Clarendon, *Life*, II, 454; III, 676–7. Pepys, *Diary*, 8 Sept. 1667. Carlyle (*E.H.R.* xxvii) argues that this difference over the role of the Privy Council in the government was the principal cause of Charles's dissatisfaction with Clarendon.

[2] James Welwood, *Memoirs of the Most Material Transactions for the Last Hundred Years* (1820), pp. 112–13; Rapin de Thoyras, *History of England* (1739), I, 879.

[3] Gilbert Burnet, *History of His Own Times* (Oxford, 1823), I, 436–7.

[4] Fr. Trans. 25 Oct./4 Nov. 1667. Sir Henry Coventry wrote to Thomas Thynne (Thynne Papers, Longleat, xvi, f. 479), 'The little love the people had for him [Clarendon] you know, and the great anger the King has against him now you can hardly think. So his station is sure very bad.'

[5] Carte, *Ormond*, IV, 306; Fr. Trans. 10/20 Oct. 1667.

reprimanding any who should dare to oppose his will.[1] He won over the Cavaliers by an appeal to their loyalty to the Crown. At the King's command, and for no other reason, Lord Ossory, the rising hope of the old and embittered Cavaliers, appeared against Clarendon. Edmund Verney, son of Clarendon's old colleague, did likewise, regarding 'a fallen minister to be necessarily wrong'.[2] When the impeachment reached the House of Lords Charles directed his energies there. He had a list given him of those lords who opposed the imprisonment of Clarendon in the Tower, and he openly berated several of them.[3] In fact, Charles's manifest displeasure weighed more heavily upon Clarendon than all the plots of his adversaries.[4] Without the King's assistance, the cabal which introduced the impeachment might never have secured its acceptance by the Commons.

The King's pleasure, or displeasure, carried little weight with either the independent country gentlemen or the Presbyterians. To win their support for the impeachment the anti-Clarendonians had to employ different tactics. They had to exploit the independent member's latent distrust of the Court and exacerbate his jealousy for the honour of the House. Above all they had to win his confidence in their leadership of the House. To this end the anti-Clarendonians asserted the privileges of Parliament at the expense of the prerogatives of the Crown. They led in the demand that the miscarriages of the late war be investigated. They were among those most eager to examine the Treasury and Admiralty books. They were the quickest to resent any affront given to the honour of the House of Commons. As a result they won the fleeting confidence of the House, secured for a time the leadership of it, and were able to carry their measures there. But this confidence, once secured, they immediately abused. They abused it by leading the House up a path from which there was no retreat with honour and no escape which did not fatally weaken the power of impeachment.

That path was the impeachment of Clarendon for High Treason upon evidence which did not exist. From the beginning the Presby-

---

[1] L. Eachard, *History of England* (1720), p. 884; Pepys, *Diary*, 16 Nov. 1667.

[2] Lord Ossory to his father, 24 Jan. 1668, Carte MSS 220, f. 327; F. P. Verney and M. M. Verney, *Memoirs of the Verney Family During the Seventeenth Century* (1907), II, 305.

[3] Egerton MSS 2539, f. 138.

[4] The Earl of Carlingford wrote to Ormond (28 Sept. 1667, Carte MSS 35, f. 737), 'I find the King angry with my Lord Chancellor, and that he believes that the greatest misfortune that can occur to him, being confident to vindicate himself from any crime can be laid to his charge.'

terians and the Country party (the term was first used in this session) showed themselves suspicious of an impeachment for High Treason. Believing Clarendon at fault for the loss of the Dutch war, they did not believe him guilty of treason. They showed this in the clearest possible manner by voting that he was not guilty of High Treason on the first article charged against him. The debate on the first article was crucial, for the anti-Clarendonians hoped to make it the basis for their accusations of High Treason. This article accused Clarendon of attempting to subvert the laws of the realm by urging the dissolution of Parliament and government by the army. That Clarendon in June 1667 urged that Parliament should not be summoned and that troops should be supported by free quarters was everywhere known to be true. But that this constituted High Treason the lawyers denied. No treason defined in 25 Edward III covered it. The anti-Clarendonians therefore fell back on the Declaratory Power; Parliament could declare that an endeavour to subvert the law was treason. Nor was this the creation of a crime *ex post facto*, for an endeavour to subvert the law had always been treason at common law.[1] But the country gentlemen and Cavaliers in the House, conscious that Strafford had been wrongly condemned for common law treasons, refused to use the Declaratory Power to play that tragedy over again. By 172 to 103 they voted that Clarendon was not guilty of treason on the first article charged against him.[2]

This unexpected check threw the managers of Clarendon's impeachment into a desperate plight. Their anxiety did not lessen as the House proceeded to the other articles. The Commons found it no treason that Clarendon had said the King was a Papist. Nor was it treason that he had taken money for passing the Canary patent, imprisoned persons in remote places, sold offices, farmed out

[1] *The Proceedings in the House of Commons, Touching the Impeachment of Edward Late Earl of Clarendon* (1700), pp. 29–30, 32–3, 42–4; Grey, *Debates*, I, 29–31. Rough notes entitled 'Authorities to prove the first Article treason' (Stowe MSS 425, ff. 86–98) set forth the case for common law treasons. According to the author of these notes (and there is every appearance that he was a manager of the impeachment or one who wished it to be rigorously prosecuted), it was treason to surrender the King's forts, to advise the alteration of the laws, to say that the King was a false man, to deny access to the King's person, to persuade the King that falsehoods were true, to rise up against the law of villeinage, to free prisoners from the Tower, to throw down enclosures, or to say that the King had not the love of his subjects.

[2] John Nicholas, who was a member of the House of Commons, wrote to his father (12 Nov. 1667, Egerton MSS 2539, f. 135), 'It was the parallel of my Lord of Strafford and I much fear we are acting that tragedy over again; the face of things look dismal.'

the customs at too low a rate, and received money from the vintners. Neither was it treason that he had acquired a large estate, introduced an arbitrary government into Barbados, failed to defend Nevis and St Christopher, advised the sale of Dunkirk, altered a letters patent, determined at the Council table disputes over land, instituted *quo warranto* proceedings, and received large sums for promoting the Settlement of Ireland Act. The Commons found no treason in any of these charges. It seemed to Buckingham and his lieutenants that the destruction of Clarendon would slip from their grasp. At this last hour, and in this desperate strait, they clutched at a straw cast upon the troubled waters of English politics by Lisola, the scheming, gregarious Imperial ambassador. Lisola had talked loudly of Clarendon's betraying the King's secrets to the French in the late war. The Dutch Pensionary, said Lisola, had intercepted a letter from Clarendon written to the French Court, informing it of the intention of the King to send troops to Flanders. These idle rumours were enough for the malefactors who sought Clarendon's life. Three of them, Sir Robert Howard, Lord St John, and Lord Vaughan, brought new charges into the House. They accused Clarendon of betraying His Majesty's counsels to the enemy during the late war. This accusation undoubtedly contained treasonous matter, and it fully satisfied the country gentlemen and Presbyterians. Along with the Courtiers and Cavaliers they voted to impeach Clarendon for High Treason. As the evidence for this charge was not at hand, the House did not send up special articles with the impeachment. Instead they sent Edward Seymour to the House of Lords, where, on 12 November, he impeached the Earl of Clarendon for High Treason and demanded his imprisonment. He accused Clarendon of treason on a general charge, presenting no particulars to prove it.[1]

The anti-Clarendonians had indeed led the Commons up a path from which there was no advance and no retreat. There was no advance because the House of Lords refused to imprison Clarendon unless the Commons brought before them special articles describing his treason. Strafford had suffered imprisonment on a general

---

[1] Fr. Trans. 14/24 Nov. 1667. John Nicholas wrote to his father (Egerton MSS 2539, ff. 135–136), 'The additional words were brought in by Lord St John of Basing, the Lord Vaughan, and Sir Robert Howard. All the testimony we heard from them is that one of them heard it from a person of honour...The business upon which they make this impeachment is a story which Baron Lisola tells of what he heard De Witt say in Holland, that the King's counsels were betrayed, and fixed it on my Lord Chancellor.'

charge, unaccompanied by special articles, and the shadow of his fate fell as long across the House of Lords as it did across the House of Commons.[1] There was no retreat because the Commons had no special articles to send up, even if they had been willing (which they were not) to surrender the cause of general impeachments. The leaders of the House, it is true, did make one attempt to secure particulars for their charge. Shortly after 12 November two of the leading anti-Clarendonians went to Lisola's house in order to ask him for proof of his accusations. The ambassador greeted them affably. For two hours he chatted amiably and discursively with them, skilfully parried all their questions, gave them no information, and sent them away empty handed.[2] That fruitless afternoon's visit made certain that the Commons would defend its right to impeach for High Treason on a general charge.

For two weeks the struggle between the two Houses of Parliament continued, and with every passing day the tension mounted. John Evelyn feared the return of a commonwealth; Pepys's friends stood amazed to see the King united with the Commons and the populace against the House of Lords—this was a government never seen before in England. Amidst this clamour and conflict the anti-Clarendonians retained the support of the Commons for two reasons: the honour of the House would not permit the admission that evidence was wanting, and the House was jealous of its right to impeach on a general charge, a right which they believed necessary for the protection of their liberties against the encroachment of over-powerful ministers. But equally firm stood the Lords, possessed of the certainty that they were on the side of law and justice, eager to vindicate their power of judicature, and unwilling to allow the Commons by frivolous impeachments to empty their House of its members.[3]

[1] To the objection that Strafford's impeachment was no fit precedent, Sir Thomas Osborne answered that Clarendon himself, then Edward Hyde, had promoted it (Danby Papers, B.M. Add. MSS 28045, f. 11). In a like manner, Osborne's role in prosecuting Clarendon was remembered against him when the Commons impeached him in 1678.
[2] Fr. Trans. 18/28 Nov. 1667; Egerton MSS 2539, f. 138.
[3] John Nicholas wrote to his father (Egerton MSS 2539, f. 145), 'If we split on this rock [commitment on a general charge] the town will then talk loudly what they now whisper, that we are glad of the occasion because we cannot prove our accusation. And if we carry this privilege it is in our power to empty the House of Lords by impeaching all those that stand in our way.' The arguments voiced in the House of Commons for commitment may be read in *Proceedings... Touching the Impeachment of the Earl of Clarendon*, pp. 51–2, 86–7, 117–23 and Grey, *Debates*, I, 42. Those voiced in the Lords against commitment may be read in Rawlinson MSS A 130, ff. 98v–100.

Only Clarendon's flight to France on 27 November ended this irreconcilable conflict. Flight was painful to Clarendon, for it suggested guilt, and he was sure of his innocence. But he knew of no other way to escape trial before a packed court; and that was the fate that Charles and Buckingham were preparing for him. Their plan was to prorogue Parliament, to appoint twenty-four peers to sit as a special court, and to try Clarendon before it. The King, by immemorial practice, would appoint the twenty-four peers; Buckingham, by reason of his great influence at Court, would most certainly nominate them.[1] Before such a court Clarendon's innocence would be a paper shield. He therefore accepted Charles's promise that his honours and estates would not be touched if he fled, and took boat for France. Three weeks later Parliament passed and the King signed a bill permanently banishing him from the kingdom.

Though Clarendon was driven to France, office came only slowly to the anti-Clarendonians. Discredited in the Commons as undertakers for the King, they were unable to carry on his business there. Disgraced with the King for their violent attacks on his prerogative, they could not persuade him to grant them office.[2] But disappointment merely whetted their appetite. By continued importunities at Court and by relentless opposition to the Clarendonians in Parliament, they slowly forced their way into office. In June 1668 Buckingham secured the position of Master of the Horse. In September 1668 John Trevor became Secretary of State, and a month later Sir Thomas Osborne and Sir Thomas Littleton became joint Treasurers of the Navy. The King appointed Sir Richard Temple a Commissioner of the Customs in 1672, at a salary of £2,000 a year. A year later he appointed Edward Seymour a Commissioner of the Admiralty. Sir Robert Howard eventually secured the lucrative office of Auditor of the Receipt in the Exchequer.

The success of the anti-Clarendonians did not go unobserved. Politicians learned from it, as the Marquis of Newcastle feared they would, that preferment could be gained by opposition, that attacking the King's ministers could be the first step to high office. It became

---

[1] Fr. Trans. 18/28 Nov. 1667. Lord Conway wrote to Ormond (P.R.O. Carte Papers, vol. 35) that Clarendon's enemies being 'somewhat diffident of the validity of evidence, do purposely decline the trial of the whole House, that he may come afterwards to a trial by commission directed only to twenty-four of such as they shall choose'.

[2] Sir Richard Temple complained bitterly at the King's refusal to bestow offices upon the undertakers (*Huntington Library Quarterly*, xx, no. 2, pp. 139–41).

the constant trade of all ambitious statesmen after 1667 to oppose the ministers then in power, that they might scramble to office over their backs. Whether it was the adherents of Arlington driving against Buckingham in 1673, or Shaftesbury and Montagu impeaching Danby in 1678, or Sir Francis Winnington and Sir Thomas Jones demanding the removal of Halifax in 1680, they all sought by their influence in Parliament to force their way into the King's service.[1]

This use of the power of impeachment to gain office distinguishes Clarendon's impeachment from those voted against Buckingham in 1626 and Laud and Strafford in 1640. Those who voted to impeach Buckingham and Laud and Strafford honestly believed that their counsels endangered the established government of the realm. This was not true of those who led in the impeachment of Clarendon. The Earl was already in disgrace and had no power to do good or ill. Even if he had enjoyed in 1667 the influence over Charles that he had enjoyed in 1660, no one really believed he would use it for any other purpose than to keep 'up the form and substance of things in the nation', a purpose which he promoted, believed Evelyn, above all other men.[2] In truth the power of impeachment as exercised in 1667 was not so much a weapon against arbitrary government as a lever for catapulting men into office. Seymour and Osborne and Howard had more in common with the Foxes and Whartons of the eighteenth century than with the Eliots and Pyms of the early seventeenth century. They were less concerned with defending the constitution than with the attainment of public office. They were driven less by a large public spirit than by a narrow personal ambition. Clarendon's impeachment marks the beginning of that struggle for office and the emoluments of office which played

---

[1] Colbert de Croissy, the French ambassador, described (Fr. Trans. 7/17 June 1669) how those who declaimed the loudest against the government and for Clarendon's destruction received offices and pensions, which led others to say openly, 'As the most factious were rewarded, so they must speak out against the present government.' So that (continues Colbert) where five or six are won over, many more join the opposition. A Country party pamphleteer (possibly Thomas Baker) wrote in the year 1681 (*The Head of the Nile: or the Turnings and Windings of the Factious Since Sixty*), 'Seeing preferment came by thwarting the King's party and designs, the whole nation, I mean their representatives, made it their constant trade. A great many got it that way and for the present were reconciled and highly offensive to us; but afterwards, being laid by for others that had the same game to play, they became disgusted and more inveterate than ever [against the Court]...'

[2] Evelyn, *Diary*, 27 Aug. 1667.

so great a role in British politics after 1714, after the great religious, constitutional, and dynastic issues had been settled. His impeachment did not continue the constitutional struggles of an earlier age: rather it opened the way to the factious political warfare of a later age.

Another consequence followed from Clarendon's impeachment: it further educated the honest country gentlemen in the art of supervising the executive. It taught them to inquire into the conduct of the King's ministers, to investigate defeats at sea, and to condemn abuses at home. The Duke of York saw more clearly than anyone that Clarendon's impeachment had injured the prerogative, that by it Parliament had regained the initiative lost in 1660. 'But the most fatal blow,' he said, 'the King gave himself to his power and prerogative...when he sought aid from the House of Commons to destroy the Earl of Clarendon...', for by that the Commons 'have grounded a pretence...of inspecting the conduct of statesmen, and indeed have fallen upon almost every minister since'.[1] Not only Charles's brother, but others expressed alarm that he should have surrendered the sceptre of government to the control of Parliament. His sister, the Duchess of Orleans, chastised him sharply for yielding so much to Parliament. The French ambassador wrote home that the King had acquired a present popularity at the expense of a real diminution of his authority. And Pepys and Ormond both came to describe Westminster as the master of Whitehall. Even Charles himself came to see the error that he had made. In 1674 the Venetian ambassador wrote, 'As His Majesty had not the heart to dismiss the late Chancellor Clarendon, Parliament was encouraged to impeach him, and the King now sees the inconvenience of having his ministers attacked by Parliament to the prejudice of his repute and authority.'[2]

For these two reasons—that the impeachment encouraged politicians to seek office by attacking the King's ministers in Parliament, and that it taught the rank and file members to condemn abuses in administration—the fall of Clarendon weakened Charles's hold on

---

[1] J. S. Clarke, *The Life of James II* (1816), I, 593, 662. The Duke of York wrote to the Prince of Orange in 1681 (Prinsterer, *Archives ou Correspondance inédite de la Maison d'Orange-Nassau*, 2nd ser. v, 481) that the Exclusion Bill would 'prove as fatal to the Crown and the lawful heirs of it, as His Majesty's calling in Parliament to destroy the late Earl of Clarendon has proved to the ministers; for you see they have still fallen on most of them since, and claim it a right so to do...'.

[2] Bryant, *Letters of Charles II*, pp. 205, 216; Fr. Trans. 2/12 Dec. 1667; Carte, *Ormond*, v, 67; Pepys, *Diary*, 22 Apr. 1668; *C.S.P. Ven. 1674–5*, p. 368.

the executive power. No doubt Charles, by ridding himself of Clarendon, escaped from the dominance of an overbearing minister and from the too-rigid forms of the Council. But the real challenge to Charles's power never came from the Council or from the great lords who sat at the Council table. The King chose his own Council, and the great ministers who served on it were expected faithfully to execute the King's commands, even though they disagreed with them. Clarendon, as Speaker Onslow later observed, drew more censure upon himself for those policies that he did not advise, but dutifully carried out, than for those that he did advise. His compliance 'wrought his ruin with the people, and put the King himself very likely upon venturing at measures he would otherwise have been afraid to have attempted'.[1] Not the Council, but a Parliament whose members the King did not choose, threatened the prerogative. Charles's dismissal of an overbearing minister may have strengthened his grasp on the sceptre; his dismissal of a minister threatened by an impeachment may have preserved it; but his joining in the impeachment indubitably weakened it.

Clarendon's impeachment had a third consequence: it gave occasion for yet another definition of the responsibilities of the King's ministers. True, there was no trial where those responsibilities could be debated, as with Strafford and Laud, but from distant France Clarendon replied to his prosecutors with *A Discourse by Way of Vindication of Myself.* In the *Discourse* he defended his innocence and defined his responsibilities in a manner made familiar to English ears by the pleas of Buckingham, Strafford, and Laud. He had negotiated the sale of Dunkirk only 'in obedience to the King's commands'; since others had advised the King to farm the customs he was 'not responsible'; he merely acted ministerially to the King and Council in issuing *quo warrantos*; Learned Counsel declared void the Earl of Carlisle's patent for the government of Barbados; the clerk in Chancery, not he, replaced 'Warwick' with 'Worcester' in Dr Crowther's patent; as required by his oath as a councillor, in discharge of his conscience, and to the best of his understanding, he gave advice at the Council Board for the maintenance of troops by free quarters and contributions. But the dominant theme of the *Discourse*, as one would expect from the apostle of conciliar government, was the concurrence of the Council in what he had done.

[1] Burnet, *History*, I, 53.

Never was there a fuller concurrence at the Board than in the grant of the Canary Patent. The rest of the Lords of the Council concurred in the Act of Settlement for Ireland. Every dispatch from Breda came before the Board. The Council Board imprisoned men in remote places, and, though present at the Board, 'I am not to answer apart for anything done by them.' To this defence the House of Commons had only one answer, that Clarendon was responsible as the chief minister. Sir Thomas Littleton, Sir Thomas Osborne, and Sir Richard Temple, in the debates on his impeachment, each declared him responsible as the King's chief minister. The last article of the impeachment explicitly charged that he had been 'the principal author of the fatal counsel of dividing the fleet'. In fact the Commons possessed no proof that Clarendon had been 'the principal author' of that counsel, and Clarendon in the *Discourse* categorically denied it. Once again the Commons found it impossible to penetrate the secrecy that prevailed at Court and in the Council.[1]

The impeachment of the Earl of Clarendon arose from the confluence of two forces: the political ambitions of the anti-Clarendonians and the anger of the Country party at the loss of the Dutch war. The fall of Clarendon satisfied neither group. The undertakers had yet to sweep all the Clarendonians from office and the Country party had not yet delved to the bottom of the mismanagement of the war. The parliamentary sessions of 1668 and 1669–70 witnessed the denouement of both these dramas.

The adherents of the Duke of Buckingham, avid for the fruits of office, sought to appease their appetites by replacing the Clarendonians at Court and in Council. Led by the Duke, they pressed Charles to dismiss Clarendon's two sons from Court, to remove Lord Ashley, the Earl of Anglesey, and the Earl of Bridgewater from the Council, to replace Secretary Morice with Sir John Trevor, to make Littleton and Osborne joint Treasurers of the Navy in Anglesey's stead, and to dismiss Ormond and Carteret from the Irish government. The massacre of the Clarendonian innocents should not stop at the Court and Council, but should extend to the Dean of the Royal Chapel and to justices of the peace. No man who had

---

[1] *A Collection of Several Tracts of the Right Honourable Edward, Earl of Clarendon* (1727), pp. 9, 18, 19, 37, 38, 65, 79; C. Robbins (ed.), *The Diary of John Milward* (Cambridge, 1938), p. 99; Grey, *Debates*, I, 23, 28.

defended the Earl of Clarendon could hope to escape the importunities of the undertakers.[1]

Yet the undertakers did not succeed. Charles possessed too much humanity and too little ruthlessness to purge his Court and Council, his Chapels and Commissions of Peace, of innocent men. He refused to remove those that the Buckingham faction designed for sacrifice. This impelled the faction to discover some means to force Charles to bend to their will. The means that they seized upon was a threat to resign from office. In late December Buckingham told Charles that if he did not dismiss men unacceptable to Parliament, he must resign, in order to avoid the precipice towards which His Majesty was driving.[2] Charles ignored the threat and called the bluff. The Duke did not resign. Yet the voltatile, vengeful Buckingham had discovered in his haphazard way a weapon which would ultimately destroy the King's independence. Clarendon, a man of integrity and probity, believed that a minister should continue to serve the King even though the King refused his advice. Buckingham, possessing no such scruples, believed that a minister might threaten to resign if the King did not employ his friends. The practice urged by the irresponsible Duke did more to promote responsible government than did the principle advocated by the more responsible Earl.

Buckingham knew that his threat to resign would carry force only if Charles required his services. He therefore sought in February 1668 to prove that his services were indispensable, particularly in the management of Parliament. In this enterprise he failed egregiously. When Parliament met on 10 February, he and his lieutenants proved quite unable to govern the House of Commons. The reason was twofold: their undertaking had discredited them in the House, and their policy of ecclesiastical comprehension met with no favour there. The Earl of Bristol had discovered in 1663 that the House of Commons detested 'the vain proposals...of pick-thank undertakers'. The Duke of Buckingham discovered the same in February 1668, when the rumour spread through the Commons that he and Temple and Howard and Littleton had undertaken to secure the King money in return for office. Members of the House proclaimed

---

[1] Fr. Trans. 9/19 Dec. 1667, 27 Dec. 1667/5 Jan. 1668, 31 Dec. 1667/9 Jan. 1668 and 6/16 Jan. 1668; Pepys, *Diary*, 30, 31 Dec. 1667, 5 Jan. 1668; Tanner MSS 45, ff. 247, 249; Carte MSS 220, f. 326; *C.S.P. Dom. 1667–68*, p. 258; Clarendon MSS 87, f. 84; B.M. Add. MSS 32499, f. 18.

[2] Fr. Trans. 31 Dec. 1667/9 Jan. 1668.

their independence of these men by refusing to listen to or follow them. For most members this was no hardship, since they detested the undertakers' plan to comprehend Protestant dissenters in the Church of England. Even before the King addressed the two Houses, the Commons resolved to ask Charles to suppress, not tolerate, religious dissent. In the face of this defeat, the undertakers deserted their own undertaking, and spent the rest of the session attacking the King's servants and opposing votes of supply. When these tactics failed to secure their redemption in the eyes of the House, they sought to exploit a dispute between the two Houses (over the question whether the Lords could act as a civil court of first instance in the case of Skinner *v.* the East India Company) in order to break up the present Parliament and secure the election of a new one. The threat of resignation proving ineffectual at Court, they resorted to parliamentary opposition; the resort to Parliament failing, they sought to appeal to the country. The anti-Clarendonians in 1668 discovered the classic moves for a politician who loses first the favour of the King and then the confidence of Parliament.[1]

The Earl of Northumberland, a leading Presbyterian peer, told the Duke of York in 1667 that the removal of the Earl of Clarendon would not satisfy the nation, that the nation also expected the redress of other grievances. The demand for the redress of grievances was not of recent origin, for in 1665 the Commons had clamoured loudly against the Earl of Sandwich for embezzling prize goods and leaving the Narrow Seas unguarded. In 1666 they had even passed an act (rejected by the Lords) for the parliamentary accounting of all money voted for the Dutch war.[2] The rivulet of 1665, the stream of 1666, became by the autumn of 1667 a torrent that swept aside all objections to the parliamentary superintendence of the executive. At the express invitation of the King, Parliament passed a bill establishing a parliamentary Commission for examining the accounts of money voted for the war. The House of Commons then appointed a Committee to inquire into the causes of the miscarriages of the war. The Commission and the Committee exercised the fullest powers of inquiry, ordered the King's servants to appear before

---

[1] B.M. Loan 29/46 No. 7; Fr. Trans. 10/20 Feb. 1668; Pepys, *Diary*, 14 Feb. 1668; Egerton MSS 2539, ff. 155, 167, 193; Shaftesbury Papers, P.R.O. Bundle 4, f. 178.

[2] Clarke, *James II*, 1, 426; Pepys, *Diary*, 25 Oct. 1665, 8 Dec. 1666. Lord Conway wrote to George Rawdon on 30 Oct. 1665 (J. Bramhall, *The Rawdon Papers*, 1819, p. 219), 'The temper of the House of Commons is strangely altered, and grown like to that in '41.'

them, interrogating them, demanded information from them, called for papers from the Secretary's office, required the production of accounts, even requested peers of the realm to send them written narratives concerning the disaster at Chatham. Never had a House of Commons so emphatically asserted its power to inquire into the King's administration. Never had a King of England so supinely defended his administration from such an inquiry.

The cause for this unprecedented exercise of the right of inquiry was the anger of the country at three years of defeat, disgrace, and mismanagement. In 1665 the Duke of York failed to prosecute his victory over the Dutch; in 1666 the division of the fleet caused the English to suffer defeat in the Channel; in 1667 the Dutch burnt and captured English vessels anchored in the river Medway. With each passing year the dishonour attendant upon English arms mounted. Defeat on the Isle of Rhé forty years before had moved Denzil Holles to write, 'Since England was England it received not so dishonourable a blow.' Defeat on the river Medway in 1667 moved John Evelyn to exclaim, 'A dreadful spectacle as ever Englishmen saw, and a dishonour never to be wiped off.'[1] Both disasters arose from the attempt of an incompetent executive to wage war with insufficient money, but in both instances the country blamed the incompetent ministers, not the Parliament which voted insufficient money. They even applauded Parliament when it called the King's servants to account for faults which its own niggardliness caused.

The Earl of Arlington, a minister deeply implicated in the mismanagement of the war, expressed the hope that the Christmas recess would cause Parliament 'to lay aside all inquisitions into men's behaviour'. His hope seemed futile, for, when the Commons assembled again in February, they resumed their inquisitions. They revived the Committee on Miscarriages and asked for reports from the Commission on Accounts. They solemnly condemned as miscarriages the failure to prosecute the Duke of York's victory, the division of the fleet, the failure to fortify Sheerness, the payment of seamen in tickets, and the lack of ships to defend the Medway. Yet Arlington's hope was not an entirely idle one, for the Commons condemned no man as the author of these miscarriages. The crucial debate occurred on 15 February, when members of the House fell on those counsellors who had advised the division of the fleet. Some

[1] Evelyn, *Diary*, 28 June 1667.

members even demanded their dismissal before voting supplies. This attack, however, came to nothing, for the Commons, though they knew that Arlington had not secured accurate intelligence of the movement of the Dutch fleet and that Coventry had not recalled Prince Rupert in time, did not know who had advised Charles to send Prince Rupert after the French in the first place. The dauntless Sir Richard Temple suggested that they ask Charles who advised him to send Prince Rupert after the French, but the House ignored his suggestion and resolved to accuse no one. Having voted that miscarriages had occurred, they seemed content to go no further.[1]

Then on 26 March the House revived the Committee on Miscarriages and within six weeks impeached Sir William Penn, Peter Pett, and Henry Brouncker. The Commons impeached these three men and not others because they had particular enemies and because they were notoriously at fault. In the reign of Charles II it required the combined force of personal envy and public hate to drive home an impeachment. The fate of these three men proved this fact.

Sir William Penn suffered from the envy of those who did not wish him to go to sea as commander of the fleet in 1668. When rumour of his appointment ran through Westminster in late March, these men, led by the Duke of Albemarle and Prince Rupert, secured the revival of the Committee on Miscarriages. The Committee then launched an inquiry into Penn's role in the embezzlement of prize goods in 1665, blithely ignoring the conduct of eight other Flag Officers who had joined in the embezzlement. The enemies of Sir William Penn had no difficulty persuading the Commons to vote an impeachment, for Penn was undeniably guilty. Nor did it help Penn to plead the commands of the Earl of Sandwich, for the Commons would have impeached Sandwich had not Charles sent him ambassador to Spain in order to remove him from Parliament's wrath and Buckingham's intrigues. The sequel to Penn's impeachment is revealing. Once Charles had decided not to send Penn to sea that summer, his enemies ceased to press his impeachment.[2]

[1] Carte MSS 46, f. 581; *C.J.* IX, 43–9; Milward, *Diary*, pp. 185–6; Grey, *Debates*, I, 71–9.

[2] Carte MSS 34, f. 488; Pepys, *Diary*, 26, 29 March, 16, 27 Apr. 1668; John Nicholas wrote to his father on 26 March (Egerton MSS 2539, f. 182), 'Sir William Penn is not a man acceptable. The Parliament have a mind to fasten some of the miscarriages in the last war on him, and upon hearing that he was to go to sea, they this day ordered the reviving the Committee for Miscarriages...' On 21 April he wrote (f. 204), 'My Lord of Sandwich is spared for this session in regard of his character abroad...'

The combined forces bearing down on Commissioner Pett were overwhelming. The wonder is he escaped so lightly. The Duke of Albemarle was his most inveterate enemy, Pett having blamed the Duke for the defenceless condition of the Medway when the Dutch sailed up it. Albemarle sought revenge by promoting Pett's impeachment in the House of Commons in December 1667. The Commons did not hesitate to vote the impeachment, for Pett had used the boats under his command to carry his private goods, rather than tow the *Royal Charles*, up the Medway. Yet the Commons did not send articles of impeachment against him to the Lords until 4 May 1668, when it was known that the session would end within a week. One possible explanation for the tardiness of the House is the fact that Charles had already dismissed Pett in June 1667. A more likely explanation is that Albemarle feared a trial that would reveal his own negligence.[1]

Henry Brouncker, Privy Purse to the Duke of York and a favourite at Court, served, as did Pett, as a scapegoat on whom Englishmen could lay the blame for the loss of the war. The Committee on Miscarriages charged him with falsely telling Captain Harman (on the night following the Duke of York's victory over the Dutch) that the Duke desired him to shorten sail. Attributing the loss of the war to this single act, the Commons expelled Brouncker from the House and impeached him before the Lords. Brouncker fled to France to escape trial. Though it appears that he fled principally from the wrath of Parliament, he actually feared more his enemies at Court. As he wrote from Paris in June, 'But that which frights me more than my trial is that I hear from several hands the probability of great alterations, which I know cannot come but at the expense of my friends, so that 'tis possible I shall find the Court as much against me as the House of Commons, in which case I will be hanged in France rather than return into England.'[2] The one prospect that frightened, and rightly frightened, every Stuart politician was to lose the confidence both of the Court and the Commons.

By their misdeeds, Penn, Pett, and Brouncker had angered the House of Commons and exposed themselves to impeachments

[1] Pepys, *Diary*, 23, 25, 31 Oct. 1667; *The Bulstrode Papers* (in *The Collection of Autographed Letters and Historical Documents Formed by Alfred Morrison*, 2nd ser. 1), p. 5; Milward, *Diary*, pp. 177–8.
[2] Henry Brouncker [to Sir William Coventry?], 9 June 1668, Halifax Papers, Box 1.

initiated by their enemies. Coventry, Ormond, and Carteret, men of higher station and greater reputation, had committed no such misdeeds and were accordingly impervious to the attacks of their enemies, the anti-Clarendonians. Of these attacks, the one which Sir Richard Temple launched against Sir William Coventry affords a classic example of Restoration intrigue. Coventry, as Secretary to the Duke of York (and therefore to the Lord Admiral), had managed the Navy so ably that his enemies could find nothing with which to charge him—except that he had sold offices. Temple, who wished to drive Coventry from the government, seized on this charge. He employed Captain Tatnall to bribe seamen to declare that they had paid Coventry for their places; they were also to sign petitions, which were to be presented to the House of Commons, charging Coventry with this crime. Captain Tatnall carried out his tasks with enthusiasm. He conspired with naval officers in King Street, travelled to Chelsea to collect names on his petitions, and offered Sir John Coventry £20 to accuse Sir William Coventry. He boasted that 'he would have Sir William's periwig from his head ere long', and rejoiced when Penn appeared at the bar of the House of Commons, predicting that Coventry would follow soon after. He dined with Sir Richard Temple at Westminster, promised promotions to those who would sign his petitions, and told his friends that Temple had 'made the Chancellor fly his country, and so he would make the rest, or else their necks must hang'. In April rumour reported that the petitions would soon be introduced into the House against Coventry for selling offices. John Nicholas wrote to his father that the Money Bill may be postponed, 'for there is an expectation that some of our undertakers will introduce some what that may be in order to the impeachment of Sir William Coventry'. The expected impeachment never occurred. Captain Tatnall confided to Gilbert Cornelius in a brandy shop near the Navy Office that Temple put off accusing Coventry in the expectation that something else would come in against him. In truth, Temple had no material charge to bring against Coventry, who had merely followed the practice of his predecessors in taking fees from those whom he appointed to office. He was prepared to plead this in a speech he composed for his defence, but never had occasion to deliver. He also mentioned in the same intended speech the reasons for his prosecution. These were, first, the anger of his enemies at their 'want of preferement', and secondly, his 'not joining to cast out Clarendon and bring in anti-Clarendonians'.[1]

The two men whom the anti-Clarendonians most persistently sought to cast out were the Duke of Ormond and Sir George Carteret. Ormond's great enemy was Buckingham, who desired to succeed him as Steward of the Household and Lord Lieutenant of Ireland. To attain this object he promoted accusation after accusation against Ormond in Parliament. In October 1667 he and his friends composed twelve articles of impeachment against the Lord Lieutenant, which they circulated among members of Parliament. In February 1668, they supported Alderman Barker's private petitions against Ormond, and secured a parliamentary investigation of Ormond's enforcement of the Irish Cattle Act. In March one of their number, Sir Charles Wheeler, accused Ormond of pocketing £20,000 of the King's money. In April the friends of Buckingham, who now included the Earl of Orrery, President of Munster, promoted a petition of the Irish Adventurers that obliquely charged Ormond with favouring Papists in Ireland.[2] But the House of Commons countenanced none of these accusations, for the Duke had committed no crime that could be justly charged against him. The Commons' restraint, however, gave Ormond little comfort, for he knew that the purpose of these accusations was only to tarnish his good name with all men. He saw clearly that the end of parliamentary accusations in the 1660's was to blast men's reputations, not to bring them to trial. Above all, he feared that these accusations would prevail with the King. 'But if the faction against me should prevail in the Parliament,' he wrote, 'it is not sure but it must upon [the King]...' Time proved Ormond's fears justified. Charles dismissed him from office in February 1669. The French ambassador wrote shortly before Ormond's dismissal, that the King would dismiss his Lord Lieutenant in order to prevent Parliament, when it reassembled, from weakening his authority by forcing him to remove the Duke.

---

[1] Coventry Papers, CI, ff. 121, 127, 133, 137–137v, 145, 157–158, 161, 225–232; Pepys, *Diary*, 24 March, 20 Apr., 24 Apr. 1668; Egerton MSS 2539, f. 206. A copy of a petition to be preferred against Coventry for selling offices is in Rawlinson MSS A 195a.

[2] Carte, *Ormond*, II, 356–9, 363–5; Carte MSS 220, f. 326–327v; Carte MSS 46, ff. 610v, 618v, 625. John Nicholas wrote to his father, 23 April (Egerton MSS 2539, f. 204), the petition of the Adventurers 'is chiefly levelled at my Lord Ormond in order to the impeaching of him, and is principally promoted by my Lord Orrery, who was formerly his creature, but now at defiance with him. It finds a great deal of countenance amongst us as do all matters of accusation.'

There is some truth in this remark, for Edward Seymour had boasted in June 1668 that he was prepared to introduce against Ormond articles of impeachment worse than those brought against Strafford. But more likely Charles dismissed Ormond for the same reason he dismissed Secretary Morice, the Earl of Anglesey, and Sir William Coventry: he could not withstand any longer the ceaseless importunities at Court of the anti-Clarendonians.[1]

The dismissal of Ormond did not end the accusations against him in Parliament. The peevish, ungovernable Earl of Meath introduced charges against him into the House of Commons in the autumn of 1669. Ormond's friends believed (though wrongly) that Buckingham and Orrery had incited the Earl of Meath to present his charges to the Commons. Therefore, in reprisal, they introduced an impeachment against Orrery, proving that two could play the game of parliamentary impeachment as well as one. As a result the ensuing session of Parliament witnessed a comedy of impeachments, in which each faction at Court extended into Parliament its intrigues against the other. The friends of Arlington and Ormond in the Commons—Samuel Sandys, Sir Thomas Meres, Sir Robert Carr, the Cavaliers, and the Clarendonians—drove on Orrery's impeachment with zeal. The friends of Buckingham and Orrery—Sir Robert Howard, Edward Seymour, Sir Richard Temple, the Presbyterians, and the anti-Clarendonians—defended Orrery and countenanced the attack on Ormond. Charles stood aghast, and commanded his servants to cease accusing one another in Parliament. Yet the indolent Charles had invited such conduct, not only by failing to rule at Court, not only by seeking Parliament's help in ridding himself of Clarendon, but also by promising Orrery in 1668 that he should not suffer if he came to England to accuse Ormond. The favour Charles showed Orrery in the next year drove Arlington to despair, and to intrigues in Parliament. Nothing came of the impeachment against Orrery or of the accusation presented against Ormond, but the story of their introduction into the House of Commons offers further

---

[1] Carte, *Ormond*, II, app., pp. 41, 46–7, 60; Fr. Trans. 1/10 Sept. and 2/12 Nov. 1668; B.M. Add. MSS 34711, ff. 105–108. Ten years later, when Ormond was again Lord Lieutenant of Ireland, Henry Coventry wrote to him (May 17 1679, B.M. Add. MSS 25125, f. 68) that he found no inclination in the King toward his removal, for 'circumstances are much altered, your danger was principally from Court, and your interest in the House of Commons was so considerable that it was that which secured you. I would . . . either you or any man of your principle had so prevailing an interest there now.'

proof that the *primum mobile* behind parliamentary impeachments in Restoration England was the intrigue of one courtier against another.[1]

The anti-Clarendonians also spent much energy in the 1669 session attacking Sir George Carteret, Treasurer of Ireland. They pursued him not only because they wished to drive him from office, but because such pursuit won them favour in the House of Commons, thereby enhancing their value to the King. In 1668 Charles had not granted the undertakers all that they had bargained for. They therefore resolved to go into opposition until he did; and they chose Carteret as their target. The 'great engine of state' (in Sandwich's words) which they turned against Carteret was the Commission of Accounts, meeting at Brooke House. The Brooke House Commissioners appeared before the Commons in the autumn of 1669 and made many damaging observations on Carteret's behaviour as Treasurer of the Navy, an office which he had held until 1667, when he parted with it to Lord Anglesey in order to escape Parliament's attention. Once the Commissioners had reported, the same old gang, Howard, Temple, Seymour, and Garroway, clamoured for Carteret's impeachment. The country gentlemen, still smarting from the failure of the war, still angry at the extravagance of the Court, still blinded by suspicion, listened sympathetically to these fiery spirits. They voted Carteret guilty of numerous misdemeanours and suspended him from the House. But Buckingham's faction did not demand his impeachment, for the House of Lords, examining the report of the Brooke House Commission, cleared him of all the misdemeanours charged against him. This forced Carteret's enemies to by-pass an impeachment, which the Lords would certainly strike down, in favour of an address, which the Commons could vote independently of the Lords. On 11 December they moved that the House vote an address to the King requesting him not to employ Carteret in any place, military or civil, in England or Ireland. The House came to no vote on the motion, for Black Rod suddenly arrived to summon them to the Lords, where Charles announced the prorogation of Parliament to February 1670.[2]

[1] Carte, *Ormond*, II, 390–1; F. R. Harris, *The Life of Edward Mountagu, K.G. First Earl of Sandwich* (1912), II, 312–17; Fr. Trans. 5/15 Aug., 18/28 Nov., 29 Nov./9 Dec., 2/12 and 13/23 Dec. 1668; Grey, *Debates*, I, 182–5, 212.

[2] Fr. Trans. 14/24 Feb. 1669, 18/28 Jan., 27 Jan./3 Feb., 14/24 Feb. 1670; Grey, *Debates*, I, 157–8, 166, 169–72, 176, 213–14; Harris, *Sandwich*, II, 311–16.

When Parliament reassembled on 14 February, Charles told them that he had examined Sir George Carteret's accounts during the recess and found them in good order. No money voted for the Dutch war had been diverted from that use, and much ordinary revenue had been used for it. This speech proved decisive. Though Buckingham spread the rumour that £800,000 remained unaccounted for, though Sir Robert Howard spoke to eighty of the Country party in a tavern, though Garroway rushed into the breach, the attack against Carteret came to nought. It did so because Carteret had committed no crime more serious than attempting to keep the fleet at sea by diverting money from wages to provisions, and because the members of the Cavalier Parliament were at heart still loyal to their King. Once Charles summoned up the courage to protect Carteret, he regained the initiative that he had lost in 1667 and restored the balance of government that had been established in 1660. The imperious tone of his speech on 14 February differed markedly from the craven notes of his speech from the throne in 1667; and with good reason, for Charles was now disillusioned with parliamentary undertakers who promised more than they could perform. He therefore deserted their counsels for the counsels of others. He announced that in the future he would favour those who had served him in the past, not those who had opposed him. He turned from parliamentary undertaking to parliamentary management, from trust in empty promises to a naked use of the power of patronage. At the same time he turned from government by Privy Councillors and a single minister to government by personal favourites and departmental heads. He divided the business of government into several channels, reserving the direction of all to himself.[1]

The long vendetta of the anti-Clarendonians against the Clarendonians brought forth, therefore, not responsible government, but personal government, the government of Charles II, abetted by his sister in France, his brother at Court, Lauderdale in Scotland, and accommodating ministers in London. Charles now governed his realm according to his personal predilections rather than the wishes of his people. He totally disregarded the principle advocated by Sir William Temple, his ambassador at the Hague, 'that a monarchy

---

[1] *C.J.* ix, 121; *Cal. of Tr. Books, 1667–68*, p. viii; Fr. Trans. 18/28 Jan. and 14/24 Feb. 1670; Harris, *Sandwich*, ii, 193; A. B. Grosart (ed.), *The Complete Works in Verse and Prose of Andrew Marvell* (1875), ii, 315.

where the Prince governs by the affections and according to the opinions and interests of his people, or the bulk of them...makes of all others the safest and firmest government'.[1]

The personal government of Charles from 1670 to 1674 wrecked the balance of government momentarily restored when the House of Commons dropped their prosecution of Sir George Carteret. The misgovernment of these years, the years of the Cabal ministry, provoked new assaults on the constitutional arrangements established at the Restoration. Those arrangements most men admired, but they soon discovered that they were wanting in one respect: they offered no way to end the sway of ministers whose policies seemed to threaten true religion and English liberty. The rank and file in the House of Commons, men of no party, men loyal to the King, had no desire to alter the constitution; they merely wished to save England from the dangerous policies pursued by the Cabal. Shaftesbury's design to tolerate Dissenters, and Clifford's to ease Papists, by a Declaration of Indulgence frightened them. Lauderdale's remark that the King's Declarations had the force of law threatened their legislative power. The Stop of the Exchequer injured their purses, and opened the way for the King to wage war without first securing their consent. Successive prorogations of Parliament raised the spectre of its extinction; while Buckingham's threat to use the army assembled at Blackheath to purge Parliament revived memories of Cromwell. The defeat of the navy at Southwold Bay disgraced English arms and ended all hopes of a profitable victory over England's commercial rival, the Dutch. Meanwhile the progress of French arms in the Netherlands frightened those Englishmen, and they were legion, who suspected that the Treaty of Dover secretly provided for the restoration of Popery in England by means of French arms.[2] The Church threatened by Indulgences, the law overthrown by the Declaratory Power, credit destroyed by the Stop of the Exchequer, Parliament over-awed by a standing army, the navy defeated by the Dutch, the country imperilled by the growth of French power—it is little wonder that the uncommitted rank and file in the Commons turned against the government in January

[1] Sir William Temple, *Works* (Edinburgh, 1754), II, 52.
[2] Ruvigny wrote to Louis XIV (Fr. Trans. 27 Dec. 1673/7 Jan. 1674), 'Parliament is certain that there are articles between Your Majesty and Charles to establish Catholicism and arbitrary government here. The opinion is so widespread and strong, that one despairs to change it.'

1674. They had little confidence in Charles, and none at all in his ministers.

Criticism of the ministers who made up the Cabal began as early as October 1669 and mounted in a crescendo to late 1673. In October 1669 some unknown factious person (believed to be a supporter of Buckingham) scattered in Westminster Hall a libel, entitled 'The Alarum', against Arlington, Clifford, and Shaftesbury (then Lord Ashley). It accused these lords of being servile placemen who clung to office from greed, who sought to establish a military model of government, who told the King that he surrendered his Crown if he failed to protect his ministers. 'As Captain Smith', observed the author of 'The Alarum', 'tied an Indian to his girdle to receive arrows shot at him, so ministers use the King to shield them from the arrows of Parliament.' 'The Alarum' spoke for a handful of disgruntled Englishmen. Dr Du Moulin's pamphlet, 'England's Appeal from the Private Cabal at Whitehall to the Great Council of the Nation', published in the winter of 1673, expressed the sentiments of the great majority of Englishmen. It portrayed Arlington and Buckingham as the dupes of France, urged that Parliament discover those who had broken the Triple Alliance, and recommended the impeachment of the King's ministers unless they broke the French Alliance.[1] A few months later, Parliament assembled again, to the terror of Shaftesbury, whom the House of Commons attacked for illegally issuing writs for parliamentary elections, and Clifford, whom Lord Cavendish denounced as unfit to be Lord Treasurer because suspect of being a Papist. Only the hasty revocation of the Declaration of Indulgence and the passage of a Test Act (requiring all office holders to take communion according to the usages of the Church of England and to declare against transubstantiation) saved the ministers of the Cabal from impeachments. During the summer the navy lost yet another campaign at sea, the Dutch seized New York, and the Duke of York refused to take the Test. When Parliament met again in the autumn, the House of Commons accordingly fell on the King's ministers, beginning with Lauderdale, the King's Commissioner in Scotland, whom they suspected of a design to destroy English liberty with Scottish troops. Lauderdale escaped

---

[1] 'The Alarum', in B.M. Add. MSS 38850, ff. 205–209; *England's Appeal from the Private Cabal at Whitehall, to the Great Council of the Nation, the Lords and Commons in Parliament Assembled*, in *State Tracts; being a Collection of Several Treatises relating to Government* (1689), pp. 11, 18, 23–5.

censure only because Charles suddenly prorogued Parliament in order to prevent the Commons from attacking his other ministers. Between the prorogation of Parliament in November and its reassembly in January 1674, the mounting wave of anger at the Cabal reached tidal proportions, and threatened to crush the King's ministers.[1]

Parliament had become an instrument of terror to the King's servants. This fact placed them in a dilemma, a dilemma which Lord Keeper Williams had first felt in 1621, but which was now many times more acute. What should they do when the King required them to execute policies hateful to Parliament? How could they retain royal favour while avoiding a parliamentary impeachment? Sir William Coventry, unable to serve with Buckingham and Arlington, avoided the dilemma by retiring from public service. Lord Keeper Bridgeman, unwilling to put the Great Seal to an illegal commission for martial law, fell victim to the dilemma when Charles dismissed him. Samuel Pepys signed the warrants presented to him, even a warrant for the sale of anchors to the French, but he read Coke at night in order to insure that he committed no treason. Fearful that they might already have committed treason, the ministers of the Cabal sued out pardons from the King and persuaded Parliament in 1673 to pass an Act of Grace protecting them. Not trusting solely to pardons and Acts of Grace, they also sought by other means to escape from their dilemma.[2]

Lord Treasurer Clifford sought to escape by hurling defiance at Parliament. Inspired by God (as he said), he told the House of Lords that the House of Commons encroached upon the royal prerogative by concerning themselves with ecclesiastical affairs. Parliament replied to these high prerogative notions by passing the Test Act, which forced Clifford to resign and retire to the country, where he soon died. Where Clifford sought safety first in defiance and then in retirement, Shaftesbury sought it in desertion. Threatened by an impeachment in the spring of 1673, he spoke in favour of the Test

[1] Grey, *Debates*, II, 2–7, 152, 222; Eachard, *History of England*, pp. 888, 891; B. D. Henning (ed.), *The Parliamentary Diary of Sir Edward Dering* (New Haven, 1940), p. 148; Stowe MSS 203, f. 161.

[2] Browning, *Danby*, I, 93, 317; Pepys, *Diary*, 4 Nov. 1667; *C.J.* IX, 280; *C.S.P. Dom. 1673*, p. 127. Sir William Coventry told Pepys (*Diary*, 28 Oct. 1667) that he desired no public employment even 'if his commission were brought to him wrapt in gold...' and that 'he would take nothing but in commission with others, who may bear part of the blame'.

Act in the House of Lords, joined the Country party in the King's Head Tavern, betrayed the King's counsels in public, and everywhere urged peace with the Dutch. But his desertion to the opposition, though it won him immunity from impeachment, earned him dismissal from office in the autumn of 1673. Buckingham sought to avoid dismissal and impeachment by simultaneously advocating Court policies and seeking Parliament's favour. He personally courted (reported Gilbert Talbot) members of Parliament, 'the debauched by drinking with them, the sober by grave and serious discourses, and the pious by receiving the sacraments at Westminster'. His efforts proved of no avail, for, though in December 1673 he suddenly rose in the King's favour, he lost Parliament's. The safety that Buckingham sought by a complete submission to the authority of the House of Commons, Arlington sought by an entire compliance with their policies. He counselled Charles to revoke the Declaration of Indulgence, accept the Test Act, rid the Court of Catholics, send away the Duke of York, and make a separate peace with the United Provinces. As a result his influence with the King diminished and his popularity in the Commons increased. The great Duke of Lauderdale disdained all such popular courses and relied solely on the protection of his sovereign. His sovereign, however, could not prevent the Commons from falling upon him with vehemence the moment Parliament met in January 1674.[1]

Parliament began by attacking Lauderdale, rather than any other minister, because he was the only member of the Cabal who had no party in the House of Commons. All the other members of the Cabal had a party there, even Clifford, who, while he lived, drew together the King's servants into a Court party. Shaftesbury, with characteristic violence, threw himself at the head of the Country party. Buckingham relied on the men who grouped themselves around his old friends, Edward Seymour, now Speaker, and Sir Thomas Osborne, now Lord Treasurer and Viscount Latimer. Frightened by the strength of Buckingham's faction in the House and shaken by Buckingham's threat to accuse him there, Arlington instructed his friends, led by Sir Thomas Littleton and Sir Charles

---

[1] Fr. Trans. 23 March/1 Apr., 26 March/3 Apr., 10/20 Nov. 1673; Roger North, *Examen* (1740), p. 40; W. D. Christie (ed.), *A Life of Anthony Ashley Cooper, First Earl of Shaftesbury* (1871), II, App. xxix; W. D. Christie (ed.), *Letters Addressed from London to Sir Joseph Williamson* (Camden Soc. n.s. VIII and IX), II, 31; Barbour, *Arlington*, pp. 220–2; O. Airy (ed.), *The Lauderdale Papers* (Camden Soc. n.s. XXXIV, XXXVI and XXXVIII), III, 3, 13.

Harbord, to work with the cabals of Ormond and Shaftesbury against those of Seymour and Osborne. The intrigues of contending ministers, none of whom believed Charles would protect them if he could profit by their fall, reached a fever pitch in January 1674. 'Your Excellencies will note', wrote the Venetian ambassador, 'that this parliamentary machine is a contrivance devised purposely by intriguing ministers to work it against each other.' Not only the anger of the nation against the government, but also the intrigues of the ministers against each other, caused the House of Commons in January 1674 to fall on the Duke of Lauderdale, the Duke of Bucking-ham, and the Earl of Arlington.[1]

The House of Commons began with Lauderdale, but they did not impeach him. Instead they voted on 13 January to present an address to the King asking him to remove Lauderdale from office and Court. The Commons chose this path because the impeachments that they had voted against Clarendon and the Clarendonians had proved more embarrassing than useful. 'Some gentlemen', observed Sir John Coventry, 'are for impeachments; we have not had good success in them hitherto.' In 1674 there was the additional obstacle of the Act of Grace of 1673, which Lauderdale and other ministers could plead in bar to an impeachment. The Commons therefore went by way of an address, which they were further emboldened to do because the Restoration had not destroyed, and the ensuing thirteen years had strengthened, the tradition that the King should dismiss ministers hateful to the people. 'All the awe you have upon the King's Council hereafter', said a member of the Convention Parliament, 'is, if they be such as the people have an ill opinion of, you may remove them...' Charles II himself gave an indirect blessing to this tradition by urging Parliament in 1667 to present him an address of thanks for the removal of the Earl of Clarendon. Andrew Marvell, poet and member of Parliament for Hull, opposed voting the address, remarking that 'Kings in their choice of ministers move in a sphere distinct from us'. But Sir William Coventry disagreed, saying, 'When the kingdom was in such consternation, I made it my request to the King that if I were any way obnoxious

[1] Fr. Trans. 20/30 Oct., 31 Oct./9 Nov., 3/13 and 17/27 Nov. 1673, 27 Dec. 1673/7 Jan. 1674; O. Airy (ed.), *Essex Papers* (Camden Soc. n.s. XLVII), I, 139, 142, 161; Christie, *Williamson Letters*, II, 29, 60–2, 77; *C.S.P. Ven. 1673–75*, p. 73. Halifax said of Charles II (Foxcroft, *Halifax*, II, 351), 'He lived with his ministers as he did with his mistresses; he used them, but he was not in love with them.'

to him or the nation he would remove me...thinking none fitting for his service that was not liking to him and his people, and those most proper that the nation most liked.' The House of Commons voted to present the address of thanks, Charles's solicitations in favour of it carrying more weight than Sir John Holland's plea that it is 'an undoubted prerogative of the King to remove his officers, his councillors, his servants, as he makes them, at his good will and pleasure'.[1]

The House of Commons next challenged the King's prerogative to remove whom he wished when he wished in December 1669. On the 11th of that month they were on the verge of voting an address asking Charles to remove Sir George Carteret from office and the Council when the Black Rod appeared at the door to ask their attendance at the Lords, where they were prorogued. No Black Rod appeared at the door on 18 March 1673 to save Colonel Richard Talbot, a Papist, a commander of a troop of horse, and an agent for the Irish Catholics, from an address asking that he 'be immediately dismissed out of all commands, either civil or military, and forbid access to Your Majesty's Court'. Mr Henry Powle justified voting such an address by appealing to the example of the first Lancastrian King. 'In 5 Henry IV complaint was made to the King in Parliament of his Confessor; the King, though he said he had nothing against him, yet upon the desire of the Commons, would put him out of his service, and remove him.' The certain fact that Talbot was a Papist forced Charles to dismiss him from his command and forbid him the Court. It is a maxim in jurisprudence that hard cases make bad law; it is an equally valid principle in politics, though Charles did not see it, that outrageous cases make new law.[2]

The Duke of Lauderdale's case was sufficiently outrageous to draw upon him the unanimous hostility of the House of Commons.

---

[1] Grey, *Debates*, II, 382; B.M. Add. MSS 35865, ff. 10–11; Pepys, *Diary*, 14 Oct. 1667; Thynne Papers XVI, f. 477; Tanner MSS 239, ff. 77v–78v. The Lords likewise passed the address of thanks at Charles's urging, though the Earls of Nottingham and Denbigh opposed it, arguing (Rawlinson MSS A 130, f. 93) that 'the King might displace his own servants at his own will, and it was not proper for the Parliament to take notice whether he had done well or ill in it...'.

[2] Airy, *Lauderdale Papers*, II, 168; Grey, *Debates*, II, 126–8, 161. Henry Coventry urged his good friend Dick Talbot to remain in retirement, writing to him (Nov. 1673, Coventry Papers, LXXXIII, f. 25), 'I believe all you say of your innocency, and that you have a good cause; but yet to speak to you as a seaman, though I knew my boat were good yet if the weather were bad and I were in port, I would not put to sea.'

Possessed of a haughty demeanour, an arrogant tongue, an avaricious wife, and vice-regal powers, he angered the Scots by his arbitrary government and frightened the English by his threatening language. In December 1673 his Scottish enemies, led by the Duke of Hamilton and the Earl of Tweeddale, came to London to inform members of Parliament of his iniquities in the north, of denials of *habeas corpus*, of salt, brandy, and tobacco monopolies, of corruption in the mint, of the sale of offices, of the engrossing of all power in his hands. These grievances, though they justified Lauderdale's boast to Charles that 'never was King so absolute as you are in poor old Scotland', did not concern England. What concerned England and frightened the House of Commons was Lauderdale's remark in Council that the King's edicts had the force of law and his promotion of a Militia Act in Scotland which gave Charles the right to order 20,000 Scotsmen to march into England. The remark was only a remark and the 20,000 militia men were never mustered; nevertheless both alarmed the English. The rumour that Lauderdale urged Charles in 1673 to summon Scottish troops to his aid rather than repeal the Declaration of Indulgence further heightened their fears. Since there were four members of the House who testified that they heard Lauderdale say that the King's edicts had the force of law, and since the Militia Act was in the statute book for all to see, the Commons with no further ado voted to address the King to remove the Duke of Lauderdale from all his employments and from the King's councils and presence for ever. Even the Cavaliers came into the vote, old hatreds being inflamed by Howe's, Garroway's, and Littleton's account of Lauderdale carrying to London in 1648 a Declaration of the Kirk for the execution of Charles I. No one remained to support the hated Duke and the motion to address the King for his removal carried *nemine contradicente*.[1]

The Duke of Buckingham's conduct was nearly as indefensible as Lauderdale's. Only the world did not regard him as arrogant and wilful; they viewed him as ridiculous and absurd. Notorious as the murderer (in a duel) of the Earl of Shrewsbury, known to be living in open adultery with the Countess of Shrewsbury, and celebrated

---

[1] Stowe MSS 203, ff. 237–238; Stowe MSS 204, ff. 38–39; R. Woodrow, *History of the Sufferings of the Church of Scotland* (Glasgow, 1839), II, 229–30; Burnet, *History*, I, 588–91; Grey, *Debates*, II, 236–44; *C.J.* IX, 292. The Earl of Shaftesbury possessed a copy (P.R.O. Shaftesbury Papers, Bundle 4, f. 180) of Lauderdale's letter to Charles containing the remark that 'never was King so absolute as you are in poor old Scotland'.

for his libertine life, he had forfeited the good opinion of mankind. Yet these sins were not the faults that undid him. The House of Commons attacked him rather for being the author of the Declaration of Indulgence, the destroyer of the Triple Alliance, and the promoter of the French Alliance. The Duke met the attack head on, by going to the House of Commons the very day they turned on the King's ministers. There he sought safety in a slavish submission to their authority. Bareheaded, clutching a ragged, scribbled-on paper, he told the Commons that he desired to stand or fall on their judgment, and that he desired never to have any employment if they had an ill opinion of him. 'No man', he said, 'ought to serve the King, whom the nation has no good opinion of.' Desperately anxious to win the House's favour, he agreed to return the next day to answer particular questions, questions which the Commons had prepared for him in the hope that he would inform against others. Who counselled the French Alliance? asked the House. Who advised the breach of the Triple Alliance, the Stop of the Exchequer, the Declaration of Indulgence, the use of the army to over-awe Parliament, and the attack on the Smyrna fleet? In violation of his oath of secrecy as a Privy Councillor, Buckingham answered the questions put to him. He exonerated himself and loaded Arlington with blame. The House listened gratefully to these revelations, but their gratitude did not extend to exculpating the Duke. They resolved, with only a few dissenting votes, to address the King to remove Buckingham from his employments and from His Majesty's presence and councils for ever.[1]

Buckingham not only loaded Arlington with blame, he had his henchmen in the Commons bring in articles of impeachment against him. Securing a copy of the articles, Arlington hurried to the House of Commons on 15 January to defend himself. He addressed the House for more than an hour, with such directness, civility, and clear reasoning, with so little servility and submission, with such elegance and nobility, that he won the universal applause of the House. If one of his own friends had not moved to declare him innocent at once, his enemies would probably have dropped their charges against him. As it was, the House debated five days on his guilt before resolving by 166 to 127 not to address the King for his

---

[1] Stowe MSS 204, ff. 36, 38v–39v, 41v; Grey, *Debates*, II, 245–9, 262–3; Christie, *Williamson Letters*, II, 114; *C.J.* IX, 293.

removal. Arlington escaped the fate of Lauderdale and Buckingham because the Court faction joined with the Country party to save him. This combination was not adventitious. The Court supported him because Charles was furious at Buckingham for having revealed the secrets of the Council table without his permission and for having reflected on his competence as a King. Arlington, on the other hand, secured Charles's permission to speak before going to the Commons, and spoke there as befitted a loyal servant of the King, which he had always been. Nor was it an accident that the Country party, now led by Shaftesbury, supported Arlington. They knew that he was essentially innocent of the charges brought against him by his enemies, that he was not the true author of the Declaration of Indulgence and the French Alliance.[1]

In the coffee houses of London it was common knowledge that Arlington was, and had long been, Spanish at heart, and that Buckingham was the friend of France. To this common report Sir John Holland, a friend of Lord Shaftesbury's, added particular evidence. He informed the House that a year ago he told Arlington that the nation regarded him as a promoter of the Dutch war and might call him to account for the issue of it. He therefore besought him to be active in promoting a peace. Arlington replied, 'I assure you, and pray assure all your friends, that I will do all I can to promote peace.' Within a month, continued Holland, every letter from London carried the news that Arlington in a Council at Whitehall had urged the King to meet his Parliament. 'When I next met the Earl in August', he said.

I took an opportunity to tell his Lordship that I was very glad that his Lordship was in the number of those counsellors that advised the King to continue the sitting of Parliament, that I could assure him that it had left impression in many members of the House of Commons to his advantage. He told me he wondered how anything he said in Council should come to be made public. He did assure me that he himself never published it, but said that it was true that it was his opinion, and ever would be his opinion, that neither the King nor kingdom could be secure or happy, but whilst there was a good intelligence maintained between him and his people in Parliament, and that he should always endeavour to preserve it.

[1] Christie, *Williamson Letters*, ii, 111, 113, 119, 130; Tanner MSS 42, f. 74v; *C.J.* ix, 296; Fr. Trans. 19/29 Jan. 1674. Maurice Lee has recently written ('The Earl of Arlington and the Treaty of Dover', *The Journal of British Studies*, i, 60–9) a convincing defence of Arlington's role in negotiating the French Alliance.

Holland solemnly assured the House of the truth of this story, and concluded, 'I have only this to add: that that man who has this principle planted in him can never be dangerous to be left about the person of the King, nor in his Councils; and therefore I do desire you not to make any address to the King to have my Lord Arlington removed.'[1]

Men knew that the Earl of Arlington had been deeply engaged in the King's affairs at the time of the Declaration of Indulgence and the French Alliance. They knew that he had clung to office tenaciously and had served the King in nefarious designs. But they pardoned him, for they believed that he had counselled against those very designs which he had helped to execute. Arlington escaped an address, not because he had the courage of a hero, but because he had the wisdom of a statesman. As he had many of those faults for which impeachments were ever introduced into the House of Commons, so he had some of those virtues which have caused statesmen to be justified in every age; he was a wise though weak man.

In his speech before the House of Commons, and in his answer to their interrogations, Arlington sought refuge in the collective responsibility of the Council. Asked who advised the many mistaken and dangerous policies pursued in the last two years, he answered with monotonous regularity that the whole Council had. 'My opinion was concurrent' in the decision to seize the Smyrna fleet. 'We all concurred in' the French Alliance. 'My opinion was concurrent' in the Declaration of Indulgence. 'All concurred in' the shutting up of the Exchequer. The war 'was the concurrent opinion of all'. Exasperated by these answers, Sir Charles Wheeler burst out, 'He is not only a concurrent counsellor, but a Prime Minister of State.' Others among his enemies accused him of engrossing all power to himself. 'Nothing', said Sir Gilbert Gerrard, 'has passed for some years but through his hands.' These unsupported accusations annoyed Daniel Finch, who replied, 'to lay the faults on the government of Lord Arlington because their origins are not known is but witchcraft'. Witchcraft it might be, but most members of the Commons preferred to call it common fame. Beginning with their address against Colonel Richard Talbot in 1673 and continuing through their addresses against Lauderdale and Buckingham, the House relied on common fame as a basis for condemning evil

---

[1] Tanner MSS 239, ff. 95–96v; Grey, *Debates*, II, 325.

counsellors, even though Secretary Coventry believed that it had 'killed more statesmen than ever the Plague did'.[1] The reliance of the House of Commons on common fame raised an important question about the nature of their addresses against Talbot, Lauderdale, and Buckingham, and their intended address against Arlington. Were such addresses judicial sentences against guilty ministers, or were they petitions to the King asking for the redress of grievances? Some members regarded them as judicial condemnations, as judgments 'by common fame in small misdemeanours'. But two considerations defeated their efforts to interpret addresses in this manner: the House of Commons had decided in 1626, during Buckingham's impeachment, that common fame extended only to the indictment and not to the condemnation of any man, and the law clearly said that the Commons had jurisdiction only over their own members or those who violated their privileges. The Commons must go to the Lords for the condemnation of anyone else, and the Lords would not condemn on common fame. The House therefore decided to regard their addresses as petitions to the King asking for the redress of grievances, not as judicial sentences. For this reason they asked that the Mastership of the Horse, being a freehold, should not be taken from the Duke of Buckingham. Common fame should not injure a man in his life or property; only an impeachment before the Lords could do that. The decisive vote in this dispute was taken on 5 February, when the House resolved not to ask the House of Lords to concur in their vote against Buckingham.[2] Few votes so seemingly unimportant have been so significant in the history of responsible government, for by this vote the Commons took a path which excluded the House of Lords—as impeachments did not—from any role in the enforcement of responsible government in England.

[1] B.M. Add. MSS 28045, ff. 21–24v; *C.S.P. Dom. 1673–75*, pp. 103–7; Grey, *Debates*, II, 271, 282, 292–3, 310, 327; Coventry Papers, LXXXIII, f. 25v. Secretary Coventry also wrote of these addresses (B.M. Add. MSS 25123, f. 13), '…the proceeding is so quick that without so much as giving them a copy of their charge they proceed to vote their removal according to the opinion they have of the person's stiffness for the Ministry'.

[2] Stowe MSS 204, f. 82; Christie, *Williamson Letters*, II, 120; Grey, *Debates*, II, 247, 255, 267–9, 287, 321–2; Tanner MSS 42, f. 74v; *C.J.* IX, 303. Arlington's enemies, defeated in their attempt to secure an address for his removal, prosecuted an impeachment against him, but floundered pathetically in their attempt to produce a witness to prove their charges. Mindful of the mistake they made in impeaching Clarendon on common fame, the Commons demanded evidence of Arlington's treasons. The impeachment died in a committee, to which it had been referred.

An address for the removal of a minister suffered from the fatal defect that the King could ignore it, as he could not ignore a sentence passed on an impeachment. The certain way to correct this defect was to label the minister a grievance to the realm, and then refuse to vote supplies until all grievances were redressed. The House of Commons pursued this course of action in 1673 and 1674, though without daring to name names. On 31 October 1673 they refused to vote supplies before 'this Kingdom be effectually secured from the dangers of Popery and Popish counsels and counsellors; and other present grievances be redressed'. On 12 January 1674 they resolved, 'That this House will, in the first place, proceed to have grievances effectually redressed, the Protestant religion, our liberties, and properties, effectually secured, and to suppress Popery, and remove all persons and counsellors Popishly affected, or otherwise obnoxious or dangerous to the government.' These votes, like the interrogations of Buckingham and Arlington, and the addresses against Buckingham and Lauderdale, drove deep into the King's prerogative to choose his own servants; but the Commons were too enraged at the ministers who had misled Charles for three years to care about the prerogative. 'They did not ponder or ascertain', said the Venetian ambassador, 'whether it became them to investigate such matters and to try peers. But everyone admits that if the King wants money he must give satisfaction to the country; and so they settle the matter without study and without confining themselves either to precedents or to constitutional law.'[1]

If the King did not need money, he need not give satisfaction. Glimpsing this truth Charles in February made peace with the Dutch, freed himself thereby from the need for parliamentary supply, and suddenly prorogued Parliament on 24 February. Freed from Parliament's demands, he did as he pleased, maintained Lauderdale in Scotland, dismissed Buckingham for his insubordination, permitted Arlington to retire to the dignity of the office of Lord Chamberlain, and issue a Proclamation forbidding his subjects 'to intermeddle in private discourse with state affairs, or the persons of the King's ministers'.[2] Charles by proroguing Parliament won

[1] *C.J.* IX, 285, 292; Grey, *Debates*, II, 213–14, 235; *C.S.P. Ven. 1673–75*, p. 201.
[2] *C.S.P. Dom. 1673–75*, p. 238. The French ambassador wrote (Fr. Trans. 26 Feb./8 March 1674), 'Parliament was prorogued, as one expected, but what surprised everyone was that it was done so suddenly, without warning Parliament of it, or consulting the Council. The King prorogued Parliament because its deliberations tended to lessen his

again what he always prized, his liberty and his ease. But this victory could not conceal the fact that the attack on the Cabal had destroyed some of his power and much of his popularity. The unsuccessful and unpopular policies he pursued from 1670 to 1674 provoked the House of Commons into actions of the most radical nature, actions reminiscent of 1641. They had questioned the King's servants about the innermost secrets of state. They had branded these ministers as grievances to the realm and had voted addresses for their removal. They had refused to vote money until they were removed. There were few precedents for such actions, but, as Sir Charles Wheeler blurted out, 'Why shall not this Parliament be a precedent to future Parliaments, as well as former Parliaments to this?'[1] Why not indeed? Charles II should have considered this possibility before he embarked on a personal government certain to alienate his subjects and to cause them to attack his ministers. He should have reflected that the more flagrant the grievances perpetrated by those possessing executive power, the greater the likelihood that those not possessing it would demand a superintendence over it.

power...and it refused to do anything towards voting supply.' Viscount Latimer's efficient management of the Treasury, as Professor Browning has shown (*Danby*, II, 114), also enabled Charles to prorogue Parliament.

[1] Grey, *Debates*, II, 309.

CHAPTER 6

THE CRISIS OF CONFIDENCE (1674–1688)

The balance of government established in 1660 seemed doomed to failure in 1674. Clarendon's impeachment had shaken it severely and the attack on the Cabal had weakened it further. Yet Englishmen persisted—at least until 1681—in their endeavours to make it work, fearing any possible alternative to it. Among these Englishmen no one strove harder to preserve the balance than Thomas Osborne, whom Charles named Lord Treasurer in 1673 and Earl of Danby in 1674. Danby saw that a Clarendonian reliance on a moribund Privy Council, to the neglect of Parliament, would not work. He also saw that a secret cabal, relying solely on the prerogative, would do no better. He therefore proposed a third solution: government by a ministry that enjoyed the confidence of Parliament and the nation. Danby's acumen allowed him to see what Clarendon and Clifford had failed to see, that a balance of government could only work if the King's ministers possessed the confidence of the Lords and Commons of England.

To win the confidence of Parliament, Danby proposed the pursuit of truly national policies, both at home and abroad. At home the King should defend the Church from Papist and Non-conformist alike. Abroad he should join with the United Provinces to put a stop to the aggrandisement of France. An alliance with Bishops at home and with the Dutch abroad would reconcile King and Parliament, would unite the greater part of the nation behind the Crown, would undo the harm perpetrated by the Cabal, and would persuade the Commons to vote the King a revenue equal to his needs. A King of England pursuing such policies would possess the love of his subjects, while his ministers would enjoy the confidence of Parliament.[1]

To restore confidence in the Crown was Danby's immediate purpose, but it was not his ultimate purpose, and herein lay his tragedy. His ultimate purpose was to strengthen the Crown (in whose service he sought to establish his fortune) in any manner that

[1] Browning, *Danby*, I, 117, 120–1, 146–7.

he could. To this end he sought to persuade Parliament to confide in the Crown; but to this end he also sought to make the Crown financially independent of Parliament and able to control its proceedings. Financial management and parliamentary management were as integral to Danby's scheme as the pursuit of national policies. By reducing expenditures at Court, by disbanding unnecessary troops, by renegotiating the Farm of the Customs, by reorganizing the Excise, and by introducing order and method into the public accounts, Danby hoped to free Charles from an unwelcome dependence on parliamentary subsidies. By the naked use of royal patronage and the covert use of secret service money, he hoped to create a Court party in Parliament which would permit the King to control its proceedings.[1] An Anglican ecclesiastical policy, a Francophobe foreign policy, an efficient management of the Treasury, and a vigorous management of Parliament, by such means Danby sought to rescue the prerogative from the threatening seas into which Clarendon's lethargy and the Cabal's folly had plunged it.

Unfortunately for the Earl of Danby, his scheme foundered under the weight of its own inconsistencies and broke on the shoals of the King's inconstancy. Danby could persuade Charles to make peace with the Dutch in 1674, even to enter into an alliance with them in 1678, but he could not persuade him to cease negotiating secretly with the French. Charles's evident attachment to the Court of France bred suspicion faster than Danby could allay it, and finally wrecked his scheme. But even before that day deep cracks appeared. His Anglican policy won over few of the opposition, for the opposition viewed it, and viewed it rightly, as less a design to guarantee a Protestant England than a plot to elect a Cavalier Parliament. His financial policy aroused even greater apprehension, for if it succeeded the King need not meet Parliament again. The closer Danby came to realizing the ideal of a King financially independent of Parliament the farther he travelled from the goal of reconciling King and Parliament. The prospect of a King ruling without Parliament spread panic and bred distrust. 'Parliament considers it

---

[1] Browning, *Danby*, I, 107, 118–19, 132, 149–50, 170–2, 177. J. R. Jones has shown ('Court Dependents in 1664', *Bulletin of the Institute of Historical Research*, xxxiv, 81–91) that though Clifford and Danby developed the techniques of parliamentary management Clarendon 'was fully aware of the vital importance of doing so', and on two occasions, in 1663 and 1664, used parliamentary management to win victories in the Commons.

high treason', wrote the French ambassador, 'for any man to advise the King to bye-pass Parliament and live on his own revenue.'[1] The creation of a Court party in Parliament also bred distrust and lessened confidence. A Parliament of Court pensioners was worse than no Parliament at all. As a result, Danby's efforts to create a Court party only served to bring into existence its antithesis, a Country party, which channelled, sustained, and organized opposition to the Court. Danby made every effort to overcome Charles's French proclivities and strove desperately to patch over the inner contradictions in his own scheme, but he failed. The history of his ministry is the story of that effort and that failure.

The first chapter in this history ended triumphantly for Danby, when the House of Commons, in the spring of 1675, acquitted him of articles of impeachment brought against him by his enemies. Chief among them was the Earl of Arlington, who sought to augment his declining credit at Court by exhibiting his superior strength in Parliament. As William Harbord remarked, ''Tis a trial of strength between Arlington and the Treasurer, with the malice of some members to either side, to let the King see which of them has the best interest.'[2] The malicious members on the side opposed to Danby were (besides Arlington's own supporters) the adherents of the Duke of Ormond, the friends of the Duke of York, and the followers of the Earl of Shaftesbury. They were a motley crew, joined by no principle, united by no ideal, and dedicated to no common purpose. Aside from the Duke of York, whose religious convictions led him to oppose Danby's anti-Catholic policy, these men acted from factious motives, desiring to drive the Lord Treasurer from the King only that they might succeed him in office.

On 26 April the enemies of Danby introduced their impeachment against him into the House of Commons. They prosecuted it vigorously for one week, but failed utterly to persuade the House to vote it. In part their want of success arose from the unwillingness of the Commons to misuse, as they had in Clarendon's case, the power of impeachment. Though Sir William Coventry warned the House, 'If you expect proof at the bar, never impeachments more...', the Commons demanded proof at the bar for each article of the

---

[1] Fr. Trans. 3/13 Aug. 1674. As early as 25 Feb. 1674, William Harbord reported (Stowe MSS 204, f. 237), 'I hear from very good hands that Osborne has proposed a way or method not to want Parliament any more.'

[2] Airy, *Essex Papers* (Camden Soc. n.s. XLVII), p. 319.

impeachment. Denied recourse to common fame, Danby's opponents set out to prove that, by procuring patents for the Customs and Excise that removed those revenues from Exchequer supervision, he had violated the law of the land. Danby's friends replied, after the manner of Strafford and Laud, that the Attorney General, the King's legal officer, had passed the patents, and therefore should answer for their illegality. Those promoting the impeachment objected that Danby was most at fault, for he had advised the King to grant the two patents. They were forced to admit, however, that they possessed no proof that he had given such advice. Neither could they demonstrate that the patents, however inexpedient, were criminal. 'Illegal and inconvenient', said Serjeant Maynard, 'are things very different, and are different questions.' Balked at every point, Danby's prosecutors asked permission to search the Exchequer books for evidence of the Lord Treasurer's delinquencies. Sir Giles Strangways replied that the Commons had taken that path before, in Strafford's case, to no good purpose. The House refused the request. Denied the right to impeach on common fame, wanting proofs that Danby had advised the patents, unable to demonstrate that they were illegal, and denied permission to impeach the offender and then search for the offence, Danby's enemies were unable to persuade the House to vote his impeachment. On the crucial division on the first article they went down in defeat, 181 to 105.[1]

Yet the clumsiness of the power of impeachment and the flimsiness of the charge against Danby do not suffice to explain his triumph. The fundamental reason for his acquittal lay in the soundness of his policies. Relieved of their worst anxieties by the fall of the Cabal, reassured further by a proclamation for the enforcement of the laws against Papists and Non-conformists, and pleased by the orderly payment of the King's creditors, the country gentlemen in the House failed to rise to the bait cast before them. Not obsequious courtiers and corrupt politicians, but Old Cavaliers like Sir Giles Strangways and Country party leaders like William Garroway spoke in defence of the Lord Treasurer. Against the testimony of these men and in face of the trust still reposed in Danby, the engine of faction was powerless. As Professor Browning observes, '...the triumphant acquittal of the Lord Treasurer was in essentials a vote of confidence

[1] Grey, *Debates*, III, 40–64, 83–90; Egerton MSS 3330, 26 Apr. 1675; *C.J.* IX, 324–6.

in the domestic policy for which he had made himself responsible, and as such it was an event of very real significance'.[1]

Though he won acquittal for himself, Danby could not win a vote of supply for Charles. This failure was particularly humiliating to Danby, for Arlington's adherents had boldly proclaimed that his employment as Lord Treasurer was the chief obstacle to the voting of supplies. Arlington's friends, wrote William Harbord, a week before the attempt to impeach Danby, 'keep their charge against the Treasurer ready in case monies be asked for shipping, as the more proper time, and in the meanwhile endeavour to wound him with the King by representing him as the obstacle to the supply, and that he dare not push for monies for fear he should be the price of it'.[2] Despite this prediction, Danby did 'push for monies', though with no success. Yet he did not fail—whatever the friends of Arlington might say—because the Commons objected to his presence at the Treasury. He failed rather because they objected to the presence of English troops in the service of Louis XIV. The presence of these volunteers in the advancing armies of France inspired in the House of Commons a deep suspicion of the intentions of the Court, and led them to refuse Charles the money he requested. Danby's acquittal was a vote of confidence in the Government's domestic policy; Parliament's refusal to grant money was a vote of no confidence in its foreign policy.[3]

The Commons also expressed in 1675 a want of confidence in the King's Scottish policy. They did so by voting a second address asking Charles to remove the Duke of Lauderdale 'from all his employments, and from Your Majesty's Council and Presence forever'. The House renewed their former address against Lauderdale because the arbitrary counsels he gave the King and the transcendent power he enjoyed in Scotland angered and frightened them. In 1675 they took the further step of annexing to their address against him reasons why the King should dismiss him. Charles should remove Lauderdale, they explained, because he had said that the King's edicts were equal to the law of the land and because he had raised a militia in

---

[1] Browning, *Danby*, I, 160.   [2] Stowe MSS 207, f. 334.

[3] Browning, *Danby*, I, 160. Otto von Schwerin, envoy for the Great Elector, reported (Leopold von Orlich, ed., *Briefe aus England*, Berlin, 1837, p. 21), 'one believes that the House of Commons will grant the King money only if he withdraws the English troops out of the service of France and dismisses Lauderdale'. Schwerin made no mention of a demand for Danby's dismissal.

Scotland which he intended to use to destroy liberty in England. Mr Dalmahoy, Lauderdale's friend, protested that the Earl of Rothes was the King's Commissioner in Scotland when the Militia Act was passed, and therefore must answer for it; but Mr Powle retorted that Lauderdale was then Principal Secretary and 'the sole manager there'. Acting on this assumption, so convenient to their purpose, the House resolved to present to the King an address asking for Lauderdale's removal, accompanied by reasons justifying the request. On 26 April, the Speaker read aloud to the King the address and reasons, and delivered them to him. A fortnight later Charles returned his answer to the address: he would not remove Lauderdale, for the Act of Grace of 1673 pardoned him from the crimes alleged against him. This reply forced the House to define more exactly the nature of their address against Lauderdale. By voting it, they said, they did not intend that the Duke should 'suffer in his life, body, honour, or fortune'. All that they sought was his dismissal from office and his removal from the King's Council and Presence, and therefore the Act of Grace could not concern their petition.[1]

Dismayed but not disheartened by Charles's answer to their second address, the House went on to vote a third. Gilbert Burnet, an opponent but formerly a confidant of Lauderdale, furnished them with the ammunition they needed. He testified that Lauderdale had on one occasion threatened to bring Irish Papists into Scotland to cut the throats of Presbyterian rebels, and, on another occasion, had boasted that the Scots would, if necessary, march into England to enforce the Declaration of Indulgence. This testimony inflamed the national and Protestant prejudices of the Commons and led them on 31 May to vote, 136 to 116, to present a third address demanding Lauderdale's dismissal. Though the sudden prorogation of Parliament prevented the House from presenting this third address to the King, there is no reason to believe that Charles would have given any more favourable a reply to it than he had to the two previous addresses. 'There was no money offered,' observed Gilbert Burnet, 'so addresses were feeble things.'[2]

---

[1] Grey, *Debates*, III, 24, 26; *C.J.* IX, 316, 323, 332; *Bulstrode Papers* (in *The Collection of Autograph Letters and Historical Documents Formed by Alfred Morrison*, 2nd ser. vol. I), p. 290.

[2] Grey, *Debates*, III, 30–2; *C.J.* IX, 348; Burnet, *History*, II, 26, 73–4, 79. Otto von Schwerin reported (above, p. 201, n. 3) that money was offered should the King dismiss Lauderdale, but Parliament never publicly espoused such an offer.

The impeachments and addresses of 1674 and 1675 prompted Marchamont Nedham, in a government-sponsored pamphlet, *A Pacquet of Advices*, to complain bitterly of the growth of 'accusatory faction' and of the popularity of parliamentary impeachments. 'And so the issue at last shall be this,' he concluded, '...the King shall never be free of his own choice [of ministers], nor secure of his ministers when he has chosen them.'[1] Danby knew this to be true, but he also knew that a King who kept the confidence of Parliament could retain the right to choose his own ministers. In the next three years, from the day of his acquittal in 1675 until the day of his impeachment in 1678, Danby struggled to create that necessary confidence, but slowly, relentlessly, the tide of battle ran against him. Instead of growing confidence in the King, he witnessed mounting suspicion, a suspicion that finally transformed the balance of government established at the Restoration into a paralysis of government in 1679.

The basic cause of this suspicion was the average countryman's belief that the Court favoured Popery, arbitrary government, and the growth of French power. In the spring of 1676 the Duke of York, heir presumptive to the Crown, openly avowed himself a Roman Catholic. At the same time Danby renewed his efforts to make Parliament subservient to the Crown by swelling the ranks of the Court party and lessening the numbers of the Country party. To this end he granted pensions on the Secret Service fund, disciplined errant Commissioners of the Customs, brought pressure on all government dependants to vote as the Court dictated, offered titles, place, and local offices to unattached members, dismissed rebellious members from office, and sought to close down the coffee houses, where the Country party recruited new members. At the same time as these actions threatened the independence of Parliament, the armies of France drove across Flanders, threatening the independence of England. In 1676 the French captured Condé and Bouchain; in 1677 they seized Valenciennes, Cambray, and St Omer. De Ruyter in 1676 suffered defeat in the Mediterranean at the hands of a French fleet, and the Prince of Orange in 1677 went down in defeat before the French at Cassel. Despite these French victories, and the urgent occasions they created, Charles

---

[1] [Marchamont Nedham], *A Pacquet of Advices and Animadversions sent from London to the Men of Shaftesbury* (1676), p. 49.

prorogued, adjourned, and again prorogued Parliament—all the time permitting Englishmen, Scotsmen, and Irishmen to serve in the armies of Louis XIV.

Danby did not approve of a foreign policy that estranged the King from his subjects, but all his endeavours to alter that policy failed. In the summer of 1675, for example, he undertook to secure Charles a vote of supply from Parliament when it met that autumn, if Charles would destroy every last vestige of the French alliance. Charles agreed to the undertaking, and Danby opened negotiations with the leaders of Parliament. But Charles, who had little faith in Danby's scheme, signed a treaty in August with Louis XIV, in which he promised the French King, in return for an annual subsidy of £100,000, to dissolve Parliament in the autumn if it should prove hostile to France. Since Charles thereby refused to destroy every last vestige of the French alliance, refused to declare himself openly against France, Danby failed to win in October the vote of supply which he had undertaken to secure. Charles therefore fell back on his French policy, which he pursued until the growing impoverishment of the Crown and the constant importunities of Danby forced him to meet Parliament again in February 1677.[1]

The Parliament of 1677 represents the zenith of Danby's fortunes, the closest he ever came to success. Though there were individual members in this Parliament who protested against French counsels at Court and who talked of removing wicked ministers, the Commons as a whole heeded Colonel Birch's admonition to proceed to 'things, not persons'. For the first time since Danby became Lord Treasurer, the House of Commons voted the King money. Frightened by the Prince of Orange's defeat at Cassell and shamed by Sir William Coventry's taunt that only a pusillanimous nation would advise the King to aid the allies and not vote him the money with which to do so, they granted Charles £600,000 for the construction of thirty ships. They also permitted him to borrow £200,000 on this supply for the immediate succour of the allies. Their trust in the King, however, did not extend to the last, full measure, for the money they voted fell far short of the amount needed to succour the allies. And when Charles in May asked that they vote him £600,000 more, declaring to them 'you shall not repent any trust you repose in me', the Commons tartly replied that they would vote him no more

---

[1] Browning, *Danby*, i, 165–6.

money until he entered into an offensive league with the Dutch. Angered by this encroachment on his right to make war and peace and fearful of being trapped in an expensive war, Charles adjourned Parliament on 28 May. This adjournment proclaimed what no one could any longer deny: King and Parliament had reached a deadlock. Parliament dared not trust the King with money before an alliance, and the King dared not enter into an alliance until Parliament voted the money to support it. Parliament feared that Charles would use the money voted to establish an arbitrary government, and Charles feared, as he told Sir William Temple, that Parliament would 'engage him in a war, and then leave him in it unless they might have their terms in removing and filling of places'.[1]

Danby perceived that only by persuading the King to enter into an alliance with the Dutch could he break this deadlock and secure for the King the final measure of confidence that he needed. He therefore strove to secure such an alliance. This time his efforts met with success, for Charles signed an offensive and defensive league with the United Provinces on 21 January 1678, a league confirmed by the marriage of the Duke of York's daughter, Mary, to the Prince of Orange. When France at the same time rejected terms of peace offered by Charles, preparations for war proceeded apace. Parliament met in February and voted to grant the King a supply to maintain the alliance with the Dutch. It seemed as if Danby's plan to reconcile all by a war with France had succeeded, but in fact the whole edifice that he had built up so patiently over the last five years collapsed in the next five months.

The edifice collapsed because of the intransigent opposition of the Country party to it and because of the feeble support of the Court party for it. The audacity and energy of the Earl of Shaftesbury promoted the intransigency of the Country party; the crypto-Catholic and Francophile sentiments of the King enfeebled the Court party.

Historical events are not to be explained independently of the personalities who make them. The course of events in Charles II's reign would have been very different had not the energy, persistence, and skill of Danby met its match in the energy, persistence, and skill of the Earl of Shaftesbury. From his place at the Treasury

---

[1] B.M. Add. MSS 28091, ff. 30–33, 39v, 41; Grey, *Debates*, 258, 349, 351, 358, 361; Temple, *Works*, I, 331.

Danby created a formidable Court party, but from his table at John's Coffee House Shaftesbury sustained a Country party which was the equal to it. Danby's purposes, perceived by many men then and understood by historians today, were straightforward: he wished to be the first minister of a powerful and popular King. Shaftesbury's purposes were an enigma to his contemporaries and a puzzle to historians since. Perhaps the source of that enigma lies in the fact that he was a hybrid politician, a cross between a John Pym and a second Duke of Buckingham. During his career he managed to exhibit the political principles of the one and the reckless ambition of the other. In 1678 the reckless ambition was most evident. He and his friends—among them Lord Holles, Lord Russell, and Buckingham himself—pursued the Lord Treasurer with a warmth and disregard for principle that suggested a desire to replace him at Court. Shaftesbury and his colleagues in 1678 cared far more for office than had John Pym and his friends in 1641.[1]

But their opposition also reflected a desire for constitutional change. Trusting neither the King nor his successor, they sought safeguards for their liberties which closely resembled those demanded by John Pym in 1641. The various pronouncements of the Country party spokesmen (both in and out of Parliament) reveal the nature of these safeguards. The King, they argued, always acts on the advice of others, whether they be private persons, Privy Councillors, or members of Parliament. Speeches from the throne, answers to parliamentary addresses, and sudden adjournments come not from the King but from his advisers, for (as Andrew Marvell wrote in *The Growth of Popery*) 'Nothing is left to the King's will, but all is subjected to his authority.' Since private persons may advise the King, even concerning war and peace, so also may Parliament; and the King ought to pay more attention to Parliament's advice than to the advice of inconsiderable, private persons, or even to that of his Privy Council. If the King, nevertheless, persists in following the advice of private persons, against the wishes of Parliament, the House of Commons should refuse to vote him supplies. The Commons should never place money in the hands of ministers whom they

[1] Barillon, the French ambassador, wrote in February 1678 (F. A. M. Mignet, *Negotiations Relatives à la Succession d'Espagne*, Paris, 1835, IV, 532), 'The opposition is composed of ambitious men who wish to overturn the Lord Treasurer, and distrustful men who fear to arm the Court against the government and religion of England.'

could not trust, nor vote the King a revenue sufficient to free him from the necessity of seeking Parliament's advice.[1] The first time that the spokesmen for the Country party sought to persuade the House to act on these principles, they failed. On 14 March 1678 they urged the House to try to find those persons who had misled the King during the past five years, that they might demand their removal. They argued that those ministers should be removed who had given the King pernicious counsels in the past, who had advised repeated adjournments, who had penned hostile replies to their addresses. Not to name persons, they said, showed a want of courage, especially since one of the main ends of Parliament was to pull down evil counsellors. A majority of the House, though a majority of only five, spurned these arguments and refused to vote an address asking Charles to remove from his councils those who had advised the answer to their address of May last.[2]

This motion of no confidence in Danby's counsels, which suffered defeat by five votes on 14 March, passed the House by 15 votes on 7 May. On that day the Commons voted an address to the King asking him to remove those ministers from his councils who had advised his answers to the Commons' addresses of 26 May 1677 and 31 January 1678. The cause for this reversal in Danby's fortune lies in the gradual erosion of the Court party. This erosion did not occur because Danby slackened in his efforts to sustain it, for on the very day of defeat his indefatigable servants rounded up 24 Court party members of Parliament from eating-houses and sent them into the lobbies to oppose the resolution. It occurred because, as Sir William Temple observed, whenever the Court strayed from 'the true interest of the nation, many of the Court party voted with those of the Country'.[3]

After the middle of March the Court strayed ever further from the true interest of the nation. That interest the House of Commons defined on 14 March, when they demanded a declaration of war against France (though they went far beyond the national interest in declaring the restoration of the boundaries defined in the Treaty of Pyrenees to be the object of that war). Charles could have

---

[1] Cobbett, *Parl. Hist.* IV, 919, 922–3; Grey, *Debates*, VI, 48–60, 94–102; *C.S.P. Dom. 1678*, pp. 159–60; B.M. Add. MSS 28091, f. 108; Carte MSS 72, ff. 346–347v, 359–362.

[2] Cobbett, *Parl. Hist.* IV, 951–5; Carte MSS 72, ff. 359–362v.

[3] *C.J.* IX, 477–9; Airy, *Lauderdale Papers*, III, 142; Burnet, *History*, II, 149–50; Temple, *Works*, I, 349–50.

declared war on France (and without committing himself to the obsolete Treaty of Pyrenees), but he refused to take this step. His refusal confirmed the widespread suspicion that he had never desired, and would never desire, war with France, that at heart he was a friend of France. Charles's past conduct told against him. He had repeatedly adjourned Parliament to the benefit of France. He had frequently consulted with the French ambassador at Whitehall. He had refused in January to lay the Treaty with the Dutch before Parliament. He had not withdrawn English volunteers from the armies of France. And he had challenged Parliament's right to advise him on matters of war and peace. All these actions provoked the jealousies and heightened the fears of the middle group in Parliament, of the members who vacillated between the Court and Country parties. By May these men, who held the balance of power, came to believe that the Court would use the money voted for a war against France to maintain a standing army in England and with it to establish an arbitrary government in the realm. Seized and possessed by these fears, they voted to condemn those ministers who had the King's ear.[1]

Charles's refusal to embark on a war against France wrecked Danby's scheme of basing the power of the Crown on the confidence of Parliament. He therefore turned to the alternative plan of making the Crown financially independent of Parliament. On 18 June he made a final, futile—pathetically futile—attempt to obtain the King a permanent, sufficient revenue. On that day Charles addressed both Houses of Parliament, asking them for an additional permanent revenue of £300,000 a year. This request had the same effect on the House of Commons that a motion in favour of gin would have on a Temperance Union. Members of the House were shocked that the subject had even been mentioned and regarded the voting of such a revenue as a vote cast for sin. The first thought of some members was to drive from the King's councils those who dared advise him to request the £300,000. 'Let us', cried Sir Francis Drake, 'get these men removed from the throne that have endeavoured to break trust and confidence betwixt the King and us. They are uneasy with a Parliament, and would have such a revenue granted the King, that they may have no more.' Sir Francis Drake

[1] Reresby, *Memoirs*, pp. 136–7; Klopp, *Der Fall des Hauses Stuart*, II, 117; Fr. Trans. 11/21 Apr. 1678.

was not the first member of Parliament to perceive that the King's ministers would be glad to see the last of Parliaments. The year before Sir Thomas Meres boldly declared, 'I am for keeping the revenue from being too big, for then you'll need Parliaments, and nothing can keep great ministers in awe but them.' Fearing to lose the power of the purse, which allowed them to keep great ministers in awe, the House resolved, without a division, to reject the King's request. In 1660 the Commons of England believed that the King ought to possess a permanent revenue sufficient to allow him to live of his own; by 1678 they ceased to believe this. The most important advance towards responsible government that occurred in Charles II's reign was not the revival of impeachment nor the resort to addresses, but the discovery (tragically forgotten in 1685) of the power of the purse.[1]

The willingness of the Commons to exercise the power of the purse, even to the paralysis of government, grew out of their sense of England's immunity from foreign invasion. In his speech on 18 June Charles had complained that his revenue was less than that of other Princes and had urged that it ought to be as great. This prompted Mr Powle to reply, 'The King desires "that his revenue may be equal to other princes". But our situation defends us, and our navy secures us. Where enemies have no sea to pass, there must be garrisons upon the frontier, and armies that must be paid.' With these sentiments Sir William Coventry concurred. During a debate on 20 May on the question of voting money to disband the army, he told the House, 'Plainly by the debate only "land forces" are meant. I desire not to be left without any navy at all.' No one dissented from this prudent advice. The same House that refused to trust the King with a standing army or a permanent revenue, gave money to defray the expenses of the navy. The Channel, and the navy which guarded it, allowed the Commons to withhold money from the King without imperilling their safety. And only by withholding supplies could the Commons persuade the King to dismiss ministers whom they distrusted. But for the Channel responsible government would have come to England a century, or two centuries, later, or not at all.[2]

The arbitrary government which the Country party feared might come to England already existed, in their opinion, in Scotland,

---

[1] Grey, *Debates*, VI, 94–102; B.M. Add. MSS 28091, f. 41.
[2] Grey, *Debates*, VI, 35, 100–1; Browning, *Danby*, I, 279.

where the Duke of Lauderdale ruled supreme. In the winter of 1678 a band of Scottish noblemen, led by the Duke of Hamilton, hurried south to assure the House of Commons that this was true, that Lauderdale was a tyrant. They told the English a story of Highland troops quartered on the King's subjects in South-west Scotland, of bonds exacted from heritors that no Conventicles be held on their land, of noblemen restricted in their movements, of other noblemen denied legal rights. The Country party welcomed these Scottish lords as true patriots; in reality they were factious politicians whose charges against Lauderdale lacked substance and merit. For only after fanatical Presbyterians had revolted in the south-west had the Privy Council sent Highlanders there, and Lauderdale's predecessors in office had inaugurated the policy of suppressing Conventicles. The power Lauderdale exercised in Scotland was vast, even arbitrary by English standards, but it was legal. Hamilton's main grievance was that he and his friends did not exercise it.[1]

Perhaps because these charges lacked substance, the Country party carefully launched their attack on Lauderdale when the House was empty of courtiers, at a time when (as a friend of Lauderdale's remarked) 'clamouring would pass for proof'. The stratagem succeeded. On 7 May the Country party persuaded a Committee of the Whole House to vote, by 137 to 92, to present the King an address asking for the removal of the Duke of Lauderdale from his councils and presence forever. Charles, deeply angered by this vote, dismissed Sir William Lowther from the Customs and drove Henry Savile from Court for supporting it. He also threatened with dismissal any servant who did not attend the House the next day (when the address came out of committee) to reverse the vote. The counter-attack ordered by the King succeeded, for the Commons on 8 May rejected by 152 to 151 the reasons offered by the Committee for removing Lauderdale, and then defeated by 161 to 151 the address itself. No worship of power alone, but respect for the law and a sense of equity besides, caused this reversal. For the Commons, as Mr Dalmahoy reminded the House, had no jurisdiction over Lauderdale's action in Scotland and had no charges before them concerning his conduct in England.[2]

---

[1] *H.M.C. Portland*, ii, 41–2, 48–9; Airy, *Lauderdale Papers*, iii, 110; W. C. Mackenzie, *The Life and Times of John Maitland, Duke of Lauderdale* (1923), p. 412.

[2] B.M. Add. MSS 32095, f. 90; *C.J.* ix, 477; Airy, *Lauderdale Papers*, iii, 131, 134–8; O. Airy, 'Lauderdale', *E.H.R.* i, 463–6.

Though the Country party could not answer Dalmahoy's clear reasoning, and though they suffered defeat in the lobbies, they did not despair. They will try again, wrote Sir Andrew Forrester to Lauderdale, 'not so much for you, as that they may, by prevailing against you, have the less difficulty in overturning all the rest of the King's ministers here.' The anticipated blow came on 10 May, when Lauderdale's enemies moved that the Commons add to their address against the King's English ministers the additional words: 'And we further humbly beseech Your Majesty that the Duke of Lauderdale may be removed from your Councils and Presence.' This motion, swiftly introduced and scarcely debated, carried by 8 votes. For a fourth time the Duke of Lauderdale stood condemned by the House. This fourth address, however, met with no more success than the previous three: Charles again refused to dismiss the Duke. But these frequent addresses did the King's reputation no good. The Dutch ambassador had the audacity to inform Charles, albeit in jest, that since Parliament had so boldly addressed against all his ministers, the foreign ambassadors in town began to wonder to whom to apply, to him or to Parliament. Charles was not amused.[1]

By the summer of 1678 the Earl of Danby saw that victory was not to be his, that he could win for the Crown neither the confidence of Parliament nor financial independence from it nor control over it. But neither had he yet suffered a major defeat: he remained the King's first minister, enjoying His Majesty's confidence and support. His energy, his passion for administration, and his love of management did not flag, nor did he contemplate resignation. Victory might have eluded him, but he had not yet lost the war. This was in the summer of 1678. Within a year he suffered total, unmitigated defeat. The Commons impeached him, the King dismissed him from office, and the Lords sent him to the Tower, where he remained for five years. His fall from power proclaimed the nation's lack of confidence in him as the King's chief minister; but it did not signify a similar want of confidence in the King. Danby suffered dismissal and imprisonment, but Charles survived the crisis with his Crown unshaken and his prerogative nearly intact.

The impeachment and imprisonment of Danby therefore poses

---

[1] Airy, *Lauderdale Papers*, III, 139, 146; *C.J.* IX, 480. Charles was no more amused when the Lord Advocate told him (B.M. Add. MSS 32095, f. 94) that 'it was said that he [Charles] said, "all he did was at the desire of his ministers merely..." To this His Majesty answered that they were base liars who said so and the contrary should be seen.'

two fundamental questions. Why was Charles forced to dismiss in March 1679 a faithful servant in whom he still confided? And why was he able, despite this, to retain for the remaining years of his reign the right to appoint and dismiss his own ministers?

The first and most obvious reason why Charles dismissed Danby was that he stood impeached for High Treason. On 21 December 1678 the House of Commons voted to impeach Danby; on the 23rd they did impeach him before the Lords, for High Treason. The majority that supported the impeachment in the Commons was an unusual amalgam of frightened Protestants and self-seeking politicians, of angry country gentlemen and discontented courtiers, of lovers of liberty and lovers of office. The weight of an angry nation had borne down Strafford; the opposition of personal enemies had largely ruined Clarendon; Danby suffered the full weight of both. Those most active against him were men driven by private resentment and personal ambition. Sir Robert Howard and Sir John Duncomb had both suffered from his omnipotence at the Treasury. Sir Henry Capell and William Herbert were angry at his support of Lord Ranelagh in Ireland, which endangered the power of their patron, the Duke of Ormond. Sir Thomas Littleton and Henry Powle, former adherents of the Earl of Arlington, continued to pursue their vendetta against him. Ralph Montagu was only the most notorious of those who opposed him in order to gain preferment at Court. Lord Shaftesbury had numerous lieutenants in the House, like Thomas Bennet, who prosecuted there Shaftesbury's quarrel with Danby. To these men who sought personal revenge and private advantage were joined others animated by party zeal: the Old Presbyterians led by Hugh Boscawen and John Swinfen and the young patriots led by Lord Cavendish and William Sacheverell.[1] Yet these known enemies of the Earl of Danby could not have carried the House of Commons against him. Their attack upon him in 1675 had failed ignominiously, in 1677 abjectly, in 1678 narrowly. The

[1] Browning, *Danby*, III, 6–9; J. R. Jones, *The First Whigs* (1961), pp. 10–18. Barillon wrote (Fr. Trans. 14/24 Nov. 1678), 'Those who desire the destruction of the Treasurer in order to profit by his disgrace and to enter into his place agitate very vigorously and with much audacity against him.' Sir William Temple (*Works*, II, 368–9), the second Earl of Chesterfield (*Letters*, p. 192), the anonymous author of *Plain Dealing* (*Somers Tracts*, VIII, 253), and the unknown author of *The Mischiefs and Unreasonableness of Endeavouring to Deprive His Majesty of the Affections of His Subjects, By Misrepresenting Him and His Ministers* (*Harleian Miscellany*, I, 40) all decried the new practice of factious men seeking employment by attacking the King's ministers.

last failure, though narrow, was particularly frustrating. In the spring of 1678 the Court and Country parties were perfectly balanced, divisions going now one way, now another, according to the merits of the question. There seemed little hope that Danby's enemies could ever persuade the independent members of the House to undertake an action so audacious as impeaching the Treasurer for High Treason.

In the summer and autumn of 1678 three events occurred which rescued them from this impasse: Titus Oates alleged that there existed a Popish Plot against the King; Danby failed to disband the army as an Act of Parliament required; and Ralph Montagu revealed how deeply Danby was implicated in Charles's Francophile policies.

Only with the greatest difficulty could the opposition direct against Danby the hysterical fears released by Oates's portentous tale, for Danby had urged the fullest investigation of the plot. Yet Danby suffered from the fear of Popery that seized Englishmen in the autumn of 1678. His friends had no ready reply to Sir Gilbert Gerrard's remark, made during the debate on the impeachment, that 'popery has increased since his management more than at any time before'.[1] Nor could his friends in the House allay the suspicions engendered by his refusal to disband the army. Parliament had voted £600,000 in May to disband the army, and it was still on foot in November. Danby might say that he kept it on foot to intimidate France, but most men believed, and not without reason, that he intended to use it to intimidate Parliament. Of the three events which precipitated Danby's impeachment, Montagu's disclosure of Danby's complicity in Charles's French negotiations proved decisive. In November the opposition were still unwilling to impeach the Lord Treasurer, because (as Sunderland said) 'the matter would not bear it', but when Ralph Montagu on 19 December read aloud Danby's letter to him of 25 March 1678, the House resolved at once to impeach the Lord Treasurer. In this letter Danby instructed Montagu, then ambassador to France, to ask Louis XIV to pay Charles six million livres annually for three years should peace be concluded, for Charles, having promoted peace with France, could not hope for supplies from Parliament.[2]

---

[1] B.M. Add. MSS 28046, f. 175v.

[2] Browning, *Danby*, II, 348; III, 9. Professor Browning (*ibid.* I, 196) writes, 'There is little doubt that at this stage [after 16 June 1678] he [Danby] considered the possibility of maintaining the royal authority and his own supremacy by means of the army.'

The Popish Plot, the standing army, and the letter to Montagu destroyed the Earl of Danby only because they crystallized fears which had long permeated English public life, and because they focused the hate occasioned by these fears on Danby. Three fears in particular were widely held: that the Court secretly promoted the growth of Popery, that the King and his ministers desired to establish an arbitrary government, and that the government looked with favour on the growth of French power. The grounds for these fears were not chimerical. Papists did find favour at Court. The heir to the Crown was a Catholic. The King and his ministers did seek financial independence from Parliament and had maintained 7,000 troops on Hounslow Heath through the summer. And England had remained neutral while the armies of France advanced across Flanders, 'the buckler of our safety', as one member of the House called it. Because Danby served a King who tolerated Papists, dreamed of establishing an arbitrary government, and acquiesced in the growth of French power, his enemies, hitherto checked, were able in December 1678 to find a majority of 63 in the Commons to impeach him for High Treason.[1]

The Earl of Danby did not believe that his impeachment by the House of Commons necessitated his dismissal by the King, for, though the Court party in the Commons had crumbled, he could fall back on three other lines of defence: his own innocence, the support of the House of Lords, and the confidence of the King. Learning of the impeachment he confided his thoughts to paper: 'The indignation great, but the innocence so great too as gives me both an inward satisfaction and a boldness to support that innocence; and that which adds still to that satisfaction is that the lordships are to be my judges, of whose great justice I have seen so many expressions.'[2] On the very day that the Commons impeached him, Danby

---

[1] Members of Parliament repeatedly voiced these fears in the debates of 19 and 21 Dec. on the impeachment. See B.M. Add. MSS 28046, ff. 15–21, 175–180v, and Grey, *Debates*, VI, 337–87. Barillon wrote (Fr. Trans. 23 Dec./2 Jan. 1678/9), 'The warmth that appeared in the Commons on the reading of the Lord Treasurer's letters has spread to London, and all those who are opposed to the Court or fear a change in the government are very excited, though many informed persons were already persuaded that the King never sincerely wanted war. Before, the people were uncertain what designs the Court had, but now they are certain that the purpose of all the talk last year was to raise a standing army. The demand for the 18,000,000 livres is seen only as a means to dispense with Parliament.' Schwerin, envoy of the Great Elector, observed (*Briefe aus England*, p. 366), 'The House of Commons were so frightened by the possibility of a change in government and religion that it would not tolerate an army dependent on the Court.'

[2] B.M. Add. MSS 28043, f. 2v.

pleaded his innocence in the House of Lords, declaring that he was guiltless of the six crimes charged against him. He had not assumed regal power by treating with France, for he possessed the King's command for all that he had done. Of raising a standing army he was no more guilty than any other lord in the House who had voted for its establishment. Had he been a friend of France, as the third article charged, he would not now stand impeached before them, for the principal informer against him acted at the instigation of France. He had not concealed the Popish Plot, but had seized Coleman's papers, the most material proof of its existence. He had not wasted His Majesty's revenue at the Treasury, but had strictly applied all monies to the uses for which they were appropriated. Finally, he had, it is true, enjoyed His Majesty's bounty, but far less than had many lesser servants of the Crown. Genuinely moved by the Lord Treasurer's defence, and persuaded that his crimes, if he had committed them, fell far short of treason, the peers refused to imprison him in the Tower, as the Commons demanded. They refused, even though their predecessors had in similar circumstances committed the Earl of Strafford to the Tower.[1]

Despite Danby's victory in the House of Lords and despite his desire to continue in office, Charles dismissed him from office on 16 March 1679. He did so, not because he had lost confidence in his Lord Treasurer, but because he saw that he could not retain Danby and yet do those things which he wished to do. To begin with, he wished to avoid a trial before the Lords in which Danby might seek to prove his own innocence by disclosing the King's guilt. He also wished to use the dwindling reserves of affection left to the monarchy to prevent the exclusion of his brother from the throne, not to save an expendable minister. Above all, he wished to gain from the House of Commons the money he needed to disband the troops and escape financial bankruptcy.

Charles did not dismiss Danby without first making an effort to save him. On 30 December 1678 he prorogued Parliament to

---

[1] Cobbett, *Parl. Hist.* IV, 1069–71. Danby was probably innocent of all the crimes charged against him, except not disbanding the army, as required by Act of Parliament. W. A. Shaw, however, asserts his innocence even here, arguing (*Cal. Tr. Books*, v, part 1, lxxx) that the money voted to disband the army was insufficient to pay the arrears owed the soldiers to 4 June, and so was simply impossible to execute. Danby wrote (B.M. Add. MSS 28047, f. 226), 'That since my time no money hath been diverted from the public uses to which it was given and though accused of the contrary about the disbanding, yet apparently false.'

4 February in the hope that the passage of time would cool the temper of the opposition and afford him an opportunity to find the money needed to pay off the army. He miscalculated grievously, for the prorogation only increased the anger of the opposition, who blamed Danby for it; and the search for money proved barren. The hopelessness of their plight drove Charles and Danby to a step which they were reluctant to take. They opened negotiations with the leaders of Parliament, more particularly with the Presbyterians, led by Lord Holles. Lord Holles and his friends, unable to divide the Court and impressed by its resoluteness, proved accommodating. They agreed to temper the fierceness of the Commons against Danby, to persuade their friends in the City to loan the money needed to disband the army, and to secure the King a vote of supply in the next Parliament. But in return for this undertaking they demanded a high price, they demanded the dissolution of Parliament and the dismissal of the Lord Treasurer. Charles, having nowhere else to turn, agreed, dissolved Parliament on 24 January, and dismissed the Earl of Danby on 16 March. The power of the purse, allied to a parliamentary impeachment, had proved too strong for the prerogative.[1]

Danby's dismissal from office did not, as the Court and Presbyterians intended, prevent his imprisonment in the Tower. It did not because Lord Holles and his friends found it extremely difficult to manage the new Parliament and because Charles's conduct made it quite impossible for them to do so. The election not only went against the Court, wiping out the Court party which Danby had built up with such care; it also resulted in a House which not even Lord Holles could lead. Alarm at the Popish Plot, fear of the Duke of York's succession, and a desire to punish Danby for his treason, led men to elect extreme opponents of the Court to Parlia-

---

[1] Browning, *Danby*, I, 310–21. One of Danby's agents among the opposition reported on 24 Dec. (B.M. Add. MSS 28049, f. 34v), 'Sir we conclude that the King must either part with him [Danby] or with his Parliament...for money matters, 'tis folly in the abstract to expect it, unless he be the peace offering.' Another agent wrote on 21 Jan. (B.M. Add. MSS 28053, f. 133), Lord Shaftesbury's party endeavours to persuade the Duke of York, 'that the Commons have resolved to do nothing for His Majesty so long as your Lordship has the Staff'. Danby wrote in 1685 (*Morrison Coll.* 1st ser. III, 119), 'Upon an assurance given to the late King by the Duke of Monmouth, that the then Parliament would give money without any condition to be made with him, but only to remove me from the place of Lord Treasurer, His Majesty was pleased to acquaint me with the proposal, and to tell me that the Duke of Monmouth did bring it to him from the chief leaders of the House of Commons, so as he did not doubt of the success of it, but yet that he would not put such an hardship upon me without my consent...' Danby consented, but predicted that the Commons would not give money even then.

ment. Danby's fate figured prominently in the election. Election pamphlets urged the return of men who would bring arbitrary ministers of state to justice, and candidates who had publicly befriended Danby were everywhere defeated. The Chancellor of the Duchy, wrote Lord Lindsey to Danby, 'goes from borough to borough liberally discoursing of your Lordship's impeachment and counting none good patriots or fit to be chosen but such who have been eminently dipped in the blood of His Majesty's most loyal subjects'. The election of February 1679 has the distinction of being the first in English history in which the character, conduct, and future of the King's first minister played an important role.[1]

Charles displayed poor tactical skill in the management of the newly elected House of Commons: his actions were tardy and his decisions unwise. He delayed Danby's dismissal too long, and then threw away most of the advantages that might have accrued from it by granting him a marquisate and a pension. He further aggravated matters by allowing Danby to name the Commissioners of the Treasury who were to succeed him and by refusing (on Danby's advice) to accept the Commons' candidate for Speaker. The worst error of all was to inform both Houses of Parliament on 22 March, when the revival of Danby's impeachment seemed likely, that Danby had done nothing except at his command, and that therefore he had granted him a pardon.[2] The King's declaration that he had pardoned Danby instantly transformed the nature of the dispute over his impeachment. What had been a political quarrel over the alleged treason of an unpopular minister, became a constitutional dispute over the right of an accused minister to plead a pardon in bar to an impeachment. The House of Commons might have considered sparing Danby's life and estates; they would never consider surrendering the power of impeachment.

To be precise, the King's speech raised two constitutional issues.

---

[1] Reresby, *Memoirs*, p. 175; Egerton MSS 3333, 15 Feb. 1679. The author of *A Character of Popery and Arbitrary Government* (1679) urged electors not to choose 'those Danbean senators', who have disturbed the peace and endangered religion and property. Barillon wrote (Fr. Trans. 27 March/6 Apr. 1679) that the leaders of Parliament 'do not know where they are, for the great number of members from the country, who have no experience, prevail against all reason, and no one dares contradict them nor oppose their motions, however irregular they may be'.

[2] Browning, *Danby*, I, 317–22; *H.M.C. Ormond*, IV, 370. The House of Lords showed their horror at Charles's speech by refusing to enter it in their journal. Lord Halifax said in the Lords a week later (B.M. Add. MSS 28046, f. 54), 'That speech of the King's pardoning him, out of respect to the King, you would not enter upon the books.'

Could a minister hide behind the King's commands? And could he seek the protection of the King's pardon? Danby would much have preferred to hide behind the King's commands rather than to seek the protection of his pardon. In December he had produced before the House of Lords a copy of his famous letter to Montagu, subscribed, 'I approve of this letter. C.R.' At the same time he told the House, 'My Lords, if my obedience to the King shall not be my crime, I think nothing else will stick upon me from these articles.'[1] The Commons never found the opportunity to reply to this plea, but if they had, they would surely have replied, as their predecessors had to Strafford, that the King can do no wrong and that his ministers must answer for all. Danby, however, would never have allowed that his case was the same as Strafford's. 'But when it is for having obeyed the King that I am to be a state sacrifice,' he wrote, 'it is without example, and beyond the case of my Lord Strafford.'[2] There is much truth in Danby's contention. Strafford had counselled the King, if Vane is to be believed, to act in an unlawful manner. Danby merely obeyed the King in a lawful command, for Charles had every right to negotiate with France for a subsidy and to prorogue Parliament whenever he wished. Furthermore, Danby had counselled against the very policies which he had obediently executed, had urged Charles to break with France and depend on Parliament. This was widely known. Yet the Commons impeached him. They impeached him because men's opinions had altered from what they had been in Strafford's time. Englishmen now believed it intolerable for a minister, not merely to give unlawful advice, but to continue to serve a King whose policies were hateful to the nation and whose commands threatened to make the Crown independent of Parliament.

On 24 March the House of Lords yielded to the torrent of hate flowing against Danby in the Commons and the country, and did what they had refused to do in December: they ordered that Danby be placed in custody.[3] For three weeks Danby avoided this fate by

---

[1] Cobbett, *Parl. Hist.* IV, 1071.

[2] Browning, *Danby*, II, 76. Danby wrote on 5 March (B.M. Add. MSS 28047, f. 413v), 'The King's command will excuse any fault or crime that is not *malum in se*, nor *malum prohibitum*, nor against some known law of the land. This [letter to Montagu] is neither of the three, therefore a just excuse.'

[3] In debates on committing Danby, Shaftesbury and Colepeper very effectively demonstrated that the Lords had refused to commit Clarendon only because the Commons had failed to produce particular charges against him, and to commit on general

hiding in London, but surrendered himself to the Lords when the two Houses passed an Act of Attainder against him, to come into effect if he did not give himself up. The Lords promptly gave him a copy of the articles of impeachment which the Commons had brought against him; on 25 April he replied to the impeachment by pleading the King's pardon. He did not wish to rely on this plea, but Charles, fearful that a trial would reveal far too much about his French negotiations, ordered him to do so. Ever obedient, Danby obeyed.

When the Lords sent Danby's plea to the House of Commons, the House refused to countenance it, declared it illegal, and refused to allow any Commoner in England (which included all the lawyers) to defend it. The ensuing controversy over the lawfulness of pleading the King's pardon in bar to an impeachment gave rise to an outpouring of words. Eloquent speeches were delivered, learned treatises written, voluminous briefs prepared, and numerous pamphlets published.[1] Those who maintained that the King's pardon could be pleaded in bar to an impeachment argued that an impeachment for High Treason was an indictment in the King's name brought by the Commons, acting as a Grand Jury. Since treason could only be committed against the King, the King could pardon the injury done him. Those who denied the legality of pleading a pardon argued that an impeachment was the appeal of a wronged nation against a criminal who had sought to subvert the laws of the realm. The King could not pardon such an appeal, for then the injured party, the nation, could have no redress. It is impossible to say which party to the dispute was correct, for one's opinion of the rightness of each argument depends upon one's philosophy of law,

---

charges would allow the Commons to imprison any lord they pleased. But the Commons had now produced particular charges against Danby (B.M. Add. MSS 28046, ff. 49–50v).

[1] The speeches may be read in Grey, *Debates*, VII, 20–30, 134–7, 152–7, 167–87, 296; and B.M. Add. MSS 28046, ff. 113–114, 116–117v, and 28047, ff. 105–106, 200–200v. Notes written by Danby and his counsel are in B.M. Add. MSS 28043, ff. 87–87v, 102, 142, and B.M. Add. MSS 28047, ff. 150–154v, 203v, 205–205v, 222–223, 246–247, 435, 482–483. Similar arguments appear in Lord Keeper North's papers, B.M. Add. MSS 32518, ff. 56–80. Arguments against the pardon are set forth in notes in the Shaftesbury Papers, P.R.O. Bundle VI, B, ff. 425–429. The ablest argument in favour of the pardon is Lord Chancellor Finch's 'Treatise on the King's Power of Granting Pardons in Cases of Impeachment', circulated in manuscript at the time (see Sloane MSS 4021, ff. 149–158v), and printed in 1791. Among the pamphlets are *A Letter to a Friend in the Country* (1679), *The Country Lawyers Address to his Friend in the City* (1679), *A New Years Gift* (1682), *Arguments of...Danby* (1682), and *A Plea for the Pardoning...* (1682).

upon whether one is a formal jurist or a legal realist. Originally impeachments had been, and formally they still were, indictments in the King's name; and by ancient statute treason only comprehended crimes against the King's person and authority. In reality impeachments were the appeal of the nation against wicked ministers, and in fact many judges and many Parliaments had extended the concept of treason to comprehend the subversion of the law.

The legal debate over Danby's pardon was not only inconclusive, it was irrelevant. Political passions decided the issue before any legal arguments could be heard. This became obvious from the day, 22 March, when Sir Francis Winnington said in the House of Commons, 'The King cannot pardon treasons against the government, for then the government cannot be safe against evil ministers...If ministers are to be pardoned for the wrongs they do, there is no security, and our pretended free and legal government is a mere cheat.'[1] Sir Francis Winnington spoke truly, and most members of the House knew that he did. They might as well surrender the power of impeachment entirely as allow the King's ministers to plead pardons in bar to impeachments. As the Commons said at a conference with the Lords on 19 May, 'The setting up a pardon to be a bar of an impeachment defeats the whole use and effect of impeachments, and should this pardon be admitted...it would totally discourage their use for the future, whereby the chief institution for the preservation of the government itself would be destroyed.'[2]

The Lords regarded the pardon with less alarm than did the Commons. They were even prepared to allow Danby's counsel to defend its validity. A sense of their responsibility as judges of the highest court of the land, a reverence for the high estate of the King, and a distaste for popular causes may have led them to show this greater tolerance. Certainly the Court still possessed, and Shaftesbury had never possessed, a strong party in the House of Lords. Furthermore, many of the lords sitting in the House hoped some day to become ministers of the King, and they knew that they also might need his royal mercy. The plight of Danby might some day be

[1] Cobbett, *Parl. Hist.* IV, 1129–30. Copies of Winnington's speech appeared in coffee houses within a week of its delivery. A fuller version than in Cobbett appears in Woodrow, *The History of the Sufferings of the Church of Scotland*, III, 27.

[2] *C.J.* IX, 631–3. Another account of the conference is in Hastings MSS, Parliamentary Papers, Box 2, in the Huntington Library.

theirs.[1] For all these reasons the Lords resolved not to condemn the pardon until they had heard Danby's lawyers defend it.

The judicial calm and the immovable resolution of the Lords goaded the Commons into furious and reckless resolves. They voted that a Committee of Both Houses, and not the Lords alone, should make arrangements for Danby's trial. They objected to the King's appointing a Lord High Steward to preside over it. Sensing that the temporal peers were evenly divided on the question of a pardon, they demanded that the Bishops, who would unquestionably support a monarchy which supported them, should not vote on the question. And until the Lords, without the Bishops, pronounced on the legality of the pardon, they refused to attend the trial of the five Catholic peers, impeached for their alleged complicity in the Popish Plot. By these actions the House of Commons sought to usurp a judicature that was not theirs, thereby forcing the House of Lords, a proud body, jealous of its privileges, and certain of its rights, to unite behind Danby and the King. On 27 May the Lords voted, 65 to 36, to stand by the right of the Bishops to vote on the legality of Danby's pardon. Charles's tactics in March may have been clumsy; the tactics of the House of Commons in May were senseless. By their recklessness they allowed Danby to retain what it had cost Strafford his life to lose, the support of the House of Lords.[2]

The Earl of Danby enjoyed a second advantage that the Earl of Strafford had lacked: his master, unlike Strafford's, could prorogue Parliament without fear of bankruptcy or revolution. Had Charles I, in order to save Strafford, prorogued Parliament in May 1641, he would certainly have gone bankrupt within a month and might have provoked a revolution within a week. When Charles II, by proroguing Parliament, prevented the House of Commons from presenting a violent remonstrance against the pardon and against the obstinacy of the Lords, he neither went bankrupt nor precipitated

[1] Browning, *Danby*, III, 140–3. The Earl of Northampton minced no words in expressing his distaste of popular causes (B.M. Add. MSS 28046, f. 53): 'They say Vox Populi is Vox Dei, but I must tell you that the greatest currs make the greatest noise in a pack of dogs.'

[2] *H.M.C. Rep. 11, Part 2, H. of L. MSS*, p. 41; *L.J.* XIII, 594; *H.M.C. Ormond*, IV, 510; Burnet, *History*, II, 219. Sir Richard Temple observed (Stowe MSS 304, f. 163) of the party that opposed the pardon: 'Although they are the great pretended assertors of liberty, yet they never come into play but they struck at any obligations of laws, oaths, liberty, or government to carry their point.'

a revolution. He did not go bankrupt because Parliament had already voted him the money he needed to disband the troops. He precipitated no revolution because Englishmen in 1679 feared few things more than civil war. 'Since the wealthy merchants', wrote Barillon, 'fear disorder, and above all civil war, I believe that it lies in the power of the King to prevent matters from being carried to an extremity.'[1] Not only because they feared civil war, but also because they did not fear Charles, the enemies of the Court did nothing. Few men believed that Charles possessed the spirit to overthrow Parliament and rule by a standing army. Nor were they frightened by the Popish Plot as their ancestors had been by the Army Plot; the one was a fabrication and was directed *at* the King, the other a reality and countenanced *by* the King. Above all, Charles II, unlike Charles I, dismissed his chief minister from office and made no attempt to rescue him from the Tower.

The parallels between Danby's and Strafford's impeachments are striking: the disclosures of a Vane and a Montagu, the threats of an Army Plot and a Popish Plot, a Catholic Queen and a Catholic successor in the wings, chief ministers charged with treason, both sent to the Tower. But the contrasts between the two impeachments are more important. No two historical events are exactly alike, and they are inescapably different when the actors in one are conscious of the outcome of the other. This was most assuredly true in 1679. Charles in that year read the history of 1641 in order not to repeat the mistakes his father had made; Court pamphleteers repeatedly accused the Country party of renewing the tragedy of '41; and the leaders of the Country party took pains to prove them wrong. If Danby lived in a more forgiving age than Strafford it was because Englishmen had learned from the Civil War the cost of intemperate zeal. Charles II knew that it was not worth risking civil war to rescue Danby from the Tower; and the most violent of Danby's enemies, even Thomas Bennet, did not really desire his death. As a result Danby spent five years in the Tower, escaped the block, and lived to serve another King another day.[2]

---

[1] Fr. Trans. 2/12 Jan. 1679; *H.M.C. Ormond*, IV, 518. Miss Behrens argues ('The Whig Theory of the Constitution in the Reign of Charles II', *Cambridge Historical Journal*, VII, 44) that the Whigs might defend revolution in theory, but the memories of '41 made it 'practically inexpedient and even socially unrespectable' to advocate it in practice.

[2] Southwell wrote to Ormond (Carte MSS 39, f. 1), ''Tis privately said that His Majesty has read much of the History of '41 and has strong apprehensions of like events and con-

This is not to say that Danby's impeachment lacked significance. It had, on the contrary, important consequences. His impeachment for obeying the lawful command of the King, simply because the House of Commons found it an objectionable command, challenged the very foundations of English monarchy. That monarchy could survive the legal doctrine that ministers of state should refuse to obey unlawful commands; but it could not survive the political principle that a minister should refuse obedience to commands which the House of Commons found objectionable. When Sir Robert Howard attacked Danby in a pamphlet entitled *An Examination of the Earl of Danby's Case*, he wrote, 'If obedience is the excuse of ill acts, it ceases to be a good duty.' He did not write, 'If obedience is the excuse of illegal acts, it ceases to be a good duty.' The difference is important, for while 'illegal' is a precise word, 'ill' is a vague one, which might mean either ill advised or unlawful. This vagueness is typical of the rhetoric of impeachments. By a studied obfuscation of what was unlawful with what was unpopular, by a constant identification of the grievous with the criminal, and by a habitual disregard for the statutory definition of treason, the House of Commons transformed the duty to disobey an unlawful command into a duty to resign before performing an unpopular one. Even a monarchist as loyal as Sir Philip Warwick could write, 'If the Prince's own counsels cast what is settled into danger, or make it to be obtained by extremities (though not illegalities) upon his own subjects, a good man would rather make his retreat and die obscurely than see His Majesty and his country run a great risk.'[1]

But no one saw the significance of his impeachment more clearly than Danby himself. In the spring of 1679 he wrote to the Duke of Lauderdale, 'Besides my own concern in this matter, I cannot but with sadness reflect upon the condition of our master, if I should any way suffer for the letters to Montagu, for he must to the world's end never blame nor expect from Secretary (or any other) to do or write anything but what must first be considered how it will be approved by Parliament.' And to Charles he wrote from the Tower,

sequences in the course of things.' Some of the Court pamphlets are *A Letter from Amsterdam* (*Somers Tracts*, VIII, 89); *A Word Without Doors* (1679), and R. L'Estrange, *The Parallel, or an Account of the Growth of Knavery* (1679).

[1] Sir Robert Howard's pamphlet is printed in *Memoirs Relating to the Impeachment of Thomas Earl of Danby* (1710), and the sentence quoted appears on p. 104; Sir Philip Warwick, *Discourse of Government* (written in 1678, published in 1694), p. 91.

'I must needs remind Your Majesty that I lie here for nothing but obeying your just commands, in which if men are not protected, there will need no other argument for their not being obeyed hereafter.' Which was precisely the reason, thought Sir John Reresby, Danby's good friend and fellow Yorkshireman, why the Commons impeached the Lord Treasurer. They desired to punish him as 'an example to others to behave themselves better in that place'.[1]

The story of Danby's impeachment throws a flood of light on the growth of responsible government during the reign of Charles II—on Parliament's growing fear of overmighty ministers, on the King's increasing inability to protect his ministers, on the clumsiness of impeachments, on the futility of pleading the King's commands, on the folly of pleading his pardon. But Danby's impeachment does not comprehend the whole story of the crisis of confidence that shook the last years of Charles's reign. Other events occurred which also illuminate the growth of responsible government during these years: the attack upon Sir Joseph Williamson, the imprisonment of Samuel Pepys and Sir Anthony Deane, the threatened impeachment of the Duke of Ormond, the half-hearted attempt to turn the Chamber of the City of London into a new treasury, the renewed address against Lauderdale, the abortive Privy Council scheme, unsuccessful parliamentary undertakings, and the fierce battles of the second Exclusion Parliament. Varied as these events were, their history serves two purposes. First, it helps to explain why Charles was able to ride out the storms raised by the Popish Plot and the Exclusion Crisis, ultimately to defeat all demands for responsible government. Secondly, it helps to explain why these same demands became part of a Whig theory of responsible government, a theory which one day would win the allegiance of all Englishmen. Charles emerged from the turmoil of these years with his hand firmly grasping the sceptre, but the Whigs emerged with a theory of the constitution that would dash that sceptre from the hands of his successors.

The House of Commons attacked Sir Joseph Williamson, the King's dull and conscientious Secretary of State, because he had obeyed the unlawful commands of the King. In November 1678 they sent him to the Tower for counter-signing commissions for

---

[1] Browning, *Danby*, II, 78; B.M. Add. MSS 28049, f. 84; Reresby, *Memoirs*, p. 173. Daniel Finch wrote (*H.M.C. Finch*, II, 48), 'But the reasons the House of Commons proceeded with so much rigour were to prevent the like abuses in government for the future by an exemplary punishment of my Lord Danby.'

Catholic officers in the army; and though Charles released him from the Tower the next day, Williamson, for fear of the House of Commons, refused in the next months to expedite many of the orders sent to him. In February, therefore, the King dismissed him from office as no longer useful to him. Williamson was not the only servant of the King who allowed Parliament's wrath to frighten him into disobeying the King. Finch, the Lord Chancellor, refused to put the Great Seal to the Earl of Danby's pardon, fearing the consequences of doing so. Charles circumvented this obstruction by seizing the Seal himself and ordering a menial servant to put it to the pardon. This was not the first time that Charles acted directly, without the mediation of a responsible official. In 1676 and again in 1678 he signed secret treaties with France in his own hand, because no minister would risk his life by counter-signing or sealing the treaties. The House of Commons, however, refused to allow the King to overthrow responsible government in this fashion. They promptly condemned Danby's pardon as irregularly obtained. Sir Thomas Clarges argued in the House, 'The law says, "That the King can do no ministerial act", but the King took the Seal from the Chancellor and sealed Danby's pardon.' Therefore it is not valid. Slowly the House of Commons tightened the knot around the prerogative. No longer could the King exact obedience from his servants in doubtful matters, for neither his commands nor his pardons offered them protection; neither could he act himself, for 'the King can do no ministerial act'.[1]

Williamson and Danby were not the only servants of the King sent to the Tower. The House of Commons also sent Samuel Pepys, Secretary of the Admiralty, and Sir Anthony Deane, an officer of the King's Yard at Portsmouth. Pepys and Deane suffered imprisonment in May 1679 because other men coveted their employments and because they were regarded as creatures of the Duke of York. Their enemies, led by William Harbord, member of Parliament for Thetford, and his agent, Colonel John Scott, accused them of betraying naval secrets to France. This momentarily satisfied the Commons, who sent the two men to the Tower, but Harbord and Scott could not substantiate their charge. The expected impeachments never materialized, partly because Pepys had already resigned

---

[1] Grey, *Debates*, VI, 216–26; VII, 282. Browning, *Danby*, I, 191, 278. *H.M.C. Finch*, II, 50–1.

as Secretary, principally because both men were innocent. Impeachments in later Stuart England remained a legal procedure, and though disreputable men could use them to blast the reputations of reputable men, they could not use them to take their lives or to deprive them permanently of their liberty. The prorogation of Parliament freed both men from the Tower.[1]

The career of the Duke of Ormond further illustrates the limitations of parliamentary impeachments. Hardly a Parliament met while he was Lord Lieutenant of Ireland without his enemies preparing articles of impeachment against him. The spring of 1679 was no exception. Two dozen articles appeared, charging him with financial mismanagement and with favouring Irish Catholics. His old enemies, Orrery and Ranelagh, were active in promoting these articles. Lord Shaftesbury in the House of Lords supported their efforts with an inflammatory speech against Ormond's administration of Ireland. But nothing came of their efforts. As the Duke of Ormond said of the two dozen articles prepared against him, 'What I think most worth the observing is that amongst them all what is averred to be most true and to be proved is most false and most impossible to be proved.'[2]

The fate of parliamentary impeachments in the spring of 1679 proved what John Pym had discovered in 1641, that the power of impeachment could not secure responsible government in England. This impelled men in 1679, as it had in 1641, to search for other means to secure responsible government. And once again the possibilities (other than impeachment) were four: the King might employ those who would undertake to manage Parliament for him, or he might govern by the advice of a Privy Council, in whom the nation confided, or he might remove from office those ministers against whom Parliament voted addresses, or he might allow Parliament to administer the kingdom through committees of its own choice. In 1678, as in 1641, no one desired the last solution—except as it

---

[1] *H.M.C. Ormond*, IV, 515; Richard Lord Baybrooke (ed.), *Diary and Correspondence of Samuel Pepys* (1875), VI, 127–9, 131; R. G. Howarth (ed.), *Letters and Second Diary of Samuel Pepys* (1932), pp. 84, 90. Sir Robert Southwell wrote to Ormond (*H.M.C. Ormond*, IV, 509), 'Many are doubtful that this constitution of the Admiralty will obstruct the giving of money and that several will quit the preferment. But Sir Henry Capel sets his heart upon it and has got very ample powers to be inserted in the Commission, and desires to have Will. Harbord for Secretary, so that Mr Pepys is to be pulled in pieces with complaints poured in, and there is a committee directed whereof he [Harbord] is the chairman, in order to effect this work.'

[2] B.M. Add. MSS 21484, f. 44.

concerned the management of money voted by Parliament. The tradition of an independent administration of parliamentary subsidies, born in 1624, survived for many decades. In November 1678 the House of Commons paid tribute to the tradition by resolving that the money voted for the disbanding of the troops should be lodged in the Chamber of the City of London rather than in the Exchequer. This was a deliberate vote of no confidence in the Lord Treasurer, who that summer had used to maintain an army money voted for its disbandment. The proposal to lodge the money in the Chamber of the City of London was not unprecedented. In the autumn of 1675, still smarting from the Stop of the Exchequer, the Country party had proposed that the money voted for the building of twenty ships be lodged in the Chamber. George Downing, the creator of the modern Treasury, objected, telling the Commons, 'You are the restorers of the government, but this about the Chamber of London is setting up a new government.' Henry Coventry added, 'He hopes never to see the day for the Parliament to have one Treasurer and the King another. He knows what will follow.' Mindful of what followed when their predecessors in 1641 had lodged money in the Chamber, the House defeated the proposal, 171 to 160. In 1675 Danby still enjoyed the confidence of the House of Commons; in the autumn of 1678 he did not, with the result that the Commons voted to set up a new government, and resolved to have a Treasury of their own. But their hearts were not in the enterprise; they really preferred to be restorers of government. When Charles replaced Danby at the Treasury with a commission headed by the Earl of Essex, they dropped their scheme for a second Treasury, and assigned the money for disbanding the troops to the Exchequer.[1]

Nor did any politician seriously propose that Parliament nominate the King's ministers for him. In the panic which seized members of Parliament in May 1679, some talked of naming the commanders of garrisons and the governors of fortified places, but it never went beyond talk. And when Charles—to head off the Exclusion Bill—proposed that Parliament should nominate ministers of state during James's reign the Commons showed no interest in the proposal, preferring a King of their own choice to ministers of their own choice. But their reluctance to name the King's servants for him

[1] Cobbett, *Parl. Hist.* IV, 772–4; *C.J.* IX, 550; Foxcroft, *Halifax*, I, 145.

did not mean that they were unwilling to name those whom he should remove. They were more than willing to do this, as they demonstrated by voting a fifth address against the Duke of Lauderdale, asking the King once more to remove him from his councils and presence forever. They voted this address in May 1679, even though they possessed no new charges to support it, unless it were the charge that Lauderdale had risen rather than fallen by the previous addresses voted against him. And they dared not publicly declare this to be a grievance, though it was the most insupportable of all. Charles, though growing weary of the Duke, refused for a fifth time to dismiss him, for he would not have the Commons lay down the law to him.[1]

The chief weakness of addresses was that the King need pay no heed to them. Charles rarely did. The obvious remedy for this weakness was to refuse supplies until he did, until he removed those against whom the Commons addressed. This fact Danby's enemies thoroughly understood. As Danby wrote of his enemies in November 1678, 'They intend to attack me shortly...but would not... address because it was to no purpose, but would pass a vote not to give any money till I was removed.'[2] The difficulty lay in persuading members of Parliament to refuse supplies for this reason, for most men regarded the use of the power of the purse for this purpose to be too naked an invasion of the King's prerogative. Men believed that the power of the purse might be coupled with an impeachment, for it was no affront to refuse supplies when the King refused justice. The power of the purse might even be allied to a parliamentary undertaking, for such negotiations went on behind the scene. But the Commons were not willing to make their grant of money to the King dependent upon his dismissal of those displeasing to them. To do so would make him a Doge of Venice.

In part Charles had himself to thank that his subjects never made him a Doge of Venice. Confronted with a crisis of confidence in the Crown in 1679 he steered dexterously through it. Unlike his stern and unbending father, he knew how to bend, to negotiate, to com-

---

[1] *C.J.* IX, 613; Ailesbury, *Memoirs*, I, 14–15. The author of *Some Farther Matters of Fact* (1679) charges (p. 3) that Lauderdale always spoke of the House of Commons with scorn, 'And after boasted among his creatures, that he had risen by their Addresses. For after one, he got himself made an Earl of England; after the other, he had a pension of £3,000 per annum in England, though he had above £9,000 per annum in Scotland of the King.'

[2] Browning, *Danby*, III, 9.

promise, to yield, and to appear to yield. Thus in the spring of 1679 he not only dismissed Danby, he also gave his assent to the revival of conciliar government and entered into a parliamentary undertaking with the leaders of the Country party.

The remodelled Privy Council, solemnly proclaimed by the King before Parliament on 21 April 1679, actually comprehended two schemes: both a revival of conciliar government and an experiment in parliamentary undertaking. This blending of two disparate elements explains much of the confusion that has surrounded discussion of the remodelled Council. Confusion disappears, however, if one realizes that Charles in remodelling his Privy Council made two separate concessions to his subjects: he brought the leaders of the Country party into his ministry and councils; and he promised henceforth to govern by the constant advice of his Privy Council.

The first concession arose out of an undertaking similar to those proposed by Neville, Saye, and Temple in earlier years. Since then the ill repute of such undertakings had diminished. The necessity of living with Parliament had taught Charles II to prize the services of those who could manage it for him. 'His Majesty thinks that no man deserves more value', wrote Sir Robert Southwell, 'than he who has...many friends in the House of Commons...who are to be relied upon when things of importance shall lie at stake.'[1] Lord Shaftesbury, for his part, did not fear the reputation of an undertaker. He wrote to Lord Carlisle in 1675, 'Neither can we fear to be accounted undertakers at the next meeting of Parliament, for I hope it shall never be thought unfit for any number of lords to give the King privately their opinion when asked.'[2] When both the King and the leader of the Country party were of a more pliable, less scrupulous temper, it is no wonder that they agreed in the spring of 1679 to work together. Secret negotiations between Charles and the opposition lords—Shaftesbury, Holles, Essex, and Halifax—began in March and were concluded by the middle of April. The Duke of Monmouth, the Earl of Sunderland, and the Duchess of Portsmouth acted as intermediaries for the opposition lords at Court. Charles, for his part, agreed to bring the leaders of the Country party into office and the Council. In March he named Essex (whose reputation suffered for coming in before the rest) first Lord of the Treasury. On 21 April he appointed Sir Henry Capell first Lord of the Admiralty

---

[1] Carte MSS 38, f. 678.   [2] Christie, *Shaftesbury*, II, 201.

and named Halifax, Holles, Russell, Cavendish, and Powle to the new Privy Council. Shaftesbury he made President of the Council. In return for preferment these leaders of the Country party undertook to secure Charles a supply sufficient both for the needs of the state and the private necessities of the King.[1]

This ambitious undertaking failed within a month. Charles, to begin with, never intended that it should succeed, regarding it merely as a stratagem for gaining time. But even had he truly given his confidence to his new ministers, it is unlikely that they could have fulfilled their part of the bargain. The moment that they appeared at Court, they lost all power and virtue in Parliament, 'so true it is', remarked Reresby, 'that the Court and Country livery can never be worn together'. The many new members of Parliament, proud of their Country livery and uninitiated into the ways of party intrigues, showed their contempt for the undertakers by ignoring their moderating counsels. They even spoke as had their predecessors in 1641, of a self-denying ordinance that would prohibit members of the House from accepting office at Court. The inability of the undertakers to guide the House demonstrated a truth of great moment, that only men who led a party that would remain loyal to them could hope to succeed in a parliamentary undertaking.[2]

The second concession that Charles made to his subjects was a promise to govern by the constant advice of his Privy Council. Sir William Temple, an elder statesman better informed about the ideals of the past than about the needs of the present, fashioned the new Council in a Clarendonian image. The Council should be only thirty in number, that it might not be unwieldy. Fifteen of its members should be chief officers of the King; ten should represent the several

[1] Fr. Trans. 7/17, 10/20, 17/27 Apr., 21 Apr./1 May 1679; *H.M.C. Ormond*, IV, 503–4; *H.M.C. Rep. XV, Part 5, Savile Foljambe*, p. 129; Burnet, *History*, II, 208–9; Temple, *Works*, I, 396–7.

[2] *H.M.C. Ormond*, IV, 502; V, 57. Reresby, *Memoirs*, pp. 177–8. *H.M.C. Rep. XV, Part 5, Savile Foljambe*, p. 129. Jones, *The First Whigs*, p. 63. The Earl of Danby wrote to the King (B.M. Add. MSS 28049, ff. 46–47) that the new Privy Council would be justified only if those men now entrusted could get money for His Majesty or protect His Majesty from harsh demands. He then added, 'But as to the former, they must prevail on Your Majesty to expect no money than to set out the fleet, and that only when the Commons are satisfied that they have everything they want. As to the second, these men are as far from protecting Your Majesty's interest in the House of Commons as are any in the whole history of the Long Parliament. And they are far from any voting power in the House of Lords.' Barillon (Fr. Trans. 1/11 May 1679) confirms Danby's judgment: 'The new ministers are in great fear of destroying their credit with the people, and are able to maintain it only by forcing His Majesty to do all that the House of Commons desires.'

ranks of the nobility; and five should be commoners. All of them, as Charles declared, should be men 'whose known abilities, interest, and esteem in the nation shall render them without all suspicion of either mistaking or betraying the true interest of the Kingdom and consequently of advising him ill'. Such a Council, named by the King but trusted by the nation, should soon, believed Temple, restore confidence in the Crown.[1]

Temple was mistaken, as he soon learned. The House of Commons received the news of the new Council with great mistrust. The Lord Mayor ordered bonfires lit to celebrate it, but there was no great concourse of people around them. The explanation for this wary reception is not hard to discover. The Country party did not desire the restoration of the Privy Council to its pristine glory: they desired its subordination to Parliament. 'What is the use of his great Council of Parliament,' said Sir Thomas Lee in 1673, 'but to inform the King he has been misled and mistaken by his Privy Council?' Five years later Sir Thomas Meres complained in Parliament, 'Our advice was not followed, but that of the Privy Council is. And can any man say, that England is in good condition? Our advice is to be taken, and is much better than theirs.'[2]

But though the Country party had little esteem for the Privy Council, they did prefer that Charles consult it rather than a Cabinet Council. 'A Cabinet Council', said Mr Powle, 'that takes things out of the hands of the Privy Council, is the complaint.' Because this was a widely shared complaint, the most warmly applauded part of the new Privy Council scheme was Charles's promise to lay aside 'any single ministry or private advices or foreign committees' and to govern hereafter by the constant advice of his Privy Council. The Country party did not applaud this promise because they believed that Privy Councillors were wiser than Cabinet Councillors. They applauded it because Privy Councillors gave their advice openly, in Council, while Cabinet Councillors whispered theirs in private. An unknown counsellor, be he a single minister, a Cabinet Councillor, or a foreign ambassador, was an irresponsible counsellor. Behind the widespread hostility to Cabinet Councils lay a fear of irresponsible counsellors, for unless ministers gave their counsels in

---

[1] W. C. Costin and J. Steven Watson, *The Law and the Working of the Constitution: Documents 1660–1914* (1952), I, 329; Temple, *Works*, I, 413–14.

[2] *Ibid.* I, 417. Fr. Trans. 24 Apr./4 May 1679. Grey, *Debates*, II, 24; VI, 83. E. R. Turner, 'Privy Council of 1679', *E.H.R.* xxx, 268.

The Crisis of Confidence

public Parliament could not discover whom to blame for misleading the King, could not answer Daniel Finch's taunt that it was 'witchcraft' to lay faults on ministers when their origin was unknown. The Earl of Shaftesbury himself, when still a courtier, wrote concerning the Stop of the Exchequer, '...it is impossible that any statesman should be so mad as to give counsel of that consequence to a junto of men...or to any but the King himself; who, it is not to be imagined, will ever become a witness against any man in such a case.'[1]

The Earl of Danby was certainly not so mad as to give the King counsel in public, with the result that the House of Commons in 1678 could only censure him in the most general terms. In May they suspected, but could not prove, that he had advised the King's answers to their late addresses, answers which scolded them for invading the King's sole prerogative to make war and peace. Since they could not prove that he had advised these answers, they could not name him; they could only ask Charles 'to remove those counsellors who advised the answers to the addresses of the 26th of May or 31st of January last, or either of them'. In the autumn they were again forced to resort to a general address. Convinced that Danby had advised Charles to refuse the Militia Act, but unable to prove it, they voted an address representing to the King the dangers to which the nation was exposed 'by His Majesty rather following private counsels than those of his Two Houses of Parliament'.[2]

Because a particular vote, naming names, carried more weight than a general vote, naming no names, the Commons were delighted when the King promised no longer to rely on 'private advices'. Now they could discover the authors of mischievous counsels, since all advice would be given in full Council, where, as Lauderdale told Charles, Your Majesty's enemies now sit. But their delight was short-lived, for Charles did not keep his promise. He was far too

[1] Grey, *Debates*, II, 310; VI, 312. Costin and Watson, *Documents*, I, 329. *The Earl of Essex's Speech* (1681), p. 1. Christie, *Shaftesbury*, II, 61–2. The opposition also sought to prevent foreign ambassadors from giving private advice. On 11 May the new Privy Council ordered that no foreign ambassador should speak to the King until he first made an appointment with the Lord Chamberlain for an audience and presented to one of the Secretaries of State a memorial of the business he wished to discuss. Charles agreed to the order, but continued to see the French ambassador privately, without appointment (*C.S.P. Dom. 1679–80*, p. 142; Dalrymple, *Memoirs*, I, 311).

[2] *C.J.* IX, 479, 551. The address voted in May complained that these answers were advised 'by some particular persons, in a clandestine way, without the participation and advice, as we conceive, of your Council Board'.

232

worldly wise to believe that men threatened by impeachments would advise him freely or fearlessly in Council. 'God's Fish!' he exclaimed to Lord Ailesbury, 'they have put a set of men about me, but they shall know nothing.' Charles was true to his word. The remodelled Privy Council knew nothing. He did not lay before it a Danish request for aid against France; he prorogued Parliament in May without consulting it; he dissolved Parliament in July against its advice; and he prorogued the newly elected Parliament in December without seeking its consent. Meanwhile he constantly took the advice of a junto composed of Sunderland, Essex, and Halifax. No wonder Roger told Humphrey, 'No, you fool, they are called the Private Council, because everything of moment is kept private from them.'[1]

The duped leaders of the Country party resented Charles's bad faith, and forged out of their anger a weapon which would ultimately enfeeble the Crown more than Charles's bad faith had strengthened it. This weapon was resignation from the King's service. Eliot in 1626 intimated that Buckingham ought to have resigned before obeying an illegal command; Howard in 1679 argued that Danby ought to have resigned before committing an ill act. These resignations, urged by Eliot and Howard, had as their design the prevention of ill or illegal acts. Resignations could, however, perform a second service: they could serve to focus responsibility for evil counsels on men who did not resign. If men regularly resigned from office or council when the King refused their advice, then those who remained might justly be held accountable for the advice upon which he did act. This new principle—and it was very new in 1679—threatened to overturn Clarendon's world (which Danby also inhabited), in which ministers ought to continue to serve their sovereign even though he rejected their advice.

In 1679 threats of resignation preceded actual resignations. Some members of the new Council threatened to resign when the Danish request for aid was not laid before them. Others threatened to resign when the King prorogued Parliament in May without asking the Council's advice. Temple and Halifax considered resigning because Charles supported Lauderdale in Scotland. Shaftesbury in

---

[1] Ailesbury, *Memoirs*, I, 35; *Plain Dealing; or a Dialogue between Humphrey and Roger* (1681), p. 7. Charles told the Privy Council in January 1679 (Stowe MSS 746, f. 7), 'I am resolved to dissolve this Parliament, and have not consulted you, knowing how vain it is when people are more afraid of it than of myself.'

July complained in Council of the King's decision to dissolve Parliament against the advice of a majority of the Council. Charles replied, 'He could not divest himself of that power of resolving without the plurality of votes...' that his predecessors possessed. By October Shaftesbury's unending complaints won him his dismissal. In November Essex resigned from the Treasury because Charles refused to give assurances that he would soon meet Parliament. In January 1680 Lord Russell, Lord Cavendish, Sir Henry Capell, and Mr Henry Powle, desiring to preserve their credit in the country and urged on by Shaftesbury, resigned in a formal, ostentatious manner from the Privy Council. Roger North saw the profound change this meant in the government of England. 'Their counsel', he wrote, 'must not only be given, but taken. It was not counselling but ruling they came for.'[1]

They came to rule, but through a King who would willingly heed Parliament's counsels, not through a Venetian Doge or a parliamentary republic. The conduct of the Whigs in the three Exclusion Parliaments proved this. They rejected all plans for limitations on a Catholic successor, whether by a regency or by the parliamentary nomination of the King's ministers. They neither desired such limitations nor believed that James would observe them. They clung to government by King and Parliament, remained loyal to the ideal of a balance of government. The harmony necessary for such a government they would secure by excluding James from the throne; placing on the throne instead a monarch in whom the nation could confide. The chief defect of this plan (aside from the lack of a suitable successor) was Charles's unalterable opposition to it. Charles would not disinherit his brother, a fact which drove the Commons in the

[1] Klopp, *Der Fall Des Hauses Stuart*, II, 202; R. W. Blencowe, *Diary of...Henry Sidney* (1843), I, 5; *H.M.C. Ormond*, IV, 530; *H.M.C. Rep. 7*, p. 741; Christie, *Shaftesbury*, II, 357; North, *Examen*, p. 78. When in June 1679 the Court persisted in its repressive policies in Scotland, 'Lord Shaftesbury and three or four more', wrote an anonymous correspondent, 'desired to withdraw themselves and not intermeddle...Mr Powle...said he thought he might hereafter by the Commons be called to account for such proceedings and desired not to be concerned in it' (*C.S.P. Dom. 1679–80*, p. 175). Sir Henry Capell justified his resignation to Colonel Sydney (7 Feb. 1680, B.M. Add. MSS 32680, f. 163) by arguing that 'the practice in affairs has been contrary to the measures declared when I had the honour to sit there; and that the dark hopes of a Parliament's sitting make men under my circumstances to have little support to the government. I conceive it most modest with the rest of those fellow Commoners who came in together humbly to be leave to retire. In short, I preserve the same principles when last we parted, and 'tis neither honour nor profit can make me desert them. To be in a station where [if] exercised [these principles] appear ill timed, and if forborne, a reproach to my honour and conscience, suits not with my temper.'

second Exclusion Parliament, which met in November 1680, to hurl impeachments and addresses against those who dared to advise the King to veto Exclusion Bills, or prorogue Parliament in order to prevent their passage.

The Commons in the second Exclusion Parliament began by voting addresses against the Earl of Halifax, whom posterity celebrates as the author of *The Character of a Trimmer*, and Sir George Jeffreys, whom posterity remembers as the 'hanging judge'. Ostensibly the Commons demanded Halifax's removal from the King's presence and councils because he had advised the dissolution of the late Parliament (which he had) and the prorogation of the present one (which he had not), but actually they demanded his removal because he had opposed the Exclusion Bill in the House of Lords and had advised the King to send a message against it to the Commons. Sir George Jeffreys's crime was that of 'abhorring', that is of abhorring or discountenancing petitions for the prompt summoning of Parliament. As Recorder of London he had called such petitions 'seditious' and had threatened the City with the forfeiture of its charter should it present one. The Commons therefore demanded his removal from public office. Being a cowardly man, as well as a bully, Jeffreys resigned, causing Charles to remark, 'Sir George Jeffreys is not parliament proof.' The Earl of Halifax, however, proved to be 'parliament proof'. Proud, aloof, and aristocratic, he refused to retreat before the rage of the Commons.[1]

Charles, equally steadfast, refused to dismiss him. He told the Commons that he did not find sufficient grounds in their address to justify removing Halifax. He went further. He told them that he would leave Halifax, and anyone else whom they impeached, 'to their own legal defence, without interposing to protect them'.[2] By this promise Charles renounced in fact, if not in principle, the right to protect his servants by granting them pardons. He now discovered what his father had learned in 1642, that the power of impeachment could be used to defend as well as to invade the prerogative.

The House of Commons were not averse to exercising the power of

---

[1] *C.J.* IX, 657, 660. Grey, *Debates*, VII, 460–71; VIII, 21–31, 34–5, 41–51. *H.M.C. Finch*, II, 95. R. North, *The Lives of...Francis North...Sir Dudley North...and John North* (1890), I, 275. Charles named Sir George Treby, a Whig, to replace Jeffreys.

[2] *C.J.* IX, 663. According to Barillon, Charles would have surrendered the power to pardon, in principle, if thereby he could have prevented Danby's trial. He wrote (Fr. Trans. 22 May/1 June 1679), 'The King agrees to a law by which those impeached in the future may have no pardon, if only Danby's is allowed.'

impeachment. In 1680 they impeached five, and threatened to impeach two more, of the King's servants. They impeached Sir Francis North, Chief Justice of the Common Pleas, Sir William Scroggs, Chief Justice of the King's Bench, Sir Thomas Jones, Justice of the King's Bench, Sir Richard Weston, Baron of the Exchequer, and Sir Edward Seymour, Treasurer of the Navy; and threatened to impeach Sir Lionel Jenkins, Secretary of State, and Sir John Davys, a Secretary of State in the Irish government. The Commons accused North of penning a Declaration published in December 1679 against tumultuous petitioning. Jones they accused of dismissing the Middlesex jury before it could indict the Duke of York as a recusant and the Oswaldston jury before it could petition for a meeting of Parliament. Weston they impeached for inveighing against the authors of the Reformation and for boasting that all power centres in the King. Against Scroggs they fired a multitude of charges: he had imposed excessive fines, refused bail, issued general warrants, defamed witnesses, discharged grand juries, and usurped legislative power by prohibiting the publication of *The Weekly Pacquet from Rome.* Seymour they nominally accused of misappropriating money as Treasurer of the Navy, but everyone knew that his real crime was to have opposed the Exclusion Bill in the Commons and at Court. Jenkins had also had the temerity to oppose the Exclusion Bill in the Commons, but the House censured him instead for apprehending a messenger sent overseas to secure information about the Popish Plot. Davys's crime was to have stifled an investigation into an alleged Popish Plot in Ireland, but Shaftesbury's lieutenants really sought his impeachment as a prelude to Ormond's.[1]

The House of Commons prosecuted none of these impeachments before the House of Lords, for none of the accused had committed a crime, except perhaps Chief Justice Scroggs. And by impeaching Scroggs for High Treason, though specifying no treasonous act that he had committed, the Commons made certain that he should escape imprisonment, for the Lords had proclaimed in Clarendon's case their unalterable opposition to commitments on general charges of treason.[2] Since the House of Lords would permit no abuse of the

---

[1] North, *Examen*, pp. 552–4, 562–7; *C.J.* IX, 658, 684, 688–92, 697–8, 700; *H.M.C. Finch*, II, 103–4; *H.M.C. Ormond*, V, 537, 542; *C.S.P. Dom. 1680–81*, pp. 623–4.

[2] Following the precedent set in Clarendon's case, the Lords refused to commit Scroggs when the Commons demanded it on 7 Jan. 1681 (*L.J.* XIII, 738).

power of impeachment, and since the King would permit none of the power to vote addresses, the House of Commons stood doubly checked.

The one move left to them, a refusal to vote supplies, proved ineffectual. On 20 December they offered to vote Charles the money he needed for retaining Tangier and setting out a fleet, if he would accept an Exclusion Bill and employ as judges, justices of peace, Lord Lieutenants, and military officers 'only men of known ability, integrity, and Protestant vigour'. The House of Commons did not, however, demand the dismissal of Halifax, Seymour, or any other minister, for they were reluctant to bargain publicly for their removal. But the leaders of the House were not reluctant to bargain privately for the dismissal of these ministers and for their own advancement. The Southampton Whigs, so called because two of their numbers, Lord Russell and Ralph Montagu, owned splendid town houses on Southampton Square, opened negotiations with the Court through the Duchess of Portsmouth. If Charles would exclude the Duke of York from the succession and employ them in the management of his affairs, they would undertake to secure him the money needed to retain Tangier and to set out the fleet. The undertakers divided the spoils before they had won them. Sir William Jones was to be Chief Justice of the Common Pleas, Sir Francis Winnington, Attorney General, Colonel Titus, Secretary of State, William Harbord, Treasurer of the Navy, Lord Russell, Governor of Portsmouth, Sir Henry Capell, a Lord of the Admiralty, and Ralph Montagu, Marquis of Chichester. This unlikely undertaking came to nought, for neither the King nor Shaftesbury nor the House of Commons would countenance it. Shaftesbury, though offered the Lord Treasurership, denounced the scheme. Charles refused an invitation to meet with the undertakers at the lodgings of the Earl of St Albans. The Commons, as ever, spurned such corrupt bargains. On 30 December they passed a self-denying ordinance which would punish with exclusion from the House any member who should accept office at Court 'without the leave of the House'.[1]

---

[1] *H.M.C. Ormond*, v, 541, 562; *H.M.C. Finch*, II, 99; Fr. Trans. 30 Dec. 1680/6 Jan. 1681, 3/13 and 6/16 Jan. 1681. Shaftesbury's opposition arose partially from his disappointment that his own undertaking in late October had failed (Prinsterer, *Archives ou Correspondance Inédite de la Maison D'Orange-Nassau*, 2nd ser. v, 423; Fr. Trans. 25 Oct./4 Nov. 1680). He also resented the fact that the leaders of the Commons had acted independently of him (Fr. Trans. 6/16 Jan. 1681; Jones, *The First Whigs*, p. 152).

This vote was not so entire a repudiation of the undertaking as might at first sight appear. During the debate on the motion, Sir Thomas Lee urged the omission of the words, 'without the leave of the House', because those most likely to be preferred could always secure such leave. Sir Francis Winnington promptly objected, 'I believe the people will be satisfied with any of your members having places whom the House thinks well of.'[1] The House of Commons followed the lead offered by Winnington, left the words in, and left the way open for the development of cabinet government in England.

The Whigs hoped that the King's necessities would force him to listen to their public and private bargains. They could not have been more mistaken, as Charles showed by telling the Commons on 4 January that he would never disinherit his brother. This peremptory message enraged the members of the House of Commons, who struck out wildly at the presumed advisers of it. On 7 January they voted addresses requesting Charles to remove Halifax, Clarendon, Worcester, Feversham, and Laurence Hyde from his councils. Since addresses carried little weight, they also voted that these men (with the exception of Hyde, who ably defended himself in the House) were 'promoters of Popery and enemies of the King and Kingdom'. These 'black votes', as men came to call them, altered the very nature of parliamentary addresses: what had been petitions for grace became violent votes of censure. Charles put an abrupt stop to this metamorphosis by proroguing Parliament on 10 January, though rumours of the intended prorogation caused the Commons to meet early on the morning of the 10th to make a last act of defiance. They resolved 'that whoever advised His Majesty to prorogue this Parliament, to no other purpose than to prevent the passing a Bill for the Exclusion of James Duke of York, is a betrayer of the King, the Protestant Religion, and of the Kingdom of England, a Promoter of the French interest, and a Pensioner of France'.[2]

---

[1] Grey, *Debates*, VIII, 222–5. Daniel Finch wrote (*H.M.C. Finch*, II, 99) that the self-denying ordinance, because it included the words 'without the leave of the House', 'did not extinguish the jealousies conceived of these great men, nay it rather confirmed them in some'.

[2] *C.J.* IX, 699, 702–3. An anonymous correspondent wrote to Ormond (*H.M.C. Ormond*, V, 562), 'Friday the 7th of January was a hot day in the House of Commons; the leaders there had a purpose to vote the Chancellor [Nottingham], the Lord Privy Seal [Anglesey], Radnor, Halifax, and Hyde evil counsellors and to be removed from the King's presence. They began with Halifax and Hyde, but others were by accidental motions introduced, against the sense of the managers, whereby the three first escaped.'

Charles was able to prorogue Parliament only because he possessed (as Laurence Hyde, first Lord of the Treasury, informed him) sufficient money to govern without Parliament. In the hope that this should prove false, the Commons voted on that terrible 7 January that any man who loaned the King money 'shall be judged to hinder the sitting of Parliament; and shall be responsible for the same in Parliament'. But the vote proved of little effect, for most Englishmen were as appalled as was Charles at the violence of these votes. Not only were they impertinent: they were also without foundation, alleging no crime and offering no proof.[1]

The want of proof was obvious, even to members of the House, but how to discover proof was not. What complicated the problem was the desire of the House to punish those who counselled, not those who executed, unpopular policies. The Attorney-General, for example, published declarations at the command of the Council. If any man should answer for the Declaration Against Tumultuous Petitioning, he should, for he published it. Yet the Commons chose to by-pass the Attorney-General and censure Sir Francis North, for North had advised the policy which the Attorney executed. But how could they prove that North had advised it? The King's counsels were sacred, advice given in the cabinet secret. Since the Commons wished to impeach North, they needed legal proof. Therefore they dragged the Attorney-General before them on four different occasions and demanded that he tell them who advised the issuing of the Declaration. Being an easily frightened man, he finally revealed to the House that Sir Francis North had advised it.[2]

In their attack on Halifax the Commons found no one craven enough to reveal the secrets of the cabinet. They therefore voted a general address, on 11 November, informing the King, 'That our difficulties... are much increased by the evil and destructive counsels of those persons who advised Your Majesty first to the prorogation then to the dissolution of the last Parliament.' The Commons then requested that for the future he not suffer himself 'to be prevailed upon by the like counsels'. But such an address lacked force, so the Commons on 22 November voted to ask for Halifax's removal by name. Possessing no evidence that he had 'clandestinely and secretly' advised the prorogation and dissolution of the last Parliament,

---

[1] Fr. Trans. 6/16 Dec. 1680; *C.J.* IX, 702.
[2] B.M. Add. MSS 32511, ff. 91–93; North, *Examen*, p. 551.

they grounded their accusation on common fame. This provoked Lord Cavendish, rarely a friend of the Court, to exclaim that it was 'mere nonsense that common fame should publish what counsels were clandestinely and secretly delivered'. His intervention did not persuade the House to abandon common fame: they simply omitted the words 'clandestinely and secretly', and presented the address to Charles.[1]

The impossibility of discovering who gave counsel 'clandestinely and secretly' drove the Whigs to despair; the same impossibility drove Charles to protect his ministers by relying more than ever on Cabinet Councils and private advices. He negotiated a treaty with France without consulting a single minister other than Laurence Hyde. Because of the threatening vote of 10 January, he took upon himself responsibility for dissolving the second Exclusion Parliament. The resolution to dissolve the Oxford Parliament, which met in March 1681, he took in a secret council held in Merton College, and this time the secret was kept. In order that no minister should be blamed for it, he published a declaration justifying the dissolution of the two last Parliaments with no superscription on it but the printer's name.[2]

Charles's conduct compelled the Whigs to devise a theory of the constitution that made the King's ministers automatically responsible for all advice upon which the King acted. This they did in two authoritative pamphlets, *A Just and Modest Vindication of the Proceedings of the Two Last Parliaments*, and *A Letter From a Person of Quality*.[3] The authors of these pamphlets began by asserting that the King always acts on the advice of others, executes nothing that is not first resolved upon in Council, for 'then 'tis the counsellors must answer for the advice they give'. Nor is there any necessity for legal proof that this or that councillor advised the King, for an address request-

---

[1] *C.J.* ix, 651, 660; *H.M.C. Ormond*, v, 503.

[2] Sir John Dalrymple, *Memoirs of Great Britain and Ireland* (1790) i, 370; B.M. Add. MSS 32680, f. 142; Ailesbury, *Memoirs*, i, 56.

[3] The authorship of *A Just and Modest Vindication* (1681) is a matter of much dispute, but the weight of evidence suggests Sir William Jones, Whig, lawyer, and manager of the Commons. The author of *A Letter from a Person of Quality* (1681) is unknown, but it might well have been Shaftesbury himself, or someone close to him. These pamphlets, one by a Southampton Whig, one by a Shaftesbury Whig, provoked royalist replies, of which the two most important were John Dryden's *His Majesty's Declaration Defended: In a Letter to a Friend; Being an Answer to a Seditious Pamphlet, Called A Letter from a Person of Quality* (1681) and Edmund Bohun, *Reflections on a Pamphlet Stiled a Just and Modest Vindication of the Proceedings of the Last Two Parliaments* (1683).

ing the removal of a councillor does not injure him in life, liberty, or estate. Common fame is sufficient where the only deprivation is loss of office. Though the King's counsels are secret, the world knows that 'those who had the administration of affairs and the King's ear' are the authors of those counsels; and common fame proclaims who they are. If men of 'honour and conscience' wish to escape responsibility for the counsels upon which the King acts, they should resign (an admonition upon which the Earl of Salisbury acted in January 1681). The logic of these fictions, for that is what they were, contributed far more to the future growth of responsible government than did schemes to revive the Privy Council.[1]

These same two Whig pamphlets also sought to answer a second objection raised against the violent votes of January 1681: that they alleged no crimes against the ministers accused. To answer this objection, the Whigs fell back on the language of the Grand Remonstrance, urging that 'there may be reasons why a man should be turned out of a service, which perhaps would not extend to subject him to punishment'. If not in law, surely in reason, they argued, the King should dismiss those ministers whom the nation hated and whom the Commons believed to be the authors of the chief grievances of the realm. Henry IV had dismissed four councillors for no other reason than that the Commons had asked him to. Dared the Commons entrust the nation's money to ministers who would misspend it? Dared they grant the King a sufficient revenue when he refused to dismiss those evil counsellors who were leading him and the kingdom to ruin?[2]

The Whig theory that the King always acted on counsel, that his ministers were responsible for those counsels, that he should dismiss those whom the Commons distrusted, and that the Commons should deny him money if he did not, horrified John Dryden. To say that the King always acted on counsel, he wrote, 'is in effect to say he can neither do wrong nor right, nor indeed anything'. 'And if His Majesty can no sooner reward the service of anyone who is not of

[1] *A Just and Modest Vindication*, pp. 1–3, 17, 46; *A Letter from a Person of Quality*, pp. 1–2.
[2] *Ibid.* pp. 2, 5, 6; *A Just and Modest Vindication*, p. 17. The author of *A Letter from a Person of Quality* (p. 5) wrote, 'I think one may affirm by law the King ought to have no person near him, that hath the misfortune of such a vote...besides is it possible the King can expect supplies of men, money, hearts...if he manages his affairs by such persons as they think they have reason to fear and hate; there are some things so reasonable that they are above any written law, and will in despite of any power on earth have their effect; whereof this is one.'

their party, but they can vote him out of his employment; it must follow, that none but their own party must be employed, and then a vote of the House of Commons is in effect the Government.' 'Here all our fore-fathers are arraigned at once for trusting the executive power of the laws in the Prince's hands.' The only use that can be made of a monarch deprived of such power, 'is for an innkeeper to set upon a sign-post to draw custom'.[1]

Ultimately the Whig theory of the constitution prevailed, but for the moment the Stuarts and their theory won the day. Charles successfully defended the prerogatives of the Crown during the Exclusion Crisis and enhanced them during the last years of his reign. He did so by procrastinating during the years of the Popish Plot, by yielding on incidentals and standing firm on fundamentals, by retrenching his expenses while augmenting his revenues with a French subsidy, and, above all, by acting moderately while his enemies acted rashly. Charles's tactical skill conspired with Whig folly to produce a reaction in favour of the Crown. This reaction, however, did not lead to the realization of Danby's ideal of a Protestant Parliament giving its confidence to a Protestant King, it did not preserve the balance of government established in 1660 and maintained so precariously since. Instead it destroyed that balance of government, replacing it with a monarchy unchecked by Parliament. The furious quarrels caused by the rise and fall of Danby and the introduction and defeat of Exclusion persuaded Englishmen (as Sir Henry Neville observed) that distrust between the King and his people could 'be laid asleep only if the King have a great deal more power, or a great deal less'.[2] Frightened by the Rye House Plot and the prospect of civil war, appalled by the republicanism of the Whigs, and calmed by a pause in the growth of French power, a majority of those Englishmen, who still possessed the franchise after the *quo warranto* proceedings of the 1680's, resolved to give the King 'a great deal more power'. On the accession of James II they elected a Parliament which perpetrated an act that Shaftesbury would have regarded as the ultimate betrayal: they voted the King a revenue sufficient to allow him to live of his own.[3] An

[1] Dryden, *His Majesties Declaration Defended* (1681), pp. 1, 10, 15–16.
[2] Sir Henry Neville, *Plato Redivivus* (4th ed. 1763), p. 221.
[3] Shaftesbury told the Lords in December 1680, 'My Lords, I hear of a bargain in the House of Commons and an Address made to the King, but this I know, and must boldly say it and plainly, that the nation is betrayed if upon any terms we part with our money

unworkable balance of government gave way to an untried royal absolutism.

The royalist reaction of the last years of Charles's reign and the financial independence granted James on his accession did not lessen the permanent erosion that the prerogative suffered during the seven years that separated the rise of Danby from the fall of Shaftesbury. For one thing, voting impeachments became a more firmly ingrained habit than ever before. Courtiers could not resist the temptation to introduce impeachments against their rivals into the House of Commons; and Country gentlemen, frightened by the Court, supported them on the flimsiest grounds. Had James II met Parliament regularly, rival courtiers would assuredly have attacked each other there, as some did threaten to attack Sunderland in 1685.[1] Because the House of Commons voted impeachments frequently, Parliaments became in these years a terror to the King's ministers. Lord Chancellors refused to seal pardons, Secretaries to sign treaties, and Treasurers to issue warrants for fear of incurring impeachments. Nor was this caution unjustified: men did suffer when impeached. As Lord Danby wrote from the Tower (where he lay under an impeachment):

Whatever Your Majesty may be informed, the lawyers do all take notice, by Mr Seymour's selling his place and by Judge Scroggs being displaced under an impeachment...that whoever is impeached by the Commons must suffer in some kind or other; and they have held out a doctrine (though with no good intent to Your Majesty) that the King can do no wrong, but all advisers must suffer, and then they vote what they please to be pernicious and illegal advice.[2]

Danby exaggerated the blow dealt to the prerogative by Scroggs's dismissal and Seymour's resignation, but he did not exaggerate the harm done to the Crown by the maxim that the King can do no wrong and by the practice of voting what they pleased to be illegal.

till we are sure the King is ours; have what laws you will, and what conditions you will, they will be of no use but waste paper before Easter, if the Court have money to set up popery and arbitrary designs in the mean while.' This speech was printed in 1681, and reprinted in 1689 as *The Speech of a Noble Peer of This Realm.* When confronted with the pamphlet in 1681, Shaftesbury refused to repudiate it.

[1] J. P. Kenyon, *Sunderland* (1958), p. 116.

[2] B.M. Add. MSS 28049, f. 166v. Sir Francis North remarked concerning the committing of great persons to prison on impeachments (B.M. Add. MSS 32520, f. 244v), 'So here is the executive part of the government taken away, and the legislative made necessary.' The fears of Danby and North were exaggerated, however, for the House of Lords refused to commit ministers unless charged with a particular treason.

The most important consequence of Danby's impeachment was that it led men insensibly to extend from illegal acts to unpopular acts the principle that the King can do no wrong, that his ministers must answer for all.

The deepest erosion suffered by the prerogative during these years did not arise from the practice of voting impeachments: it arose from the practice of voting addresses against the King's ministers. For from this practice emerged the Whig theory of responsible government, the most lasting legacy of the parliamentary battles fought between 1674 and 1681. The theory maintained that the King always acts on the counsels of others, of those who served him in high office and at Court; only by resigning could those officials and courtiers escape responsibility for the counsels upon which the King acted. If they gave pernicious advice, the House of Commons might demand their removal; if the King refused to remove them, the Commons might refuse supply. That the power of the purse be not destroyed, Parliament should withhold from the King a sufficient, permanent revenue. This Whig theory of the constitution did not commend itself to many Englishmen in 1685; they resolved instead to put their trust in a strong monarch. But the theory, a product of the political strife of these years, existed, to be seized upon when Englishmen no longer put their trust in Princes.

CHAPTER 7

THE LOGIC OF PARLIAMENTARY
SUPREMACY (1688–1697)

Had James II met Parliament oftener during his reign, the exercise of the power of impeachment would have made unnecessary the Glorious Revolution of 1688. But James, who had no intention of allowing Parliament to attack his ministers, never met Parliament after the autumn of 1685. Ministers of state, he believed, owed unquestionable obedience to him; in return he owed them protection. James repeatedly told his servants that he was King, and would be obeyed. He brought the same autocratic temper to the problem of taking counsel. He not only ignored the Privy Council, but the Cabinet Council as well; if he sought advice at all he sought it from a secret junto of Catholic counsellors meeting at Mr Chiffinch's office. And from those who counselled him he expected agreement, not opposition; he turned out any man whose sentiments he found opposed to his. James not only intended to be a King, but to be seen to be a King. During his short reign he took counsel from anyone or no one, dismissed any man who opposed him, granted a pardon to any man who obeyed him, directed all, and assumed responsibility for all. Never since the reign of Richard II had the government of England been so wholly contained in the person of the King; neither Henry VIII nor Charles I ever asserted so fully the King's right to rule his realm directly and personally.

For this reason the Convention Parliament of 1689 made no attempt to define, or redefine, the responsibilities of ministers of state. Those who sat in the Convention knew only too well that James himself had threatened their laws, their liberties, and their religion. In their Declaration of Rights they openly charged him with an endeavour to subvert the laws and religion of England. The Jacobites might—and did—cry out that the King can do no wrong, that his ministers are responsible for all, but the authors of the Revolutionary Settlement conveniently forgot this ancient maxim. It did not serve their immediate purposes, which were to define the succession, to destroy the suspensive power, to grant toleration to

The Logic of Parliamentary Supremacy

Protestant Dissenters, and to mitigate the dangers of a standing army. Furthermore, Parliament did not wish to endanger its attempt to declare old law by an hasty endeavour to create new law. In order to avoid unnecessary controversy, it dropped from the Declaration of Rights the one clause that redefined the responsibilities of ministers of state, the clause which denied them the right to plead the King's pardon in bar to an impeachment.[1] Because Parliament in 1689 sought to undo the harm that James had done, and not the harm that his or Charles II's ministers had done, it erected safeguards against royal, not ministerial, irresponsibility.

The principal safeguard which Parliament erected against government by an arbitrary King was financial. By refusing to vote William a sufficient revenue for life, it made the Crown dependent upon Parliament. The decision to deny the King a sufficient revenue was deliberate. In 1660 Parliament had (as Sacheverell reminded the Commons in 1689) voted 'such an extravagant revenue' that Parliaments were 'kicked out at pleasure'. No man needed to be reminded what it had cost England to surrender the power of the purse in 1685; but an aged servant of Charles II pungently summed up the experience of his generation. We have learned, said Sir Joseph Williamson, 'that when Princes have not needed money, they have not needed us'. In order to guarantee that the King should have need of them, the two Houses deliberately voted him an inadequate revenue.[2]

The House of Commons desired to meet frequently not merely to pass needed legislation, but also in order to act as a check on the executive. As William Harbord said, 'You have an infallible security for the administration of the government: all the revenue is in your own hands, which fell with the last King, and you may keep that back. Can he whom you place on the throne support the government without the revenue? Can he do good or harm without it? It is reasonable that you should be redressed by laws; but unless you preserve your government, your papers cannot protect you.'[3]

Parliament hoped to check the executive in two ways: by impeaching errant ministers of state and by demanding the redress of

[1] Leopold von Ranke, *History of England* (Oxford, 1875), IV, 513–14.
[2] Cobbett, *Parl. Hist.* V, 55, 554. Though Andrew Browning ('The Stop of the Exchequer', *History*, XIV, 333) has shown that views such as Sacheverell expressed give a distorted picture of the financial settlement at the Restoration, these views determined men's actions in 1689. [3] Cobbett, *Parl. Hist.* V, 57.

246

grievances—including the removal of hated ministers—before voting supplies. Though impeachments had proved a frail reed in the past, Englishmen still put their trust in them, believing with John Locke that the mere restoration of 'our ancient government' afforded a sufficient safeguard for English liberty. This reliance on impeachments, however, did not preclude the voting of addresses against ministers of state found obnoxious to the nation. Both means of opposing evil ministers were in the minds of parliamentarians in 1689 and 1690, and for both frequent Parliaments were necessary. In the critical debates on the voting of revenues to the Crown (which occurred in March of 1690) Sir John Lowther urged that they demonstrate their trust in William by voting him a sufficient revenue for life. John Guise objected, '"Tis said, "Put no distrust on the King", but I would not have all ill management laid on the King, which ought to be laid on the ministers.' Only, he continued, if you keep the revenues in your hands can you punish those who 'have done amiss'. Colonel Austen concurred with him, 'A Parliament will secure you from other ill persons, as well as ill kings, I mean the ministers. Granting it for life will prevent any ill ministers being called in question, and you can never reach them.' The House heeded these sentiments by granting William the customs for only four years, though previous Parliaments had granted it for life. The Commons did not, by this act, seek to usurp new powers: they sought only to vindicate their ancient right to impeach, or vote addresses against, evil ministers of state.[1]

By retaining the power of the purse, Parliament secured to itself the power to censure those who misused the executive power. Members of Parliament found justification for exercising this power of censure in the increasingly popular doctrine that supreme power, sovereignty, resides in the legislature, which then entrusts executive power to the King. John Locke enunciated this doctrine in his *Second Treatise on Government*, where he explicitly spelled out its consequence. 'When the legislative', he wrote, 'has put the execution

[1] B. Rand (ed.), *The Correspondence of John Locke and Edward Clarke* (1927), p. 288; Cobbett, *Parl. Hist.* v, 556, 560. Sir John Somers later remarked (*ibid.* p. 713), 'The only thing besides giving money [possessed] by the Commons is right of impeachments.' To prove the antiquity of the right to address against evil ministers, Thomas Wharton reminded William III (Dalrymple, *Memoirs of Great Britain and Ireland*, II, 200) and Sir Thomas Atkyns reminded the nation (*The Power, Jurisdiction, and Privilege of Parliament*, 1689, p. 38), that Henry IV had dismissed four servants for no other reason than that the House of Commons had asked him to.

of the laws they make into other hands, they have a power still to resume it out of those hands when they find cause, and to punish for any maladministration against the laws.'[1] Many lesser writers, with less precise pens, proclaimed the supremacy of the legislature and the subordination of the executive.[2] But not only in pamphlets, in practice also Englishmen testified to the supremacy of the legislature. In December 1688 the peers and Commoners then assembled in London temporarily entrusted 'the administration of public affairs' to William, Prince of Orange; in February 1689 the Convention Parliament, by naming him King, entrusted it to him permanently. As the idea of a balance of government characterized the Restoration Settlement, so the idea of government as a trust from the people characterized the Revolutionary Settlement. The one idea justified the grant of an independent revenue to Charles II; the other vindicated the financial supremacy of Parliament declared in 1690. The Revolutionary Settlement made little formal alteration in the government of England, but the financial and ideological changes accompanying it placed supreme power in Parliament.

The two Houses of Parliament had no intention of exercising this latent supremacy except in circumstances of extreme peril, such as the succession of another James II would create. For the moment they placed their trust in a Protestant Prince, and granted him the same executive powers that his predecessors had enjoyed. No one suggested that Parliament name the King's ministers and counsellors for him. This right they allowed him in as full plentitude as ever any

[1] John Locke, *Second Treatise on Government* (New York, 1949), p. 198. The seeds of this doctrine may be found in the principle, clearly recognized by legal authorities in the reign of James I, that Parliament possessed a power beyond the law itself, for Parliament (and only Parliament) could alter the Common Law. William Hakewill maintained this in a speech in 1610 against impositions (W. Hakewill, *True Libertie of the Subject*, 1641, p. 98) and Edward Coke asserted it in *The Second Part of the Institutes of the Laws of England* (1797 ed.), pp. 97, 619. Citing both these legal authorities, the anonymous author of *An Introduction to a Treatise Concerning the Legislative Power* (1708) commented (p. 50), 'Therefore the supreme authority of a nation ultimately and properly belongs to those that have the legislative authority reserved to them, but not to the Prince who hath only the executive; for that is merely a trust, and no more, whenever it is separated from the power legislative.'

[2] The doctrine that sovereignty resides in the legislature may be found in *Questions of State Concerning the English Constitution*, in *Reflections Upon the Great Revolution*, in *Political Aphorisms*, and in *A Brief Justification of the Prince of Orange's Descent*. These pamphlets are printed in *A Collection of State Tracts, Published on Occasion of the Late Revolution in 1688, and During the Reign of King William III* (1705-7). See pp. 169, 254, and 388 in vol. I and p. 138 in vol. II. By the time of Swift, Addison, and Steele the doctrine had become a commonplace.

King of England possessed. Nor was their trust misplaced. William exercised the executive power according to the law of the land and according to the will of the people. He pursued policies with which the nation sympathized, he named men of talent to high office, he gave no unlawful orders, he surrendered his will to no Court minion, he protected no man from impeachment, and he met Parliament often. Yet all was to no avail. Parliament attacked his ministers as frequently and noisily, if not as bitterly, as had earlier Parliaments attacked the ministers of Charles II. He knew no more peace than had his predecessors from the incessant clamours of the Commons against his servants. His ministers, if anything, suffered more censures from Parliament than had earlier ministers. Why Parliament persisted in attacking the ministers of a law-respecting, liberty-regarding Protestant Prince is a question of critical importance in the history of responsible government in England.

Losses in Ireland in 1689, losses at sea in 1690, the employment of Dutchmen in the army—all these angered Englishmen and gave occasion for attacks upon the King's ministers. But these abuses were remedied, and still criticism of the King's ministers continued. Defeats at Londonderry and La Hogue, and General Ginkel's conduct at Steenkirk genuinely offended the pride of Englishmen, but the clamours which they occasioned were quite peripheral to the central discord which disturbed William's reign, a discord which arose from the violent personal ambitions and the passionate party jealousies of English politicians in the age of King William. Williamite politicians thirsted for the power and emoluments which high office conferred, and, if denied office, opposed the government until rewarded to their satisfaction. But isolated, disgruntled individuals could inflict little damage on the government unless allied with others, unless joined together in party. Lord Lonsdale observed with astonishment and pain the revival of the names of Whig and Tory in the Convention Parliament.[1] But that Parliament witnessed much more than the revival of the names of party: it witnessed also the resurgence of the passions and jealousies of party. Whigs distrusted Tories and Tories despised Whigs. Most members of Parliament belonged to no party, but enough members belonged to some party to drive William to distraction. William's chief difficulty lay in the demand which each party made for a monopoly of offices.

[1] *E.H.R.* xxx, 93–4.

The extreme Whigs in particular, led by the Earl of Monmouth and Thomas Wharton, clamoured for such a monopoly. The effrontery of their demand, voiced in an age which still believed in monarchy, prevented their stating it baldly. Wharton and his friends had to couch their demand for one party government in the plausible assertion that men of the Church party could not be trusted because they were at heart loyal to James II. This was their constant refrain.[1] Some among them may have sincerely believed it, but for most of them it was mere rhetoric. It justified their demand that William remove churchmen and employ them, that they might then enjoy the fruits of office and promote at Court policies which they favoured. Personal ambition was a powerful force in the decade after the Revolution, but it would have dissipated itself in all directions had not party distinctions, based on contending principles in Church and State, channelled the many rivulets of personal ambition into the larger stream of party opposition.

In order to gain a monopoly of office, the extreme Whigs did not limit themselves to importunities at Court or appeals to the country. They also sought to use the House of Commons as an instrument for driving their enemies from office. Since they had nothing remotely like a majority in the Commons they adopted the strategy of embarrassing their enemies by inflaming the House against those who had served James II and Charles II in their tyrannous schemes. Their chief effort was to transform a Bill of Indemnity designed to bury the past into a Bill of Pains and Penalties designed to resurrect the quarrels of the past. They sought to do this by excepting from the Bill of Indemnity not particular persons, as Sunderland or Jeffreys, but any person guilty of one or more of a whole catalogue of crimes, a catalogue so broad, remarked Roger North, as to 'comprehend all mankind'. By this means the Whigs hoped to leave their enemies in constant fear of prosecution. The Tories replied to this strategy by urging the House to except from the Bill particular persons, by name, thus giving security to all else. Over the question whether to except from the Indemnity any man guilty of certain

---

[1] H. C. Foxcroft, *Supplement to Burnet's History of My Own Time* (Oxford, 1902), p. 313; Dalrymple, *Memoirs of Great Britain and Ireland*, II, 187–200; Col. Laughton to Thomas Wharton, Carte MSS 228, ff. 188v, 194v; *The Works of the Right Honourable late Lord Delamer and Earl of Warrington* (1694), pp. 48–9, 82–6; *H.M.C. Rep. VII*, pp. 230–1; John Sheffield, Earl of Mulgrave and Duke of Buckingham, 'Humanum Est Errare', B.M. Add. MSS 27382, ff. 91v–92; *Plain English* (in *State Tracts, William III*, II, 91).

crimes or only certain persons named in the Bill, the two parties wrangled and disputed for more than a year, until in January 1690 the Tories sought to force the passage of a meaningful Indemnity Bill. 'There will be terrible debates over this affair,' wrote William on 17 January, '...the Tories wish to pass it [the Indemnity Bill], the Whigs oppose it, or at least wish a great many exceptions.' The decisive debate occurred on 21 January, when the Tories moved that the House name particular persons who should be excepted from the Bill. The Whigs opposed the motion and carried the House with them, 190 to 173. This proved, however, to be the last victory for the Whigs in their continuing effort to keep their enemies in continual fear. William, who desperately wanted a Bill of Indemnity that would bury all past quarrels, dissolved Parliament in February 1690. In the new Parliament, which met in March, the Whigs possessed a much diminished voice, and could not prevent the passage of an Act of Grace which excepted, by name, only the more notorious of James's servants—Sunderland, Jeffreys, and two dozen others.[1]

The interminable debates over the Indemnity Bill revealed clearly that the deeper purpose of the Whigs was not to punish the dying Jeffreys and the exiled Sunderland, but to proscribe from public life the Marquis of Halifax and the Marquis of Carmarthen (as the Earl of Danby was now known). They cared less about the former servants of James II, none of whom had employment at Court, than about the former servants of Charles II, the most famous of whom did enjoy employment at Court. Though many servants of James II remained in London, a few even in Newgate, the House of Commons impeached none of them, neither the wicked solicitors Philip Burton and Richard Graham, nor the Attorney-General Sir Robert Sawyer, nor the Chief Justices Lord Herbert and Lord Wright. Ultimately all were released from custody.[2] But the Whigs in both Houses continued to pursue their vendetta against Halifax and Carmarthen. Led by Howe, Garroway, Guise, Hawles, and Strickland, they showed a greater interest in the Fitzharris case than in the Hales

---

[1] North Papers, B.M. Add. MSS 32524, f. 2; N. Japikse, *Correspondentie van Willem III en van Hans Willem Bentinck, eersten Graaf van Portland* (Hague, 1927–35), I, 81; *C.J.* x, 338, 423–4.

[2] The House of Commons did impeach the Earls of Peterborough and Salisbury, Privy Councillors in the reign of James II, for reconciling themselves to Rome. However, in October 1690 the Lords, with no protest from the Commons, ruled that the prorogation and dissolution of Parliament had discharged them from their impeachments (*C.J.* x, 275; Cobbett, *Parl. Hist.* v, 652; *L.J.* xiv, 538).

case, in *quo warranto* proceedings than in the proceedings of the ecclesiastical commission, in the great councillors behind the judges than in the judges themselves. In the opening debate on the Bill of Indemnity, Sir William Strickland publicly declared, 'I would look for what is to come, and address the King that those who have been the authors of our former miscarriages, may be removed from his councils.' Sir John Guise immediately added, 'Everybody is satisfied that we are governed by a sort of people who may come within the Indemnity. I know not but our misfortunes are from the same hands still.'[1] The attempt of the Whigs to use the Bill of Indemnity as a lever to dislodge Carmarthen and Halifax failed, but it was not the only weapon in their arsenal. There were at least three others: the legality of Carmarthen's pardon, the complicity of Halifax in the execution of Lord Russell, and the miscarriages in Ireland.

On assuming the Crown, William named the Marquis of Carmarthen Lord President of the Council. The appointment vexed the Whigs, who promptly cried out that he lay under an impeachment. In June Jack Howe, who refused to allow a place at Court to silence him, moved an address requesting His Majesty to remove from his Council any man who stood impeached. He spoke pointedly of those who had taken money in order to put off Parliaments and who had fled to pardons for protection against impeachments. But his motion failed, for he lacked the courage, when challenged the next day, to name names. The most that he and his friends could do was to carry a resolution to add to the Bill of Indemnity a clause declaring that the King's pardon was no bar to an impeachment. Since the House never passed the Bill of Indemnity, this clause did Carmarthen no harm. Nor did the Bill of Rights injure him, for in May the House of Lords removed from it a clause declaring the King's pardon no bar to an impeachment. The Commons acquiesced in this action, but a group of wilful Whigs in the House of Lords did not. In November, on the third reading of the Bill of Rights, they sought to add a rider declaring null and void any pardon pleaded to an impeachment. By a vote of 50 to 17 the Lords rejected the rider.[2] Few actions illustrate better the conservative character of the Revolutionary Settlement than the refusal of the two Houses to

[1] Cobbett, *Parl. Hist.* v, 285.
[2] *C.J.* x, 162; Carte MSS 79, f. 220; A. Boyer, *The History of King William the Third* (1702), II, 119; *H.M.C. Rep. XII, Part 6*, pp. 345-7.

diminish the King's prerogative of pardon, even when it seemed to endanger the power of impeachment. Though in part their refusal arose from an awareness of the particular services that Carmarthen had performed in driving out James II and bringing in William III. In 1689 Carmarthen had many friends in the Commons and even more in the Lords, and they did not intend to allow the Whigs to oust him from office by declaring illegal the pardon he had once pleaded.

William gave the Privy Seal to the Marquis of Halifax, but his appointment proved no more popular with the Whigs than Carmarthen's. The Whigs in the Commons had not forgotten, and refused to forget, his alleged complicity in the attack upon the Charters and the prosecution of the Rye-House conspirators. However, the long-awaited exhuming of Halifax's past misconduct came, in the end, not from the Commons but from the Lords. In November 1689 the peers named a committee, popularly known as the Murderers Committee, to discover who were the authors of the *quo warranto* proceedings, the advisers of the Dispensing Power, and the judicial murderers of Lord Russell and others. But this 'deepest laid of party mines', as the historian Ralph called it, failed to explode. The mine was a dud, for Halifax's accusers possessed no proof of his complicity in Russell's death. The work of the committee came to naught, forcing the personal and political enemies of the Marquis to look elsewhere for charges to justify their attacks upon him.[1]

In fact they had been searching for such charges all summer, and they believed they had found them in the present misgovernment of the kingdom. This was likewise true of the enemies of the Lord President, for against him the Whigs also brought an indictment of mismanagement. And the mismanagement which they regarded as most grievous was the delay in sending succour to Ireland. Throughout June and July the House of Commons sought to discover those responsible for this delay. The obvious candidate was Colonel Lundy, whose treachery had left Londonderry defenceless and whose misinformation had turned back a fleet coming to its rescue. But there were members of both Houses who wished to blame Halifax and Carmarthen, not Lundy, for the delay—who would turn to political account the military reverses in Ireland. The greatest obstacle facing them was the secrecy of the Council, for unless they

[1] *H.M.C. Rep. XII, Part 6*, p. 283; J. Ralph, *History of England* (1744), II, 177; Burnet, *History*, IV, 59–60; Foxcroft, *Halifax*, II, 91–105.

had knowledge of the advice given there, they could not prove Halifax and Carmarthen culpable. To solve this problem they turned to the right of inquiry, as Eliot had in 1626, Pym in 1640, and the enemies of the Cabal in 1674. They examined Colonel Lundy and others; they inspected the Admiralty Books; and twice they asked William for permission to inspect the Privy Council Books and the Minute Books of the Committee on Irish Affairs. When William gave them procrastinating answers, their tempers snapped. On 13 July the Commons resolved that those who were the occasion of delay in sending relief to Ireland and those who had advised delay in allowing members of the House to examine the Privy Council Books were enemies of the King and kingdom. A further motion to address the King to remove Halifax and Carmarthen from his Council failed only because both sides were so equally matched that they postponed putting the question. The general vote of censure, however, frightened William into allowing the Commons to examine the Privy Council Books and the Minute Books of the Irish Committee. The inquiry proved disappointing, for they discovered nothing that cast any guilt on any minister. This did not deter the enemies of Halifax, who, on 2 August, moved an address for his removal. The motion, made by Sir John Guise, provoked a long debate which ended in a close division. By 11 votes the House declined to vote an address for his removal. Sir Edward Harley, writing of Halifax's triumph, concluded, 'But I think his wound will not heal.' He proved a true prophet. Harassed by his personal enemies in the Lords, distrusted by the Tories as a Trimmer, hated by the Whigs as the enemy of Exclusion, unsure of Carmarthen's support, and unwilling (in Nottingham's words) to 'remain an object of his enemies' envy and resentment', he resigned the Speakership in October 1689 and the Privy Seal in February 1690. William wished him to keep the Seal, but the Marquis, who had refused in 1680 to retreat before an address of the House of Commons, insisted on retreat before the possibility of such an address in 1690. He saw, if no one else did, the logic of the supremacy that Parliament had seized in 1689.[1]

In the autumn of 1689 the Commons turned their attention from

---

[1] *C.J.* x, 217, 224; Cobbett, *Parl. Hist.* v, 381–2; Ralph, *History*, II, 133; Sir Edward Harley to Robert Harley, B. M. Loan 29/140, No. 8; W. A. Aiken, *Conduct of the Earl of Nottingham* (New Haven, 1941), pp. 52–3; Foxcroft, *Halifax*, II, 113.

the siege of Londonderry and the treachery of Colonel Lundy to the miseries of the English army in Ireland and the delinquencies of John Shales, Commissioner General of Provisions. The House had no difficulty discovering the faults of Shales, who had failed to send the army good meat, good drink, and sufficient Ordnance. But the House was not satisfied with punishing Shales alone: they wished to punish the minister who had recommended his appointment and to whom he was accountable. 'In plain English,' said Mr Smith, 'knaves and villains are employed...I would desire the King to tell us, who were the occasion of putting these men in.' Sir Christopher Musgrave added, 'You should know to whom Shales is accountable. If these miscarriages are of so great a date as August last, you must know why this was never examined nor punished. It must rest upon these persons whom the King has entrusted. If this House examines all miscarriages, you must be a perpetual Parliament. I know Shales's employment is Commissary of the Stores; certainly some persons are superintendents.'[1]

The House agreed that the departmental head, the minister who recommended men to employment, should be accountable for all miscarriages. But how could they discover who recommended Shales for employment?

The Commons began by asking William directly who had recommended Shales's appointment as Commissioner General of Provisions; but William was no more inclined than Charles I before him to play the role of a common informer. On 2 December he replied to the House, 'Gentlemen, it is impossible for me to give you an answer to this question.'[2] Unlike Charles, however, William did not leave the matter there. He seized the initiative by inviting the House of Commons to name seven Commissioners of their own choosing to manage the sending of provisions to Ireland. The

---

[1] Cobbett, *Parl. Hist.* v, 453–5. In March Sir Robert Howard objected to Burton's and Graham's plea that 'they were but ministerial' and in June Sir Thomas Lee denounced the plea of Sir Robert Sawyer, James's Attorney General, that 'I was but a ministerial officer'. Perhaps because the House, at bottom, did regard them as 'merely ministerial', they never prosecuted Burton, Graham, or Sawyer (*ibid.* pp. 159, 326, 356).

[2] *C.J.* x, 295, 300. Andrew Newport wrote to Robert Newport on 20 Nov. (B.M. Add. MSS 7080, f. 20v), 'Yesterday we had a very long debate whether we should address to the King to let the House know who recommended Commissary Shales to him and advised his being employed. Many thought it to be very indecent, and that 'twas not to be expected a private gentleman should name a man in such a case...' In 1694 Mr Jeffreys proposed that they ask the King who advised him to veto the Place Bill, 'but there was', reports Anchitell Grey (*Debates*, x, 377), 'a general "No" thereto'.

extreme Whigs—Howe, Guise, Birch, Williams, and Hawles—favoured accepting the offer, even to the extent of naming members of their own House to serve on the Commission. But their allies, the Hereford Whigs led by Foley and Harley, and the Country Tories led by Musgrave and Seymour, opposed accepting the offer. 'We have no part of the executive authority of the government,' said Edward Seymour, 'but we may advise the King.' Paul Foley concurred, 'Though not fit for us to nominate; yet, as a state of the Kingdom, you may advise the King with qualifications.'[1] In fact the House had no wish to assume responsibility for the proper exercise of the executive power. 'Just as the people', observed Hoffman, the Imperial envoy, 'attribute these miscarriages, and with good reason, to the King's ministers, so they would, in case the Commissioners found no remedy, attribute the mismanagement to the House of Commons.' Nor did the Commons wish to invite a new tyranny by giving executive power to those who should act as a check on the executive power. It is 'too great a temptation to human frailty,' wrote John Locke, '...for the same persons who have the power of making laws, to have also in their hands the power to execute them, whereby they may exempt themselves from obedience to the laws they make, and suit the law, both in its making and execution, to their private advantage...'[2] The principle of the separation of powers, joined to a fear of responsibility, prevented the Commons in 1689 from lodging executive power in Parliament. On 2 December the Commons humbly desired to be excused from recommending any person to serve in Ireland and left it to His Majesty's great wisdom to nominate fit persons to serve there.[3]

This did not mean that the Commons chose to surrender their role as critics, a role that they notably enjoyed playing. After Seymour had told the House that they had no part of the executive,

---

[1] *C.J.* x, 299; Cobbett, *Parl. Hist.* v, 468–72, 480.

[2] Klopp, *Der Fall Des Hauses Stuart*, v, 65; Locke, *Second Treatise on Government* (in E. Barker, *Social Contract*, 1948, p. 85). Sir John Thompson urged the Commons to refuse the King's offer, for their commissioners might also fail for want of money; Sir Thomas Clarges added, 'If the commissioners fail, the House will make but faint prosecution of it' (Cobbett, *Parl. Hist.* v, 468, 471).

[3] *C.J.* x, 300. Though the Commons refused to name commissioners for sending provisions to Ireland, they did name Commissioners for Wool, who were to enforce the laws against the exportation of wool. This departure from the principle of the separation of powers worked badly, led to conflict with the King's officers over the seizure of wool from a French vessel, and was abandoned in 1702 (Robert Lees, 'The Constitutional Importance of the Commissioners for Wool of 1689', *Economica*, XIII, 147 ff. and 264 ff.).

Sir Thomas Lee rose to remind them that they had a duty to inform the King of faults in the administration. 'Show him the fault,' said Lee, 'and the persons, and not in generals, lest you throw out the King and Kingdom together.'[1] But there lay the rub. How could they inform the King of faults except in generals, since they did not know who in particular counselled him? The examination of minute books had proved fruitless, and William would not testify as an informer. The Commons therefore fell back on common fame, on the notoriety of the fact, even though Roger North deplored its use by legislative assemblies. It was, they said, notorious that Carmarthen had frequent access to the King; it was common report that he had nominated Shales. Why should he not bear the blame? This censure without proof gained a semblance of equity from the practice of attributing responsibility to those who held office and served in the King's councils. 'If there be ill management,' said Sir John Guise, 'it must be from those in employment.' 'We must', urged Mr Smith, 'attribute all the miscarriages and misfortunes to the Committee for the Affairs of Ireland.' These private opinions received a public endorsement in the Commons' address of 21 December 1689, which marked the culmination of six months' opposition to William's ministers. The address warned of imminent dangers to the kingdom caused by 'the want of ability or integrity in those who have the direction of affairs', and complained of the mismanagement of affairs caused by 'the ill advice of those who have undertaken the management of them'. The address concluded with a request that William 'appoint affairs to be managed by persons unsuspected, and more to the safety of Your Majesty, and the satisfaction of your subjects'. This was assuredly an address expressed in generals, the kind Lee warned against, but it differed from similar addresses voted in the reign of Charles II by placing responsibility on those 'who have the direction of affairs' and on those 'who have undertaken the management of them'. The address was an augury of the day when men would automatically hold the ministry or cabinet responsible for all advice upon which the King acted.[2]

[1] Cobbett, *Parl. Hist.* v, 418.
[2] R. North, 'A Letter in Answer to an Inquiry about the Act of Pains and Penalty, &c.', B.M. Add. MSS 32524, ff. 5–6; Cobbett, *Parl. Hist.* v, 446, 456. A Committee of the Whole House resolved on 14 Dec. to present this address to the King. The House debated their recommendation on the 21st, when they voted to recommit it to Committee, where it died (*C.J.* x, 308–9, 317).

The Logic of Parliamentary Supremacy

The House of Commons never formally presented their address of 21 December to William, for those members who thought it too audacious joined with those who thought it too weak to secure its return to committee, where it died. But the censure implied in the vote on the 21st led Halifax to propose to William that 'we' (by whom he presumably meant Carmarthen, Nottingham, Godolphin, and himself) 'might go off according to the intended address'. William, however, refused his advice, for he had no wish to grant the Whigs a monopoly of his counsels. Neither had he any wish to exclude them from his counsels. His aim was to create a balance of counsel between Whig and Tory, excluding from his presence no man who could give him good advice and from office no man who could give him good service. He instinctively recoiled from being a prisoner of a party. He saw that the prerogative to name his own ministers could have no meaning if he must name them from one party. He therefore declined Halifax's advice, urged him not to resign, refused to dismiss Carmarthen, Nottingham, and Godolphin, and dissolved the Parliament which sought to drive them from him. In dissolving Parliament, William had a clear purpose: to free himself from those extreme Whigs who attacked his Tory ministers, drove on Bills of Pains and Penalties, promoted parliamentary addresses, and sought to exclude Tories from the corporations for seven years. William had had enough, and therefore he resolved to summon another Parliament, which would support his desire for a mixed ministry.[1]

For seven years, from 1690 to 1697, William strove to govern England with moderate men, with men drawn from both parties or from none (which he much preferred). He sought to create a motley administration, with the Whig Shrewsbury as one Secretary and the Tory Nottingham as the other, with the radical Earl of Monmouth presiding over a Treasury Commission which also included the able Lord Godolphin, with an Admiralty Commission which comprehended both outspoken Whigs like William Sacheverell and moderate Tories like Sir John Lowther of Whitehaven. But William's

---

[1] Foxcroft, *Halifax*, II, 203–4, 206, 232, 242–4. William Heylar wrote to Dr Arthur Charlett in January 1690 (Ballard MSS 38, f. 125), 'The King said, "I am neither for a Commonwealth after my decease, neither will I be a Doge of Venice, while I live."' Godolphin followed Halifax's example by resigning in the face of the vote on the 21st, but he returned to the Treasury in November 1690. William expressed his confidence in Godolphin by telling Halifax in March 1689 (Foxcroft, *Halifax*, II, 205), '...if he had a mind to keep Lord Godolphin, who should hinder him?'.

brave experiment in government by a ministry of all the talents failed. By the year 1697 the Whigs wholly dominated his government; no Tory of importance, neither Carmarthen nor Nottingham nor Godolphin, held office. In the struggle between those who advocated a balance of counsels and those who demanded a monopoly of counsels, the advocates of monopoly won out. The course of this struggle was confused and complicated; the battle lines were ever shifting; the issues were never explicitly stated, if even comprehended; and the lines of party were criss-crossed by personal animosities and aristocratic connections. But gradually and indisputably the Whigs gained a monopoly of office; William found he must rely on them alone. The history of this seven-year struggle, confused as it is, takes on some clarity if broken down into six separate campaigns. (1) From March 1690 until March 1692 an alliance of extreme Whigs and High Tories harassed the government until William bought off the High Tories with office. (2) From March 1692 until April 1693 the Whigs, by petulant resignations, committees of inquiry, parliamentary addresses, and private intrigues, forced their way back into the government. (3) Between April and November 1693 the Whigs in the House of Commons waged a remorseless campaign against the Earl of Nottingham, which ended in his dismissal. (4) In 1694 the Whigs demanded and secured the purge of Tories from the Excise and Customs Commissions. (5) In the year 1695 the Whigs drove Carmarthen, now Duke of Leeds, from the Presidency of the Council by an impeachment. (6) And finally, in 1697, by an artful ruse, they secured the resignation of Godolphin. In each of these campaigns there is one paramount question that demands an answer: what drove William to retreat from his ideal of balanced counsels and to surrender to demands for a monopoly of his counsels?

In one sense William himself, by dissolving Parliament in February 1690, endangered the balance of parties upon which depended a balance of counsels, for the dissolution delighted the Tories and outraged the Whigs. Nor did he help matters by openly showing his favour towards the Church party in the ensuing months, a display which may well have helped it secure considerably more seats in the new Parliament than it had held in the old.[1] But at heart he

---

[1] William wrote to Portland of the dissolution (Japikse, *Correspondentie*, I, 95), 'The Tories are pleased, but not the Whigs.' According to divisions on disputed election

The Logic of Parliamentary Supremacy

remained a Trimmer, resolved to discountenance the Tories in their turn if they demanded a monopoly of office; and quite unwilling to trust the High Tories who would surely demand it. There is no denying that he dismissed from office the more radical Whigs, as the Earl of Monmouth and Lord Delamer, but he put moderate Tories in their places, and retained the services of moderate Whigs. The result was a government of moderate men, of able administrators, of loyal servants of the Crown. Such a government, however, failed to satisfy those in Parliament who were consumed, as was Sir Edward Seymour, with ambition for office, or who were driven, as was Sir John Guise, by party passion, or who distrusted, as did the Harleys and Foleys from the west of England, any courtier whatever, even if he served a Protestant Prince. These men, High Tories, extreme Whigs, and Country patriots, had, as early as October 1689, formed an unholy alliance against the King's ministers. In the next two years, with the help of disillusioned Whigs and sullen Jacobites, they waged relentless guerrilla warfare against the government.[1]

The intentions of the Whigs soon became known throughout London. 'I perceive', wrote James Johnston in June 1690, 'that the Whigs are turned against my Lord Carmarthen, I wish he make up with them before winter, otherwise they will take the King at some disadvantage, and by uniting with discontented Tories make a majority against his Lordship, and necessitate the King to part with him.' The intentions of the Court were no less clear: it would never dismiss Carmarthen simply to please the Whigs. As Queen Mary wrote to William concerning Monmouth's complaints against the present ministry, 'I told him in the same freedom he seemed to speak to me, that I found it very strange you were not thought fit to choose your own ministers; that they had already removed Lord Halifax, the same endeavours were used for Lord Carmarthen, and would they now begin to have a bout at Lord Nottingham too; it would show they would pretend to control the King in his choice,

returns in the new Parliament (divisions which the Prussian resident, Bonnet, regarded as 'simply an affair of Whig versus Tory'), the Tories had a majority of 197 to 182 over the Whigs (Ranke, *History*, vi, 156).

[1] Foxcroft, *Halifax*, ii, 243–4, 247. Lord Lonsdale, whom the Whigs and High Tories attacked on frivolous charges, wrote to his son (*E.H.R.* xxx, 93–4) that they attacked all men in authority, in order 'either to carry on faction or gain employments'. The jealousies harboured by the Country members for courtiers found perfect expression in Sir William Whitlocke's remark (Cobbett, *Parl. Hist.* v, 642), 'If an angel came from heaven that was a Privy Councillor, I would not trust my liberty with him one moment.'

260

which, if I were he, I would not suffer, but would make use of whom I pleased.' 'Upon this,' she added, 'he said...that he thought it necessary the nation should be satisfied.'[1]

The extreme Whigs and High Tories, in order to drive Carmarthen and Nottingham from office, sought the support of the independent Country members. This they did by denouncing the mismanagement of the war, by complaining of corruption at Court, and by opposing the grant of money to those who wasted it. In March 1690 Seymour, Guise, and Foley complained once again of waste and mismanagement in the government, provoking Richard Hampden, Chancellor of the Exchequer, to reply, 'inquire into the ill usage [of ministers]...If you think persons undermine the government and waste the treasury, you are to give the King counsel...If any objection of mismanagement remain, remove them that have been faulty...If any officer be to blame, let him be named.' Hampden's challenge embarrassed the opposition, for they had no proof of mismanagement and could not name those who were at fault. The most they could do was to reply, as Sir John Guise replied: the greatest grievance is that 'people do not own the counsels they have given'.[2]

The right of inquiry was the accepted means of discovering faulty ministers and the Court invited the opposition to use it. On 14 April the ministry moved that a bill be brought in to appoint commissioners to take an account of all monies voted since December 1688. Despite the known ineffectiveness of the Brooke House Commission of the 1660's, both Houses passed the bill; and continued to pass similar bills throughout the reigns of King William and Queen Anne. To these Commissions of Public Accounts the House of Commons invariably named the leaders of the country gentlemen: Robert Harley often came at the top of the poll, Paul Foley never far behind. But in all the years spent scrutinizing the public accounts, the Commissioners never discovered the proof of waste and corruption that they sought. Their efforts may have forced Treasury officials to attend to their duties, but they never elicited any information that could be used to censure the King's ministers.[3]

---

[1] J. Johnston to Sir William Colt, B.M. Add. MSS 34095, f. 9; Dalrymple, *Memoirs of Great Britain and Ireland*, III, 94.

[2] Cobbett, *Parl. Hist.* V, 563–70.

[3] *C.J.* X, 378; Burnet, *History*, IV, 113–14; *Cal. Tr. Books*, XI, clv. John Colt, accused of corruption by the Commissioners in April 1692, wrote to Robert Harley (B.M. Loan, 29/131), 'all this malice is Whig and Tory, and a trial of skill' between the two.

The Logic of Parliamentary Supremacy

The House likewise used its right of inquiry to investigate naval disasters. Lord Torrington appeared before them in 1690 to justify his refusal to engage the French at Beachy Head and Sir Edward Russell in 1691 defended his tardiness in putting to sea that summer.[1] On this latter occasion Seymour, Clarges, Musgrave, and Foley attempted to wrest from the King the right to name the officers of the fleet. They were thwarted in their endeavour by a powerful speech made by Sir John Guise, rarely a friend of the Court. Sir John told the House that 'it was certainly enough that they had the liberty to investigate the actions of the officers whom the King chose, without wishing further to seize one of the greatest prerogatives of the Crown, which is to name to offices'. Still loyal to the principle of the separation of powers, a majority of the House supported Sir John Guise, causing the proposal to fall.[2]

One question still remained. Did 'the liberty to investigate' extend to the Council table? Clearly it did not, a fact which provoked numerous diatribes against secret Cabinet Councils and frequent demands for the revival of the Privy Council. As in 1679, so in 1692, these demands for the revival of the Privy Council signified no deep veneration for an ancient institution, afforded no illustration of what Toynbee calls the 'idolization of an ephemeral institution'. For the true demand of the opposition was not to resurrect conciliar government, but to insure that counsellors publicly owned what advice they gave the King. 'There are no books or records to be seen,' complained Goodwin Wharton, 'and you cannot punish them, because you have no light into their actions. I move that a part of your advice be that the King call his Council, and that they do set their hands to their advice, or their dissent.' Wharton made this motion for the written responsibility of Privy Councillors on 21 November 1692, but Paul Foley had voiced a similar demand two years earlier, on 13 May 1690. Prompted by Goodwin Wharton's motion of the 21st, Foley now, on the 23rd, renewed his earlier demand, but to no effect. On none of these

[1] Narcissus Luttrell, *A Brief Historical Relation of State Affairs* (Oxford, 1858), II, 128; *H.M.C. Rep. XIV, Part 2*, p. 481. The failure of the Commons to impeach Lord Torrington, guilty of the gravest naval miscarriage of the reign, demonstrates convincingly that political partisanship, and not genuine anger at naval miscarriages, lay behind parliamentary attacks on the King's ministers in William's reign. Bonnet wrote of Torrington (Ranke, *History*, VI, 148), 'The fact that the Whigs wish to destroy him suffices to persuade the Tories to attempt to save him.'
[2] Ranke, *History*, VI, 162; *H.M.C. Rep. 7*, p. 206.

occasions did the Commons support the proposal that the King's councillors put their hand to advice which they gave His Majesty.[1]

In large measure, the Commons refused the proposals of Wharton and Foley because they knew that the publicity of advice which they demanded consorted ill with the secrecy of counsels which the conduct of the war required. 'The House', observed Sir Richard Temple, 'has always complained that the secrets of the Council are not kept; how much more might they reckon on the disclosure of secrets if by this motion thirty or forty separate persons shared them?' There did exist, however, a means to reconcile the requirements of secrecy with the requirements of responsible government. The perspicacious but anonymous author of six 'Humble Proposals' discovered that means. His Majesty, he proposed, should inform Parliament that he will advise in all emergencies with five men, whom he should name, and who should then be 'accountable to the Parliament for any mismanagement or pernicious advice'.[2]

William did not accept this radical proposal; nor is there any reason to believe that public opinion, which preferred innovations wrapped in the fustian of old ideas, would have welcomed it. Yet the slow evolution of political practice prepared the way for its ultimate triumph. In the heat of denouncing the Cabinet Council in 1691, Lord Brandon suddenly added, and 'those who have composed it during the Regency are responsible for everything'. The Earl of Shrewsbury, for one, did not oppose this idea. In 1694 he told William that it was desirable that 'some people do meet to take the lead', otherwise responsibility would 'lie upon one'. This was not, he added, to be a formal council, but one composed of those active in administration. 'You are in the right', Sunderland wrote to Portland at the time, 'to believe Shrewsbury is for a Cabinet Council, but it is for the five officers who now meet, excluding all others...' A month later Sunderland added, 'I can say only what I have said already, there must be either no Cabinet Council, or one composed of the great officers only...' This union of administration with counselling, of the great offices of state with the Cabinet Council, slowly created a visible body which Parliament, without exposing

---

[1] Cobbett, *Parl. Hist.* v, 643, 723–33; a full account of Foley's demand may be read in Harleian MSS 1243, f. 197, 'A Proposal at a Committee of the Whole House A° 1690 to prevent Ministers giving Ill Advice'.

[2] Klopp, *Der Fall des Hauses Stuart*, vi, 148; Ranke, *History*, vi, 187–8; P.R.O. S.P.D. King William's Chest, 8/6, no. 51.

The Logic of Parliamentary Supremacy

the secrets of the Council table, could hold accountable. At the same time members of Parliament grew more willing to accept such a solution because they no longer sought to deprive faulty ministers of their liberty, their property, or their lives. They were satisfied merely to deprive them of their offices. As Sir William Anson has observed, '...the suppression of the privy council by the cabinet marks a stage in which criminal responsibility enforceable by impeachment begins to give way to moral responsibility enforceable by loss of office'.[1]

All this lay in the future. In the meantime, in the autumn of 1691, the enemies of Carmarthen and Nottingham failed to find any proof that the Lord President or Secretary had caused ill management in the Treasury, delays in sending out the fleet, or the losses inflicted on English shipping by French corsairs. Undeterred by their lack of success, the opposition continued to examine Commissioners of the Treasury, to denounce Cabinet Councils, and to delay voting of supplies. But all to no effect. The lack of any real grievance to exploit, disunion in their own ranks,[2] and Carmarthen's shrewd exploitation of the Preston plot, broke the back of their movement. The House of Commons generously voted William the money he needed to continue the war. Nevertheless, William in March 1692 brought two of the most vocal enemies of the ministry, Seymour and Rochester, into the government, appointing Seymour a Commissioner of the Treasury and naming both men to the Privy Council. William did not bring them into the government because he wished to, for he distrusted Rochester and despised Seymour. Neither did he bring them into office in order to embark on an experiment in party government, for, though the Tories now en-

[1] *H.M.C. Rep. 7, Denbigh*, p. 205; W. Coxe (ed.), *Private and Original Correspondence of Charles Talbot, Duke of Shrewsbury* (1821), p. 35; Sunderland to Portland, 13 July and 5 Aug., Portland Papers; Sir William Anson, 'The Cabinet in the 17th and 18th Centuries', *E.H.R.* xxix, 56. The author of *A Dialogue Betwixt Whig and Tory*, in *State Tracts, William III*, II, 371, wrote in 1692, 'For though the House of Commons, seconded by the House of Lords, cannot reach the life or estate of any person, but by a full proof in form of law; yet because it is so difficult a matter to come at such proof, a vote of the House of Commons against any minister, has always been esteemed by all Kings (who were well with the people) a sufficient reason for the removing them from Court.'

[2] There was not only disunion, but confusion. The High Tories opposed Carmarthen, but not Nottingham, whom the Whigs hated. The Whigs sought to blame Carmarthen, the Tories Russell, for naval miscarriages (*H.M.C. Downshire*, I, 389–90), 'Our factions are still great, but Whig and Tory endeavoured to unite or mix at the beginning of the session, yet so soon as the mouse appeared the lady turned cat again, I mean the parties flew out for their interests and hopes of prey.'

joyed a marked ascendancy in the Cabinet (made certain by Henry Sidney's dismissal as Secretary of State), William brought two Whigs into the government, Sir John Somers as Attorney-General and Charles Montagu as a Commissioner of the Treasury. The most probable motive guiding William in March 1692 was a desire to weaken the opposition in Parliament by buying off the Tories who followed Rochester and Seymour. At the same time he hoped to placate the Whigs and reward merit by employing the ablest among them. The Earl of Sunderland, who had returned to England in May 1690, advised William to rely more heavily on the Whigs than on the Tories, for they enjoyed more support in the House of Commons, but William refused his advice. He could not rid himself of the belief that the Whigs wished to make him a Doge of Venice; he preferred to bring into office gentlemen who believed in monarchy.[1]

William's decision had an unexpected effect: by bringing the High Tories into the government he gave a party character to the opposition in Parliament. It became a Whig opposition. For five years, from the spring of 1692 until the spring of 1697, the Whigs used their power and popularity in the Commons to expel Tory ministers from office and to replace them with Whigs, until finally the government became a Whig government.

The Whigs were not a homogeneous party nor did the various factions called Whig enjoy a majority in the House of Commons. But they soon learned the advantages to be gained by acting together and by sedulously advocating popular causes in the House. In 1692 the extreme Whigs, who followed Monmouth and Delamer, joined with the moderate Whigs, led by Somers and Montagu, and the Country Whigs, led by Harley and Foley, to launch a virulent attack upon the Earl of Nottingham, the King's sole Secretary of State. By branding the Secretary as a Jacobite and by blaming him for naval miscarriages, they won over many members of the House who were genuinely alarmed by Jacobite plots, by the want of convoys, by the lack of a descent on France, and by the escape of part of the French fleet at La Hogue. No member, for example, dared oppose a motion on 21 November which obliquely censured Nottingham for meddling in naval affairs. Without a division the House resolved that His Majesty 'be desired to constitute a Commission

---

[1] Kenyon, *Sunderland*, pp. 251–2; J. P. Kenyon, 'The Earl of Sunderland and the King's Administration, 1693–1695', *E.H.R.* LXXI, 580–1.

of the Admiralty of persons of known experience in maritime affairs, and that all orders to the Fleet may for the future go through the Admiralty so constituted'. The Commons also, on 26 November, passed a resolution, no man dissenting, which urged His Majesty in the future 'to employ men of known integrity and ability', since the great affairs of the government have 'been for the time past unsuccessfully managed by those that have had the direction thereof'. Again, on 30 November, no one, apart from Sir Richard Temple, spoke against a motion to ask William to employ 'only those persons whose principles engaged them to defend the rights of their Majesties against King James'. This last motion was obviously aimed at Nottingham, who persisted in recognizing William as *de facto* but not *de jure* King of England. Temple alone believed, or had the courage to say, that the faults of the administration arose not from the remissness of those who distinguished between a *de facto* and a *de jure* King, but from the violence of those who distinguished between a Whig and a Tory party. And he proposed an address requesting the King 'to employ none whom he has or shall observe more zealous for a party than for promoting the public interest of the nation and government'. The House ignored Temple's motion, and voted the earlier one. Too many members, perhaps, agreed with Lord Wharton's retort to Temple, that 'he scorned the thought of knowing of any party but King William's and King James's'.[1]

Members of the Commons might unanimously condemn mismanagement and censure disloyalty, as preachers universally condemn vice and censure wickedness, but not all members would condemn a particular minister on insufficient evidence. They demonstrated this on 5 December, when they nearly defeated a Whig motion to censure Nottingham for not having ordered Russell to execute a landing in France that summer. By only 1 vote, by

---

[1] Grey, *Debates*, x, 274; *H.M.C. Rep. 14, Part 2*, pp. 507–8; Ranke, *History*, vi, 191–2; Aiken, *Conduct of the Earl of Nottingham*, pp. 105–7. The author of *Short Considerations upon the Present State of Affairs* (in *State Tracts, William III*, ii, 301) likewise accused the Whigs of seeking a monopoly of office, remarking that they are 'so fully satisfied that theirs is the proper talent for business that they think it is being injurious to the public not to employ them...They don't pry but rake into the actions of great men, as if they had an interest they should be faulty, and were to share in the forfeiture or composition... They ought to be contented to share the favours of the Government, without engrossing them...when a nation is unhappily divided into parties...matters should be managed by balanced counsels.' The author of *A Dialogue Betwixt Whig and Tory* (*ibid.* ii, 371) replied, 'Have not mismanagements multiplied by your changing the ministry from Whig to Tory in the last two years?'

156 to 155, were the Whigs able to carry a resolution 'that the want of necessary and timely orders in those who should have given them occasioned that miscarriage'. And the Lords gave the resolution a harsh reception. The Earl of Nottingham in particular seized on the occasion to defend himself. As Secretary of State, he pleaded, he had obeyed the Queen's orders, issued on the advice of the Council. Even if those orders had been improper, he added, 'it would have been an unpardonable presumption in him and inconsistent with the administration of the government if he had pretended to over-rule the opinion of so many great men entrusted with it'. Because he had concurred in those counsels, he continued, he was prepared to share the blame for them, but he was not solely responsible. Like Strafford, Laud, Clarendon, and Arlington before him, Nottingham sought refuge in the collective responsibility of the whole council. Nothing in Stuart England promoted the acceptance of this principle more than the determination of every accused minister to plead it. In the autumn of 1692 the Lords, predominantly Tory in sentiment, indirectly sanctioned the principle by acquitting the minister who pleaded it; they found Nottingham innocent of the charges brought against him.[1]

In the autumn of 1692 the House of Lords examined the naval failures of the past summer with the same thoroughness as had the Commons, only party rancour led them to search into the delinquencies of Edward Russell, who, though the victor of La Hogue, was also a Whig stalwart. When they sent papers to the Commons reflecting on Russell, the Commons replied by voting that 'Admiral Russell, in his command of the Fleet during the last summer's expedition, has behaved himself with fidelity, courage and conduct.' By this vote the Commons proved that they could express their confidence in, as well as vote their censure against, the King's servants. Both became the currency of parliamentary life and party strife during William's reign. Insensibly the Commons came to regard their addresses for and against the King's servants less as humble petitions to the King and more as votes of censure and confidence, to be read by the whole kingdom. The votes of 21, 26, and 30 November against Nottingham occurred in committee, and the House was content to let the last two die there. Only the first came to a vote before the full House, and the House then rejected

[1] *H.M.C. Rep. XIV, Part 2*, p. 509; Aiken, *Conduct of the Earl of Nottingham*, pp. 108–9.

it. This is not to say that the Whigs did not strive to secure its passage, but the Court proved stronger. William regarded all these votes as 'impertinent and untenable', and strongly supported Nottingham and the Admiralty. As a result the Commons refused (by a margin of 23 votes) to condemn the Admiralty. Though the division caught many members at dinner, it was none the less a defeat for the Whigs and a rebuke to Russell.[1] Edward Harley, writing in December, foresaw this defeat and the reason for it. That the ministry 'shall be altered by Parliament', he wrote, 'is hardly to be expected where so much inconsistency and unsteadiness prevails'.[2] The moral was clear: the Whigs needed unity, steadiness, and a majority.

Edward Russell responded to this vote and the continuance of Nottingham in office by resigning, both as Admiral and as Treasurer of the Navy. In resignation he found the means to wreck all the King's schemes for government by balanced counsels; but he was not the first of William's servants to discover this weapon. The Earl of Shrewsbury before him had resigned from office in 1690 because he could not concur in the counsels which William then followed. He openly declared, to William's anger, that he must quit because 'the King was engaged in measures in which he could not concur'.[3] Shrewsbury's action—and even more the reason he gave for it— destroyed the Clarendonian world in which ministers loyally served their monarch even though their counsels were refused. The last person ever to enunciate this principle hardly brought credit to it. The Earl of Sunderland in 1689 defended his conduct as James's principal minister by arguing, 'my greatest misfortune has been to be thought the promoter of things I opposed and detested,' adding, 'I was often foolishly willing to bear what my master would have done, though I used all possible endeavours against it'.[4] Shrewsbury for one, Russell for another, elected not to bear responsibility for measures they opposed or to act with men whom they distrusted.

---

[1] *C.J.* x, 759; Klopp, *Der Fall des Hauses Stuart*, VI, 150, 153–5, 160; B.M. Add. MSS 34096, f. 242v; Ranke, *History*, VI, 202. The House obliquely censured Nottingham by humbly counselling His Majesty to have all orders for the fleet in the future issue from the Commissioners of the Admiralty (*ibid.*).

[2] *H.M.C. Rep. XIV, Part 2*, p. 510. The House further demonstrated its trust in William's ministers by voting five million pounds for the conduct of the war in early December rather than in the spring (Klopp, *Der Fall des Hauses Stuart*, VI, 150–1).

[3] Foxcroft, *Halifax*, II, 250–1. Lord Carberry, a staunch Whig, likewise resigned office in 1690, in fact he did so at Shrewsbury's behest (*ibid.* p. 91). The measure to which Shrewsbury particularly objected was the King's opposition to a Triennial Act.

[4] Kenyon, *Sunderland*, p. 234.

Clarendon's principle deserved the allegiance of any man who truly believed in monarchical government, who truly believed that the sceptre belonged in the King's hands, but such men were becoming increasingly rare by the reign of William. The 1690's differed substantially from the 1660's, and in no way more markedly than in the increasing willingness of men to lay down conditions for serving the King. By 1689 Clarendonianism was dead. The years from the Restoration to the Revolution present no lacuna in the development of the English constitution, for during those years the world of the Earl of Clarendon disappeared, to be replaced by a quite different one.

The career of one fascinating man bridged the divided and distinguished worlds of the Earl of Clarendon and the Earl of Shrewsbury. That man was the Earl of Sunderland, who as minister to James II represented the old order and as counsellor to William III exemplified the new. In the spring of 1692 Sunderland became the confidential adviser of the King, and as such urged William to bring the Whigs back into the government, for only they could carry on his business in Parliament.[1] Sunderland saw that the parliamentary supremacy created by the Revolutionary Settlement demanded continual attention to the management of Parliament. He himself became the most skilful of parliamentary managers. But he did not clearly distinguish between parliamentary management and parliamentary undertaking, between the minister's use of royal patronage to influence the proceedings of Parliament and the politician's use of parliamentary support to wrest office from the King. In actual fact, Sunderland's agile mind was receptive to both: the King should persuade men to support his policies by offering them preferment; he should also accommodate his policies to, and offer office to, those who could manage Parliament for him. The historian, however, unlike the politician, has an obligation to distinguish between these two principles of government, for only then can he assess accurately the relative power of King and Parliament during the century and a half between the Revolution and the Reform Bill. Indeed, during these years the history of responsible government is largely the history of the struggle between these contending though intertwined principles.

William and his ministers never totally ignored the power of patronage. In 1689 Nottingham sought to buy off Sir John Knatchbull

---

[1] Kenyon, *Sunderland*, p. 255; Kenyon, 'Sunderland and the King's Administration', *E.H.R.* LXXI, 580; Burnet, *History*, IV, 187–8.

with the promise of preferment; Sir John Trevor, the Speaker, became in 1690 the dispenser of pension and place; both Jack Howe and Sir Rowland Gwynn lost places at Court for opposing the government. The practices which Danby had raised to a system in the 1670's were not forgotten after the Revolution. By December 1692 the Commons became sufficiently alarmed at their revival to pass a Place Bill which would prevent any man from sitting in the House who received place or pension at Court. The Lords, however, rejected the Bill. The Commons expressed great anger at its rejection, but they had little reason to, for the King's servants in the Commons were neither well organized nor well heard nor well instructed.[1]

This was Sunderland's constant complaint, the want of management in the House of Commons. By 1693 he concluded that only the employment of Whigs, who spoke with effect in the House, could remedy this defect; he therefore again advised the King to bring them into the government. William heeded his advice, at least to the extent of naming Sir John Somers Lord Keeper and Sir John Trenchard Secretary of State. William turned to the Whigs in March 1693 for various reasons. In part personal inclination led him to give office to the Whigs, for they shared, as the Tories no longer shared, his desire to wage war against France in Flanders. But he also acted out of prudence, seeking to mollify with office those Whigs whom he had angered by vetoing the Triennial Bill. Not prudence alone, but necessity also, forced him to prefer the Whigs, for they had displayed great strength in Parliament that winter. One purpose he did not harbour: a wish to give the Whigs a monopoly of his confidence, for he kept Nottingham in office and named three of Nottingham's nominees as Admirals of the Fleet. The ministerial changes of 1693 marked only another move in the perpetual balancing act that William performed during the early years of his reign. As Gilbert Burnet observed, 'The King studies only to balance them...that so he might oblige them all to depend more entirely on himself.'[2]

The Whigs, however, were not content with the balance created in March, 1693. They wanted a monopoly of the King's counsels;

---

[1] Diary of Sir John Knatchbull, B.M. Add. MSS 33923, ff. 465v–466v; Dalrymple, *Memoirs of Great Britain and Ireland*, II, 182–4; R. J. Kerr and I. C. Duncan (eds.), *The Portledge Papers* (1928), pp. 133–5, 156.

[2] Burnet, *History*, IV, 279.

more particularly, they wanted the Earl of Nottingham dismissed from office. But how could they persuade Parliament to demand his dismissal when, as Edward Harley had observed, so much 'inconstancy and unsteadiness' prevailed there? The fate of the Smyrna fleet that summer, attacked with heavy losses by the French fleet at the Bay of Lagos, offered the Whigs the solution they needed. Throughout the summer they voiced their rage at the losses inflicted on the fleet, demanded an inquiry into the disaster, and whispered of the treachery of the Secretary of State.[1] Parliamentary censure of Nottingham that autumn seemed inevitable. But it came not, for William forestalled it by dismissing Nottingham from office on 6 November, the day before he opened Parliament. The same day he threw himself into the hands of the Whigs by naming Edward Russell Admiral of the Fleet.

Personal inclination, respect for merit, and the pursuance of a balance between parties may have led William to give office to Somers and Montagu in 1692 and to Trenchard in 1693, but neither inclination nor respect nor a balancing act led him to dismiss Nottingham and employ Russell in the autumn of 1693. William admired and trusted Nottingham and had little respect for Russell, a fiery Whig and crypto-Jacobite. He dismissed the one and gave office to the other only because he believed that nothing else would secure him the support he needed in Parliament to carry on the war.[2] The counsellor who persuaded him that nothing else would do was the Earl of Sunderland. Sunderland was not a party man; he was simply a realist. The King's business in Parliament must be carried on. There was a moment in the spring when Sunderland believed that careful parliamentary management would suffice to carry on the King's business the next year. In May he met with Somers and Trenchard, and together 'they looked over and

---

[1] Burnet, *History*, iv, 203.
[2] William wrote to Nottingham (P. Finch, *History of Burley-on-the-Hill*, 1901, p. 192), 'I thank you for your services. I have nothing to complain of in your conduct. It is only from necessity that I part with you.' Queen Mary wrote shortly before Nottingham's dismissal (R. Doebner, *Memoirs of Mary, Queen of England*, 1886, pp. 58–60), 'When I saw one who had served him [the King] longest and most faithfully so discouraged that he was ready to leave him, and when I saw himself forced to disoblige the party he thinks alone will support the throne, and court those who use him ill and will never be satisfied, 'twas impossible not to be extremely melancholy.' She added a few days later, 'At his [the King's] coming, all the world was almost despairing; himself thought his case so bad that he was forced to part with Lord Nottingham to please a party whom he cannot trust.'

considered the list of Parliament men and agreed upon the best means of persuading them to be reasonable'. In June he met with Henry Guy of the Treasury and with the Speaker, Sir John Trevor; together they took 'measures to fix men for Parliament'. Mulgrave was to have a Marquisate, Brandon a regiment, and Stamford money. Even in July Sunderland hoped that the King's affairs could be set right 'without doing anything dishonourable, anything that interferes between Whig and Tory, or that shall lessen the prerogative'. But later that month he came to London, viewed the public rage at the losses suffered by the Smyrna fleet at the Bay of Lagos and by English troops at Neerwinden, and changed his mind. 'I think', he wrote to Portland on 7 August, 'that the measures which were resolved on before...must be pursued...with this difference, that the King must do abundance more than if these dismal accidents had not happened.'[1]

What he meant by 'abundance more' Sunderland made clear a week later. 'I am persuaded the King may yet cure all if he pleases, but it must not be done by patching, but by a thorough good administration, and employing men firm to this government, and thought to be so.' Since Sunderland had repeatedly told William that all the Whigs but only one-fourth of the Tories were firm to the government, his meaning was clear: William should employ Whigs in the administration. In June Sunderland had played the role of a master parliamentary manager; in August he became the great parliamentary undertaker. He ceased to follow the ways of Bacon, Clifford, and Danby, and adopted the tactics of Neville, Saye, and Temple. Or more precisely, he assumed the role played by Hamilton in 1641 and Buckingham in 1667; he became the broker at Court for those who would undertake to manage the House of Commons for the King. That there was a parliamentary undertaking in the offing, the world learned from a meeting of the Whigs with Sunderland at Althorp in late August. As Professor Kenyon has shown in his life of Sunderland, the Earl invited the Whigs to Althorp in order to inform them that the King had finally agreed to appoint Edward Russell Admiral of the Fleet. In return Sunderland gained from Charles Montagu and Lord Wharton an undertaking to support the government in the Commons. This undertaking made

---

[1] Sunderland to Portland, 3 May, 20 June, 10 July 1693, Portland Papers; Japikse, *Correspondentie*, II, 38–40; Kenyon, *Sunderland*, p. 259.

at Althorp proved a success. As Gilbert Burnet observed, being given office 'the Whigs expressed new zeal and confidence in the King. All the money that was asked for the next year's expenses, was granted very easily.' Sunderland was not the first of the great undertakers in English history—Sir Henry Neville deserves that title—but he was the broker for the first *successful* undertakers in English history, the Court Whigs of 1693.[1]

The success of their undertaking was not, however, complete. The Country Whigs, led by Robert Harley and Paul Foley, regarded it as rustic squires had always regarded undertakings, with opprobrium. In 1614, again in 1641, and then again in 1680, the House of Commons had passed, or had threatened to pass, self-denying ordinances. Now in December 1693 the House once more passed a Place Bill that would prevent its members from accepting places at Court. The Lords amended the Bill to permit the re-election of place men to Parliament, but William vetoed the Bill, amendment and all. William's rejection of the Bill provoked an explosion of wrath in the Commons, where Country Tories like Clarges and Musgrave joined Country Whigs like Harley and Foley to secure the passage of an address condemning 'as an enemy of their Majesties and Kingdom' any man who advised the rejection of the Bill. But as Robert Rich once said in the House of Commons, 'A general address is none at all.' And William, who in 1689 had ordered Halifax to seek to make an intended address as general as possible, shared this opinion. He therefore dismissed the Commons' address of December 1693 with a polite, evasive answer. But the answer only goaded Robert Harley to propose yet another address, demanding from the King a further answer to their earlier address. Harley's motion brought the Court Whigs, Montagu and Russell, to their feet, to defend the King's prerogative to veto bills that he found unacceptable. In the division on Harley's motion the Court Whigs defeated the Country Whigs by 229 to 88 votes, but the split in the Whig party occasioned by the unwillingness of Harley and Foley to support the Althorp undertaking proved irreparable.[2]

---

[1] Kenyon, *Sunderland*, pp. 250, 260–1; Burnet, *History*, IV, 215.

[2] Cobbett, *Parl. Hist.* V, 466; Foxcroft, *Halifax*, II, 243; Grey, *Debates*, X, 375–86. The weakness of the Tory party in the House of Commons was further revealed by Lord Bellomont's abortive attempt to impeach Lord Coningsby and Sir Charles Porter, two former Whig Lord Justices of Ireland. Bellamont introduced eight articles of impeachment against the two men on 16 Dec. 1693; on 29 Jan. 1694 the House acquitted them,

The Logic of Parliamentary Supremacy

Nottingham's dismissal did not, as William had hoped, prevent a lengthy, passionate, and partisan inquiry into the disaster suffered by the Smyrna fleet. The Commons examined at the bar of the House the three Admirals of the Fleet, Killigrew, Delaval, and Shovell; and the House exposed, with the King's permission and the assistance of the Lords, the innermost secrets of the Cabinet. But the deeper they dug, the more they undermined their own case. On 17 November the Whigs had persuaded the House to vote, by 140 to 103, that there had been 'treacherous mismanagement'. But their investigations unearthed no treachery, not even negligence, except in Trenchard, the Whig Secretary of State. Nottingham, it turned out, had informed the Council that the French fleet, sixty-eight vessels strong, had put to sea, but Trenchard, whose duty it was to forward the information to the admirals, had failed to do so. Unwilling to indict innocent men, the House on 6 December acquitted the admirals, by 185 to 175. But despite their acquittal, William dismissed them from all their employments; irresistible political considerations drove him to it. Meanwhile Trenchard, who was the most at fault, remained in office. Few episodes in William's reign so sharply etch the partisan nature of politics in the 1690's as the dismissal of the innocent admirals and the survival of the faulty Trenchard.[1]

Observers as diverse as the Prussian resident, Friedrich Bonnet, Dykveld's correspondent, Monsieur Blancard, the Imperial resident, Herr Hoffmann, the churchman Edmund Bohun, and James II himself concluded in November 1693 that William had surrendered the government of England to the Whigs.[2] The only men who disagreed were the Court Whigs, who pressed for the dismissal of more Tories and the employment of more Whigs. The office they most coveted was the Secretaryship left vacant by Nottingham's dismissal. Sunderland intended the office for Shrewsbury, but Shrewsbury

article by article (C.J. xi, 33–4, 73). It is possible that Coningsby was guilty of hanging a man, named Gaffney, without a proper trial; a fact which led Anne Pye to write to Abigail Harley (H.M.C. Rep. XIV, Part 2, p. 549), 'Lord Coningsby, by the public news, has met with good friends amongst the Commons to be so acquitted.'

[1] C.J. xi, 5, 21, 91; Aiken, Conduct of the Earl of Nottingham, p. 117; C.S.P. Dom. 1693, p. 426. When Admiral Russell chastised Lord Ranelagh for defending the three admirals, Ranelagh replied affably that 'next year he would do the same for him, since one of the parties will not fail to attack him in turn' (H.M.C. Rep. 7, p. 217).

[2] H.M.C. Rep. 7, p. 213; Ranke, History, vi, 217; Klopp, Der Fall des Hauses Stuart, vi, 244; S. W. Rix (ed.), The Diary and Autobiography of Edmund Bohun (Beccles, 1853), p. 122; Macpherson, Original Papers, i, 453.

hesitated to serve a King who vetoed Triennial Bills and employed Carmarthen. Rumour announced that the post would go to Sir John Lowther, a friend of Nottingham's, but Lowther replied that 'he would never accept it, for he preferred to be the companion, not the successor, of his friend'. Finally, in March, Shrewsbury reluctantly accepted the seals. In April William dismissed Seymour from the Treasury and named Charles Montagu Chancellor of the Exchequer. The scheme devised by Sunderland and the Whigs had reached fruition.[1]

Then in the summer of 1694 the authors of the scheme fell out. They fell out because the scheme hatched at Althorp in the summer of 1693 possessed not one nature, but two natures, a fact which no monophysite interpretation of it can long conceal. It was a Court scheme and a party scheme; it was an attempt at parliamentary management and an experiment in parliamentary undertaking. Present at Althorp were not only Whigs like Montagu and Wharton, but courtiers like Godolphin and Marlborough. The courtiers did not believe that the scheme entailed a surrender of their control of royal patronage. The Whigs believed it did, and proceeded to act in this sense. In the summer of 1694 they sought to sweep the Tories out of the Commissions of Excise and Customs. Godolphin, who held that the Treasury Board should govern these Commissions, protested. 'I cannot think it for your service', he wrote to William, 'to make changes in the management of your revenue, to gratify party and animosity...' Godolphin spoke as a civil servant and a courtier, anxious to defend efficient administration and the King's prerogative. The Whigs spoke as politicians, who sought to manage the Commons and to win elections. 'That which we had chiefly regard to in this representation', Trenchard wrote to the King, 'is that those branches of the revenue may be advanced, or at least kept from sinking; that your affairs in Parliament relating to the revenue may be always well explained, and the debate concerning it well supported, as often as there shall be occasion...' Sir John

---

[1] Ranke, *History*, VI, 218; Kenyon, *Sunderland*, p. 261; *H.M.C. Rep. 7, Denbigh*, p. 213. Lord Capell was annoyed with Shrewsbury for laying down conditions. He wrote to Lord Russell in January (Dalrymple, *Memoirs*, III, 57), 'But I am infinitely surprised at my Lord Shrewsbury...We have been often blamed as men contented with nothing; and if the church, the law, the fleet, the army (in regard to Talmash's great station), and the offering of both seals to be in the hands of our friends (the obstacle to common safety, my Lord Nottingham, being removed) will not give content, what will the world say of us?'

Somers then added, 'Those Commissioners have yearly the disposition of £100,000 in salaries to inferior officers...and if this great sum be distributed to the worst men which can be picked out, and it be considered how great an influence these inferior officers have upon great numbers of your subjects, and how they are spread in every part of the Kingdom, it will be plain that nothing can tend more to the poisoning of the people.'[1]

The conflict between the courtiers and the politicians grew so heated that Sunderland had to intervene to resolve it. His personal predilections were clear: he hated party and believed that all men, irrespective of party, should serve the King loyally. 'The Whig party', he wrote to Portland, 'makes me weary of my life.' But the courtier was also a realist, who had a healthy respect for power and a quick perception of where it lay. The Sunderland who served James II and the Sunderland who counselled William III were at bottom the same man, a man whose ambition made him infinitely servile before power and whose intelligence made him acutely sensible where it resided. In 1685 he saw that James possessed power and served him accordingly; in 1694 he saw that the Whigs possessed power and therefore spoke for them at Court. In a letter to Portland he expressed his sympathy for Godolphin's position, then added, 'But this is certain, if those Commissions are not changed which are so necessary, it was to no purpose to do anything else...they must be made, or the government cannot be right.' William again yielded to his advice, seeing that he could not secure from Parliament (or the City) the money he needed unless he altered the Commissions. In August 1694 he named to the two Commissions those persons whom the Whigs had nominated (with the exception of two men personally unacceptable to him). Not Godolphin alone, but the Tories resented the changes. 'That maxim of nominating Commissioners,' wrote Musgrave to Harley, 'if anything will be resented, it will.'[2]

When it came to a test, the power of the dominant party in the Commons had proved greater than the power of patronage. This does not mean that the power of patronage was negligible in the

---

[1] *C.S.P. Dom. 1694–95*, pp. 179, 184–6.
[2] Sunderland to Portland, 13 June and 5 Aug. 1694, Portland Papers; Kenyon, *Sunderland*, pp. 265, 270–1; Kenyon, 'Sunderland and the King's Administration', *E.H.R.* LXXI, 592–3; S. Baxter, *The Development of the Treasury* (Cambridge, Mass., 1957), pp. 97–9; Christopher Musgrave to Robert Harley, 24 Sept. 1694, B.M. Loan, 29/312.

England of William III. The scramble for office, title, and pension which graced or disgraced his reign made the author of these gifts a real power in the land. But in the summer of 1694 the political party dominant in the Commons partially wrested the power of patronage from the Court; Whig managers, such as Wharton, Montagu, and Somers, replaced Court managers, such as Godolphin, Guy, and Trevor. They became dispensers of office and favour; and, though their control of patronage was far from entire, it was substantial. And it possessed a multiplier effect, for the greater the dominance of a party in Parliament, the stronger its grip on patronage; and the stronger its grip on patronage, the greater its dominance in the House. After 1694 the King was not free to dispense patronage as he pleased, particularly if he were the prisoner of a party that governed in Parliament.[1]

The fall of the courtiers became irreparable in the spring of 1695, when the House of Commons, urged on by Montagu and Wharton, committed Henry Guy to the Tower for taking a bribe from an army agent and censured Sir John Trevor for taking £1,000 from the City in return for securing the passage of the Orphans Bill. Guy lost his post as Secretary to the Treasury and Trevor, who had been Speaker and corrupter of the House since 1690, lost all influence, for good or ill. But the House did not stop its inquiries into bribery with these men: it went on to bigger game. In April it impeached the Marquis of Carmarthen, now Duke of Leeds, of High Crimes and Misdemeanours, accusing him of accepting a bribe of 5,500 guineas from the East India Company in return for espousing their cause before the Council. The Duke of Leeds protested his entire innocence, and declared to the Lords that the storm which now descended upon him 'was some time a gathering' and 'was promoted by a faction and a party' that had a pique against him.[2]

---

[1] The power of patronage during William's reign was strong enough (in conjunction with military victories abroad) slowly to erode the power of the Jacobites. James Brydges's letter to his father on 8 July 1694 (Huntington Library S.T. 57, I, f. 20) explains why. 'I am very glad to understand that your Lordship is pleased to give me leave to follow my own desires as touching public affairs. It being the opinion of most persons here, as well as of strangers abroad, that the present government is so firm, and if not well settled, nevertheless settled so well of King William's advantage, that there's no likelihood of its ever changing in favour of King James: and that therefore consequently if I have any thoughts of raising my fortunes by preferment, my only way is to strike in with the government before it is too late, and in order thereto to get myself presented to Her Majesty and kiss her hand.'

[2] *C.J.* XI, 226, 271, 328; *A Collection of the Debates and Proceedings in 1694 and 1695 Upon the Inquiry into the Late Briberies and Corrupt Practices* (1695), p. 55.

The Logic of Parliamentary Supremacy

His complaints contain some truth. The Whigs had sought to drive him from the government on one pretext or another ever since 1689. But the urgency of their opposition to him had declined with his declining influence in the government. Honoured by a dukedom in April 1694, he had ceased from that moment to play a central role in government, though remaining Lord President. There is no evidence that his enemies planned to introduce an impeachment against him in 1695. Only the accidental discovery that his servant, Robart, had received 5,500 guineas from the East India Company led them to do so. And the subsequent flight of Robart to Switzerland with (some said) the connivance of Leeds himself, hardly spoke for his innocence. The Commons voted to impeach him on 26 April, and on the 29th Lord Wharton, in the name of the whole House, impeached him before the Lords. The flight of Robart in late April and the prorogation of Parliament in early May prevented the Commons from prosecuting their impeachment, but the mere fact that they had voted it compelled William to drop Leeds from the list of Lords Justices whom he named to govern England that summer. This slight did not discourage the Duke of Leeds, who now (as he always had) clung to office like a limpet to a rock. In the autumn he even sought to resume his seat in the Cabinet, to the embarrassment of William, who had to ask him to attend no longer. No contempt for Leeds's counsel led William to exclude him from the Cabinet; he did so only from necessity, or rather from fear that his return to the Cabinet would precipitate the revival of his impeachment in the Commons, with all the attendant disruption of business there.[1]

Lord Wharton and Charles Montagu won a great victory over their rivals, Sir John Trevor and Henry Guy, but victory went to their heads like strong wine. They lost all sense of proportion and decency. Montagu offended all men, but particularly the Harleyite Whigs, by an open display of treachery. In February he had promised Trevor immunity from attack if he would furnish the information needed to send Guy to the Tower. Trevor furnished the information,

[1] *C.J.* xi, 328; L'Hermitage, B.M. Add. MSS 17677PP, ff. 255v–256. William told Shrewsbury (Coxe, *Shrewsbury Correspondence*, p. 399), that 'he had done a hardship to my Lord President [Leeds] in hindering him coming to Council, which he could not easily persuade himself to do'. He then went on to urge Shrewsbury and Somers to prevent renewed inquiries into corruption. Somers (*ibid.* p. 400) agreed that such inquiries would 'spoil the session' but added 'if this is to be prevented, it is the King himself who must enter into it; otherwise it cannot be brought to pass...'.

278

but Montagu nevertheless led the attack against him in the House in March. Wharton matched Montagu's treachery with an equally indefensible arrogance. He boasted publicly that he had a list of fifty members whose re-election the Court would prevent and stated openly that the King had vowed never to give preferment to the two Harleys. Both Montagu and Wharton boasted of their influence at Court, in Parliament, and throughout the country. Their confidence reached such an extravagant pitch in July that they concluded that they could do without Sunderland, that they needed no intermediary between themselves and the King.[1]

But these two Whig *enragés* overreached themselves. William still clung to his power to dispense patronage as he wished and the members of the House of Commons still clung to their independence and self-respect. William gave the lie to Wharton and his confidence to Sunderland; and the House of Commons repudiated the new managers by refusing to elect their nominee, Sir Thomas Littleton, to succeed Trevor as Speaker. Instead they chose the Country party stalwart, Paul Foley. Wharton himself nominated Littleton, but discovered, as Lowther had in 1690 and Seymour in 1692, that preferment at Court did not make one better heard in the House. The Whigs were saved from the ham-fisted management of Wharton and Montagu only by the good sense of Shrewsbury and Somers and the great patience of Sunderland. In August, guided by Shrewsbury and Somers, the Whigs acknowledged their dependence on Sunderland, the confidant of the King. Even Wharton and Montagu beat a retreat, denying that they had ever intended to manage Parliament without Sunderland's help and making unstinted promises of loyalty to him in the future.[2]

On one point Wharton and Montagu were reluctant to retreat. They wanted the present Parliament, in which they thought they had a majority, continued. But William had no wish to continue a Parliament which they dominated. On the advice of Sunderland,

[1] Henry Guy to Portland, 31 May, 14 and 18 June, and 12 July 1694; Sunderland to Portland, 29 July 1694, Portland Papers. Kenyon, *Sunderland*, pp. 271–4.

[2] L'Hermitage, B.M. Add. MSS 17677PP, ff. 193–194; Guy to Portland, 12 and 30 July 1694; Sunderland to Portland, 18 Aug. 1694, Portland Papers. Kenyon, *Sunderland*, pp. 274–5. Henry Guy wrote to the Earl of Portland (6 Aug. 1694, Portland Papers), 'Sunderland is gone out of town this day; but before he went, he hath settled all things amongst these people [the Whigs]; and all or most of them have assured him, that they will be totally governed by him; and will do as he shall direct...I think it may hold, because I find they are sensible enough, that they do not well know how to stir without him.'

Somers, and Shrewsbury he dissolved Parliament in the autumn of 1695 and issued writs for the election of a new one. Sunderland hoped for the return of men loyal to the King, men of no party; Somers hoped for the election of loyal Whigs. Neither saw his wish fulfilled. The new Parliament had a majority of Whigs, but of Country and Court Whigs together, not of Court Whigs alone.[1]

Paul Foley and Robert Harley now became political powers deserving respect. Endlessly flexible, undismayed, ever resilient, Sunderland opened negotiations with Paul Foley who led the Country elements in the House—Tory squires, Whigs who distrusted all courtiers, and the solid phalanx of Herefordshire and Worcestershire members. Sunderland even went so far as to support a Country party proposal to grant Parliament, and not the King, the right to name the members of the newly created Council of Trade; but the attachment of the House to the principle of the separation of powers proved too great even for Foley and Sunderland. With the full support of William, the Court Whigs secured the defeat of this proposal, the last ever made in England for the parliamentary nomination of the King's servants.[2]

This minor defeat did not destroy Sunderland's new scheme for managing Parliament with the assistance of Foley and Harley. Two other events in 1696 destroyed the scheme: the Assassination Plot and the failure of the Land Bank. The attempted assassination of William III at Turnham Green gave Lord Keeper Somers an opportunity which he was quick to grasp. He at once drew up an association for the King's protection, in imitation of that drawn for Queen Elizabeth's protection in 1585, which members of Parliament and officials everywhere were to subscribe. The association effectively split apart the Country Whigs and their Tory allies, for ninety-three Tories in the House of Commons refused to sign it. Then came the failure of the Land Bank, which Harley and Foley had promoted and Sunderland covertly supported.

This was a far worse blow, for the Land Bank was designed to free

[1] Sunderland to Portland, 29 July 1694, Portland Papers; Kenyon, *Sunderland*, pp. 274–6. William possessed little power to determine the outcome of the election, for, as Speaker Onslow observed some years later (Burnet, *History*, IV, 279), William never possessed the power his successors did to influence 'the choice of a Parliament'.

[2] Kenyon, *Sunderland*, pp. 277–8; Burnet, *History*, IV, 287–9. Though John Locke in his *Second Treatise on Government* opposed placing executive power in the legislature, he was quite willing to accept an appointment on a Council of Trade named by Parliament (Lord King, *Life and Letters of Locke*, 1884, p. 240).

William from a dependence on the financial power of the Whigs. In the years 1693 and 1694 the Whigs wrested office from the King not only because they could secure him votes of supply in Parliament, but also because they could secure him loans in the City. Hoffmann in 1693 wrote home that the King was obliged to employ the Whigs because only they could finance the war. The creation of the Whig-dominated Bank of England in 1694 further augmented their financial power. In order to free the King from this dependence on the Whigs, Edward Harley and Paul Foley in 1696 organized a Land Bank, which landed men should control and which should lend the government £2,564,000.[1] The venture was a complete failure; only three subscribers, bringing a mere £2,100, supported the scheme with their cash. The failure of the Land Bank threw William back on the Whig money interest, a fact which Sunderland quickly perceived. He came up to London in August 1696 and let his opposition to the Land Bank be known. By this act he signalled his return to the service of the Whig party, a party whom he could never love but whose power in Parliament and the City he respected.[2]

The first service that the Whigs asked of him was the removal of Godolphin from the Treasury. The Court Whigs did not desire his removal because they were dissatisfied with his performance at the Treasury. They desired it because they hoped his fall would appease the clamours occasioned by Sir John Fenwick's confessions, and thereby save Shrewsbury and Russell. In the summer of 1696 Fenwick accused Godolphin, Shrewsbury, and Russell of corresponding with James II at St Germain. The accusation struck terror into Shrewsbury's heart, who foresaw an impeachment against him in Parliament. In his terror he wrote to Wharton that many men were sufficiently angry at Godolphin to bring down everyone implicated by Fenwick in order to destroy the Treasurer. He therefore

---

[1] Keith Feiling, *A History of the Tory Party 1640–1714* (Oxford, 1924), pp. 310, 319–21.

[2] Klopp, *Der Fall des Hauses Stuart*, VI, 242; J. K. Horsefield, *British Monetary Experiments* (Cambridge, Mass., 1960), pp. 205–7. Francis Gwin wrote to the second Marquis of Halifax on 3 Aug. (Halifax Papers, Althorp, Box 4), 'My Lord Sunderland...came to town by particular summons; whether he thinks the encouraging these subscriptions will set up one party of men too high, and too much pull down Montagu &c., or whether my Lord Keeper has prevailed with him, I cannot tell, but he seems rather against these new subscribers than for them...In the meantime my Lord Portland is to go away satisfied that Mr Montagu &c. have acted very wisely in refusing the Land Bank, since they are not able to furnish £200,000; and therefore, though the Foleys and Harleys were at the head of it, all that Land Bank is called a cheat...The animosity of Land Bank and Old Bank seems to me almost as high as Jacobite and Williamite.'

suggested that the King should remove Godolphin in order to save the rest. The Whigs and Sunderland adopted this strategy. Sunderland even agreed to serve as the hatchet-man. He persuaded Godolphin to offer his resignation to the King in order that William, by refusing it, might show his confidence in him. Godolphin fell for the ruse, offered his resignation, and stood aghast when William accepted it. By engineering Godolphin's fall Sunderland helped save the Whigs, for there was no attack upon them in Parliament that winter, but he did so at the cost of betraying a friend, an able administrator, and an advocate of government by loyal civil servants. Nottingham's dismissal marked the triumph of the Whigs over the Tories; the removal of Godolphin proclaimed their victory over the administrators. It is ironical that Sunderland, who believed in government by the King's friends, should have been instrumental in its overthrow.[1]

Godolphin's removal opened the way for Charles Montagu's advancement. In May 1697 the King made him first Lord of the Treasury. At the same time he gave Wharton a seat at the Admiralty and bestowed peerages on Russell and Somers. But he did not give the Junto (as Somers, Russell, Montagu, and Wharton were now called) his full confidence: he reserved that for Sunderland and Shrewsbury. To them he wrote asking whom he should name ambassadors to negotiate peace at Ryswick. To them he entrusted the power of patronage. To them he voiced his complaints and his disappointments. But these two lords, as closely as they worked together, did not draw their power from the same source. Sunderland drew his from the King's favour, a fact which William advertised by naming Sunderland Lord Chamberlain in April. Shrewsbury drew his from both the King's favour and the support of the Whig party, and when in April he had to choose between the two he chose the party. In April William told Shrewsbury that 'those of both denominations' who had opposed the government must be

---

[1] Kenyon, *Sunderland*, pp. 284–5. Shrewsbury wrote to Lord Wharton, who had succeeded to his father's peerage in February (Carte MSS 233, f. 27, 30 Oct. 1696), 'I think the only difficulty is what your Lordship has stated, that many people are fond it [Fenwick's charge] should not be thought a false accusation upon all...' He then added, 'Most people [probably meaning the Country Whigs] are so much more eager against their enemies than for their friends, that rather than spare some, they will load all. The best way I think to get over this, is that whoever is in this circumstance, and that people are inclined to believe this of [presumably Godolphin], the King should order it so that they would retire...'

removed from the Customs and Excise Boards, and insisted 'that if no punishment were made, no government could be expected for the future'. Shrewsbury answered that His Majesty ought to distinguish between those who had but once done wrong, through ignorance, and those 'who, in the whole course of business, had continually opposed'. Shrewsbury later wrote to Somers that his answer to William met 'with so cold a reception, that I think it is not hard to guess what was meant by that speech; though I think if it be intended against Sir Walter Young and Mr Clarke, we are obliged (I am sure I think myself so) to stand by them'. Then he added, 'A meeting will soon be pressed by Lord Sunderland. It would be well if you, Montagu, Russell, and myself could meet first.'[1] That final sentence exactly defined Sunderland's relation to the Whigs. He did not participate in their inner councils; his indispensable role was to act as a broker for them at Court, where he interpreted their wishes to the King. And real power resided in the Whigs, not their broker, as the disposal of offices in the summer of 1697 proved. Sir Walter Young and Edward Clarke, whom the Whigs meant to stand by, remained in office, but Sunderland could not secure places for Arnold and Colt, though his protégé, Sir William Trumbull, threatened to resign as Secretary of State if he did not—and in fact resigned for that reason in December.[2] Shrewsbury at bottom was more powerful than Sunderland, because he had behind him a party as well as a King.

By the summer of 1697 William had surrendered to the Whigs, who now enjoyed a monopoly of his counsels. The paramount question remains: what led him, between 1692 and 1697, to retreat from the ideal of a mixed ministry and to surrender to the Whig demand for a party ministry? In part he yielded to the Whigs because he respected their ability, shared their enthusiasm for a land war in Flanders, and believed them loyal to the Revolutionary Settlement. But principally he yielded to them because he was compelled to, because they alone could successfully manage his business in Parliament, could win him votes of supply, could secure him loans in the City. Only slowly, reluctantly, and painfully did he come to see that the logic of parliamentary supremacy required

[1] Hardwicke, *State Papers*, II, 431.
[2] Trumbull's Diary, ff. 8–9, 11, 20–21, Berkshire Record Office. I am indebted to Mr Peter Hills for loaning me photostats of Trumbull's Diary.

him to employ ministers in whom Parliament could confide. It was also his unhappiness to discover that Parliament would not confide in a ministry composed of men drawn from all parties: party passions were too vehement to allow this. He therefore had to choose his ministers from the dominant party in Parliament. Parliamentary supremacy joined to the vehemence of party passions proved too much for the royal prerogative.

Between 1689 and 1697 England moved steadily towards responsible government, but the form which responsible government took would have surprised those early Stuart politicians who first demanded it. In the year 1641 five possible solutions had emerged to the problem of securing a more responsible government for England. They were reliance upon impeachments, the voting of parliamentary addresses, conciliar government, government by parliamentary committees, and government by parliamentary undertakers. In the year 1689 Englishmen still cherished the right to impeach iniquitous ministers of state, but they discovered that the House would only impeach ministers who were either clearly guilty or so passionately hated that their innocence offered no armour. Impeachments were too clumsy and attended with too much violence to be practicable; yet they lurked in the shadows throughout William's reign to put fear into men's hearts.

Parliamentary addresses proved far more useful than impeachments. From the meeting of the Convention Parliament until William's death, both Houses resorted to them. In 1692 and 1693 the Commons went far towards turning such addresses into votes of censure and votes of confidence. But votes of censure had two drawbacks: they offered no proof that the ministers censured had in fact given the King pernicious advice and they did not inform the King whom he ought to employ in their place.

A desire to correct the first of these drawbacks led to a clamour for the revival of the Privy Council. This clamour signified no wish to resurrect conciliar government as Clarendon envisaged it; government by the full Privy Council enlisted no man's enthusiasm in the 1690's. What did enlist the enthusiasm of some men was the requirement that councillors give their advice in full Council, even putting their hands to it, so that Parliament could know whom to hold responsible for advice given the King. However, most members of Parliament, conscious of the necessity for secrecy of government in time of war, ignored the demand. Instead they countenanced the idea of a collective responsibility residing in those who possessed office, sat in the Cabinet Council, and enjoyed 'the direction of affairs'.

The obvious way to correct the second drawback attendant upon votes of censure was to nominate the King's ministers for him. But members of Parliament remembered too vividly the history of the Commonwealth to accept this solution. Therefore they refused in 1689 to name Commissioners of Supplies for Ireland and in 1696 to nominate the Council of Trade. True, they did nominate the Commissioners for Wool, but the experiment proved a failure, thereby confirming men in their opinion that the legislative and executive power should be kept apart.

Englishmen came instead to believe that the King should employ those who could manage his affairs in Parliament and who could undertake to secure him a vote of supply from the two Houses. No King of any mettle would willingly accept this limitation, least of all William III, who once said, 'I will be a King of my people and not a party.'[1] He therefore sought, by drawing on the loyalty that men owed the Crown and by exploiting the patronage that he possessed, to build a party of the King's friends in the two Houses, a party that would serve him and heed his wishes. But the power of patronage and the loyalty felt for the Crown, great as they were, proved feeble when confronted by suspicious country gentlemen given to voting Place Bills and party politicians given to voting addresses against any minister, however able, however innocent, who happened to belong to the opposite party. All men bewailed the revival of party distinctions in 1689, but their lamentations only testified to the reality of party. In the continuing battle between the power of patronage and the power of party, between parliamentary management and parliamentary undertaking, the opposing combatants advanced and receded according to the unity and strength of the prevailing party in Parliament. The more broken that party and the weaker its numbers, the stronger the King; the more united the predominant party and the greater its numbers, the weaker the King. This rule offers the surest guide to eighteenth-century politics and to the growth of responsible government after 1697.

[1] John Oldmixon, *The History of England during the Reigns of King William and Queen Mary, Queen Anne, and King George I* (1735), p. 105.

CHAPTER 8

THE TORY CONVERSION TO
RESPONSIBLE GOVERNMENT (1697–1702)

In December 1697 the high tide of Whig ascendancy began to ebb and to flow towards a Tory predominance. That change was marked by the fall from power of the Earl of Sunderland, a politician who enjoyed neither the full trust of the once ascendant Whigs nor the support of the now revived Tories. Both parties joined against him in 1697, forcing him to resign as Lord Chamberlain. That resignation illustrates both the argument of the last chapter and the theme of the present one, for Sunderland's resignation in the face of Whig hostility proclaimed the final defeat of the parliamentary managers at the hands of the parliamentary undertakers, and his retreat before Tory threats of impeachment began four years of Tory opposition to the King's ministers. Sunderland was too much a Whig to satisfy Musgrave and Seymour and too little a Whig to satisfy John Smith and Lord Wharton; as a result he lost the confidence of Parliament and fell from office.

Sunderland, though his intelligence informed him that government by party was often necessary, much preferred government by the King's friends. In November he testified to this preference (and to his undoubted skill at management) by persuading William to appoint James Vernon, an industrious clerk, as Secretary of State, rather than Lord Wharton, an unswerving Whig. It was undoubtedly a skilful manoeuvre, but it turned the Whigs irrevocably against him. As a result when William, hearing that Lord Norris intended to attack Sunderland in Parliament, asked Lord Wharton 'to engage his friends to stand by my Lord Chamberlain', Wharton refused. Bereft of Whig support, attacked by the Tories, and unwilling to depend upon a feeble Court party led by Henry Guy, Sunderland resigned. As James Vernon wrote on the 27th, 'my Lord Sunderland would not stay to be addressed from Court, and therefore last night he delivered up his key and staff'.[1]

Three months later Sunderland, regretting his decision to resign,

---

[1] *Vernon Corr.* I, 446, 448.

sought to return to public life, but the Whigs adamantly refused to countenance his return. William sadly admitted to the Earl of Portland, 'I see that there is no hope that I can secure Sunderland's return with the agreement of the Whigs; thus I no longer dream of it, at least as long as this Parliament lasts, whose end I cannot foresee.'[1] The King prized the counsels of Sunderland much, but he valued the support of the Whigs more.

The Whigs played only a passive role in Sunderland's fall; the Tories took the initiative in attacking him. They spoke in the Commons of impeaching or voting an address against him. They blamed him for advising the King to rule by a standing army. They—John Granville, Sir Thomas Dyke, Lord Norris—never let a day pass without attacking him. To escape from the range of their gunshot Sunderland resigned and retired to Althorp. But he did not retreat only from their volleys: he retreated also from the universal applause that greeted them. When Sir Thomas Dyke first attacked Sunderland in the House, the members, few of whom could have forgotten the Earl's services to James II, cried out, 'Hear! Hear!' And among those who shouted, few, probably, were more vocal than the members of the Country party. This party may be said to have had its birth on the day in 1694 when the Whig Robert Harley opened a correspondence with the Tory Sir Christopher Musgrave. Both men spoke for the country squire against the servile courtier; both spoke against the Bank, the Debt, high taxes, and expensive alliances; both distrusted the Court and those who served at Court. By 1697 the Country Whigs had formed a close alliance with the Old Cavaliers. Not only Tories like Granville and Dyke, but Whigs like Jack Howe and Sir Francis Winnington, spoke against the Earl of Sunderland in 1697. Sunderland ought, in fact, to be counted the first victim of the Country party's determination to drive the Court Whigs from office.[2]

The determination of the new Country party to drive the Junto

---

[1] Japikse, *Correspondentie*, I, 273–4. William refused, however, to allow the Whigs to intimidate him into naming Lord Wharton Lord Chamberlain. As he wrote to Portland (*ibid.* p. 297), 'They urge me to make Lord Wharton Lord Chamberlain, to which I am as little inclined as to make him Secretary of State. The Whigs pretend that they will not be satisfied, and that my affairs will not be concluded to my satisfaction in Parliament if I do not gratify them. You see how far they carry matters.'

[2] Klopp, *Der Fall des Hauses Stuart*, VIII, 11; *C.S.P. Dom. 1697*, p. 534. Robert Walcott (*English Politics in the Early Eighteenth Century*, Cambridge, Mass., 1956, pp. 86–8) carefully traces the growth of the Country party and accurately describes its composition.

from office was incontestable—four years of relentless opposition testified to it. More problematical were the motives that led them to oppose the King's ministers at every opportunity. One motive was surely love of liberty. The backwoodsmen of Worcestershire and Herefordshire, the Tory squires of Westmorland and Cumberland, the burgesses of Abingdon and Gloucester no doubt feared government by a standing army and a corrupt Parliament. Another motive was hatred of taxes, taxes whose necessity they attributed to the peculations of the King's ministers and lavish grants of land in Ireland. A third was fear of foreigners, for xenophobia permeated the land. But these fears and hatreds explain principally the conduct of the rank and file in the new Country party. They do not sufficiently explain the sustained fury with which the leaders of the party, the Harleys, Musgraves, Seymours, Foleys, and Rochesters, drove against the Junto. These men knew that Somers and Montagu had no wish to govern by a standing army, that an expensive war made necessary high taxes, and that not a single foreigner served in high office. Not fear for English liberty, but ambition for office and passion for party lay behind their conduct. They wished to drive the Junto from Court so that they might secure offices of profit and power for themselves and might promote the interests—fiscal, social, and economic—of the country gentlemen whom they represented.[1]

The means by which the Tories and their allies sought to drive the Junto lords from office proved more unusual than the purpose itself. They did not intrigue at Court against Wharton and Russell (there was hardly any need). They did not seek to persuade William that they could administer the Chancery better than Somers and the Treasury better than Montagu. They did not promise to serve him more faithfully or to promote his policies in Parliament more sedulously. Instead they relentlessly opposed his measures in the Commons, persistently attacked his ministers there, and sought, by dominating Parliament, to make themselves indispensable to the King. They adopted the tactics of the Shaftesbury Whigs and acted on the principle recently enunciated by James Vernon, that those 'who are the strongest in the House of Commons and in possession

---

[1] As Matthew Prior wrote in March 1699 (*H.M.C. Bath*, III, 324), 'most of those... who compose...the Country party...are and have been always Whigs; on the other side the Tories in these last affairs have voted against their principles because the chiefs of their party...are against the Court, right or wrong, because they are not of it.'

of the management' of it, are not in danger of being disregarded at Court.[1] Pursuant to these tactics and in obedience to this principle, they spent the next three years espousing popular causes and attacking the King's ministers.

They began by attacking Charles Montagu, financial wizard and leader of the Court party in the House of Commons. The new Country party chose Montagu because, as Somers observed, 'They are sensible how useful and indeed how necessary' he is to the Court in the management of the Commons. They also began with him because they believed they could condemn him for falsely endorsing Exchequer Bills, in order to draw interest upon them. Unfortunately for their cause, Montagu was innocent of this crime. When Robert Harley on 18 January 1698 moved that the House proceed by impeachment against those who had falsely endorsed Exchequer Bills, Montagu had no difficulty demonstrating his innocence. He then carried the war into the enemy's camp. Suspecting that Sunderland's friends had promoted the attack on him, he exposed the guilt of one of them, Sir Charles Duncomb, who had in fact falsely endorsed Exchequer Bills. As a result the House voted a Bill of Attainder against Duncomb, not against Montagu, as Harley had intended. Montagu's triumph was complete and deserved, but it was not politic. By securing the condemnation of Duncomb, he irreparably split the Whig and Sunderland factions of the Court party, thereby making it more difficult, not easier, to manage Parliament for the King. No doubt the spirited Montagu enjoyed his hour of victory; a more prudent man would have thought on the future.[2]

The Country party did not give up upon this initial defeat. On 16 February they charged Montagu with unlawfully procuring two grants from the King, one for cutting timber in the Forest of Dean, the other for collecting forfeited recognizances in Ireland. The debate on this charge grew heated; nothing less than an impeachment would satisfy the opposition. They moved, as a forerunner to sending him to the Tower, that Montagu withdraw from the House. Against this motion the friends of Montagu rallied their

---

[1] *Vernon Corr.* I, 474.

[2] C. Cole (ed.), *Memoirs of Affairs of State* (1733), p. 22; *Vernon Corr.* I, 469; *C.S.P. Dom. 1698*, pp. 40–1, 44, 46, 54, 71, 89, 144; *Shrewsbury Corr.* pp. 516, 527–8. The Tories in the House of Lords, led by Rochester, Leeds, and Bolton, threw out the Bill of Attainder against Duncomb.

forces in the House, defeating the proposal by 209 to 97. They then carried without a division a motion that Montagu 'for his good services to this government does deserve His Majesty's favour'. Not deterred by this crushing defeat, the leaders of the Country party returned to the attack a third time. On 22 February Musgrave, Seymour, and Harley sought to persuade the House that it was illegal for the Treasury to receive Exchequer Bills in discharge of Bills of Exchange payable in gold. The Commissioners of the Treasury replied that they had only sought to serve the public by maintaining the credit of Exchequer Bills. The House accepted this explanation by rejecting, by 170 to 88, a motion that receiving Exchequer Bills in this manner was illegal and a loss to the public.[1]

The Earl of Portland, contemplating the successive vindications of Montagu, was prompted to write to William, 'If those who compose one party [the Whig] were also of one mind on public business, the affair of Montagu would be a proof that the men of that party could do what they like.'[2] Portland was in error. The ability of the Junto to defend Montagu did not mean that they could, on behalf of the King, defeat Triennial and Place Bills and secure a standing army of 30,000 men, with a Dutch Guard. Most members of the House did not count themselves members of any party, whether Whig or Tory. They regarded themselves as independent members, perhaps Country in their sympathies, perhaps royalist, but certainly not partisan. This does not mean that a Whig party and a Tory party did not exist. There were steadfast Whigs in the House, and steadfast Tories, but on every particular issue and on each given occasion they had to court the independent members, who voted according to the merits of the question or their own individual prejudices.[3] Thus the Whigs could secure the acquittal of an obviously innocent Montagu, yet fail to secure the King a standing army. Portland was a very obtuse observer of the political scene not to see this.

[1] *C.J.* xii, 116; *C.S.P. Dom. 1698*, pp. 94–6, 102, 105.
[2] P. Grimblot (ed.), *Letters of William III and Louis XIV and Their Ministers* (1848), I, 216.
[3] The Prussian envoy, Friedrich Bonnet, wrote (17/28 Dec. 1700, B.M. Add. MSS 30000 D, f. 363), 'Though the English are nearly all divided into Whigs and Tories, there are many members of Parliament from the country who do not sit with either party, in order to espouse none. They vote according to their own light, which does not reach beyond the shores of this island. The principles which guide them are (1) the religion of the country, (2) the liberty of the individual, (3) the promotion of their manufactures, and (4) the profitable cultivation of their land. Whichever party rules and however eloquent it may be, it will never win if it attacks one of these.'

Shrewsbury and Montagu, shrewder judges of the political scene, did see, or rather foresee, the imminent dissolution of the Junto ministry. Shrewsbury had sought to resign as early as the autumn of 1697, when Sunderland and the Junto split; now that he saw that their reconciliation was impossible he did resign, in the autumn of 1698. His retreat is comprehensible, for he was ill, weary of office, and angry at the Whigs for their treatment of Sunderland. Montagu's retreat is a profounder mystery. He began it in September 1698, by preparing a safe and lucrative place for retirement. He secured the office of Auditor of the Exchequer for his brother, Christopher, to be held in readiness for himself. During the 1699 session of Parliament he made little effort to manage the House successfully for the Court. In June 1699 he resigned as Chancellor of the Exchequer and in November as First Commissioner of the Treasury, in order to become Auditor. Why did he retreat so ingloriously in 1699 after so glorious a victory in 1698? He did so because he wished to avoid the cruel dilemma of advocating royal policies that he knew to be unpopular in the House and in the country. The English elected a new Parliament in the summer of 1698, whose members, though they chose a Whig to be Speaker, proved more hostile than ever towards the Court. Above all, they refused to vote William a standing army of more than 7,000 men. James Vernon most exactly expressed the dilemma that this created for the Whig managers:

At present we are under great perplexity. Those that are convinced in their judgments that a greater force is necessary are apprehensive of the ill consequences if such a question be carried against them upon a division, which fixes people in a party, so that no good is to be expected during the rest of the session. If it be not attempted, the King will be disobliged, and may be told, if there were not more troops it was because nobody pressed it. This dilemma is a little staggering.[1]

So staggering, indeed, that Montagu chose to retreat from it, first by securing the Auditor's place for his brother, then by refusing to take upon himself the management of the Commons, finally by resigning as Chancellor and Treasurer to become Auditor.

Having devoted the year 1698 to repeated assaults on Montagu, the Country party spent the year 1699 attacking Lord Orford, the

---

[1] *Vernon Corr.* II, 224. In March Vernon wrote (*ibid.* 268) that Somers and Montagu 'are still called the ministers, though there are none that I see who take upon them any management'.

victor of La Hogue and an intractable Whig. Robert Harley and Paul Foley instigated and guided the attack by means of a Committee on the State of the Navy, but they were careful not to seek the condemnation of Orford until after the House had first divided on a motion to limit the standing army in England to 7,000 men. They hoped that the Junto's opposition to this limitation would discredit it in the House, that a majority won in a division on the size of the army would hold together on other questions. Their strategy met with little success, for the King's ministers remained silent when Harley moved that the army be limited to 7,000 men. They chose to desert the King rather than invite the wrath of the House. Their choice enraged William, but it saved Orford. On 15 March the Committee on the State of the Navy laid before the House an account of the mismanagements which it had discovered in the navy. The committee condemned the delay in sending out the Straits Fleet the previous summer, the perquisites enjoyed by Captain Priestman, the high salaries paid to navy officers, the introduction of new and unnecessary charges, the passing of victualling accounts without proper vouchers, and the joining of the offices of the Treasurer of the Navy and of the first Commissioner of the Admiralty in one person. Though these abuses were not flagrant abuses, the House agreed to present them to His Majesty with a request that he take measures to prevent such mismanagements in the future. But the House rejected by 4 votes an amendment requesting William to 'place the administration of the Admiralty in such hands' as would prevent these mismanagements hereafter. Robert Harley was unhappy that the desertion of 'our friends' had occasioned Orford's acquittal, but he need not have been. Weary of being the target of the House and vexed that William would not dismiss the Tory Sir George Rooke from the Admiralty Board, he resigned all his offices on 15 May 1699.[1]

Somers's turn came next, in the year 1700, but the task of driving him from office proved far more difficult than the task of driving out Montagu and Orford: for where Montagu by his avarice and Orford by his dissolute life had offended many men, Somers appears to have been a paragon of virtue. But the necessity of driving Somers from

---

[1] *Vernon Corr.* II, 238–9; *C.J.* XII, 618; *H.M.C. Rep. XIV, Part 2*, p. 603. Captain Priestman ran before the storm by resigning from the Admiralty Board in March (*C.S.P. Dom. 1699–1700*, p. 115).

office outweighed all the difficulties, for he was, as Sunderland said, 'the life, the soul, and the spirit of his party'. Furthermore, he was the only Whig left who had any credit with the King. For these reasons the Country party resolved to use their power in the House of Commons to drive him from office. They first sought to censure him for his complicity in the Captain Kidd affair, for Somers had joined with others to commission this faithless captain to seize pirates in the Indian Ocean. That Captain Kidd had turned pirate himself certainly made Somers look ridiculous, but it did not make him criminal. The Commons reached the same conclusion, for on 6 December 1699, by a majority of 56, they cleared him of all fault in the commissioning of Captain Kidd.[1]

Thwarted in this endeavour, the opponents of Somers turned to the more promising question of the Irish land grants. Somers as Lord Chancellor had put the Great Seal to many of the lavish grants which William had made to his favourites out of forfeited Irish estates. In the winter of 1700 a motion that the Crown should resume these grants preoccupied most of Parliament's time. Though the lands were worth only £1¾ million and the public debt stood at £18 million, the Tories persuaded the House to vote that the grants had occasioned the debt. They also spoke of punishing those who had occasioned the debt by passing the grants. Charles Davenant, economist and Tory publicist, proclaimed in his *Discourse of Grants and Resumptions* the principle, first enunciated by Sir Robert Cotton in James I's reign, that in England the impeachment of ministers who passed illegal grants should precede the resumption of those grants. If this principle were followed now, Somers was doomed to an impeachment. But doomsday never broke, for, though the Country members were keen on resumptions that promised to take a shilling in the pound off their taxes, they believed Somers innocent of wrongdoing. On 13 February 1700, by a majority of 50 votes, they rejected a motion that any minister concerned in passing a grant to his own benefit had violated 'the trust reposed in him'.[2]

---

[1] Hardwicke, *State Papers*, II, 440; *Vernon Corr.* II, 378–9, 381; Burnet, *History*, IV, 421-4, 431. In December 1699 the Tories also moved an address for the removal of Gilbert Burnet, Bishop of Salisbury, as preceptor of the Duke of Gloucester, but were defeated by 173 to 133 (*C.J.* XIII, 56).

[2] 'Report of the Commissioners for Enquiring into Irish Forfeitures', Lansdowne MSS 660, f. 16; *C.J.* XIII, 208; Sir Charles Whitworth (ed.), *The Political and Commercial Works of...Charles Davenant* (1771), III, 231–2; Manchester Papers, P.R.O. 30/15 Box 4, no. 684, xii, and Box 5, no. 686, lxxi; Bonnet, B.M. Add. MSS 30000D, ff. 51v–56v, 144v.

Still the party of Musgrave and Harley refused to give up. They waited patiently until the Whigs should anger the Country members by opposing the Bill for Resuming the Irish Land Grants; but this Somers and Montagu resolutely refused to do, much to William's anger. The Bill passed easily through the Commons, and went to the House of Lords. William's hatred for the Bill now led him to bring all his influence to bear on the ministerialists in the Lords to reject it. They yielded so far as to amend it, which was a blunder, for their action provoked a crisis deeper than any that had occurred since the rejection of the Exclusion Bill in 1680. Though the amendments merely sought to protect the Lords' right of judicature and the King's prerogative, Harley spoke as if they imperilled the nation.[1] Seymour adroitly turned the crisis against Lord Somers, initiating a debate in which several members of the House charged the Lord Chancellor with procuring exorbitant grants for himself, putting the Seal to grants for others, advising the King to give sharp answers to their addresses, and promoting opposition to the Resumption Bill in the Lords. This attack on Somers was patently partisan, arising from no true concern for the public good, from no genuine hatred for exorbitant grants. Somers's single grant of £400 was trifling by the side of the £5,500 enjoyed by the Duke of Leeds; and Seymour and Godolphin had sat on the Treasury Board which had approved many of the grants which the Tories condemned Somers for sealing. Nor did the House possess any proof that Somers had advised William's sharp answers to their addresses; and it was notorious that being ill at home he could not have promoted opposition to the Resumption Bill in the Lords. Because the attack was unmistakably partisan, because Somers's probity, affability, and genius were widely admired, and because the lawyers in the House stood by him, the attack failed. It also was of no help that Musgrave altered Sir John Leveson's motion for an impeachment into a motion for an address for his removal from the King's presence and councils for ever. The House on 10 April rejected the latter motion by a majority of 61. The next day the King prorogued Parliament.[2]

---

[1] B.M. Add. MSS 28053, f. 402. In 1695 Robert Harley told Henry Guy that he wondered the country gentlemen of Wales should make such a noise about the Earl of Portland's grant, 'for it was as much in the power of the King to give to whom he pleased, as it was of any gentlemen in England to dispose of any part of his own estates' (Japikse, *Correspondentie*, II, 60–1).

[2] *Vernon Corr.* II, 5–6, 19–24, 413; Bonnet, B.M. Add. MSS 30000 D, ff. 14, 123v–126v, 137–139; L'Hermitage, B.M. Add. MSS 17677 VV, ff. 207–208v, 210–211. L'Hermitage

The Tories were not downcast. 'Some of them', reported James Vernon, 'said afterwards they did not value that question, since they expected the same effect by his voluntarily retiring.' Their confidence was fully justified by events, though not in the exact manner they expected. Somers refused to retire voluntarily, believing that it would be a sign of guilt; therefore William was forced to dismiss him, which he did on 26 April. Rumour said that he had dismissed him on Sunderland's advice to employ those who governed in the House of Commons. Sunderland himself believed that William dismissed Somers in a fit of pique, caused by the refusal of the Whigs to oppose the Resumption Bill. Wherever the truth resides, one fact is indisputable: party passion would not allow William to govern with balanced counsels, as he wished. In February Robert Harley refused to enter a government containing Lord Somers; in April Somers refused to desert his party by serving with Tories. 'The Court', wrote Count Tallard on 26 April, 'seeks in every way to make the House of Commons more favourable to it next year. At first it sought to mix Churchmen and Presbyterians in the administration, but neither party would consent.' Since a ministry of all the talents was impossible, William heeded the advice allegedly given by the Earl of Sunderland, and turned to the party which governed in the House of Commons. One wit celebrated this event by nailing a placard on the door of the Chancery, 'House for Rent, Enquire of Lord Sunderland.' But a more discerning humorist posted over it, 'House for Rent, Enquire of the House of Commons.'[1]

The Country party, by their incessant clamours and obstructive tactics, drove the Junto from office, but they did not secure preferment for themselves. William was too much in love with moderate counsels to employ men filled with the spirit of party. When Shrewsbury laid down the seals, William gave them to the Earl of Jersey, a courtier and brother of Lady Orkney. To replace Orford at the

reported (*ibid.* f. 211) that the Commons resolved to go by an address rather than an impeachment because an examination into the laws of the land showed that there was no law that would condemn him for the fault imputed to him.

[1] *Vernon Corr.* III, 22; Bonnet, B.M. Add. MSS 30000 D, f. 164; L'Hermitage, B.M. Add. MSS 17677 VV, ff. 228–228 v. Count Tallard wrote (26 Apr./7 May 1700, Fr. Trans.), 'Sunderland...proposes that the King allow Parliament to do what it wishes, in order to win it to the King's interest. This strategy is very dangerous to the King and will force him to see all his ministers chased from him...A lord, to whom an office was offered some time ago, replied that he did not wish it, since he could not decide whether he served a King or a Republic.'

Admiralty he named the Earl of Bridgewater, and to replace Montagu at the Treasury the Earl of Tankerville; Bridgewater was a mere cipher in politics, Tankerville a protégé of Sunderland's. The Great Seal, which William took from Lord Somers, he gave to Sir Nathan Wright, an undistinguished and inconspicuous Tory. When the Duke of Leeds resigned in 1699 as Lord President, William replaced him with the Earl of Pembroke, a moderate Tory; and he gave the Privy Seal laid down by Pembroke to Lord Lonsdale, a respected elder statesman. Though these men were not declared Whigs, though they threatened no man's liberty, though they served the King loyally and lawfully, their preferment did not satisfy those who governed in the House of Commons. 'Some people', wrote the Bishop of Norwich to Dr Charlett, 'think the alterations will stop at present with my Lord Chancellor but others with more reason are of opinion that the whole ministry will be changed, that... Leeds, Rochester, Sunderland, Godolphin, and that party [must] come into play again.'[1] William had no desire to bring 'that party' 'into play again', but before the year was out he had. Why had he?

William turned to the Tories in the summer and autumn of 1700 because the only two other possibilities—a Whig ministry and a balanced ministry—turned out to be impossibilities. In May and June William, regretting his haste in dismissing Somers, asked Sunderland to negotiate the return of Shrewsbury and the Whigs to his service, but Shrewsbury had no heart for further employment and the Whigs refused to deal with Sunderland. An enterprise hopeless to begin with quickly came to nothing. Hopes of creating a ministry in which both parties were equally balanced proved equally ephemeral. The indefatigable James Vernon, Secretary of State, sought earnestly to create such a ministry, urging it on Robert Harley throughout late June and early July. But Harley only replied, 'The King ought long since to have been convinced, that the persons he employs are not capable of carrying on his service... the King's business must miscarry while blasted men have the conduct of it... It was now a general complaint we had no ministry, no right management of public affairs; and if the King did not mind it, a reformation would be wrought in a more disagreeable manner.' William himself invited Harley to Hampton Court in June, only to meet with the same intransigence. He therefore gave up the idea

[1] Ballard MSS X, f. 39v.

of employing any able man, irrespective of party, who manifested a zeal for his service. Party hatreds in 1700 made a balanced ministry about as feasible as a one-way pendulum.[1]

William therefore opened negotiations with the Tories, the only group of men who could undertake to manage his affairs in Parliament with success and the only group who could secure him the supply he needed to wage a war which he believed imminent. The death of the Duke of Gloucester in July increased the necessity of turning to the party of Rochester and Seymour, of Godolphin and Harley, for only if the Tories established the succession in the House of Hanover would the whole country accept it. But the Tories placed a price on their willingness to undertake the management of the King's affairs in Parliament. They wanted preferment at Court, a new Parliament, and the meeting of Convocation. William acceded to their demands, but not wholeheartedly. He named Godolphin First Commissioner of the Treasury, but refused his demand that the Whig John Smith be removed from the Treasury Board. He made Rochester Lord Lieutenant of Ireland, but Rochester wanted to be President of the Council. He named Sir Charles Hedges, a stalwart Tory and ally of Nottingham, as Secretary of State in Lord Jersey's place, but he gave no other office to the Tories. He agreed to use the Court's influence to secure the election of Harley as Speaker and to remove the troublesome Montagu to the Lords by creating him Baron Halifax, but he did not, as was rumoured, give Harley office at Court. He dissolved Parliament, but too late in the year to allow the Tories to prepare an electoral victory in the country. Convocation met in the winter of 1701, but by that time the attention of the nation was focused on Parliament, where the Tories had not won the great majority they had hoped for. Only because William prevailed upon Sir Thomas Littleton, a Court Whig, to step down, could the Tories elect Harley Speaker.[2]

Nevertheless they did win the contest for the Speakership, a contest which John Locke believed to be 'a leading point showing

[1] Kenyon, *Sunderland*, pp. 316–18; *Vernon Corr.* iii, 88–91. Vernon was not deceived by Harley's pretence to be of no party. 'Mr Harley professes himself to be of no party, and yet finds fault with the new reform of the Commissions, as if it were done by halves' (*ibid.* p. 91). The 'new reform of the Commissions' was the return to the Commissions of Peace of some of the Tories whom Somers had removed two years before.

[2] Burnet, *History*, iv, 454, 458, 506; B.M. Add. MSS 4107, f. 226; Bonnet, B.M. Add. MSS 30000D, ff. 307–308v, 332–333v, 357, 361. Harley defeated Sir Richard Onslow, the nominee of the Country Whigs, 249 to 125.

the strength of the parties'. And they won despite the fact that they were, as the third Earl of Shaftesbury observed, 'esteemed undertakers' throughout the land.[1] In the past the reputation of being an undertaker for the King had proved fatal; but Rochester, Godolphin, and Harley escaped this hazard because they had a party behind them, a party admittedly composed of many factions, but a party which had learned from the Whigs the value of party unity. William Bromley, observing the tyranny of the Whigs over the gentlemen and clergy of England, wrote to Robert Harley in August, 'We see plainly how this is brought upon us, and how those who are the smaller part of the nation have made themselves formidable and terrible to the greater. They have taken advantage of the mistakes of others, and though they hate one another yet they unite together to carry on their designs. Why may not the same thing preserve the whole...which they do to destroy and overturn everything?'[2] Bromley's rhetorical question was unnecessary, for Harley understood as well as any man the need for unity. In June James Vernon had found him 'bent upon having the superiority the next session, whether it be a new Parliament or the same again'.[3] Earlier yet, in April, Harley had begun drilling his troops. His whips scoured the countryside to bring up members to vote in the crucial divisions of 10 April. Upon the prorogation of Parliament he devoted his labours to unity, meeting with the clergy at Oxford, negotiating with Seymour in the west, and reconciling Godolphin, the leader of the Court Tories, with Rochester, the head of the Country Tories.[4] Sir Henry Neville in 1614, Lord Saye in 1641, Sir Richard Temple in 1668, and the Southampton Whigs in 1680 had made no such preparations to support their undertakings to manage Parliament for the King; they led no parties upon whose allegiance they could count. Only the growth of political parties made successful parliamentary undertakings possible in England,

---

[1] Peter Lord King, *Life and Letters of John Locke* (1858), p. 256; T. Forster, *Original Letters of John Locke, Algernon Sydney, and Anthony Lord Shaftesbury* (1830), pp. 109–10.
[2] B.M. Loan 29/127, Bromley to Harley.
[3] *Vernon Corr.* III, 104.
[4] Bonnet, B.M. Add. MSS 30000 D, f. 143; B.M. Add. MSS 34515, f. 6; Feiling, *Tory Party*, pp. 341–2. Thomas Foley wrote to Harley on 10 Apr. 1700 (B.M. Loan 29/316), 'I received a command from some of your officers, but having none from the General, I thought there was no occasion to return to my post. I suppose there is no need of numbers to dispute the Lords amendments, but in good earnest I would have come up, could I hope to be in time enough and if you had intimated your pleasure.'

for without parties behind them the undertakers could not fulfil the promises they made the King.

What these promises were in 1701 is a matter of surmise. They certainly included an undertaking to pass a Bill of Succession; they probably included an undertaking to secure William the money needed to resist French designs on the Spanish monarchy; possibly they included a promise not to revive the quarrels which had disgraced and disrupted the last Parliament. Whatever the extent of these promises, it is certain that William employed the Tories in the hope that they would guarantee the succession, vote money for a possible war with France, and keep civil peace at home. Of these three tasks the Tories performed the first satisfactorily, the second belatedly, and the third not at all.

The Tories faithfully fulfilled their promise to establish the succession of the Crown of England in the House of Hanover, but not before they tacked to the Act of Settlement a new bill of rights severely limiting the prerogatives to be enjoyed by Queen Anne's successors. Unlike the rights set forth in the Petition of Right and the Bill of Rights, the rights established by the Act of Settlement were concerned less with guaranteeing individual liberty than with securing responsible government. Four of the eight clauses in the Act directly or indirectly sought to secure responsible government for England. The fourth clause required the King to transact important affairs of state in the Privy Council and required Privy Councillors to sign all resolutions to which they assented. The sixth clause sought to prevent the King from corrupting Parliament by prohibiting placemen from sitting in the House of Commons.[1] The seventh clause made judges irremovable except upon a parliamentary address. And the eighth clause declared it illegal to plead the King's pardon in bar to an impeachment. Though the Tories of the Exclusion Crisis had sabotaged the Privy Council scheme of 1679, defeated the self-denying ordinance of 1680, defended the judges impeached by the House of Commons, and supported the validity of Danby's pardon, their successors in 1701 resolved to embrace the cause of conciliar responsibility, place bills, removable judges, and sovereign impeachments.

[1] Place bills both promoted and obstructed the growth of responsible government. They promoted it by making it impossible for the King to support irresponsible ministers by corrupting Parliament; they obstructed it by making it impossible for the leaders of the House of Commons to serve the King in high office.

The Tory Conversion to Responsible Government

The fourth clause of the Act of Settlement reads: 'All matters and things relating to the well governing of this kingdom, which are properly cognizable in the Privy Council by the laws and customs of this realm, shall be transacted there, and all resolutions taken thereupon shall be signed by such of the Privy Council as shall advise and consent to the same.' Parliament, by adding this clause to the Act of Settlement, finally inscribed on the statute book the written responsibility of ministers, demanded by the Commons in 1642, defended by Neville in 1681, and urged by Foley in 1690 and 1692. The measure, asserted one publicist, 'amounts to as much as if there were a standing Committee of Parliament to manage all the great affairs of the Kingdom, since what is signed by the Privy Council is cognizable in Parliament'.[1] Why did Parliament pass so revolutionary an act?

A desire to resurrect the Privy Council was not the reason for its passage: the true reason was a desire to establish foolproof machinery for discovering who had misled the King. The followers of Pym in 1642, the adherents of Shaftesbury in 1679, and the friends of Paul Foley in 1692 had all found it difficult to discover who had given the King bad advice. The new Country party in their turn encountered the same difficulties. Infuriated at the King's address from the throne in 1699, Jack Howe moved that His Majesty be asked to inform them who advised him that he was unkindly used by Parliament and that the nation was defenceless. But the House refused to ask the King to become a common informer. Undeterred by this defeat, a member proposed in November 1699 that William be asked to name those ministers who had advised the address from the throne last May. This motion received more support than Howe's motion in February, but it did not receive a majority.[2]

The King's answer of 21 February 1700 to the House's address of 15 February provoked a third, and greater, outpouring of wrath in the Commons. In his answer William openly justified his Irish land grants and assumed entire responsibility for them. Faced with such blunt talk, the Tories sought refuge in the theory of the constitution espoused by the Whigs during the Exclusion Crisis: the King never acts on his own advice, but always on that of his ministers,

---

[1] A. Browning (ed.), *English Historical Documents, 1660–1714* (1953), p. 134; *Claims of the People of England Essayed in a Letter from the Country*, in *State Tracts, William III*, III, 21.

[2] *C.S.P. Dom. 1699–1700*, p. 43; Klopp, *Der Fall des Hauses Stuart*, VIII, 438.

who are answerable for all. The King can do no wrong, cried Musgrave and Howe in February 1700, for he always acts on the advice of counsellors who must bear the blame. It is a crime, they added, to advise the King to say that he made these grants on his own volition. Howe then moved that the Commons brand as enemies to the King and kingdom those who had advised this answer to their address. Musgrave softened the censure to read, 'Resolved that whosoever advised His Majesty's Answer to the Address of this House presented to His Majesty on Wednesday last has used his utmost endeavour to create a misunderstanding and jealousy betwixt His Majesty and his people.' The Whigs in the House offered no opposition to the motion and refused to divide the House when the Speaker ruled, upon an equal cry on a voice vote, that the motion had carried. They made no opposition because they knew that there was little danger in a general vote. In 1693 the House had condemned as 'enemies to Your Majesty and your government' those who had advised the King to veto the Place Bill, but the condemnation, naming no particular man, had no effect. The King's ministers feared personal votes, but they had no fear of general votes. This fact above all others explains why the Commons desired them to put their counsels in writing. As Sir John Thompson complained in 1694, 'All debates should be in Council; now all things are huddled up.'[1]

The vote in 1693 against those who had advised William to veto the Place Bill also illustrates how little respect the Commons bore the Privy Council. That vote did not ask the King to hearken to his Privy Council rather than to particular persons: it asked that 'for the future Your Majesty should graciously be pleased to hearken to the advice of your Parliament, and not to the secret advices of particular persons'. The Commons showed the same disrespect for the Privy Council on 24 March 1701. Four days earlier the House of Lords had condemned the King's ministers for assenting to the second Partition Treaty without first seeking the advice of the Privy Council. The Commons now also condemned the ministers who had assented to the Treaty, but they did not blame them for not seeking the Privy Council's advice: they blamed them for not seeking Parliament's. The last thing in the world the Commons

---

[1] *C.J.* xiii, 228; *Vernon Corr.* ii, 446–7; Bonnet, B.M. Add. MSS 30000D, ff. 69–70; L'Hermitage, B.M. Add. MSS 17677VV, f. 169; Cobbett, *Parl. Hist.* v, 829; Grey, *Debates*, x, 376.

wanted in 1701 was the revival of a powerful, independent Privy Council.[1]

What they wanted was a council responsible to Parliament—as the debates on the clause made manifest. Opponents of the measure, a powerful party of eloquent, well-informed Court Whigs, denounced it as introducing into England the maxims of the Turkish Court, where one judged the wisdom of advice by the outcome of events. No person of any sense would accept the position of councillor if held responsible for the good success of his advice, for the best laid plans miscarried. To these objections advocates of the clause answered that many pernicious measures had been taken in the past, but the House had been unable to discover their authors. It was necessary therefore that all affairs be laid before the Privy Council and that all councillors who assented to its resolves should record their assent in writing. Otherwise a Prime Minister or cabal of ministers might seize the management of affairs and seek safety in the secrecy of their counsels. Since the King can do no wrong, Parliament must bridle his ministers. These arguments enjoyed the applause of the Country Whigs, the friends of Harley, and the Country Tories, all of whom cheerfully voted for the clause. The High Tories in the House, some verging on Jacobitism, also voted for the clause, but only in order to defeat the Bill of Succession by so overloading it with limitations on the prerogative that the Lords would reject it, or the King veto it. The placemen in the House voted for the clause because they believed that Harley's advocacy of it betokened Court support for it. In the end even the Court Whigs in the House of Lords swallowed the measure, for they dared not risk the passage of the Act of Settlement by amending it. Rather than endanger the succession in the House of Hanover they would accept a folly which they could later undo.[2]

The House of Commons, having made certain that they could discover those who gave the King pernicious advice, went on to ensure that the King could not pardon them. They declared in the

[1] *C.J.* xi, 72; xiii, 419. Cobbett, *Parl. Hist.* v, 1238. *L.J.* xvi, 625, 628. Wolfgang Michael wisely observes ('Die Entstehung der Kabinettsregierung in England', *Zeitschrift für Politik*, vi, 561), 'I do not really believe that the legislators of 1701 held it possible to make the Privy Council once again the government of the land.'

[2] Bonnet, B.M. Add. MSS 30000E, ff. 63v–64, 67–70, 73v–74, 77–78v, 205; L'Hermitage, B.M. Add. MSS 17677WW, ff. 183–185; Klopp, *Der Fall des Hauses Stuart*, ix, 260–1, 266–8; Tallard, Fr. Trans. 6/17 March 1701.

Act of Settlement that 'no pardon under the Great Seal of England be pleaded to an impeachment by the Commons of England'. Thus twenty-two years after Danby's impeachment, the Commons persuaded the King and the Lords to concur in their resolution of 1679 that the King's pardon was no bar to an impeachment. The victory was tardy and unnecessary, for there existed no likelihood that an impeached minister would ever again rely on the King's pardon. More injurious to the prerogative was a clause declaring that judges could only be removed upon an address from both Houses of Parliament. While the main purport of the clause was to guarantee an independent judiciary, it also enhanced the weight of a parliamentary address. Justice Scroggs would not long have remained on the Bench had such a power resided in the two Houses of Parliament in 1680. Writing to Frederick I of Prussia concerning the eight clauses in the Act, Bonnet felt obliged to comment on their significance. 'If I may be allowed to add my own sentiments, as a disinterested person, I find that these limitations devolve power almost entirely on the people, or rather, on the leaders of the House of Commons.'[1]

This may have been true, but the champions of liberty in the House, especially the Country Tories, did not intend that their leaders exercise that power personally. They also added to the Act of Settlement a clause declaring that 'no person who has an office or place of profit under the King...shall be capable of serving as a member of the House of Commons'. The chief purpose of this provision was to prevent the King from destroying the independence of the House by corrupting its members with place, but the addition of this clause to the Act of Settlement also proves how little the House of Commons envisaged the growth of cabinet government. Such a self-denying ordinance would have prevented members of the House from becoming responsible ministers to the King, sitting in the House, answering the questions of the House, and defending royal policy before the House. The limitations on the Crown contained in the Act of Settlement were the product of extended deliberations, but this did not make them any less archaic. The Elizabethan flavour of the Privy Council clause, the irrelevancy of the clause against the pardon, and the anachronism of the self-denying ordinance, all betokened the constitutional battles of

[1] B.M. Add. MSS 30000 E, ff. 79–80.

yesteryear. They richly illustrate, in fact, the wisdom of Sir Lewis Namier's observation that 'in the earlier stages the growth of constitutional monarchy was impeded rather than aided by conscious political thought'.[1]

The Tories, albeit they added a bill of rights to the Act of Settlement, fully honoured in that Act their promise to settle the succession in the House of Hanover. The same cannot be said of their promise not to revive the quarrels which disrupted the previous Parliament, for the Tories would not cease attacking the Whigs. That they persisted in attacking them is the more puzzling because the Whigs no longer enjoyed office or influence. Yet the Tories had their reasons—the two chief being a fear that William would once again turn to the Whigs should war break out over the Spanish Succession and an uneasiness at their own weakness in Parliament and the country. The Tories, insecure in their tenure in office, wished to make it more secure by discrediting the Junto so completely that their re-employment would be unthinkable, alike to William, to Parliament, and to the country.[2]

Nothing demonstrated more clearly the unwillingness of the Tories to live at peace with the Whigs than their refusal to drop the affair of Captain Kidd. Captured in 1699, William Kidd was, at the behest of the House of Commons, examined before the Admiralty in April 1700, at which time he testified that his crew had forced him to turn pirate and that he had never seen Lord Somers in his life. Hearing of this Musgrave concluded, 'I suppose the examination of Kidd was not very strict.'[3] The parliamentary inquiry that this remark portended duly took place when the House of Commons assembled in 1701. On 27 March Captain Kidd appeared before the House; but to no purpose, for he refused to implicate in his

---

[1] Act of Settlement, printed in Trevelyan, *Blenheim*, p. 120; Sir Lewis Namier, 'Monarchy and the Party System', *Crossroads of Power* (1962), p. 213.

[2] Count Tallard wrote (Fr. Trans. 9/20 Feb. 1701), 'The Whigs proposed nothing less than to regain the office of Lord Chancellor for Lord Somers...and to remove the Earl of Rochester from the office of Lord Lieutenant of Ireland. The Anglicans promise that they will cut off the head of Lord Somers for having sealed the Partition Treaty without informing Parliament.' Later he wrote (22 March/2 Apr.), 'The two parties oppose each other because each wishes to govern during the war.' Both L'Hermitage (B.M. Add. MSS 17677WW, f. 201v) and Bonnet (B.M. Add. MSS 30000E, f. 113) agreed that the Tories wished to remove the Whigs from office forever by destroying their reputations with the King and country.

[3] *H.M.C. Portland*, IV, 1. Though the Commons asked that Kidd be examined before the Admiralty, they also asked that he not be tried, discharged, or pardoned until the next session (Cobbett, *Parl. Hist.* V, 1216).

piracy the lords who had commissioned him to destroy piracy. The Tories therefore sought to condemn as illegal the commission itself, which Montagu had drawn up and Somers sealed. But on the 28th the Commons, by 13 votes, defeated a motion declaring the commission to be illegal. 'So this matter', John Ellis wrote, 'is ended to the satisfaction of the Whigs, as we term them, and it is likely this day's work will take off the edge of many of the fierce men in the House, and abate of their intentions to prosecute and impeach, and consequently make the sessions shorter as well as calmer.'[1] But John Ellis did not take the true measure of Sir Edward Seymour. Hearing from a coffeeman, Kitsdale, that Captain Kidd had said in Newgate, 'He would hang for nobody, and was resolved to speak all he knew', Seymour had the captain brought before the House a second time, only to hear him refuse once again to accuse Halifax, Orford, Shrewsbury, or Somers. 'The fellow is a fool as well as a rogue', muttered Sir Edward. But still Seymour did not rest. Ten days later he wasted a whole day of the Commons' time inquiring into a rumour, which proved false, that Halifax and Somers had tampered with Kidd the morning before his second appearance in the House.[2] There the affair finally ended, an affair that is not without significance, for it reveals the fierce partisanship of the men who, in the same session, bitterly attacked the Junto lords for negotiating the two Partition Treaties.

That the Tories desired to use the Partition Treaties to blast the reputations of the Junto lords is incontrovertible, but this does not preclude the possibility that they had other motives for attacking the Treaties and those who made them. They may have objected to the matter contained in the Treaties and the manner in which they were negotiated.

The opposition of Tory England, and of nearly all England, to the Partition Treaties (which gave Naples, Sicily, and part of Tuscany to France) was genuine. Few Englishmen dared defend the second Partition Treaty when its provisions became public in the summer of 1700, and many Tories, once again led by Charles Davenant, loudly condemned it. Both Houses of Parliament in March 1701 voted that it was of 'ill consequence' to the peace of Europe. But

---

[1] B.M. Add. MSS 7074, f. 8v.
[2] *A Full Account...in Relation to Captain Kidd*, in *State Tracts, William III*, III, 231–56.

though Tory opposition to Partition was genuine, it was not notably reasonable, in fact it was downright contradictory. Tory publicists and politicians criticized the Treaty because it enhanced the power of France, yet they simultaneously advocated giving the entire Spanish monarchy to Louis XIV's grandson, the Duke of Anjou. They condemned the Treaty because it caused the King of Spain to draw up a will leaving all his realms to the Duke of Anjou, yet they urged William to accept the will and recognize the Duke. They objected to the Treaty because it augmented the power of France, yet favoured giving the whole Spanish monarchy to a French prince. The Tories truly hated the Treaty, but their quarrel was not so much with its provisions as with reality. Not the Treaty but the facts of international life forced the English to choose between a costly war and a more powerful France; neither William nor the Junto lords, but Louis XIV, imposed this choice on England. Indeed, William negotiated both Partition Treaties in order that a war-weary England might escape the choice, and his Whig ministers assented for the same reason. Faced with a deafening clamour for peace and low taxes, largely raised by the Tories, William and his ministers sought to avoid both war and the Duke of Anjou's succession to the whole Spanish monarchy by negotiating the Partition Treaties. For those who raised that clamour now to condemn that choice was either an act of opportunism or of irrationality. One is inclined to accuse Charles Davenant of the one and Jack Howe of the other.[1]

Far more Englishmen objected to the manner in which William negotiated the Treaties than to the substance of them; and there were good reasons for their objections, for William had negotiated the Treaties by himself, seeking only the advice of his Dutch counsellors, Dykveld, Heinsius, and Portland. He had asked the advice of his English counsellors only after the Treaties were made, and then he consulted only a few select counsellors, not the

---

[1] C. Davenant, 'An Essay upon the Balance of Power', *Works*, III, 346–60. Klopp, *Der Fall des Hauses Stuart*, VIII, 75–6, 219, 628; IX, 113–17, 192. Bonnet, B.M. Add. MSS 30000 E, ff. 44, 66–66 v, 90 v. William wrote to Heinsius in 1698 (Grimblot, *Letters of William III and Louis XIV*, I, 348) that 'there seems so great an aversion to war at present, that should France make any kind of plausible proposals of accommodation, and I should ask the opinion of Parliament respecting them, there is no doubt that they will be inclined to accept them, without considering much the security of them'. Vernon wrote to Portland in 1698 (Japikse, *Correspondentie*, II, 97), 'I think the time is past and will not come again very soon that the Parliament shall find fault with the Government for not entering into war with France.'

Privy Council, not even the Cabinet Council. There was nothing extraordinary in this. After the Revolution of 1688 politicians of every stripe had tacitly agreed to leave the conduct of foreign affairs to William. Secretaries of State became his clerks, but did not share in his secrets. William personally corresponded with the Emperor; William alone signed the Grand alliance of 1689; William alone renewed it in 1695. Neither Shrewsbury in 1696 nor Vernon in 1700 knew of the existence of the Grand Alliance of 1689. Foreign ambassadors in London dared not speak freely with the King's English ministers, for fear of betraying secrets those ministers should not know. It might be true that the King could do no wrong, but it was most assuredly false that he could do nothing, for in the conduct of foreign affairs he did nearly everything.[1]

With the publication of the second Partition Treaty all this came to an end. Both Houses conducted searching inquiries into the manner in which the two Treaties had been negotiated, inquiries which were not partisan, for the Whig Duke of Devonshire was as indignant as the Tory Earl of Nottingham; and members of the new ministry, like Pembroke and Jersey, were as deeply implicated as Somers and Halifax. The fruits of these inquiries were two addresses presented to the King demanding that in the future he consult English ministers, convene his Privy Council, and take the advice of Parliament before negotiating treaties and alliances. The Lords presented their address, asking that he heed the advice of the Privy Council, on 21 March; the Commons presented theirs, urging him to seek the advice of Parliament, on the 26th.[2] The inquiries and the addresses were not without effect. William took care to use English counsellors in negotiating a treaty with the Dutch and he asked Parliament's advice concerning the treaty.[3]

Had the affair of the Partition Treaties come to an end with these two addresses, one could argue that the chief motive of those who drove it on was to extend to the King's conduct of foreign affairs

---

[1] Klopp, *Der Fall des Hauses Stuart*, IV, 491–2, 529; VII, 28, 30, 117, 206; VIII, 17, 217, 220–5, 385, 431–2; IX, 94. William told Count Wratislaw in 1700 (*ibid.* IX, 110) that he could not entrust an Englishman with the secrets of foreign negotiations because it was a characteristic trait of Englishmen to tell their fellow countrymen all the secrets they knew.

[2] *L.J.* XVI, 628–9; *C.J.* XIII, 425–6. Originally the Lords intended to condemn as 'not agreeable to our Constitution' the manner in which the Treaty was negotiated, but then dropped the phrase (*H.M.C. H. of L. MSS*, n.s. IV, 220).

[3] Bonnet wrote (B.M. Add. MSS 30000E, f. 99), 'His Majesty's message asking the Commons' advice on the Treaty with the Netherlands has caused unhappiness among the malcontents there.'

those maxims of responsible government which already guided his conduct of domestic affairs. But these addresses did not mark the end of the affair: they marked the beginning of it.

The Tories in the House of Commons demonstrated a flagrant partisanship in their choice of men to impeach for negotiating the Partition Treaties. They introduced an impeachment against the Earl of Portland, who signed the second Treaty, but not against the Earl of Jersey, who also signed it, but found safety by deserting to the Tories. They promoted the impeachments of Halifax and Orford for assenting to the second Treaty, but not of Pembroke and Marlborough, who also assented to it. They demanded the impeachment of Somers for putting the Great Seal to a commission empowering plenipotentiaries to negotiate the first Treaty, but not against James Vernon, who prepared the commission, but found safety in being a civil servant rather than 'the life, the soul, and the spirit' of the Whig party. The conclusion is inescapable that Musgrave, Seymour, and Howe introduced these impeachments in order to destroy their political opponents, not to save Europe or the constitution. Because their partiality was so manifest, the problem how to persuade the House to vote the impeachments was all the greater.[1]

The strategy chosen to solve this problem was to begin with the least popular among the authors of Partition, the Earl of Portland, whom all Englishmen distrusted as a foreigner. The strategy was well advised, for Englishmen of every party viewed with anger and jealousy William's reliance upon Dutchmen in general, and Portland in particular. In 1692 both Houses of Parliament voted addresses requesting William to replace Dutch officers with English officers and entreating him never again to allow a foreigner to command Englishmen. In 1693 the House of Lords asked William to remove two Dutchmen, Colonel Goor and Mr Meesters, from the Ordnance. In 1696 the wrath of the English, or rather the Welsh, turned on the Earl of Portland. William had granted him, over the protests of thirty Welsh gentlemen, land in Denbigh worth £1,800 a year. When Parliament met the Welsh members expressed their intense displeasure, the Court party sat in silence, and no man said a word in defence of Portland. The House unanimously voted an address

[1] Bonnet wrote (B.M. Add. MSS 30000 E, f. 130v), 'Though the Earl of Jersey also signed the Treaty of Partition, as Secretary of State, no one has spoken of him, nor is it likely that anyone will, for he has made a secret composition.'

requesting the King to resume the lands which he had granted to Portland, and the entire House accompanied the Speaker to present the address to the King. There was little that William could do but yield to the will of the Commons; he revoked the grant. As Sir Edward Seymour said to Lord Galway, another foreigner in the service of the King, 'your misfortune is not to be bone of our bone and flesh of our flesh'.[1]

The decision to begin with Portland proved a wise one. When Simon Harcourt on 29 March accused him of high crimes and misdemeanours for negotiating the second Partition Treaty, the whole House, with the exception of a solitary Captain of the Guard, supported the impeachment—though not before the Speaker, Robert Harley, threw his weight behind it. Dropping the guise of moderation which he had worn until then, he endeavoured to win over those who deferred to his judgment. He began his speech by regretting that the matter of the Partition Treaties had arisen at all, but then declared that since it had, since the question was now before them whether those who had negotiated the Treaties were guilty, 'they would put the axe to the roots of their liberties if they failed to vote them guilty'. 'If this crime remained unpunished,' he said, 'one could date from this moment the destruction of English liberty.' Harley's dire warnings helped cement Portland's fate, but they failed to provoke Lord Somers's condemnation. The vote against Portland being taken, Jack Howe rose and urged that he who had sealed the Treaty was as guilty as he who had signed it, that Lord Somers was as criminal as the Earl of Portland. He then moved the impeachment of Lord Somers. But the respected Lord Chancellor, the able leader of the Whigs, the indubitably English counsellor, found many friends in the Commons, friends who reminded the House that Somers had advised against the Treaty as a Privy Councillor, and had only sealed it as Chancellor because it contained nothing illegal. His friends, joined by the Court dependants (to the anger of the Tories), proved numerous enough to secure his acquittal by 7 votes, 189 to 182. For the fifth time in two years the Commons voted their confidence in Lord Somers. But still his indefatigable enemies would not rest, and an indiscretion

[1] B.M. Add. MSS 34096, ff. 221–232 v. Luttrell, *Historical Relation*, II, 628, 639; III, 42. Japikse, *Correspondentie*, II, 64, 66. Klopp, *Der Fall des Hauses Stuart*, VII, 151–2. Bonnet, B.M. Add. MSS 30000 D, f. 364.

by the Earl of Portland gave them a sixth chance to impeach him, a chance which they did not neglect.[1]

Without friends in either House, Portland defended himself in the only way he could, by merging his individual responsibility in the collective responsibility of all. He told the Lords that he had agreed to negotiate the Treaty only after Vernon had written to him that Somers and the other ministers approved his doing so. The Commons pounced on this remark and demanded to see Vernon's letter, only to be told by Portland that he had burned his correspondence. Undeterred by this disappointment and determined to discover damaging evidence against Lord Somers, they demanded that Vernon turn over to them his correspondence with Portland. Vernon expressed a willingness to go to the Tower rather than deliver up the correspondence, but William, fearing a hostile address from the Commons, ordered him to deliver the letters to the House of Commons, which command he obediently performed. The Commons read the letters on 14 April and the enemies of Somers found there the damaging evidence they had searched for so long. Both Portland and the King, the letters revealed, had sought the advice of Cabinet Councillors concerning the wisdom of England's adhering to the first Partition Treaty, and Somers, Halifax, and Orford had failed to seize the opportunity to oppose it. They had merely written to William, who was then in Holland, that it was a delicate affair.[2]

Informed that the Commons might impeach him that very night, Somers followed the example of Buckingham and Arlington in 1674 —he hurried to the Lower House to defend himself. Standing bareheaded while the members of the House remained covered, Somers spoke modestly and eloquently for half an hour. His defence was not unlike Strafford's in 1641 and Clarendon's in 1668. As a Privy Councillor he had given his advice to the best of his ability and as a servant of the King he had obeyed a lawful command. He had advised against many particulars in the Treaty, as his letter to the

[1] Fr. Trans. 20 March/9 Apr. 1701; L'Hermitage, B.M. Add. MSS 17677WW, ff. 211–213v; Bonnet, B.M. Add. MSS 30000E, ff. 120–121v. Herr Hoffmann wrote (Klopp, *Der Fall des Hauses Stuart*, IX, 208), 'The fact that the Court dependants joined with the Whigs in this vote gave rise to a special meeting of the Tories, where it was said that the King named Tory ministers only for appearance sake, at heart he still had an understanding with the Whigs; but unless he broke from this party they would not vote him a farthing for the war.'

[2] Fr. Trans. 2/13 Apr. 1701; B.M. Add. MSS 17677WW, ff. 218, 225, 228; Bonnet, B.M. Add. MSS 30000E, ff. 138, 141–142; Klopp, *Der Fall des Hauses Stuart*, IX, 208–9.

King of 28 August 1698 (a copy of which he laid before the House) amply testified. Having failed to dissuade the King from entering into the Treaty, he had sealed it at his command, knowing that treaties depend upon the King and that this Treaty contained nothing against the laws of England.[1]

The modesty, candour, and substance of Lord Somers's speech swayed the House in his favour, as Robert Walpole, a new recruit to the House, later asserted. But the favourable impression which Somers made was allowed to fade. Somers spoke at eight in the evening to a House which had been sitting since ten in the morning; but despite their exhaustion a long, acrimonious debate ensued. It was nearly ten before Robert Harley, the Speaker, could put the question for an impeachment before the House, and by then most members had forgotten the eloquence of Lord Somers. Furthermore, Harley gave a malicious turn to the proceedings of the House, by framing the question in a manner highly disadvantageous to Somers. He did not propose the question: had Lord Somers advised the first Partition Treaty?—a question which might have led to Somers's acquittal. Instead he assumed the fact and asked only for a judgment at law. He put the question in these words: having advised the first Partition Treaty, by which great parts of Spain were surrendered to France, was Lord Somers guilty of a high crime and misdemeanour? Confronted with this question, 198 members of the House voted that he was guilty, 188 that he was not. The Tories followed up their victory by impeaching Halifax and Orford that same night, sitting until eleven. Though no one could charge the two lords with any crime more serious than knowing of the first Partition Treaty without opposing it, they impeached them by majorities of 40 and 50 respectively. The long campaign to prevent the Whigs returning to power by discrediting them in Parliament had finally issued, on the night of 14 April, in a decisive victory.[2]

One redoubt, however, remained to be captured: the House of Lords. Having voted impeachments against Portland, Somers, Halifax, and Orford, could the Commons prove before the Upper

---

[1] Cobbett, *Parl. Hist.* v, 1245–6; L'Hermitage, B.M. Add. MSS 17677WW, f. 229v; Bonnet, Add. MSS 30000E, ff. 142–142v.

[2] W. Coxe, *Memoirs of the Life and Administration of Sir Robert Walpole* (1798), I, 14; L'Hermitage, B.M. Add. MSS 17677WW, ff. 230–231v; Bonnet, B.M. Add. MSS 30000E, ff. 143v–144v. Somers did himself great harm, as Vernon observed (*Vernon Corr.* III, 145), by producing his own and the King's letter, for the King in his letter asked Somers to seal the Treaty if it appeared convenient to him.

House that these lords were guilty of high crimes and misdemeanours for negotiating and assenting to the Partition Treaties? The answer, which could hardly have escaped the notice of any politician in London, was 'probably not'. There were three good reasons for believing that the Commons could not successfully prosecute their impeachments: first, the House of Lords had already resolved in March that Somers had no choice but to seal the Partition Treaties, since the King possessed the right to make treaties; secondly, the Court and Whig peers enjoyed a majority in the Upper House; and thirdly, none of the impeached lords had violated the law of the land, for, though the Partition Treaties may have been imprudent, they were not unlawful. It is true that Somers had violated the formalities of his office when, without any warrant other than a letter from the King, he had put the Great Seal to a commission granting full powers to the negotiators of the first Partition Treaty. He also acted irregularly by sealing that commission though it contained blanks in which William was to write the names of the two plenipotentiaries. The Treaty itself also contained a blank page allowing for last-minute emendations. But most men knew that the need for speed and secrecy, not an intent to commit a crime, caused Somers to commit these irregularities. Knowledge of Somers's offences helped persuade members of the Commons to vote his impeachment, but these offences were not the stuff from which one made convincing articles of impeachment. The crimes which the House could charge against Halifax and Orford were even flimsier. In fact they had to revive the old charges of Halifax's exorbitant grants and Orford's naval accounts. Against Portland they had nothing. Considering these facts, it is not surprising that the Commons chose not to prosecute their impeachments before the House of Lords, but rather to address the King to remove these lords from his councils and presence forever.[1]

---

[1] Fr. Trans. 17/28 March 1701; Bonnet, B.M. Add. MSS 30000E, f. 94; Cobbett, *Parl. Hist.* v, 1266–8. L'Hermitage wrote at the time (18/29 Apr., B.M. Add. MSS 17677WW, ff. 234v–235), 'The committee which is charged with the task of drawing up articles of impeachment finds itself very embarrassed, not discovering in the two Partition Treaties any matter for their articles, so that it is said that they desire to have recourse to other subjects, which they will intermix with the former, and thereby embroil matters further; for they see clearly that the lords, being innocent, will have no difficulty absolving themselves. They have therefore resolved not to push for a judgment.' Poussin and Bonnet agreed that the Commons had no intention to prosecute their impeachments (Fr. Trans. 9/20 June 1701; B.M. Add. MSS 30000E, ff. 233–234).

On the very morning after the night that they had voted their impeachments, the House of Commons voted an address asking William to remove the four accused lords from his councils and presence for ever. By voting impeachments against the accused lords, the Tories in the House of Commons proclaimed their belief in the legal responsibility of ministers; by voting an address against them they announced their conversion to the doctrine that ministers are also politically responsible to the House of Commons. And the address was a political act, for the leaders of the House originally omitted Portland's name from it, he being of no political party. Only when a young member of the House advertised the omission did the managers of the House add Portland's name. Another member then proposed that Lord Jersey's name be added, for he was as guilty as Portland, but Sir Edward Seymour prevented this with a piquant sally: they ought assuredly to make it criminal for Lord Jersey to judge badly the modes of a beautiful peruke or a handsome attire, but they would do him an injustice to blame him for mistakes in affairs of state. The House added Portland's name to the address, but not Jersey's, and presented it to William on 23 April. William replied, 'you may depend upon it that I will employ none in my service but such as shall be thought most likely to improve...mutual trust and confidence between us...', an answer which the Countess of Rutland jubilantly interpreted to mean that William 'would employ none that was disagreeable' to the House of Commons, and would continue 'to adhere to the strongest party'. Bonnet, a shrewder judge, observed that the King's reply 'accorded all without according anything'. 'It seems', he continued, 'that His Majesty has resolved to confide in the Tories...but without entirely abandoning the Whigs. The Tories, who do not wish His Majesty to divide his confidence, are not wholly satisfied, and desire a more positive answer, one which will destroy all prospects of the future employment of the four lords.' For this reason the House of Commons, on 13 May, voted, by 134 to 111, to ask William to give 'a more effectual answer' to their earlier address, and by 'effectual' they meant the removal of the impeached lords from the Privy Council. William answered this second address with silence, for he had no wish to become the prisoner of the Tories by repudiating the Whigs, particularly at a time when the movement of public opinion in the country and the conduct of the lords in the Upper House offered him an opportunity to escape that servitude.[1]

It is doubtful whether the peers, even under the most favourable circumstances, would have looked with favour on the impeachments sent up by the Commons, but the Commons' action in addressing William to remove the four accused lords from his council and presence for ever made certain their hostility to the impeachments. The Lords regarded the address as a judgment before trial and as a palpable invasion of their right of judicature; and promptly sent William an address requesting him not to remove the impeached lords until they had been tried. Nor did they rest content with this action. They also sought to bring the impeached lords to an immediate trial. On 5 May, five weeks after the Commons had voted the impeachments, they asked the Commons for articles of impeachment against the accused lords. On receiving articles against Orford, Somers, and Halifax, they immediately sent back the replies of these lords. When the Commons continued to delay, they set a date for Orford's trial. When the Commons protested that they wished to proceed with Somers first, the Lords agreed, and set a day for his trial.

The Commons replied to all this prodding with protests and obstruction. They suddenly demanded a Committee of Both Houses to arrange the trials. They insisted that the four accused lords should not be judges in each other's case. And when Lord Haversham reminded the Commons that they themselves had set a precedent for guilty men judging each other's case by not accusing Vernon, Williamson, Jersey, Marlborough, and Pembroke, the Commons replied by demanding justice against Haversham. Seizing upon these disputes as pretexts for avoiding the trials which they feared, the Commons informed the Lords that they would not prosecute their impeachments until the peers granted them a Committee of Both Houses, promised that the four lords would not sit as judges in each other's case, and gave satisfaction for Haversham's scandalous remarks. Convinced of their right to regulate trials upon impeachments and determined that the accused should have swift justice, the Lords imperturbably proceeded to the trials. At their bidding Sir Christopher

---

[1] *C.J.* xiii, 492, 539; L'Hermitage, B.M. Add. MSS 17677WW, f. 233; Luttrell, *Historical Relation*, v, 42; *H.M.C. Rutland*, p. 167; Bonnet, B.M. Add. MSS 30000E, ff. 155–156v; *Vernon Corr.* iii, 145.

Wren prepared the scaffolding in Westminster Hall, with a commodious section for the foreign ambassadors. They then appointed 17 June for Lord Somers's trial. The ladies came with their fans, but the Commons did not come with their witnesses. Despite their absence, the President of the Court proceeded to the trial, even warning the peers to listen attentively to the witnesses, which caused the assembled peers to burst into laughter. But laughter or no, they went through the forms of a trial and finally resolved, by 56 to 31, that Lord Somers stood acquitted of his impeachment. On the 23rd they similarly acquitted Lord Orford; and the next day they declared that all peers whose impeachments had not been tried in the session in which voted stood acquitted. In resolving to impeach their Whig rivals, the Tories had failed to take into account the jealous determination of the Lords to protect their own members from frivolous impeachments.[1]

Against the King's stubborn silence and the Lords' firm resolve to see justice done, the Tories had only one weapon, to withhold supplies. 'The Lords have right on their side,' observed Bonnet, 'but the Commons force, for they hold the purse strings.' And a disgruntled member of Parliament told Poussin, the French ambassador, that 'even though Holland were harder pressed than it is, even though a French army were at the gates of London, the Commons would not vote one man or one shilling to the King unless he explained his intentions about the four lords'. These were brave but idle words. Exactly because the armies of Louis XIV pressed hard on Holland, exactly because the English feared the growth of French power, the Tories dared not oppose a vote of supply to the King. This was particularly true because the Whigs were busy in the country exploiting this fear of French power in order to regain their reputation.[2]

In January 1668 the Duke of Buckingham had decided that he and his friends should demand the election of a new Parliament if their power in the existing House of Commons proved insufficient

[1] *L.J.* xvi, 654, 667, 730–1, 735, 739, 755–6, 767–9; *C.J.* xiii, 600, 635; L'Hermitage, B.M. Add. MSS 17677WW, ff. 233, 295v; Bonnet, B.M. Add. MSS 30000E, ff. 276v–277v.

[2] Bonnet, B.M. Add. MSS 30000E, f. 152v; Fr. Trans. 15/26 and 19/30 May 1701. Poussin wrote on 19 May, 'The Commons persist to this hour in their resolution not to discuss the subsidy for 10,000 men promised to Holland until the King satisfies their demand concerning the four impeached lords.'

to force Charles to grant them preferment at Court. In February 1679 the Earl of Danby agreed to the dissolution of Parliament in the pathetic hope that an appeal to the country would save him. Now in 1701 the Whigs adopted the tactics of Buckingham and Danby: they appealed from the Parliament in Westminster to the electors of England. On 8 May the Grand Jury and Freeholders of Kent implored the House of Commons to vote His Majesty the money needed to assist his allies. A week later Defoe's *Legion's Memorial* appeared, branding addresses based 'upon bare surmises' as unlawful and castigating as illegal impeachments designed 'to blast the reputation of the persons [accused], without proving the fact'. Jack Howe received a letter from Gloucester ordering him to vote for war, or never be chosen again; other constituencies sent similar letters to their representatives. By a single vote the Whigs failed to persuade the Common Council of London to petition Parliament to end its divisions and to defend Europe. Elsewhere in the country they successfully promoted petitions for the dissolution of Parliament. Only the sudden prorogation of Parliament on 24 June prevented the House of Lords from likewise urging William to dissolve Parliament. By exploiting the growing clamour for war against France and by denouncing the dilatory preparations made to wage that war, the Whigs sought to re-establish their ascendancy in the country, in Parliament, and at Court.[1]

The Tories responded to this counter-attack in three ways: by redoubling their efforts to crush the Whigs, by posing as the champions of a war against France, and by setting their best pamphleteers to work justifying the impeachments that they had voted. Nothing seemed to abate the desire of the Tories to drive the Whigs from office and prevent their return. No man was too inconspicuous and no office too unimportant to escape their attention. They imprisoned or declared fugitive the five gentlemen who brought the petition from the Grand Jury of Kent. They accused Lord Stamford, Chancellor of the Duchy of Lancaster, of alienating forest lands, and they voted an address to the King requesting his removal. In order to drive from office those whom Lord Somers had appointed to the Commissions of Peace, they introduced a bill, rejected in the Lords, which would require justices of the peace to own land worth

---

[1] Cobbett, *Parl. Hist.* v, 1251–4; L'Hermitage, B.M. Add. MSS 17677 WW, f. 254; Klopp, *Der Fall des Hauses Stuart*, ix, 274.

£500. But though they continued their attacks on the Whigs, they sought at the same time to persuade the country that they, the Tories, were staunch enemies of France and enjoyed the King's confidence. To this end, Rochester, Godolphin, Abingdon, Seymour, Musgrave, and Harcourt met in secret conclave at Nottingham's house, where they proposed that William come to the House of Lords, pass the Bill of Succession, and publicly thank both Houses for supporting him in those alliances that were so necessary for the security of England and the preservation of the liberties of Europe. In response to this public approbation of their conduct, the Commons would vote an address promising to support His Majesty in those alliances which he thought fit to make with the Emperor and the States General. William obliged the Tories by executing his part; the Commons duly performed theirs. They also voted the supplies necessary to prepare for a war against France. The Whigs fumed at this royal approbation of their enemy's conduct, but the Tory members of the House, who feared (said the Whigs) being stoned to death on their return to their constituencies, heaved a sigh of relief.[1]

The Tories, once the Whigs had appealed to the electors of England against the majority in Parliament, had no alternative but to justify their conduct to the country. Harley himself wrote a pamphlet; Davenant (with Harley's assistance) wrote several; and Rochester commissioned others. But the pamphlet most prized by the Tories was Sir Humphrey Mackworth's *A Vindication of the Rights of the Commons of England*, published in August 1701. William Bromley wrote to Harley that it was 'our best written book and [written] with most pains'. Henry St John, though he thought its style and invention 'barren and dry', thought its argument splendid. 'It contains', he wrote to Sir William Trumbull, 'a great deal of plain truth, and exposes to the eyes of the people a just draught of our admirable constitution.' This may have been true, but it was a draught of the constitution borrowed almost entirely from the Exclusionist Whigs.[2]

Sir Humphrey Mackworth opened with a classic description of

---

[1] Cobbett, *Parl. Hist.* v. 1294–5; *L.J.* xvi, 757; Bonnet, B.M. Add. MSS 30000E, ff. 222v–223, 259v–261v, 278, 283v–284. Bonnet wrote concerning Stamford (f. 223), 'He holds his office of the Old Ministry, and therefore it is not surprising that the New Ministry seeks to destroy him.'

[2] Bromley to Harley, B.M. Loan 29/127; *H.M.C. Downshire*, I, 806.

the English government, a description as acceptable to the age of Coke as to the age of Blackstone. The powers of government were vested in the King, Lords, and Commons, and the good government of England depended on their harmony. In order to maintain this harmony the King possessed 'the power of appointing public officers at his will and pleasure', the Commons 'a power of impeaching them for any mismanagement and breach of trust', and the Lords 'the power of judging whether their actions are justifiable or not'. No Englishmen would have contested this view of the constitution, but Mackworth then skilfully turned the argument towards conclusions that robbed the King of his power to appoint 'public officers at his will and pleasure'. The King, he argued, can do no public act himself, for if any mismanagement occurred his subjects would have no remedy. Since nothing can be imputed to the King, all must be imputed to those officers who executed his commands and to those ministers who advised him in council. Nor could these officers and ministers plead the King's command, for that would throw the blame on the King. 'Whoever', wrote Mackworth, 'affirms that the King's command does justify the minister in doing an unlawful act maintains a proposition that destroys the original frame and constitution of the government.' And Mackworth held it unlawful to pass a grant which injured the public interest or to seal a treaty which had not been laid before Parliament.[1]

Not only were councillors responsible for the advice upon which the King acted, they were answerable to Parliament for the wisdom of that advice. In England, maintained Mackworth, the people are protected from misgovernment, 'because the Privy Councillors being upon oath, and being answerable to the Parliament, have reason to take care to give such advice as shall be advantageous for the public good'. And in great matters of state, as war and peace, and summoning and dissolving Parliament, the King must consult with his Privy Council. If the King refuses to heed the advice of his Privy Council, if he spurns the counsels of his ministers, if he orders them to execute unlawful commands, his councillors and

[1] Sir Humphrey Mackworth, *A Vindication of the Rights of the Commons of England* (1701), pp. 1–11. The Earl of Rochester went so far as to tell William that 'Princes must not only hear good advice, but must take it', which caused William, on Rochester's withdrawal, to stamp about the room repeating 'must, must, must', several times over (Dartmouth's note in Burnet, *History*, IV, 506).

ministers have only one recourse: to resign. A councillor, Mackworth insisted, should 'argue and plead hard to convince his Prince of the unlawfulness of an action', but if the Prince nevertheless persists in it the councillor must either resign or risk impeachment. Should the councillor choose to risk impeachment, he could not count on the protection of the King's pardon, for the King's high prerogative of pardoning offenders cannot defeat the power of impeachment, 'which is appointed as a check upon the prerogative itself, and is the great bulwark of the rights and liberties of the people against an evil ministry and arbitrary power'.[1]

Mackworth did not regard the power of impeachment as the sole bulwark against arbitrary power: equally important was the right of the Commons of England to vote addresses against evil ministers.

What had become of this nation in former reigns, when evil ministers had almost ruined the King and Kingdom by secret intrigues and private counsels, if the Commons of England had not had a power to censure them upon even Common Fame? How often had England been undone, if it had been necessary to make the proofs public before the Commons impeached evil ministers, or made any Address to the King to remove them from his council and presence?...If evil ministers are to be continued till such proofs can be regularly produced, upon trial of an impeachment, the nation in that time may be ruined and undone.

As if frightened by the arbitrary power he assigned to the House of Commons, Mackworth hastily added that no man can suffer injustice from the Commons, for they 'are a branch of the legislative authority, representative of all the people, guardians of their liberties, and patriots of their country, and...it is not to be imagined that a majority of so numerous a body of gentlemen can be influenced against reason and justice'. Though he began with the classic picture of a balanced constitution, and throughout celebrated the separation of powers, Mackworth ended by pleading the infallibility of the House of Commons.[2] Sir Humphrey Mackworth's *Vindication of the Rights of the Commons of England* was not an isolated statement of the Tory view of the constitution. Other writers repeated his arguments or went beyond them. Robert Harley, in *A Justification of the Proceedings of the House of Commons*, urged that all matters cognizable in the Privy Council should be transacted there and should be signed by the councillors. Charles Davenant in *Parliamentary*

---

[1] Mackworth, *Vindication*, pp. 8–15, 18.   [2] *Ibid.* p. 30.

The Tory Conversion to Responsible Government

Authorities cited innumerable precedents from the reign of Richard II to prove that the Commons possessed the right to address the King to remove persons of ill fame and to refuse supplies until he did remove them. The author of *The Ballad*, an answer to Defoe's *Legion's Memorial*, insisted that the King's removing men who were impeached was not an execution before judgment since it entailed no fine or imprisonment, the sentences which followed judgments upon impeachments. James Drake added that to suppose any man accused by the House of Commons to be innocent, before a trial showed him to be so, was an affront to the honour of the House. James Drake also argued, in his *History of the Last Parliament*, that the King acts not upon 'his own wisdom alone', but upon that of his ministers, who, 'if they advise, they are answerable with their heads for the damage the nation may suffer by their advice; if they do not advise, they ought to resign their places'. And if they will neither give good advice nor resign, the King should, upon the representation of the House of Commons, remove them.[1]

The Whigs read these pamphlets with amazement and could not restrain a cry that the Tories had embraced their principles. The author of *The Dangers of Europe* even concluded that the union of both parties in 'Whiggish principles' had destroyed 'the very notion of Toryism'. But not all the Whigs relished these popular doctrines. The Court Whigs denounced these Tory pamphleteers for embracing a popular government that destroyed the ancient English balance of government.

Have they not destroyed our very constitution, [wrote Lord Somers in *Jura Populi Anglicani*] and made our government plainly popular?...Is it not a popular government, and a very intolerable one, where they have usurped the power of the King and Lords, and broken in upon the rights of the people, by taking the execution and legislation upon themselves and punishing contrary to law? Have they not assumed the power of the King, both executive and legislative, when they are grown to that exorbitancy of power that they expect he will do whatever they require of him, though it be to punish some, who have long toiled in support of his government, and turn out others from places of public trust, who have appeared with a warmth and extraordinary zeal in his and their country's service?

---

[1] [R. Harley], *A Justification of the Proceedings of the House of Commons* (1701), p. 13; C. Davenant, *Parliamentary Authorities* (1701), pp. 1–2; *The Ballad...With the Memorial, alias Legion, replied to Paragraph by Paragraph* (1701), p. 33; [J. Drake], *The History of the Last Parliament* (1702), pp. 162, 188.

Jonathan Swift, who in 1701 applied his great talents to the Whig cause, agreed wholeheartedly with Somers. In *A Discourse of the Contests and Dissensions Between the Nobles and the Commons in Athens and Rome*, he praised the ideal of a balanced government (which he denied to be a Gothic invention) and accused the Tories of destroying that balance of government in England, in order to establish a *dominatio plebis*. The author of *The Candidates Try'd* put the case more directly when he remarked that 'there's nothing more to be dreaded than a popular assembly taking upon itself an Executive as well as a Legislative power'.[1]

The Country Whigs, led by John Toland, replied to the Tories in a very different manner. They accepted and echoed the principles of Mackworth and Davenant, but turned them against Tory ministers like Rochester. In his *Art of Government by Partys*, Toland preached the duty of ministers to resign 'if the King should go about to put them on any indirect measures', and asserted the right of the House of Commons to choose the King's ministers. 'If therefore our future Kings either want the mind or the ability to choose the fittest persons into their ministry to serve the nation, the Parliament will be obliged to recommend such as shall be answerable to the public for their actions.' The anonymous author of *The Duke of Anjou's Succession Further Considered* agreed that 'our legislators ought in all reason to be thought the most proper judges as to persons duly qualified to administer' the realm. The same refrain occurred in *The Dangers of Europe*, whose author observed, ''Twas never reckoned any diminution to the Prerogative of the English Crown for our Princes to ask and take the advice of their Privy Council in the disposal of public offices; much less ought it to be accounted such, when they take the advice of the Great Council of the Nation.' The same author strongly urged on ministers of state the duty of resignation if their advice were refused. 'It is evident', he wrote, 'that ministers of state and Privy Councillors in England ought not only to be so honest as not to concur with those that give ill advice to their prince,

---

[1] *The Dangers of Europe from the Growing Power of France* (1701), p. 356; [Lord Somers], 'Jura Populi Anglicani', in *State Tracts, William III*, III, 261; Jonathan Swift, *A Discourse of the Contests and Dissensions Between the Nobles and the Commons in Athens and Rome*, in *State Tracts, William III*, III, 222; *The Candidates Try'd* (1701), p. 4. The Whig author of *Some Queries* (1701), p. 1, demanded of the Tories, 'By what law the executive power of government has been transferred' to the House of Commons; and the author of *A Letter from Some Electors* (1701), p. 21, observed, ''Tis the business of the legislative power to make rules and laws and of the executive to apply those rules or laws to particular cases.'

but likewise to have so much fortitude and self-denial, as to quit any post whatever in the prince's service, rather than be obliged to concur in anything that may be to the dishonour and disadvantage of the Crown or Country.' The Country Whigs dared to urge these doctrines, which the Tories so recently embraced, because they anticipated the imminent dissolution of Parliament and an appeal to the people. The difficult choice, whether by dissolving Parliament to allow such an appeal, rested on William alone.[1]

Neither the Whigs nor the Tories knew what decision William would ultimately reach, for he had preserved a sphinx-like silence and a studied impartiality throughout the spring of 1701. He had prudently kept out of the violent quarrels between the two Houses and had patiently allowed events to force Parliament to support the policies he favoured. The immediate purpose of William's silence and impartiality was to encourage both parties to support the alliances which he had negotiated with the Dutch and the Emperor; but the ultimate purpose was to avoid becoming the prisoner of either party. William sought now, as he had throughout his reign, to keep an even balance between the two parties, so that he might tip the scales as he wished. In order to maintain that balance, William in 1701 looked with equal favour on both Whigs and Tories. He gave a favourable answer to the Tory's address against the four impeached lords, but refused to dismiss them from the Privy Council. He tolerated Tory delays in supporting the alliances he had made, but told them flatly he would count no man his friend who opposed supporting those alliances. He remained silent while the Tories sought to take £100,000 from the Civil List, but secured from them a Supply Bill placing 3s. on the pound. Upon the Earl of Tankerville's death in June, he named three Tories as Commissioners of the Privy Seal, but refused a Tory demand to purge the government of those Whigs still remaining in it. When proroguing Parliament he praised the work of the Tory House of Commons, but at the same time he graciously received the four impeached lords at Court. With the patience of Job and the delicacy of a trimmer, he steered safely through the furious party quarrels of the spring of 1701.[2]

[1] John Toland, *The Art of Governing by Parties* (1701), pp. 102–10; *The Duke of Anjou's Succession Further Considered*, in *State Tracts, William III*, III, p. 55; *The Dangers of Europe*, in *State Tracts, William III*, III, 351.

[2] Bonnet, B.M. Add. MSS 30000E, ff. 147, 155, 176, 203, 259v, 266, 297–299; Klopp, *Der Fall des Hauses Stuart*, IX, 164, 274–6.

Upon the question whether to dissolve Parliament William brought the same habits of procrastination and trimming. Not until 11 November did he finally resolve upon a dissolution, and then only after much hesitation. Three events appear to have tipped the balance in favour of a dissolution: Sunderland, whose advice he sought, informed him plainly that the Whigs were his friends and that the Tories could never be; public opinion, angered by Louis XIV's recognition of the Pretender as James III of England, swung around fully for war; and the Tories refused to give up their designs to drive the Whigs permanently from public office. Of these events the last carried the greatest weight. Had the Tories agreed to live peacefully with the Whigs and not to revive their impeachments, William would probably have kept his Tory ministers and the existing Parliament. But their demand for a monopoly of his counsels and a proscription of the Whigs continued unabated. In June the leaders of the Tory party told Bonnet that they would grant no subsidy in the next Parliament unless the House of Lords gave the House of Commons satisfaction concerning the impeached lords. In August Sunderland wrote to William that the Tories would be satisfied with nothing less than the ruin of Lord Somers. Hoffmann discovered in October that the Tories intended to renew their quarrel with the House of Lords, and would hold back supplies until given satisfaction. When William arrived back in England early in November he asked the leaders of the Tory party whether they would agree to an amnesty for the impeached lords when Parliament assembled. They refused to agree to such an amnesty. William therefore dissolved Parliament. But he had no intention of throwing himself into the hands of the Whigs, who demanded a monopoly of his counsels as imperiously as did the Tories. He therefore refused to dismiss the Tory ministers before the elections, fearing that their dismissal would lead to a decisive Whig victory. Stubbornly, determinedly, silently, he pursued the dream which he had cherished all his reign, the dream of governing England with a mixed ministry of talented men, supported by a Parliament of loyal men.[1]

The politicians did not help him realize his dream. Lord Somers agreed to write for William a speech to be delivered at the opening

[1] Bonnet, B.M. Add. MSS 30000E, ff. 291, 381–382v, 392v–393; Hardwicke, *State Papers*, II, 445; Klopp, *Der Fall des Hauses Stuart*, IX, 422, 498.

of the new Parliament, but he refused to accept office unless the King's other ministers approved of his appointment, a condition which angered William, for he knew they would never approve.[1] Godolphin, though reputed to be a politique, likewise acted in a manner that precluded government by a mixed ministry. He resigned the moment he heard that William had dissolved Parliament. At the Admiralty the Tory Rooke refused to sit with the Whig Haversham, so William removed Haversham. Despite these rebuffs, William persevered in his scheme. He replaced Godolphin with the Earl of Carlisle, a man identified with no party. The Sunday before the new Parliament met he dismissed Secretary Hedges from office for refusing to promise to vote for the Court candidate for Speaker, and replaced him with the more pliant Earl of Manchester. Three weeks later, on 25 January, he dismissed the Earl of Rochester, the highest of the High Tories and a declared enemy of mixed ministries. He named the Duke of Somerset, a peer of sturdy independence, Lord President of the Council in Pembroke's place, moving Pembroke to the Admiralty. That Manchester was a Whig and Pembroke a Tory meant much less than the fact that they were moderate, tractable, and loyal. By skill and persistence William finally secured at the very end of his reign a ministry composed of men more zealous for the public good than for party. He achieved this success, however, only because the electors of England returned a Parliament evenly divided between both parties and purged of the worst extremists among the Tories.

In December 1701 the electors of England expressed their distaste at the violent conduct of the more extreme Tories by refusing to elect Davenant, Howe, Hammond, and Musgrave to Parliament; but the high hopes of the Whigs for a great victory at the polls were disappointed. When the critical vote for the Speakership came, their candidate, Sir Thomas Littleton, though supported by the Court, could not prevail against Robert Harley, whom the House re-elected Speaker. But neither could the Tories take satisfaction in the composition of the new Parliament, for Harley won re-election by only 4 votes; and the party lacked 14 votes when it sought to revive the

---

[1] W. M. Torrens, *History of Cabinets* (1894), I, 35. Sunderland advised William to dismiss his Tory ministers, to place Somers at the head of affairs, and to follow his advice in forming a ministry (Hardwicke, *State Papers*, II, 446). And Somers advised the King (*ibid.* p. 455) that 'to set himself and his people at ease, he must trust those whom the body of the people do not distrust'. He should quit the Tories and 'depend upon the affections of the Whigs'.

impeachments of the Junto lords. This day, 26 February 1702, was one of those climactic moments in the history of the Commons, when the fate of parties are determined by a packed House sitting late into the night. The order of the day was a debate on the privileges of the House, which augured the revival of their quarrel with the Lords over the four impeached lords. Four hundred and fifty-six members, more than had ever before attended the House, were present; even the sick were carried in. They met without recess from noon until nine in the evening. A young member from Wootton Basset, Henry St John, later to become Viscount Bolingbroke, moved the question which occasioned the debate: resolved, 'that the House of Commons had not right done them in the matter of the impeachments in the last Parliament'. The Whigs opposed the motion with spirit, reminding the House that there were at least five other persons as guilty as the Junto lords, whom they had not accused, and suggested that they would do better to impeach those ministers who had advised the King to recognize the Duke of Anjou last spring. Since the debate occurred in committee, Robert Harley could speak. In his characteristically soft, gentle voice he defended St John's violent resolution, only to hear a Whig member, imitating his voice perfectly, publicly ridicule him, to the merriment of half the House. Because justice and the public good, as well as superior wit, lay on the Whig side, they persuaded the House to reject the proposal by 235 to 221. Thus the Whigs and moderates defeated a measure closer to the hearts of the Tory leaders than any other measure. Had they carried the day, wrote L'Hermitage, they would have introduced attainders against the Junto lords and attached them to the Supply Bill in order to force William to accept them. Their embittered plan failed, and left William free to govern England during the last weeks of his life with a ministry of his own choice. Because the parties were evenly balanced in Parliament, William could rely upon the 80 or 90 Court dependants in the House to carry on his business there. In the last month of his reign William seems to have won the independence which he had always desired.[1]

---

[1] L'Hermitage, B.M. Add. MSS 17677XX, ff. 210, 234–238v; Klopp, *Der Fall des Hauses Stuart*, IX, 497, 503–5. The third Earl of Shaftesbury wrote of this debate (Forster, *Original Letters*, p. 174), 'Mr Harley betrayed his passions and showed that private animosity and revenge prevailed over all other obligations (I am sorry to say it) and even over the assurances he gave to us his friends, to the King, and I believe also to many of you abroad, who have heard of his engagement to lay aside all resentment and let the matter of last year sleep.'

Yet his triumph was ephemeral. The violence of party, momentarily quelled, would soon revive and make a Cabinet of moderate men impossible. Nor could the King fall back on his prerogative powers, for they were much abated. William had stubbornly fought to maintain his prerogative powers intact throughout his reign, but during the last four years he had seen them substantially reduced. The most apparent diminution, but the least important, was the Act of Settlement, which limited his Hanoverian successors' right to seek counsel in secret, to grant pardons to impeached ministers, to win men by places, and to remove judges at pleasure. Far more serious was the conversion of the Tory party to Whiggish principles, for now there was no party dedicated to the defence of the prerogative and devoted to the sovereign who possessed it. Rochester, Nottingham, Seymour, and Harley in 1701 behaved no differently from Shaftesbury, Salisbury, Russell, and Winnington in 1679; and Mackworth and Davenant propagated the very principles advocated by Sir William Jones in 1681. Men of both parties openly used their power in Parliament to force the King to give them office, thereby severely circumscribing the King's right to choose his own servants. Who should win preferment became the central political issue of the day. As the author of *The Claims of the People of England Essayed* observed in 1701, 'The royal prerogative of place-giving has been the occasion of all the jealousies between the King and people that I can remember.'[1]

Bishop Burnet saw and declaimed against the encroachment of parties on the King's right to name his own ministers. In the year 1708, looking back over the reign of William III, he wrote, 'One of the most detestable and the foolishest maxims, with relation to our government, is to keep up parties and a rivalry among them; to shift and change ministers, and to go from one party to another, as they can be brought in their turns to offer the Prince more money, or to give him more authority.' Burnet believed that William had freely chosen to pursue this maxim of government, but Speaker Onslow saw that necessity not choice drove him 'to shift and change ministers, and to go from one party to another'. 'He did it', wrote Onslow, 'from necessity, not from maxims of policy. I am persuaded such were his times, that without it he could not have carried on his

---

[1] *The Claims of the People of England Essayed in a Letter from the Country*, in *State Tracts, William III*, III, 6.

government or held his Crown. His Parliaments forced him into it...'[1]

But the most serious check to the King's power, and the clearest victory for responsible government, came in the sphere of foreign affairs. At the Revolution men tacitly agreed to leave the conduct of foreign affairs, the formation of alliances, and the conclusion of treaties to William. In domestic affairs Parliament demanded to be informed, inquired into all mismanagements, and punished those ministers of state found at fault. Into the conduct of foreign affairs they made no inquiries and held no minister of state responsible: this sphere of government they left to the King alone. After the impeachment of the four Junto lords the King lost his ability to answer for the conduct of foreign affairs. The House of Commons, to be sure, failed to prosecute their impeachments successfully before the House of Lords, but they won their main point: the King could no longer act in foreign affairs without the intervention of an English minister or the advice of English councillors. No longer could a Cabinet Councillor say (as Devonshire said) that he possessed less knowledge of the contents of a treaty than a porter in the street. No longer would a plenipotentiary sign a treaty before the ministers at home had deliberated upon it. No longer would the ministers at home deliberate upon it without considering how Parliament would receive it. And the ministers knew, as Marlborough in the Hague negotiating the Grand Alliance knew, that Parliament would hold them accountable for negotiating a treaty injurious to the realm. The impeachments of the Junto lords arose out of party passion, proceeded along an arbitrary course, and came to no good end, but none the less they took from the King the last important sphere of action in which he could act personally and bear responsibility for his own decisions. After 1701 ministers of state served the King in the conduct of foreign affairs and bore responsibility for the legality and the wisdom of his decisions. The passionate resentment of the Tories against the Whigs may have had other consequences, but there is no denying that its principal effect was to deprive the monarch of the last significant field of action in which he could act without the intervention of a responsible minister.

These changes prompted the author of *Anglia Libera* to write in 1701, 'But at length by an insensible progress...power fell into the

---

[1] Burnet, *History*, VI, 219.

scale of the Commons, where it seems to be now wholly fixed, and according to which the government is in a manner new modelled (yet by unobserved degrees), though the ancient names and customs generally continue still the same. *Arcanum novi status, imago antiqui,* says Tacitus: "The secret of setting up a new government is to retain the image of the old."[1]

[1] *Anglia Libera* (1701), p. 19.

CHAPTER 9

POLITICAL PARTIES AND RESPONSIBLE GOVERNMENT (1702–1714)

'A coach may as well be driven with unequal wheels', wrote Henry St John in September 1701, 'as our Government be carried on with such a mixture of hands.'[1] The mixture of hands to which he adverted was the presence of a remnant of Whigs in a predominantly Tory government, and the principle of government which he recommended was government by a single party. The young, mercurial St John, the future Viscount Bolingbroke, knew the facts of political life better than most Englishmen, but he did not voice their sentiments about political parties. Most Englishmen abominated political parties and believed it wrong to base governments upon them. As Marlborough said to Count Wratislaw, while accompanying him to Kensington Palace to visit the dying King, 'Believe me, the Princess will never as Queen rely upon one of the two parties, but will, if she finds it impossible to gain the services of both parties, employ those persons who show the greatest inclination for her and the kingdom.'[2] Marlborough, not St John, justly expressed the sentiments of the nation, the hopes of men of affairs, and the intentions of the Queen.

Above all he expressed the intentions of the Queen, who, though personally inclined to the Tories, had no wish to become their prisoner, or the prisoner of any other party. 'I shall always wish', she told Parliament in May 1702, 'that no difference of opinion among those that are equally affected to my service may be the occasion of heats and animosities among themselves.'[3] It was a prudent wish, for nothing could more swiftly limit her prerogative to choose her own servants than party passion, nothing more surely circumscribe her freedom of choice than the refusal of members of one party to serve with those of another. Throughout her reign Queen Anne struggled to govern with balanced counsels, to employ moderate men from all parties, but every experiment foundered on

---

[1] *H.M.C. Downshire*, I, part 2, 807.
[2] Klopp, *Der Fall des Hauses Stuart*, IX, 483.   [3] *C.J.* XVII, 150.

the shoals of party passion. On three occasions, in 1702, again in 1705, and yet again in 1710, she embarked on experiments in mixed ministries, only to see each experiment collapse before the jealous demand of one party that the other be proscribed. By refusing to serve in cabinets with their enemies or by resigning when the Queen employed those whom they hated or by using their power in Parliament to drive their opponents from office, Whig and Tory politician alike destroyed the Queen's hopeful schemes to govern her realm by a mixed, not a party, ministry.

Queen Anne's first government, formed in 1702, was an alliance of administrators, courtiers, and Tory politicians. The presence in the government of experienced administrators like Marlborough and Godolphin assured Englishmen that the Queen's affairs would be well managed; the presence of courtiers like Pembroke, Somerset, and Devonshire assured them that they would be conducted with moderation; and the presence of Tory politicians of every specie, whether adherents of Rochester or friends of Nottingham or allies of Harley, assured them that the Queen's business would not miscarry in Parliament. Though predominantly a Tory, it was none the less a mixed ministry, with Marlbourugh and Godolphin at the centre of it. In the parliamentary elections of 1702 the electorate, aware that the Queen favoured the Tories, returned a House of Commons largely in sympathy with the new ministry. The wonder is therefore all the greater that this ministry collapsed before the life of the Parliament had run its course.[1]

Equally astonishing is the fact that the thirst of the Tories for office, not the desperation of the Whigs at being denied it, brought down this composite administration.[2] Tory members of the House of Commons would not temper their anger at or forget their quarrels with the Whigs. The first act of the House was to vote, by 189 to 81, 'that right has not been done the Commons' in the matter of the

---

[1] Professor Walcott has written the best analysis of the composition of this ministry and of the Parliament elected in 1702 (*English Politics in the Early Eighteenth Century*, pp. 97–110).

[2] Admittedly, there was little the Whigs could do to bring down the government, having little influence at Court and no majority in the Commons. But one Whig, the Duke of Devonshire, did protest the proscription of Whigs by threatening to resign. He refused to continue as Lord High Steward in the new ministry unless Lord Wharton should continue as Comptroller of the Household. Queen Anne, however, refused to tolerate Lord Wharton's presence at Court, and Marlborough, through the good offices of Count Wratislaw and the Duke of Somerset, finally persuaded Devonshire to continue in office even though Wharton was dismissed (Klopp, *Der Fall des Hauses Stuart*, x, 38).

four impeached lords. Their next act was to address the Queen to remove the Bishop of Worcester from the office of Lord Almoner to Her Majesty. The Bishop had opposed a Tory candidate for Parliament from the county of Worcester, saying of him that he 'had all the vices of the males of his family without the virtues of the females'. For this crime the Commons requested his dismissal. The Lords promptly asked the Queen not to dismiss him until he had been heard in his defence. The Queen replied, 'I agree that every peer and lord of Parliament, and indeed every other person, ought to have an opportunity of being heard to any matters objected against him, before being punished...but I look upon it as my undoubted right to continue or displace any servant attending upon my own person, when I shall think proper.' And she thought it proper to dismiss the Bishop of Worcester that very day, 21 November. In a rage, the Duke of Devonshire and the Duke of Somerset offered their resignations, but the Queen refused to accept them, and the two Dukes continued in her service.[1]

The removal of the Bishop of Worcester was a mere squall. The main storm struck those ministers and officials who had managed the kingdom's treasury in the preceding reign. Partly to discredit the Whigs and partly to vindicate their own claim that the public debt arose from past mismanagement of the revenue, the Country Tories, in March 1702, appointed a new Commission for Taking the Public Accounts. They elected four Harleyites, two Nottinghamites, and an adherent of Sir Edward Seymour to the Commission, which duly reported its observations to the House in October 1702.[2] The Commons seized upon them avidly, finding in them proof that the Earl of Ranelagh, as Paymaster General, had misapplied public money, and that the Lord Halifax, as Auditor of the Exchequer, had not, as required by law, examined the vouchers for paying annuities every three months or transmitted the imprest roll to the King's remembrancers every six months. Ranelagh sought safety in resignation, but resignation did not save him from expulsion from the House, where he had long proved a useful friend to Lord Godolphin. Because Lord Halifax stood firm, the Commons asked the Queen to order the Attorney General to prosecute him for his

---

[1] *C.J.* xiv, 12, 37; *L.J.* xvii, 168, 169; W. Nicolson, 'Diary', *Transactions of the Cumberland and Westmorland Antiquarian and Archaeological Society*, n.s. ii (1902), p. 188; Klopp, *Der Fall des Hauses Stuart*, ix, 220.

[2] Walcott, *English Politics in the Early Eighteenth Century*, p. 101.

crimes. The Queen, despite an address from the House of Lords clearing Halifax of all fault, ordered the prosecution. The next year, in 1704, the Commons censured Lord Orford for neglecting to make up his accounts properly when Treasurer of the Navy, again requested that the Attorney-General bring Halifax to trial, and asked the Queen to bring similar prosecutions against Philip Papillon, Cashier of the Victualling Office, against two Commissioners of Prizes, John Parkhurst and John Paschall, and against Lord Ranelagh. None of these prosecutions came to anything. Halifax, it is true, came to trial in June 1704, but when the Court of Exchequer ruled in favour of the defendant in a disputed point of law, the Attorney-General entered a *nolle prosequi*. This provoked the 'wild faction in the House' (to use Harley's phrase) to demand in November 1704 the retrial of Halifax and the impeachment of William Cowper and Sir Joseph Jekyll for daring to serve as his counsel; but Harley, now dedicated to moderation, persuaded the House to drop the whole matter. The only tangible result of the high expectations raised by the examination of the public accounts was the replacement of Lord Ranelagh with Jack Howe and Sir Stephen Fox as Paymasters General.[1]

The truth now became apparent that parliamentary addresses and commissions of accounts were not the weapons for driving the Whigs from the Court, the Council, the Treasury, Commissions of Peace, and borough corporations. Far more effective for this purpose were threats of resignation and bills against Occasional Conformity. The Earl of Rochester, Lord Lieutenant of Ireland and the leader of the High-flying Tories in Parliament, saw this as early as February 1703. Uneasy at Marlborough's ascendancy at Court and vexed that not he but Godolphin was Lord Treasurer, Rochester persistently obstructed the government's work, even demanding the removal of men he disliked from the Treasury. Godolphin replied that he would rather resign than remove persons upon whom he could rely. Apprised of Rochester's obstructive conduct, Marlborough urged the Queen to remove him. The Queen softened the blow: she merely ordered her uncle to Ireland, to attend to his duties as Lord Lieutenant. But Rochester, unmindful of his father's precept that a minister should serve even though his advice were

---

[1] *C.J.* XIV, 70, 140, 143, 170–1, 369, 376, 388, 428; *L.J.* XVII, 270–1; Luttrell, *Historical Relation*, v, 438–9, 488; *H.M.C. Portland*, II, 188.

spurned, preferred resignation to service in a ministry he could not dominate. He told the Queen that he would rather give up his office than the leadership of his party in Parliament.[1]

The Earl of Nottingham, a High Churchman and Secretary of State, made the same choice in April 1704, when the Queen refused to expel his enemies from the Cabinet. These enemies, among them Somerset and Devonshire, had secured the defeat in the House of Lords of the Occasional Conformity Bill, the favourite device of the High Church party for depriving dissenters of office and all hope of office. At the same time the Lords obliquely censured Nottingham by taking into their own hands an investigation into a Jacobite plot in Scotland, an investigation which the Secretary of State ought to have undertaken. Angered by these affronts and unconsoled by a vote of confidence in his conduct from the Commons, he told the Queen that she must dismiss Somerset and Devonshire from the Cabinet Council or he would resign. But Anne did not dismiss Somerset and Devonshire; instead she removed from office Lord Jersey and Sir Edward Seymour, two close friends of Nottingham. The next day the Earl resigned as Secretary of State.[2] Though celebrated in his age as a zealous defender of the prerogative, Nottingham in 1704 placed party above prerogative.

The predominantly Tory ministry which began the Queen's reign now gave way to a Triumvirate, a ministry composed of the Duke of Marlborough (as Lord General), the Earl of Godolphin (as Lord Treasurer), and Robert Harley (as Secretary of State). The Triumvirate demonstrated its undoubted abilities that summer by preparing, financing, and conducting the campaign that ended in the Battle of Blenheim, but there still hung over its head the question whether it could find the support it needed in Parliament. The Court party in Parliament was, as Godolphin confessed to Harley, small; and the moderate Tories, or Sneakers, as the true gentlemen of England called them, had no majority. The ministry feared an attack that autumn by the High-flying Tories, supported by the Junto Whigs. The Tory attack came in November, when Lord Haversham,

---

[1] Klopp, *Der Fall des Hauses Stuart*, x, 235–6.

[2] *Ibid.* xi, 32–3, 38–9. Robert Harley wrote to Edward Harley on 22 April (B.M. Loan, 29/70), 'Thursday Lord Nottingham brought the Seals to the Queen, told her he could not serve her with that Cabinet &c. She persuaded him to carry them back. This day at one o'clock he has finally delivered them; the manner of it can never be justified, if he had had reason.'

seconded by Nottingham and Rochester, denounced the Act of Security in Scotland as a bill designed to exclude the House of Hanover, and urged the Lords to censure Lord Godolphin for advising the Queen to accept it (though he had no proof that Godolphin had given such advice). Lord Halifax, for the Whigs, began to join in the attack, when Lord Wharton, after consulting first with Lord Godolphin and then with Somers, joined with Somers to caution Halifax. Thereafter Halifax spoke in a milder strain, and the Whigs went on to defend as necessary the Queen's approval of the Act of Security. The attack upon Godolphin in the Lords failed; so also did a similar attack upon him in the Commons in December. In both instances the Whig party parried the stroke which the High Church party directed against Godolphin. They also helped defeat an attempt to tack to the Supply Bill a Bill against Occasional Conformity. But their reward for these services to the government proved meagre. When in March the Triumvirate drove the Duke of Buckingham and other notorious 'tackers' from office, they replaced them, not with Junto Whigs, but with moderate Whigs like the Duke of Newcastle. The Triumvirate had no desire to desert the system of balancing parties for an unwelcome reliance upon one party.[1]

The ministry formed in the spring of 1705, resting on moderate Whigs rather than High Tories, represents the second major attempt by the Queen to govern with mixed hands. It too failed in the end; but in the spring of 1705 Harley and Godolphin and Marlborough still cherished the hope that the careful management of a loyal Parliament would preserve the ministry. Their hopes centred on the election that spring of a House of Commons in which neither party had a majority. Superficially they won the victory they desired, for the 100 or more servants of the Queen held the balance between 190 Tories and 160 Whigs.[2] But in fact, as the Imperial envoy, Hoffmann, saw, this victory was no victory at all. 'The Court', he wrote, 'guides itself according to the maxim, *divide et impera*: it would hold the balance between the two parties, in order to decide as it wishes in any given instance. But experience proves that he who

---

[1] *H.M.C. Portland*, IV, 75, 118, 146–9. Burnet, *History*, V, 179. L'Hermitage, B.M. Add. MSS 17677ZZ, ff. 531v–532, 571–572; AAA, ff. 210–213, 271. Patricia Ansell ('Harley's Parliamentary Management', *Bulletin of the Institute of Historical Research*, XXXIV, 92–7) has shown that Harley's careful management of Parliament helped defeat the Tack in 1704.

[2] *H.M.C. Portland*, IV, 291; Walcott, *English Politics in the Early Eighteenth Century*, pp. 114–16.

would work with both parties can rely upon neither.'[1] Godolphin and Harley, for all their balancing schemes, knew this as well as Hoffmann. They must choose to go with the Whigs or the Tories.

With the Tories, however, they could not go, for the Tories promptly priced themselves out of the market by countenancing a violent pamphlet by Dr James Drake, entitled *The Memorial of the Church of England*. In his pamphlet Dr Drake defended party government, urged the employment of Churchmen only, demanded the proscription of Whigs and 'neuters', justified those who had resigned because their advice was refused, and called on all true Englishmen to oppose the present ministry.[2] The ministry therefore turned to the Whigs, whose price, though modest, was unpalatable enough, especially to the Queen. They demanded the election of John Smith as Speaker and the appointment of William Cowper as Lord Keeper. Queen Anne saw at once the danger of replacing the High Church-man Sir Nathan Wright with Cowper. 'I wish very much', she wrote to Godolphin, 'that there may be a moderate Tory found for this employment. For I must own to you that I dread falling into the hands of either party, and the Whigs have had so many favours shown to them of late that I fear a very few more will put me insensibly into their power.'[3] But the Whigs remained obdurate: unless the Queen named Cowper Lord Keeper and the Queen's servants supported Smith for Speaker, they would not support the government against the anticipated Tory attack. The Court gave way. Godolphin in July instructed the Queen's servants to support Smith and the Queen in October named Cowper Lord Keeper.[4]

The outraged Tories attacked the ministry in December. In the House of Lords Rochester, Nottingham, and Buckingham charged that the present administration endangered the Church, for it had approved the Act of Security, had failed to invite Princess Sophia to

[1] Klopp, *Der Fall des Hauses Stuart*, xii, 19.
[2] *The Memorial of the Church of England* (1705), pp. 4–7, 23–6, 56.
[3] Winston Churchill, *Marlborough* (1947), ii, 31.
[4] Addressing thirty principal officers of the Crown at the Chancellor of the Exchequer's, Godolphin said that 'there was a party that nothing would satisfy but wresting the administration out of the Queen's hands, with the Tackers; that he thought in such a conjuncture they could not do the Queen or their country better service than in choosing Mr Smith for their Speaker'. He added 'that it might be objected that he [Mr Smith] was of the Whig party, but assured them that he found those under that character, though under no obligation to this government, yet to have been hearty friends to it and for supporting Her Majesty's administration' (Mr Eyles to the Earl of Portland, 2 July 1705, Portland Papers, University of Nottingham).

England, and had opposed the Occasional Conformity Bill. Rochester cleared the Queen from all suspicion, even maintaining that they must suppose the ministers to have composed her speeches. The same problem of separating the Queen from her administration emerged in the Commons, where Harley urged that it had once been declared criminal to distinguish between Her Majesty's person and government. But Mr Ward refused to allow the Secretary to screen himself behind the Queen, insisting that ministers were accountable for the acts of the sovereign. The debates in both Houses revealed how well the Tories had learned the rhetoric of responsible government and how willing any minister was to use the Queen's name to ward off censure. The debates also revealed the strength of the government in both Houses. By 61 to 30 in the Lords and by 212 to 162 in the Commons the two Houses resolved that whosoever declared that the Church is in danger under her Majesty's administration was an enemy to the Queen, the Church, and the kingdom.[1]

In this same session of Parliament the Court and the Whigs used their strength in both Houses to remove two major obstacles to the growth of responsible government in England: the clause in the Act of Settlement requiring Privy Councillors to put their hand to advice given the monarch and the clause forbidding placemen to sit in the Commons. The one clause would make Cabinet government unworkable by destroying that secrecy of counsel necessary to any form of government; the other clause, by excluding ministers of the Crown from the House of Commons, would make necessary the emergence of an executive separate from it. Yet it must not be thought that these considerations explain why the Court and the Whigs joined to repeal these clauses in January and February 1706. Their motives were more practical, just as the occasion for repeal was more fortuitous than the logic of history ought to allow.

The story begins with the attempt of the Tories to embarrass the Court by proposing to invite Princess Sophia to England, alleging that her visit would guarantee the Hanoverian Succession. The Court replied by introducing a Regency Bill into the House of Lords, a Bill which would provide for the swift accession of the House of Hanover on the Queen's death. When this Bill reached the House of Commons on 12 January, Mr Freeman observed that by

[1] Abel Boyer, *History of the Reign of Queen Anne digested into Annals* (1703–11), IV, 203–4; Anonymous Parliamentary Diary, C.U.L. Add. MSS 7093, f. 22; *C.J.* xv, 58; *L.J.* xviii, 43.

the Act of Settlement no placeman was to sit in the House of Commons after the Queen's death, but by this Bill the existing Parliament, placemen and all, should continue for six months. Not only did he see this anomaly; he also observed that the Regency Bill did not require, as did the Act of Settlement, that the councillors who were to govern on the Queen's death should sign their advice. Except for Sir Richard Onslow, who found the obligation of councillors to sign their advice most objectionable, as exposing men to faction, the House paid no attention to this question. They focused their attention instead on a proposed amendment to the Regency Bill which would explain further the clause in the Act of Settlement forbidding placemen to sit in the Commons. The amendment, finally driven through the House by a coalition of Tories and Old Whigs on 24 January, provided that on the death of the Queen all but forty-seven placemen should be excluded from the House. Among the forty-seven who were permitted to remain in the House were the Treasurer of the Household, the Chancellor of the Exchequer, the two Secretaries of State, the Attorney-General, the Secretary at War, five commissioners of the Treasury, five commissioners of the Admiralty, and ten Privy Councillors. Clearly the intent of the clause was to prevent the Crown from corrupting the House, not to preclude Commoners from serving the Queen.[1]

To the Whig and Court peers in the Upper House the exclusion of all but forty-seven of the Queen's servants from the House of Commons was intolerable. On 31 January they rejected the Commons' amendment. They then seized upon the occasion to make some constitutional changes of their own, changes which the Junto Whigs particularly had desired to make ever since the passage of the Act of Settlement. By 68 to 25, the peers added to the Regency Bill amendments which repealed those clauses in the Act of Settlement that declared that no officer should sit in Parliament after the Queen's death and that required all Privy Councillors to put their hands to their advice. The Court peers and the Junto peers joined their forces to secure this victory. But then no one really defended the requirement that Privy Councillors sign their advice, it being found, as L'Hermitage observed, 'too delicate a matter in this country to

---

[1] Anonymous Parliamentary Diary, C.U.L. Add. MSS 7093, ff. 72–73; Luttrell, *Historical Relation*, VI, 5, 8–9; L'Hermitage, B.M. Add. MSS 17677 BBB, ff. 49–50, 57, 81. Harley, Walpole, and St John opposed adding the amendment to the Regency Bill (Anonymous Parliamentary Diary, ff. 78, 82–83).

assume responsibility for one's opinions by signing them'. Bishop Burnet reached the same conclusion as L'Hermitage, writing that 'it was visible that no man would be a Privy Councillor on those terms'. An immediate regard for their own safety, not a prophetic vision of the future development of the English constitution, led politicians of all parties to join to repeal this impracticable requirement. When the House of Commons received the amended Regency Bill on 4 February, they accepted the repeal of the Privy Council clause without a division. Unanimously and silently the representatives of the English nation acknowledged the usefulness of cabinet secrecy and the legitimacy of Cabinet Councils.[1]

No such unanimity greeted the Lords' amendment repealing the clause in the Act of Settlement which prohibited placemen from sitting in the Commons. The High Churchmen in the Commons, joined by many Whigs, denounced the Lords' action, arguing that it would allow a wicked prince to fill the House with his corrupt creatures. By a vote of 205 to 183 the House refused to accept the Lords' amendment. There followed two weeks of conferences, compromises, and political bargaining. While the Lords declared in a formal conference that the exclusion of placemen was incompatible with the nature of the English government, a few peers met privately with some leaders of the Commons (whom Godolphin called 'the heads of the Whimsicals') to work out a compromise. The peers proposed that at the conclusion of the present Parliament, Commissioners of Wine Licences, Governors of Plantations, Commissioners of the Navy in Out Ports, as also all pensioners, should be excluded from the House of Commons; they also proposed that members of the Commons who accepted any other office from the Crown should offer themselves for re-election. Satisfied by these concessions, the Whimsicals returned to the government fold and voted with the Court to accept the Lords' amendment repealing the clause in the Act of Settlement that would exclude all servants of the Crown from the Commons upon the accession of the House of Hanover. The vote was 220 to 197.[2] Throughout the crisis the

---

[1] *L.J.* xviii, 83–4; *C.J.* xv, 127; Burnet, *History*, v, 234; L'Hermitage, B.M. Add. MSS 17677BBB, ff. 81v, 88. L'Hermitage does mention (f. 87v) that the Tory peers, when debating the Regency Bill on the 31st of January, insisted that the House ought not to discuss the clause touching the signatures of Privy Councillors; but others replied that it was proper to repeal the clause now, in order to put everything into the best order possible.

[2] Boyer, *History of Queen Anne*, IV, 222; *C.J.* xv, 127; *L.J.* xviii, 94–6; Luttrell, *Historical Relation*, vi, 13, 16–18; *Bulletin of the Institute of Historical Research*, xiv, no. 40, pp. 29–33.

independent Whigs (presumably those whom Godolphin called the Whimsicals) held the balance, and though they voted with the Church party in early February and the Junto Whigs in late February, their position remained unchanged: to admit to the House ministers of state who could inform the House of the Queen's affairs, but to exclude those pensioners and placemen who could only impair its independence. Unlike John Pym in 1641, the Whigs in 1705 wanted no self-denying ordinance which would keep their leaders from office. They merely wanted a Place Bill which would lessen the power of the Court to corrupt the House of Commons.[1]

And well they might, for the struggle for responsible government in the reign of Queen Anne had become a battle between party and patronage, or rather between the Crown's use of patronage to seduce men from party and the party's use of Parliament to appropriate to themselves the power of patronage. The fate of George Clark in 1705 offers an instructive example of both. In October Prince George, the Queen's husband and Lord High Admiral, ordered Clark, who was Secretary of the Admiralty, to vote for John Smith as Speaker. Clark replied that he had a high esteem for Smith, but that Smith was of a different party. Clark thereupon placed party above office and voted for Bromley, not Smith, to be Speaker. Two days later Prince George dismissed him from office, but it would be hard to say whether his dismissal was a triumph for the Court or for the Whigs, for patronage or for party, since Clark suffered as much for not being a Whig as for not being a courtier. An event which occurred a month later suggested that perhaps the Whigs,

Godolphin wrote to Harley at this time (B.M. Loan 29/64), 'I have had this morning an account of a long, tedious meeting between the heads of the Whimsicals and some Lords of our House. The sum of it was that they would agree to the method proposed by the Lords provided they might exclude several offices besides the prize office; the Lords told them they might exclude negatively whatever they would in the next reign. This obliged them to take off their mask and they fairly told them, that was doing nothing at all, and they should be laughed at; in short, after much wrangling they agreed to some additional heads to those I mentioned last night, none very material, but some very foolish.'

[1] In the remaining years of Queen Anne's reign the Country members in the Commons made three further attempts to prohibit placemen from sitting in their midst. In 1710, 1711, and 1712 they persuaded the House to pass Place Bills, which were duly sent to the House of Lords. The Lords summarily rejected all of them. During the debates on the Place Bill of 1710 Robert Harley, now bereft of office, spoke in favour of the Bill, only to be silenced by Mr Dolben's story of the King of Beasts, who, having lost his tail, thereupon used all his rhetoric to persuade the other beasts to cut off theirs, but could prevail with none but a few monkeys and jackanapes (*Wentworth Papers*, p. 106). Once again in office after the summer of 1710, Harley opposed the Place Bills of 1711 and 1712.

and not the Court, held the upper hand. In December the Whigs discovered that many Court Tories, though voting with them in general matters, opposed them in divisions on disputed election returns. They immediately complained to Godolphin, who gave them only honeyed words; so they sat silent the next time the High-flyers attacked the Lord Treasurer in the House. Their silence had the result they wished. In the next division on a disputed election return the Court Tories voted with the Whigs. The compliance of both Houses with Court measures may have been, as Evelyn observed, greater than had been known for many years, but this compliance was purchased at a steep price.[1]

The ministry of the Triumvirate could only last as long as the coalition between the Queen's servants and the Whigs lasted, and the Whigs threatened to destroy that coalition by constantly raising the price of it. In the summer of 1706 they demanded the dismissal of Sir Charles Hedges, a Tory, as Secretary of State and the appointment of the second Earl of Sunderland, a Whig, in his place. Queen Anne balked at paying the price. She wrote to Godolphin that such a change were to throw herself into the hands of a party and to Marlborough that such a surrender would make her but Queen in name, not in reality. The Queen spoke truly, for by embracing one party she would become 'but their slave'. However, there was no alternative. Without Whig support the government could not carry the Act of Union or win (as Marlborough wrote to her) the 'five million for carrying on the war'. And without Sunderland's appointment they could not count upon Whig support. Marlborough and Godolphin, perceiving this, even threatened to resign if the Queen did not name Sunderland Secretary of State in place of Hedges. Sadly, despairingly, despondently, the Queen gave way, dismissed Hedges, and appointed Sunderland. 'During the autumn and early winter of 1706,' observes G. M. Trevelyan, 'the Queen lost the decisive battle in the war that she waged all through her reign for the independence of the Crown in the choice of its ministers.'[2]

One member of the Triumvirate, Robert Harley, believed that the Queen need not lose the freedom to choose her own ministers,

---

[1] L'Hermitage, B.M. Add. MSS 17677AAA, ff. 497, 502; Klopp, *Der Fall des Hause Stuart*, xii, 18–19; Evelyn, *Diary*, 2 Dec. 1705.

[2] William Coxe, *Memoirs of the Duke of Marlborough* (1893), ii, 3; Churchill, *Marlborough*, ii, 205, 209; G. M. Trevelyan, *Ramillies and the Union with Scotland* (1932), p. 167.

that she could name whomever she wished to serve her and then win support for them in Parliament by uniting into one body all men who placed loyalty to the Crown above party allegiance. 'I dread the thought', he wrote to Godolphin, 'of running from the extreme of one faction to another, which is the natural consequence of party tyranny, and renders the government like a door which turns both ways to let in each party as it grows triumphant.'[1] To escape the tyranny of party by relying on the Queen's friends was the heart of the scheme which, at the Queen's bidding, Harley pursued in the autumn of 1707. The scheme failed, and failed because Godolphin and Marlborough did not believe that the government could manage Parliament without forming an alliance with either the Whigs or the Tories; which meant in effect with the Whigs, for a Tory alliance meant moving the main theatre of the war from the Low Countries to Spain, a strategy wholly unacceptable to Godolphin and Marlborough. But the most remarkable fact about Harley's scheme, and the ministerial crisis to which it led, was not the loyalty of Godolphin and Marlborough to the Whigs, but the steadfastness of the Queen to Robert Harley. Neither the threatened resignations of Marlborough and Godolphin in February 1708 nor the refusal of the Cabinet to conduct business in their absence caused her to desert the Secretary. She capitulated only when Harley told her that he could not form a government to carry on her business. And he was forced to tell her this because the moderate Tories had given him little help in managing the House of Commons that winter and because the moderate Whigs refused to enter the scheme. The result was his enforced resignation, followed at once by those of his friends, Sir Simon Harcourt, Henry St John, and Thomas Mansell. Marlborough would have liked to have kept Harcourt, St John, and Mansell in the administration to counter-balance the Junto Whigs, but these three men, as James Brydges observed, regarded Harley's dismissal 'as a full declaration of the ministry's intention to join entirely with the Whigs' and as inconsistent with the assurances frequently 'given to the Tories that no such thing should be done'.

---

[1] Churchill, *Marlborough*, II, 294. Where Harley dreaded running from one extreme to another, Godolphin dreaded being left defenceless in Parliament. On an earlier occasion, when Harley's friends supported an opponent of Godolphin in a disputed election return, Godolphin wrote to Harley (B.M. Loan 29/64), 'It is the sole business of an inveterate party in both Houses to tear me to pieces, and 'tis the business of all my most particular friends to take every occasion of disobliging those who are unwilling to protect me.'

Party zeal on both sides made impossible government by mixed hands.[1]

The Whigs gained by the fall of Harley and his friends. Henry Boyle and Robert Walpole, both Newcastle Whigs, replaced Harley and St John as Secretary of State and Secretary at War. The Earl of Cholmondeley, a Whig, took Mansell's place as Comptroller of the Household and Halifax's brother, Sir James Montagu, over the loud protests of the Queen, succeeded Harcourt as Attorney General. Yet the Whigs were still not satisfied; their appetite merely grew with eating. In April Devonshire and Newcastle carried to the Queen a Whig demand that she name Lord Somers President of the Council. The Queen refused the demand, and seized upon the occasion to declare the principle that guided her in the choice of ministers: she would favour none who opposed her in Parliament, but would countenance any who served her there.[2] It was the same principle that the Marquis of Newcastle had urged on Charles II: reward your friends, do not seek to buy off your enemies. Unfortunately for the Queen it did not work, for there was no necessity to reward those who were already loyal, but there was a great necessity to buy off those who could do her mischief. In fact the Queen had no choice but to employ those whose services were indispensable to her, and there were few better ways to prove one's indispensability in the early eighteenth century than by opposing the government when out of office.

The Junto Whigs—Somers, Halifax, Orford, Wharton, Sunderland, and their allies in both Houses—were not blind to this truth, and acted according to its dictates in 1707 and 1708. Forgetting for the moment the deep principles that divided them from the 'Tackers', they joined with them to attack the government for losses at sea and defeats in Spain. In the Lords they launched, with the support of Rochester and Nottingham, a violent attack on the Admiralty for

[1] Godfrey Davies, 'The Fall of Harley in 1708', *E.H.R.* LXVI, 246–54; Burnet, *History*, v, 341–5; 'Lord Coningsby's Account of the State of Political Parties', *Archaeologia*, XXXVIII, 709; Japikse, *Correspondentie*, 2nd ser. II, 567; Brydges Papers, Huntington Library S.T. 57, II, f. 18.

[2] Churchill, *Marlborough*, II, 322. James Brydges wrote to Cadogan, 24 Dec. 1707 (Huntington Library S.T. 57, II, f. 7), Her Majesty has 'given Mr Secretary Harley, as my Lord Treasurer has the Attorney General and others, authority to say that she is for the future firmly resolved to govern upon such principles as will incline her to side with the violence neither of Whig nor Tory; that she will never make bargains with either party to persuade them to do that which a sense of their duty alone ought to lead them to, but that those shall always be the object of her countenance and favour, who, without expecting terms, come voluntarily into the promoting of her service'.

failing to protect English shipping. In the Commons they also sought to censure the Admiralty for negligence. At the same time they joined with the Tories to vote an address asking Her Majesty why there were insufficient men at the Battle of Almanza. Since the port of London alone had lost 1,100 merchant ships during the war and since only 8,660 of the 29,395 men voted for the war in Spain were present at Almanza, the Junto Whigs had genuine grievances to exploit. But their real desire was not to redress grievances, it was to win office. The Junto Whigs, wrote James Brydges, 'when they found their representations and importunities with the ministry would not prevail...attempted to force themselves into it, and entered into a conjunction in both Houses with the hottest Tories'.[1] The attack on the Admiralty came to nought because the Newcastle Whigs refused to join it and because the Tories, fearing that it was only a scheme for replacing Admiral George Churchill with Lord Orford, deserted it. The attack on the government for the want of men at Almanza, led by the Tories, tolerated by the Harleyites, and supported by the Country Whigs, likewise failed, for the Junto Whigs, appeased by Harley's dismissal, rallied behind the government in late February, dragging many Country Whigs with them. By 55 votes they secured the defeat of a motion in the Commons to censure the government for having insufficient men at the Battle of Almanza; they then secured an address thanking Her Majesty for the care she had taken in the management of the war in Spain. Having raised enough mischief to prove that they had a capacity for doing harm, the Junto Whigs now came to the government's support in order to prove that they had an equal capacity for doing good.[2]

The General Election of 1708 considerably enhanced the power of the Whigs to do both good and ill. 'The elections are now in a great measure over,' a good Whig wrote to the Earl of Manchester in May, 'with a considerable alteration, in the main for the better, so that we already call it a Whig Parliament. When the bustle is passed, 'tis thought the old attack will be renewed to obtain Lord

[1] Huntington Library S.T. 57, II, f. 6.
[2] Klopp, *Der Fall des Hauses Stuart*, XIII, 28–9; L'Hermitage, B.M. Add. MSS 17677 CCC, ff. 322v–323v; *C.J.* xv, 569. Of this debate on the want of men at Almanza, Joseph Addison wrote (*H.M.C. Rep. VIII, App. II*, p. 95), 'We look upon the debate... as that which has fixed all men in their proper parties, and thoroughly established the present ministry.'

Somers and Sir James Montagu for President of the Council and Attorney-General, both which have been very hard pressed and long depending.'[1] The hard-pressed Queen in early October yielded so far as to name Montagu Attorney-General, but held out against naming Somers President of the Council, regarding his appointment as utterly destructive of her prerogative. The Whigs, she wrote to Marlborough in August, were 'designing to tear that little prerogative the Crown has to pieces' and to 'have none in employment that does not entirely depend upon them', in short, she concluded, either 'I shall submit to the five tyrannizing lords, or they to me'.[2] The history of the next year of her reign was the story of her unhappy submission to the five tyrannizing lords. Upon the death of Prince George, whose resignation the Junto lords had long sought, the Earl of Pembroke became Lord High Admiral, resigning his office of President of the Council to Lord Somers and his post as Lord Lieutenant of Ireland to Lord Wharton. A year later the Queen, again yielding to Whig demands, named Lord Orford to head the Admiralty in Pembroke's place. The Triumvirate ministry of 1705, a ministry of mixed hands, had become by 1709 a Whig ministry, based solidly on the strength of the Whig party in Parliament.

Marlborough and Godolphin, who would hardly treat Lord Somers with common civility, urged these appointments on the Queen most unwillingly. But they saw the clear necessity for them, and their calculations proved correct. In 1709 the Whigs defeated, by 231 to 97, a Tory motion to censure Godolphin for laxness in collecting the land tax; in 1710 they expressed their confidence in Marlborough by voting, by 182 to 101, to thank the Queen for employing him as a general and ambassador; in both sessions Parliament voted the money needed to carry on the war.[3] Distasteful as party government was to them, they preferred it to a Parliament that would obstruct the war effort abroad.

[1] S. Edwin to Manchester, P.R.O. 30/15, Box 7, no. 695, xvii.

[2] Coxe, *Marlborough*, II, 292.

[3] *C.J.* XVI, 126, 394; Klopp, *Der Fall des Hauses Stuart*, XIII, 207, 379. Robert Walpole wrote to James Brydges (Huntington Library S.T. 57, V, f. 124) of the address expressing confidence in Marlborough, 'Sir G. Heathcote moved for an address to hasten the Duke of Marlborough to be assisting at the negotiations for the peace that are now renewing. Mr Annesley, Bromley, etc., fired at this motion and treated it as if the Duke had been or were to be laid aside...Lord Marlborough's friends came zealously into the motion, among the rest your humble servant took his part very freely; upon the division yeas 184, noes 101. In short, 'twas a pitched battle, and I think the best day's work I have seen in a good while.'

Robert Harley, now in opposition, reached a different conclusion. He viewed with dismay the triumph of the five tyrannizing lords and their party. Not loss of office alone, but sympathy for the Queen, drove him to this opinion. 'Do they not', he confided to a memorandum in April 1708, 'tear everyone from her who would treat her like a Queen or obey her?...It is now complained of that the Queen presumes to argue with her ministers...The power of the Crown ought to protect against the violence of men or party; now the power of the Crown is given to a party to destroy others.'[1] Harley's private reflections (like Strafford's seventy years before) contained many unpalatable truths which the fictions of responsible government and the language of the Court served to conceal. The Whig party had torn from the Queen those who would obey her; Godolphin and Marlborough had resented the Queen's opposition to policies they regarded as necessary; and the Whigs had used the power of the Crown (particularly the power of patronage) to destroy other men. From this tyranny of party Robert Harley resolved to rescue the Queen, a resolve which was as honourable as his reflections on the political scene were honest. The only problem was how to accomplish the task, how to use the power of the Crown 'to protect against the violence of men or party'. In 1708 Harley had possessed the unreserved support of the Crown and had failed. How could he now succeed?

The strategy which Harley finally adopted proved paradoxical: create a party for the Queen in Parliament—rescue the Queen from party by giving her a party. The reverse side of the coin was to weaken—by dividing—the party in Parliament which would tyrannize over her. Unite the Queen's friends and divide her enemies became Harley's strategy, and the political history of the year 1710 testifies to its brilliance, and to the author's supreme tactical skill in carrying it out. But the political history of the next three years of the Queen's reign illustrates the danger inherent in the strategy: what should the Queen do if her friends proved not to be her friends, if her party proved not to be her party?

In January 1710 a deep fissure appeared in the Junto ministry. Godolphin and Somers refused to join Marlborough and Sunderland in demanding Mrs Masham's dismissal from the Bedchamber. The demand originated with Marlborough, who had grown tired of

[1] B.M. Loan 29/10, no. 22.

serving a Queen who acted on the advice of an irresponsible coun-sellor. As early as 1708 he had written to the Queen his opinion that 'to continue in your Council to advise, without credit enough to prevail with you to follow good advice, would only expose myself and my reputation in the world, by making myself answerable for other people's follies, or worse'.[1] The folly that finally provoked Marlborough to demand that either he or Mrs Masham go was the Queen's decision to give the command of a regiment to Colonel Hill, Mrs Masham's brother. For Marlborough the question was far greater than Hill's incompetence: it was the question of the Queen's persistent reliance on Mrs Masham's rather than his counsels. For that reason he threatened to resign unless the Queen dismiss her favourite. Sunderland supported him unreservedly, even promoting (allegedly against Marlborough's wishes) a parlia-mentary address for Mrs Masham's removal. Henry Mordaunt was prepared to urge the Commons to vote no supplies unless she were dismissed. But the Whigs deserted Marlborough, though he had long served them as an intercessor with the Queen. At a meeting held in late January, Godolphin and Somers spoke heatedly against a proposal that 'all the great officers' should, 'as Sir Simon Har-court and Sir Thomas Mansell did when Harley and St John were turned out', resign with Marlborough.[2] The assembled Whigs rejected the proposal; and Marlborough backed down, agreeing to continue in the Queen's service even though Mrs Masham continued at Court. The House of Commons voted no address against Mrs Masham, the moderate Whigs not wishing to dictate to the Queen whom she should employ in her Bedchamber. 'By this neglect to take action,' writes Sir Winston Churchill, 'not only the Whigs but Godolphin settled their own speedy downfall.'[3]

The failure in January to drive Mrs Masham from Court was the first step in the fall of the Junto ministry. The second step was Shrewsbury's appointment as Lord Chamberlain in April; the third was Sunderland's dismissal in June; the fourth was Godolphin's dismissal in August. The beauty of Harley's tactics lay in the gradual movement from the more moderate to the more extreme measure,

---

[1] Coxe, *Marlborough*, II, 293.
[2] J. Cartwright (ed.), *The Wentworth Papers* (1883), pp. 103–4, 108.
[3] Churchill, *Marlborough*, II, 665; J. H. Plumb, *Sir Robert Walpole* (1956, 1960), I, 152 n. Hoff-mann wrote (Klopp, *Der Fall des Hauses Stuart*, XIII, 376), 'In the Commons many were for an Address, but the moderates held back. In the Lords Godolphin hindered a similar proposal.'

from the more acceptable to the least acceptable alteration at Court, from the partial change to the total change. But these tactics would not have worked had not Harley enjoyed three indispensable advantages: the Queen was his, the Whigs were divided, and the electorate favoured his cause. All of these advantages, the Queen's confidence, the division of the Whigs, and the country's support, were requisite for success, not any one of them, or two, but all three.

The appointment of the Duke of Shrewsbury as Lord Chamberlain illustrates this truth. Distrusted by the Whigs for his conduct in the Sacheverell trial and for his intrigues with Harley, he won office only because Harley could persuade the Queen to employ him at Court and admit him to the Cabinet. And he remained in office only because the disunited Whigs failed to protest against an appointment made without their knowledge or consent and because the Queen prorogued Parliament a few days before the appointment, thus preventing an explosion there. The moment the news of the appointment was out the jubilant Tories (as well as the downcast Godolphin and the observant Hoffmann) concluded that a new Parliament was inevitable. In fact the Whigs dared not protest too vigorously against the appointment for fear that their protest would cause the Queen to dissolve the present Parliament, thereby leaving them a Samson shorn of his locks.[1]

Godolphin and Marlborough could not in good conscience protest against Shrewsbury's appointment, for they had previously urged the Queen to give him office. But they could, and Marlborough did, protest vehemently against Sunderland's dismissal in June. For Marlborough, Sunderland's dismissal was the decisive event. 'If the Whigs', he wrote to his wife, 'suffer Lord Sunderland to be removed, I think, in a very short time, everything will be confusion.' And Marlborough had a ready prescription for avoiding this confusion. 'Of all things', he wrote, 'the Whigs must be sure to be of one mind, and then all things, sooner or later, must come right.' To their cost the Whigs were not of one mind. James Brydges did hear that the most considerable Whigs in the Commons had 'resolved to lay down the minute my Lord Sunderland is out', but none did. When the Queen took the seals from Sunderland on 14 June, Godolphin and

---

[1] Huntington Library S.T. 57, III, f. 228; Klopp, *Der Fall des Hauses Stuart*, XIII, 429; [Nathaniel Hooke], *An Account of the Conduct of the Dowager Duchess of Marlborough* (1742), pp. 248–52.

the leading Whigs (Somers, Cowper, Halifax, Orford, and New-castle) not only remained in office, but wrote to Marlborough urging him to remain at his post. Marlborough had no choice but to acquiesce in their advice, but it is ironical that he, the one time protégé of James II, the former Tory, the courtier and the general, should see more clearly than the Whigs themselves that party unity was the surest means of preserving power in Parliament and therefore at Court.[1] The paralysis of the Whigs had at least two causes. One was the skill with which Harley detached first Somerset and Shrewsbury, then Halifax and Newcastle, and finally Somers and Cowper, from the main body of the Whigs, playing skilfully on the individual hopes, fears, and jealousies of each man. But equally important was the dread the Whigs harboured of a dissolution of Parliament. Fearing new elections they dared not precipitate them by taking united action against the Queen. In their letter urging Marlborough to remain at his post, the leading Whigs flatly confessed, 'This we look upon as the most necessary step that can be taken to prevent the dissolution of this Parliament.'[2] But while the Whigs accepted Sunderland's dismissal in order to avoid a dissolution, the political pundits of the day regarded it as a sure harbinger of a dissolution, believing that Harley had gone too far ever to meet the old Parliament again. 'The dissolution of the Parliament', James Brydges wrote to Lord Stair on 3 July, 'is very confidently reported, and that a new one will be called the middle of August. And truly in my opinion I am very much inclined to believe it will, for they who had credit enough with the Queen to persuade her into the measures she has taken, will hardly think themselves safe in a House of Commons, when the majority is against them, and when by a dissolution they think they shall have as considerable an one on their side.' Marl-borough, though he agreed not to resign, had no illusions that his remaining at his post would prevent a dissolution, observing that 'Mr Harley and his friends know the whole depends on that'.[3]

[1] *Private Correspondence of Sarah, Duchess of Marlborough* (1838), I, 352; Coxe, *Marlborough*, III, 68; Huntington Library S.T. 57, IV, f. 3. Walpole also reported (Plumb, *Walpole*, I, 155) that the Whigs in the Cabinet considered resigning in a body.
[2] Churchill, *Marlborough*, II, 718. Sarah, Duchess of Marlborough wrote to Mr Maynwaring (*Private Correspondence*, I, 324), '...but as long as the Whigs fear an ill Parliament, nothing can be done...'.
[3] Huntington Library S.T. 57, IV, f. 43; Churchill, *Marlborough*, II, 719. Hoffmann wrote on 18 July (Klopp, *Der Fall des Hauses Stuart*, XIII, 458), 'But the fear they have of Parliament, because of the steps hitherto taken, prevails over all other considerations;

Robert Harley was a supremely skilful political tactician, but he had not thought deeply about the future. Through the spring and summer he won skirmish after skirmish, won Whig after Whig over to his scheme for a 'motely ministry', as Lord Wharton called it. But he had not considered how these skirmishes could help him win the final battle for a mixed administration, supported by the Queen's friends in Parliament, or even whether such a victory were possible. In fact by August of 1710 he suddenly discovered that his splendid tactics had led him to the centre of the battlefield, in which position he was exposed to a withering cross-fire from both sides. The root of all his difficulties lay in his refusal to face up to the problem of the future of the present Parliament. The Whigs, including those whom he had won over to his scheme, were unalterably opposed to its dissolution. Newcastle led a delegation from the Bank to petition the Queen against its dissolution; Shrewsbury said he did not know who could answer advising the Queen to dissolve Parliament; Halifax threatened not to go as a plenipotentiary to Holland should the Queen dissolve Parliament; Orford violently opposed a dissolution at the Council table, in the Queen's presence; and Somers, Cowper, Devonshire, and Godolphin all threatened to quit if Parliament were dissolved.[1] In the face of this massive opposition from his newly won allies it is astonishing that Harley even considered the dissolution of Parliament, for thereby he threw away his best, perhaps his only, opportunity to create a mixed ministry. Since no Whig would serve the Queen if she dissolved Parliament, and since the expected Tory victory at the polls would make a Tory ministry unavoidable, the question inevitably arises, why did Harley advise the Queen to dissolve Parliament? Even more important, why did he advise her to dismiss Godolphin before dissolving Parliament, thereby throwing the Court's interest against the Whigs in the ensuing elections?[2]

and they regard themselves as insecure until a new Parliament has been summoned, in which they hope to have a Tory majority.'

[1] Huntington Library S.T. 57, f. 65; Cartwright, *Wentworth Papers*, p. 123; Churchill, *Marlborough*, II, 731.

[2] Klopp, *Der Fall des Hauses Stuart*, XIII, 457. If John Drummond was a good prophet, Harley's decision seems even more unwise. Drummond wrote to Brydges on 25 July (Huntington Library S.T. 58, VI, ff. 145–146), '...neither do I see any necessity which the new party lies under to have a new Parliament. If any mischief, impeachment, or violent votes or addresses happen, the Parliament can for such crying reasons be more plausibly dissolved than now; but I am of opinion a great many gentlemen would be upon their good behaviour, and that there would neither be that majority amongst the Lords nor the Commons as was last session.'

In some measure Harley acted from hope, from a hope that the Whigs would continue to support his scheme even though Parliament were dissolved, and from a hope that the electorate would return moderate men, loyal men, to the new Parliament. But necessity more than hope drove him to ask the Queen to dissolve Parliament. All negotiations to form a composite ministry, supported in Parliament by both moderate Whigs and moderate Tories, collapsed in August. Nor could those Whigs who were negotiating with Harley—Somerset, Halifax, Newcastle, and Cowper—demonstrate to his satisfaction that they were able to manage the old Parliament for the new ministry; and Harley knew as well as any man that the Queen's servants in Parliament were too few in number to carry on the Queen's business alone. There was no alternative but to seek a new Parliament, whose members might prove more loyal to the Queen than to party.[1]

The decision to dissolve a Parliament in which the Whigs predominated and to seek a Parliament in which no party predominated meant the dismissal of Godolphin, for he adamantly opposed a dissolution and resisted all attempts to remodel the Lord Lieutenancies and Commissions of Peace in favour of men loyal to the Queen. Yet more than necessity contributed to Godolphin's dismissal on 8 August. The Queen and Harley desired it for personal reasons. The Queen could no longer abide his arrogance, though that arrogance amounted to no more—and no less—than an insistence that Her Majesty consult him, and not her secret cabal, before naming men to public office. For his part Harley would have been less than human had he not desired the dismissal of the man who had engineered his disgrace in 1708; and he would surely have been less than the politician he was had he not sought to win control of the Treasury for himself. Through the summer of 1710 Godolphin used all his power as Lord Treasurer and all his influence with the Queen to oppose Harley's schemes. He spurned all accommodation with Harley and his allies, accused Shrewsbury of 'French counsels',

---

[1] The negotiations between the various parties were very secret and quite hopeless, as St John suggested in a letter to Brydges on 1 Aug. (Huntington Library S.T. 58, vi, f. 157), 'The treaty you mention I was not let into the secret of. I can only say that it seems to me very difficult, if not utterly impossible, to carry on with success a negotiation of that kind between parties amongst whom there is not the least confidence remaining.' Five days later Harley wrote to Newcastle (*H.M.C. Portland*, ii, 213), 'It is impossible to bring Lord Cowper and Lord Halifax out of general terms to particulars, nor will they tell how Parliament is practicable.'

and harangued the Queen on the evils of secret cabals. There was really little else Harley could do but advise the Queen to dismiss her intractable Lord Treasurer. But the decision proved costly to Harley's plans for a 'motely' ministry, for it angered most Whigs. The Duke of Devonshire, for example, ceased supporting moderate Tory candidates at the hustings, an action which led Harley to lament, 'it is plain they are striving if they can to drive us into a party'.[1]

Yet even at this moment Harley refused to be driven into a party, refused to surrender his dream of a composite administration; and the failure of the Whigs to resign as a body upon Godolphin's dismissal gave some substance to his dream. Even though Harley took over the management of the Treasury, even though Anglesey and Poulett entered the Cabinet, even though the Queen began to remodel the Lieutenancies and Commissions of Peace, the Whigs still clung to office—Somers as Lord President, Cowper as Lord Chancellor, Devonshire as Lord Steward, Wharton as Lord Lieutenant of Ireland, Orford as First Lord of the Admiralty, and Boyle as Secretary of State. But their presence in the government only infuriated the Tories, who sent Francis Atterbury to Harley in mid-August with a demand that he forthwith dismiss the Whigs and dissolve Parliament. Harley protested that he would rather resign than be directed by anyone but the Queen; but the Tories would not relent.[2] Rochester boldly told the Queen that 'the plan to form a government which would remain independent of party was unworkable. Neither he nor any other member of the High Church party would serve with men who did not agree in principle with them.'[3] These Tory fusillades found Harley, defenceless and alone, in the middle of the battlefield. He had no choice but to capitulate. On 20 September

---

[1] *H.M.C. Portland*, II, 215. In a long letter to Mr Drummond (Huntington Library S.T. 57, IV, ff. 110–117), James Brydges describes Godolphin's fall, concluding, 'Thus passed this great affair, and after this I presume nobody can question but Her Majesty is resolved to go through the scheme that is laid, and we are in daily expectations of the alterations ... that are said to be intended in the several Commissions of Lieutenancies and Justices of Peace throughout the Kingdom, in order to influence the ensuing elections, for which we expect every week the writs ... That which I am told occasions a delay is the various opinions there are amongst the new ministers themselves, some being for a mixed administration, consisting of an equal number of Whigs and Tories in each Commission; others thinking matters driven to so great a height of animosity betwixt the two parties, that there can be no subsisting for the new ministry without giving it entirely to the Tories.'

[2] Felix Salomon, *Geschichte des letzten Ministerium Königin Anna von England* (Gotha, 1894), p. 36.

[3] Hoffmann's report of Rochester's interview with the Queen, Klopp, *Der Fall des Hauses Stuart*, XIII, 486.

the Queen dismissed the Whigs from office and named Tories—Rochester, Buckingham, Ormond, St John, and Harcourt—in their place. The next day she announced her intention to dissolve Parliament. Through it all Harley clung pathetically to his dream of making the Queen the centre of a new ministry. To Newcastle he wrote, 'As soon as the Queen has shown strength and ability to give the law to both sides, then will moderation be truly shown in the exercise of power without regard to parties only.'[1]

To be precise, the Queen dismissed Somers, Devonshire, and Boyle on the 20th; Orford, Wharton, and Cowper resigned two days later. Cowper's resignation was a particularly cruel blow to Harley, for he had sought desperately to keep him in the government. But Cowper told him, 'things were plainly put into Tory hands; a Whig game, either in whole or part, impracticable; that to keep in, when all my friends were out, would be infamous', that it was impossible he should serve when measures were adopted which he 'could not but think hurtful to the public and contrary to the true interest of the country'.[2] Lord Cowper was an esteemed lawyer and a man of moderate views, not a reckless Whig politician like Wharton. When a man of his probity embraced the cause of party unity and refused to accept responsibility for measures he believed unwise, there was no going back to the age of Queen Elizabeth. And it was to the age of Queen Elizabeth that Robert Monckton, son of the distinguished royalist Sir Philip, now urged Harley to return. 'I cannot but again remind you', he wrote to Harley in August, 'of Burleigh, who never suffered one party to be too superior to the other and thereby rendered them both subservient to his mistress.' Two weeks later Monckton, a Whig, told Peter Wentworth that 'he'll be no Whig any longer, for... he angered... some of his old friends by being so reasonable as to maintain 'twas fit the Queen should use her pleasure in disposing of employments as she pleases'. Not a gulf, but an ocean, separated the world of Queen Elizabeth from the world of Queen Anne.[3]

---

[1] *H.M.C. Portland*, II, 219.

[2] *The Private Diary of William First Earl Cowper* (Eton, 1833), p. 44. Even Somerset, who had been the first to join with Harley, offered to resign as Master of the Horse, which led Peter Wentworth to observe (Cartwright, *Wentworth Papers*, p. 143), ''Tis odd for him that has been running down those that would be telling the Queen, upon every rub they met to their will, they must lay down, that he should so soon be at the same game.'

[3] *H.M.C. Portland*, IV, 576; Cartwright, *Wentworth Papers*, p. 141. Queen Anne was no less royal in her conduct than her predecessor, but it did her less good. When Richard Hampden refused to serve as a Commissioner of the Treasury unless the Queen promised

To the historian of responsible government two important truths concerning the political crisis of 1710 stand out: Whigs and Tories would not work together in a mixed administration; and all men regarded it as axiomatic that there must be a new Parliament if the Queen turned to the Tories. Recognition of the first truth finally drove Harley to a reliance upon the Tories; and an awareness of the second led him to advise the Queen to dissolve Parliament. Not Parliament now, but the electorate, was to decide who should serve the Queen, the Whigs or the Tories. As Lord Wharton told Lord Dartmouth, 'If you have the majority we are undone, if we have the majority, you are broke.'[1]

Robert Harley did not see it this way. He used all the instruments of propaganda at his disposal to persuade the electorate to return men loyal to the Queen, not to party. At the same time his pamphleteers sought to answer the clamour of the Whigs against those who had advised the Queen to dismiss a ministry which had conducted the war with unparalleled success and to dissolve a Parliament which had supported it with unprecedented generosity. The most important of the pamphlets written under Harley's direction was *Faults on Both Sides*, a pamphlet which may even have been written by Robert Harley himself. In the pamphlet Harley (or his scribe) maintains that 'the change in the ministry was not a result of caprice, but of necessity to check the formidable power of a few men, who seek to govern both the Queen and the nation'. These few men possessed formidable power because, by allying with the 'unanimous Whigs, they had so large a majority in the House of Commons that they had assurance of carrying everything there according to their own minds'. The dissolution of Parliament was therefore also necessary. But the way to free the Queen from the tyranny of the Whigs was not to turn to the Tories, to the 'bigoted party-men' who in 1703 had sought to make the Queen their prisoner; but to turn to 'a coalition of the honestest men of both sides', for the Queen was resolved to admit into the ministry all men who would support 'moderate measures', and intended 'that the names of parties and factions be buried in oblivion'.[2]

not to dissolve Parliament, the Queen replied (*ibid.* p. 138), 'though she offered him an employment yet she did not ask his advice'. Hampden thereupon declined the office.
[1] *H.M.C. Portland*, II, 219.
[2] *Faults on Both Sides*, in *Somers Tracts*, XII, 695–6, 700 (where Sir Walter Scott quotes Oldmixon's attribution of the pamphlet to Harley, but suggests that it may have been Defoe; Speaker Onslow in Burnet, *History*, VI, 12, attributes the pamphlet to Mr

353

Political Parties and Responsible Government

The Tories, in their replies to *Faults on Both Sides*, agreed that the insolence of the late ministers justified the Queen in dismissing them and dissolving Parliament. For Jonathan Swift nothing exemplified that insolence better than the new phrases that had crept into use at Court.

They usually run in the following terms: [he wrote in *The Examiner*] 'Madam, I cannot serve you while such a one is in your employment. I desire humbly to resign my commission if Mr _____ continues Secretary of State. I cannot answer that the City will lend money unless my Lord _____ be President of the Council. I must beg leave to surrender except _____ has the Staff. I must not accept the Seals unless _____ comes into the other office.' This [concluded Swift] has been the language of late years from subjects to their Prince. Thus they stood upon terms, and must have their own conditions to ruin the nation.[1]

To free herself from this tyranny, argued the Tories, the Queen had to dissolve a Parliament in which her insolent ministers possessed such strength. 'For in our political constitution,' wrote Abel Boyer, summarizing the arguments of the Tories, 'if the ministerial part of the government and the Parliament be not of a-piece, nothing can be expected from them but continual jars and misunderstandings, each contending to put the other in the wrong, and obstructing what the other moves for the public good.' James Brydges, though not yet the Tory he was to become, fully concurred with this view of the constitution. Writing to his Dutch correspondent after the elections, he said, 'The Tories hitherto have carried it two to one in the elections...and I believe you gentlemen are not dissatisfied with it, for to have a ministry one way and the Parliament another would have created such confusion and disorder, as would have been inconsistent with carrying on the war.'[2]

But though Tories joined with Harleyites in justifying the dismissal of the late ministry and the dissolution of Parliament, they did not support Harley's call for a coalition government, moderate measures, and an end to party distinctions. 'Common reason tells

Clements working under Harley's direction). Arguments similar to those in *Faults on Both Sides* may be found in *The Secret History of Arlus and Odolphus* (1710), whose author observes (p. 6), 'that as long as men tenaciously keep up their distinction of parties...no statesmen can propose to support themselves that are not openly at the head of a party, in defence of whose principles they must declare themselves resolved to stand or fall'.

[1] *The Examiner*, no. 19, in H. Davis (ed.), *The Prose Works of Jonathan Swift* (Oxford, 1940), III, 37.

[2] Abel Boyer's summary of Tory arguments in favour of the dissolution, *Annals*, IX, 235; Huntington Library S.T. 57, IV, f. 178.

us', wrote Joseph Trapp in *Most Faults on One Side*, 'that a Coalition of Contrarieties can tend to nothing but corruption; and common experience assures us of the same truth in the very instances we are now speaking of.'

I lay no more stress [he continued] upon the words Whig and Tory than he [the author of *Faults on Both Sides*] does; but I lay a great deal upon the principles, which are really as distinct and opposite as East and West... Those things are plain and visible; and 'tis jest to say that all the difference lies in party names: those words, no doubt, are used in a very loose signification, and are often applied to persons that don't deserve them; but still there is a real and visible distinction in men's principles and practices, whatever names are put upon them.

Joseph Trapp then asserted that moderate measures were only a disguise for bringing in the Whigs, whom nothing but reigning alone would content.[1]

The Whigs could hardly join with the Tories in justifying the dismissal of the late ministry and the dissolution of Parliament, but they could and did agree with them that a coalition government was an impossibility. 'A Tory can no more be a moderate manager', wrote the author of *A Supplement to Faults on Both Sides*, 'than the elements can cease to put forth their complete vigour when left to nature and freed from constraint.' The author of *The Medley* was particularly indignant that the author of *Faults on Both Sides* had sought to 'confound Whig and Tory, by dividing the Whigs into Old and Modern, a wicked distinction invented by their enemies to ruin those by divisions' whom they could not destroy when united. Even Defoe, who sought to win Whig support for the new ministry by calling it Whiggish, declared that the Queen ought not to employ High-flying Tories, for they were all traitors. Both Swift and Defoe opposed party government, but Swift would not have the Queen employ Whigs for they were republicans and Defoe would not have her employ High-flying Tories for they were traitors.[2]

The earliest returns in October 1710 seemed to answer Harley's

[1] [Joseph Trapp], *Most Faults on One Side* (1710), pp. 18, 21, 23. Robert Ferguson argued in a pamphlet which he dedicated to Robert Harley (*Of the Qualifications Requisite in a Minister of State*, part II, p. 63) that the Queen should not expect those 'whose principles are irreconcilable to concenter in the same designs and actions', for that were 'no less impracticable...than the making two contradictories to agree'.

[2] *A Supplement to the Faults on Both Sides* (1710), p. 8; *The Medley*, no. 18; *The Examiner*, no. 36; *The Review*, VII, no. 65, 75, 101. Defoe (*ibid.* no. 99) likewise regarded the distinction between Old and Modern Whig as a 'hateful, and indeed foolish, distinction'.

expectations, for the number of Whigs elected appeared to equal the number of Tories, thereby allowing the Queen's servants to carry the House for moderate measures. But the final results proved a calamity for Harley and his purposes. Alarmed by the republican notions proclaimed by the Whigs in Sacheverell's trial, the electors of England turned against them, returning 350 Tories to Parliament, to only 186 Whigs. Of the 350 Tories, 140 were High Churchmen.[1] These results proved calamitous to Harley's purposes, for he was no longer, as he had been in William's reign, a party leader who wished to tyrannize over his monarch; he had become a courtier who wished to serve his Queen. Harley now aspired to the role of a favourite who dispensed his mistress's power, took upon himself her faults, and promoted her interests. He detested the minister who over-valued his own services and undervalued his sovereign's under-standing, who laid down the law to the sovereign rather than receiving it from her. The greatest glory of which he could conceive was to have served Henry VIII or Queen Elizabeth or Henry IV of France as a chief minister.[2] The political career of Robert Harley after 1702 cannot be understood if one regards him as the leader of a political party or represents him as a parliamentary undertaker. Parliament he knew well, most assuredly, and his happiest hours were probably spent whispering advice to the Speaker or passing notes to Foley or consulting with Bromley or creating majorities out of the endless permutations and combinations that a House of Commons without parties afforded. But under Anne he was a parliamentary manager, not a parliamentary undertaker; he was the successor of Bacon, Danby, and Sunderland, not Neville, Saye, Temple, and Wharton. Sunderland he resembled most of all, for like William's confidant he appreciated the importance of royal

---

[1] Boyer, *History of Queen Anne*, ix, 248; Mary Ransome, 'The General Election of 1710', University of London Master's Thesis (1938), pp. 6, 199–201. Miss Ransome's belief that the passions loosed by the Sacheverell trial overwhelmed both Court and family influence in the elections finds confirmation in a remark Brydges made to Godolphin (Huntington Library S.T. 57, ii, f. 29), 'but the violence of parties have rendered most popular and numerous elections (such as mine consisting of near 100 voices) so uncertain, that no family interest hardly is to be depended on'.

[2] These thoughts of Harley's may be found in a memorandum in praise of court favourites, which he wrote in July 1710 (B.M. Loan 29/10, no. 20). In this same memo-randum he echoed Queen Elizabeth's words to Parliament in 1584 by writing, 'A sovereign would be in a much worse condition than any of his subjects, if he...could not deliver himself from a servant who is grown dangerous by his excessive power or intoler-able by his presumption and restless ambition.'

patronage, detested the passions of party, and desired to serve his monarch by skilfully managing Parliament. But Harley, like Sunderland before him, saw his carefully laid plans to govern by a Court party swept away by the passions of contending parties. As Swift observed, Harley's 'moderating schemes...were by no means reduceable to practice'.[1]

Soon after Parliament met in November, Harley discovered that the Queen's friends possessed no majority, not even the numbers to balance between Whig and Tory. In repeated divisions the Tories outvoted both the Whig and Court interests. Nor were these fortuitous majorities, for the Tory gentlemen in the House had organized themselves into the October Club, and had sworn to vote in the Commons as the majority in the Club resolved. Against party discipline of this nature, there was no hope of burying party distinctions. Harley therefore trimmed his sails to the prevailing wind and sought Tory support for the new ministry. He gave them a Land Qualification Bill, a bill to build fifty churches in London, the expulsion of the Palatines, a Commission of Account, and an investigation into the debts of the navy. But he refused to surrender to their demands for the impeachment of Godolphin and a purge of all Whigs in subaltern employments. And the members of the October Club, though they inwardly fumed, acquiesced in Harley's leadership, for they had not forgotten the fatal consequence of their clamour for a monopoly of office in 1704. They also knew that Harley enjoyed the confidence of the Queen, whose favour was the first step necessary to office. Harley was thus able with their help successfully to manage Parliament for the Queen.[2]

But he did have to pay a price. He had to allow the Tories to examine into the alleged maladministration of the late ministry, inquiries bound to exacerbate party animosities. Their first inquiries resulted in the expulsion from the House of Thomas Ridge, a Whig

---

[1] Swift, 'An Enquiry into the Behaviour of the Queen's Last Ministry', *Works*, VIII, 160. In late October 1710 Harley wrote a Plan of Administration (Hardwicke, *State Papers*, II, 485–8), which sets forth the art of parliamentary management in a manner reminiscent of Bacon's advice to James and of Sunderland's to William.

[2] George Lockhart, *The Lockhart Papers* (1817), I, 320–5; Cartwright, *Wentworth Papers*, pp. 161, 180; Klopp, *Der Fall des Hauses Stuart*, XIV, 673. A High Tory, William Bishop, wrote to Dr Charlett on 22 Jan. (Ballard MSS 31, f. 89), 'I was this day before a Committee in my cousin Norwood's affairs, where I thank God...we have had better success than I expected, three to one for us, against the Court and Whigs. I am sorry to mention them together, but all people grumble on the high-side that there is no alteration made, nor likely to be made, as I can hear of.'

member and a victualler of the navy, who had pocketed interest on government money in his possession. These same inquiries led to a resolve that the Commissioners of the Victualling Office were guilty of negligence, and to an address requesting the Queen to order the Attorney-General to prosecute Mr Player and five other brewers for frauds in victualling the navy. But none of these matters touched Godolphin, who was the true object of their inquiries. His turn came on 4 April when Edward Harley, brother of Robert, charged that £35,000,000 spent by the Treasury remained unaccounted for. Though no one offered proof of embezzlement, the House of Commons voted on 28 April that those who possessed the management of the revenue had, by not 'compelling the several accomptants duly to pass their respective accounts', done an injustice to the nation. The vote passed by 181 to 119. Many of those who supported the censure probably agreed with Swift, who had written in *The Examiner* two days before, 'it is possible, that many great abuses may be visibly committed, which cannot be legally punished'. Only two weeks earlier the House had exhibited the same readiness to censure men for mere errors of judgment; they had resolved that whoever counselled the admission of the Palatines into this kingdom was an enemy to the Queen and kingdom. The vote was aimed at the Earl of Sunderland, for though the House could not prove that he had counselled the Queen to admit them, common fame proclaimed it. None of these votes, not even that against Thomas Ridge, led to a successful prosecution in a court of law, but they were not intended to. They served their purpose, which was to justify the clamour raised in the country against the corruption of the late ministry.[1]

In the House of Lords the Tories launched a far more formidable attack upon the late ministry, for it concerned the war in Spain, which had not been waged successfully. They began by censuring the Earl of Galway, Lord Tyrawley, and General Stanhope for advising, at a Council of War in Valencia in January 1707, an offensive war in Spain, advice which caused the defeat at Almanza and the failure to capture Toulon. The Tories had no personal animus against Galway, Tyrawley, or Stanhope; they censured them only as a prelude to an attack upon the late ministry, an attack which they initiated on 12 January. On that day the clerk read aloud a letter from the Earl of Sunderland to General Stanhope,

---

[1] *C.J.* xvi, 502, 525, 598, 619; *The Examiner*, no. 38, Swift, *Works*, iii, 141.

informing Stanhope that the Queen entirely approved of the advice which he had given for an offensive war in Spain. When the clerk had finished, the Earl of Scarsdale promptly moved, 'That it appears by the Earl of Sunderland's letter to Mr Stanhope, that the design of an offensive war in Spain was approved by the Cabinet Council...which contributed to our misfortunes in Spain and to the disappointment before Toulon.'[1] The Whigs opposed the motion, their opposition giving rise to a debate which revolved around three important, but not new, constitutional issues. Was it permissible for ministers to use the Queen's name to shelter themselves from parliamentary censure? Was it proper for Parliament to censure ministers in general, without naming names? And was it right to judge the wisdom of counsels by the success of events?

Sunderland's letter spoke of the Queen's approval of an offensive war in Spain; Scarsdale's motion referred to the Cabinet Council's approval. This disparity caused Lord Cowper to remark that he saw no connection between the premise in the letter and the inference in the question. To this remark the Earl of Rochester replied heatedly, 'He knew very well the meaning of that objection, that for several years past they had been told, "That the Queen was to answer for everything", but he hoped that time was over; that according to the fundamental constitution of this Kingdom, the ministers are accountable for all, and therefore he hoped nobody would, nay dared, name the Queen in this debate.' The most remarkable fact about Rochester's outburst is not that a fierce old Tory should have uttered such sentiments, but that no man in the entire house should have contradicted him; not one man, not even Cowper. Even though Sunderland's letter unmistakably referred to the Queen, the assembled peers chose to believe that the Secretary of State wrote on behalf of the Cabinet Council, not the Queen. As the Earl of Ferrers said, 'a Secretary of State gives no directions but from the Cabinet Council'.[2]

A curious debate did follow Rochester's remarks; it concerned the

---

[1] *History and Defence of the Last Parliament* (1713), p. 43. Hoffmann wrote (Klopp, *Der Fall des Hauses Stuart*, xiv, 36), 'The intention of the new ministry is to wrest from Galway the confession that the previous ministry had commanded him to offer battle on every occasion. If this proves true, they can build an accusation on it against the late ministry ...The present ministry requires a vindication for the dismissal of the previous ministers, because their credit now, as before, is sinking.'

[2] *History and Defence of the Last Parliament*, pp. 45–6, 53–4.

question whether the phrase 'the ministers' or the words 'Cabinet Council' should appear in the motion. Originally Lord Scarsdale had spoken of the 'Cabinet Council', but later he substituted the phrase 'the ministers'. When the Duke of Devonshire protested against the change, Lord Scarsdale replied that he thought 'ministers' better known than 'Cabinet Council'. But L'Hermitage reported a different reason for the change. 'One lord', he wrote, 'directed the motion against the "Cabinet Council", and said that it was to blame for ordering an offensive war, but as they wished to envelop all in the blame, others of the same party urged that the blame be imputed to the ministers in general; after much debate they changed the motion to ministers.' What speaks against L'Hermitage's clear analysis is the actual muddle of the debate. The Duke of Beaufort urged that the phrase 'Cabinet Council' 'does not imply all ministers', while the Duke of Argyle opined that 'all ministers were of the Cabinet Council, but that all the Cabinet Council were not ministers'. Earl Poulett, a close friend of Harley's, probably spoke more accurately than either of the Dukes when he said, 'There is no distinction between the ministry and the Cabinet Council; for those who were of the Cabinet were ministers.'[1]

The debate over the relative merits of 'ministers' or 'Cabinet Council' was inconclusive and unimportant, but the decision to condemn the ministry as a whole, whether under the rubric 'ministers' or 'Cabinet Council', was profoundly important. For a century Parliament had sought to discover the particular counsellors who had misled the King, and invariably had failed, for the secrecy of the Council table and the privacy of the Bedchamber had concealed their identity. Now it abandoned the enterprise altogether. Parliament could afford to do this because it, or rather the Tories in both Houses, now desired to discredit an entire ministry, not particular ministers. The two Houses could also afford to abandon the enterprise because they no longer sought a legal condemnation of any man. As parliamentary censure replaced parliamentary impeachment, as political responsibility superseded legal responsibility, as dismissal from office took the place of death at the block, the need for legal proof disappeared. Common fame sufficed to censure men. And the appearance of a visible ministry, a group of men possessing

[1] *History and Defence of the Last Parliament*, pp. 43–7; L'Hermitage, B.M. Add. MSS 17677 EEE, f. 46v.

the chief employments, meeting weekly as a Cabinet Council, and acting together according to common interests, made it easy for common fame to declare who had misled the sovereign.

The word 'ministry' first appeared in English political discourse at the Restoration. The word then meant what 'administration' means today, that is the daily care of the realm, entrusted by the King to his great officers. Sir William Temple spoke in 1674 of 'the ministry of the late Cabal' and four years later he praised Danby for the negotiations achieved 'under your ministry'. But insensibly 'ministry' came to mean the persons entrusted by the King with the administration of the realm, not the trust itself. Sir William Temple in 1669 referred to 'the King's present ministry' and Sir Richard Temple in 1679 wrote that a majority of the House of Commons favoured 'the ministry'. James Vernon in 1699 wondered if he was rightly informed of Mr Harley's irreconcilableness 'to the ministry', and Henry Withers in 1701 wrote to Thomas Pitt concerning 'our new ministry, as we call them'. In the age of Queen Anne every kind of modifier was joined to the word: there was 'the late ministry', 'the present ministry', 'the new ministry', 'the reigning ministry', and 'the Whig ministry'. Because the ministry became so real, so palpable, so familiar an entity, Parliament decided to place responsibility upon it, rather than upon particular ministers.[1]

Two particular developments gave reality to the ministry: the Cabinet Council and the administration became one, and the growth of political parties gave unity to the ministry. In 1680 Sir Henry Neville had ridiculed the Privy Council scheme of the previous year because those admitted to the new Council were not admitted to office. In the reign of William III both Shrewsbury and Sunderland urged that counselling and administering be joined. In November 1701 Sunderland wrote to Somers, 'None to be of the Cabinet Council, but who have, in some sort, a right to enter there by their

---

[1] T. P. Courtenay, *Memoirs of the Life, Works, and Correspondence of Sir William Temple* (1836), I, 425. Temple, *Works*, III, 368; IV, 383. *Vernon Letters*, II, 267. Henry Withers to Thomas Pitt, B.M. Add. MSS 22851, f. 131. The first use of the adjective 'ministerial' to mean the responsible rather than the subordinate part of the administration occurred in 1710 when Abel Boyer wrote (*History of Queen Anne*, IX, 235), 'For in our political constitution, if the ministerial part of the government and the Parliament be not of a-piece, nothing can be expected from them but continual jars and misunderstandings.' The usual meaning of 'ministerial' continued to be 'subordinate', as when James Brydges wrote to Mr Drummond (17 Nov. 1710, Huntington Library S.T. 57, IV, f. 217), 'as I have been but a ministerial officer...there is nothing I am answerable for...'.

employment.' He then listed ten great officers, among them the Lord Treasurer, the Lord Keeper, and the two Secretaries of State, who should sit in the Cabinet. By the accession of Queen Anne those who counselled the Queen were also those who administered the realm; they sat in the Cabinet and they governed the great departments of state. They were the ministry. Queen Anne, it is true, objected. She insisted that no office automatically carried Cabinet rank and she refused to admit the Duke of Devonshire to the Cabinet in order to prove that a seat there was not inherent in the office of Lord Steward. But it was to no avail. The moment the Queen named Earl Poulett First Commissioner of the Treasury, the entire political world gave him a seat in the Cabinet, and the Queen soon fulfilled their prophecy. In subsequent years Kings of England occasionally admitted to the Cabinet men who did not possess high office, but they never excluded those who held the highest offices.[1]

Only if the ministry had some semblance of unity could Parliament, in equity, censure every member of it by a general vote. Clarendon hated the notion that all the King's ministers should agree in their counsels, but Sunderland in 1698 wrote to Portland that 'whoever is counted a minister cannot serve unless he is supported by other ministers'.[2] William himself told Rochester in 1702 that those men only should sit in the Council who can agree in their advice.[3] The history of Cabinets under Anne gives ample testimony to the wisdom of William's remarks; balanced counsels and mixed ministries proved unworkable. Inexorably they became either Whig or Tory. The very debate over the late ministry's counselling an offensive war in Spain revealed the extent of Cabinet unanimity. Lord Cowper testified that all the Council were for an offensive war in Spain; Somers owned freely that he had given such counsel; and Godolphin said, 'all the ministry were unanimous in their opinions for an offensive war'. Only because this was true could Parliament condemn the ministry in general without perpetrating an injustice against innocent men. Even the Whigs agreed that a ministry could rightly be blamed for counsel given the Queen. When some months later Lord Scarsdale attributed a message for adjourn-

---

[1] *H.M.C. Portland*, II, 200; J. H. Plumb, 'The Organization of the Cabinet in the Reign of Queen Anne', *Transactions Royal Historical Society*, 5th ser. VII, 145–6.
[2] Kenyon, *Sunderland*, p. 310.
[3] L'Hermitage, B.M. Add. MSS 17677 XX, f. 191v.

ment to the Queen, Sunderland cried out, 'anything that was done irregularly could never be imputed to the Crown, but to the ministry'.[1]

The ministers who counselled an offensive war in Spain never seriously sought to hide behind the Queen's name or seek refuge in cabinet secrecy. Their principal defence was their innocence. They had given their advice to the best of their ability and with a sincere intention to serve their country. 'God Almighty has blessed my endeavours with success,' said Marlborough, 'but if men are to be censured when they give their opinions to the best of their understanding, I must expect to be found fault with as well as the rest.' Lord Somers insisted that the ill success of the Battle of Almanza was no argument against the counsel for an offensive war, for no man would be safe 'if they judged of opinions by events'. The plea was not new—Strafford, Laud, Clarendon, and Danby had voiced it in their defence—but the objection was now of much less political significance, for Parliament did not intend to execute or imprison the late ministry for criminal conduct. They wished only to censure them for unwise counsels. As the author of *The Old and New Ministry Compared* wrote, those who

give either weak or pernicious counsels...should answer for it, and not plead in excuse, 'That they had given the King counsel after the wit and grace God had listed to give them.' For if they were unknowing in affairs of state, and through notorious ignorance erred often, why did they undertake great employment? It being necessarily true, that ignorance and want of foresight in ministers, is as pernicious to the Commonwealth they govern, as malice or corruption.[2]

Many moderate peers, agreeing with the sentiments expressed by the author of *The Old and New Ministry Compared*, joined with the High-flying Tories and newly elected Scottish peers to censure the late ministry. By 68 to 48 they carried a resolution, 'That it appears, by the Earl of Sunderland's letters, that the carrying on the war offensively in Spain was approved and directed by the ministers,

[1] *History and Defence of the Last Parliament*, pp. 47–8, 53; Cartwright, *Wentworth Papers*, p. 240. The first attempt to lay responsibility on a ministry actually occurred in November 1707, when the Tories sought to blame 'the ministry' and the 'Cabinet Council' for the mismanagement of the fleet. The Whigs made no objection to the expressions 'ministry' and 'Cabinet Council'; they only insisted that the Admiralty, not the ministry, was at fault, for the Secretaries of State had often warned the Admiralty of negligence in the management of the fleet (Burnet, *History*, v, 336–7).

[2] *History and Defence of the Last Parliament*, pp. 50, 53; *The Old and New Ministry Compared* (1711), pp. 31–2.

notwithstanding the design of attempting Toulon, which the ministers at that time knew was concerted with the Duke of Savoy; and therefore are justly to be blamed, for contributing to our misfortunes in Spain, and to the expedition against Toulon.' Two weeks later they voted a second resolution, which censured 'the ministers' for 'not supplying the deficiencies of men given by Parliament for the war in Spain'. With a third vote censuring Galway for surrendering the post of honour to the King of Portugal, they ended their inquiries into the war in Spain. The purpose of their inquiries had not been to drive the Queen's ministers from office, but only to justify the changes in the ministry which the Queen had made. Swift observed 'with infinite pleasure' that a great part of what he had charged against the late ministry 'is now confirmed by resolutions of Parliament'.[1]

The Earl of Rochester's death in April offered Robert Harley an opportunity to consolidate his power and gave the Queen an occasion to reward him for his loyal services. In May she bestowed upon Harley the Earldoms of Oxford and Mortimer and appointed him Lord Treasurer in a reconstituted ministry. Men everywhere wrote to congratulate him upon his new honours. One of these correspondents, John Chamberlain, reported that 'all the philosophers and unprejudiced' believe that while the new Lord Treasurer 'holds the scales of the contending parties he will produce harmony out of discord'. It was also the prayer of 'the philosophers and unprejudiced', he added, that the Earl of Oxford 'may long hold the balance, and always have weight enough to make an equilibrium; and then he may be able to stop that party tide even with his thumb, which has hitherto borne down all the ministers before it'. James Brydges reported the same general applause for Oxford's moderate conduct, but wondered how the Earl could maintain his ground 'if one party, not satisfied, and the other, incensed, should join to oppose his measures'. He held out little hope that moderate measures could purge the fevers of party strife. 'The gentlemen known by the name of October Men are already alarmed, and give out... that they expected every man who had been under the suspicion of being a Whig should have been turned out before this time, and threaten how uneasy they'll make the winter to be to those who have neglected the gratifying these their passions.' 'And 'tis cer-

[1] *L.J.* XIX, 192, 213; *The Examiner*, no. 40, Swift, *Works*, III, 148–9.

tain', he concluded, 'that the Administration cannot be carried on if the Court does not exert itself and the ministry find some way to get strength enough to keep the determining power in their own hands.'[1]

The Earl of Oxford, unwilling to drive every Whig from office, yet mindful of the need to appease the October Club, decided that his best hope lay in bringing to a swift conclusion the long, expensive, and now unpopular war with France. But to make peace with France meant the dismissal from office of the Duke of Marlborough, the one remaining member of the old ministry who still sat in the Cabinet. The deep hatred which both the Queen and Oxford bore Marlborough undoubtedly contributed to the decision to dismiss him, but the principal reason for his removal was his irreconcilable opposition to a peace with France.

> I am very free to acknowledge [he wrote to the Queen] that my duty to Your Majesty and country would not give me leave to join in the counsels of a man, who in my opinion puts Your Majesty upon all manner of extremities. And it is not my opinion only, but the opinion of all mankind, that the friendship of France must needs be destructive to Your Majesty, there being in that Court a root of enmity irreconcilable to Your Majesty's government and the religion of these kingdoms.[2]

True to his word, Marlborough refused to sit in the same Cabinet with Oxford and voted against the peace in the House of Lords; the Queen therefore had no choice but to dismiss him from office on 31 December 1711. At the same time she dismissed Robert Walpole as Treasurer of the Navy and the Duke of Somerset as Master of the Horse, telling Somerset that, since he had chosen another party and since her service required unity among her ministers, she must dismiss him. On hearing of these dismissals, the Whigs cried out that Oxford was altering the constitution, but the Tories rejoiced that he was now in earnest. It is doubtful whether

[1] *H.M.C. Portland*, IV, 697; Brydges to Sir David Dalrymple, 15 July 1711, Huntington Library S.T. 57, V, ff. 132–134.
[2] Coxe, *Marlborough*, III, 281. A year before Marlborough's fall, James Brydges wrote to Mr Drummond (16 Jan. 1711, Huntington Library S.T. 57, IV, f. 259), that Marlborough had 'given assurances he will enter into the measures of the Queen and the ministry...but notwithstanding these fair appearances it is my opinion [that]...my Lord Godolphin and my Lord Somers will entangle him still in correspondence with the Junto, the professed enemies to be sure to the present ministry, and consequently keep up a distrust of him, which is inconsistent with that harmony that ought and must be kept amongst ministers who intend to keep the power.'

either were right, but it is certain that Oxford's plan for a composite administration lay in shambles.[1]

In former times the House of Commons voted impeachments and addresses against ministers of state in order to drive them from office; in Queen Anne's reign the House voted them in order to justify the previous dismissal of ministers from office. A monarch possessed of the prerogative in its fullest extent needed no such vote to justify the dismissal of a minister of state, but Queen Anne exercised a much diminished prerogative. She felt the need to justify by a vote of Parliament the dismissal of a popular servant. Therefore she gave as the reason for her dismissing Marlborough the fact that the Commissioners for Taking the Public Accounts had presented information against him to the House of Commons.[2] The Commissioners had indeed presented information against him, as also against the recently dismissed Robert Walpole. They charged Marlborough with wrongly taking £5,000 a year from the Bread Money voted for the provisioning of the army in Flanders, and 2½ per cent from the subsidies voted for the payment of foreign troops. They charged Walpole with accepting a 500-guinea bribe from the recipients of a forage contract. Marlborough replied that the £5,000 was a perquisite enjoyed by every commander in Flanders since Prince Waldeck and that he had the Queen's warrant, countersigned by a Secretary of State, for the 2½ per cent; furthermore he had used the money for the purpose for which it was given him, to pay the cost of secret service. Walpole pleaded that the 500 guineas had gone to one of the original contractors, Mr Mann, and not to himself, which Mr Mann swore to in an affidavit. Walpole and Marlborough were innocent, but Marlborough's dismissal had to be justified to the people; and Walpole's exclusion from the House of Commons, where his skill and daring embarrassed the government, had to be secured. Therefore a Tory majority, on 17 January 1712, found Walpole guilty, expelled him from the House, sent him to the Tower, and kept him there for the rest of the session. On the

---

[1] Salomon, *Geschichte des letzten Ministerium Königin Annas*, p. 134. The Earl of Strafford observed to Princess Sophia in February 1712 (Macpherson, *Original Papers*, II, 350), that '...the Queen saw that reigning by one party was but being a slave to the heads of that party; and therefore when she first made her change, it was positively resolved not to stick to parties, but to those who served her best. However, the other party's opposition and violence may have made her change her mind, for the mere necessity, at this conjuncture.'

[2] Coxe, *Marlborough*, III, 280.

24th the Commons found Marlborough guilty of both charges brought against him, but declined to vote an impeachment against him. 'One cannot reach him in a legal way,' wrote Hoffmann, 'furthermore the purpose of the entire attack is only to blacken him before the nation and justify his removal.'[1]

The desire to heap obloquy on the old ministry did not end with the expulsion of Walpole and the censure of Marlborough. In February the House of Commons expelled Adam de Cardonnel, Marlborough's faithful secretary, for accepting a gratuity of 500 ducats from a government contractor. More importantly, they exhumed the Barrier Treaty of 1709 between the Dutch and the British, condemned it as destructive to the commerce of Great Britain and injurious to the Queen's honour, and declared Lord Townshend an enemy to the Queen and kingdom for signing it. Lord Townshend, it is true, had exceeded his instructions by yielding to the Dutch several towns which he had no authority to yield, but the Tories were far less anxious to censure him for this oversight than to condemn the late ministry for pursuing an intransigent policy of war against France. 'Consider', said Arthur Moore in the debate, 'in whose hands the Treasury, the Seals, the Admiralty, and the great offices were at this time, when the French were ready to give reasonable concessions for a peace.'[2]

Unlike the old ministry, the new ministry had no intention of spurning reasonable concessions for a peace. They desired, needed, and sought peace with France. And their urgent pursuit of peace gave the Whigs the occasion they sought to oppose the Queen's government. Though men in the age of Queen Anne often talked of the loyalty which they owed the Queen, they willingly opposed her administration if excluded from it. The leaders of the Whig party, observed Swift, often quarrelled with each other, but 'they perfectly agreed in one general end, of distressing by all possible methods the new administration; wherein if they could succeed so far as to put the Queen under any great necessity, another Parliament must be called, and perhaps the power devolve again into their own hands'. One need not agree with Swift that the defence of principle had nothing to do with the resolve of the Whigs to oppose the peace, in order to recognize that the Whigs were willing (as Swift charged)

---

[1] *C.J.* xvii, 30, 38; Klopp, *Der Fall des Hauses Stuart*, xiv, 254.
[2] *C.J.* xvi, 92, 97; Cartwright, *Wentworth Papers*, p. 266.

to oppose the Queen simply because they could not choose her ministry for her. Court rhetoric cannot conceal the fact that men during Queen Anne's reign readily went into opposition in order to force their way back into office—as did even the Earl of Nottingham, furious that the Queen had not made him Lord President of the Council or Lord Privy Seal.[1]

The Whigs, allied with Nottingham, systematically opposed the Queen's government during the last three years of her reign. The opening barrage was dramatically successful. In December 1711 they carried, with Nottingham's help, a vote in the House of Lords 'that no peace can be safe or honourable to Great Britain or Europe if Spain and the West Indies are to be allotted to any branch of the House of Bourbon'. But Oxford secured the reversal of this vote by persuading the Queen to name twelve new Tory peers. Strengthened by these new peers in the House of Lords and supported by the October Club (who were pleased at the new Commissions of Victualling and Customs) in the Commons, the government carried all before it. When the Whigs in May 1712 denounced the Restraining Orders sent to the Duke of Ormond, the government repulsed the attack by 68 to 40 in the Lords and 203 to 73 in the Commons. A month later the government prevailed again when the Lords voted their confidence in the Queen's endeavours to negotiate a peace. During the spring of 1713 the government met no check to its affairs in Parliament, causing William Bishop to write to Dr Charlett, 'Affairs in both Houses go on fairly and softly—I am told the present ministry have interest enough in both Houses to carry what they please, notwithstanding the outcry and petitions raised by the Whigs to hinder it, so that there is no danger from the Whiggish attempts, as I am assured, which time will show.'[2]

William Bishop's complacency was premature, as time rapidly showed. He wrote to Dr Charlett on 11 June; a week later, on the 18th, the House of Commons rejected by 11 votes a Bill to Confirm the 8th and 9th Articles of the Commercial Treaty with France. It was a humiliating defeat for the government. Defoe wished that the ministry had not supported the Articles, so that their rejection would not have discredited the government. All the members from the City but one opposed the Bill, as did half the Scottish members; but

---

[1] Swift, *Works*, VI, 128, 131; VII, 4, 16, 18.
[2] *L.J.* XIX, 399, 461, 474; *C.J.* XVII, 246; Ballard MSS 31, f. 102.

what really caused amazement was the opposition of thirty Hanoverian Tories, led by Sir Thomas Hanmer. Their opposition was caused less by solicitude for English trade than by anger at Oxford's past conduct. They complained that he had not, despite repeated promises, removed Whigs from the Lord Lieutenancies, the Deputy Lieutenancies, and the Commissions of Peace, nor dismissed them from the Customs and Excise commissions. They objected to his behaving like an absolute minister, whose management no one should criticize. They wished him to cease negotiating with the Whigs, as rumour said he did, and to cease countenancing the Pretender, as suspicion reported. They wished him to cease being 'an ambidexter', a man who used both parties to serve his own ends. To make him heed their demands they resolved to shake him to the roots by opposing the Treaty of Commerce. 'You see what becomes of trimming it betwixt two parties,' wrote William Bishop, 'neither cares for you.' And John Plunket, a Jacobite agent, concurred, 'The truth on't is he thinks if the government is lodged in the hands of the Tories only, he is not long lived in it, and therefore he aimed at a mixture; but now, to his cost, it won't do.'[1]

Oxford reacted to this threat to his continuance in office as he had reacted to earlier threats: he brought more Tories into office. Sir Thomas Hanmer was promised the position of Speaker in the next Parliament, and Bromley, the former Speaker, became Secretary of State in the place of Lord Dartmouth, who became Lord Privy Seal. Sir William Wyndham became Chancellor of the Exchequer, Francis Atterbury became Bishop of Rochester, and Arthur Moore replaced the most loyal of courtiers, James Brydges, as Paymaster of the Foreign Troops. In many lesser offices Tories replaced Whigs. In fact never before had a ministry so swiftly purged so many of its political opponents from the administration.[2]

Yet the purge still failed to satisfy Henry St John, now Viscount

---

[1] *C.J.* xvii, 430; Defoe, *Letters*, 418–19; William Bishop to Dr Charlett, 20 June 1713, Ballard MSS 31, f. 104v; John Plunket to Sir William Ellis, 22 June 1713, in Macpherson, *Original Papers*, ii, 417. In a letter to Sir William Ellis, Ralph Wingate summarizes the complaints of the rebel Tories (*ibid.* p. 419).

[2] The author of *The Right of the Sovereign in the Choice of His Servants* (1714) lists 95 offices whose occupants the new ministry purged between 1710 and 1714, giving the names of those expelled and those who replaced them. The offices range from Lord Treasurer and Lord Chancellor to Commissioners of the Wine Office and Clerks of the Ordnance.

Bolingbroke, who had never believed in driving a coach with unequal wheels. He now outdid Hanmer in demanding a total proscription of Whigs everywhere and the passage of measures that would insure a perpetual ascendancy for the Church party in the political life of England. He informed Oxford in July that if he would not lead the Church party someone else must. Faced with this ultimatum, Oxford had three choices: to find a Court party in the next Parliament, to resign as Lord Treasurer, or to govern as the leader of the Tory party. The elections in August made futile the search for a Court party that could hold the balance in the Commons; by Oxford's own computations the Tory majority was 89 and the number of placemen 50 or 60 at most. As a result Oxford contemplated resignation. On 19 March 1714 he wrote to Sir Simon Harcourt, 'I have found myself a burden to my friends and to the only party I ever have or will act with. Ever since this was apparent, I have withdrawn myself from everything but where neglect would be inexcusable.' But he did not resign; instead he remained at the Treasury, confiding his disappointments to paper on 26 March. 'The first complaint was he did all...the same persons complain he is indolent and unacting...who hinders him from heading the Tories but those who complain?' In this pathetic, indolent, bitter mood Oxford confessed that only as the leader of a party—the role he had always eschewed—could he remain in office.[1]

The most remarkable fact about the quarrel that raged between Bolingbroke and Oxford in 1714 was its confinement to Court. It never erupted into parliamentary impeachments. The Duke of Buckingham in 1667 and the Earl of Orrery in 1669 showed no such discipline, but they lived before men realized that all depended on party unity. In the spring of 1714 the Queen knew, Bolingbroke knew, even Oxford knew, that once the Tories split the Whigs would return to power. But perhaps no one saw more clearly than Jonathan Swift the importance of party unity. In his *Advice to the October Club* he marvelled at the unanimity displayed by the Whigs and deplored the disagreements rife 'among ourselves'. In his *Letter to a Whig Lord* he observed with wonder that in the vote condemning a peace without Spain there was not a 'single negative in your whole list,

---

[1] 19 March 1714, B.M. Loan 29/138, No. 5; 26 March 1714, B.M. Loan 29/10. Oxford estimated (19 March 1714, B.M. Loan 29/10) that there were 240 Tories, 151 Whigs, and 50–60 Court dependants.

not above one Whig-lord guilty of a suspicious absence...'.[1] And when Richard Steele, newly elected to the House of Commons as a Whig, announced that he would 'follow no leaders, but vote according to the dictates of his conscience', Swift replied, 'He must, at that rate, be a very useless member to his party.' For Swift little judgment joined to great unanimity was preferable to great wisdom joined to little unanimity.

What Swift urged in theory, the Tory ministers strove to achieve in practice. In April 1714 Oxford, Bolingbroke, Harcourt, and Hanmer, fearful of a revolt of the backbenchers, met with thirty of them. They proposed, wrote Sir Edward Knatchbull, 'that we should...not let a majority in Parliament slip through our hands, and that we should meet twice a week for a mutual confidence...'. And they declared that 'the Queen was determined to proceed in the interest of the Church, etc., and my Lord Bolingbroke farther added afterward that he would not leave a Whig in employ.'[2]

But the unity of the Tories in Parliament did not dissuade the Whigs from attacking the government. In the spring of 1714 they moved resolutions in both Houses that the Protestant Succession was in danger from the present administration. In the House of Lords they opposed a resolution declaring the Peace of Utrecht to be safe, honourable, and advantageous. They also sought in the Lords to censure the government for deserting the Catalans, for allowing the Pretender to remain in Lorraine, and for paying subsidies to Jacobite Highlanders. Their fiercest attack was on Arthur Moore (and indirectly upon Bolingbroke) for negotiating a disadvantageous commercial agreement with Spain. None of these attacks succeeded, for, as one Tory said of the debate on the peace, 'We did not trouble ourselves to say much, for we knew our numbers, and so did the Whigs.'[3] But these attempts to censure the government did give the Whigs the opportunity to embrace once more the cause of responsible government, and allowed the Tories to revert

---

[1] Swift, *Works*, VI, 77, 134; VIII, 16, 88. Swift's pamphlet against Richard Steele is the source for the remark allegedly made by Steele (*ibid.* VIII, 16).

[2] A. N. Newman (ed.), 'Proceedings in the House of Commons, March–June 1714', *Bulletin of the Institute of Historical Research*, XXIV, 213. A week later Thomas Strangways, while dining at Arthur Moore's, objected 'that the keeping in the Whigs in places, was an alloy to the spirit of the Tories', upon which 'Lord Bolingbroke swore it was not his fault, and that to show he was in earnest, if there was one Whig in employment at the rising of this session he would give any one leave to spit in his face if he would keep his seals two months after the session' (*ibid.* p. 214).   [3] Cartwright, *Wentworth Papers*, p. 379.

to a traditional royalism. On 5 April, for instance, Sir Simon Harcourt, the Lord Chancellor, proposed to substitute 'under Her Majesty's administration' for 'under the present administration' in the motion declaring the Protestant Succession in danger. But the Whigs would have none of it, protesting that the Queen should not be mentioned, 'for by our constitution, the sovereign can do no wrong; and, if anything be done amiss, the ministers alone are accountable'. But the Tories, by 77 to 63, substituted 'under Her Majesty's administration'. The House of Commons used the same expression, despite the objections of Sir Robert Walpole and Sir Thomas Hanmer that the ministry should not screen itself behind the Queen's name.[1] Not only did the Whigs maintain that ministers of state were accountable for what they did, they also insisted that they were responsible for what they advised. And the Queen was always presumed to act on their advice. In the debate on the Highlanders, Lord Wharton demanded that the ministers should not shelter themselves behind the Queen's name, 'for whatever the Queen did the ministers that advised it were to answer for it'.[2] But what should Parliament do if the Queen acted alone, upon her own counsels, without asking advice? This possibility the Whigs would not allow, as they demonstrated in their attack upon the Treaty of Commerce with Spain. Appended to that treaty were three Explanatory Articles which bore no signature but the Queen's. 'It was using the Queen ill,' argued the Whigs, 'to advise her to sign what none of them durst.'[3] The Whig lords in the Upper House gave point to this argument by persuading the House to vote an address requesting the Queen to send them an account of the manner in which the Explanatory Articles 'were proposed, treated, and agreed, in order to the ratification of them'. The Queen answered that she had consented to the ratification of the Explanatory Articles because she judged them not materially different from the Treaty of Commerce with Spain

[1] Cartwright, *Wentworth Papers*, pp. 364, 370–1; Cobbett, *Parl. Hist.* VI, 1335, 1346; *L.J.* XIX, 647, 659; *C.J.* XVII, 574.
[2] Cartwright, *Wentworth Papers*, p. 374. When the Queen, in an answer to an address from the Lords, said that she would not, as they requested, issue a Proclamation for seizing the Pretender, Lord Wharton remarked (*ibid.* p. 373), 'He knew Her Majesty's goodness was such that she would never take anything ill from her House of Lords unless some bold whisperer had misrepresented their debates and intentions, therefore the ministry ought to answer for this.'
[3] *Ibid.* p. 379.

negotiated at Utrecht. But she did not say who had 'proposed, treated, and agreed' to the Explanatory Articles. Her refusal provoked the Earl of Sunderland to say that if the House received such answers from the Crown, they were of no use and might as well never meet again. But the House of Lords did not press her to name names. They did not wish to make her a common informer: they merely wished to establish the principle that she always acted on the advice and by the instrumentality of ministers of state.[1]

That the Queen could do no wrong because she always acted on the advice of others became during Queen Anne's reign orthodox constitutional doctrine, though not without some protests from unreconstructed royalists. In 1703, for instance, the author of *The Unanimous or Consentient Opinions* sought to establish the orthodoxy of the maxim that the King can do no wrong by citing eighteen authorities, from Sir Edward Coke to Mr Edmond Hickeringill, who agreed that the maxim meant that the King's ministers must answer for all. The publication of *The Unanimous or Consentient Opinions* led John Byrdall to protest in a pamphlet, *Noli Me Tangere*, which appeared that same year. Byrdall argued that the maxim that the King can do no wrong merely means that a sovereign Prince is not accountable to his subjects. He made no mention whatever of the accountability of his ministers, but he roundly condemned 'the damnable opinion' of the Despensers that the King's political capacity could be distinguished from his natural person, and that greater allegiance was owed to him in his political capacity than in his personal.[2]

Jonathan Swift, ten years later, voiced similar sentiments in his quarrel with Richard Steele over the meaning of the maxim that the King can do no wrong. In *The Englishman* for 14 November 1713 Steele confidently asserted,

In Kingdoms where an absolute and tyrannical government prevails, the Prince and his ministers are in effect the same; but, God be praised, it is not so with us. Our laws have fenced the person of the Prince, as it were, with a wall of brass: he is by them secured from violence, or any imputation of wrong; but his ministers are by the same laws left as open to accusations of all kinds, as any other of their fellow subjects. Nay, what

---

[1] *L.J.* xix, 741, 746; Cartwright, *Wentworth Papers*, p. 396.

[2] *The Unanimous or Consentient Opinions of the Learned...in the Explication or Exposition of that Celebrated Maxim in the Laws of England, the King can do no Wrong* (1703); [John Byrdall], *Noli Me Tangere* (1703).

is more, an Englishman may, as I take it, have the utmost horror for what may be done by ministers, at the same time that he has the greatest veneration and duty for his Prince.[1]

To Swift these sentiments echoed the damnable opinion of the Despensers. 'You are to understand', he wrote to the Bailiff of Stockbridge (where Steele was standing for Parliament), 'that in the great rebellion against King Charles I there was a distinction found out between the personal and political capacity of the Prince; by the help of which, those rebels professed to fight for the King, while the great guns were discharging against Charles Stuart. After the same manner Mr Steele distinguishes between the personal and political prerogative.' And he will not allow the Queen to exercise the political prerogative, for 'Providence has given her will, pleasure, and passion.' Neither shall her ministers be held to act by her command, 'for then Mr Steele will cry out, What? Are Majesty and Ministry consolidated?' And Swift concluded that at that rate the prerogative might as well be lodged with the Crown in the Tower, to be shown for 12*d*. But Swift would have the Queen act otherwise. He would have her say to Mr Steele, 'My ministers were of my own free choice; I have found them wise and faithful; and who-ever calls them fools or knaves, designs indirectly an affront to myself.'[2]

But even Swift could only face reality momentarily. Having exposed the constitutional fictions embedded in the maxim that the King can do no wrong, having shown its kinship to the doctrine of the Despensers, having shown how it reduced the Queen to a cipher, he promptly embraced the doctrine himself, albeit hesitantly.

There is a very good maxim, I think it is neither Whig nor Tory, that the Prince can do no wrong; which I doubt is often applied to very ill pur-poses. A monarch of Britain is pleased to create a dozen peers, and to make a peace; both these actions are, for instance, within the undisputed prerogative of the Crown, and are to be reputed and submitted to as the actions of the Prince: But as a King of England is supposed to be guided in matters of such importance by the advice of those he employs in his Council; whenever a Parliament thinks fit to complain of such proceedings, as a public grievance, then this maxim takes place, that the Prince can do no wrong, and the advisers are called to account.

---

[1] Rae Blanchard (ed.), *The Englishman. A Political Journal by Richard Steele* (Oxford, 1955), p. 76. In a later *Englishman* (*ibid.* p. 131), Steele maintained that an English King could not be said to have acted 'in his single person, without evil counsellors to advise and wicked agents to put such advice in execution'.

[2] Swift, *Works*, VIII, 17, 19.

Swift squared his adherence to constitutional orthodoxy with his attack upon Steele by concluding that the maxim justifies parliamentary criticism of the Queen's ministers, but not criticism by mere pamphleteers.[1]

While Swift and Steele argued in print and while the Whigs and Tories quarrelled in Parliament, Bolingbroke and Oxford contested for power at Court. The ironical result was the victory of the party politician over the loyal courtier—of the man who would have the Queen rely upon a triumphant Tory party over the man who would have her hold the balance between both parties. Bolingbroke won his victory, however, because he was the better courtier. He secured Mrs Masham's support at Court by promising her a share in the Asiento contract and he won the Queen's favour by his intrepid opposition to a proposal, offensive to her, to send a parliamentary writ to George, Duke of Cambridge, Princess Sophia's son. But no sooner had Bolingbroke won his victory at Court, than he saw it endangered in Parliament. Throughout the session the number of Tories joining the Whigs against the government mounted. On 15 April, for instance, eighty Tories joined the Whigs in the Commons to vote that the Succession was in danger.[2] But the real crisis came in the House of Lords in July, when the Whigs raised a hue and cry against the authors of the Explanatory Articles, whom they believed to be Arthur Moore and Bolingbroke himself. The danger for Bolingbroke was very great, for had Oxford publicly declared in the Upper House what he had privately told the Whigs—that Bolingbroke had negotiated and secured the ratification of the Explanatory Articles without the knowledge and authority of the Cabinet Council—he could have brought down his rival with a parliamentary impeachment. But he made no such public declaration, fearing to lose the Queen's favour at a time when he had so few friends in Parliament. His timidity insured

---

[1] Swift, *Works*, VIII, 23. The controversy surrounding Steele's writings occasioned the republication of Thomas Rymer's treatise, *Of the Antiquity, Power, and Decay of Parliaments*, a treatise which the late historiographer-royal originally published in 1681. In this treatise he perfectly expressed (p. 8) what was to become the orthodox view of the constitution: 'Now since, for the conduct and sway over men, the world is not furnished with any specie more noble than man, art supplies what was wanting in nature; an artificial man is framed, a politic creature, a King that never dies, that can do no wrong, that cannot be deceived, whose counsels and determinations are the result of the joint experience and wisdom of a whole nation.'

[2] L'Hermitage, B.M. Add. MSS 17677 HHH, f. 187v.

his fall from power, for Bolingbroke only awaited the prorogation of Parliament before advising the Queen to dismiss her Lord
Treasurer.[1]

Bolingbroke not only eagerly awaited, he precipitated, the prorogation of Parliament. On 8 July the Lords read letters written by
Bolingbroke, which showed that he had arranged for grasping
courtiers (rumour pointed to Mrs Masham, Arthur Moore, and
himself) to appropriate the Queen's share of the Asiento contract.
Witnesses the same day brought serious charges of corruption against
Arthur Moore, Bolingbroke's agent.[2] Frightened by these disclosures, which angered Tories as well as Whigs, Bolingbroke advised
the Queen to prorogue Parliament the very next day. Her sudden
arrival on the 9th prevented a possible censure of Arthur Moore;
her final speech infuriated her subjects. 'But I must tell you plainly,'
she said to both Houses, that liberty, tranquillity, and true religion
cannot be secured 'unless you show the same regard for my just
prerogative, and for the honour of my government, as I have always
expressed for the rights of my people.'[3] However much all else may
have changed since 1603, the last words to Parliament of the last
Stuart rang out no less imperiously than the first words of the first
Stuart.

The Queen dismissed the Earl of Oxford on 27 July, but her death
on 1 August extinguished all hopes that Bolingbroke may have had
of establishing a Tory ascendancy on the basis of the Queen's favour
at Court and the operation of the Schism and Occasional Conformity
Acts in the country. There is no reason to believe that Bolingbroke
could have succeeded in his scheme even had the Queen lived, for the
Tory party was in disarray and the Queen's favour was no substitute
for the control of Parliament. If there was any lesson that Bolingbroke ought to have learned during his many years in politics it was
this: no minister could survive the sustained hostility of Parliament.
The Queen's favour was important to a minister, but Parliament's
support was indispensable. The Queen, for all her stubborness,
had not been able to force Robert Harley on the nation in 1708,
but Parliament, despite Anne's bitter hatred for the Whig Junto,
had forced the Junto on her in 1709. Bereft of parliamentary
support in 1708, Robert Harley had failed; possessed of Parliament's

[1] Klopp, *Der Fall des Hauses Stuart*, xiv, 617–19; Macpherson, *Original Papers*, ii, 633.
[2] Cartwright, *Wentworth Papers*, pp. 398–9.   [3] *L.J.* xix, 760.

support in 1710 he had succeeded. The explanation for Parliament's superiority lay in party, or rather in the power of party allied to the power of the purse. Together these two proved greater than the power of patronage allied to the prerogative. At no time in the reign of Queen Anne did the Court party possess a majority, and often it did not even hold the balance. James Brydges, the most astute as well as the most successful placeman in the reign, understood perfectly well the weakness of the power of patronage. The popularity of those who exercised it, he wrote in 1714, 'must diminish, it being a truth confirmed by experience that they who are possessed of great power disoblige more than they can possibly oblige, and are compelled to do so many hardships, and to such numbers, as easily reconcile men to those who formerly enjoyed their favour'. The Marquis of Newcastle in 1660 had likewise seen that the bestower of place disobliges more men than he obliges, but Brydges went beyond Newcastle in observing that patronage also divides the political party that exercises it. After every great change in government, he wrote,

the strongest side runs into subdivisions and quarrels about the distribution of power, of which none thinks he has such a proportion as his merits demand. And in this low state to which our factions of late years have reduced the regal authority, very few [men] contain their pretensions within the limits of modesty, and as many as are disappointed detach themselves from the main body; so that where every one thinks he has a just title to whatever the Crown can possibly give, it must needs disunite such a number of pretenders, who think their deserts equal.[1]

Party unity, and only party unity, could prevent the strongest side, which had captured the power of patronage, from running into subdivisions and quarrels. William Oldisworth saw this truth, declaring in *The Examiner* in January 1714:

In general, whoever among the Tories, at this time of day especially, endeavours at any thing that may divide his own party, or create misunderstanding between them, takes the shortest, the surest, and the only way to ruin them. The Whigs in a body, though everyone of them were a

[1] James Brydges to the Duke of Marlborough, 9 Jan. 1714, Huntington Library S.T. 57, x, ff. 31, 32. Or as Joseph Addison observed in *The Freeholder* (*Works*, 1901, v, 76), '...by the nature of our constitution it is in the power of more particular persons in this kingdom, than in any other, to distress the government when they are disobliged. A British minister must, therefore, expect to see many of those friends and dependants fall off from him, whom he cannot gratify in their demands upon him; since, to use the phrase of a late statesman..."the pasture is not large enough."'

Guiscard, are not half so formidable. Unity and concord must perfect the good work; and by these arts the Tories will for ever flourish and be immovable. Unity and self-preservation are the same thing to them, and so far as this virtue goes, I would have every Tory a downright Dutchman.[1]

And from party unity came the power that could support a parliamentary undertaking. From the time of Neville through the age of Shaftesbury the independent country gentlemen had condemned party and repudiated undertakers. But the growth of parties during the reigns of King William and Queen Anne altered this situation. Those who won office because they could undertake to manage Parliament now led parties there; and the loyalty of those parties insured that they could succeed in their undertaking. Furthermore, the sway of party clearly overbalanced the influence of the Crown in the deliberations of Parliament, just as the power of the purse outweighed the prerogative in the government of the realm. For these reasons the parliamentary undertaker who used his majority in Parliament to secure office came to eclipse the parliamentary manager who sought to use his influence at Court to control Parliament. The triumph of the parliamentary undertaker over the parliamentary manager—the most important single step taken towards responsible government in the reign of Queen Anne—rested solidly on the triumph of party over patronage in the management of Parliament.

[1] *The Examiner*, v, no. 11.

CHAPTER 10

THE END OF IMPEACHMENT (1715–1717)

When *The Flying Post*, in May 1712, reported that the government was negotiating a separate peace with France, the Earl of Oxford rose in the House of Lords to deny it, declaring, 'Such a peace would be so foolish, so knavish, and so villainous a thing, that every one who served the Queen knew they must answer for it with their heads to the nation.'[1] The Whigs, who believed that the government sought such a peace, would have been more than human had they forgotten Oxford's words. In fact they did not forget them. Three years later, in June 1715, a Whig House of Commons impeached, not only the Earl of Oxford, but also Viscount Bolingbroke, the Duke of Ormond, and the Earl of Strafford, for negotiating a separate peace with France. They likewise impeached them for endeavouring to secure the Pretender's succession to the throne. On receiving these impeachments, the House of Lords imprisoned Oxford in the Tower, attainted Bolingbroke and Ormond (both of whom had fled to France), and demanded that Strafford answer the charges brought against him. But, as so often in the past, these impeachments came to nothing. The House of Lords acquitted Oxford in 1717, the House of Commons declined to prosecute Strafford's impeachment, Parliament pardoned Bolingbroke in 1725, and would have pardoned Ormond had he not chosen to spend his remaining years in the Pretender's service.

The events of these years raise two obvious questions: why did the Whigs impeach the late Queen's ministers, and why were they unable to prosecute successfully their impeachments against them? But beneath these two superficial questions lie two more profound ones: what responsibilities lay upon ministers of state at this time, and what caused the practice of impeaching ministers of state to fall, after 1717, into desuetude? The first two questions deserve answers,

---

[1] Cobbett, *Parl. Hist.* VI, 1138. After Oxford had finished, Lord Wharton rose and besought the Lords to bear in mind those words 'foolish, villainous and knavish', and also the words, 'answer for it with their heads'. In 1715 a Whig pamphlet, entitled *An Address to the Good People of Great Britain Occasioned by the Report of the Committee of Secrecy* (p. 38), reminded the English people of Oxford's words in 1712.

but chiefly for the light they throw upon the responsibilities borne by ministers of state at the accession of George I and upon the reasons for the end of impeachment as a means to secure responsible government.[1] The Whig ministers of George I—Stanhope, Sunderland, Townshend, Walpole, Cowper, and Marlborough—resolved in the spring of 1715 to impeach the ministers who had negotiated the Treaty of Utrecht. Among the motives which prompted them, a desire to revenge past Tory attacks upon themselves cannot have been absent. Between 1710 and 1714 the Tories had sent Walpole to the Tower, had accused Marlborough of corruption, had censured Townshend for negotiating the Barrier Treaty, and had driven many other Whigs from office. 'I shall one day revenge what I heartily despise', wrote Walpole when in the Tower, and the day had now arrived.[2] But it is unlikely that men as shrewd as Walpole or as wise as Cowper would have embarked on the path of parliamentary accusation merely to gratify a passion for revenge. A far more practical motive drove them to the impeachment of their Tory opponents: a desire to proscribe them from public life forever. By impeaching Oxford, Bolingbroke, Ormond, and Strafford, the Whigs sought to accomplish what the Tories in 1701 had hoped to gain by impeaching Somers, Halifax, Orford, and Portland. They hoped to drive their enemies from Parliament, to discredit them with the nation, and to prevent their ever again serving their sovereign. The Whigs feared Oxford's talent for management, Bolingbroke's brilliance in debate, Ormond's popularity with the populace, and Strafford's knowledge of foreign Courts. Bolingbroke in particular they feared. 'Many believe', wrote the French ambassador of the Whig effort to frighten Bolingbroke into flight, 'that the purpose of the Whigs is no other than to be rid of an antagonist whom they have reason to fear...for there are no other lords in the Upper House capable of forcefully sustaining his party'.[3]

---

[1] The House of Commons subsequently impeached seven Jacobite lords in 1716, Lord Macclesfield in 1725, Lord Lovat in 1747, Warren Hastings in 1787, and Lord Melville in 1805. But the Commons did not vote these impeachments in order to enforce responsible government. The Jacobite lords, Lord Lovat, and Warren Hastings were not ministers of the Crown; and the Commons only accused Macclesfield and Melville of personal delinquencies, not of giving the King pernicious advice or obeying unlawful orders.

[2] Plumb, *Walpole*, I, 215.

[3] Fr. Trans. 18/29 Sept. 1714. The French ambassador's remarks find confirmation in the fact that when Parliament pardoned Bolingbroke in 1725, it did not (at Walpole's insistence) allow him to resume his seat in the House of Lords.

The desire of the Whigs to proscribe their opponents from public life was a genuine but not a sufficient motive for impeaching them. Oxford no longer had any credit with his party; Bolingbroke's schemes lay broken; Ormond possessed no political judgment; and Strafford possessed no reputation. Far more important to the Whigs than the proscription of these men was the destruction of the party which they led. The Whigs hoped by exposing to the world the treachery of the late ministry to discredit the Tory party for all time. And while destroying the Tories they hoped simultaneously to justify themselves, to vindicate their past opposition to the Queen's ministers, to prove that their cries of perfidy and betrayal had not been baseless. As the Earl of Nottingham said to Count Bothmar, 'An inquiry into the previous ministry's conduct of affairs is necessary in order to show the nation that one had not complained of it without cause.'[1]

The Earl of Nottingham sought to justify his own opposition to the previous ministry, but the Whigs had more to justify than past opposition to Tory ministers. They sought also to justify a present Whig monopoly of all places in government. Walpole, Townshend, and Cowper had no use for a mixed ministry or a 'motely' administration, but they knew that the popular cant of the day favoured them. Count Bothmer gave expression to that cant when he wrote to George I that His Majesty should give office to men according to their merits, not according to whether they were Whig or Tory. Yet Bothmar immediately added that His Majesty should not employ those who in the previous reign had endangered Europe and the Protestant Succession by their counsels.[2] In effect Bothmar proclaimed what most Englishmen believed, that it was wrong to exclude a man from office because he was a Tory, but permissible if he were a traitor. For the Whigs the logical deduction to be drawn was clear: if they wished to justify a monopoly of office for themselves they must persuade the King, the Parliament, and the electorate that the Tory party was the party of treason, that by their treachery in the previous reign the Tories had proved themselves unfit for office in the present one.

[1] R. Pauli, 'Aktenstücke zur Thronbesteigung des Welfenhauses in England', *Zeitschrift des historischen Vereins für Niedersachsen* (1883), p. 67. Lord Bathurst wrote similarly to Strafford (Cartwright, *Wentworth Papers*, pp. 438–9), 'Those who have blamed every thing which has been done abroad for these four years last must in their own justification endeavour all they can to oppress the principal actors in those affairs.'

[2] Pauli, 'Aktenstücke', p. 85.

The End of Impeachment

There is no denying the determination of the Whigs to secure a monopoly of office for themselves. Their purge of Tory officeholders went beyond the Cabinet and the Court to the remotest corners of the administration, to Deputy-Treasurers of Chelsea Hospital and to Commissioners for Appeals in the Excise.[1] But thirst for office, though the primary, was not the sole cause for excluding Tories from the government: the Whigs also believed that a government composed of both Whigs and Tories could not work. Lord Cowper in September 1714 advised George I that it was 'not possible so to distribute your royal favours, but that one or other of the parties will appear to have a superior degree of trust reposed in them: and if such a perfect equality was possible to be observed, perhaps it would follow that an equal degree of power, tending at the same time different ways, would render the operations of government slow and heavy, if not altogether impracticable'.[2] Lord Bolingbroke, the Tory, concurred fully with Lord Cowper, the Whig. He told the French ambassador that he would not remain Secretary of State if other offices were filled with Whigs, 'for there could be no compatibility between them'.[3]

There never was any chance that the new King would ask Bolingbroke to remain in office, but George I did so far seek to escape from the domination of one party as to offer lucrative employments, if not places of trust, to the Hanoverian Tories. In late September he offered the Chancellorship of the Exchequer to Sir Thomas Hanmer and a place as Teller in the Exchequer to William Bromley. Both men, unwilling to lose the support of their Tory friends, refused office. Sir Thomas told his intimate friends that he could not in prudence accept a place 'which would lose him the dependence of

---

[1] Plumb, *Walpole*, I, 205. Pleading with the Earl of Halifax not to dismiss a Commissioner for Appeals brought in by Oxford, James Brydges wrote (Huntington Library S.T. 57, XI, f. 202), 'I hope there will nothing be suggested to Your Grace against him and, if he should have been guilty of errors in the former part of his life, relating to party matters, I dare answer for him, he'll endeavour to make amends by his future conduct.'

[2] Costin and Watson, *Law and Working of the Constitution*, I, 361.

[3] Fr. Trans. 8/19 Aug. 1714. Lord Egmont shared Cowper's and Bolingbroke's sentiments, writing (B.M. Add. MSS 47087, Oct. 1714), 'The hatred which the Whigs and Tories bore one another was (as it still continues) so insurmountable, that His Majesty soon became convinced of the impracticableness of taking into his intimate councils the heads of both parties.' Only Oxford among practising politicians clung to the ideal of a mixed ministry, writing to Dartmouth at the end of August 1714 (*H.M.C. Rep. II, Part 5*, p. 321), 'Neither party of the two denominations (Whig and Tory) separately can form any such [ministry] as is practicable...It is therefore plain there must be an understanding between those who wish a settlement in England...'

his friends and then leave him at the mercy of his enemies'.[1] He preferred, as did Bromley, to throw in his fortune with the Tories who were determined to remain united, to win a majority in Parliament, and to distress the government until the King gave them office. 'From this time', wrote Lord Egmont, 'the Tories resolved to unite their strength and if possible to gain a majority in the ensuing Parliament as the only means left to support their declining party, hoping the King might be prevailed on to dismiss his new ministers when he should be convinced that the sense of the nation ran in favour of the Church party.' The Tories, he added, hope 'after distressing the government to have their choice of the best offices'.[2]

The refusal of Hanmer and Bromley to accept offices angered George I, who had come to England resolved to make no distinctions as to party in the bestowal of employments. But the refusal of two principal Tories to serve with the Whigs forced him to change his mind, caused him to incline more than ever to the Whigs. He now agreed to a total change in all the Commissions and to the removal of Tories from the meanest of places.[3] Like William and Anne before him, George knew that a sovereign who employed men drawn from a single party must submit to the dictates of that party, but he had even less power than his two predecessors to escape from the coils of party government.

A desire to avenge wrongs done them in the past, a wish to proscribe men dangerous to them in the present, a determination to discredit the Tory party irreparably, and a wish to justify a Whig monopoly of offices—these were the motives, sufficient and powerful, that led the Whig ministers of George I to introduce impeachments against Oxford, Bolingbroke, Ormond, and Strafford. Only one consideration caused them to hesitate: could they carry their impeachments in the Commons and prosecute them successfully before the Lords? Above all, could they find evidence to prove these men guilty of treason?

From the moment of George's accession the Whigs industriously sought the evidence that would convict the late ministry of negotia-

---

[1] Lord Egmont's Journal, B.M. Add. MSS 47087, Oct. 1714.

[2] *Ibid.* L'Hermitage (B.M. Add. MSS 17677 HHH, ff. 406 v–407, 416), Herr Hoffmann (Klopp, *Der Fall des Hauses Stuart*, xiv, 670), and Peter Wentworth (Cartwright, *Wentworth Papers*, p. 430) agreed with Lord Egmont that Hanmer and Bromley chose to place their trust in a party which hoped to win a majority in Parliament.

[3] Brydges Papers, Huntington Library S.T. 57, xi, ff. 157–158.

ting a separate treacherous peace and of seeking to bring in the Pretender. They seized, locked, and sealed Bolingbroke's office before he could carry away his papers. They forced a reluctant Strafford to surrender papers which he believed should remain in his possession. They asked the Bishop of Bristol to deliver up his papers. Their search met with some success; rumour reported in January 1715 that the ministry had made great discoveries. And they had, but their discoveries concerned only the haste with which the late ministers had made peace, not the fact that they had sought to bring in the Pretender. Yet it was proof concerning the design to bring in the Pretender that the Whigs most wanted. In its absence they could only rely upon suspicion, a suspicion, however, that a timely event in November seemed to confirm. In that month the Pretender published a manifesto, in which he lamented the Queen's untimely death, particularly because 'for some time past he could not well doubt his sister's good intentions towards him'. The effect of this remark upon most Englishmen was to persuade them that there had been a secret correspondence between the Queen's ministers and the Court of St Germain. Bolingbroke stood amazed at the Pretender's folly in publishing the manifesto, saying that this single act should persuade the world that the Pretender was truly the son of his father.[1]

The King's ministers were emboldened to proceed on suspicion rather than proof because the Court, the Whig party, and the nation clamoured for impeachments. The Court made clear its intentions in December, when Baron von Bernsdorff (through Lord Cowper) informed the Earl of Halifax that the King, hearing that Halifax would not do his part at the Treasury to promote a parliamentary inquiry into the old ministry, expected that he should. Halifax had indeed sought a reconciliation with Oxford in order that he might become the head of a mixed ministry, but he now dropped the scheme and promised to do his part in the prosecution of the late ministry.[2] It was well he did, for not only the Court, but also the publicists of the Whig party, took him to task for being lukewarm in the pursuit of the late ministry. Of all the pamphlets calling for the impeachment of the Queen's Tory ministers, none met with more success than *The Necessity of Impeaching the Late Ministry in a Letter*

---

[1] *H.M.C. Rep. XI, Part 4, Townshend MSS*, p. 157.
[2] *Diary of Mary Countess Cowper* (1864), p. 30.

to the Earl of Halifax, written by Thomas Burnet, son of Bishop Burnet. In his pamphlet Burnet sought to justify impeaching the late ministry by cataloguing the black crimes which they had committed. His tract was only one of many Whig demands for the impeachment of the late ministry.[1] What alarmed the Tories most and most encouraged the Whigs was the enthusiastic reception these pamphlets received in the country. In coffee houses men threatened Bolingbroke with impeachment and in the streets the crowds hissed Oxford. Whig-inspired addresses poured into Parliament demanding an inquiry into the conduct of the late ministry and the punishment of those at fault. Moderate men deplored the Woodstock address, calling for fire and faggot, but they applauded 'The Instructions Given by the Citizens of London to their Representatives', which called for the discovery and punishment of those who had advised a separate peace with France and who had prepared the way for the Pretender.[2] When Parliament assembled on 17 March, the ministry could hardly have withstood the popular demand for impeachments, even had they wished to.

This was particularly true because the Whigs had won a decisive majority in the new Parliament, a majority of 150.[3] The Whig victory came as no surprise, for the King's Proclamation summoning a new Parliament called for the election of only those men who had been firm to the Protestant Succession. Men who sought preferment and

[1] Thomas Burnet, *The Necessity of Impeaching the Late Ministry* (1715). Other pamphlets demanding justice against the late ministry were John Oldmixon, *The False Steps of the Ministry after the Revolution* (1714); John Dunton, *Neck or Nothing* (1714); *An Inquiry into the Miscarriages of the Last Four Years* (1715); *The Happy Crisis* (1715); *Mr Burnet's Defence* (1715); and *Reasons Without Passion for the Accusation of Corrupt Ministers* (1715).

[2] William Bishop wrote to Dr Charlett (Ballard MSS 31, f. 129), 'The Woodstock address calls for revenge, no less than fire and faggot. The moderate Whigs think it overdoing and scandalous.' L'Hermitage wrote (B.M. Add. MSS 17677 III, f. 71), 'A newspaper has published the Instructions of the Citizens of London to their four representatives, which, though not authentic, as not coming from the Court of Aldermen or Common Council, yet...is a précis of daily complaints and will certainly give rise to similar instructions in other places, in a more authentic form. One does not doubt that in the next Parliament the conduct of the previous ministry will be investigated.' 'The Instructions' are printed in Abel Boyer, *A Compleat and Impartial History of the Impeachments of the Last Ministry* (1717), p. xxiv.

[3] Wolfgang Michael, *England under George I; The Beginnings of the Hanoverian Dynasty* (1936), p. 116. James Brydges wrote to Lord Bolingbroke (7 Feb. 1715, Huntington Library S.T. 57, XI, f. 250), '...the elections growing more Whiggish than I am apt to think even the Court itself desires, there will in all probability be some violent measures set forward which the ministry will not be able (should they be willing) to avoid giving into. The steps they have taken...have so raised the expectation of the Whigs that they'll be soured and dissatisfied to the last degree if there is not care used to provide a sacrifice for them.'

favours from the Court naturally voted Whig, for the Whigs were in favour at Court; men who desired civil peace and domestic tranquillity likewise voted Whig, for a Tory parliament might provoke domestic strife and civil war. These two groups—joined by confirmed Whigs—easily carried the day, a fact immediately evident when the reunited Tories, Jacobite and Hanoverian, suffered defeat (by 224 to 138 in the Commons and 66 to 33 in the Lords) in their attempt to reject Addresses of Thanks for the King's speech from the throne. The Tories had no choice but to oppose the addresses, for they condemned the late ministry in a manner which led men to regard them as the prelude to impeachments. And the prelude to impeachments they proved to be. A fortnight later, on 9 April, Secretary Stanhope delivered to the House of Commons twelve folio volumes of papers concerning the negotiations of the peace, and proposed that, because the papers were so voluminous, a select, secret committee examine them. The House agreed, and named a Committee of Secrecy of twenty-one, all of them Whigs, seventeen of them in the ministry.[1]

The Committee of Secrecy elected Robert Walpole as their chairman, divided into four subcommittees, met eight hours a day, laboured through the Easter holidays, and spent the month of May preparing a lengthy report for the House. The Committee read the correspondence of Bolingbroke and Torcy, the letters of Matthew Prior, the memorials of the Earl of Oxford. Nothing that they could lay their hands on escaped their scrutiny. No witness whom they could apprehend escaped their vigilant questioning. That right for which the House of Commons had fought for a century, the right to inquire into the conduct of the King's ministers, was now triumphantly asserted. Yet it was not so much the House as the party that governed the House that won the victory, for in the same month that the Committee of Secrecy prepared their report, the Commons rejected by 61 votes a bill to establish a Committee for Taking the Public Accounts. For twenty-four years the House had established such committees in order to harass the executive, but now the Whigs had the strength to prevent it. Committees to inquire into the misconduct of Tory ministers were acceptable, but not committees to inquire into their own misconduct.[2]

---

[1] *C.J.* xviii, 22, 57; *L.J.* xx, 32.

[2] L'Hermitage, B.M. Add. MSS 17677III, ff. 168–169v, 173v–175, 229–229v; *C.J.* xviii, 138.

On 9 June Robert Walpole read to the House the Report of the Committee of Secrecy; the next day, without dividing, the House voted to impeach Viscount Bolingbroke and the Earl of Oxford for High Treason. On 21 June the House voted to impeach the Duke of Ormond for High Treason, by a vote of 234 to 187; the next day, by a vote of 268 to 100, they voted to impeach the Earl of Strafford for high crimes and misdemeanours. The hatred of the Whig members for the late ministry sufficiently explains their support for these impeachments, but it does not explain the decisive majorities which the House gave them. These majorities arose from something more than party zeal: they arose from astonishment at the sordid tale of betrayal, duplicity, and dishonour revealed by the Report. 'The blackest things that can be imagined', wrote Lord Egmont, 'are come out in relation to the making the peace...The charge was so bad upon them that the Tories would not divide in their favour, nor did any of their leaders speak in the whole debate.'[1]

Of the many black indictments in the Report the blackest was the charge that the late ministry had deserted the allies in order to make a separate peace with France. In 1712 the Earl of Oxford had declared that any minister who made a separate peace with France ought to pay for his villainy with his head. The Report of the Committee of Secrecy revealed that the late ministry had made such a peace. They had initiated overtures to France for peace in July 1711 and then signed Preliminary Articles of Peace with France in October. When the allies in 1712 bridled at accepting these terms, the ministry withdrew British armies from the allied camp (thus disrupting the siege of Quesnoy), occupied Bruges and Ghent, and signed a suspension of arms with France. At the ensuing peace negotiations at Utrecht the British plenipotentiaries worked hand and glove with France to embarrass the allies. In form the Treaty of Utrecht was a general peace, but its outward form could not conceal the fact that Britain had, by negotiating Preliminary Articles of Peace with France and by withdrawing its troops from the war, made a separate peace. Neither could the Treaty signed at Utrecht conceal the duplicity and perfidy with which the ministry had driven on their negotiations. Matthew Prior kept secret his negotiations in

---

[1] Lord Egmont to his brother, 11 June 1715, B.M. Add. MSS 47087. Lord Egmont added, 'I have met with Tory members since, and so likewise have others, who, upon the discoveries of the Committee made, own themselves astonished at the late ministry's proceedings, and think them justly chargeable with High Treason.'

25-2

France by burning Oxford's letters to him and the ministry clumsily sought to authorize their negotiations with Ménager in London by ante-dating a warrant empowering them to meet with him. The government sent Strafford to the Hague with instructions not to allow Spain and the West Indies to fall into the hands of Philip V, but the ministry had already accepted Philip V's guarantee that Gibraltar and Port Mahon should remain British. Not until seven months after the beginning of negotiations with France did Bolingbroke ask Torcy for France's demands on the allies. In December 1711 the ministry prevailed upon the Queen to tell Parliament that the States General had concurred in a general peace, when in fact they had not. In January 1712 they prevailed upon her to deny to Parliament that a separate peace was being negotiated, when in fact such negotiations were being carried on. The Duke of Ormond's public instructions required him to act in concert with the allies, his private instructions required him to act in concert with Marshall Villars. Yet even this long catalogue of duplicity Parliament might have excused had the peace brought advantage and honour to Britain, but it brought neither. The ministry admitted France to the Newfoundland fisheries, ceded Cape Breton to France, allowed Spain to lay duties as high as 29 per cent on British goods, failed to secure the expulsion of the Pretender from France, deserted the Catalans, and allowed the Duke of Anjou to ascend the throne of Spain as Philip V, even though Torcy had declared that the Duke's renunciation of the Crown of France had no force in law. In short, the Report chronicled an unedifying story of allies betrayed, Parliament deceived, and the realm dishonoured, a story which left the Tories powerless to stand against the impeachment of the late ministry.[1]

In one important respect the Report disappointed the Whigs: it contained no proof that the late ministry had sought to bring in the Pretender. It offered only circumstantial evidence that they had, circumstantial evidence based on Abbé Gaultier's unexplained journeys back and forth across the Channel. Normally the House of Commons would have hesitated before acting on such flimsy evidence, but Bolingbroke's flight to France had prepared them to believe the worst. Disguised in an ordinary surtout coat and black wig, Bolingbroke had slipped out of London on the evening of

---

[1] *The Report of the Committee of Secrecy*, reprinted in *Reports from Committees of the House of Commons* (1803), 1, 3–43.

27 March. He had good reason for flight. As Secretary of State he had conducted the peace negotiations with heedless abandon, fully informing Mênager of Instructions given to Lord Strafford, exhorting the British plenipotentiaries at Utrecht to act more closely with France, advising the French how they might gain Tournay, and writing to the Bishop of Bristol that the Dutch 'though they kick and flounce like wild beasts caught in a toil, yet the cords are too strong for them to break; they will soon tire with struggling, and when they are tired grow tame'.[1] But even more frightening to Bolingbroke than the probable disclosure of these follies was the possible discovery of his plans to bring in the Pretender, plans which he boasted to the French ambassador in August 1714 would have reached fruition had the Queen lived six weeks longer. Nor was it an accident that he fled England the day after Matthew Prior landed at Dover, for Prior knew too many secrets and was thought too willing to reveal them. The certain knowledge that the ministry intended to impeach him (conveyed to him by Marlborough), joined with a fear that Prior would reveal all, compelled Bolingbroke to flee from justice; but by fleeing from justice he made it impossible for his Tory friends in Parliament to oppose his impeachment.[2]

The Earl of Oxford did not fly from justice, nor did the Report reflect upon him as it had on Bolingbroke, yet the House voted, without dividing on the question, to impeach him for High Treason. There are a number of reasons why they did. He was unpopular; as the Queen's first minister he bore a special responsibility for the peace; common fame, always sufficient in an impeachment, held him to be the author of the peace; and the ministry promised to furnish the House further proof of his treason. Oxford, never a popular minister, had earned for himself a reputation for deviousness and bad faith. In June 1715 that reputation caused him irreparable harm. Though the Report contained no proof that he had advised a separate peace with France or negotiated with the Pretender, his many enemies, Whig and Tory alike, were quite prepared to believe that he had. They were all the more inclined to believe this because his ascendancy in the late ministry had been unmistakable. He possessed the favour of the Queen, reigned at the

---

[1] *Reports from Committees*, I, 7, 8, 22, 25.

[2] Klopp, *Der Fall des Hauses Stuart*, XIV, 640–1; Boyer, *Impartial History*, xliv; Churchill, *Marlborough*, II, 1023. H. N. Fieldhouse has published (*E.H.R.* LII, 678–81) the French ambassador's account of Bolingbroke's flight.

Treasury, and sent his creatures, Prior, Gilligan, and Tom Harley to France, Spain, and Utrecht. In introducing the impeachment against Oxford, Lord Coningsby argued that if a subordinate minister were found guilty of these crimes, he who had the principal administration of affairs could not be less guilty. The Report itself urged that one could not suppose that Bolingbroke had acted 'without the advice and approbation of the Lord Treasurer, as first minister'. Common fame proclaimed that a treacherous peace had been made and common fame proclaimed that Oxford had presided over the ministry that made it. For most members this was proof enough, especially when the Attorney-General reminded them that common fame, though insufficient to convict a man, offered reason enough to impeach him. But for others common fame was not reason enough, and to assuage their doubts the ministry offered as proof of Oxford's guilt a letter of Bolingbroke's in which he declared that Oxford had advised giving Tournay to France. To the great annoyance of the ministry, Sir Joseph Jekyll, a Whig, a lawyer, and a member of the Committee of Secrecy, destroyed the efficacy of this evidence, by doubting whether it was valid in law, since the letter only contained an allegation by Bolingbroke about Oxford. To retrieve the ground lost by Sir Joseph's intervention, Secretary Stanhope rose and declared (as Lord Vaughan had declared in Clarendon's impeachment) that there was a person who would corroborate the evidence offered by Bolingbroke's letter. This promise swept away the last remaining doubts of the sceptical; the House, without troubling to divide, voted to impeach the Earl of Oxford for High Treason.[1]

Though the Report of the Committee of Secrecy blackened the good name of the Duke of Ormond by revealing that he had acted contrary to the Queen's instructions, had withdrawn the British army from the siege of Quesnoy, and had revealed to Marshall Villars the movement, numbers, and disposition of the allied troops, neither the ministry nor the House wished to impeach him. The ministry even offered him clemency if he would submit to the King and cease to countenance riots and tumults against the government, but the proud Duke would make no submission to George I, would

---

[1] *Reports from Committees*, I, 12; L'Hermitage, B.M. Add. MSS 17677 III, f. 262v; S.P.D. Geo. I, 35, III, ff. 58 following. In the debate on Oxford's impeachment, Walpole concluded his speech by quoting Oxford's words in 1701, when the impeachment of Somers was before the Commons: 'They would put the axe to the roots of their liberties if they did not impeach the lord before them' (*ibid.*).

not discountenance the riots and tumults carried out in his name, and would not cease counselling with notorious Jacobites like Bishop Atterbury. As a result the ministry introduced an impeachment against him into the House of Commons. Because the Report made it certain beyond question that Ormond had exceeded his instructions by informing Marshall Villars of what passed in the Allied Council of War, the House voted to impeach him for High Treason, though 187 members, among them twenty Whigs, stood loyally by the hero of Vigo Bay and voted against the impeachment.[1]

Far fewer members stood by the Earl of Strafford when his impeachment came before the House, for he was as notorious for his vanity and pettiness as Ormond was celebrated for his splendour and generosity. Furthermore the Report of the Committee of Secrecy showed him to have been an adventurous, intriguing, meddlesome politician, who had advised the cessation of arms in 1712, had counselled the seizure of Bruges and Ghent by Ormond, had lied to the Dutch, and had insulted the ministers of Hanover and their Prince. Archibald Hutchinson, a Tory, valiantly sought to defend Strafford by pleading that he had done nothing at Utrecht that his fellow plenipotentiary, the Bishop of Bristol, had not also done; and yet the ministry did not impeach the Bishop. Were they, he asked, extending benefit of clergy to the Bishop of Bristol? John Aislabie answered, no, that they impeached Strafford and not Bristol because the Bishop had merely obeyed orders while the Earl, exceeding his instructions, had advised the most pernicious measures. There is much truth in this, but it is likewise true that the Whigs, mindful of what the impeachment of Sacheverell had cost them, had no intention of committing that error again. Fearing to provoke the cry 'the Church in danger', they did indeed extend benefit of clergy to the Bishop of Bristol. But Strafford's impeachment they wanted— and on 22 June secured, by a vote of 268 to 100.[2]

---

[1] *Reports from Committees*, I, 14–16, 18–19; L'Hermitage, B.M. Add. MSS 17677 III, ff. 272, 274v, 276. Lord Egmont wrote in his Journal (31 May 1715, B.M. Add. MSS 47087), 'Last night being the 30th, the mob were up again, some of them crying out nonsensically, King Ormond, no King George...The riots committed in London, Oxford, and other places are but too plain marks of the dissatisfaction the common people have taken at the King's choice of his ministry.' Lord Egmont's remark emphasizes a truth that might easily be forgotten: whatever ministerial responsibility there was in 1715 was to Parliament, not to the people.

[2] *Reports from Committees*, I, 14, 18, 20, 66; L'Hermitage, B.M. Add. MSS 17677 III, f. 276v. Strafford's impeachment led the Earl of Chesterfield to write to Matthew Prior (*H.M.C. Bath*, III, 448) that 'the wise Earl of Strafford, who had his head cut off by a

The House of Lords appeared to be as willing as the House of Commons to promote the impeachment of the late ministry. When Lord Coningsby impeached the Earl of Oxford before the Lords on 9 July and demanded that he be placed in custody, the Lords sent him to the Tower. In August when the Commons impeached Bolingbroke and Ormond, the Lords ordered the two peers to be placed in custody, and, finding them absent from the Kingdom, informed the House of Commons of the fact. When the House of Commons then sent up Bills of Attainder, condemning the two peers unless they appeared by 10 September, the Lords passed both Bills. In September when the Commons impeached the Earl of Strafford, the Lords demanded that he answer the charges brought against him. But at the same time the House of Lords remained on guard, as they had for a century, against any abuse of the power of impeachment. They agreed to Oxford's imprisonment only because the House of Commons produced, as they had not produced when demanding the imprisonment of Strafford, Clarendon, and Danby, particular articles of impeachment, one of which (the eleventh, concerning Tournay) contained a particular treason. They agreed to Attainders against Bolingbroke and Ormond because both had fled from the justice of their peers, Bolingbroke in March, Ormond in July, when at four in the morning of the 21st, concealed in a hackney coach, he drove east from Richmond. Ormond's flight thoroughly demoralized the Tories, one of whom confessed, 'The Report of the Committee of Secrecy had begun to open his eyes, and that the Duke of Ormond's flight had fully convinced him that the heads of the Tory party were a set of knaves and villains, who designed to have ruined their country.'[1] As for Strafford, whom the Commons had only accused of high crimes and misdemeanours, the Lords neither sequestered him from the House nor placed him in custody; he remained at liberty and continued to sit in the Lords.

company of knaves as well as fools, advised his son never to aspire to a higher employment in the service of his country than that of justice of peace. Perhaps the present Earl of Strafford (notwithstanding his excess of bloated pride) may have wished more than once that he had followed the maxim.' The present Earl was the son of Sir William Wentworth, nephew of the first Earl of Strafford.

[1] Quoted by Boyer, *Impartial History*, p. 233. L'Hermitage wrote (B.M. Add. MSS 17677 III, f. 367) 'that many who had opposed Ormond's impeachment have declared since his flight to France they have nothing more to say to excuse him, and are persuaded he was guilty of High Treason'.

In the end not one of these impeachments was brought to a full trial. Bolingbroke and Ormond did not return by 10 September; instead they entered the Pretender's service. The House of Commons made no attempt to prosecute their impeachment against Strafford, and made only a half-hearted attempt to prosecute Oxford's, an attempt which failed almost before it began. But though the House of Lords did not try these men, public opinion did. In sitting-rooms in Camden Town, in coffee houses in London, in Senior Common Rooms in Oxford, in pamphlets innumerable, in speeches before both Houses of Parliament, in articles of impeachment, in answers to them, and in legal briefs, the enemies and friends of the late ministry indicted, defended, and passed judgment upon them. The legal arguments which they marshalled for and against the im- peached lords are of interest, but of far greater interest are the constitutional arguments which they brought forward. For these constitutional arguments cast a flood of light upon the ideas which men then held concerning the responsibilities of ministers of state. Could a minister of state defend himself by pleading the sovereign's commands? Could he take refuge in the secrecy of the Cabinet or screen himself behind the commands of a superior minister or find safety in the concurrence of others? Must a great officer of state accept responsibility for what occurred within his department? Did the Prime Minister bear a special responsibility for the good govern- ment of the realm? Was a minister obligated to oppose counsels of which he disapproved and to resign if his opposition were ignored? Might he justify his conduct by pleading the approval of Parliament for what he had done? In the public debate that raged around the four impeached lords, men were not reluctant to give their answers to these questions.

Though not central to their defence (as it had been to Laud's and Strafford's), all four impeached lords pleaded obedience to the Queen in a lawful command. Bolingbroke in his letter to Lord Lansdowne, Oxford and Strafford in speeches before the Lords, and the Duke of Ormond through the pen of Bishop Atterbury, all made this plea.[1] The late Queen had possessed an undoubted right

---

[1] *A True Copy of a Letter from the Right Honourable the Lord Viscount Bolingbroke* (*Somers Tracts*, XIII, 627); Cobbett, *Parl. Hist.* VII, 105; L'Hermitage, B.M. Add. MSS 17677 III, f. 399. Bishop Atterbury argued, in *English Advice to the Freeholders of England* (*Somers Tracts*, XIII, 527) that Ormond's conduct was 'the result of his obedience to his Queen;

to make war and peace; she had in her great wisdom resolved to make peace; and they had obeyed her in negotiating it. 'As Her Majesty', wrote the author of *An Account of the Conduct of Robert Earl of Oxford*, 'found reason to resolve to put an end to the war; her ministers, whether they entered into Her Majesty's reasons or not, would find themselves obliged to enter into her measures for bringing it to pass.'[1]

The Whig opponents of the impeached lords refused to countenance this plea. When the Earl of Oxford's answer to his impeachment was read in the House, Walpole attacked it as 'a false and malicious libel, laying upon his royal mistress the blame of all the pernicious measures he had led her into against her honour and the good of his country'. He hoped, he continued, that 'the Earl's endeavouring to screen himself behind the Queen's name, would avail him nothing. That it is indeed a fundamental maxim of our constitution, that Kings can do no wrong, but...at the same time it is no less certain, that ministers of state are accountable for their actions, otherwise a Parliament would be but an empty name; the Commons should have no business in that place; and the government would be absolute and arbitrary.' Walpole blithely ignored, as did every Whig pamphleteer, any possible distinction between obedience to a lawful command and obedience to an unlawful one. Obedience to either was wrong, if the consequence proved pernicious to the kingdom. By 1715 the legal maxim that the King cannot be held responsible for an unlawful act had become the political principle that he cannot be held accountable for an unwise act. As the anonymous W.R. wrote in *Mr Burnet's Defence*, 'Our constitution...expressly makes ministers accountable for all transactions contrary to the interest and honour of their nation.'[2]

and obedience to one's Prince will not, I presume, be thought bad doctrine in this reign, whatever it might have been in the last'. In their answers to the articles of impeachment against them, both Oxford and Strafford repeated the plea that they had negotiated the peace at the Queen's command (Cobbett, *Parl. Hist.* VII, 174–5, 204–5, 259–60).

[1] *An Account of the Conduct of Robert Earl of Oxford* (1715). A similar statement occurs in a memorial written by Oxford, or by one of his counsel (B.M. Loan, Portland Papers, no. 8), 'It is known that the Queen was resolved to make the peace, and that her orders were positive, and if they were not manifestly unlawful her ministers were bound by their allegiance to execute them; and in equity they are not presumed to will themselves what they did in obedience to their sovereign.'

[2] Boyer, *Impartial History*, 334–5; W.R. *Mr Burnet's Defence, or, More Reasons For an Impeachment* (1715), p. 33.

Not only could the King do no wrong, he could do nothing by himself. He always acted upon counsel and through his ministers. He could not be said to have dissolved Parliament or created peers or composed speeches or sent emissaries abroad. Despite this doctrine the Earl of Oxford averred that the late Queen had performed these acts. So also did Matthew Prior. When the Committee of Secrecy asked him, 'Did the Lord Treasurer send you to France?', he answered, 'No, I was sent by the Queen.' This infuriated the Committee, but they could hardly punish Prior for affirming what the evidence before them proved. His instructions, not countersigned by a Secretary of State, bore only the initials A.R. But the Committee did declare their opinion concerning this practice. It is very remarkable, they observed in the Report, 'that there is not one paper or powers or instructions throughout the whole affair countersigned by any one minister, but the Queen's name exposed to cover all'.[1]

But in truth the Committee had little desire to discover the ministers who obeyed the Queen's commands or countersigned her orders; their real interest was to discover who had counselled her to issue those commands and orders. A close reading of the articles of impeachment against Bolingbroke, Oxford, Ormond, and Strafford demonstrates this concern. The Commons did not charge one of these lords with obeying an illegal command or executing an unlawful order. They did not accuse Bolingbroke of obeying the Queen's orders to sign the Preliminary Articles; they accused him of advising the Queen to issue such orders. They did not charge Oxford with obeying a warrant from the Queen to pay an annuity to James II's consort: they charged him with advising the Queen to issue such a warrant. They did not impeach Ormond for obeying the Restraining Orders of June 1712: they impeached him for disobeying the Queen by agreeing to a cessation of arms before France had performed the conditions prerequisite to it. They did not impeach Strafford for obeying the Queen's commands, though he was her plenipotentiary at Utrecht: they impeached him for advising separate negotiations with France, counselling a cessation of arms, and recommending the seizure

[1] Cobbett, *Parl. Hist.* VII, 161, 165, 187; Churchill, *Marlborough*, II, 879; *Reports from Committees*, I, 5. The author of *Observations on the Report* (1715) maintained (p. 15) that the Queen's speech in June 1712 concerning the peace 'was entirely the work of the Treasurer, Secretary, etc., so are they answerable for all the mistakes in it....'.

of Ghent and Bruges.[1] If the Commons had only sought to punish criminal conduct, they would simply have impeached those who acted criminally. But they really sought to condemn policies which they believed pernicious to the realm, and a sense of equity told them that those who counselled such policies, not those who executed them, were primarily responsible. A minister had no right to refuse obedience to a lawful command, however unwise he thought it, but neither did he lie under any obligation to give the Queen unwise counsel.

The desire to punish those who counselled rather than those who executed unpopular policies made far more difficult the discovery of the person or persons most at fault. The Commons could easily discover who had sealed an unlawful charter, issued an illegal warrant, or signed an unauthorized diplomatic instruction. It was another matter to discover who counselled the Queen, for the Queen might deny that anyone had counselled her or refuse to say who had counselled her. The first possibility most Englishmen refused to allow, affirming that the Queen always acted on the advice of others. Among the few who denied this, who believed that she might follow the dictates of her own judgment as well as the counsel of others, the most notable was the Earl of Oxford, who prided himself upon having rescued the Queen from the tyrannous counsels of the Whigs. In his answer to the articles of impeachment against him, he solemnly declared that 'everything relating to transactions of the peace was communicated to Her Majesty and maturely considered by her before any thing was determined thereupon'.[2] And the publicists who came to Oxford's defence painted a similar picture of the Queen presiding at Council, listening to debates there, seeking every man's advice, and then resolving according to her own judgment. The Earl of Oxford's purpose in 1710, wrote the author of *Memoirs of Some Transactions*, was to

restore Her Majesty to an entire freedom of acting; that all her affairs should be explained and laid before Her Majesty; that she should no

---

[1] Cobbett, *Parl. Hist.* VII, 120, 132, 140, 149–55. The author of *The Method of the Proceedings in the House of Lords and Commons in Cases of Impeachments for High Treason* (3rd ed. 1715) observed, 'That almost in every considerable and legal impeachment since Charles the First, the giving of "evil advice" to the Prince has been the foundation of the accusation and has bore hardest upon the persons accused.'

[2] Cobbett, *Parl. Hist.* VII, 204. Thomas Burnet observed (*The Necessity of Impeaching*, p. 19), 'And any man who will but consider the ancient maxim, that the King can do no wrong, will find the only reason upon which that maxim is founded to be because the monarch's counsellors are answerable for all his actions.'

more wear the Crown without the Sceptre, that the doors should be open to all her subjects, and a free access to her person be given to all; that causes of consequence might not come covered with the representation of the ministers; but everything be laid before the Queen, that she might act with open eyes, see for herself, and give to, not receive commands from, her ministry.[1]

The Whigs would have none of it. They presumed that the Queen was always advised, though few of them chose to express it as harshly as the pamphleteer who wrote that, whenever he spoke of her late Majesty, he meant her late ministry, 'for 'tis plain she, poor lady, knew nothing of the mysterious part of their management, but considering the natural infirmities of her sex, submitted herself and power to her late servants...'.[2] The thought was not very gracious to the late Queen, but neither was it entirely unjust to her. Queen Anne did lean heavily upon the counsels of her ministers. As the Jacobite politician, George Lockhart, observed, the Earl of Oxford showed the Queen great respect, laid all matters submissively before her, and seemingly took her directions in them, but in fact he 'managed and disposed of her will as absolutely as did his predecessors'.[3] When political reality lends support to a constitutional maxim, men are likely to act upon it.

The House of Commons found it comparatively easy to believe that the Queen always acted on advice; they found it more difficult to discover who had advised her. And the Earl of Oxford fully exploited their difficulties. No single refrain occurs oftener in his answer to the articles of impeachment against him than the plea that he had not given the Queen the counsel which the articles charged him with giving. On twenty-four different occasions he categorically denies giving the Queen the advice which he is charged with giving.[4] Oxford could voice these denials with impunity because, though in the past a great apostle of the written responsibility of ministers of state, he had never put his advice to the Queen

[1] *Memoirs of Some Transactions during the Late Ministry of Robert Earl of Oxford* (1717), p. 27.

[2] *A Letter to the Honourable House of Commons: Shewing the Necessity of Impeaching The Principal Agitators of the Late Ministry* (1715), p. 28.

[3] Lockhart, *Lockhart Papers*, I, 377. Even Oxford admitted in a private memorial (B.M. Loan, Portland Papers, no. 8) that the Queen acted on the advice of her ministers: 'But admit they [the ministers] were the counsellors, authors, executors of the peace (for a peace was never made without the advice and aid of ministers) what law of the kingdom prohibited them to make peace without the consent of foreigners.'

[4] Cobbett, *Parl. Hist.* VII, 165–86, 188–207.

in writing. The Committee of Secrecy soon discovered, to the fury of the chairman, that they possessed not a single letter proving that Oxford had given the Queen wicked counsels. Their embarrassment, however, did not cause them to resurrect that clause in the Act of Settlement (repealed in 1706) which required councillors to put their hand to advice given the King. During the entire debate over the impeachment of the late ministry, no one, not a single member of Parliament, nor a single pamphleteer, demanded that ministers of state henceforth put their advice in writing. Englishmen now had the sophistication to know that secrecy was necessary to the good government of the realm and to the successful conduct of foreign policy. They also realized that there were other, less formal ways to focus responsibility upon those most at fault.

Chief among these was the practice of blaming those who sat in the Cabinet, for they were in a position to give wicked counsels. This procedure, however, suffered from one drawback: equity demanded that Parliament condemn the whole Cabinet, not one or two members of it. In their time Strafford, Laud, Clarendon, Arlington, and Danby had understood this, and had argued in their defence that the whole Council had concurred in the advice for which they were condemned. Bolingbroke, before he fled to France, had a mind to make the same defence. He told Bothmer that he could only be charged with having negotiated the peace, and that in this he had done nothing of himself, but had only 'executed what was decided upon in the Council'.[1] But had Bolingbroke remained to make this defence, he would have found that it would do him no good, for the House of Commons in 1715 decided that the complicity of others should aggravate, not mitigate, the faults of a councillor. Unlike all previous articles of impeachment, those against Bolingbroke, Oxford, Ormond, and Strafford explicitly accused them of conspiring 'with other evil counsellors' to mislead the monarch.[2] The Report of the Committee of Secrecy repeatedly and explicitly held 'the late ministry' responsible for the faults, follies, and crimes committed during the past four years. The House of Commons

[1] Klopp, *Der Fall des Hauses Stuart*, xiv, 659.

[2] Cobbett, *Parl. Hist.* vii, 81–2, 129–30, 131, 150–1. This fact led Oxford to write (B.M. Loan 29/10, no. 24), '...yet I cannot but observe that the impeachment is founded on a conspiracy; and the first article expressly says—"maliciously and wickedly formed a confederacy with other evil disposed persons, then also of Her Majesty's Privy Council". Query, can any Privy Counsellor be obliged to be examined in this affair where he most effectually accuses himself?'

could now afford to blame a whole ministry and to admit that an entire cabinet had conspired in wicked advice, because they sought to discredit the party which dominated both, not to blame some men and exculpate others. No doubt written evidence or the testimony of witnesses was necessary to secure the condemnation of an impeached minister, but his collective guilt as a member of the Cabinet sufficed to destroy his reputation, for most men believed that those who sat in the Cabinet should answer for the wisdom of the advice upon which the sovereign acted. And since the main purpose of an impeachment in 1715 was to destroy a man's reputation rather than cut off his head, further proof was unnecessary.

The articles of impeachment voted against Bolingbroke, Oxford, and Strafford differed in another respect from those voted earlier. They condemned councillors (as earlier impeachments had not) for failing to remonstrate against the advice upon which the monarch had acted. As members of the Cabinet they ought to have opposed the advice upon which the Queen acted. Bolingbroke had failed in his duty by not advising against speeches from the throne which contained falsehoods, and Strafford by not advising against a treaty with France that was dishonourable.[1] The House of Commons did not say that these men ought to have resigned, but they presumed that since they did not resign they were friends of the counsels upon which the Queen acted. The author of *The Method of the Proceedings* said of Oxford, 'If he did not advise of these matters, yet he failed to remonstrate against them, as his office demanded.' And the author of *Memoirs of Some Transactions* defended Oxford's withdrawal from affairs in 1714 with the argument that otherwise he 'was sure to bear the scandal' of measures he opposed.[2]

The Commons held Cabinet Councillors collectively responsible for the counsels upon which the Queen acted, but this did not prevent them from holding departmental heads individually responsible for the proper functioning of their departments. In their articles of impeachment against them, they held Oxford responsible, as Lord Treasurer, for the management of the revenue, and Bolingbroke, as Secretary of State, for the conduct of diplomacy. And this responsibility extended beyond their own actions, to those who

[1] Cobbett, *Parl. Hist.* vii, 99, 131, 151.
[2] *The Method of the Proceedings...in Cases of Impeachments*, pp. v–vi; *Memoirs of Some Transactions*, p. 43.

acted under them. Perceiving this, Strafford argued in his defence that he had merely acted ministerially, had merely obeyed the orders of the Cabinet in London. As he wrote in his answer to the articles of impeachment against him,

he looked upon himself as a ministerial officer, whose duty it was to pursue such instructions as he should from time to time receive; and...since he could not doubt but that all orders sent him...had been first maturely weighed and digested, he humbly apprehends your Lordships will think it had been too great a presumption in him to advise against or oppose such orders, which carried not in themselves any apparent illegality, when he knew not the springs or reasons of them.[1]

In fact the Commons had anticipated his plea by impeaching him for advice he had given the Queen and for acts done without her warrant, not for his obedience to commands sent by her ministers. Though in 1715 a person could not plead the King's commands, he could plead a superior minister's commands, for the Commons desired to make ministers of state responsible for the acts of their subordinates. They wished to blame Oxford for what Prior and Gilligan had done, and Bolingbroke for the actions of Moore and Hill. The responsibility of the departmental head was political rather than legal, but it was no less real for that. The first publicist in England to advocate it explicitly was Mr Tutchin, the Whig publisher of the *Observator*. In 1702 he wrote in his paper:

In all public frauds, cheats, embezzlements, treasons, and other crimes committed by men in offices, I think the recommenders are the greatest criminals, and pity it is we have no law to punish such men as the principals in the cheat who recommended men of such morals to the favour of the Prince...If persons recommending were answerable for the sins of ignorance of the persons they recommended, and were to be punished for the same, they would be more careful and sparing of their recommendations.[2]

Parliament passed no laws making the recommender the principal in any cheat, but they saw the convenience and desirability of placing political responsibility on the departmental head. They had no time to inquire into and punish the misconduct of every minor official; and the opposition much preferred to use such misconduct as a stick with which to beat the government.

---

[1] Cobbett, *Parl. Hist.* VII, 248–9.

[2] Tutchin, *Observator*, no. 2 (8 Apr. 1702) and no. 87 (20 Feb. 1703). The articles of impeachment against Oxford described Matthew Prior as 'an instrument and creature' of the Lord Treasurer (Cobbett, *Parl. Hist.* VII, 118).

Nothing disconcerted the Whigs more—unless it was the destruction of Oxford's letters to Prior—than the fact that the negotiations of the peace did not fall within the province of the Treasury. To circumvent this difficulty they boldly charged that Oxford, as Prime Minister, was chiefly responsible for the peace. Oxford denied that he was, asking his fellow peers how he could 'with any colour of equity be made answerable for advising and conducting the peace', when the 'advice of all those in high trust about Her Majesty' was taken.[1] When this plea was read in the Commons in September 1715, Robert Walpole replied that 'it was notorious that the Earl of Oxford, as Prime Minister, was the chief adviser, promoter, and manager of the matters charged upon him in the articles'.[2] Oxford pleaded the injustice of the Commons' holding him chiefly responsible for the peace; Walpole pleaded the notoriety of the fact that he was chiefly responsible. Their opposing pleas pose two questions concerning the English constitution at that time: was there in fact, among the Queen's servants, a Prime Minister; and did men hold him chiefly responsible for the government's actions?

Whether a Prime Minister existed in early eighteenth-century England depends entirely upon how one defines 'Prime Minister', upon whether one regards him as a courtier who monopolizes the King's counsels, or as a civil servant who dominates his administration, or as a parliamentary manager who dispenses his patronage, or as a parliamentary undertaker who governs the House of Commons for him. If one defines 'Prime Minister' as a courtier who possesses a monopoly of the King's favour, there have always been Prime Ministers in England, though the name did not appear until the Restoration, when it was applied to Clarendon (who, however, rejected it as too recently translated out of the French). But if one defines 'Prime Minister' to mean a great officer of state who owes his ascendancy to his dominance over the administration, then perhaps the Earl of Danby, whom Sir John Reresby called the 'Chief Minister', deserves the title of the first Prime Minister in England. The additional power he enjoyed because of his control of patronage also recommends him to that title, though he never enjoyed the power of patronage in the full plentitude that the Earl

---

[1] Cobbett, *Parl. Hist.* VII, 204. The author of *An Account of the Conduct of Robert Earl of Oxford* argued (pp. 82–3) that 'as it was not his [Oxford's] province to correspond with ministers abroad, so he is not to answer for those that did'.

[2] Boyer, *Impartial History*, p. 334.

401

of Godolphin did in 1705. Because he had a firmer grip on patronage than any previous minister in English history, Godolphin might well be regarded as the first Prime Minister; some of his contemporaries called him by that name. But he governed no party, and if leadership of the party which enjoyed a predominance in Parliament be the defining characteristic of a Prime Minister, then Lord Somers in the year 1708 comes nearer to being the first Prime Minister in England. Jonathan Swift described him as 'the life and soul, the head and heart' of the Whig party, and the Whig party in 1708 laid down the law to Godolphin, to Marlborough, and to the Queen herself.[1]

But historians commonly regard neither Clarendon nor Danby nor Godolphin nor Somers as the first Prime Minister in England: they reserve that distinction for Robert Walpole. And they probably do so because Walpole joined in his own person all four possible defining characteristics of a Prime Minister. He monopolized the counsels of the King, he closely superintended the administration, he ruthlessly controlled patronage, and he led the predominant party in Parliament. But if these four qualities make a Prime Minister, it is not fanciful to maintain, as Walpole himself did, that Oxford in the years 1711 and 1712 was a Prime Minister. For the influence which he then exercised over the Queen was unmistakable; no one then questioned it. Equally evident was his dominance over the administration, for he superintended the restoration of credit, corresponded with foreign courts, sent emissaries abroad, and kept in his own hands the threads of peace negotiations. When in 1711 Oxford lay near death, stabbed by Guiscard, Bolingbroke told Swift that his death 'would be an irreparable loss', for he alone was 'master of the scheme by which they were to proceed'.[2] And a year later Auditor Harley wrote to his brother, 'As your Lordship is the spring of everything so it is not possible they should move aright without your continual direction....'[3] In part Oxford was 'the spring of everything' because he spurned Defoe's advice that 'the Secretary's office well discharged makes a man Prime Minister', and

---

[1] *The Continuation of the Life of Edward Earl of Clarendon* (Oxford, 1761), II, 89; Reresby, *Memoirs*, p. 174; Swift, *Works*, VI, 152. Wolfgang Michael argues (*Englische Geschichte*, III, 538), that under Godolphin one 'could observe the characteristic features of the latter [Prime Minister's] office for the first time; he already could choose his colleagues himself...'.

[2] Swift, *Works*, VIII, 145.

[3] Auditor Harley to Robert Harley, 9 Feb. 1712, B.M. Loan 29/143, no. 4.

went to the Treasury, where he controlled its extensive patronage.[1] This patronage not only gave him a superiority over his colleagues, it also allowed him to influence Parliament, upon whose successful management so much depended. Yet Oxford's success in managing the Queen's affairs in two successive Parliaments arose far more from the strength of the Tory party in the two Houses than from the votes of the Queen's servants. Through a long parliamentary career, Oxford, though no friend of party government, had ever attended to the needs of party organization. And now that he was the Queen's chief minister, he found leadership of the Tory party thrust upon him. 'As all parties have a head,' observed a writer in 1702, 'so that party which has the Prime Minister on their side, naturally rank themselves under him.'[2] By timely concessions to the October Club, by withstanding their demands on other occasions, Oxford proved that he could preserve, unite, and lead the Tories in Parliament, at least during the early years of his ministry. During those years Oxford, as the Queen's favourite, as Lord Treasurer, as the disposer of office, and as leader of the Tories, enjoyed an ascendancy in the ministry which his contemporaries apostrophized by calling him Prime Minister—and the expression had now been sufficiently long translated out of the French to be (as Swift observed in 1715) accepted usage.[3]

Walpole therefore spoke truly when he said it was notorious that Oxford, as Prime Minister, had the chief direction of affairs. But should he for that reason bear the chief responsibility for the government's actions? In Strafford's and Clarendon's impeachments the Commons had suggested that the King's favourite ought to bear a special responsibility; and when Arlington in 1674 pleaded the concurrence of the whole council, Sir Charles Wheeler retorted, 'He is not only a concurrent counsellor, but a Prime Minister of State.' In a similar fashion the Commons held Danby particularly responsible for the growth of Popery and French power during his ministry. This practice of holding the chief minister particularly responsible did not go unnoticed by those who served the King.

---

[1] Defoe, *Letters*, p. 31. The Earl of Oxford's refusal in 1710 to make 'a thorough change in employment' and 'a general removal' caused Swift to observe (*Works*, VIII, 143), 'This manner of proceeding in a prime Minister, I confess appeared wholly unaccountable, and without example.'

[2] *A Short Defence of the Last Parliament, Answered* (1702), p. 24.

[3] Swift, *Works*, VII, xxxv.

26-2

Barillon in 1686 observed that Sunderland, 'since he is not chief minister', fears less than Rochester the consequences of a French alliance.[1] But during William's reign and the early years of Anne's no single minister emerged who notoriously dominated the monarch's counsels—instead, a junto of ministers prevailed. Consequently the idea of a chief minister, bearing a chief responsibility, faded into the background. For this reason there is much truth in Oxford's plea that the Commons could not in equity hold him chiefly responsible for a peace which all those in places of high trust had advised. There existed no convention of the constitution that placed chief responsibility upon a Prime Minister. But Oxford's very career altered this. He notoriously dominated the Queen's counsels, with the result that L'Hermitage could write that the nation held him, as Prime Minister, responsible for the counsels he had given the Queen; and the Commons could express their astonishment that he dare deny being concerned in matters of state that were confessedly 'done under an administration wherein he was notoriously the first minister and chief director'.[2] In the year 1710 few Englishmen, if any, believed that a Prime Minister should bear a special responsibilty for the counsels upon which the sovereign acted, but by the year 1715 many Englishmen believed he ought to. Oxford himself acknowledged this change when he told the House of Lords that his misfortune in falling under the displeasure of the House of Commons was the heavier because he had 'had the honour to be placed at the head of the late ministry, and must now, it seems, be made accountable for all the measures then pursued'.[3]

Oxford's plea that the Queen had commanded and the Council concurred in the peace caused his enemies little unease, but his plea that two successive Parliaments had approved of it discomfited

---

[1] Quoted in Kenyon, *Sunderland*, p. 116.

[2] L'Hermitage, B.M. Add. MSS 17677III, f. 146v; Cobbett, *Parl. Hist.* vii, 213. The author of *The Method of the Proceedings* urged (pp. i–ii) that there should be no scruple at impeaching Oxford, 'For let us only first consider what has been done during... his ministry, and of which he must necessarily be either the director or conductor.' Swift observed (*Works*, viii, 160) that though Oxford often could not persuade the Queen to take his advice, he 'would needs take all the blame on himself, from a known principle of state prudence, that a first Minister must always preserve the reputation of power'.

[3] Cobbett, *Parl. Hist.* vii, 105. A defence of Oxford entitled 'The Fate of Favourites' (Rawlinson MSS D37, p. 12) first defends his conduct 'as Lord High Treasurer only, abstracted from the Prime Minister of State'. Then later defends him 'as Minister in his public and almost single and universal administration of the affairs of state'.

them. Oxford could voice this plea because the impeachment of the Partition Treaty lords had taught him (as it had taught Marlborough) that no minister dare negotiate or conclude a treaty of peace without first securing Parliament's approval for it.[1] He had sought and won Parliament's consent to negotiations with France and approval for the final treaty. In 1712 Parliament asked Her Majesty to negotiate peace on the basis of the Preliminaries and in 1713 and 1714 a newly elected Parliament approved of the final peace.[2] As Oxford said in the House of Lords on 9 July 1715, 'This is certain, that this peace, as bad as it is now represented, was approved by two successive Parliaments.' He repeated the plea in his answer to the articles of impeachment against him. Strafford voiced the same plea in his answer. Sir William Wyndham and Edward Harley echoed it in the House of Commons.[3] And hardly a single Tory pamphleteer failed to publicize it. 'The Parliament', wrote one of them, 'advised the peace, and approved the terms, as well before as after it was done, in the strongest manner. The Queen, pursuant to their advice, concluded it; and the ministry were the servants of both in transacting it; which if they can be called to account for, then no human power can protect a British subject in the service of the British nation.'[4] Another Tory publicist asked, 'If then the command of the Sovereign, after mature deliberation in Council...followed by the approbation of two Parliaments, be not sufficient justification for ministers employed in a treaty, acting against no known law, nor charged with any corruption, whose life, whose property is safe in Great Britain?'[5]

The Whigs could give no convincing answer to this plea. According to *The Examiner* some of them dared to argue 'That Acts of Parliament are no security for bad peace makers', but this argument too openly contradicted the Whig doctrine of the supremacy of

---

[1] Marlborough wrote to Godolphin in 1710 (Churchill, *Marlborough*, II, 682 n.), during negotiations for peace at Getruydenberg, '...I think it is absolutely necessary for the Queen's service that the Parliament should be sitting, for should it [the peace] be refused or granted without knowledge of Parliament; I fear it might cause very great uneasiness...'.

[2] *C.J.* XVII, 259–60, 437; *L.J.* XIX, 659.

[3] Cobbett, *Parl. Hist.* VII, 105, 206–7, 260; Boyer, *Impartial History*, p. 123.

[4] *Reasons against Impeaching the Late Ministry* (1715), p. 11. The author of *A Letter to a Young Gentleman* (1715) admired these two sentences so much he quoted them in his pamphlet (p. 24).

[5] *Weekly Journal* (2 July 1715), p. 156, summarizing a late pamphlet entitled *The State of the War and the Peace*.

Parliament.[1] Far more useful to the Whigs was the argument that Oxford had packed the House of Lords and corrupted the House of Commons. The articles of impeachment brought against Oxford accused him of 'having on all occasions used his utmost endeavours to subvert the ancient established constitution of Parliaments'. They particularly charged him with having advised the creation of twelve peers after the Lords had voted that no peace would be safe that left Spain in the House of Bourbon; they also accused him of boasting to the Queen that he 'had used all his skill and credit to keep the House of Commons from examining' into the £28,000 voted for the Quebec expedition.[2] 'A Prime Minister', argued one Whig, 'would be highly criminal, if he, finding the majority of twelve judges to be above corruption, added such a number to them as would outvote these unbiased judges.'[3] Other Whig authors maintained that the ministry had only won the Commons' approval for the peace 'by corruption', by 'a stratagem', by asking for a vote on a mere abstract of the peace terms, in a noisy House, after no debate.[4] In their desperation to find some answer to Oxford's plea these authors absurdly exaggerated the corruption of the Commons and the servility of the Lords, but they did touch upon a political issue—the use of royal influence to win majorities in Parliament—which was to dominate the history of responsible government in the eighteenth century as impeachments had dominated it in the seventeenth.

Had his case been fully tried before the Lords, Oxford would have had little difficulty answering Whig complaints that he packed and corrupted Parliament. In the first place the government carried by 13 votes, not 12, the resolution in favour of negotiating an immediate peace, one more vote than the number of peers newly created. In the second place no one really believed that the late ministry had corrupted two successive Parliaments within two short years. Knowing that the plea of parliamentary approval was unassailable,

---

[1] *The Examiner*, VI, no. 19 (26 July 1714). Swift in 1711 accused the Whigs of screening themselves behind parliamentary addresses, writing in *The Examiner* (no. 39) that to defend a desperate counsel they 'procure a majority' for it—form it 'into an address which makes it look like the sense of the nation. Under shelter they carry on their work, and lie secure against after-reckoning.'

[2] Cobbett, *Parl. Hist.* VII, 102, 115–16.

[3] *An Address to the Good People of Great Britain, Occasioned by the Report From the Committee of Secrecy* (1715), p. 44.

[4] *Mr Burnet's Defence* (1715), p. 28; *A Letter to the Honourable House of Commons* (1715), p. 31.

Oxford was prepared to press it to the utmost. In notes preparatory to his defence, either he or his counsel put it in the sharpest possible language:

But the Great Council of the Kingdom was likewise the counsellor of the Peace; the two Houses advised the Sovereign to make it, and when it was made, approved it; wherefore if counselling was a crime in the Cabinet it was also a crime in the Parliament...And who can prove that there was malice in the ministers and none in the Parliament?...The majority in Parliament should in equity be impeached. For whatever foreigners may think of British Parliaments; with us their authority is inviolable, and the separate peace is approved and ratified by that authority; though not by an express statute, yet by what is equivalent, the declared will of the legislative power: and if such a ratification will not warrant a peace and indemnify the makers, so far the authority of Parliament is nothing.[1]

That the Earl of Oxford could plead in his defence that 'the majority in Parliament should in equity be impeached', marked not only the certain defeat of his prosecutors, but also the end of an epoch. Impeachments ceased to be necessary when the purpose for which they had been voted for a century had been attained. The impeachment of the authors of the Partition Treaties had taught ministers of the Crown to be responsive to the will of Parliament. The impossibility of condemning the Earl of Oxford upon an impeachment proved that Queen Anne's ministers had truly learned that lesson.

Oxford's plea that Parliament had approved the peace embarrassed the Whigs and heralded the end of the age of impeachments. His plea that he had committed no criminal act in negotiating the peace proved equally embarrassing to them and contributed equally to the demise of impeachments. For the House of Lords in 1715 (as it had for a century) insisted that impeachments concern criminal acts, not political faults, that impeachments remain a legal procedure and not become a political weapon. Aware of this, both Oxford and Strafford denied forthrightly that they had committed any crime or violated any law.[2] And a chorus of speeches and pamphlets supported their plea. If there was any treason, said Mr Hungerford in the Commons, it was 'committed against the Dutch and our allies, who, he hoped, were not to be looked upon as our

---

[1] B.M. Loan, Portland Papers, the Impeachment of Robert Harley, no. 8.
[2] Cobbett, *Parl. Hist.* VII, 164–72, 179, 194, 196, 208–9, 263–4.

sovereign'. 'The Statute Books', observed the author of *A Letter to the Lord Bishop of Salisbury*, 'nowhere prescribe what articles of peace are always to be entered into with France.' And the author of *A Second Letter from a Country Whig* asked, how can the King ever find ministers willing to conclude a peace if the late ministers are punished for entering into peace negotiations and hung for not making 'so wise a bargain' as they ought to have? For who knows, remarked the author of *Britons Strike Home*, but our present King may be engaged in war and obliged to make peace? 'Shall he then by a precedent so black, make it impossible for his ministers to be safe in serving him?'[1] But no one expressed better than Lord Oxford himself (or his counsel) the injustice of impeaching men for mere faults or saw more clearly the deleterious effect which such impeachments would have on the good government of the realm:

The peace itself is not condemned. The method according to law and common practice in all treaties. The event happy, which the nation now enjoys, thankful for and rejoicing.

If there was a fault, it is only an error in judgment, of a thing lawful. A man must not be criminal, because another person judges better or otherwise than he when there is no fraud, no corruption objected. If otherwise every judge upon the Bench who differs from another is liable; and a Privy Council must be all of one mind. This introduces arbitrary power.[2]

And elsewhere he (or his counsel) observed:

But admit they were the counsellors, authors, executors of the peace (for a peace was never made without the advice and aid of ministers) what law of the Kingdom prohibited them to make a peace without the consent of foreigners?...Infinite are the errors and evils which are not punished by law, especially in public counsels and acts of government, but these are tolerated evils arising from the necessity of things, and the defects of

[1] S.P.D. Geo. I, 35, III, ff. 58ff; *A Letter to the Lord Bishop of Salisbury* (1715), p. 14; *A Second Letter from a Country Whig* (1715), pp. 28–9; *Britons Strike Home* (1715), p. 18. Speaking for the Tory party the author of *Britons Strike Home* observed (pp. 19–20), 'But in the making of this peace...has there anything illegal been done? Anything against the constitution or contrary to an Act of Parliament? Let but this one question be proposed in Westminster-hall to the judges of England; and if they give it against Her late Majesty's servants, then we must all of us to a man choose to share in the punishment.'

[2] B.M. Loan 29/10, no. 24. William Bromley in the House of Commons said (B.M. Add. MSS 17677III, f. 276v), 'All Princes make separate peace when they judge it necessary, and for a hundred years Holland has done the same.' He then cited the Treaties of Munster, Nimuegen, and Ryswick. Eleven precedents of princes making separate peace, from Philip Duke of Burgundy in 1435 to Charles II in 1674, are found in 'Collection of Separate Treaties', B.M. Loan, Portland Papers, Impeachment of Robert Harley, no. 5.

human nature, and to punish them without law will be a remedy worse than the evil, will deprive princes of ministry and council, and will leave the body politic without arms to act, nor feet to move, without eyes or ears to inform the understanding...If actions commanded by the Sovereign, justified by Parliament, forbidden by no law of the Kingdom can be made criminal and penal, in such a government there can be no security, not to the most innocent, not even to inspired prophets who may forsee the danger but cannot prevent it.[1]

The use of the power of impeachment to attack innocent men for their political errors cast that power into disrepute. 'Before we run too hastily into impeachments,' wrote Daniel Defoe in *A Letter to a Merry Young Gentleman*, 'let us consider what the nation has ever got by them.' Those which the Commons voted in Richard II's reign, he maintained, are no example for today, for 'time has varied the face of affairs' and no longer does every lord who receives the least disgust draw his sword to punish a Court favourite. The present age being a 'more lawful and considerate' one, parliamentary impeachments 'are not so useful'. And least useful of all are 'party impeachments', such as those in 1701, which go beyond 'the common rules of justice', and are based not on fact, but 'on party politics'.[2] The same broad historical view informed the argument of *A Second Letter from a Country Whig*. Its Tory author, thinly disguised as a Whig, confessed that he had a great aversion to impeachments, for they seemed 'to take the executive power from those to whom it is wisely committed by our laws and constitution...'. The beginnings of this encroachment upon the prerogative he placed in the reign of James I, when Buckingham, unable to crush Cranfield by his own power, revived the power of impeachment. From that day to this, he argued, impeachments have been abused, being prosecuted in order to vent 'personal pique and party interest', not to enforce justice. With impeachments properly used to defend the people's liberties against the encroachments of evil counsellors the author of *A Second Letter* had no quarrel. But to vote them 'to gratify our own revenge and cement our power with the blood of our adversaries' can only create new divisions and endless confusion. 'And may not another Parliament be as ready to impeach on the other side?...The chief business of every ministry will be to rip up and unravel the conduct of those whom they have supplanted',

---

[1] B.M. Loan, Portland Papers, Impeachment of Robert Harley, no. 8.
[2] *A Letter to A Merry Young Gentleman, Intituled, Tho. Burnet* (1715), pp. 19, 23.

and the King will be able to stop this butchering of his subjects only by proroguing or dissolving Parliament.[1]

These attacks on parliamentary impeachments provoked a reply from the anonymous author, probably a Whig, of *The Method of the Proceedings...in Cases of Impeachments*. Plundering the journals of both Houses, he presented a series of potted histories of the impeachments of Strafford, Clarendon, Danby, and the Partition Treaty lords. Though defending impeachments when voted against arbitrary ministers, he condemned them when they were prosecuted 'with passion, violence, and personal resentments'. Only when impeachments acted as a check on arbitrary power, ought they to be voted, only when they were 'the last resort left open for honest men to interpose in preventing the ruin of their country'.[2] The same plea of the right of self-preservation appeared in the far more violent pamphlet by Richard West, lawyer and playwright, entitled *A Discourse Concerning Treason*. The late ministers, he argued, claim that Parliament cannot in law punish them capitally, but 'it is nonsense to talk of laws and constitution, if any man may commit what is notoriously most prejudicial to the country, and yet escape with impunity by screening himself behind formalities'. Parliament has always adjuged it treason to endanger the safety of the realm. Furthermore, it is 'treason by the very nature of things, for any man to attempt the subversion of that law he is born subject to. No law can justify such an action. The punishment of it is absolutely necessary to the preservation of government; and if it cannot be done in the ordinary method of proceeding, the law of self-preservation legitimates any other, though never so extraordinary.'[3]

From the lips of John Pym the argument of self-defence had some meaning. With Lord Strafford still counselling the King, Parliament had some reason to strain the law in order to preserve it, to vote an arbitrary impeachment in order to secure English liberty. But such a justification for voting unjust impeachments had no meaning whatever when the Earl of Oxford, in disfavour at Court, out of office, discredited with his party, had no power to do ill. They speak,

---

[1] *A Second Letter from a Country Whig* (1715), pp. 4–12.
[2] *The Method of the Proceedings...in Cases of Impeachments*, p. 58.
[3] [Richard West], *A Discourse Concerning Treasons and Bills of Attainder* (1716), pp. 3, 22, 66, 80, 103–4. The author of *Rocks and Shallows Discovered* (1716), concluded (p. 9) that the words of the *Discourse* 'deserve to be inscribed upon the tomb-stone of Magna Carta'.

wrote the Tory author of *A Second Letter from a Country Whig*, of the public treasure despoiled, of the people loaded with taxes, of laws and liberties endangered, 'but what is all this to the present case? The men we have now to deal with are possessed of no more power than the rest of the people.' If the late ministers have acted criminally, nothing obstructs their prosecution in the ordinary courts of law. Only if a new junto of ministers threaten to subvert our laws and liberties ought Parliament to resort to impeachments, and then only 'if proper addresses to the Throne shall be tried in vain'.[1]

Only 'if proper addresses to the Throne shall be tried in vain': this prerequisite for the voting of impeachments meant the end of impeachments, for no minister could any longer survive such an address. And lest any Englishman doubted it, Daniel Defoe in *The Secret History of the Scepter* proclaimed it to the world by relating how the sceptre, the symbol of the King's executive power, had fallen from the hands of the monarch into the grasp of the House of Commons. 'By the Scepter,' he wrote, the King 'is supposed to administer all the parts of civil government in times of peace.' By surrendering it to favourites earlier Kings of England had promoted the growth of faction and provoked the Barons' War and the Great Rebellion. By entrusting it to priests James II had provoked the late Revolution:

But with this disadvantage, that custom had naturalized the method of demitting the Scepter by the Sovereign into the hands of the servants; and in the next reign [William's] the courtiers did not so much labour to have the practice continued as to form themselves into parties, to secure it to themselves, and keep it from the other; taking it for a received maxim of government, that the King would keep the Crown upon his head, and perhaps being a martial prince would take the management of the Sword into his own hand; but for the Scepter, that was their province, and they were sure of it.

Not that William III wished to surrender the sceptre, but, being a new King on the throne, and lacking a knowledge of England, he was powerless to prevent it. Hence the choice of those who were to hold the sceptre became 'the subject not of the King's free will only,

---

[1] *A Second Letter from a Country Whig*, pp. 8, 12. The author of *A Letter to the Lord Bishop of Salisbury* observed (p. 21), when Mr Burnet 'said, "The security of our whole constitution for the future depends on a speedy impeachment", I am afraid he had not well considered the number of the criminals that must be impeached to secure the constitution as he would have it. The Tory faction is large, and will send up new leaders as soon as one is cut off.'

but of the whole kingdom's agency, and this put the nation into that flame of parties which has never yet been extinguished, and which it is feared never will'. Denzil Holles in 1646 had prophesied that taking the sceptre from the King would promote the growth of faction; Daniel Defoe in 1715 recorded it as an historical fact. The King's entrusting the sceptre to others, he wrote, 'has been the foundation of all the factions which have agitated these Kingdoms for some ages, and by which we are devolved almost entirely into the government of parties'.[1]

With parties growing ever stronger and the monarch ever weaker, the sceptre 'became at last subjected entirely to one of these two incidents: first, to the party who had the money, and, secondly, to the majority of the House of Commons'. By the first the Crown became mortgaged to the City; by the second the Crown found it 'absolutely necessary' to regard who governed in the House of Commons. 'And as the High or Low [Church] interest prevailed there, so gradually they got hold of the Scepter; this too often obligated the King to depute the Scepter to those whom otherwise he would not by his choice have been concerned with.' But the growth of parties and the scramble for possession of the sceptre had a second untoward consequence: the party which was out of power sought to make an interest in the nation by raising a hue and cry against the corruption of those in power. By exploiting these complaints they won a majority in the House, 'and by that means made their way to the Scepter'. This was the reason why in William's reign the sceptre changed hands oftener than ever before.[2]

Queen Anne, continued Defoe (who may be regarded as the earliest of all historians of responsible government), proved no abler than William to retain the sceptre in royal hands. Being a woman, she had not the authority to stand against the insistent demands of party. 'Alas! the Scepter was out of her hands; and it was for Her Majesty to act by the former rules, viz., That as the majority guided in Parliament, so the Court steered in proportion; and the Moderate Party seeming to get the better there, by twice rejecting the Occasional Bill, they got the better at Court, and the Scepter into their hands, for the first time.' But despite victory abroad and good administration at home the parties fell to quarrelling, 'the foundation of all their quarrels being chiefly...who

[1] [Defoe], *The Secret History* (1715), pp. 7–9, 11–12.   [2] *Ibid.* pp. 17, 19–21.

should get the Scepter into their hands'. The fight over Occasional Conformity really concerned the winning of office—not the preservation of the Church or the securing of toleration. And in 1708 the Whigs, however much they talked of maladministration, really desired office, not the reformation of abuses. Two years later a new ministry (whom Defoe does not criticize, thereby revealing his Harleyite bias) had to make a hasty peace and to rely upon Jacobites because the previous ministers refused to serve the Queen unless they alone held the sceptre. But ultimately divisions among the Tories themselves ruined their plans to keep the sceptre, and it was falling from their hands at the Queen's death.[1]

Defoe did not, in *The Secret History*, conceal his dislike of that 'flame of parties' which transformed the regal government of England into a 'government of parties', but, the deed being done, he found some reason for preserving parties in England. 'Nay, such is the fate of this unhappy island,' he wrote, 'that it is hard to say whether it would be well at this time that this fire should be totally extinguished or no. Such is the natural propensity of mankind to exercise power in a tyrannical manner, to the prejudice of those whom they have in subjection to that power, that it is doubtful whether the check every party is to each other is not needful to the whole, in order to restrain from tyranny and oppression.' The perspicacious Defoe saw, however regretfully, that the balance of government extolled in 1660 no longer existed, that the executive power had fallen into the hands of the legislature. This being true, a balance of parties must replace a balance of government as the palladium of English liberty; party must check party that government might be kept within its due bounds.[2]

By the year 1715 impeachments were doomed, for they had become obsolescent, unjustifiable, and unnecessary: obsolescent because Parliament could remove by an address any minister of whose conduct they disapproved; unjustifiable because political errors were not criminal acts; and unnecessary because the purpose for which impeachments had been voted in the past—to make ministers responsive to the will of Parliament—had been achieved. But the final blow destroying impeachments in England was the fiasco of the Earl of Oxford's trial, for that farce proved that impeachments were no longer useful even as a political weapon. As

[1] [Defoe], *The Secret History*, pp. 25, 27–8, 30, 31–4, 44, 46.   [2] *Ibid.* p. 13.

Defoe remarked, 'It is besides requisite to the reputation of a party, to be pretty sure of making their impeachments good, otherwise they sink in the opinion of those who are lookers on.'[1] Of this truth, Walpole, Townshend, and Stanhope could not have been ignorant; they must have been as conscious as Defoe of the danger of voting frivolous impeachments. Yet they went ahead with the impeachment of the late ministry. Why? Besides wishing to blacken the reputation of the late Queen's ministers by innuendo and villification, with no intention of convicting them, they must have acted from the hope of finding proof of a design to bring in the Pretender, or of some other treason, such as surrendering territory to the enemy without the Queen's authority. Impeachments had not become so obsolescent that they could not be voted against ministers who had actually committed treason.[2]

But the problem was to discover proof of the treason. That the Earl of Oxford had in fact committed treason by negotiating with the Pretender, many men then suspected and historians now know for certain. The correspondence of Torcy, Ilberville, and the Duc d'Aumont proves it conclusively. As George Macaulay Trevelyan has written, 'Their correspondence, now open to historians in the French Foreign Office, was not available to the Whigs when they impeached Oxford and Bolingbroke in 1715. If it had then been published, it would have proved what was so strongly suspected, that the two English ministers, from the Treaty of Utrecht to the death of Anne, were in constant communication with the Pretender, and were plotting with the French Ministers to bring him to the throne on the Queen's death.'[3] That Oxford entered into these negotiations only to win Jacobite support in the 1713 elections and to insure himself against a Jacobite Restoration, which he feared rather than desired, would have made no difference to the Whigs, for they wanted his conviction and they knew that a statute passed

---

[1] *A Letter to a Merry Young Gentleman*, p. 21. Defoe also observed (p. 23), 'but if I remember rightly, the party which impeached them [Partition Treaty lords] never recovered the credit lost by it, during that reign at least'.

[2] Or other known crimes; which is the reason the Commons continued to impeach those whom they knew to have committed unlawful acts, as Lord Macclesfield in 1725, Lord Lovat in 1747, and Lord Melville in 1805.

[3] G. M. Trevelyan, *The Peace and the Protestant Succession* (1934), p. 249. The French Foreign Office papers also show that Oxford lied when he said that proposals for peace first came from Torcy in April 1711; in reality these proposals, months before, were 'collusively arranged between Jersey, Harley, and Shrewsbury on the one side and Louis's Minister Torcy on the other' (*ibid.* p. 176).

in William's reign declared it treason to promote the Pretender's succession and that another statute passed in Queen Anne's reign made it treason in any manner to seek to prevent the succession of the House of Hanover. But the Committee of Secrecy found not a scrap of evidence that any of the late ministers had promoted the Pretender's succession, which is not surprising for they had more sense than to put anything in writing. More disappointing was the refusal of either Matthew Prior or Thomas Harley to reveal any of the secrets they may have known about Abbé Gaultier's mysterious trips. Thomas Harley even had the audacity to deny that he had ever seen Gaultier, though one of St John's letters proved that he had. For his contumacious attitude, the House of Commons threw him in the Gatehouse where he remained until Parliament was prorogued.[1]

Thwarted in their search for proof that Lord Oxford had corresponded with the Pretender, the Whigs sought proof that he had advised the King of France how he might acquire Tournay. Since a single allegation in one of Bolingbroke's letters hardly sufficed to condemn Oxford, the Whigs placed their hopes in the testimony of Matthew Prior, whom they interrogated for nine hours on 16 June 1715. Walpole put the crucial question to Prior: had the Earl of Oxford ever said anything about Tournay? Prior replied that he was not certain, but believed that about 1711 Lord Oxford said it must go to the Dutch. 'Here', wrote Prior, 'Walpole and Stanhope grew mightily perplexed; one in a sullen, and the other in an unbounded, passion. Coningsby raved outright. I may justly protest that I could not conceive the cause of this disorder, for I did not know that they had already founded their High Treason upon the Article of Tournay.'[2] When in July the Commons carried their articles of impeachment to the House of Lords, Oxford categorically denied that he had advised the French how they might secure Tournay; and in September he repeated his denial in his answer to the articles, adding that he had not at any other time during the said war aided, helped, assisted, or adhered to the French King.[3]

---

[1] 13 William III, Cap. vi and 6 Anne, Cap. vii, *Statutes at Large* (1764), x, 406; xi, 308–9; *The Whole Proceedings* (1715), pp. 88–97.

[2] L. G. Wickham Legg, *Matthew Prior* (Cambridge, 1921), pp. 241–2. The House of Commons likewise imprisoned Matthew Prior, and kept him in prison until the prorogation.

[3] Oxford's speech before the House of Lords, B.M. Loan 29/1; Cobbett, *Parl. Hist.* vii, 179. Oxford probably never advised the cession of Tournay, but he lied when he said he had never assisted France. In October 1712 he and Bolingbroke (as Trevelyan writes,

Conscious that they possessed no proof that Oxford had advised the French King how to gain Tournay, the Whig managers of the House of Commons grew faint in their prosecution of his impeachment. 'By what I can understand', wrote James Brydges in December 1715, 'we shall open our sessions on the 9th of next month with a trial of Lord Oxford, but I am apt to think the House will give up the point of Treason, and that the Court will be inclined to bring it to Crimes and Misdemeanours only.'[1]

But when January came, Parliament found itself too busy impeaching the seven Jacobite lords who took part in the '15 to have time to prosecute Oxford's impeachment. And when Parliament next met, in the autumn of 1716, the Whig ministers of George I had dropped all plans to prosecute Oxford for treason. 'With respect to Lord Oxford's trial,' Lord Townshend wrote to Secretary Stanhope, 'the Lords [of the Council] are of the opinion, that the charge of High Treason should be dropped, it being very certain that there is not sufficient evidence to convict him of that crime.'[2] Townshend then recommended his prosecution for misdemeanours, but the ministry made no move to prosecute the impeachment.

In the end the Earl of Oxford petitioned, the Commons did not demand, that the Lords set a day for his trial. Oxford's timing of his petition was exemplary, proving that he had not lost his skill in political tactics. He presented his petition two years after his impeachment, thereby allowing resentments against him to abate, and two months after the Whig ministry had split apart, thereby exploiting their differences and the desire of Walpole and Townshend to find Tory allies. Because of the divisions among the Whigs, the Court party in the House of Lords could not prevent the peers from setting 13 June for Oxford's trial. The Tories naturally supported an early trial; what carried the day was Viscount Townshend's open advocacy of setting the earliest possible day for the trial.[3]

Peace and Protestant Succession, p. 218) 'together sent word through Gaultier to Torcy "That they have been informed this morning by a courier that Prince Eugene has resolved to surprise Nieuport or Furnes. This advice has been given by a spy they have about the Prince, whose services he is to use on the expedition." "I am warning Marshall Duke of Villars of it," Gaultier takes care to add. This letter would have proved a useful piece, if the Whigs had got hold of it for the impeachments.'

[1] Huntington Library S.T. 57, XII, f. 222.   [2] Coxe, *Walpole*, II, 123.

[3] William Harlwick, *The History of the Third Session of the Present Parliament* (1717), p. 69. Hugh Thomas wrote (*H.M.C. Stuart*, IV, 355), 'All the Tory lords in England are either come or coming up for the Earl of Oxford's trial, against which the Court used all their interest, but on a division in the House of Lords the Court party were but 47 against 85,

When the Lords' message appointing 13 June for the Earl of Oxford's trial reached the House of Commons, the House asked the Committee of Secrecy to recommend an answer. The Committee recommended that the House ask the Lords to delay the trial, in order that the Commons could inspect again the treaties, letters, papers, and records concerning the impeachment. On hearing this recommendation the House fell into a two or three minute silence. Then several members complained that delay would work a hardship upon Lord Oxford and discredit the House of Commons. Samuel Tufnell delivered a moving speech, in which he said that he would never have voted to prosecute Oxford for treason had not an honourable gentleman (meaning Walpole) undertaken to prove a fact (concerning Tournay) which the house had already adjudged treason and promised 'living and legal evidence to support the charge'. 'This', he concluded, 'and this alone swayed my opinion.' Then William Shippen suggested, 'after all, those who had first begun the impeachments ought to be satisfied with having got the places of those who were impeached, which indeed seemed to be what they had principally in view'. That this was their view, he added, should now be evident, since those (meaning Walpole and Townshend) who are now out of office no longer have any interest in prosecuting the impeachments. John Hungerford then told the House, 'That for his own part, he ever was against impeachments, because he had observed that they generally came to nothing.' In reply to these reflections upon him, Walpole made only the faintest apology; but Nicholas Lechmere, for the government, made so persuasive a speech in favour of delay that the Commons, ever mindful of their right to demand judgment upon an impeachment whenever they chose, resolved to ask the Lords to delay the trial.[1]

The Lords acquiesced in the Commons' request to the extent of postponing the trial to 24 June. The Commons in return for this courtesy agreed to prosecute their impeachment against Oxford on the 24th. When that day arrived, the Commons appeared in Westminster Hall; the Earl of Oxford, looking unconcerned, arrived by

a vast majority for the trial, and like to be more.' However, the Lords were unwilling to reduce the power of impeachment to a nullity by allowing the King to end an impeachment by proroguing Parliament. They voted, even the Tories, even Oxford's friends, against Lord North and Grey's motion that the late prorogation had ended Oxford's impeachment (*ibid.* p. 330).

[1] Harlwick, *History of the Third Session*, pp. 72–5; B.M. Loan, Portland Papers, no.10(1).

water from the Tower; the Lord High Steward, the patent being read naming him to that dignity, took his place as presiding officer; and the trial began. Through the long afternoon the clerk of the Parliament read the twenty-two articles of impeachment against the Earl of Oxford and the Earl's answer to them, omitting half his answers, occasionally skipping ten sides at a time. The preliminaries completed, Richard Hampden opened for the prosecution with an acrimonious speech, in which he accused Oxford of betraying the Queen's counsels, deserting the allies, treacherously surrendering strongholds to the enemy, and opposing the Protestant Succession. Sir Joseph Jeckyll then appeared at the bar to make good the first article, only to be interrupted by Lord Harcourt who moved that their Lordships adjourn to their own House. Once in their own chamber, Lord Harcourt proposed that they require the Commons to prosecute the charge of treason first, and only after they had finished with it to proceed to the misdemeanours. Oxford himself conceived of this strategy in early June, knowing that the Court had long since despaired of proving the treason charged against him, but hoped to make good the misdemeanours. Though Lord Parker insisted that in all courts of law it was customary to proceed through all the evidence before giving judgment on any part of the accusation, the Lords preferred Harcourt's argument that no peer innocent of treason should be tried for misdemeanours while outside the bar and without counsel as to fact. In reality these legal arguments counted for little. Political motives led the peers, after four hours' debate, to vote, by 88 to 25, to demand that the Commons proceed first to the charge of treason. The Tories naturally supported Harcourt's motion; the ministerial peers as naturally opposed it; what carried the day were the dissident Whigs, among them the Dukes of Devonshire, Argyle, Grafton, and Rutland, the Earls of Bristol, Islay, Derby, and Dorset, and Viscount Townshend himself. Had they not sought to embarrass the government, Oxford's strategy would have failed.[1]

When at nine in the evening the Lords filed back into Westminster

---

[1] Accounts of the trial may be found in Harlwick, *History of the Third Session*, pp. 76–9, 91–5; B.M. Loan 29/266, no. 2; L'Hermitage, B.M. Add. MSS 17677 KKK (2), ff. 212–213; *H.M.C. Polwarth*, 1, 283–4; Ballard MSS 32, ff. 32–32v. A memorandum entitled 'Querys to consult Lord Trevor, Lord Harcourt, and the Duke Shrewsbury' (B.M. Loan, Portland Papers, no. 10, 1) suggests that Oxford conceived of the strategy, which Lord Harcourt so effectively executed—and even formulated the arguments which Harcourt used before the Lords.

Hall and informed the Commons that they must proceed first to the charge of treason, they proclaimed, as their predecessors had before them, a determination not to allow the Commons to abuse the power of impeachment. In 1701 the Lords had prevented the Commons from voting impeachments that they never intended to prosecute; now they prevented them from charging men with treason when they only intended to prosecute them for misdemeanours. Now, as in 1701, the House of Commons protested and blustered, but in vain. On hearing the decision they first protested that they had an undoubted right to proceed to misdemeanours first, then they marched from the Hall. In subsequent days there followed conferences, messages, and protestations, but neither House would yield. Finally the Lords, refusing to meet the Commons in a Free Conference, resolved that Oxford's trial should resume on 1 July. When that day arrived, the Earl of Oxford appeared, knelt at the bar, listened as a proclamation summoning the Commons was read three times over; but no member of the House of Commons appeared, for the Commons preferred not to prosecute the impeachment at all rather than proceed first to the charge of treason. After fifteen minutes of silence, the Lords withdrew to their own chamber to consider how they should proceed. Lord Harcourt moved that they discharge Lord Oxford from the treason charged against him, the Commons having failed to appear to prosecute him, but the Earl of Sunderland, now presumably weary of the whole affair, proposed instead that they discharge him from all the crimes charged against him, misdemeanours as well as treasons. Thus one of the most inveterate foes of the Earl occasioned his complete rather than partial discharge from his impeachment, for the Lords adopted Sunderland's proposal. Returning to Westminster Hall, the Lord High Steward asked each lord whether, the Commons not prosecuting their impeachment, he believed the Earl of Oxford discharged from his impeachment. Of the 107 lords present all answered yes, for the thirty ministerial peers who opposed Oxford's acquittal had withdrawn. That night the Earl of Oxford went free and the next day he resumed his place in the House of Lords.[1]

[1] Harlwick, *History of the Third Session*, pp. 78, 81–3; B.M. Loan, Portland Papers, Impeachment of Robert Harley, no. 5; B.M. Add. MSS 34515, f. 182; L'Hermitage, B.M. Add. MSS 17677 KKK (2), ff. 220–222. There are two lists of the peers who voted to discharge the Earl of Oxford, B.M. Loan 29/266, no. 2, and Harlwick, *History of the Third Session*, pp. 101–2.

While these farcical events transpired in Westminster Hall,[1] the Commons fell into a furious debate over the conduct of the Lords. Secretary Stanhope and Samuel Tufnell vented their rage in inflammatory speeches, others counselled moderation, Solicitor General Lechmere proposed that they proceed as the Lords desired, and Sir William Strickland moved that they vote an Act of Attainder against Oxford. But the House heeded none of these proposals: instead they did nothing, nothing, that is, but adhere to their resolution not to appear in Westminster Hall unless they could prosecute the charges in the manner they wished. There is every reason to believe that many in the Commons welcomed the quarrel as an excuse not even to prosecute the misdemeanours charged against Oxford, for the House never prosecuted the Earl of Strafford's impeachment, though it was for misdemeanours only. In truth, the House could not have convicted either lord of misdemeanours, for neither had committed any. In 1717 the Whigs suffered the same retribution of shame for voting baseless impeachments that the Tories had suffered in 1701. They now learned the lesson the Tories then learned: that voting unjust, arbitrary, and groundless impeachments against one's political enemies was far more productive of embarrassment than profit. The refusal of Sir Robert Walpole's enemies in 1742 to impeach him proved that politicians had learned the lessons of 1701 and 1717.[2]

The acquittal of the Earl of Oxford on 1 July 1717 marked the end of an epoch that had begun on a summer's day in 1610, but two other events in 1717 signalled the end of the age of impeachment. Robert Walpole resigned as Chancellor of the Exchequer because he would not accept responsibility for actions of which he disapproved. And George I withdrew from the Cabinet because he was not allowed to bear responsibility for decisions reached there. Both men acted on the assumption that the King's ministers, not the King himself, must answer to Parliament for the good government of the realm.

---

[1] One wag posted-up a paper, in the form of a Play House Bill, which read, 'The Lord Oxford's Tryal Comes On etc., or a Farce Between the Lords and Commons' (*H.M.C. Report 12, Part 9*, p. 97).

[2] Harlwick, *History of the Third Session*, pp. 82, 97–8; L'Hermitage, B.M. Add. MSS 17677 KKK (2), ff. 221 v–222; *H.M.C. Report 2, Part 9*, p. 97. The Commons asked the King, and the King agreed, to except the Earl of Oxford from an Act of Grace passed that session (*C.J.* xviii, 616, 618), but as Dr Stratford wrote to Lord Harley (*H.M.C. Portland*, vii, 224), 'I suppose your father, who has stood an impeachment, will not fly an exception in the Act of Grace.'

Walpole resigned on 10 April 1717, informing the King in a private audience that

it was impossible to serve him faithfully with those ministers, to whom he had lately given his favour and credit. For that they would propose to him as Chancellor of the Exchequer, as well as in Parliament, such things, that if he should agree to and support, he should lose his credit and reputation in the world; and should he not approve or oppose them, he should lose His Majesty's favour. For he, in his station, though not the author, must be answerable to his King and country for any extraordinary measure.[1]

To the House of Commons he justified his resignation by suggesting that he could not comply with the measures of the present ministers.[2] What these measures were any member could surmise: war credits against Sweden, an increase in the standing army, the employment of German mercenary troops, and an aggressive diplomacy in the Baltic that threatened a costly war. Rather than answer for these policies Walpole resigned.

But a far stronger motive than a desire not to answer for an unpopular foreign policy led Walpole to resign. He resigned because others enjoyed that ascendancy in the King's counsels which he himself coveted. A German ministry composed of irresponsible courtiers like Robethon, the Duchess of Munster, Bothmer, and Bernsdorff, he could not brook. With Walpole's unwillingness to serve a King who listened to German counsellors most Englishmen would have concurred, but fewer of them would have concurred with his refusal to serve a King who listened to other Englishmen, to Whigs like Stanhope and Sunderland. Yet it was unquestionably Stanhope's and Sunderland's willingness to acquiesce in the dismissal of Viscount Townshend from office that led Walpole to resign. When he first heard that the King intended to dismiss Townshend, his close friend and political ally, Walpole wrote a blistering letter to Stanhope, who replied that the King was determined to be rid of Townshend. 'Ought I,' continued Stanhope, 'either in my own name or in the name of the Whiggish party, to have told the King, that my Lord Townshend must continue to be Secretary of State, or that I, nor any other of our friends, would have anything to do? I really have

---

[1] Coxe, *Walpole*, II, 169–70. Another account of this audience, presumably based on Hoffmann's dispatches, appears in Wolfgang Michael, 'Walpole als Premierminister', *Historische Zeitschrift*, CIV, 505.

[2] Cobbett, *Parl. Hist.* VII, 448.

not yet learned to speak such language to my master.'[1] Secretary Stanhope may not have learned to speak such language, but it was Swift's opinion, as also the opinion of others, that such language was commonly heard at Queen Anne's court.[2]

What is certain is that Walpole had learned to speak such language, however artfully he wrapped it up in the rhetoric of a courtier. Throughout the last months of 1716 he sulked because George I would not have Townshend as Secretary of State and in 1717 he resigned because the King would not have Townshend as Viceroy of Ireland. He not only resigned himself, but took with him Devonshire, Orford, Pulteney, St Quintin, and Edgecombe. Nor did Walpole resign merely in order to retreat to his seat in Norfolk; he immediately went into opposition. He now adopted the strategy that he had threatened to adopt all winter, to use his strength in Parliament to make himself indispensable at Court. He did not invent this strategy, the second Duke of Buckingham did in 1667, but he pursued it with a relentless purpose that neither Buckingham nor Shaftesbury nor Wharton had ever exhibited. He opposed the Septennial Act, which he had once favoured; he favoured the Schism Act, which he had once opposed; though a Whig, he opposed measures to make the universities less Tory; and though he had impeached their leaders, he now sought an alliance with the Tories.[3] 'Mr Walpole', wrote Thomas Foley to the Earl of Oxford in November 1717, 'seems more convinced that they [the ministry] will not be reconciled to him, and consequently more fixed to oppose them than last session.'[4] Whatever other men may have thought, Walpole and his friends concluded that they might oppose the King until he entrusted them with office.

What other men did think soon became evident in a pamphlet war over the propriety of the conduct of Walpole and his friends. The author of *An Answer to the Character and Conduct of Robert Walpole* drew the battle line by proclaiming, 'My allegiance is due to King

---

[1] Coxe, *Walpole*, II, 154.

[2] Swift, *Works*, III, 37. The author of *Memoirs of Some Transactions* (1717) wrote (p. 27), 'Her Majesty had, with some regret, received the former importunities of some about her, in the case of placing or displacing of persons; and especially that unpleasant, uncomely, as well as undutiful expression of, "I cannot serve Your Majesty unless, etc.". . . .'

[3] Plumb, *Walpole*, I, 249–50. According to Hoffmann (quoted in Michael, 'Walpole als Premierminister', *Historische Zeitschrift*, CIV, 523), Walpole had no use for a House of Commons so divided that it could be governed by the Court; he preferred one in which a superior party could govern.

[4] B.M. Loan 29/136, no. 7.

George, whoever he is pleased to make choice of for his servants.'
'There is no man in England', he continued, 'that can think it
right to quarrel with a neighbouring gentleman for changing his
servants, and yet most of Mr Walpole's friends think themselves at
liberty to distress the King through his ministry, and to act as contrary as they please to their past principles, if the King takes a
servant in Mr Walpole's room, even though he has put himself out
of place, by refusing to serve the King any longer.' This Mr Walpole
'has the impudence to say, that though a person was recommended
by the King himself, he must not expect to succeed, if he did not
come into certain measures'. With this sense of rage at Walpole's
conduct, Matthew Tindal was in full sympathy. In *The Defection
Considered* he roundly denounced those ministers who, rather than
allow His Majesty to dismiss their friends, resign, and scruple not
'to embroil the public affairs, in order to make themselves necessary;
and to force the Prince to part with those whom he judges best
deserve his kindness, and to employ none but them and their
creatures'. 'Quitting places', he continued, 'is no crime; but if
several cabal to throw up, when the government has most occasion
for their services, in order to force it to comply with their unreasonable demands, this is a very criminal conspiracy.'[1]

The enemies of Robert Walpole rightly charged that his conduct
effectively destroyed the King's liberty to choose whom he wished to
serve him. As a counter to this argument Walpole's friends asserted
the minister's liberty of judgment. 'Ministers of state', wrote Daniel
Defoe in *Some Persons Vindicated*, 'have always a right of preserving
their own principles, and a liberty of adhering to what in their
judgment they think is for the service of their country, and the
interest of the master they serve; otherwise they were slaves by
office.' Since His Majesty's servants possessed a right to liberty of
judgment, even when their judgment differed from the King's, how
much more should they enjoy that right when their judgment merely
differed from a fellow servant's. Lord Townshend and Mr Walpole
'found themselves under the misfortune of seeing others of His
Majesty's servants to have different sentiments of things from themselves, and those such as they could not reconcile to their opinions'.
Surely their libellers will 'not contend that a minister of state is

---

[1] *An Answer to the Character and Conduct of R_____ W_____* (1717),
pp. 32–3, 38; Matthew Tindal, *The Defection Considered* (1718), pp. 23–4.

obliged to submit his opinion or his principles on all occasions...
to any arbitrary notions of others his fellow servants in the same
ministry...'. George Sewell, for one, agreed that no minister
should have to submit to the arbitrary notions of others. When there
are 'ill designs in hand', he wrote in *The Resigners Vindicated*, it concerns a minister of state to guard his honour 'from any share in the
management of them'. The author of *The Defection Detected* also
defended the liberty of judgment of the King's ministers, giving a
long-awaited answer to those who had claimed from the time of
Elizabeth that a monarch had as much right as any gentleman of
England to dismiss an unwanted servant. 'But I hope it may without offence be said that according to customs in practice with
Englishmen, it lies as much in the breast of a servant to quit an
employment under the best of masters, as it does in that of the
masters to discharge and turn off the servant.'[1]

To defend the resignation of a minister who would not embark
upon ill designs was a comparatively simple task in the England of
George I; to defend Walpole's unprincipled opposition to the
government because the King dismissed his friend Townshend was
more difficult. But the author of *The Defection Detected* bravely
essayed the task. 'Men divested of prejudice', he argued, 'will
conclude with Machiavelli, that for a minister of state to keep the
helm, while "his friends and relations are in disgrace is to run the
risk of the same fate himself".' In former reigns, he added, great
favourites ever behaved in the same manner. The Whigs turned
against the Court upon the dismissal of Godolphin. 'It was thought
no crime in them to go over to the Country party, who were averse
to the measures set on foot by the Court.'[2]

An age in which half the Cabinet resigned from office because the
King would not employ a man whom they wished him to employ

---

[1] Daniel Defoe, *Some Persons Vindicated against the Author of the Defection* (1718), pp. 14–16;
George Sewell, *The Resigners Vindicated* (1718), p. 9; *The Defection Detected* (1718), p. 7.

[2] *Ibid.* pp. 18–19. Had the author of *The Defection Detected* perused his Machiavelli
more closely, he might have read this passage in the *History of Florence* (New York, 1901,
pp. 114–15), a passage which affords an equally apt, though less charitable, commentary
on Walpole's conduct: 'From proceedings such as these [hatreds, quarrels, banishments]
arise at once the attachment for and influence of parties; bad men follow them through
ambition and avarice, and necessity compels the good to pursue the same course. And
most lamentable is it to observe how the leaders and movers of parties sanctify their base
designs with words that are all piety and virtue...Thus laws and ordinances, peace and
war, and treaties are adopted and pursued, not for the public good...but for the convenience and advantage of a few individuals.'

bore little resemblance to the age of Charles I, when Edward Hyde continued to serve Charles though Charles did not even keep faith with his own servants. Walpole's resignation in 1717 is an event of unusual significance, for as destructive as impeachments were to the prerogative, more destructive yet was the practice of resigning when one's friends were not employed. In the long run not the willingness of Parliament to vote impeachments but the willingness of ministers to resign when their counsels were refused dealt the most fatal blow to the King's power. Resignations, in fact, had a twofold effect: they circumscribed the monarch's freedom of choice in his ministers, and they justified Parliament in holding those who continued to serve him responsible for the counsels upon which he acted. The King could only employ those who would serve together and they must answer to Parliament for their advice.

Robert Walpole resigned from the Cabinet in order to avoid responsibility for its decisions; George I withdrew from the Cabinet because he was denied responsibility for its decisions. The story that George I withdrew from the Cabinet because he could not speak English is mere legend, for he regularly attended the Cabinet for two years, conversing with his ministers in French, and he continued throughout his reign to meet with his ministers in the Closet, conversing in German, French, or Latin.[1] Not difficulty of language, but embarrassment at possessing so little authority drove him to absent himself from the Cabinet. He was not asked to make, but to sanction, decisions. As the Prussian Resident, Bonnet, wrote in January 1718, 'I have observed in the two former reigns how one discussed serious questions in the Cabinet. In the present reign the Cabinet is only seldom held, the ministers of state design everything, and only leave it to the King to authorize the matter.'[2]

The ministers had good reason to design everything, for they must answer to Parliament for decisions reached in the Cabinet. Stanhope

[1] E. R. Turner, *The Cabinet Council of England* (Baltimore, 1930–32), ii, 94–5; W. Michael, *Englische Geschichte*, iii, 568–76. Michael maintains (*ibid.* p. 576) that no historian in the eighteenth century ever mentioned George's inability to speak English as a reason for his withdrawal from the Cabinet. The legend arose when later historians misinterpreted a remark made by Henry Hallam.

[2] Quoted in Michael, 'Die Entstehung der Kabinettsregierung', *Zeitschrift für Politik*, vi, 576. J. N. Plumb has shown ('The Organization of the Cabinet in the Reign of Queen Anne', *Transactions of the Royal Historical Soc.* 5th ser. vii, 137–57) that during Anne's reign the Cabinet, meeting at the Palace with the Queen, merely revised, reconsidered, and gave royal authority to acts and decisions reached by her ministers, meeting without her, at the Cockpit.

discovered this fact in the spring of 1717 when, in the name of the King, he asked the Commons to vote supplies for a possible war against Sweden. He offered no estimate of expenses, nor any description of the need, but merely asked that they leave to the King 'the management of what money should be thought necessary for his service'. He then added 'that none would refuse compliance with this message but such as either were not the King's friends, or who distrusted the honesty of his ministers'. This gave great offence to the House, and particularly to Gilfrid Lawson, who replied 'that if every member of this House that used freedom of speech on any subject of debate must be accounted an enemy to the King when he happens not to fall in with his ministers, he knew no service they were capable of doing for their country in that House; and therefore it was his opinion, that they had nothing else to do but to retire to their country-seats, and leave the King and his ministers to take what they pleased'.[1] The House voted the supplies asked, but Stanhope never again sought to screen himself behind the King's name. A year later he told the House of Lords (where he now sat) 'that both with relation to Sir George Byng's instructions, and in all other respects, in this whole affair [the negotiation of the Quadruple Alliance], His Majesty had acted on the advice of his Privy Council; that he was one of that number, and he thought it an honour to have advised His Majesty to these measures...'. And when Walpole in the Commons said on the same day that he hoped all men would distinguish between His Majesty and his ministers, James Craggs, lately named Secretary of State, 'readily admitted of the distinction'.[2] A long chapter in the history of responsible government came to a close when the ministers in power, as well as the politicians out, agreed to distinguish between the King and his ministers.

This was particularly true because the King himself accepted the distinction. In March 1718 George I told Pentenrriedter, the Imperial Envoy, that his ministers were answerable to the nation, and that he could not protect them.[3]

Conscious that he was unable to protect his ministers and aware that he could not override their determinations in the Cabinet, George I resolved to withdraw from the Cabinet. This does not

---

[1] Cobbett, *Parl. Hist.* VII, 435–6.   [2] *Ibid.* pp. 561, 565.
[3] Report of Pentenrriedter, 27 March 1718, quoted by Michael, 'Die Entstehung der Kabinettsregierung', *Zeitschrift für Politik*, VI, 579.

mean that his influence on the government of Great Britain came to an end; he merely transferred it from the Cabinet to the Closet. He preferred to meet his ministers individually rather than collectively, informally rather than formally. In the secrecy of the Closet he could make known his pleasure, threaten the withdrawal of his favour, appeal to the reverence owed the Crown, and use to the utmost his power of patronage. As a result his will often prevailed, but always within the limits of action set for him by his ministers, ministers who must in turn answer to a Parliament that controlled the purse strings. Rather than consent to measures which they believed unwise or illegal or unlikely of success, the King's ministers would first resign, for they must answer to Parliament for the wisdom, the legality, and the success of the King's measures. That they and not the King must assume this responsibility all Englishmen agreed. Parliament insisted upon it, the King's ministers acknowledged it, and the King himself admitted it. The epoch which opened on a summer morning in 1610 when James I refused to allow Parliament to prosecute his servants ended in the summer of 1717 when George I declined to attend the Cabinet regularly because, as he later told the Imperial Ambassador, his ministers were answerable to the nation, and he could not protect them.

CONCLUSIONS

To explain how the present grew out of the past, how one age grew out of another, is one of the central tasks of the historian. But to perform it he must do three things. He must ascertain in what ways the present differs from the past. He must trace how these changes came about. And he must discover why they came about. This study has sought to answer each of these questions as they concern the growth of responsible government in Stuart England. How did the responsibilities of ministers of the Crown at the accession of George I differ from what they had been at the death of Queen Elizabeth? How did these changes come about—by what steps, by what decisive events, by what trials, and by what errors? And why did they occur—what motives led men to demand them and what circumstances allowed them to win their demands?

The most striking difference between the two ages lies in the inability of George I to assume responsibility, as the Tudors did, for the good government of the realm. Admittedly Elizabeth could not, in a court of law, assume legal responsibility for her commands; but for the political wisdom of her commands she could and did (though answerable only to God) assume full responsibility. And her ministers could disarm criticism by pleading obedience to their sovereign's commands. The ministers of George I could not. Against neither impeachment, censure, nor criticism could they plead the commands of the King; nor could they use the King's name to justify the illegality, the imprudence, or the ill success of their actions. Not only was George I powerless to protect his ministers by assuming responsibility for commands given them, he was likewise powerless to protect them by acting alone. Powers, warrants, instructions, proclamations, and treaties must be countersigned by a responsible minister. And though the King might dissolve Parliament in person, might address both Houses from the throne, and might meet with foreign ambassadors and foreign princes, Englishmen in the eighteenth century insisted that he do so upon the counsels of others, never upon his own judgment. Denied the right to assume responsibility for commands given his ministers, denied the right to act without them, the King had only one means left to protect them, by granting them a pardon when impeached by the House of Commons. But the Act of Settlement in 1701 took this power from him. Whatever else the King of England could do in the eighteenth century, he could not assume responsibility for the actions of his government; his ministers must bear that responsibility, and he could not protect them from the censure of Parliament.

The maxim that the King can do no wrong and the principle that the monarch is always advised left unsolved the problem of discovering the servants who did wrong and the councillors who gave bad advice. In the eighteenth century, however, Parliament possessed far more resources for discovering errant ministers and evil councillors than it did in the sixteenth. Elizabeth's Parliaments possessed no right of inquiry—could not demand papers, examine accounts, question servants of the Crown, or imprison contumacious witnesses. The first Hanoverian Parliament exercised all these rights to the fullest. But these inquiries, though pursued with all the energy exhibited by the Committee of Secrecy in 1715, rarely uncovered the authors of ill counsels. Those who advised the King did so in the secrecy of the Cabinet and the Closet. To discover these men and to lay on them the faults of misgovernment, Parliament gave up the search for legal proof (which the replacement of impeachments with addresses permitted) and settled on common fame. Common fame in turn pointed an accusing finger at those who sat in the King's council, at those who governed the various departments of state, and at those who enjoyed a pre-eminence in the King's counsels. These ministers common fame could justly blame, for should the King follow the advice of other men, of irresponsible counsellors, these ministers ought to resign, thereby escaping responsibility for the advice upon which the King acted. At the accession of George I the collective responsibility of the Cabinet, the particular responsibility of the departmental head, and the special responsibility of the Prime Minister were ideas yet in their infancy; but under Elizabeth they were not yet dreamed of.

Parliament sought to focus responsibility on ministers of state, not that they should then answer to the King for the good government of the realm, but to Parliament. Elizabeth's ministers need not answer to Parliament for their actions. They feared neither impeachment, remonstrance, address, nor vote of censure. They need not fear dismissal because the House of Commons would refuse supplies unless they were removed or because they could no longer carry on the Queen's business successfully in Parliament. The ministers of George I had good reason to fear all these possible calamities. The House of Commons could impeach them for any criminal acts or unlawful counsels. If they lacked evidence of criminal conduct or unlawful counsels, they might yet brand them —if angry enough—'enemies of the King and Kingdom'; or they might vote an address asking the King to remove them from his councils and presence for ever. Far more likely the Commons would censure them by condemning the policies which they pursued or by rejecting proposals for additional supplies for the King. But the greatest danger facing the ministers of George I was the possibility that they should fail to manage the King's affairs in Parliament successfully, and that the King would then turn to those men who could. No group of ministers could hope to serve the King long who regularly met defeat in the House of Commons; nor could the King long employ those who consistently met defeat there. Henry VIII had said that 'it pertains nothing to any of our subjects to appoint us our Council'. But the House of Commons in the eighteenth century would not permit the King to appoint men to his Cabinet who did not enjoy their confidence.

Despite the gulf that separates the responsibilities borne by Burghley from those borne by Walpole, responsible government was far from achieved in 1714. The Hanoverian Kings retained a real, though much weakened, grasp on the sceptre throughout the eighteenth century. They retained it because ministers of state were reluctant to thwart the King's will and because Parliament was reluctant to challenge his right to choose his own ministers. In the secrecy of the Closet the Hanoverian Kings hectored their ministers, argued with them, appealed to the obedience they owed their sovereign, disregarded their advice, and threatened their dismissal. And the threat of dismissal carried weight, for the King might prevail upon Parliament to give its confidence to other ministers. By appealing to the reverence men owed the Crown, by influencing elections to the House of Commons, by astutely distributing place, pension, and title, and by holding out the hope of preferment to others, the Hanoverian Kings could (when parties lay in disarray) win support in Parliament for ministers of their own choice. How much obedience did ministers render the King in Georgian England?

How reluctant were they to use their power in Parliament to enforce their wishes on His Majesty? How much latitude did Parliament give the King in his choice of ministers? How deep was the reverence then paid to the Crown? How great was the royal influence in Parliament? These are questions which only the historian of the eighteenth-century constitution can answer. The most that the historian of Stuart England can safely say is that men in the Stuart epoch laid the foundations upon which Hanoverian and Victorian politicians later built. Hanoverian and Victorian politicians merely showed a greater willingness to exercise powers and adopt expedients which Stuart politicians had secured and discovered. As the eighteenth century waned and the nineteenth century unfolded ministers of state exhibited an increasing readiness to contest the royal will, Parliament a growing willingness to challenge the King's choice of ministers, and politicians a mounting love for party and suspicion of patronage. More and more Englishmen came to accept the collective responsibility of the Cabinet and the special responsibility of the Prime Minister. But there was nothing new in all this. The shape which responsible government took in these years followed the shape of the foundations laid down in the previous century. It was the special contribution of Stuart politicians to have laid down these foundations, and to have laid them down solidly.

No architect in Stuart England designed these foundations with an eye to the future development of the constitution. Seventeenth-century Englishmen possessed no blue-print for the building of responsible government. The historical process by which responsible government developed was erratic, experimental, labyrinthine, and myopic. It was marked by trial and error, by a search for expedients, by the stress of immediate political quarrels, by the exigencies of party and personal strife, by present fears and proximate hopes. Furthermore, these changes occurred gradually, step by step, with no thought beyond the immediate demand of the moment. Precedent succeeded precedent, claim followed claim, but no one consciously strove to transfer the sceptre from the King's hands to Parliament's. Instead they sought to win immediate political demands, and sought to weaken the King's control of executive power only when that control obstructed the winning of their demands. But though the process was devious, faltering, and repetitive, it was also cumulative. Men finally ceased perpetrating the same errors over and over again, and finally stumbled upon expedients that would work.

The story is complex, but certain themes can be discerned. Among them are (1) the revival and initial failure of impeachment, (2) the rise and fall of the demand that Parliament name the King's ministers, (3) the failure of conciliar government, (4) the return to impeachment and the triumph of the maxim that the King can do no wrong, (5) the end of impeachment and the emergence of parliamentary addresses, (6) the beginning of Cabinet responsibility, departmental responsibility, and the special responsibility of the Prime Minister, and (7) the ultimate victory of parliamentary undertakings.

Englishmen first sought to make the executive responsible to Parliament by reviving the power of impeachment. They began hesitantly. In 1610 they asked and were denied permission to arrest and sue the King's servants. They acquiesced in James's veto of their wish; but in 1621 they demanded what in 1610 they had only requested. They imprisoned, interrogated, impeached, and tried the King's servants. They took the first bold step towards the winning of responsible government. But in one important respect it was a modest step, for they impeached Mompesson, Michell, and Bacon for personal delinquencies, not for obeying the King's commands or giving him evil counsel. In 1624 the House of Lords compelled the Commons to maintain the same distinction when they impeached the Earl of Middlesex; but the anger of the Commons against Buckingham in 1626 caused them to impeach him, not for corruption alone, but for misleading the King by his counsels and by his obedience. Charles I at once interposed his authority between Buckingham and his accusers. He asserted that he had commanded Buckingham to act as he did; and he insisted that he followed his own judgment as well as the counsels of others. He sought to protect Buckingham by assuming responsibility for his actions. The House of Commons refused to permit him to do so, proclaiming that the King can do no wrong and that therefore his ministers must answer for all. The impeachment of Buckingham for misleading the King, far more than the impeachment of Bacon for taking bribes, proved the decisive event in the revival of the power of impeachment in Stuart England. Here was a direct confrontation between a King who assumed responsibility for his minister's conduct and a House of Commons who denied him that responsibility.

Buckingham's assassination ended the confrontation, but Strafford's dark counsels and suspect conduct renewed it in 1640. Once again the House of Commons insisted that no command of the King could excuse his ministers and that his ministers must answer to them for their treasonous counsels. But Strafford's trial revealed the limitations of the power of impeachment, for the Commons could not prove that his counsels had been treasonous. The law and the House of Lords prevented the Commons from transmuting a medieval legal instrument into a modern political weapon. They therefore destroyed Strafford, and Laud after him, by Acts of Attainder. But the more radical members of the Commons wept few tears over the failure of Strafford's and Laud's impeachments, for they saw that the power of impeachment, even though it could be used to drive a hated minister from the King's side, could never ensure that the King replaced him with a man in whom they could confide.

The Commons, under John Pym's guidance, therefore turned to the parliamentary nomination of the King's councillors. They incorporated this demand in the Nineteen Propositions which they presented to Charles in June 1642. But Charles had no more intention of surrendering the sceptre to Parliament than he had of giving up the government of bishops in the Church. He therefore refused the demand—at least until the autumn of 1648, when his desperate situation forced him to accept it, in the guise of the Isle of Wight conditions. But the hour was too late. Executive power had come to reside immediately in Parliament, and the army was momentarily content with this arrangement. But the Englishmen whom they ruled were not. Government by parliamentary committees proved unpopular, for if the executive resided in Parliament, who would check the abuse of executive power? *Quis custodit custodem?* By 1660 Englishmen had little use for either the parliamentary nomination of the King's councillors or government by parliamentary committees. Both destroyed that separation of powers which Englishmen now came to view as the bulwark of their liberty. Though the Presbyterians in 1660 sought to revive the Isle of Wight conditions, though the House of Commons in 1675 and 1678 talked of a parliamentary treasury, and though William III urged the Commons to name commissioners to supply the army in Ireland and allowed them to name commissioners to collect the wool tax, Parliament made no serious effort to secure the parliamentary nomination of the King's ministers or to place executive power in Parliament itself. The prejudice against such proposals, a prejudice nurtured on men's memories of the Interregnum, proved too powerful.

Though Englishmen rejected the parliamentary nomination of the King's ministers in 1660, they did not wish to go back to the royal absolutism which Strafford threatened or to the irresponsible government which Buckingham exercised. They therefore turned to a balance of government, in which the Privy Council should play a central role. Legislative power should reside in Parliament; executive power in the King. But in exercising the executive power the King should heed the advice of councillors in whom the nation could confide. As early as the year 1625 the House of Commons asked Charles to choose 'a wise, religious, and worthy Council', and to advise with it upon every important act of state, but Charles replied that he would employ 'one or many or nobody' in his government, as he wished. Not until the autumn of 1641 did Charles, at Edward Hyde's urging, agree to seek the advice of Privy Councillors in whom the nation could confide; and he deserted his undertaking within two months. At the Restoration Edward Hyde, now Earl of Clarendon, sought to persuade the martyred King's son, Charles II, to rely upon a Privy Council composed of men in whom the nation could confide. But this experiment likewise proved short-lived. The Privy Council which advised Charles II in the 1660's was not the efficient instrument which it had been during Elizabeth's reign; nor did Charles II often seek, much less heed, its advice. The impeachment of the Earl of Clarendon, the great apostle of concilar government, brought this unreal experiment to an end. Sir William Temple in 1679 might urge Charles II to govern by the advice of thirty grave and learned councillors, named by the King, yet representing the various ranks of Englishmen, but no one else, least of all the King or his opponents, put any faith in such a scheme.

Since Charles II had no more desire than his father to govern by the advice of 'a wise, religious, and worthy Council', Parliament during his reign resorted once again to voting impeachments against unpopular counsellors. By an impeachment they drove Clarendon into exile; by the threat of impeachments they disrupted the Cabal ministry; by another impeachment they drove the Earl of Danby from the King's side. Danby's impeachment in 1678 was fraught with greater constitutional significance than any other in Stuart history, except Buckingham's in 1626. The Commons impeached Danby because he acquiesced in Francophile policies of which he was known to disapprove. His only crime was obedience to the King in a lawful, though most unpopular, command, a command to seek a subsidy from Louis XIV in order that Charles might prorogue Parliament for three years. Charles II at once avowed his minister's actions by writing on Danby's incriminating letter to Montagu, 'I approve this letter. C.R.' He then further avowed Danby's conduct by granting him a pardon. The gage which Charles threw down the Commons picked up. They declared that the King's commands offered no justification for the performance of an ill act—that since the King can do no wrong his ministers must answer for everything. With equal vehemence they condemned the pardon, for were they to allow it the King could utterly destroy the power of impeachment, the only means they had for punishing errant ministers. The fury of their attack upon the pardon gave them the victory they sought: no minister after Danby dared to plead a pardon in bar to an impeachment and the Act of Settlement made it impossible for them to do so. But future ministers did plead the King's commands in answer to impeachments. Lord Somers did so in 1701 and the Earl of Oxford in 1715, but on both occasions the House of Commons denied the validity of the plea, maintaining that the King could do nothing unlawful, nothing unwise, nothing unsuccessful. For the illegality, folly, or ill success of the government's actions his ministers must answer. Impeachments were a violent instrument for enforcing responsible government and fell into desuetude after 1715, but not before their frequent employment had transformed the legal maxim that the King can do no wrong into the political principle that he could not assume responsibility for the unpopular and unsuccessful actions of his ministers. Insensibly the doctrine that the King could not be sued in his courts became the principle that he could not be censured in Parliament. Gradually the King's inability to protect his ministers in illegal acts became an inability to protect them in ill acts. The transformation of this legal doctrine into a political principle was the most profound of all the consequences that followed from the frequent voting of impeachments in Stuart England.

But impeachments themselves had no future. They ceased to be voted against unpopular (as distinct from criminal) ministers after 1715. The House of Lords bears the chief responsibility for bringing impeachments to an end. In 1667 they refused to imprison the Earl of Clarendon on a general charge of treason, unaccompanied by articles of impeachment charging him with a particular treason. In 1679 they insisted that Danby's counsel might plead the validity of his pardon and that the bishops in the House might vote on its validity. In 1701 they insisted that the House of Commons prosecute their impeachments within a reasonable time. In 1717 they demanded that the House of Commons proceed first to the treason charged against Oxford, then to the misdemeanours. The Lords would not allow the Commons, by voting impeachments which they did not intend to prosecute, to imprison ministers in the Tower or destroy their reputation with the people. Standing sentinels to the law, they prevented the Commons from turning a legal procedure for punishing criminals into a political instrument for censuring ministers.

The watchfulness of the Lords forced the Commons to seek other means to censure ministers of state. When in 1626 it seemed likely that the Lords would not find Buckingham guilty upon an impeachment, the Commons prepared an address, or remonstrance, to the King asking for the Duke's removal. Charles prevented the Commons from presenting the remonstrance by hastily proroguing Parliament, but two years later the Commons presented a second remonstrance, which not only asked for Buckingham's removal, but also censured Bishop Neile and William Laud. In the crisis of 1641 the Commons repeatedly requested the King to remove hated judges, bishops, and ministers, maintaining in the Grand Remonstrance that they often had just cause for demanding the removal of a minister, even though they could not impeach him for criminal conduct. The Civil War and the rule of the army did not cause parliamentary addresses to fall into that disrepute into which parliamentary nominations fell. Though the right to tell the King whom he must dismiss appears to differ little from the right to tell him whom he must appoint, the difference was crucial. As a member of the Convention Parliament observed in 1660, 'All the awe you have upon the King's Council hereafter is, if they be such as the people have an ill opinion of, you may remove them, and it is better for us than to name them, for [then] we must be responsible for them.'

The Commons wished, not to govern, but to criticize those who governed. During the reign of Charles II they displayed their delight in playing the critic by voting numerous addresses against the King's ministers, most notably against the ministers of the Cabal in 1674 and the opponents of Exclusion in 1680. But these addresses suffered from the defect that the King need not heed the advice contained in them. Lauderdale survived five addresses asking for his removal.

The obvious remedy was to refuse to vote the King supplies until he removed the minister against whom the address was voted. As early as August 1625 the Commons withheld supplies because they objected to the monopoly of the King's counsels which Buckingham enjoyed. In their remonstrance of 1626 the Commons made the removal of the Duke a condition for the voting of supplies. And in 1642 they declared that they could not settle a revenue on the King 'till he shall choose such counsellors and officers as may order and dispose it to the public good'. The Commons justified using the power of the purse to drive ministers from the King by appealing to the Lancastrian tradition that supplies shall not be voted until grievances have been redressed—and then by branding as the 'grievance of grievances' the ministers surrounding the King. But the justification satisfied few men in 1660. The Restoration Settlement, at least nominally, granted the King a revenue adequate to his ordinary needs. This revenue, though at times embarrassingly inadequate, allowed Charles II to ignore parliamentary addresses against his ministers. James II, given an even greater revenue, enjoyed an even greater immunity from parliamentary addresses. Not needing to meet Parliament, he could employ Jesuits in his councils. For this reason the authors of the Revolutionary Settlement deliberately voted William an inadequate revenue. They intended to make it impossible for him to protect his ministers by governing without Parliament. As a result William was unable to retain any minister against whom the House of Commons voted an address. Halifax in 1689, Nottingham in 1693, Sunderland in 1697, the ministers of the Junto from 1698 to 1701, all retired from office because Parliament either voted or threatened to vote addresses requesting their removal. During the reign of Queen Anne Parliament preferred to censure ministers by condemning the policies which they advocated, rather than by requesting their dismissal, but whatever the form a vote of no confidence took, no minister could long survive the hostility of the Commons.

The power of the purse removed one weakness of parliamentary addresses—how to force the King to heed them—but there remained a second, how to discover what councillors had given the King evil advice. The right of inquiry, a right which the necessity of prosecuting impeachments had placed in the House of Commons, might suffice to discover proof of a Treasurer's peculation or an Admiral's incompetence, but it could not discover who whispered evil advice to the King—and throughout these years the House of Commons desired to punish those who advised the King, not those who obeyed him. But those who advised the King did so in the secrecy of the Cabinet and the Closet. Therefore a cry arose that councillors should give their advice in full Council, even that they should put their hands to the advice they gave. Such a demand was part of the Nineteen Propositions presented to Charles I in 1642, but he would not admit of it. His son, however, promised Parliament in 1679 that he would lay aside 'any single ministry or private advices or foreign committees' and govern by the advice of his Privy Council. It proved an empty promise. In 1690 and 1692 Paul Foley and Goodwin Wharton again demanded that councillors acknowledge in writing the advice they gave the King; and their demand became a part of the Act of Settlement in 1701. But the proposal was impracticable, for cabinet secrecy was too important to the good government of the realm to be thus sacrificed. Nor would men serve the King under those conditions. In 1706 Parliament repealed the clause in the Act of Settlement which required the King to seek the Privy Council's advice and required Privy Councillors to put their hands to the advice they gave.

Parliament was willing to repeal the clause because it discovered a more informal means to focus responsibility on faulty ministers. It would no longer demand legal proof of a minister's delinquency, but would merely hold him guilty when common fame pointed an accusing finger at him. This could offend no principle of equity, for Parliament did not seek his life, liberty, or estate, only his dismissal. Furthermore it was notorious that those who presided over a department of state were responsible for its efficient management, that those who sat in the Cabinet counselled the King, and that he who enjoyed the King's favour most prevailed most in his counsels. In 1689 the Commons explicitly proclaimed that they would hold the departmental head responsible for the mistakes of his subordinates, for he recommended their employment, as Carmarthen did Shales's. The collective responsibility of the Cabinet the Commons were more reluctant to accept, for every impeached minister from Strafford to Somers had pleaded the concurrence of the whole council in the crimes charged against them. But in 1711 the Lords set the Commons an example by censuring the whole Cabinet for advising an offensive war in Spain; and in 1715 the Commons impeached Oxford for conspiring with other councillors to make the Treaty of Utrecht. The particular responsibility of the Prime Minister the Commons had asserted in every important impeachment voted in the seventeenth century, but they most explicitly proclaimed it in their impeachment of the Earl of Oxford. As Walpole cried out, 'It was notorious that the Earl of Oxford, as Prime Minister, was the chief adviser, promoter, and manager of the matters charged upon him in the Articles.' By 1715 the King's ministers knew that the Commons would hold all of them responsible for any advice upon which the King acted; and lest any minister complain that it was unjust to tax him for counsels which others gave, the Commons were ready with the rejoinder that he ought to resign if he could not concur in the counsels upon which the King acted.

By voting parliamentary addresses the Commons could drive ministers from the King, but to drive one minister after another from the King until he chose one in whom they could confide was a clumsy way to secure responsible government. It would be more sensible to tell the King in whom the House did confide. The problem was how to do this without incurring responsibility for the actions of the ministry then formed; the solution was to have the King choose his ministers, but to choose them from those who could carry on his business in Parliament. He should name his own servants, but they should have the confidence of Parliament. Sir Henry Neville in the summer of 1612 stumbled on this expedient for reconciling King and Parliament. Knowing 'the inwardest thoughts' of the principal gentlemen in the House of Commons, he undertook to win their support for the King if the King would give employment to Winwood, Southampton, and himself. The proposal came to nothing, for James would not have a Secretary of State imposed upon him. But James's opposition did not end the history of this 'pragmatical invention', as the Earl of Northampton called it. Bishop Williams in 1625, the Earl of Bedford and Lord Saye in 1641, Sir Richard Temple in 1663, the anti-Clarendonians in 1668, Shaftesbury and his allies in 1679, the Southampton Whigs in 1680, all sought to secure office by undertaking to manage Parliament successfully for the King. But these undertakings failed, for Charles I and Charles II regarded them merely as stratagems for winning men by the offer of place, and the undertakers could not, once they had put on the Court livery, retain the support of the independent country gentlemen in the Commons. The growth of political parties obviated both these difficulties and made possible the triumph of parliamentary undertaking. In the first place, party distinctions led men to refuse to serve in a Cabinet if their opponents also sat there, a practice which forced the monarch to choose between groups of men, rather than to play them off against each other. Secondly, party loyalties made it possible for the undertakers to retain support in the House of Commons even though they accepted preferment at Court. The Junto Whigs in 1693, with Sunderland as their broker at Court, first demonstrated that the road to power was the ability to manage Parliament successfully for the King— and to prevent any other party from doing so. But the Tories under Queen Anne showed that they too could play the game, that they also knew how to resign from Cabinets and to organize power in the Commons. By the accession of George I both parties had mastered the art of parliamentary undertaking, and it was this art which finally brought responsible government to England, not impeachments or Privy Council schemes or parliamentary addresses. If there is a hero to the story of the growth of responsible government in Stuart England, it is Sir Henry Neville, the obscure Berkshire gentleman who first saw that responsible government could best be attained by the King employing those who could undertake to manage Parliament for him.

To trace is to explain, but only to explain in part. Having traced the historical process by which any change occurred, having delineated the decisive events in that development, the historian must then examine each step in the process, each decisive event, in order to discover what motives drove men on each separate occasion to voice the demand they did. What motives led the Commons to ask

James for permission to arrest and sue his servants? What motives led the Commons to impeach Buckingham, attaint Strafford, demand the removal of Halifax, deny William an adequate revenue, and refuse Queen Anne the liberty to govern through mixed ministries? To these particular questions, particular answers must be sought, but where similar motives guided men through many decades, generalizations may be made. There are at least three that emerge from this study: that under James I and Charles I anger at incompetent, arbitrary, and unrepresentative government drove men to demand responsible government; that under William III and Queen Anne ambition for office and party passions led men to grasp at the sceptre; and that under Charles II both sets of motives operated, in nearly equal balance.

Though the House of Commons in the early seventeenth century contained many ambitious politicians, though Robert Carr in 1610 stirred up the Commons against Salisbury, and Buckingham in 1624 promoted Middlesex's impeachment, the true cause for the growth of responsible government in these years was the universal anger at James's incompetence, Buckingham's arrogance, Charles's indifference to his subjects' wishes, and Strafford's predilections towards royal absolutism. Indignation at the prodigality of James's administration, at the extortions of the monopolists whom he tolerated, and at his failure to enforce the penal laws against Catholics, drove the House of Commons to attack his ministers in 1610, 1614, and 1621. They were the readier to do this because they had no confidence in James's ability to end the waste, corruption, and oppressions that characterized his reign. The Commons's argument with Charles concerned less his fitness to govern than the fitness of the minister in whom he reposed his entire confidence. The follies perpetrated by Buckingham impelled the Commons to impeach him and demand his dismissal. The unanimity of the whole nation in censuring the Duke's arrogant, foolish conduct ought to have persuaded Charles to dismiss him, but the proud and stubborn Charles preferred to invite a challenge to his sole control of executive power than to surrender a favourite. The assassination of Buckingham did not end the challenge to the King's power, because Charles chose to use that power to promote Arminians, reprieve Papists, and collect tonnage and poundage, policies anathema to a majority in the House of Commons. The efficiency of the English government during the years of prerogative rule did nothing to diminish the Englishman's hatred for the policies pursued by the Court and his fear of the arbitrary counsels that prevailed there. By pursuing personal rather than national policies and by seeking to raise the prerogative above Parliament, Charles provoked the Commons to impeach his judges, his bishops, and his ministers. By countenancing army plots, by hearkening to the advice of Digbys and Murrays, and by attempting to arrest the five members, he persuaded men that no confidence whatever could be reposed in him. As a result the Commons demanded in the Nineteen Propositions that he surrender the sceptre wholly to Parliament.

To argue that James's incompetence and Charles's narrowness provoked the Commons to demand responsible government is not to argue that there were no men in Parliament who would not have sought it for other reasons. Coke needed no provocation to seek to make the executive accountable to the high court of Parliament. Eliot idealized the Commons of England and would have sought under the most virtuous of Kings to enhance their power. Pym, the political leader of the Puritans, sought to place executive power in the Commons in order to promote those financial, economic, diplomatic, and religious policies which he and his friends thought best for England. But these men, though numerous enough to lead, were not numerous enough to carry the House. They would have met defeat in their endeavours had not the arbitrary, incompetent, and unrepresentative government of the Stuarts driven a majority of the Commons and those who elected the Commons to support them. In time an ambitious gentry and a puritan clergy might have sought responsible government from the best of Kings, but in fact an enraged and fearful Commons demanded it from the worst of Kings.

The motives which led men to attack the King's ministers during the reign of Charles II were more complex. Two forces, for example, led to Clarendon's impeachment: the political ambitions of those who sought preferment at Court and the anger of the nation at the loss of the Dutch war. The lethargy displayed by Clarendon and the disgrace suffered at Chatham were undeniable, but it is unlikely that Clarendon would have suffered impeachment had not Buckingham and his friends desired to replace Clarendon and the Clarendonians at Court. The attack upon the Cabal arose largely out of the fury of the Commons at the Stop of the Exchequer, the Declaration

442

of Indulgence, and the alliance with France, but the party of Buckingham intrigued in Parliament against Arlington, and Arlington's party replied by attacking Buckingham. Courtiers knew well how to extend their intrigues against each other into Parliament, exploiting there the country gentlemen's fear of popery, arbitrary government, and the might of France. In 1678 that fear reached fever pitch, allowing Shaftesbury and Montagu to drive Danby from office by exploiting it. There was much cynicism in their conduct, but there was likewise much truth in the allegation that Charles II was prepared to tolerate Catholics, to govern by a standing army, and to countenance the growth of French power. By pursuing, or appearing to pursue, these policies, Charles II invited attack upon his ministers. He also invited such attacks by surrounding himself with ministers who were opposed to the exclusion of his Catholic brother from the throne. But at least some of the vehemence of the Shaftesbury Whigs against Halifax, Seymour, and the Hydes arose from their disappointment at being excluded from high office. In many ways the reign of Charles II was transitional, but perhaps in none more than in the motives that drove men to attack the King's ministers. In part these motives arose from a desire to defend English liberty, parliamentary government, and the Protestant religion; in part they reflected a desire for office and the emoluments of office.

Though Robert Harley in 1701 told the House of Commons that the axe would be put to English liberty if they did not impeach Lord Somers, it is hard to believe that either under William III or Queen Anne English liberty, parliamentary government, and the Protestant religion were ever seriously threatened. During these years the main force behind attacks upon the King's ministers was the ambition of unemployed politicians to replace them at Court. To win the support of the independent country gentlemen in the House they exploited their hatred for foreigners, dread of high taxes, anger at naval defeats, and suspicion of courtiers; but increasingly they relied upon the passions of party to win a majority in the House of Commons. By Queen Anne's reign the hatred of Whig for Tory and Tory for Whig replaced fear of foreigners or fear of popery. Desire for the power and wealth that high office conferred drove men to seek to gain it by making themselves indispensable to the monarch in the management of Parliament. And only by maintaining party unity in

Parliament could they prove to the monarch that they alone, and no one else, could manage it. No doubt many men gravitated into that party which advocated principles in Church and State congenial to them, but others, like James Brydges, adhered to the party which could best promote their careers. In 1715 the Whigs expressed shock at the Treaty of Utrecht, but their chief purpose in impeaching the authors of the Treaty was to remove them from public life, not to undo the alleged harm that the Treaty inflicted on England. No attempt was made to re-negotiate the Treaty; but every attempt was made to prevent its authors from attaining high office again.

The motives of men explain why they put forward the demands they do; but their motives do not explain why they are able to secure those demands. Circumstances must explain their success. In Stuart England one can discern at least four circumstances that explain why Parliament repeatedly won its demands from reluctant Stuart monarchs. These circumstances were the weight of numbers, the power of the purse, the existence of the Channel, and the superior attraction of party solidarity over royal patronage.

In the seventeenth century royalist historians were quick to charge that those who sought to rob the King of his right to choose his own ministers were a mere faction of self-seeking men. But the universal hatred of Buckingham, the unanimous votes against Strafford and Laud, the overwhelming opposition to the Cabal, and the general detestation of Danby suggest that no mere faction swayed the counsels of the House of Commons. The truth is the insensitivity of the first four Stuart Kings to the wishes of their subjects drove most men of property and rank to oppose them. Thus whenever these Kings appealed from Parliament to the electorate, as Charles did in 1628 and Charles II in 1679, the electorate returned men as opposed to the King's ministers as were those who sat in the previous Parliament. And when in 1642 Charles I appealed to arms, his enemies in the Commons found enough Englishmen ready to fight for their cause to defeat the King.

Only twice, in 1642 and 1688, was there an appeal to arms; more often the appeal was to majorities, both in Parliament and at the hustings. But only the insufficiency of the King's ordinary revenue, joined to the tradition that Parliament must consent to all extra-ordinary revenues, compelled the King to meet Parliament. The opponents of Buckingham, Strafford, Clarendon, and Danby all profited from the King's financial difficulties and from the tradition, held sacred by all Englishmen, that the King shall not tax their property without their consent. Sensing that the power of the purse was their most effective weapon, Englishmen in 1690 denied their sovereign an independent revenue equal to his needs. Thereafter no monarch could withstand the demands of Parliament, if Parliament chose to refuse supplies until granted its demands.

A country beset by foreign enemies can ill afford the paralysis of government that a refusal to supply the King occasions. As a royal spokesman asked in 1626, 'Shall we be talking of grievances until the enemy comes upon us?' To which the ready answer was, the navy and the Channel will defend us. Because Kent was not contiguous to Flanders, the Commons could talk of grievances and deny the King supplies, even in time of war. As Henry Powle observed in 1678, 'The King desires "that his revenue may be equal to other Princes". But our situation defends us and our navy secures us. Where enemies have no sea to pass, there must be garrisons upon the frontier, and armies that must be paid.' The Commons kept the navy in repair, but beyond that they were quite prepared to refuse the King money until he met their demands.

After 1689 the King could not hope to govern without Parliament; therefore he must seek to govern through Parliament. Sunderland saw this, as did Harley; but before either of them Danby had perceived it and Bacon glimpsed it. By appealing to the reverence owed to the Crown and by using the patronage at its disposal, the King should win for himself a party in Parliament. But William III and Queen Anne soon discovered that party loyalty took precedence over loyalty to the Crown and that the control of patronage must be shared with the party which governed in the Commons. As a result all efforts to build up a sizeable Court party in the two Houses of Parliament failed. At no time between 1689 and 1714 could William or Anne have supported a ministry by such a party. The parliamentary undertaker, who appealed to party loyalty and who promised that office could be won by opposing the King, proved stronger than the parliamentary manager, who appealed to the allegiance men owed the King and who promised that office could be won by supporting the King. Nothing weakened William more than Sunderland's failure to create a Court party for him; nothing circumscribed the power of Queen Anne more than Oxford's inability to persuade men to serve her irrespective of party. Under William and Anne party proved stronger than patronage.

Given an island secured by a navy, given a Crown dependent on parliamentary revenues, given a people impatient of injustice and unhappy at constraint, given a succession of Kings inept at governing and insensitive to the wishes of their subjects, and given a race of politicians eager to secure office by proving that they could govern in the Commons, no other result could be expected than a struggle for the sceptre that would issue in the eventual triumph of responsible government.

INDEX

Abbot, George, 66
Abbot, Wilbur C., 162 n.
Abernathy, George R., 158 n.
Abingdon, Montagu Bertie, second Earl of, 317
Account of the Conduct of Robert Earl of Oxford, An, 394
Accounts, parliamentary, examination of: proposed, 175; adopted, 175–6; consequences of, 182–3; in William's reign, 261, 261 n.; in Anne's reign, 331; rejected, 386
Act of Grace (1673), 186, 188, 202
Act of Settlement (1701), 326, 398, 429, 435, 438
Addison, Joseph, 343 n.
Addresses, parliamentary, for removal of the King's servants: at Restoration, 120–1; and common fame, 193–4; nature of, 194–5, 194 n.; Whig acceptance of, 241, 241 n., 244; and Revolutionary Settlement, 247, 247 n.; general addresses, 273; and Act of Settlement, 299, 303; Tory acceptance of, 319–20; in George I's reign, 415, 430, 436–7; for addresses against particular persons, *see* Commons, House of
Advice to the October Club (Swift), 370
Agreement of the People, The, 146–7, 150
Ailesbury, Robert Bruce, first Earl of, 233
Aislabie, John, 391
'Alarum, The', 185
Albemarle, first Duke of, *see* Monck, George
Alford, Edward, 51
Almanza, Battle of, 343, 358, 363
Althorp, meeting at, 272–5
Anarchy of a Limited or Mixed Monarchy, The, 150 n.
Andover, Charles, Lord, *see* Berkshire, second Earl of
Anglesey, Arthur Annesley, first Earl of, 173, 181–2, 238 n.
Anglesey, Arthur Annesley, fifth Earl of, 351
Anglia Libera, 327–8
Anjou, Philip, Duke of (afterwards Philip V of Spain), 306, 321, 325, 388

Anne, Queen: for government by mixed hands, 329, 334, 396–7; refuses to employ Wharton, 330 n.; dismisses Bishop of Worcester, 331; dismisses Rochester, 332–3; resists Junto, 335, 340, 341, 342; capitulates, 344; and Tory ministry, 346–8, 350–2, 364, 365–6, 370, 376; real weakness of, 445–6; mention of, 412–13, 437, 443
Annesley, John, 344 n.
Ansel, Patricia, 334 n.
Anson, Sir William, 264
Answer to the Character and Conduct of Robert Walpole, An, 422–3
Anti-Clarendonians, the; impeach Clarendon, 158–62, 165–6; as undertakers, 168–9, 440; attack Clarendonians, 173, 175, 179–83.
Apsley, Sir Allen, 23 n.
Argyle, Archibald Campbell, seventh Earl of, 108
Argyle, John Campbell, second Duke of, 360, 474
Arlington, Henry Bennet, first Earl of: and Clarendon, 155–7, 161; opposes Orrery, 181; unpopularity of, 185; compliance with Parliament, 187; impeachment introduced against, 191, 194 n.; his defence, 191–3; mention of, 170, 176–7, 186, 188, 199, 201, 267, 310, 398, 403, 443
Army Plot of 1641, 97 n., 222
Arnold, Michael, 283
Arrest of Five Members, 107, 110, 111
Art of Government by Partys, The (Toland), 321
Arundel, Thomas Howard, 21st Earl of, 64, 66
Arundel, Thomas, Archbishop of Canterbury, 8 n.
Ashburnham, John, 96
Ashley, Lord, *see* Shaftesbury, first Earl of
Ashton, Ralph, 125
Asiento contract, 375–6
Atkyns, Sir Thomas, 274 n.
Attainder, Act of: origins of, 8–9; against Proctor, 13, 13 n., 14; against Strafford, 92–8, 433; against Laud, 130–1; discredited, 133; against Danby, 219;

447

Attainder (*cont.*)
against Duncomb, 289; threatened against Portland, Somers, Halifax, and Orford, 325; against Bolingbroke and Ormond, 392; motion for against Oxford, 392
Atterbury, Francis, Bishop of Rochester, 351, 369, 391, 393, 393 n.
Aumont, Duc d', 414
Austen, Colonel, 247

Baber, John (Recorder of Wells), 67–8
Bacon, Sir Francis: as parliamentary manager, 18–20, 445; impeachment of, 23, 26–9; guilt of, 26, 29, 30, 34; pardon of, 35; compared to Middlesex, 36; mention of, 60, 79, 155, 272
Bagshaw, Edward, 82 n., 132
Baker, Thomas, 170 n.
Baillie, Dr Robert, 103
Ballad, The (answering Defoe's *Legion's Memorial*), 320
Bampfield, Thomas, 147 n., 153 n.
Banbury, Battle of, 141
Bank of England, 281, 287, 349
Barillon, Paul, 212 n., 214, 222, 404
Barker, William, 180
Baron, Hartgill, 143
Barrier Treaty, 367, 380
Bassano, Paul, 27
Bastwick, John, 128
Bate, Charles, 157 n.
Bate, George, 132
Bathurst, Allen, first Baron, afterwards first Earl of, 381
Baxter, Richard, 105 n., 158
Bayley, Lewis, Bishop of Bangor, 65
Baynes, Captain, 152
Beachy Head, Battle of, 262
Bealknap, Sir Robert, 8 n.
Beauchamp, Sir John, 8 n.
Beaufort, Henry Somerset, second Duke of, 360
Bedford, Francis Russell, fourth Earl of: his undertaking, 100, 102–5; mention of, 146, 272, 440
Behrens, B., 222 n.
Bellomont, Richard Coote, first Earl of, 273 n.
Bennet, Sir Henry, *see* Arlington, first Earl of
Bennet, Sir John, 23, 23 n. 31–2
Bennet, Thomas, 212, 213
Berkeley, Sir Maurice, 19
Berkeley, Sir Robert, 100 n., 101, 101 n.

Berkshire, Charles Howard, Viscount Andover and second Earl of, 160
Berners, Sir James, 8 n.
Bernsdorff, Andreas Gottlieb, Baron von, 384, 421
Bill of Rights, 252–3
Birch, Colonel John, 144, 204, 256
Bishop, William, 357 n., 368–9, 385
Blackstone, Sir William, 150, 318
Blake, John, 8 n.
Blancard, M., 274
Blenheim, Battle of, 333
Blundell, Sir Francis, 23 n.
Bohun, Edmund, 240 n., 274
Bolingbroke, Henry St John, Viscount: on Mackworth, 317; moves 'that Commons had not right done them', 325; on party government, 329; resigns, 341–2, 346; given office, 352; for proscribing Whigs, 369–70, 371, 371 n.; failure of, 375–6; refusal to serve with Whigs, 382; impeachment of, 379, 383–7; flight, 388–9; attainder of, 392–3; charges against and defence, 393, 395, 398–9, 400; mention of, 337 n., 350 n., 380, 390, 402, 415, 415 n.
Bolton, Sir Charles Paulet, second Duke of, 289 n.
Bonnet, Friedrich, Prussian resident, 259 n., 262 n., 290 n., 303, 304, 307 n., 308 n., 313, 315, 317 n., 323, 425
Book of Sports, 127, 128
Bordeaux, Antoine de, 136
Boscawen, Hugh, 212
Boteler, Major-General, 133 n.
Bothmer, Casper, Baron von, 381, 398, 421
Bouchain, capture of, 203
Boyer, Abel, 354, 361 n.
Boyle, Henry, 342, 351, 352
Bracton, Henry de, 61
Brandon, Lord, *see* Macclesfield, Charles Gerard, second Earl of
Bray, Dr William, 126
Bridges, Giles, 23 n.
Bridgewater, John Egerton, first Earl of, 66
Bridgewater, John Egerton, third Earl of, 173, 296
Bridgeman, Sir Orlando, 78, 133, 186
Bristol, George Digby, second Earl of: on Triennial Act, 97–8; as an undertaker, 160, 174; as a secret counsellor, 104, 107, 112, 115 n.; impeachment of, 113 n., 116; mention of, 78, 82 n., 83

Bristol, John Digby, first Earl of: quarrel with Buckingham, 57, 64, 66, 82; as counsellor to Charles I, 94, 103, 103 n., 104; removal desired, 107

Bristol, John Harvey, first Earl of, 418

Bristol, Dr John Robinson, Bishop of, 384, 389, 391

Britain, Sir Henry, 23 n.

Britons Strike Home, 408, 408 n.

Broderick, Alan, 135

Bromley, William: on party unity, 298, 317; refuses office, 382–3; mention of, 339, 344 n., 356, 369, 408 n.

Brooke, Christopher, 19

Brooke House Commission, 182

Brouncker, Henry, 177–8

Brown, John, 125 n.

Browning, Andrew, 196 n., 200, 213 n., 246 n.

Bruges, occupation of, 387, 391, 396

Brydges, James, afterwards first Duke of Chandos: on Harley's dismissal, 341; on Queen Anne and the Junto, 342 n., 343, 347; on 1710 crisis, 351 n., 354, 356 n.; replaced as Paymaster, 369; on patronage and party, 277 n., 364, 377, 385 n.; on Oxford's trial, 416; mention of, 382 n., 444

Buckingham, George Villiers, first Duke of: and 1621 Parliament, 23, 28, 29–31; attacks Middlesex, 36–7, 441; promotes Subsidy Bill, 40; as court favourite, 35, 41, 42–3, 66; faults of, 53, 56–8, 76; attack upon (1625), 44–9; impeachment of (1626), 59–64; remonstrance against (1628), 68–70, 436; assassination of, 71; mention of, 75, 79, 82, 127, 170, 172, 194, 233, 409, 432–3, 435, 437, 445

Buckingham, George Villiers, second Duke of: promotes Clarendon's impeachment, 159–63, 169, 442; as an undertaker, 160 n., 173–5; attacks Ormond and Carteret, 180–3; unpopularity of, 184, 185, 187; address for removal of, 188, 190–2, 194; mention of, 170, 177, 185, 272, 310, 315–16, 370, 422, 443

Buckingham and Normanby, John Sheffield, first Duke of, 272, 334, 335, 352

Burgess, Richard, 67

Burgh, Sir William, 8 n.

Burghley, William Cecil, first Baron of, vii, 352, 430

Burlamachi, Philip, 69

Burley, Sir Simon, 8 n.

Burnet, Gilbert, 144, 202, 270, 273, 326, 338

Burnet, Thomas, 384–5, 396 n., 411 n.

Burton, Philip, 251, 255 n.

Byng, Sir George, 426

Byrdall, John, 373

Byron, Sir John, 111

Cabal, the: discontent with, 184–6, 197; parties within, 187; attack upon, 196, 200, 434, 437, 442, 444; as a ministry, 361

Cabinet, the: hostility to, 231, 262, 264; acceptance of, 263–4, 285, 338; meaning of, 359–60; responsibility of, 84, 360–1, 363 n., 398–9, 429, 431, 438–9

Cambray, capture of, 203

Candidates Try'd, The, 321

Cape Breton, cession of, 388

Capell, Sir Henry, first Baron, 212, 226 n., 229, 234, 234 n., 237, 275 n.

Carberry, John Vaughan, third Earl of, 160, 167, 167 n., 268 n., 390

Carleton, Sir Dudley, 16

Carlingford, Theobald Taaffe, first Earl of, 165 n.

Carlisle, Charles Howard, first Earl of, 172, 229

Carlisle, Charles Howard, third Earl of, 324

Carlisle, John Hay, first Earl of, 47 n.

Carlyle, E. I., 138, 164 n.

Carmarthen, first Marquis of, *see* Danby, Thomas Osborne, first Earl of

Carr, Robert, *see* Somerset, first Earl of

Carr, Sir Robert (M.P.), 181

Carrickfergus, 111, 116 n., 117 n.

Carteret, Sir George, 173, 180, 182–4

Cary, Sir John, 8 n.

Cassel, defeat at, 203, 204

Castlemaine, Barbara Palmer, Countess of, 156 n., 164

Catalans, the, 371, 388

Cavaliers, the: at Restoration, 143; and Clarendon, 158–9, 162, 165, 167; support Ormond, 181; acquit Carteret, 183; oppose Lauderdale, 190; support Danby, 200

Cavendish, Lord, *see* Devonshire, William Cavendish, first Duke of

Cecil, Robert, *see* Salisbury, first Earl of

Cecil, William, *see* Burghley, first Baron

Censures, votes of, *see* Commons, House of

Chamberlain, John, 364

Chamber of the City of London, 224, 227
Channel, importance of, 62–3, 209, 445
Charles I: as Prince, 28, 36 n., 37–8;
reliance on and support of Buckingham, 43, 45, 50, 54–64, 66, 69–71,
432; defends Montagu, 51; protects
Sawyer, 68; and Petition of Right, 66,
68; answer to 1628 remonstrance, 71;
and 1629 Parliament, 72–4; unpopular
policies of, 80–1, 441–2; and Strafford,
83–4, 96–8; accepts Triennial Act, 98;
refuses to be a constitutional monarch,
100; and undertaking, 102–4, 134,
440; rejects conciliar government,
106–7, 434; refuses the parliamentary
nomination of ministers, 108–17,
433, 438; and peace negotiations,
141–2; trial and death of, 131–2;
mention of, 155, 221–2, 245, 255, 425,
444
Charles II: at Restoration, 120, 142–3,
437; and Clarendon's impeachment,
155–7, 160, 163–5, 169, 171–2, 188;
and the anti-Clarendonians, 174–5;
permits examination of accounts,
177–8; dismisses Ormond, 180; allows
Court intrigues, 181; protects Carteret, 182–3, 186; and the Cabal, 188,
188 n., 192, 195–6; attachment to
France, 198–9, 204, 208; failure to
win supplies, 201, 204–5, 208–9;
preserves the prerogative, 211–12;
and Danby's impeachment, 215–16,
435; avoids civil war, 221–2, 222 n.,
242; dismisses Williamson, 225; acts
without ministers, 225, 240; and
parliamentary nomination, 227; and
Privy Council, 139, 228–33, 233 n.,
234, 434, 438; and parliamentary
undertaking, 229–30, 237, 440; dismisses Shaftesbury, 234; on Jeffreys,
235; retains Halifax, 235; protects
Lauderdale, 195, 202, 210–11, 228,
437; refuses Exclusion, 238–9; mention
of, 134, 154, 248–9, 250–1, 443–4
Charlett, Dr Arthur, 258 n., 296, 368
Chatham, disgrace at, 163, 176, 442
Chesterfield, Philip Stanhope, second Earl
of, 212 n.
Chesterfield, Philip Stanhope, third Earl of,
391 n.
Chevreux, Duke of, 50
Chiffinch, William, 245
Choke (Serjeant-at-law), 5
Cholmondeley, Hugh, first Earl of, 342
Churchill, Admiral George, 343

Churchill, John (Deputy Registrar in
Chancery), 23 n.
Churchill, John, *see* Marlborough, first
Duke of
Churchill, Sir Winston, 346
Claims of the People of England Essayed, The,
326
Clarendon, Edward Hyde, first Earl of:
(as Edward Hyde) on inconstancy of
Commons, 46; for impeaching Strafford, 78; on constructive treason, 95;
on undertakings, 104; favours government by Privy Council, 100, 106–8,
434; opposes parliamentary nomination, 109–10, 113; author of *A Full
Answer*, 132–3, 133 n.; and Restoration, 135–9, 143, 154; mention of, 96,
115; (as Earl of Clarendon) dismissal,
156, enemies of, 157–60; impeachment of, 155, 161–8, 172–3, 442;
flight of, 169; defence, 172–3; address
of thanks for removal of, 188–9; as a
Prime Minister, 401–2; mention of,
21, 175, 188, 197, 198 n., 199, 212,
233, 236, 236 n., 267–9, 310, 362–3,
390–2, 398, 403, 410, 425, 436
Clarendon, Henry Hyde, second Earl of,
173, 238
Clarendonians, the, 162, 172–3, 181, 183,
188, 442
Clarges, Dr Thomas, 135
Clarges, Sir Thomas, 225, 256 n., 262, 273
Clark, George, 339
Clarke, Edward, 283
Clements, Mr (Secretary to the Earl of
Peterborough), 353 n.
Clifford, Sir Thomas, first Baron: favours
Declaration of Indulgence, 185; attacked, 184–5; resigns, 186; as a
parliamentary manager, 20, 187,
198 n.; mention of, 197, 272
Coke, Sir Edward: on the King's inability
to do wrong, 5, 7, 35, 50, 70; on
precedents for removing ministers,
9 n., 47; for condemning Mompesson,
25; against commission to try Bacon,
28; pleads concurrence of others, 34;
on sovereignty of legislature, 34;
248 n.; opposes Buckingham, 45–6,
48, 69–70; on foreign ambassadors,
50–1; motives of, 24, 443; mention of,
82, 98–9, 122, 138
Coke, Sir John, 88 n.
Coke, Sir Robert, 39
Coleman, Edward, 215
Colepeper, Sir John, 106, 110, 113

Collective Responsibility
  of Cabinet: asserted, 263–4; pleaded by Portland, 310; defined, 360–1; accepted, 398–9, 429, 431
  of Council: pleaded by Yelverton and Coke, 34; by Williams, 39; by Buckingham, 57–8; by Strafford, 84–5, 91; by Laud, 124–5; by Clarendon, 172–3; by Arlington, 193; by Nottingham, 267
  of ministry: asserted, 257; defined, 362–4; accepted, 372
  of Regency, 263
Colt, John, 261 n., 283
Commission to Take the Public Accounts, 331, 357, 366; *see also* Accounts, parliamentary examination of
Commissioners of Supplies for Ireland, 255–6, 285, 433
Commissioners of the Victualling Office, 358
Commissioners for Wool, 256 n., 285, 433
Committee of Both Houses: to prepare Strafford's impeachment, 83; for Removing Evil Counsellors, 110–11
Committee of Both Kingdoms, 120, 145
Committee of Safety, 118, 120
Committee of Secrecy, 386, 395, 398, 415, 417, 429; Report of, 387–92, 398
Committees, parliamentary, government by: as an alternative, 100; emergence of, 118–19; discredited, 145–51; at Restoration, 120–1
Common Fame: precedents for, 7; invoked against Proctor, 12; asserted by Turner, 56, reliance on in 1620s, 69, 74–5; invoked against Strafford and Laud, 79, 79 n.; under Charles II, 193, 199–200, 240, 241; and Revolutionary Settlement, 257; defended by Mackworth, 319; sufficiency of, 360; and Oxford, 389–90; under George I, 429, 438
Commons, House of
  addresses introduced into, but not voted, for the removal of: Carteret, 189; Arlington, 191–3; Halifax and Carmarthen, 254
  addresses of thanks: for the removal of Clarendon, 188–9, 189 n.; for the employment of Marlborough, 344, 344 n.
  addresses by recommending the employment of: Salisbury and Pembroke, 108; Conyers, 111; 'men of known ability, integrity, and Protestant vigour', 237; men of experience in the Admiralty, 266–8; men 'of known integrity and ability' and opposed to James II, 266–8; English officers in place of Dutch, 308
  addresses requesting: that Parliament might arrest the King's servants, 1; that the Tower and forts be placed in the hands of those in whom Parliament can confide, 111–12; that Carteret not be employed, 182; that the Attorney General prosecute Halifax, Papillon, Parkhurst, Paschall, and Ranelagh, 331–2; resumption of lands granted Portland, 308–9
  addresses voted by, for the removal of: Harvey, 39; Wren, Laud, and impeached judges, 101; Talbot, 189; second Duke of Buckingham, 190–1; Lauderdale, 188–90, 201–2, 210–11, 228; those who advised King's answer, 207; Halifax, 235, 238; Clarendon, Worcester, Feversham, and Hyde, 238; Burnet, 293 n.; Goor and Meesters, 308, Portland, Somers, Halifax, and Orford, 312–14; Stamford, 316; Bishop of Worcester, 331
  censure voted by, against: Richmond, 116; those who misled the King (1642), 116 n.; private counsellors (1678), 232; those who advised the dissolution of the last Parliament (1680), 239; opponents of Exclusion, 238–9; 'those who have the direction of affairs' (1689), 257–8, 257 n.; those responsible for the want of timely orders, 266–7; those who advised veto of Place Bill, 273, 301; those guilty of 'treacherous mismanagement' (1693), 274; Trevor, 277; Admiralty, 292; those who advised the King's answer (1700), 301; those who assented to Partition before seeking Parliament's advice, 301; Orford, 332, Commissioners of the Victualling Office, 358; those who possessed the management of the revenues, 358; those who admitted the Palatines, 358; Marlborough, 366–7; Townshend, 367; censure, introduced into but not voted against, Somers, 293–4; Godolphin, 344
  impeachments introduced into, but not voted against: Ormond and Orrery, 181; Arlington, 191, 194 n.; Danby

Commons, House of (*cont.*)
(in 1675), 199–200; Coningsby and
Porter, 273 n.; ministers who passed
illegal grants, 293
impeachments voted by, against: Bacon,
23, 23 n., 26–9; Mompesson, 23–5;
Michell, 23 n., 31–2; Bennet, 23 n.,
31–2; Field, 23 n., 32; Harris, 32;
Bishop of Norwich, 39; Buckingham,
59–64; Montagu, 65; Mohun, 67;
Burgess, 67; Manwaring, 68; Strafford, 77–9, 78 n., 82–3; Laud, 77–9,
78 n.; Finch, 77–9; Windebank, 77–9,
78 n.; Radcliffe, 83; Ship,Money judges, 100; bishops who passed Canons,
100; bishops who questioned the authority of Parliament, 133 n.; Herbert,
115, 115 n.; Digby, 116; eight Army
Plotters, 133 n.; Inigo Jones, 133 n.;
nine lords and twenty-two commoners
opposing Parliament, 133 n.; Gardner, 133 n.; Henrietta Maria, 133 n.;
Ormond, 133 n.; Lord Mayor and
five Aldermen, 133 n.; Maynard and
seven peers, 133 n.; Howard, 133 n.;
Boteler, 133 n.; Clarendon, 155–73;
Penn, 177–8; Pett, 177–8; Brouncker,
177–8; Danby, 212–24; North, 236;
Scroggs, 236; Jones, 236; Weston,
236; Seymour, 236; Peterborough,
251 n.; Salisbury, 251 n.; Leeds
(Danby), 277–8; Portland, 308–15;
Somers, 308–15; Halifax, 308–15;
Orford, 308–15; Oxford, 379–94;
Bolingbroke, 379–94; Ormond, 379–
94; Strafford, 379–94
remonstrances voted by: asserting the
right to question persons grievous to
the Commonwealth, 58, 62; demanding Buckingham's removal, 63–4;
censuring Buckingham, Laud, and
Neile, 69–70; condemning those who
introduce innovations in religion or
advise the taking of tonnage and
poundage, 74; the Grand, 102
votes by arresting or imprisoning,
Proctor, 1, 13; Michell, Mompesson,
Fowle, Dike, Geldard, Churchill,
Bennet, 23 n.; Montagu, 51; Williamson, 224–5; Pepys and Deane, 224–6;
Walpole, 366–7; Thomas Harley and
Matthew Prior, 415 n.
votes by expelling or suspending from
the House: Floyd, Mompesson, Bennet, and Bridges, 23 n.; Brouncker,
178; Carteret, 182; Ranelagh, 331;
Ridge, 357–8; Walpole, 366–7; Car-
donnel, 367
votes of confidence in: Russell, 267–8;
Delaval, Killigrew, and Shovell, 274;
Montagu, 290; Nottingham, 333
Conciliar government, *see* Privy Council,
reliance upon
Condé, capture of, 203
Coningsby, Thomas, later first Earl of,
273 n., 390, 392, 415
Conventicle Act, 157
Convention Parliament (of 1660), 143–4,
153, 436
Convention Parliament (of 1689), 245, 248,
249
Conway, Edward, first Viscount, 50
Conway, Edward, second Viscount, 94, 127
Conway, Edward, third Viscount, 161 n.,
163 n., 169 n., 175 n.
Conyers, Sir John, 111
Cooper, Anthony Ashley, *see* Shaftesbury,
first Earl of
Corbett, Dr Richard, 127
Cork, Richard Boyle, first Earl of, 78
Cornelius, Gilbert, 179
Corriton, William, 72, 74
Cortes, the, 49
Cosin, Dr John, 72, 133 n.
Cottington, Francis, first Baron, 92, 103
Cotton, Sir Robert, 47, 293
Council of War (of 1624), 10, 39–40, 48–9,
55
Court of High Commission, 65, 130
Coventry, Henry, 143, 143 n., 164 n.,
181 n., 189 n., 194, 194 n., 227
Coventry, Sir John, 179, 188
Coventry, Thomas, 126
Coventry, Sir William, 155–7, 161, 177,
179–80, 181, 186, 186 n., 188, 199,
204, 209
Cowper, William, first Baron and Earl of:
named Lord Keeper, 335; remains in
office, 348–51; resigns, 352; mention
of, 332, 359, 362, 381–2, 384
Craddock, Dr John, 32, 39
Craggs, James, 426
Cranfield, Sir Lionel, *see* Middlesex, first
Earl of
Crew, Sir Thomas, 19, 21
Crisly, Walsingham, 57
Crofts, Sir William, 68
Croissy, Colbert de, 170 n.
Cromwell, Oliver, 146, 147–8
Cromwell, Thomas, fourth Baron, 52
Crosby, Sir Pierce, 84 n., 85, 86
Crowther, Dr, 172

Dalmahoy, Thomas, 202, 210–11.

Danby, Henry Danvers, first Earl of, 127.

Danby, Thomas Osborne, first Earl of (afterwards Marquis of Carmarthen and Duke of Leeds): opposes Clarendon, 159–60, 168 n., 170; becomes Treasurer of the Navy, 169, 173; strategy as Lord Treasurer, 197–8, 199 n., 205–6; failure of, 204, 207–8; impeachment of, 211–14; dismissal, 211–12, 214, 216; defence of, 215, 218; pardon, 217–18; significance of impeachment of, 223–4, 243; want of confidence in as Treasurer, 227–8; opposition to in William's reign, 251–4, 257–8, 260–1, 264, 264 n., 270, 272, 275; impeached as Duke of Leeds, 277–8; resignation, 296; mention of, 20, 187–8, 259, 289, 294, 316, 356, 361, 363, 401–3, 410, 434–6, 439, 444–5

Dangers of Europe, The, 320, 321

Darcy, Lady, 39

Dartmouth, William Legge, first Earl of, 353, 369

Davenant, Sir Charles, 293, 305–6, 319, 321, 324, 326

Davies, Godfrey, 144

Davys, Sir John, 236

Deane, Sir Anthony, 224–6

Declaration of Causes and Remedies, 112

Declaration of Rights, 245–6

Declaration of Indulgence (of 1662), 158 n.; (of 1672), 184–5, 187, 190–3, 202, 442–3

Declaration of the Lords and Commons of 19 May 1642, 112, 115

Defection Considered, The (Tindal), 423

Defection Detected, The, 424, 424 n.

Defoe, Daniel, 316, 320, 353 n., 355, 368, 402, 409, 411–14, 423

Delamer, Henry Booth, second Baron (later Earl of Warrington), 260, 265

Delaval, Admiral Sir Ralph, 274

Denbigh, Basil Fielding, second Earl of, 189 n.

Denwit, Thomas, 85

Departmental Responsibility: asserted by Eliot and Selden, 57–8, by Coke, 69; during the 1620s, 75; in Strafford's trial, 87–9, 88 n.; in Laud's trial, 126–7; by Clarendon, 172; in Shales's case, 255–6, 255 n., 257; in Oxford's trial, 399, 400, 401 n.; acceptance of, 429, 431, 438–9

Derby, James Stanley, tenth Earl of, 418

De Ruyter, Admiral, 203

Despensers, doctrine of, 122, 133 n., 373–4

Devonshire, William Cavendish, first Duke of, 185, 212, 230, 234, 240

Devonshire, William Cavendish, second Duke of: on Partition, 307, threatens to resign, 330–1, 330 n.; enemy of Nottingham, 333; and 1710 crisis 342, 349, 351–2; and definition of Cabinet, 260, 362

Devonshire, William Cavendish, third Duke of, 418, 422

D'Ewes, Sir Simonds, 80, 93, 97 n., 101 n., 109 n., 117

De Witt, Jan, 167, 167 n.

Dialogue Between a Counsellor and a Justice o, the Peace, A (Raleigh), 61

Digby, George, *see* Bristol, second Earl of

Digby, John, *see* Bristol, first Earl of

Digges, Sir Dudley, 19, 59, 63, 122–3, 141, 146

Discourse by Way of Vindication of Myself, A (Clarendon), 172

Discourse of Grants and Resumptions, A (Davenant), 293

Discourse Concerning Treason, A (West), 410

Dixon, Robert, 23 n.

Doddington, John, 160 n., 163 n.

Dolben, Sir Gilbert, 339 n.

Dorset, Sir Edward Sackville, fourth Earl of, 24–5, 66, 127

Dorset, Lionel Cranfield (Sackville), seventh Earl and first Duke of, 418

Dover, Treaty of, 184, 192 n.

Downing, George, 227

Drake, Sir Francis, 208–9

Drake, Dr James, 320, 335

Drummond, John, 349

Dryden, John, 159, 240 n., 241–2

Dudley, Edmund, 9, 9 n., 15

Duke of Anjou's Succession Further Considered, The, 321

Du Moulin, Peter, 185

Duncomb, Sir Charles, 289, 289 n.

Duncomb, Sir John, 212

Dunton, John, 385 n.

Dutch War
second, loss of, 156–7, 163, 166, 173, 175, 442
third, loss of, 184–5, 192–3

Dyke, Sir Thomas, 287

Dykveld, Everard van Weede, 274, 306

Edgecombe, Richard, 422

Edgehill, Battle of, 141

Edward, I, 126

Edward, II, 8
Edward III, 3–4, 6–7
Edward IV, 5, 68
Eglisham, Dr George, 23 n.
Egmont, John Perceval, first Earl of, 382 n., 383, 387, 387 n., 391 n.
Eliot, Sir John: guides Commons, 55, 57–9, 61; imprisoned, 63; attacks Weston, 73–4; Wentworth's contempt for, 77; motives of, 442; mention of, 56, 69, 75, 80, 99, 155, 233, 254
Elizabeth, Queen: responsibilities of ministers under, vii, 2–3, 9, 14; mention of, 43, 130, 138, 280, 352, 356, 356 n.
Ellesmere, Sir Thomas Egerton, first Baron, 21, 27
Ellis, John, 305
Elton, G. R., 9
Empson, Sir Richard, 9, 9 n., 15
Englishman, The, 373
Erskine, Sir Thomas, 95
Essex, Arthur Capel, first Earl of, 227, 229, 233, 234
Essex, Robert Devereux, second Earl of, 3
Essex, Robert Devereux, third Earl of, 96–7, 103, 103 n., 104, 145, 161
Estates General, 49
Evelyn, John, 168, 176, 340
Examination of the Earl of Danby's Case, An (Howard), 223
Examiner, The, 354, 358, 377, 405, 406 n.
Exclusion Bills, 227, 234–8, 242, 294
Explanatory Articles (of Treaty of Commerce with Spain), 372–3, 375

Fairfax, Thomas, third Baron, 142
Falkland, Lucius Cary, second Viscount, 78, 80, 106, 110, 113
Faults on Both Sides, 353–5
Felton, John, 71
Felton, Thomas, 11–13
Fenwick, Sir John, 281
Ferguson, Robert, 355 n.
Ferne, Dr Henry, 122
Ferrar, John, 23 n.
Ferrers, Robert Shirley, first Earl of, 359
Fevershan, Sir George Sondes, first Earl of, 238
Field, Dr Theophilus, Bishop of Llandaff, 23 n., 32
Fiennes, Nathaniel, 95
Finch, Daniel, *see* Nottingham, second Earl of
Finch, Sir Heneage, *see* Nottingham, first Earl of

Finch, John, first Baron, 77–9, 78 n., 80, 100–1, 101 n., 133 n., 155
Fitzharris case, 251
Flanders, French conquest of, 203, 214
Fleetwood, Sir Miles, 36
Floyd, Sir Robert, 23 n., 34
Flying Post, The, 379
Foley, Paul: as leader of the Country party, 256, 260–1, 265, 273; demands written responsibility of councillors, 262–3; elected Speaker, 279; and Land Bank, 280–1, 281 n.; attacks Orford, 292; mention of, 300, 356
Foley, Thomas, 298 n., 422
Forrester, Sir Andrew, 211
Fortescue, Sir John, 6
Fowle, Mathias, 23 n.
Fox, Charles James, 20
Fox, Sir Stephen, 332
Fox's *Martyrology*, 126
Frankenthal, 43
Freeman, Ralph, 336–7
Fulthorp, Sir Robert, 8 n.

Galway, Henri de Massue de Ruvigny, first Earl of, 184 n., 309, 358, 359 n., 364
Gardiner, Sir Thomas, 113 n.
Garroway, William, 182, 183, 190, 200, 251
Gaultier, Abbé, 388, 415 n.
Geer, Captain, 54
Geldard, George, 23 n.
George I: as Duke of Cambridge, 375; offers office to Tories, 382–3; promotes impeachments, 384; and Ormond, 390; dismisses Townshend, 422; withdraws from Cabinet, 420, 425–7; responsibility of ministers under, vii, 428
George of Denmark, Prince Consort, 339, 344
Gerard, Sir Gilbert, 136, 142, 193, 213
Getruydenberg, negotiations at, 405 n.
Ghent, occupation of, 387, 391, 396
Gibraltar, 388
Gilligan, Emanuel Manasses, 390, 400
Ginkel, General, 249
Gloucester, William, Duke of (Queen Anne's son), 297
Glynn, John, 89, 116
Godolphin, Sidney, first Earl of: as minister of William III, 258, 258 n., 259, 275–7, 281–2, 282 n., 294; as a Tory ally, 296, 297–8, 317, 324; as Anne's Lord Treasurer, 330–3, 335, 335 n., 340–1, 341 n., 344–5; dismissal,

345–51; attack upon, 357–8; as Prime Minister, 402, 402 n.; mention of, 362, 365 n.

Goldsmith, Henry, 23 n.

Gondomar, Sarmiento de Acuna, Count of, 43

Good Parliament of 1376, the, 7

Goodwin, Sir Francis, 34

Goodwin, Robert, 109

Goor, Colonel John Wyant, 308

Gorges, Colonel, 151

Gough, J. W., 149

Grafton, Charles Fitzroy, second Duke of, 418

Graham, Richard, 251, 255 n.

Grand Alliance (of 1689), 307; (of 1702), 327

Granville, John, 287

Great Contract (of 1610), 14, 14 n., 16

Green-Cloth, officers of, 13

Grimstone, Sir Harbottle, 78, 82 n., 239

Grocers' Hall Committee, 105, 107, 110, 111, 113, 117

Grotius, Hugo, 80

Guiscard, Marquis de, 402

Guise, Sir John, 247, 251–2, 254, 256–7, 260–2

Guistianian, Giovanni, 84

Guy, Henry, 272, 277–9, 279 n., 286

Gwin, Francis, 281 n.

Gwynn, Sir Rowland, 270

Hakewill, William, 8, 15, 25, 32, 248 n.

Hale, Sir Matthew, 131, 144

Hales case, 251–2

Halifax, Charles Montagu, first Baron: as one of the Junto, 265, 271–3, 275, 277–9, 281 n., 282–3, 288; Tory attack upon, 289–92, 291 n.; resignation, 292, 296–7; and Kidd, 305; impeachment of, 308–15; attack upon, 331–2; defends Godolphin, 334; minister under Anne, 342, 348, 350, 350 n.; and Oxford, 384; mention of, 380

Halifax, George Savile, first Marquis of: on Charles II, 188 n.; for committal of Danby, 218 n.; as a Privy Councillor, 230, 233; attacks upon during Exclusion crisis, 235, 238–40, 238 n.; attacks upon under William, 251–4, 254, 258, 258 n., 260; mention of, 170, 217 n., 237, 273, 437, 443

Hallam, Henry, 425 n.

Hamilton, Sir Frederick, 88

Hamilton, James, third Marquis of (afterwards first Duke of), 92, 103

Hamilton, William Douglas, third Duke of, 190, 210

Hammond, Anthony, 324

Hampden, John, 78 n., 103–4

Hampden, Richard, 261, 418

Hanmer, Sir Thomas, 369–72, 382–3

Hanoverian Tories, 369, 382

Harbord, Sir Charles, 187–8

Harbord, William, 199, 199 n., 201, 225, 226 n., 237

Harcourt, Sir Simon, first Earl of, 309, 317, 341–2, 346, 370–2, 418–19

Hardy, Thomas, 95

Harley, Sir Edward, 254, 268, 271, 358, 402, 405

Harley, Robert, *see* Oxford, first Earl of

Harley, Thomas, 415

Harman, Sir John, 178

Harrington, James, 151, 154

Harris, Alexander, 23 n., 32

Harvey, Sir Simon, 38–9, 51

Haselrigge, Sir Arthur, 78, 152

Hastings, Sir Francis, 11

Hastings, Warren, 380 n.

Hatton, Christopher, first Baron, 137–8

Haversham, John Thompson, first Baron, 314, 324, 333–4

Hawles, Sir John, 251, 256

Heath, Sir Robert, 46, 49, 72–3, 103

Heathcote, Sir Gilbert, 344 n.

Hedges, Sir Charles, 297, 324, 340

Heenvliet, Baron de, 112 n.

Heinsius, Anthony (Grand Pensionary), 306

Henrietta Maria (Queen Consort of Charles I), 46, 50, 72, 102, 112, 116, 133

Henry IV: precedents from the reign of, 6, 62; references to his dismissing servants at Parliament's behest, 9, 62, 140, 189, 241

Henry IV of France, 356

Henry VI, 7, 49

Henry VII, 5

Henry VIII, 2, 9, 130, 138, 245, 356, 430

Herbert, Sir Edward (Attorney General), 115, 133 n.

Herbert, Sir Edward (Chief Justice), 251

Herbert, William, 212

Hertford, William Seymour, first Marquis of, 103–4, 136

Heylar, William, 258 n.

Heylyn, Peter, 46, 127

Heywood, Dr William, 126

Hibbots, Lady, 85

Hickeringill, Edmund, 373
Hill, Colonel Jack, 346, 400
Hill, Richard, 264 n.
History of the Last Parliament, The (Drake), 320
Hoffmann, Johann Philip (Imperial Resident), 218, 256, 274, 310, 323, 334–5, 346 n., 347, 348 n., 367, 383 n., 422
Holborn 'patriots', 30
Holland, Henry Rich, first Earl of, 84 n., 94
Holland, Sir John, 107, 143 n., 189, 192–3
Holles, Denzil, first Baron: on defeat at Isle of Rhé, 66; on subversion of religion and liberty, 80; to be Secretary of State, 103–4; and Nineteen Propositions, 113; on secret counsels, 116; undertaking of, 216–17; named to Privy Council, 230; mention of, 118, 136, 142, 176, 229, 412
Holles, John, afterwards first Earl of Clare, 19
Holt, Sir John, 8 n.
Hoskyns, John, 16, 21–2
Howard, Sir Edward, first Baron Howard of Escrick, 133 n.
Howard, Sir Robert (M.P. in 1621), 65
Howard, Sir Robert (M.P. in Cavalier Parliament): opposes Clarendon, 159, 167, 167 n.; Auditor of the Exchequer, 169; mention of, 170, 212, 223, 255 n.
Howe, Sir George, 190
Howe, Jack: attacks ministers, 251–2; for naming commissioners, 256; loses place, 270; impeaches Somers, 309; defeat of, 316, 324; Paymaster General, 332; mention of, 256, 287, 300, 306, 308
Humble Petition and Advice, 138
Humble Proposals (of 1692), 263
Hungerford, John, 407, 417
Huntingdon, Henry Hastings, fifth Earl of, 14 n.
Hunton, Philip, 121–3
Hussey, William, 6
Hutchinson, Archibald, 391
Hyde, Edward, *see* Clarendon, first Earl of
Hyde, Laurence, *see* Rochester, first Earl of
Hyde, Lawrence (M.P. in 1610), 13
Hyde, Sir Nicholas, 19, 72–3

Ilberville, Marquis d' (French Ambassador), 382, 414
Impeachment, power of: origins of, 7–8, 8 n.; revival of, 22–5, 32, 32 n., 41, 432–3; acceptance of, 75, 81, 113;

failure of, 100–2, 119; at the Restoration, 120–1, 133–4; in the reign of Charles II, 188, 226, 235, 243, 434–5; and Revolutionary Settlement, 245, 246–7, 247 n., 284; justified in Tory pamphlets, 316–19; in the reign of Anne, 366–7; in George I's reign, 380, 394–406, 430; end of, 407–14, 416–20, 435–6; for impeachments of particular persons *see* Commons, House of
Indemnity, Bill (of 1689), 250–2
Infanta Isabella, 43
Inojosa, Marquis d' (Spanish Ambassador), 43
Inquiry, Right of: asserted, 30, 32–3; exercised in 1620 Parliaments, 55–7, 69, 72–3, 75; in Strafford's impeachment, 81–4; under Charles II, 175–6, 191–2, 200, 239; under William III, 254, 257, 261–2, 274, 304, 307; under Anne, 331; vindications of, 383, 386, 415; limitations of, 438
Institutes of the Laws of England, The (Coke), 7, 82, 248 n.
Instructions of the Citizens of London, 385, 385 n.
Instrument of Government, 138, 146, 151
Irish Land Grants, Bill for Resumption of, 293–4
Islay, Archibald Campbell, first Earl of, 418
Isle of Rhé, 66, 69, 176
Isle of Wight conditions, 131, 136, 140, 142–4, 433

Jacobite lords (of the '15), impeachment of, 380 n., 416
Jacobites, 245, 265–6, 277 n., 302, 369, 386, 413–14
James I: refuses permission to arrest his servants, 1, 13–14, 17 n., 432; rejects Neville's undertaking, 18–19, 439–40; reflects on Salisbury, 21; dissolves Addled Parliament, 22; protects his servants, 23, 24–6, 28–9, 32; and Yelverton, 31; and Middlesex's impeachment, 35–8, 40; reliance on favourites, 42–3, 441–2; mention of, 34, 35, 409, 427
James II: (as Duke of York) supports Clarendon, 157, 161–2, 164, 171; advises Charles, 183; opposes Danby, 199; becomes a Catholic, 203; attempted Exclusion of, 234–8; mention of 175–6, 178, 205, 225; (as King) granted a sufficient revenue, 242,

437; personal government of, 245, 248; servants of, 250–1; on William's government, 274; mention of, 253, 268–9, 276, 283, 287, 348, 411
Jeffreys, Sir George, 235, 250–1
Jeffreys, John, 255 n.
Jekyll, Sir Joseph, 332, 390, 418
Jenkins, Sir Lionel, 236
Jermyn, Henry, 96
Jersey, Edward Villiers, first Earl of, 295, 297, 307–8, 308 n., 313, 314, 333, 414 n.
Johnstone, James, 260
Jones, Inigo, 133 n.
Jones, J. R., 198 n.
Jones, Sir Thomas, 170, 236
Jones, Sir William, 20, 237, 242 n., 326
Junto Ministry (of William's reign), 282, 287–8, 290–2, 295, 304–6, 325, 327, 437; (of Anne's reign), 343–7, 365 n., 376
Junto Whigs, 333–4, 337, 339, 341–4, 440
Just and Modest Vindication, A, 240–1, 240 n.
Justification of the Proceedings of the House of Commons, A (Harley), 319.
Juxon, William, Lord Treasurer, 92

Kearney, H. F., 94 n.
Kemp, Betty, 153
Kenyon, J. P., 272
Kidd, Captain William, 293, 304–5
Kildare, George FitzGerald, sixteenth Earl of, 85
Killigrew, Admiral Henry, 274
Kimbolton, Lord, *see* Manchester, Edward Montagu, second Earl of
King can do no wrong
  asserted: by Coke, 35; by Digges, 59; by Wentworth, 68; by Phelips, 69; by Corriton, 74; in the 1620s, 39, 41, 75; in Strafford's trial, 88–9; in Commons' Declaration of 19 May 1642, 115; in Laud's trial, 128; in pamphlets, 121–4; in Charles's trial, 131–2; at the Restoration, 133; in Danby's case, 218, 223, 225; in Exclusion crisis, 240–4; by Musgrave and Howe, 301; by Mackworth, 318; by Roches-ter, 336, 359; by third Earl of Sunderland, 362–3; in *The Unanimous or Consentient Opinions*, 373; by Swift and Steele, 373–5, 374 n.; by Rymer, 375 n.; in George I's reign, 393–6, 428–9
  origins of, 4–7

secured by frequent impeachments, 432–3, 435
King, Colonel, Edward, 144
Kingdom's Brief Answer, The, 132, 149
Knatchbull, Sir Edward, 269–70, 371

Lake, Sir Thomas, 17 n.
Lambe, Dr John, 32, 39
Land Bank of 1696, 280–1
Land Qualification Bill, 357
Lane, Thomas, 78
Lansdowne, George Granville, first Baron, 393
Lapsley, Gaillard, 7
La Hogue, defeat at, 249, 265
La Rochelle, 47–8, 66
Latimer, William, fourth Baron, 3, 8 n., 15
Latimer, Viscount, *see* Danby, Thomas Osborne, first Earl of
Laud, William: forebodings of attack upon, 16, 65; remonstrance against, 70–1, 436; letter to Strafford, 77 n.; impeachment of, 77–80, 133 n., 433, 444; failure to prosecute, 100–1; trial of, 124–30; attainder of, 130–1; mention of, 72, 75, 99, 170, 172, 200, 267, 363, 393, 398
Lauderdale, John Maitland, first Duke of: as courtier, 183–4; first address against, 185–90; second, 201–2; third, 202; fourth, 210–11; fifth, 224, 228; letter to, 223; on new Privy Council, 232; Charles support for, 233, 437
Lawes Subversion, The, 150
Lawson, Gilfrid, 426
Lechmere, Nicholas, 417, 420
Lee, Maurice, 192 n.
Lee, Sir Thomas, 231, 238, 255 n., 257
Legion's Memorial (Defoe), 316, 320
Leicester, Robert Dudley, first Earl of, 2–3
Lepton, John, 23 n.
Les Mains Sales (Sartre), 82
L'Estrange, Sir Roger, 133, 151, 152
Letter from a Person of Quality, A, 240–1, 240 n.
Letter to a Merry Young Gentleman, A (Defoe), 409
Letter to a Whig Lord, A (Swift), 370
Letter to the Lord Bishop of Salisbury, A, 408
Levellers, 149, 151
Leveson, Sir John, 294
Lewis, William, 136, 142
L'Hermitage (Dutch Agent in London), 304 n., 325, 337, 338 n., 360, 385, 392 n., 404
Lilburne, John, 148, 152

Lincoln, Bishop of, *see* Williams, Dr John
Lindsey, Robert Bertie, third Earl of, 217
Lisola, Baron, 157 n., 167–8
Littleton, Edward, 68
Littleton, Sir Thomas, 160, 169, 173–4, 187, 190, 212, 279, 297, 324
Locke, John, 152, 247–8, 256, 280 n., 297
Lockhart, George, 397
Loftus, Adam, first Viscount, 85, 88
Lokton, John, 8 n.
Londonderry, defeat at, 249, 253, 255
Long, Walter, 69
Lonsdale, Sir John Lowther, first Viscount, 247, 249, 260 n., 275, 279, 296
Lords Appellant, 8
Lords, House of:
    addresses voted by: of thanks for Clarendon's removal, 189 n.; censuring ministers for assenting to Partition, 301, 307; clearing Halifax of all fault, 332
    assert right of judicature, 11–12, 25, 29, 32–3, 38, 41, 64; denied right to join Commons in voting addresses, 194
    prevent abuse of impeachment: in Buckingham's case, 61; in Strafford's, 91–2, 101; in Clarendon's, 167–8; in Danby's, 215, 218 n., 220–1; in Scroggs's, 236–7, 236 n.; in Somers's, 312–15; in Oxford's, 392, 407, 416–19; in general, 432–3, 436
    votes of censure against: Nottingham, 267; the ministers for ordering an offensive war in Spain and having insufficient men at Almanza, 363–4; Galway, 364
    votes of confidence in: Nottingham, 267; the Queen's endeavours to negotiate peace, 368
Lords Ordainers, 8
Lorkin, Thomas, 20
Louis XIV, 201, 204, 213, 306, 315, 323, 435
Lovat, Simon Fraser, eleventh Baron, 380 n., 414 n.
Lowther, Sir John, *see* Lonsdale, first Viscount
Lowther, Sir John of Whitehaven, 258
Lowther, Sir William, 210
Lundy, Colonel, 253–5
Lunsford, Thomas, 107, 111
Lyndsell, Dr Augustine, 127
Lyons, Richard, 3, 8 n., 15

Macaulay, William Babington, vii
Macclesfield, Charles Gerard, Viscount Brandon and second Earl of, 263, 272

Macclesfield, Thomas Parker, first Earl of, 380 n., 414 n.
Machiavelli, Niccolo, 424, 424 n.
Mackworth, Sir Humphrey, 317–19, 321, 326
Magna Carta, 4
Mallory, Sir John, 11–12
Manchester, Charles Montagu, fourth Earl of, 324
Manchester, Edward Montagu, Lord Kimbolton, Viscount Mandeville, and second Earl of, 103, 109, 115, 135–7, 142, 146
Manchester, Henry Montagu, Viscount Mandeville and first Earl of, 26, 29, 34, 79 n., 82, 92
Mandeville, Edward Lord, *see* Manchester, Edward Montagu, second Earl of
Mandeville, Henry Lord, *see* Manchester, Henry Montagu, first Earl of
Mann, Robert, 366
Mansell, Thomas, 341–2, 346
Mansell, Sir Thomas, 49
Mansfeld, Count, expedition of, 41, 47, 52
Manwaring, Dr Roger, 68, 72, 127–9
Marat, Jean-Paul, 82
Markham, Sir John, 5, 68
Marlborough, John Churchill, first Duke of: at Althorp, 275; negotiates Grand Alliance, 327; on parties, 329; works with Whigs, 330, 330 n., 332, 333–4, 340–2, 344–5; vote of confidence in, 344, 344 n.; and 1710 crisis, 345–6, 347; on censuring men for ill-success, 363; dismissal and attack upon, 365–7; mention of, 308, 314, 380, 389, 402, 405
Marlborough, Sarah, Duchess of, 348 n.
Martin, Sir Henry, 16, 19, 51, 126, 135
Marvell, Andrew, 188, 206
Mary II, Queen of England, 205, 260–1, 271 n.
Masham, Mrs (Abigail Hill), 345–6, 375–6
Matthew, Roger, 57
May, Sir Humphrey, 45, 49
Maynard, Sir John, 78, 86–9, 90 n., 130, 133, 150, 200
Meath, Edward Brabazon, second Earl of, 181
Medley, The, 355
Medway, defeat in, 176, 178
Meesters, William, 308
Melville, Henry Dundas, first Viscount, 380 n., 414 n.
Memoirs of Some Transactions, 399
Memorial of the Church of England, The, 335

Index

Mênager, Nicolas de Baillif, Comte de Saint-Jean, 388–9

Mende, Bishop of, 58, 62, 63 n., 64

Meres, Sir Thomas, 181, 209, 231

Method of the Proceedings...in Cases of Impeachment, The, 399, 404 n., 410

Michael, Wolfgang, 302 n., 402 n., 425 n.

Michell, Sir Francis, 25, 31–2, 35, 432

Middlesex, Lionel Cranfield, first Earl of: becomes Lord Treasurer, 35; impeachment of, 36–8; object of intrigue, 409, 441; mention of, 60, 79, 432

Militia Act, Scottish, 190, 202

Milton, John, 151

'ministry', origin of the concept, 361–2, 362 n.; responsibility of, 362–4, 363 n., 372 n.

Mohun, Lord John, 67

Moir, Thomas, 18

Mompesson, Sir Giles, 23 n., 23–5, 29–30, 36, 432

Monck, George (afterwards first Duke of Albemarle), 135, 143, 177–8

Monckton, Robert, 352

Monmouth, Earl of, *see* Peterborough, Charles Mordaunt, third Earl of

Monmouth, James Scott, first Duke of, 229

Montagu, Charles, *see* Halifax, first Baron

Montagu, Christopher, 291

Montagu, Sir James, 342, 344

Montagu, Ralph, 170, 212–13, 222–3, 237, 435, 443

Montagu, Richard, 51–2, 65, 69, 127–8

Montereul, Comte de, 94 n., 98

Montesquieu, Baron de, 150

Moore (a Jesuit), 73

Moore, Arthur, 367, 369, 371, 371 n., 375–6, 400

Mordaunt, Henry, 346

Mordaunt, John, first Viscount, 136, 143

Morice, Sir William, 144, 173, 181

Morley, Dr George, 143

Moseley, Sir Edward, 67

Most Faults on One Side (Trapp), 355

Mountnorris, Francis Annesley, first Baron, 78, 85, 87–8, 88 n., 89

Mowden (High Constable of Kingston), 67

Moyle, Walter, 5

Mr Burnet's Defence, 394

Mulgrave, Lord, *see* Buckingham and Normanby, John Sheffield, first Duke of

Munster, Mlle Schulenburg, Duchess of (afterwards Duchess of Kendal), 421

Murray, Will, 107

Musgrave, Sir Christopher, 255–6, 262, 273, 276, 286–8, 294, 304, 308, 317, 324

Namier, Sir Lewis, 304

Narrative of the Late Parliament, A, 146

Neale, Sir John, 10

Necessity of Impeaching the Late Ministry, The (Burnet), 385

Nedham, Marchamont, 203

Neerwinden, losses at, 272

Neile, Richard, Bishop of Winchester (later Archbishop of York), 70, 436

Neville, Christopher, 22

Neville, Sir Henry: meets with Salisbury, 15; undertakes to manage Parliament, 17–20, 439; mention of, 100, 102–3, 160, 229, 272–3, 298, 356, 378, 440

Neville, Sir Henry (author of *Plato Redivivus*), 242, 300, 361

Neville, John de, third Baron, 8 n.

Newcastle, negotiations at, 131, 141

Newcastle, William Cavendish, first Earl, Marquis, and Duke of, 134–6, 169, 342, 377

Newcastle, John Holles, first Duke of, 334, 348–9, 350, 352

Newcastle, Thomas Pelham-Holles, first Duke of, 20

Newfoundland fisheries, 388

New Gagg for an Old Goose, A (Montagu), 51, 65

Newport, Mountjoy Blount, first Earl of, 116

Nicholas, Sir Edward, 78 n., 115, 134, 136–9

Nicholas, John, 166 n., 167 n., 168 n., 177 n., 179, 180 n.

Nichols, John, 39

Nineteen Propositions, 105, 107, 112–14, 117, 138, 140–2, 433, 438, 442

Noli Me Tangere (Byrdall), 373

Nomination of the King's servants: in Subsidy Bill, 39–40; advocated by Pym, 100; attempts to secure, 108–12; in Nineteen Propositions, 113–14; growing distrust of, 119, 139–44, 432–4; rejection of, 227, 234, 248, 255–6, 262, 280, 285; urged by Toland, 321

Norris, James Bertie, Baron (afterwards first Earl of Abingdon), 286–7

North, Sir Francis, 236, 239, 243

North, Roger, 234, 250, 257

North and Grey, William North, fifth Baron, 417 n.

Northampton, James Compton, third Earl of, 221 n.

Northampton, Henry Howard, first Earl of, 14, 20, 22, 440

Northumberland, Algernon Percy, fourth Earl of Northumberland, 79 n., 113–14, 136, 142, 175
Norwich, John Moore, Bishop of, 296
Norwich, Samuel Harsnet, Bishop of, 39
Nottingham, Daniel Finch, second Earl of: on Common Fame, 193; as minister under William III, 258–9; Whig attacks upon, 260–1, 264, 264 n., 265–8, 268 n., 269–71, 271 n., 274, 282, 437; in Queen Anne's reign, 330–1, 333, 333 n., 334–5, 342, 368; mention of, 224 n., 232, 238 n., 275, 275 n., 381
Nottingham, Heneage Finch, first Earl of, 219 n., 225, 238 n.
Nottingham, Charles Howard, third Earl of, 189 n.
Noy, William, 8, 25, 34, 56–7, 126

Oates, Titus, 213
Observations upon Some of His Majesties Late Answers and Expresses (Parker), 121
Observator, The, 400
Occasional Conformity, Bill of, 332–3, 334, 336, 376, 412–13
October Club, 357, 364–5, 368, 403
Old and New Ministry Compared, The, 363
Oldisworth, William, 377
Oldmixon, John, 353, 385 n.
Onslow, Arthur, (Speaker), 172, 280 n., 326, 353 n.
Onslow, Sir Richard, 153 n., 337
Orford, Edward Russell, first Earl of: quarrel with Nottingham, 262, 264 n., 266, 268; as Admiral, 271–2, 273, 274 n., 281–3, 288; Tory attacks on, 291–2, 295, 305; impeachment of, 308–15, 380; under Anne, 332, 342, 344, 348–9, 351, 352; resigns, 422
Orkney, Elizabeth Villiers, Countess of, 295
Orleans, Duchess of, 171, 183
Ormond, James Butler, twelfth Earl and first Duke of: impeachment of, 133 n.; opposed by Buckingham, 173, 180–1, 181 n.; threatened impeachment of, 224, 226, 236; mention of, 137, 157–8, 160 n., 165 n., 169 n., 171, 199, 212
Ormond, James Butler, second Duke of: given office, 352; Restraining Orders sent to, 368; impeachment of, 379, 383, 387–8, 390–5, 398
Orrery, Roger Boyle, first Earl of, 180–1, 180 n., 266, 370
Osborne, Sir Edward, 87–8

Osborne, Sir Thomas, *see* Danby, Earl of
Ossory, Thomas Butler, styled Earl of, 160 n., 165
Overton, Richard, 132, 152
Oxford, Robert Harley, first Earl of: as leader of Country party, 256, 260–1, 265, 273, 276, 280–1, 281 n., 287–8; leads attack on Junto, 289, 292, 294, 294 n., 295–6; as Speaker, 297–8, 297 n., 303, 309, 311, 324–6, 325 n.; author of *A Justification,* 317, 319; enters government under Anne, 330–6; and Place Bills, 337 n., 339 n.; dismissal, 340–2, 346; secures dismissal of Whigs, 345–51; fails to form a mixed ministry, 351–3, 353 n., 355–7; as Lord Treasurer, 364–6, 368–71; dismissal, 375–6; impeachment of, 379, 383, 385–92; defence of, 393–8, 405–9; as Prime Minister, 401–4, 403 n.; guilt of, 414–15, 415 n.; trial of, 416–20; mention of, 361, 382, 422, 435, 439, 443, 445–6
Oxford, Treaty of, 131, 141

Pacquet of Advices, A, 203
Palatinate, Frederick, Elector of, 42
Palmer, Geoffrey, 86, 87
Papillon, Philip, 332
Pardon: granted to Bacon, 35; to Manwaring, Montagu, Cosin, and Sibthorpe, 72; sued out by Cabal, 186, 188; dispute over Danby's, 217–21, 224–5; Charles willing to declare invalid in bar to an impeachment, 235 n.; Revolutionary Settlement silent on, 246, 252–3; declared invalid in bar to an impeachment in Act of Settlement, 299, 302–3, 326, 435; declared invalid by Mackworth, 319; and George I, 429
Paris, Matthew, 4
Parker, Henry, 102, 121–3, 132, 140–1, 144, 148, 152
Parker, Sir Thomas, *see* Macclesfield, first Earl of
Parkhurst, John, 332
Parliamentary Authorities (Davenant), 320
Parliament's Right to Elect Privy Councillors, Great Officers, and Judges, The (Pym), 141
Parry, Henry, 85
Parry, Sir Thomas (Chancellor of the Duchy of Lancaster), 20
Parties, political: force behind parliamentary attacks, in

William's reign, 251–3, 265, 288, 304–5, 307–8; in Anne's, 330–1, 357–8, 367–8; in George I's, 380–2

make mixed ministries impossible, in William's reign, 249–50, 258–9, 284, 297, 323–4, 326; in Anne's, 329–30, 334–5, 341, 351–3; in George I's, 382–3, 443

power of greater than patronage, 276–7, 285, 339, 377, 445

as the necessary support of under-takings, 273, 298–9, 378, 440, 444

Partition Treaties, 305–12

Paschall, John, 332

Patronage, power of: under James I, 19–21; under Charles I, 104–5, 105 n.; at Restoration, 135–6; under Charles II, 198–9, 206, 210; under William III, 269–72, 275–7, 277 n., 279, 385; under Anne, 333–4, 339–40, 345, 350, 370, 370 n., 377–8, 445; under George I, 430–1; in the eighteenth century, 406

Peel, Sir Robert, vii

Pembroke, Thomas Herbert, eighth Earl of, 296, 307–8, 314, 324, 330, 344

Pembroke, William Herbert, third Earl of, 7, 37, 44, 49, 54

Penn, Sir William, 177, 177 n.

Pennyman, Sir William, 87

Pentenrriedter, Christopher, 426–7

Pepys, Samuel: comments by, 159, 168, 171, 186; attack upon, 224–6, 226 n.

Percival, Edmund, 79 n.

Percy, Henry, 96

Peterborough, Charles Mordaunt, first Earl of Monmouth and third Earl of, 250, 258, 260, 265

Peterborough, Henry Mordaunt, second Earl of, 251 n.

Petition of Right, 67, 68, 89, 129

Pett, Sir Peter, 177–8

Petty, Sir William, 133 n.

Phelips, Sir Robert, 25, 36, 45–6, 48–9, 69, 97

Philip V of Spain, *see* Anjou, Duke of

Pierrepont, William, 136, 142

Pitt, Thomas, 361

Place Bills: in William's reign, 270, 273, 285, 290; provision for in Act of Settlement, 299, 299 n., 303, 326; repeal of, 336–9; under Anne, 339 n.

Player, Mr (a brewer), 358

Plucknett, T. F. T., 7

Plumb, J. N., 425 n.

Plunket, John, 369

Pocklington, Dr John, 126

Popish Plot, 213–16, 221–2, 224, 236, 242

Porter, Sir Charles, 273 n.

Portland, William Bentinck, first Earl of: grant of land to, 294 n.; negotiates Partition, 306; impeachment of, 379–94; mention of, 272, 276, 287, 290, 362, 380

Portland, Sir Richard Weston, first Earl of Portland, 46, 72, 74, 127

Port Mahon, 388

Portsmouth, Louise Renée de Keroualle, Duchess of, 229, 237

Poullett, John, first Earl, 351, 360, 362

Poussin (French Envoy), 315

Powle, Henry, 189, 202, 209, 212, 231, 234, 445

Preliminary Articles of Peace, 387, 395, 405

Presbyterians: oppose Strafford, 78; under-taking of, 135–7; and Isle of Wight conditions, 141–3, 433; and Claren-don, 157–8, 162, 165–7, 169; defend Orrery, 181; oppose Danby, 212, 216

Preston, battle of, 142

Preston Plot, 264

Pretender, 323, 369, 371–2, 379, 384–5, 388–9, 393, 414–15

Pride's Purge, 132

Priestmann, Captain Henry, 292, 292 n.

Prime Minister, responsibility of: asserted by Eliot, 57–8; by Coke, 69; in the 1620s, 75; in Strafford's trial, 85–6, 91; in Clarendon's impeachment, 173; by Wheeler and Gerrard, 193; by Powle, 202; in Oxford's trial, 390, 401–4; in eighteenth century, 429, 431, 438–9

Prior, Matthew, 288 n., 386–7, 389–90, 395, 400–1

Privy Council

Charles II's disregard of, 164, 172, 183, 241, 434

oath of secrecy of, 84, 191–2

publicity of advice in urged: in Nineteen Propositions, 114–18; in the 1670s, 231–3, 232 n.; in the 1690s, 262–3, 284; by Harley, 319; conceded in the Act of Settlement, 299–303; repealed in the Regency Act, 336–8, 438

reliance upon urged: by Williams, 44; by the Commons, 47–9; by Hyde, 100, 106–8; at the Restoration, 120–1, 137–9; by Temple, 224, 226, 229–33; by Shaftesbury, 233–4; by the Lords, 307; by Mackworth, 318

Privy Council (*cont.*)
  use of: in Tudor times, 42; in the 1630s, 75
Proctor, Sir Stephen, 1, 11–12
Protectorate, the, 138, 144 n., 146, 147 n., 148 n., 150
Prynne, William, 77, 127
Pulteney, Sir William, 422
Purveyors, 1, 13
Pym, John: motives of, 24, 442; on revival of impeachment, 33; in 1620 Parliaments, 55, 61, 65, 69; and Strafford's impeachment, 78, 78 n., 82 n., 82–3, 90, 92; urges Parliamentary Nomination, 100, 103, 105–6, 108–12, 109 n., 113–14; treatise by, 141, 141 n.; mention of, 56, 63, 75, 99, 118, 206, 226, 254, 300, 339, 410, 433
Pyrenees, Treaty of, 207–8

Quadruple Alliance, 426
Quesnoy, siege of, 387, 390

Radnor, John Robartes, first Earl of, 136, 142, 238 n.
Raleigh, Sir Walter, 43, 61
Ralph, James, 253
Ranelagh, Richard Jones, first Earl of, 212, 226, 274 n., 331
Ranelagh, Roger Jones, first Viscount, 78
Ransome, Mary, 356 n.
Refusal to serve with others: in William's reign, 274–5, 275 n., 295–6, 324; in Anne's, 332–3, 351, 365; in George I's, 381–3, 382 n.; comments on, 354–5
Regency Act, 336–9
Remonstrance, Grand, 102, 105, 106, 110, 241, 436
Reresby, Sir John, 224, 230, 401
Resignation: before executing an illegal command, 58, 68, 68 n., 233, 241, 244, 318–22, 399, 423–4, 429, 439; because advice refused, 233–4, 234 n., 268–9, 268 n., 324, 331–3, 335, 341, 346–8, 348 n., 352, 354, 421–5, 422 n.
Resigners Vindicated, The (Sewell), 424
Restoration Settlement, 120–1, 153–4, 183–4, 188, 197, 242, 248, 437
Restraining Orders, 368, 395
Revolutionary Settlement, 245–8, 252–3, 283, 437
Rich, Sir Nathaniel, 44, 48–9
Rich, Robert, 273
Rich, Reverend Samuel, 125
Richard II, 7–8, 29, 40, 61, 245, 409
Richelieu, 58

Richmond, Charles Stuart, third Duke of, 164
Richmond, James Stuart, first Duke of (second creation), 116, 136
Richmond, Ludovic Stuart, first Duke of, 27 n.
Ridge, Thomas, 357–8
Right of the Sovereign in the Choice of His Servants, The, 369 n.
Robart, John, 278
Robartes, John Lord, *see* Radnor, first Earl of
Robinson, Dr John, *see* Bristol, Bishop of
Rochester, Laurence Hyde, first Earl of: as Clarendon's son, 173; attacked, 238, 238 n.; at Treasury, 239–40; in William's reign, 264, 296–8, 304, 317, 324; in Anne's, 330–2, 334–6, 342–3, 351–2, 359; mention of, 21, 288, 289 n., 326, 362, 364, 404, 443
Rolle, John, 73
Rooke, Sir George, 292, 324
Rossetti, Count, 103
Rothes, John Leslie, seventh Earl of (afterwards first Duke of), 202
Rudyard, Sir Benjamin, 62, 78, 82 n., 83, 93, 100
Rump Parliament, 146
Rupert, Prince, 177
Rushook, Bishop of Chichester, 8 n.
Russell, Conrad, 95 n.
Russell, Edward, *see* Orford, first Earl of
Russell, William, Lord, 206, 230, 234, 237, 253, 326
Rutland, Katherine, Countess of, 313
Rutland, Robert Manners, second Duke of, 418
Ruvigny, Henri de Massue, Marquis de, *see* Galway, first Earl of
Rye-House Plot, 242, 253
Rymer, Thomas, 375
Ryswick, Peace of, 282

Sabran, Marquis de, 131
Sacheverell, Dr Henry, trial of, 347, 356, 356 n., 391
Sacheverell, William, 212, 246, 258
Sackville, Sir Edward, *see* Dorset, fourth Earl of
St Albans, Henry Jermyn, first Earl of, 237
St Alban, Viscount, *see* Bacon, Sir Francis
St John, Henry, *see* Bolingbroke, first Viscount
St John, Oliver, 78, 78 n., 95–6, 96 n, 103–4, 105 n., 136

St John, Paulet, Baron St John of Bletso (afterwards third Earl of Bolingbroke), 160, 167
St Omer, capture of, 203
St Petre de Havre Grace, seizure of, 55, 59, 60
St Quintin, Sir William, 422
Sales, Francis de (Saint), 126
Salisbury, James Cecil, third Earl of, 241, 251 n., 326
Salisbury, Robert Cecil, first Earl of, 14–16, 16 n., 17, 21, 21 n., 42, 441
Salisbury, William Cecil, second Earl of, 66, 108
Salisbury, Sir John, 8 n.
Salvetti, Amerigo (Tuscan Envoy), 30 n., 31 n., 40 n., 73 n., 79 n., 105
Sandwich, Edward Montagu, first Earl of, 175, 177, 177 n.
Sandys, Sir Edwin, 15, 19, 21, 36, 38
Sandys, Samuel, 181
Sartre, Jean Paul, 82
Savile, Sir Charles, 157 n.
Savile, George, *see* Halifax, first Marquis of
Savile, Henry, 157 n., 210
Savile, Thomas, Lord, 103
Sawyer, Edmund, 67–8
Sawyer, Sir Robert, 251, 255 n.
Saye and Sele, William Fiennes, first Viscount: on gratuities, 27; as an undertaker, 103–5, 105 n.; at Restoration, 142; mention of, 160, 229, 272, 298, 356, 440
Scarsdale, Robert Leake, third Earl of, 359–60, 362
Schism Act, 376, 422
Schwerin, Otto von, 214 n.
Scot, Thomas, 152
Scott, Colonel John, 225
Scroggs, Sir William, 236, 236 n., 243, 303
Seals, royal, use of to express the royal will, 5–6, 9
Searle, George, 134 n.
Second Letter from a Country Whig, A, 408, 409, 411
Second Part of Vox Populi, The, 148
Secret History of Arlus and Odolphus, The, 354 n.
Secret History of the Scepter, The (Defoe), 411–14
Security, Act of, 334–5
Selden, John, 55–7, 78, 117
Self-Denying Ordinances, 103, 146–7, 147 n., 230, 237–8, 273
Separation of Powers: during Interregnum, 145–51, 153; in reign of Charles II, 226–7, 242; and Revolutionary Settlement, 255–6, 256 n.; in William's reign, 262, 280, 285; celebrated in pamphlets, 319–21; end of, 413; importance of, 433
Septennial Act, 422
Settlement, Act of, 299, 300, 302–4, 336–9
Sewell, George, 424
Seymour, Sir Edward: as an anti-Clarendonian, 159, 161, 167, 169, 170, 181–2, 187–8; impeachment of, 236–7, 243, 443; in William's reign, 256, 260–2, 264, 275, 279; attacks Whig lords, 294, 297–8, 305, 308–9; defends Jersey, 313; dismissal, 333; mention of, 279, 286, 288, 316, 326, 331
Seymour, Sir Francis, 45–6, 48, 50, 70–1, 82 n.
Shaftesbury, Anthony Ashley Cooper, first Earl of: at Restoration, 142; as a member of the Cabal, 173, 184–7; as leader of the Country party, 187–8, 190 n., 192, 199, 205–6, 212; denounces Ormond, 226; as an undertaker, 229–30, 232, 233–4, 237, 237 n.; on danger of voting James money, 242, 242 n.; mention of, 170, 218 n., 300, 326, 378, 422, 440, 443
Shaftesbury, Anthony Ashley Cooper, third Earl of, 298, 325 n.
Shales, John, 255, 439
Shaw, John, 143
Shaw, W. A., 215 n.
Ship Money judges, impeachment of, 100–1, 133 n.
Shippen, William, 417
Shovell, Sir Cloudesley, 274
Shrewsbury, Anna Maria Brudenell, Countess of, 190
Shrewsbury, Charles Talbot, twelfth Earl of: resigns, 268–9; refuses office, 274–5, 275 n.; as Secretary of State, 275, 279, 280–3; resigns again, 291, 295–6; and Kidd, 305; and Grand Alliance, 307; as minister in Anne's reign, 346–50; mention of, 258, 263, 414 n., 418 n.
Shrewsbury, Francis Talbot, eleventh Earl of, 190
Sibthorpe, Robert, 72, 128
Sidney, Henry (later Earl of Romney), 265
Skinner *v.* East India Company, 175
Skelton, Richard, 69
Smith, John, 255, 257, 286, 297, 335, 335 n., 339
Smith, Sir Thomas, 145
Smyrna Fleet, attack on, 191, 193, 271–2

'sneakers', 333

Somers, Sir John, first Baron: on impeachments, 247 n.; as one of the Junto, 265, 270–2, 276–7, 278 n., 279–83, 288–9; Tory attacks upon, 292–6, 304–5, 304 n.; impeachment of, 308–15; as author, 320; advice to William, 323, 324 n.; as minister under Anne, 333, 342, 344–6, 348–9, 351–2; on Cabinet, 363–4; as Prime Minister, 402; mention of, 291 n., 380, 435, 439, 443

Somerset, Robert Carr, Viscount Rochester and first Earl of, 17, 42, 441

Somerset, Charles Seymour, sixth Duke of, 324, 330–1, 333, 348, 350, 352, 365

Sophia, Electress of Hanover, 335–6, 375

Southampton, Henry Wriothesley, third Earl of, 18, 28, 30, 102, 439

Southampton, Thomas Wriothesley, fourth Earl of, 136

Southampton Whigs, 237, 298, 440

Southwell, Sir Robert, 226, 229

Southwold Bay, defeat at, 184

Sparrow, John, 23 n.

Spiller, Henry, 1, 11–14

Stamford, Thomas Grey, second Earl of, 316

Stanhope, James (afterwards Lord Mahon), 358–9, 380, 386, 390, 414–16, 420–1, 425–6

Steele, Richard, 371, 373–5, 374 n.

Steenkirk, Battle of, 249

Steward, Henry, 85–6

Stop of the Exchequer, 185, 191, 193, 227, 232, 442

Strafford, Thomas Wentworth, first Earl of: on Mompesson's impeachment, 33; opposes Buckingham, 46, 83 n.; and Petition of Right, 67; letter to Laud, 77; political philosophy of, 81, 94 n., 99, 441; impeachment of, 77–9, 82–3, 84 n., 444; trial of, 84–92, 84 n., 89 n., 439; attainder of, 92–8; stumbling block to Bedford's undertaking, 103; mention of, 21, 21 n., 61, 72, 75, 100, 128, 131, 133 n., 166–7, 168 n., 170, 172, 200, 212, 215, 218, 221, 267, 310, 345, 363, 391–3, 398, 403, 410, 433–4

Strafford, Thomas Wentworth, first Earl of (third creation): letter from, 366 n.; impeachment of, 379, 383–4, 387–9, 391–3; defence of, 393–6, 394 n., 398–400, 405, 407; prosecution of dropped, 420

Strangways, Sir Giles, 200

Strangways, Thomas, 371 n.

Stratford, John, Archbishop of Canterbury, 7

Stratford, Dr William, 420 n.

Strickland, Sir William, 251–2, 420

Strode, William, 109–10, 118

Stroud, Sir William, 44

Stuart, Francis, 164

Subsidy Bill of 1624, 39–40, 55

Suckling, Sir John, 96

Suffolk, Thomas Howard, first Earl of, 14

Suffolk, Michael de la Pole, first Earl of, 8 n.

Suffolk, William de la Pole, first Duke of, 8 n., 49

Suffolk House Cabal, 136, 142–3

Sunderland, Charles Spencer, third Earl of: as Secretary of State under Anne, 340, 342, 345–6; dismissal of, 346–8, 358; letter from 358–9; on responsibility of ministry, 362, 373; minister of George I, 380, 419, 421

Sunderland, Robert Spencer, Earl of Sunderland: threatened attack on, 343; on Cabinet, 263, 361–2; as parliamentary manager, 265, 268–9, 270–5, 279–82, 281 n., 445; as Lord Chamberlain, 282–3, 286–7, 437; continues to advise William, 289, 293, 295, 295 n., 296, 323, 324 n.; mention of, 20, 213, 229, 233, 250–1, 291, 356–7, 404

Supplement to the Faults on Both Sides, A, 366

Supplies, withholding of: in the 1620s, 49, 61–3, 75, 437; until Strafford's attainder accepted, 97; urged by Pym, 109; in the 1670s, 195, 201, 201 n., 206–9, 216 n., 228; ineffectual in 1680s, 237, 239; part of Whig theory, 241, 241 n., 244; made effective by Revolutionary Settlement, 246–8; and City, 281; justified by Davenant, 320; threats of, 276, 310 n., 315, 325, 346; consequence of, 412

Swift, Jonathan: on balance of government, 321; on laying down conditions for employment, 354, 422; on Whigs, 355; on Harley's scheme, 357; on censure of Whig ministry, 358, 364; on motives of Whigs, 367; on party unity, 370–1; quarrel with Steele, 373–5; on Somers, 402; on Prime Minister, 403, 403 n., 404 n.; on parliamentary addresses, 406 n.

Swinfen, John, 212

'tackers', 334, 334 n., 335 n., 342
Talbot, Colonel Richard, 189, 189 n., 193, 194
Talbot, Gilbert, 187
Tallard, Count, 295, 295 n., 304 n.
Talmash (or Tollemache), General Thomas, 275 n.
Tangier, 237
Tankerville, Forde Grey, first Earl of, 296, 322
Tatnall, Captain, 179
Temple, Sir Richard: as an anti-Clarendonian, 159–60, 169, 181–2, 440; memorandum of, 160 n., 162 n., 169 n.; intrigue by, 179; on opposition to Danby, 221 n.; on need for secrecy, 262; mention of, 20, 173–4, 177, 229, 266, 272, 298, 356
Temple, Sir William: on monarchy, 184; Privy Council scheme of, 230–1, 434; considers resigning, 233; mention of, 205, 207, 212 n., 361
Ten Heads (of 24 June 1641), 105, 108, 110
Test Act, 185–7
Thelwall, Sir Eubule, 23 n.
Thelwall, John, 95
Theobalds, confrontation at, 1, 14
Thomas, Hugh, 416 n.
Thompson, Sir John, 25, 301
Thornall, Mr, 67
Thurborne, James, 23 n.
Thurloe, John, 133
Thynne, Thomas, 16 n.
Tilliers, Count Leveneur de, 31 n.
Tindal, Matthew, 424
Titus, Colonel Silas, 237
Toland, John, 321
Tooke, John Horn, 95
Torcy, Marquis de, 386–7, 414, 414 n.
Torrington, Arthur Herbert, first Earl of, 262, 262 n.
Toulon, siege of, 358–9, 364
Tournay, cession of, 389, 390, 392, 415–17
Townshend, Charles, second Viscount, 380, 381, 414, 416–18, 421–3
Townshend, Sir John, 23 n.
Toynbee, Arnold, 262
Trapp, Joseph, 355
Treason, concept of: in Strafford's impeachment, 91–6, 95 n.; in Laud's, 310–11; in Clarendon's, 166 n; in Danby's, 215, 223; in Scrogg's, 236; in Oxford's, 410, 415–16
Treasury, want of confidence in, 40, 118, 227; Danby's management of, 196 n.,

198, 215; as basis of Prime Minister's power, 403
Treasury, parliamentary: attempts to establish (in 1624), 39–40, (in 1641), 118–19, (in 1675 and 1678), 224, 226–7
Treatise of Monarchy (Hunton), 121
Treaty of Commerce (with France), 368–9, (with Spain), 371–3
Trenchard, Sir John, 270–2, 274–5
Trevelyan, George Macaulay, 340, 414, 414 n., 415 n.
Trevor, Sir John (Baron of the Exchequer), 100 n.
Trevor, Sir John (M.P.), 160, 169, 173, 270, 272, 277–9
Trevor, Thomas, first Baron, 418 n.
Triennial Bills: (in 1641), 97–8; William's opposition to, 268 n., 270, 275, 290
Triple Alliance, 185, 191
'Triumvirate', 333–4, 340
True State of the Case, A, 150
Trumbull, Sir William, 283, 317
Tufnell, Samuel, 417, 420
Turner, Dr Samuel, 56
Turnham Green, attempted assination at, 280
Tutchin, John, 400
Tweedale, John Hay, second Earl of (afterwards first Marquis of), 190
Twysden, Sir Roger, 140, 141 n., 144
Tyrawley, Charles O'Hara, first Baron, 358
Tyron, Sir Samuel, 23 n.

Unanimous or Consentient Opinions, The, 373
Undertaking, parliamentary: origins of, 17–20; by Sandys and Phelips, 36; by Williams, 48; by Bedford and Saye, 100, 102–5; inadequacy of, 119; at Restoration, 120–1, 134–7; by Temple and Bristol, 160, 174; by the anti-Clarendonians, 163, 169, 173–5, 182; Charles II turns from, 183; by Holles, 216–17; by Shaftesbury, 224, 226, 229–30, 230 n.; by Southampton Whigs, 237–8; by Junto, 269, 272–5, 285; by Tories, 297–9; by Harley, 356; triumph of, 378, 439–40
Uniformity, Act of, 157
United Provinces, Treaty with, 205, 208
Usher, James, Lord Primate of Ireland, 94
Usk, Thomas, 8 n.
Utrecht, Treaty of, 371, 380, 387, 395, 439, 444
Uxbridge, Treaty of, 131, 141

Valenciennes, capture of, 203
Vane, Sir Henry (the elder), 92, 94, 119, 218, 222
Vane, Sir Henry (the younger), 151–2
Vaudry, John, 27
Vaughan, John Lord, *see* Carberry, third Earl of
Verney, Edmund, 165
Vernon, James: seeks a mixed ministry, 296; on Harley, 297 n., 298; on Partition, 306 n.; ignorant of Grand Alliance, 307; not impeached, 308, 314; his letter, 310; mention of, 286, 288, 290, 295, 361
Vigo Bay, 391
Villa Clara, Marquis of, 50
Villars, Duc de, Marshall of France, 388, 390–1
Villiers, Christopher, 30–1
Villiers, Sir Edward, 30–1
Villiers, George, *see* Buckingham, first Duke of
Vindication of Parliament, A, 148
Vindication of the King, A, 149
Vindication of the Rights of the Commons of England, A (Mackworth), 317

Walcott, Robert, 287 n., 330 n.
Waldeck, Prince, 366
Walker, Sir Edward, 45, 135 n.
Waller, Sir William, 59
Walpole, Sir Robert: on Somers, 311; and Regency Act, 337 n.; as Secretary at War, 342, 344 n., 348 n.; attack upon, 365–7; against ministers hiding behind Queen, 372; as minister of George I, 380, 380 n., 381; manages Oxford's impeachment, 387, 390, 394, 401, 415–17, 439; as Prime Minister, 402; and end of impeachment, 414, 420; resignation, 420–6; distinguishes between His Majesty and his ministers, 426; responsibilities assumed by, vii, 430
Walsingham, Thomas, 4
Warwick, Sir Philip, 45, 83, 223
Weekes, Dr John, 126
Weekly Pacquet from Rome, The, 236
Welby, Sir William, 67
Wentworth, Peter (of Elizabeth's reign), 22
Wentworth, Peter (of Anne's reign), 352, 383 n.
Wentworth, Sir Thomas, *see* Strafford, first Earl of
Wentworth, Sir William, 392 n.

West, Richard (later Lord Chancellor of Ireland), 410
Weston, Sir Richard (Lord Treasurer), *see* Portland, first Earl of
Weston, Sir Richard (Baron of the Exchequer), 236
Wharton, Goodwin, 262–3, 438
Wharton, Thomas, fifth Baron, first Earl, and first Marquis of: for Whig monopoly of office, 247 n., 250, 266; as undertaker, 272, 275, 277–9; impeaches Leeds, 278; named to Admiralty, 282; defends Godolphin, 334; as minister under Anne, 342, 344, 349, 351–2; and 1710 elections, 353; in opposition, 372, 379 n.; mention of, 281, 286, 330 n., 422
Wheeler, Sir Charles, 180, 193, 196, 403
Whig theory of responsible government, 240–2, 244
'Whimsicals', 338–9
Whitelocke, Bulstrode, 86, 89
Whitelocke, James, 3, 4, 15, 21
Whitlocke, Sir William, 260 n.
Wickins, Nathaniel, 127–8
Wildman, John, 132, 150, 152
William III: marriage of, 203, 205; and Revolutionary Settlement, 247–9; seeks to govern by a mixed ministry, 249, 251–5, 258–9, 264–5; and power of patronage, 269–70, 445–6; dismisses Nottingham, 271, 271 n.; vetoes Place Bill, 273; turns to Whigs, 274–5, 278–80, 282–3; hatred of party, 283; seeks to save Sunderland, 286–7; against Wharton, 287 n.; turns to Tories, 294–7; refuses to be an informer, 255, 300; assumes responsibility for Irish grants, 300; conducts foreign affairs, 306, 306 n., 307; relies on Dutchmen, 308–9; tactics in 1701, 310, 313, 315, 317, 322–3; final independence of, 325; mention of, 361–2, 411–12, 433, 437, 443
Williams, Dr John, Bishop of Lincoln: advice to James and Buckingham, 26–7, 30; as Lord Keeper, 35, 39; intrigues of, 44–5; as an undertaker, 48–9, 440; dismissal, 50; driven from Council, 66; on Strafford's attainder, 98; mention of, 102, 186
Williams, Sir William, 256
Williamson, Sir Joseph, 224–5, 246, 314
Willson, David, 17
Wilmot, Henry, 96

Windebank, Sir Francis, 77–80, 100–1, 133 n.
Winnington, Sir Francis, 170, 220, 237–8, 287, 326
Winwood, Sir Ralph, 18, 439
Withers, Henry, 361
Woodstock Address, 385, 385 n.
Worcester, Edward Somerset, fourth Earl of, 14
Worcester, Henry Somerset, third Marquis of (afterwards first Duke of Beaufort), 238
Worcester, William Lloyd, Bishop of, 331
Wormald, B. H. G., 106

Wotton, Sir Henry, 22–3, 46
Wratislaw, Count, 329, 330 n.
Wren, Sir Christopher, 314–15
Wren, Matthew (Bishop of Norwich), 101
Wright, Sir Nathan, 296, 335
Wright, Sir Robert, 251
Wyndham, Sir William, 369, 405
Wynn, Sir John, 45

Yelverton, Sir Henry, 19, 23 n., 30–1, 33–4, 34 n., 35
York, Presidency of the Council at, 93–4
Young, Sir Walter, 283